Marshall

Hero for Our Times

Books by Leonard Mosley

Nonfiction
Marshall: Hero for Our Times   1982
The Druid   1981
Blood Relations: The Rise and Fall of the du Ponts of Delaware   1980
Dulles: A Biography of Eleanor, Allen, and John Foster Dulles and Their
     Family Network   1978
Lindbergh: A Biography   1976
The Reich Marshall: A Biography of Hermann Goering   1974
Power Play: Oil in the Middle East   1973
Backs to the Wall: London in World War II   1971
On Borrowed Time: How World War II Began   1969
Hirohito: Emperor of Japan   1966
The Battle Of Britain   1965
Haile Selassie: The Conquering Lion   1964
Faces from the Fire: Biography of Sir Archibald McIndoe   1962
The Glorious Fault: The Life of Lord Curzon   1962
The Last Days of the British Raj   1961
The Cat and the Mice: A German Spy in Cairo   1960
Duel for Kilimanjaro   1959
Castlerosse: The Life of a Bon Vivant   1956
Gideon Goes to War: A Biography of Orde Wingate   1948
Report from Germany, 1945   1945
Downstream, 1939   1939
So Far So Good: A Fragment of Autobiography   1934

Fiction
The Seductive Mirror   1952
Each Had a Song   1951
War Lord   1950
No More Remains   1938
So I Killed Her   1937

Marshall

Hero for Our Times

Leonard Mosley

Hearst Books
New York

Grateful acknowledgment is extended for permission to quote from previously copyrighted materials:

Excerpts from *Present at the Creation* by Dean Acheson reprinted with permission of W. W. Norton & Company, Inc.

Excerpts from *The Turn of the Tide* by Sir Arthur Bryant reprinted with permission of Doubleday & Company, Inc.

Excerpts from *Master of Sea Power* by T. B. Buell reprinted with permission of Little, Brown and Company.

Excerpts from *The Eisenhower Diaries* by Dwight D. Eisenhower reprinted with permission of W. W. Norton & Company, Inc.

Excerpts from *Memoirs of General Lord Ismay* by Hastings L. Ismay reprinted with permission from Viking Press, Inc. © 1960 by The Viking Press, Inc.

Lines from the song "How're Ya Gonna Keep 'Em Down on the Farm" Copyright 1919 Mills Music, Inc. Copyright renewed. Used with permission. All rights reserved.

Excerpts from *American Caesar* by William Manchester reprinted with permission of Little, Brown and Company.

Excerpts from *Memoirs of My Service in the World War 1917–1918* by George C. Marshall. Copyright © 1976 by Molly B. Winn. Reprinted by permission of Houghton Mifflin Company.

Excerpts from the book *General Marshall Remembered* by Rose Page Wilson. © 1968 by Rose Page Wilson. Published by Prentice-Hall, Inc., Englewood Cliffs, New Jersey 07632.

Continued on p. v

Mosley, Leonard, 1913–
    Marshall, hero for our times.

    Includes bibliographical references and index.
    1. Marshall, George C. (George Catlett), 1880–1959.
2. United States—History, Military—20th century.
3. United States. Army—Biography. 4. Generals—
United States—Biography. I. Title.
E745.M3767   973.918′092′4 [B]   82-1065
ISBN 0-87851-304-3   AACR2

10 9 8 7 6 5 4 3 2

MANUFACTURED IN THE UNITED STATES OF AMERICA

Grateful acknowledgment is extended to the following for permission to reproduce pictures:

The George C. Marshall Research Foundation for photographs of George Catlett Marshall Sr., Laura Bradford Marshall, the three Marshall children, Marshall at age 17 in Uniontown, Marshall and his family on the day of his marriage to Lily Coles, Marshall with General Pershing in World War I, Marshall at Fort Myer in 1923, Lily Marshall at Tientsin railroad station, Marshall with fellow officers and their wives on a North China beach in 1926, Katherine Tupper Brown, Marshall with his wife, step-daughter, and stepsons, Marshall with General MacArthur in 1943, Marshall at the Cairo Conference in 1943, Marshall with Brigadier General Frank McCarthy, Churchill, Roosevelt, Stalin, Cunningham, Portal, Leahy and Marshall at the Yalta Conference in 1945, the round table at Yalta on the first day of the conference, Attlee with Truman, Acheson, and Marshall during the Korean war crisis.

Life Magazine for photographs of: Marshall at a cookout with Katherine in 1939, by Thomas McAvoy, © 1939, Time Inc.; Marshall on maneuvers in 1941, by Thomas McAvoy, © 1940, Time Inc.; Marshall with Stimson, by Thomas McAvoy, © Time Inc.; Marshall with De Gaulle in 1944, by George Skadding, © Time Inc.; Admiral King, Marshall, and Eisenhower, by Frank Scherschel, © Time Inc.; Marshall with Molotov in 1947, by N. R. Farbman, © 1949, Time Inc.; Mme Chiang Kai Shek in 1958, by Carl Mydans, © Time Inc.; Marshall with Chang Chun and Chou En Lai in 1946, by George Lacks, © 1947, Time Inc.; Queen Frederika of Greece in 1958, by Joe Schershel, © 1958, Time Inc.; Marshall and wife Katherine, in retirement, by Mark Kaufman, © Time Inc.

Life Picture Service for photographs of: Marshall at a VMI reunion; and the Anglo-U.S. conference at Quebec on August 18, 1943.

The Imperial War Museum for photographs of Marshall with Sir John Dill; and Marshall with Churchill and Montgomery in 1943.

Bill Mauldin for his cartoon showing "Willie" and "Joe" mourning General Marshall, © 1959 Bill Mauldin.

Contents

PART THREE:
The Statesman

PART FOUR:
Recall

Acknowledgments

At the end of this book will be found Source Notes giving in detail the research institutions, documents, books, and authorities I have consulted for this study of the career of General George Catlett Marshall. It is here, however, that I would like to thank those who have been particularly helpful to me in my quest for information and enlightenment about both Marshall and the momentous events in which he was involved.

I have stated in the Source Notes how grateful students of Marshall's life should be to the labors of Dr. Forrest C. Pogue, but I would also like to add a note of personal thanks to him for his cordial reception of my project and for the help he gave to me and my fellow researcher, my wife, in order that we should find the richest possible sources of material both in Washington and in Lexington, Virginia, where the Marshall Research Foundation is situated. It was he who gave us an introduction to Ambassador Fred L. Hadsel, director of the foundation. For a research sojourn there which was to last several months, it was Mr. Hadsel who put the resources of his pleasantly efficient library and its staff at our disposal. His deputy, Mr. Royster Lyle, Jr.; his archivist, Mr. John Jacob; and the whole of the foundation staff were kind, willing, and most intelligently perceptive of our needs, and were unflagging in their efforts to assist us.

Working at the Marshall Foundation is a pleasant chore for a researcher, for it is situated on the grounds of the Virginia Military Institute, adjacent to the campus of Washington and Lee University, and within easy walking distance of one of the most attractive and hospitable small cities in the United States. Anyone staying in Lexington for more than a month is welcomed as a neighbor and made to feel at home, and doors to very delightful homes swing open. Many of those who made our stay pleasant were also able to reward us with useful information about Marshall, and among those to whom we owe double thanks in this regard are: General and Mrs. George R. E. Shell (superintendent emeritus of the VMI); Colonel Henry S. Bausum, professor of history at VMI, and his wife; Major Jeffrey A. Gunsburg, assistant professor of history at VMI; Colonel George M. Brooke, professor of history at VMI, and his wife; Colonel B. McCluer Gilliam, professor of political science at VMI, and his wife; Dr. and Mrs. Barry Machado, Dr. and Mrs. Roger Jeans, Dr. and Mrs. John R. Handelman, Mr. and Mrs. C. Carrington Tutwiler; Mr. Gerald L. Nay, associate director of the Marshall Foundation, and his wife; Dr. Larry I. Bland, editor of the Marshall Papers, and his wife; Mrs. William W. Old III, in charge of public information at the foundation, and her husband, Dr. Old, a Lexington surgeon and VMI physician; and Mr. Joseph D. Neikirk, now consultant to the VMI Foundation, and his wife, a noted local artist.

In Washington I not only made use—once again—of the vast resources of the National Archives and manuscripts division of the Library of Congress but renewed acquaintance with two distinguished public men who have helped me with previous books: Mr. Paul Nitze and Mr. Lucius D. Battle, both of whom worked with Marshall and willingly shared their experiences with me. A week or two previously I had been to San Antonio, Texas, to talk with General William Simpson, former commander of the Ninth Army in World War II, and General Thomas Handy, who was Marshall's right-hand man in the Chief of Staff's department. General Simpson, who was in his late eighties, got up from his sickbed to talk, and if his body was frail, his mind was as quick and vivid as ever, and he gave a graphic and colorful picture of what it was like along the Elbe River in Germany in the last chaotic days of World War II. He sent me a signed picture of himself as a memento of the visit, and I am sad to say that it arrived after the news of his death reached me. There are other pictures from General Simpson's collection in this book, and I would like to thank his charming and devoted widow, Mrs. Kay Simpson, for having gone through his files and picked them out for me.

I have, of course, long known that soldiers—like orchestral conductors—keep clear and orderly minds right on into old age, and General Handy* proved that with his amusing and detailed

---

*I am sad to report that he died at age 90 in San Antonio on April 14, 1982.

memories of life in Washington and on the battlefronts of the world with his old chief. So did General Albert C. Wedemeyer, who talked frankly and at length into my tape recorder about his sometimes stormy associations with Marshall when we visited him at his Maryland farm. My wife and I would like to thank Mrs. Wedemeyer for so pleasantly entertaining us afterward.

Another of Marshall's old aides, Brigadier General Frank McCarthy, gave up a large chunk of valuable time—it was just after the election of his old friend President Ronald Reagan—to talk about his chief. We met him in his hilltop home in Beverly Hills, which looks down on the scene of some of his greatest triumphs as a film producer, and he provided not only some amusing stories about life with Marshall but some invaluable leads to further information. In Chevy Chase, Maryland, General James Moore was good enough to check the information about the Ninth Army which General Simpson, his old commander, had given me.

I had researched and written at length about the admission of Israel to the United Nations in previous books, but there had always been gaps in the information which could be filled in only by those Israelis who were present at the creation of the Israeli state. One of the two most important is Mr. Abba Eban (the other, Moshe Sharett, is dead), and my wife and I arrived in Israel to talk to him at a moment when there was a fierce political crisis in the Israeli Labor party, to which Eban belongs. Nevertheless, he cut short several meetings in order to talk to us at his home near the seashore at Herzlia, and that made the long journey to see him more than worthwhile.

There are many others who deserve most grateful thanks for their help, in this country, in Britain, France, and Germany, but I have room here to mention only two from nearly a hundred. One is Mrs. Joan Bright Astley, who looked after the British side of the great wartime conferences in Quebec, Cairo, Teheran, and Yalta and became a good friend of Marshall and his staff as a result of these meetings. (At one time the general turned matchmaker and tried to marry off Joan to one of his favorite aides.) Joan provided me with some amusing and enlightening glimpses of the human side of Marshall in his rare moments of relaxation. The other will never read these words because he is dead, but I would like to write them just the same—to say how much I miss the long talks I used to have with the late General Sir Frances "Freddy" de Guingand, who once held the unenviable job of chief of staff to Field Marshall Viscount (Bernard) Montgomery. We were friends and companions for many years in London and at our homes in the south of France, and his confidences about Marshall and other great wartime commanders have helped, I hope, to give a special flavor to this book.

It goes without saying that I have used many other institutions and sources of material for my research, in addition to the Marshall Library, and they include the National Archives and the Library of Congress in Washington; the Dwight D. Eisenhower Library in Abilene, Kansas; the Harry S. Truman Library in Independence, Missouri; the British Library and the Wiener Library in London; the Bibliotheque Nationale in Paris; the Institut für Zeitgeschichte in Munich, among others. In addition, my own not inconsiderable files now include—because of research for previous books—much material from the private collections of the two Dulles brothers, John Foster and Allen Welsh, at Princeton University. John Foster Dulles worked closely with Marshall while he was secretary of state and took over his job under the Eisenhower administration. Allen Dulles, as head of the CIA, handled the correspondence between Marshall and Queen Frederika of Greece after Marshall had discovered that his go-between in the Greek Embassy in Washington was not secure. Other documents have come to me through sources which would be too complicated to specify here, and they will be found at the back of this book.

I should add that this book would probably not have seen the light of day had it not been for the devoted collaboration I have had in its production by my editor, Bruce Lee, who not only shares my enthusiasm for my subject but is an expert on the wartime periods with which I have dealt; and that goes too for my agent, John Cushman, who knows whereof I write and has constantly and amiably looked over my shoulder.

Finally, I would like to say thank you with all my heart, once again, to my wife and fellow researcher, Deirdre, for her constant vigilance and encouragement.

Introduction

As a soldier, as a statesman, and as a human being, General George Catlett Marshall is not an easy man for modern, skeptical Americans to accept. For those who have grown wary of heroes and look for the hidden vices in so-called great men, he had qualities present-day cynics may find hard to swallow. He had to scrape and scratch his way to the top of the tree in the U.S. Army. He had to fight for this nation's interests—sometimes its very life—both as U.S. Chief of Staff during World War II and as secretary of state in the raw, cold, hungry postwar world that followed.

Yet this was what makes Marshall both remarkable and special: He never lied in either his own cause nor his country's. He was a superb negotiator and a brilliant public speaker. He could manipulate the most stubborn, difficult, and politically agile men, including Roosevelt, Stalin, Churchill, Truman, and Eisenhower. He had wit, persuasion, and charm—loads of charm, as a number of famous and beautiful women discovered.

But when General Marshall was buried in Arlington National Cemetery in 1959, you could truly have written across his tombstone: "Here lies an honest man." He never tricked anyone. He never made a promise, to a man, woman, or child, that he did not keep. In a world of overpaid heroes and untrustworthy politicians, is it possible that one great American made it to the peak and still kept his principles?

Not without pain and struggle and suffering, he didn't. And that is what has made the writing of this biography so fascinating. In a more innocent age it used to be preached that honesty, modesty, and virtue would get you everywhere. But in the world in which George Catlett Marshall grew up, these were the qualities which, far from polishing the path to the top, made the journey ten times more difficult. The only return Marshall got out of the struggle was that when he finally made it, he just felt better about the means he had used to get there.

Marshall never got around to writing his own autobiography; he was the only wartime general and postwar statesman who failed to do so. He turned down an offer of $1 million from the *Saturday Evening Post* to tell his story because, he said, he didn't want to embarrass the generals who had served under him and the statesmen with whom he had worked by recounting the mistakes they had made and the scandals they had gotten into.

I suspect that in addition, he did not wish to lay bare the anguishing personal incidents in his own life—about his first wife, his stepsons, and his relations with fellow soldiers and other famous men and, in particular, two celebrated women.

It was a mistake, I think, for him to neglect to tell his story because it has created a gap in U.S. contemporary history and deprived modern Americans of knowledge of the facts about one of their greatest men—probably the greatest man since Lincoln. It has been both a privilege and an adventure for me to search out those facts and be able to tell his full story at last.

There is not likely to be another man like him, neither in our time nor in the generations to come. It is time that America—and the world—learned everything there is to know about what he did for them, and at what cost to himself.

PROLOGUE

Call from the President

On August 20, 1945, General of the Army George Catlett Marshall sat down at his desk in the Pentagon, read the latest dispatches from the Far East, and then took up his pen to write a letter to President Harry Truman. He wrote:

> Now that hostilities have terminated, the demobilization of the Army is actively under way, the major military decisions regarding cut-back in war production have been taken and postwar military planning is in an advanced state, I feel free to propose my relief as Chief of Staff.
>
> I have been on duty in the War Department continuously for more than seven years, six as Chief of Staff. Aware of the wear and tear of the job, I am certain it would be advantageous to make a change.
>
> If I may be permitted to propose a successor, I suggest that General Eisenhower is unusually well qualified for the duties of Chief of Staff at this particular time.

It was a letter that took people's breath away when they heard about it in official Washington. And when news spread to foreign chancelleries and Army posts around the world, no one, at first, took it seriously. Why, peace was less than a week old. It was just six days since the Japanese government, its armies in retreat, its navy destroyed, Tokyo burned, two of its cities atomized and others threatened, had agreed to surrender unconditionally and brought World War II to an end. True, Adolf Hitler's Nazi German Reich had already been annihilated, and Allied troops were in occupation of its smoking ruins. How could General Marshall be planning to go now—when there were still the fruits of victory to be savored, a victory it was generally recognized he had done most to plan and achieve?

Not for nothing had the British prime minister, Winston Churchill, blessed his name and called him the "organizer of victory." After the defeat of the Nazis, he had written him:

> It has not fallen to your lot to command the great armies. You have had to create them, organize them, and inspire them. Under your guiding hand, the mighty and valiant formations which have swept across France and Germany were brought into being and perfected in an amazingly short space of time. Not only were

xvii

the fighting troops and their complicated ancillaries created but, to an extent that seems almost incredible to me, the supply of commanders capable of maneuvering the vast organisms of modern armies and groups of armies, and of moving them with unsurpassed celerity, were also found wherever they were needed. . . .

There has grown in my breast through all these years of mental exertion a respect and admiration for your courage and massive strength which has been a real comfort to your fellow toilers, of whom I hope it will be recognized that I was one.

Churchill's words were echoing in every Allied capital, for it had long since been generally acknowledged that without Marshall's genius, energy, determination, and, especially, patience, World War II might not have been won by the democracies. With superb skill and control, he had curbed jealous and arrogant generals, calmed squabbling politicians, soothed xenophobic and suspicious Allies, and, at the same time, tirelessly fostered the strategies that had defeated the mighty German and Japanese war machines. Even the haughty chiefs of the U.S. Navy had saluted Marshall's soldierly qualities.

"I simply thank God for you from the bottom of my heart," one admiral wrote in 1945. "I don't know how we would have gotten along without you."

Most citizens who had endured the rigors of war at home and most soldiers who had borne the brunt of the battles overseas would have been inclined to endorse those words. Though the full story of his wartime administration had yet to be released, it was rightly suspected that his contribution to victory had been even greater than the official bulletins had suggested. He was a genuinely self-effacing man who had never tried to steal the limelight from the generals who had served under him. Yet as Chief of Staff of the U.S. Army he could hardly have avoided becoming a public figure. Every crisis of World War II, with its concomitant Big Four conferences, confabulations at the White House, and appearances in front of congressional committees, had inevitably put him into the headlines. Somehow the feeling had gotten around that he was a new kind of warrior, a global strategist of genius, in whose judgment, skill, and probity America and its allies could place their trust.

Once the war was won, therefore, no one had expected Marshall to fade away. There had been a movement around the country to sponsor him as a presidential candidate in the next election, and a lot of well-meaning people had been surprised (and a little hurt) when he had quashed such a suggestion in crisp and definitive terms. It was presumed he would probably write his memoirs, as many another general and admiral were already doing. But Marshall pointed out to those colleagues who urged him to do so that he would have to tell the truth as he had experienced it and that therefore, some wartime scandals and controversies would inevitably surface, to the detriment of the statesmen and generals with whom he had had to deal. Such controversies would garner all the headlines when the book came to be reviewed, and that was the last thing he wanted to see. Therefore, though he was not by any means a rich man, he rebuffed all offers.

Nor was he fooling about his resignation. When President Truman asked him to reconsider, he refused. He was not interested in staying on. He and his wife, Katherine, he told the President, had bought an old colonial mansion, Dodona Manor, at Leesburg, Virginia, and it was to this haven that he proposed to retreat—and literally cultivate his garden. He did not wish to consider any other offers.

It took him some time, but Truman finally accepted Marshall's decision. All Truman asked was that he stay on in office until the fall, to give General Eisenhower time to clear things up in Europe before returning to become the new Chief of Staff. To this, though exhausted in body, mind, and spirit from his wartime exertions, Marshall finally agreed. He waited impatiently for the summer to end and his time of departure to come around.

In November 1945 the President held a ceremony at the White House. It was to bid farewell to his Chief of Staff and to pin on his uniform an oak leaf cluster to his Distinguished Service Medal. The President himself read out the citation:

> In a war unparalleled in magnitude and in horror, millions of Americans gave their country outstanding service. General of the Army George C. Marshall gave it victory. . . . His standards of character, conduct and efficiency inspired the entire Army, the Na-

tion and the world. To him, as much as to any individual, the United States owes its future. He takes his place at the head of the greatest commanders of the world.

When the ceremony was over, the President drew Marshall to one side. He wished him a long, happy life in the comfort and ease of his retirement, and added that he was making him a promise: "General, you have done so much for your country, I will never disturb you in your retirement. You have earned your rest."

That was on November 26, 1945. A few days later there was a political crisis. The ambassador to China, a political general named Patrick J. Hurley, had returned home for consultation with the President. After paying his respects at the White House, he went on to an engagement at the National Press Club, where, in an excess of Irish exuberance, he proceeded to criticize the administration's policy on China and make some indiscreet remarks about Truman.

"These really got my dander up," the President said later, adding, "He made a terrible statement about my inability to run things. So I fired him."

But as a result, the President had a crisis on his hands. Hurley had powerful friends in the Congress and in the Republican party. He could raise a fuss over his abrupt dismissal. In addition, his departure left an awkward vacuum in China, where trouble was brewing that threatened peace in the Pacific. Therefore, Hurley had to be replaced without delay.

Who was big enough, popular and prestigious enough, to take the political heat off in Washington and at the same time bring new hope of a solution to the troubles in China? There was only one man, and Truman knew it. He did not hesitate. Ignoring his earlier promise, he picked up the telephone and called General Marshall.

"General," said the President, "I told you last week that I would never interrupt your retirement. I don't like to interrupt you now, but it is urgent."

Truman reminded Marshall that the situation in the Far East was crumbling and a disastrous civil war was spreading through

China. Only the firm intervention of the United States could bring it to a halt and prevent a dreadful tragedy.

"Will you go to China for me?" he asked.

It so happened that George and Katherine Marshall had moved into their new home at Dodona Manor that very afternoon. The general and his wife were in their bedroom, unpacking their clothes.

There was a long pause after the President asked his question. What he did not know was that Marshall was looking across the bedroom at his wife, who was gazing through the window at the gardens spread beneath her, a smile of great contentment and satisfaction on her face. His instinct was to say a curt "No!" and hang up. Yet this was the President of his country speaking, his Commander in Chief, and he was a soldier who had spent a lifetime obeying orders. There was an unspoken appeal to his patriotism in Truman's voice, and it was a call that was instinctive and irresistible to him. Yet what was he going to say to Katherine if he obeyed his instincts? He looked at her again and just could not bear to tell her—not yet anyway—what the President was asking of him.

"Are you there, General?" asked the President again. His tone was pressing. "Will you go to China for me?"

"Yes, Mr. President," Marshall said, and quietly put down the telephone.

A few moments later Katherine Marshall came away from the window and put on the portable radio by the bed. An announcer came on the air with a special bulletin: It had just been announced from the White House that General of the Army George Marshall was going to China as the President's special ambassador.

Katherine Marshall turned around to look at her husband, standing in the shadows.

"Oh, George," she said, "how *could* you?"

I

The Road to the Top

1

A Disgrace to the Family?

When George Marshall was a boy in Uniontown, Pennsylvania, his biggest ambition was to own a dog. His parents always refused him. One of his father's uncles had been bitten in the leg by a hunting dog and had died in agony from rabies, and the description of his death throes had become a family horror story.

So the boy lavished his affections, instead, on a scrub-haired terrier owned by a schoolmate, who despised the dog because he was disobedient, scared of fights with bigger dogs, and apt to howl loudly whenever he was beaten, as was frequent. Young Marshall would sneak the dog out of his schoolmate's yard and take him on long walks through the countryside; he taught him to swim in the local streams, nose out rabbits from their lairs, and flush quail, bobwhites, and wild turkeys. They became such good companions that whenever his schoolmate came around to complain that his dog was missing, all Marshall needed to do was whistle, and Trip, as the terrier was called, would appear from the hiding place where he had been watching.

Years later, when Marshall left Uniontown, leaving Trip behind was the most painful wrench of his departure. While he was away for one period of several years, he learned that his schoolmate had died, and on his next visit to Uniontown he went around ostensibly to sympathize with his friend's mother, but secretly to find out what had happened to Trip. He was delighted to find Trip, a very old terrier now, lying out in the yard in the sun. But when he called to him, the dog paid him no attention, didn't even bark, but just gazed at him with blank indifference.

"That was quite a blow to me," said Marshall later, "because Trip was one of the companions of my youth. So I sat down on this long flagstone that was around the pump and succeeded in petting him, although he rather resented it."

He talked to him for a long time, anxious to stir some memory in the old dog's mind, distressed that he was not remembered at all. "After, I suppose, five or ten minutes," he said, "he took a careful sniff of me, then he sniffed at me two or three times, and then he just went crazy. He had finally gotten a scent in his old nostrils and he remembered me. That was the most flattering thing that occurred to me on that short visit home after many years of not being there."

Uniontown was the place where George Catlett Marshall was born, on December 31, 1880, but except for Trip, its memories were not exactly sentimental. The youngest of three children,* he was four years the junior of his sister, Marie, and six years younger than the elder son, Stuart Bradford Marshall. Neither brother nor sister appears to have welcomed the addition to their family circle. Marie, a bright, selfish, noisy child, was always in a temper over her small brother. Stuart was his father's favorite son and very jealous of it, never hesitant about cashing in on paternal indulgence. It might have been easier for George if he had been able to outshine either of them. But sad to relate, as a child he was a slow learner.

George Catlett Marshall, Sr., and his wife, Laura, had been married for slightly more than seven years when their younger son was born. They had first met as teenagers in Augusta, Kentucky, a small town on the Ohio River some fifty miles from Cincinnati. The time was the Civil War, and they had shared a traumatic experience which appears to have cemented their feeling for each other. Both their families were living in Augusta at the time, and so far as the War Between the States was concerned, it was a divided town, and they were on opposite sides. Laura's father, Dr. Jonathan Bradford, was, like the rest of his family, a fervent abolitionist with no sympathy at all for the southern cause. The Marshalls, on the other hand, already had two sons fighting with the Confederate Army. There was a great gulf between the two fam-

---

*There had been a fourth, the Marshalls' firstborn, but he had died at the age of six months.

ilies, and they did not mix. Nevertheless, both sides were agreed on one thing. They must try to keep Augusta and its citizens from becoming involved in the war. So when the Bradfords persuaded the Augusta City Council to raise a town militia pledged to protect them from attack and keep them neutral, George Catlett Marshall, Sr., then only sixteen years old, volunteered to carry a rifle. Laura Bradford, who was fourteen, joined the older women in running messages, learning to load rifles, and getting bandages ready for the wounded. Not that fighting was expected. It was true that two Federal gunboats had sailed down the Ohio River and tied up at the wharves in Augusta, to block any Confederate attempt to ford the river and threaten Cincinnati, but the Augustans convinced themselves that their presence would deter rather than invite conflict, especially since the boats carried formidable twelve-pounder cannons.

But in September 1862, as part of the southern attempt to drive the North out of Kentucky, Confederate General Edmund Kirby Smith detailed Colonel Basil Duke to take 450 cavalry and some light artillery and occupy Augusta, cross the Ohio, and threaten Cincinnati. When the detachment reached a hill overlooking the town on September 27, they observed the Federal gunboats in the river and positioned howitzers, ready to open fire. Dr. Bradford, apprized of this move, rushed down to the captains of the gunboats and urged them to destroy the Confederate artillery before they could do any damage. The northern captains had no intention of doing any such thing. Instead, they fled to safety, and the southerners rode triumphantly into the town. Bradford, realizing he was heavily outnumbered, at once raised the white flag to surrender Augusta to the Confederacy. But by an oversight he neglected to inform his militiamen that he was surrendering, and they had hidden themselves in the houses and stores along Augusta's Main Street, guns cocked and ready. When the cavalry trotted into the town and reached Main Street, the militia opened fire. Young Marshall, Sr., was among them. A tragic, unnecessary skirmish followed during which 21 Confederate soldiers were killed and 18 wounded. The town militia suffered 7 killed and 15 wounded when Colonel Duke ordered up artillery to blast them out. Enraged by the useless slaughter, the Confederates were all for shooting every man and boy in the town. Duke decided otherwise, but to mollify his soldiers, he allowed them to take away 100 militiamen as hostages.

Among them was Marshall, Sr., the youngest rifleman of them all. The last sight he saw as he marched away was the tearful face of Laura Bradford, hand raised to wave good-bye to him. He was back in town a few weeks later, but it took him another ten years to overcome the snobbish reluctance of the Bradfords to accept him as a son-in-law. It was not until 1873 that he and Laura were married.

By the time their youngest child, George, was born the Marshalls were prospering. Marshall, Sr., had become president of a coke and furnace company and owned tracts of rich coal lands in Pennsylvania. They had moved to Uniontown, and he became a popular member of the local Democratic party. Everyone liked him. Only his younger son knew that his father possessed a fiery temper and was a firm believer in corporal punishment for recalcitrant small boys. There was a long willow stick in the basement of the family home, and young George came to feel its stinging bite on his bottom only too often. But though his father did not believe in sparing the rod, George noticed that never once was Stuart beaten in similar fashion, and he came to the conclusion that his older brother was either a paragon, which he was certainly not, or the favored son who was allowed to get away with it.

Admittedly young Marshall merited the punishment he frequently suffered. He stoutly insisted in later life that his father never beat him undeservedly. On the other hand, he resented the fact that Stuart so frequently got off scot-free for behavior which, in his own case, would have brought on a beating so severe that he would not have been able to sit down for days. "But maybe that was because Stuart was smarter," he said later.

"Smart" was the one word Marshall would never have used about himself. In his first years at Miss Thompson's prep school in Uniontown, he discovered that learning did not come easily. For one reason or another, he lacked a sense of application, and when, time and again, he emerged from tests toward the bottom of his class, he was mortified and ashamed. He confessed later that he decided early on that he was destined to be "one of the dull ones," as he put it. He made up his mind about this when he was nine years old and was taken by his father to see the head of the Uniontown public school, to which an application had been made for his transfer from Miss Thompson's establishment. In his father's presence he was given an oral test and abysmally failed to answer most of the "rather simple questions." He remembered that his father "suffered very severely" from this public exhibition of his son's ignorance and made it plain that he was ashamed to have such a dolt in the family. This hurt young George deeply. But having decided that he was not the learning type and that no amount of effort would improve his mental capabilities, he made up his mind that there was only one way to avoid the bitter disappointment of future failure, and that was not to try and, moreover, to demonstrate that he just did not care. And beware anyone who dared laugh at him and suggest that he didn't try because he couldn't.

His sister, Marie, discovered the danger of mocking his failure in school. She made the mistake of calling him the "dunce of the class" and found a frog in her bed the next night when she turned back the sheets. He also climbed to the roof of the house and dropped water bombs on Marie's beaux when they came to visit her. Once, when she was giving a party for her girl friends and persuaded her mother to keep her brother out of the house, he went into a wood nearby, stirred up a wasps' nest until the infuriated wasps chased him across the field and into the yard, then dashed into the house with the insects in hot pursuit. At the open door of the parlor where the party was taking place, he swerved neatly and disappeared into a closet. The wasps went on and took it out on Marie's friends.

He got a severe beating for that, but it didn't stop him. His persecution of his sister did not cease until the day when he waited by the front door of the house with a garden hose in his hand, waiting for the moment when Marie appeared through the door in her party dress. His mother came out instead and got the full frontal jet. Laura Marshall forgave him, of course; she adored her

7

younger son and lavished on him all the affection he failed to get from his father. But his brother, Stuart, did not fail to report the incident to George Catlett, Sr., and it was down to the cellar again.

Meanwhile, the sorry school record continued, and the boy was beginning to get a reputation as something of a scallywag as well as a layabout.

His mother always forgave her younger son when he got into a scrape and tried her best to keep his transgressions from the knowledge of her husband, knowing what steps he would take to curb his wayward son. She even connived to protect him when he started breeding game cocks and, having entered one of his birds in an illegal cockfight, had to hide out after a raid by the police. She never reprimanded him, seeming to sense that he learned a lesson from each misadventure and was not likely to repeat a foolish misdemeanor. But she could not always keep young Marshall's transgressions quiet, with the result that the seats of her younger son's pants were only too often in need of patching, and not because he wore them out from sitting around. One of his severest beatings came not simply because his father was mad at him but because a lot of local mothers joined in demanding his punishment, and that happened when some of the local girls dared to laugh at him.

Running near the Marshall house was a small tributary of the Ohio known locally as Coal Lick Run, and if you could get across it without taking the long way around by the bridge, it saved quite a distance in the morning walk to school. George Marshall tried to build a raft to cross the shallow stream but couldn't find the right kind of wood, and a local shopkeeper came up with a flat-bottomed boat which he presented to the lad. Thenceforth young Marshall set himself up as a ferryman and charged pennies—or sometimes pins—for the fare across the stream, printing his own tickets and punching them with his mother's laundry stamper. Most of his passengers were local schoolgirls, who regularly, if reluctantly, paid their fares for the journey. But one day they apparently ran out of pennies and, when he demanded their fares, tried to bluff him into allowing them across, jeering at him and mocking his poor scholastic record when he insisted he be paid.

"I was terribly humiliated," Marshall said in later years, "and what made it worse, my chum Andy began laughing at me. And there I was—the girls in the flatboat all jeering at me and my engineer and boon companion laughing at me and I was stuck. Just then my eye fastened on a cork in the floor of the boat which was utilized in draining it. With the inspiration of the moment I pulled the cork, and under the pressure of the weight of the passengers a stream of water shot up in the air. All the girls screamed, and I sank the boat in the middle of the stream. They all had to wade ashore. I never forgot that because I had to do something and I had to think quickly. What I did set me up again as the temporary master of the situation."

When the girls straggled home in their soaked and mud-stained dresses, a cry of anger rose up among the mothers around Coal Lick Run. Useless for him to point out that their darling daughters were never in any danger and that he knew to an inch the shallowness of the water. His father marched him down to the basement and this time told him to drop his pants, and George Marshall resolved, after that painful experience, never to make a fool of a female again.

But nothing seemed to goad him into doing better at school, and this infuriated his already impatient father. George Catlett, Sr.'s, only encounter with the armed forces had, as we have seen, been catastrophic, but instead of disenchanting him, it had proved to be the highlight of his life, about which he never ceased to reminisce. He was sadly regretful that the only military action he had seen during the Civil War was that single day's massacre in the streets of Augusta, and his ambition was to see one of his sons become what he had never been allowed to—an officer in the United States Army. At first his elder son and the apple of his eye, Stuart, had looked as if he would fulfill his father's dream. He had been accepted as a cadet at the Virginia Military Institute in Lexington, Virginia, and had done well at that venerable old college. But when he reached his final year, it became apparent that Stuart's ambitions were more scientific than martial, and he had concentrated his efforts on the chemical and physics courses in which VMI also specialized. When he was graduated, he left the parade ground for good and joined a big local ironworks as a chemist. Disappointed, his father turned regretfully toward his younger son.

But what earthly hope was there of getting this feckless lad into a decent military school? And then it came about that Marshall's own ambitions were fired, and suddenly he could not rest until he persuaded his parents to send him to his brother's alma mater, VMI. It was not so much a sudden love affair with the Army that galvanized him, nor even the thought of himself strutting around in uniform. His ambition was much meaner than that, as he later admitted. It was simply a burning determination to put one over on his sneering, superior, and hypercritical elder brother. For one day, after Stuart had heard his parents talking about sending George to VMI, he burst out with objections. What? Send that worthless shaver to his old college? Not if he could help it! He rushed to talk to his mother, and Marshall overheard them.

"He was trying to persuade her not to let me go [to VMI]," Marshall said later, "because he thought I would disgrace the family name. Well, that made more impression on me than all the instructors, parental pressure, or anything else. I decided then and there that I was going to wipe his eye."

He had found the goad at last, and even while admitting that it was not a very worthy one, Marshall recognized it as the spur that changed his whole attitude toward life. He did not, of course, blossom immediately afterward into a scholar or a genius nor become the brightest student in his class. But his brother's gibes made him resolve never to take the easy way out again and never to refuse a challenge. And at the end of a life in which he had wrestled successfully with problems concerning the fate of the world, it was probably this which gave him the greatest sense of achievement, of being able to say, "I did finally get ahead of what my brother had done. That was the first time I had ever done that, and it was where I learned my lesson. The urgency to succeed came from hearing that conversation."

He enrolled at VMI in September 1897, still only sixteen, and shortly afterward learned another lesson—at the end of a bayonet.

The Virginia Military Institute sits on a hill overlooking the friendly old red-brick town of Lexington, amid some of the softest and pleasantest countryside in the nation. At the crossroads of U.S. 11 and U.S. 60, its valleys unfold south toward the Smokies, north to the verdant banks of the mighty Shenandoah, west to the pine-clad slopes and bubbling hot springs of the West Virginia spa country, and east across the Blue Ridge Mountains to the sea. It is a land of browsing cattle and prosperous farms, where even today the air is clear of all but wood smoke, and rarely is the vapor trail of an airplane to be seen in the sky.

Lexington came off lightly in the Civil War, and few of its precious old buildings were damaged. But when northern troops under General David Hunter occupied the town in 1864, they proceeded up the hill and turned their cannons on the main buildings of the VMI, burning them to the ground. It was not necessary for military reasons, so perhaps it was an act of revenge for the part the cadets had played in the Battle of New Market. There 450 cadets, in what came to be known as the Baby Battalion, fought side by side with the soldiers of General J. D. Imboden and turned back northern troops attacking across the Shenandoah. They took 100 prisoners but lost 10 cadets killed, whose deaths were commemorated every year at a ceremonial on the VMI parade ground. Marshall, like his fellow cadets, had a constant reminder of them in the unstitched, unhemmed lower half of his uniform jacket, symbolizing the uniform cloth the cadets had torn up at New Market to make bandages for their wounded.

Unlike West Point, VMI gave no guarantee to its graduates that they would automatically be officers in the U.S. Army. To northern eyes, the school seemed to be living on its Confederate past, hero-worshiping its old instructor Stonewall Jackson (who

11

is buried in the town) and the South's greatest general, Robert E. Lee (who had become president of the adjacent university, Washington and Lee). Thus, VMI could only strive to make its graduates worthy of selection by turning them into better potential soldiers than West Point could graduate. And to do that, its superintendent, General Scott Shipp (a Civil War veteran himself), insisted on unending toil, ceaseless application, and rigid discipline. Compared with the duties expected of a VMI cadet, life at West Point was effete. Term lasted from September to June without a break save for Christmas Day, New Year's Day, Washington's Birthday, and the commemoration of the Battle of New Market.

A cadet's day started with reveille at first light and ended long after dusk. Saturday afternoon was free for visits to Lexington, but only into that area in the vicinity of the institute; downtown, where the taverns were, was out of bounds. Sunday, once church parade was over, was a day free to roam the countryside, climb trees, practice woodlore, swim in the rocky mountain streams, but Lexington itself was forbidden territory. Life was not only tightly disciplined but uncomfortably austere, particularly since living quarters for the cadets were still being rebuilt after the depredations of Hunter's men. There was no running water in the buildings, it had to be fetched from faucets in the yard; lavatories were of the old nonflush variety, and one of the penances freshmen had to face was the noisome task of cleaning them out. The new cadets were known as "rats" to the seniors, who ran them ragged. They were forced to sleep with their windows wide open even in bitter Virginia winters, and snow was sometimes piled on their cots when they woke up in the morning. The staple food was a notorious dish called growlie, a hash of suspicious origin which earned its name for its effect on youthful stomachs. Both by instructors and by seniors, punishments were freely given for the lightest infraction of the rules. A rat never had any time of his own because he was endlessly engaged in drills, exercises, running errands, in addition to which he was frequently subjected to that specialty of U.S. academic institutions, hazing. Because it was a military establishment and therefore proud of its toughness, VMI's form of hazing could be unpleasant.

George Marshall was late in enrolling at VMI because, a few weeks before the year started, he came down with a bout of typhoid, which, though much less rare a disease in those days, was serious in its potential consequences. He was quite ill, and it was not until a week after the other cadets had been enrolled that Marshall arrived, still pale, weak, and convalescent. He never complained about it later, but his first few weeks at VMI must have been one of the nastier periods of his life. Almost immediately his accent attracted the attention of the seniors, who complained of being offended by his "appalling Pittsburgh twang" and dubbed him the "Yankee rat." He was heaped with unpleasant and arduous chores, and he admitted later that he scrubbed more toilets in his first month at VMI "than a cleaning lady did in a lifetime." He stood up to it with patient, if hardly cheerful, fortitude, helped, no doubt, by the dire warnings his brother had given him beforehand of what he would have to endure. It did not occur to him to rebel against it or ask for quarter on account of his physical condition. As he said later, "I think I was more philosophical about this sort of thing than a great many boys. It was part of the business, and the only thing to do was accept it as best you could."

But then came the moment when he had to measure up to the worst test, calling for extra endurance, to which the rats were subjected by their seniors, especially those who didn't measure up or fit in—as Marshall, with his Yankee accent, didn't. This was the bayonet test. A bayonet blade was planted point-up in the floor, and the rat to be tested was forced to squat naked over it for ten minutes, being prevented from moving out of the blade's way and knowing what would happen to him if and when he collapsed. The senior cadets did not seem to be aware that Marshall was still weak from his bout with typhoid, and he certainly did not mention it to them. The result was that after a couple of minutes he crumpled and collapsed on the point of the bayonet. He was hastily pulled free and lay on the floor, pumping blood. Finally, he was taken down to the medical officer, Dr. Young, who cleaned up the wound in his groin and sewed it up. In his weekly bulletin for September 29, 1897, Young noted that he had

13

treated Cadet Marshall for what he called "a buttock wound." And it was as a stab in that part of his anatomy that Marshall always referred to it in later years, but he did add, "I had a very narrow escape from serious injury." It may have been narrower than he thought.

The senior cadets waited with some apprehension for Marshall's explanation to the medical officer of how he had come by his unusual wound, but to everyone's satisfaction and approval, he said not a word. He hobbled painfully around the parade ground for some days, and the instructors, who were (albeit unofficially) aware of what had happened, went easy on him until he had recovered from both his wound and his illness. By that time, like some tribal aspirant, he found that he had emerged from the ordeal of initiation with flying colors. If he was not yet a fully fledged warrior, he was at least regarded by his peers as a full-fledged cadet. He had no more trouble. He had won his spurs. And as one of his ex-classmates put it later, "The way he kept a stiff upper lip about what we all knew was a very stiff upper leg got him good marks from everybody. By the time that episode was over nobody cared about his accent. He could have talked double Dutch and they'd have accepted it. He was in."

He finished his first year at VMI as first corporal of cadets and two years later was named captain of the institute, taking command of the assembled cadets at all the big ceremonials, including Washington's Birthday and the New Market Commemoration. On these occasions he discovered he had a voice which must have been the envy of many a top sergeant because when he raised it to shout a command, the resonant tones seemed to carry for miles and bounce back off the surrounding hills. At the same time he discovered one of the great pleasures of soldiering: the thrill of actually commanding men and seeing them move, march, and drill exactly according to his orders. He found himself, whether in command or not, relishing the solid slog, the backbreaking routine, the painful effort of parade ground drill. And in his case it had been, literally, painful. Among the other physical disadvantages with which he had come to VMI was a torn ligament in his right arm which he had ripped in a game of football. He had refused to see a doctor about it despite the fact that each time he raised his arm or was jostled by someone, an excruciatingly agonizing pain shot through his whole body. Life for a cadet at any military college is one long succession of saluting one's superiors, and since Marshall could not lift his arm above his elbow without wincing, his first two years at VMI (which was as long as the injured ligament took to heal) must have been a continuous torture. But no one would have guessed it from watching him. He never dodged a salute. On the parade ground he was grim-faced but proudly efficient, getting the best out of his well-disciplined cadets as they drilled and wheeled in the sunlight. His instructors came out to watch him and regarded his adeptness with approval.

So did one nonmilitary spectator. Whether by coincidence or not, it was often when Marshall was taking drill on the VMI parade ground that a pony and trap would pass along the perimeter road, and up in the driver's seat, a whip held in her hand, face flushed and eyes sparkling, was an extremely pretty young woman.

Her name was Elizabeth Coles Carter, and she lived with her widowed mother in the family house on the edge of the VMI campus. Lily Carter was mad about young men in uniform, and very soon afterward George Marshall was mad about her.

2

Shavetail

There were a number of remarkably attractive and talented women who figured in George Marshall's later life—they included a couple of British duchesses, a famous Chinese beauty, and a reigning European queen—but none of them, not even his beloved second wife, had quite the impact on his heart as Lily Carter of Lexington. She was his first grown-up love, and his devotion to her lasted through her lifetime and beyond, though she was a burden to him from the day of her marriage.

Lily Carter had a reputation among the cadets at VMI and among the matrons in Lexington as a tease and a flirt. She was ravishingly pretty, with rose-red cheeks and vivid violet-blue eyes, and as someone who knew her in later life said, "When she smiled at you, your defenses crumbled. Young men thought her something special."

Lily was four years older than First Captain of Cadets George C. Marshall, and he was by no means the first young man at VMI with whom she had had a flirtation. One of her most serious beaux, in fact, though Marshall didn't know about it until later, had been his elder brother, Stuart. Stuart had paid assiduous court to her in his last two years at VMI, acted as her escort at a number of college dances, and even asked her to marry him in his final year. She had turned him down. Since he had a large opinion of himself, this had been a considerable affront to Stuart's pride, and he did not forgive her for his rejection.

His decision not to have anything more to do with her certainly did not seem to cause Lily any particular concern. She was so attractive that not only did most senior cadets moon over her when she passed by, but several eligible members of the faculty got dreamy over her, too. And since she was a cool, self-confident beauty, and an elegant one as well, there is little doubt that they would have come running at the snap of her shapely fingers. But the truth was, Lily was looking for someone special. The qualities in a husband-to-be for which she was searching were not quite those which the run-of-the-mill students at VMI possessed. On the other hand, she had watched George Marshall show off his leadership qualities on the VMI parade ground. In her mother's salon, where members of the VMI staff were often entertained, she had heard gossip about his behavior under hazing, his fortitude, his quiet acceptance of ordeal by pain, and though he was certainly not the only cadet who was talked about, he was the one toward whose activities and exploits she cocked a delicate ear.

It was by no means unusual in those days for a young lady to perform charmingly on the piano, but it so happened that Lily played excellently and with innate good taste and discrimination. She must have felt she knew exactly what was likely to capture the untutored ear of this handsome young captain of cadets, and when he and a group of classmates took a stroll one evening past her house at the end of a long VMI day, it was the strains of a Chopin nocturne which floated through the open window on the soft evening air. The next night, when he walked by alone, she was singing a little something by Heine, self-accompanied, of course. By the end of the week he was coming by every evening, and her cattier critics in Lexington afterward whispered that she must have been getting toward the end of her repertoire. At any rate, the music stopped, the front door opened, and dimpling, the young lady asked him whether he would like to join her inside. He went in entranced and came out besotted.

As some observers have pointed out, the regimen at VMI was not designed for a young man in love. "Even the comparative privileges of a first classman who was first captain to boot," one of them has written, "did not provide nearly enough liberty. To be sure, Lily was close by: Marshall could see her often, driving her 'little horse and Stanhope trap' along the parade ground."

She sometimes invited him to drive with her, and he joyfully accepted and proudly took the reins from her when they reached the grounds where the less fortunate cadets were drilling. "But that was not often enough. And so the austere young first captain took to 'running the block,' or, in plain English, ducking out of the Institute after hours. The maneuver was apparently not too difficult, but the penalty for being caught would certainly have been loss of his cadet rank and possibly even expulsion."

He admitted as much years later and, when asked why he had taken such a risk, voiced the only defense he had: "I was in love."

He was not caught—except by Lily. From the first time he walked by her house and she went over to the piano, she had known unerringly that here was the man she wanted—and needed.

"That is the man I am going to marry," she had told her mother as she sat down to play the opening bars of the Chopin nocturne.

By the time graduation arrived at VMI, the young couple had reached an understanding. George Marshall had come in eighth in his class, which was much higher than he had dared to hope (but, as he said later, "by that time ambition had set in"), and he was eager to embark on an Army career. Lily had made it plain that she was willing to share it with him. He had proposed, and she had accepted. They would marry the moment he received his commission in the U.S. Army. In the meantime, they considered themselves secretly engaged.

George Marshall went back home to Uniontown to tell his father and mother the good news and urged them to rally their Democratic friends and campaign to get him his commission. Marshall, Sr., checked with General Shipp, the superintendent at VMI, and was told that he had already written to President McKinley recommending a commission for Cadet Marshall. Shipp assured his father that "if commissioned in the Army, young Marshall will in all respects soon take his stand much above the average West Point graduate." Marshall, Sr., thereupon set about pulling strings among his party cronies and began writing congressmen in Washington.

In the meantime, he questioned his son about the rumors he had heard. What was all this about a girl in Lexington and a secret engagement? His son told him all about Lily Carter.

As ill luck would have it, his elder brother, Stuart, happened to be in the room when he broke the news about Lily. Marshall would never afterward say exactly what remarks Stuart made when he learned that his little brother had corralled the belle of VMI. They were certainly not complimentary, and Marshall's anger was such that he never forgave Stuart for them. He also refused to talk about his brother from that day on. The only person who ever succeeded in persuading him to break his silence was, many years later, his goddaughter, Rose Page Wilson, of whom he became extremely fond. One day she plucked up enough courage to ask him about his relations with Stuart. She wrote later:

> I had heard a lot of rumors of the falling out between the two, and so one day I asked Colonel Marshall: "Is it true that you and your brother got mad at each other because he was in love with Lily too, and you won out?" "Certainly not," he answered coldly. "You know perfectly well we were never congenial, and that Stewart [sic] opposed everything that I wanted to do, including my marriage to Lily. It had absolutely nothing to do with him. I've told you before that I was too young and too poor to marry. And when he made unkind, unfair remarks about Lily, I cut him off my list." He never mentioned his brother again.

Nor did he ever mention to Lily that Stuart had made "unkind" and "unfair" remarks about her.

In the meantime, his father's friends had done their best for him by bombarding the War Department with letters recommending his son. One recommendation came from the president of VMI itself: John Wise, the son of the governor of Virginia, who wrote to Major General John R. Brooke, commanding the U.S. Army, Eastern District, commending Marshall and adding, "General Shipp regards him as one of the fittest pieces of food for gunpowder turned out by this mill for many years."

Cadet Marshall was called to New York to sit for his examination for a commission in September 1901 and romped through the test. But by an oversight it was not until the end of that year, when he reached the age of twenty-one, that he was informed that he had passed, an agonizing and unnecessary wait of nearly three months. He took the oath as a second lieutenant in the United States Army on February 3, 1902, before a notary public in Uniontown. Five days later he received notice that he was being posted to the Philippine Islands, where he would join the command of General Arthur MacArthur and help put down the national insurrection, still simmering in the Philippine jungles after years of guerrilla warfare. He was due to report to Fort Myer, near Washington, on February 13, meaning that he had four days left in which to get married.

The ceremony took place on the evening of February 11, 1902, in the same room in the Carter family home in Lexington from which Lily had played her siren music. The bride was all in white but seemed calm, composed, and content, local guests afterward said, and much less nervous than the bridegroom. Her brother, Edmund, gave her away, and Andy Thompson, an old friend of George's from Uniontown, was best man. Marshall, Sr., and his wife were there, of course, but so was an unsmiling Stuart Marshall. Since Marshall had carefully not mentioned his brother's rudeness toward her, Lily was not at all discomposed, and the bridegroom recognized it as a moment to forget family feuds and treated his brother as if nothing unpleasant had ever passed between them.

The next day the young couple left by train for a honeymoon at the New Willard Hotel in Washington, D.C., where they were given the news that in view of the marriage, Marshall's leave was being extended for another five days. As it turned out, this was not the good news it at first appeared. For on the first night of their honeymoon Lily had given her new husband something of a shock. He had always known she was a delicate girl, forbidden by her doctors to undertake any strenuous exercise. She had not even been allowed to dance at college parties. At the time she had told him this was only a temporary condition brought on, she said, by too much "social activity" in the years before he had met her.

But now she told him the truth. She explained that she was

suffering from a heart condition known as mitral insufficiency, which, when he looked it up in the medical dictionary, he found was "an abnormal closure of the mitral valve resulting in regurgitation of blood into the atrium and leading to heart failure." She could never risk having children, and she would have to be treated as a semi-invalid.

In the circumstances, it was perhaps as well that the newlywed lieutenant was leaving his wife behind while he served overseas. But the extra five days' leave could hardly have been anything but dreadfully difficult since it was both too agonizingly short and too painfully long for a young man desperately in love with his beautiful new bride to adapt to this unexpected marital situation. But if Lily had had her special reasons for choosing Marshall as the man she had decided to marry, he more than justified the unerring percipience of her decision. For he said not one word to anyone about the appalling emotional blow which had been dealt him on his first night of his honeymoon, nor did he show any sign of being less devoted—or less in love—with Lily because of the prospect with which she had confronted him.

He was due to sail on the troopship *Kilpatrick* from San Francisco on April 12, 1902, for a two-year hitch in the Philippines. Lily said good-bye to him in Washington, and it was fond and affectionate on both their parts. Then she went back to her mother, and her piano, in Lexington, Virginia.

This is no place to go into the history of the U.S. occupation of the Philippines, except for the effect it had in shaping Marshall's character and military career. The United States had taken over the islands as one of the prizes won in the Spanish-American War and had soon discovered that being in the colonial business has its liabilities as well as its rewards. Many of the American administrators who had flocked to Manila, eager to bring the benefits of Yankee civilization to the backward Filipinos, were discovering that the natives were by no means pleased by this flood of alien knowhow. Not, at least, as long as it was the aliens who administered it and ruled their lives. As the British had long ago discovered, foreign rulers, no matter how enlightened they endeavor to

21

be, are not loved. In Balfour's words, "people, alas, seem to prefer self-government to good government."

The result was that the United States soon had a national insurrection on its hands. Under the ruthless command of General Arthur MacArthur, whose son would one day fight on the same soil against very different enemies, the U.S. Army appeared to have crushed the rebels. The best known of their leaders, in fact, surrendered while Marshall was still aboard ship in the Pacific, and President Theodore Roosevelt officially proclaimed peace on July 6, 1902, a few weeks before the young lieutenant landed in Manila. Actually, however, sporadic guerrilla warfare continued and went on both during his hitch and long after.

"Peace" of a sort was maintained by the U.S. army of occupation, which, while reduced from an original force of 70,000 men, still numbered 35,000, and if the Americans had originally landed with symbolic olive branches in their hands and received symbolic hibiscus blossoms in return from the smiling natives, now there were scowls all around and rancor and hatred on both sides. From the moment he landed, Marshall was met by tales from his fellow Americans of the savagery, treachery, and cunning of the Filipinos and of the "necessary" reprisals which had to be taken to keep them in check. "I distinctly remember one officer reporting that he had three men wounded in an encounter, and he had burned the town down," he said later.

One or two of his fellow officers were surprised and not a little indignant when he characterized the troops as being just as bad as the guerrillas. Near Manila a cathedral containing a precious religious library was burned down in reprisal for guerrilla attacks, and some of the troops, dressed in stolen priests' robes, danced outside, brandishing silver from the chancel. To the indignation of his immediate superior, Marshall expressed the opinion that they should be arrested and court-martialed.

He agreed that "it showed how men are likely to get out of hand when they are on their own in critical situations" but thought they ought to be made an example of. Active service, he told a fellow officer, was a dangerous situation in which to countenance emotional and hysterical behavior. This officer, Captain (later

General) Walter Krueger, was astounded at the cool, calm, impartial composure of the young lieutenant.

"He was neither shocked at what we considered the brutality and thoughtless cruelty committed against American troops by the Filipinos," said Krueger later, "nor was he appalled that his fellow Americans could be equally ruthless and destructive. It was the way people behaved under stress. In crisis situations, so-called civilized Americans and ignorant jungle warriors acted in exactly the same way. There was only one way to control them. Strict discipline and example."

He once said to Krueger, "Once an army is involved in war, there is a beast in every fighting man which begins tugging at its chains, and a good officer must learn early on how to keep the beast under control, both in his men and himself."

Krueger added, "It was a remarkable statement to come from such a youngster. U.S. officers didn't think like that in those days, and if they did, they certainly didn't talk about it. He was just about the most self-contained lieutenant I ever met in the U.S. Army. There he was, all of twenty-two years old, and he made us senior officers feel like kids. Yet he wasn't a prig. He mixed in with everybody. At concerts he was right in there, laughing at the crude jokes, joining in the singsongs. But somehow you got the feeling he'd been through things we hadn't even experienced, not even those of us who'd fought in the jungle. He had a sagacity and thoughtfulness far beyond his years. Or at least I think he had. When you really tried to find out what he was like, he clammed up, and you never discovered what he was really thinking."

They all knew, of course, that Marshall had got married just before he shipped out, and he was joshed about his wife, especially when the regular weekly letter arrived from her. After he had shown them a photograph of Lily, they were suitably impressed by her looks, and attempts were made to find out what sort of things she said to him in her letters. All Marshall would reveal was that she had put herself on a diet, so she would be really slim for him when he got back.

"How's Lily doing?" they would ask after he had finished perusing his weekly letter.

"She's lost another three pounds," he would say.

After this had gone on for several months, some wag hung a picture of a female scarecrow wearing boxing gloves in the mess. "Mrs. George Marshall," it said. "Lightweight Champion of the World, Weighing in at Minus 25 Pounds."

The war had simmered down by the time Marshall arrived in the Philippines; but there were other little local difficulties to be experienced and overcome, and not all of them were human. He learned almost at once what it was like to cope with an Oriental typhoon, for within days of landing in Manila he was ordered to join a regiment in occupation of the island of Mindoro, and that involved another sea journey. This time it was made aboard an Army coastal charter vessel named the *Isla de Negros,* which turned out to be an unseaworthy tub even in normal weather conditions but a positive floating coffin when a storm came. The *Isla de Negros* was struck by a full-scale typhoon soon after passing Corregidor, and the steamy-flat calm of the hot afternoon was instantly turned into a maelstrom.

Marshall was no Conrad, but the ordeal was such that he remembered it vividly for the rest of his life.

"I am not exaggerating when I say that the boat," he recalled, "would tilt over until the longboats on the upper deck would go into the water. It would just poise there for a little bit as if it would never go back again; then it would roll to the other side. The captain got frightened—or sick. Anyway, he left the bridge and went to his stateroom, where he knocked about in a sea chest which was rolling from one side to the other. The Filipino at the wheel got his ribs smashed, and he was gone. That left nobody to steer and nobody to command. So a young fellow, Lieutenant Daly, who was going back to his station at Calapan [on Mindoro], and I took over the boat. The two of us got the wheel and, of course, turned it in the wrong direction. We were heading towards a forbidding-looking mountain before we got straightened out and turned the other way.

"We battled it until about three o'clock in the morning. Then the first mate came up from the lower deck. He climbed up on the stanchions on the outside and would go underwater every time the boat tilted over. The water also poured into the engine room through the open ventilated space in the middle section of the deck. During the worst of it the Filipinos started to leave the engine room. We leaned over the hatch and with our guns threatened them and, as I recall, shot once or twice. I wouldn't have stayed myself if I had been in that position. It was a nerve-racking experience, but finally, with this Spanish mate we made it."

Life on Mindoro seemed boringly calm after such a journey, despite the fact that the troops with whom he had to deal turned out to be among the wildest and most recalcitrant in the U.S. Army. They ate rookie lieutenants for breakfast and quickly sized up Marshall as a tasty victim. The first time he took them out for a jungle patrol, they were wading across a sizable stream when someone yelled, "Crocodiles!" and the troop proceeded to race and flounder for the far bank, treading Marshall down into the water and mud as they stamped their way to safety. He was a sorry sight when he finally stumbled to his feet and made it to the bank, and the men howled with laughter. In some ways it was an adult version of the incident with the schoolgirls at Coal Lick Run. Once more he urgently needed to restore discipline and control.

"I realized that this wasn't a time for cussing around," he said. He was also well aware that the jungle stream was, in fact, a haunt of crocodiles, and even though he had been the victim of a false alarm, it might have been genuine. All the more reason to teach the jokers a lesson.

"I ordered them to fall in on the far bank," he recalled, "gave them 'Right shoulder arms,' and then faced them towards the river they had just crossed. I gave the order to march. Down we went, single file, into the river, I at the head, and across it and up the other bank. Then, as soon as we were across, I shouted, as though we were on a drill field, 'To the rear—march!' Again we crossed the crocodile river. When we were back on the far bank, I halted them, faced them towards me, inspected their rifles, and then gave them 'Fall out!' That was all."

The soldiers never tried to fool around with their green lieutenant again.

Early that summer a great cholera epidemic swept through Manila, wiping out thousands in the city, around which a strict *cordon sanitaire* was thrown by the U.S. Army. But some fishermen managed to slip through the sea patrol instituted by the U.S. Navy and, unable to go back to Manila, landed with their catches at Mindoro. They brought not only fish but the pestilence, and soon the island's inhabitants were threatened by the disease that had already claimed 120,000 in the capital. Marshall saw his first cholera victim while visiting the village of Calapan with the district quarantine officer, Dr. Victor Heiser, a theatrical type who loved to dramatize man's helplessness in the struggle with tropical disease. He listened with chilled fascination as Heiser leaned over the dying man and exclaimed, "See the cold, clammy sweat on his face and the way his skin is shrinking! Note the dark gray color of the complexion—that comes from violent diarrhea! Listen to his groans, because he has agonizing cramps in his calves and his arms! He is crying for water, but it's no use—because his thirst is unquenchable! As to his circulation, it is so sluggish that—why, if you cut him, he wouldn't even bleed!"

The regiment on Mindoro had been told to look after its own welfare and take meticulous precautions against the spread of the disease. It became Marshall's task to oversee the rigid rules of cleanliness, to make sure every soldier washed his hands before touching food or preparing meals, to inspect rations to see that all food and water had been boiled. But he also shared his tent with the regimental doctor, Lieutenant Fletcher Gardner, who was trying to help the stricken civilian population by setting up an isolation camp outside Calapan. In between his other duties, Marshall spent his spare time helping the doctor, as did a group of U.S. troops who had volunteered for the duty.

"The first time I went [to the camp]," he recalled later, "I found the soldiers peacefully eating their supper off a pile of coffins. Later on there weren't any coffins. The deaths came too rapidly, and they were buried by dozens in a trench. A sheet was put over them, and disinfectant poured on them. It was a tragic sight. The sides of the tent were rolled up so you could see the patients on these gold metal cots without any sheets, their legs drawn up almost under their chins, generally shrieking from the agony of convulsions. But they didn't last long."

Soon there were so many bodies they had to be burned.

He was twenty-two years old and fighting fit, but the humid heat, the oppressive nature of the jungle setting, the need to be constantly vigilant to preserve cleanliness and discipline among the men, and the omnipresent sound of human torment and smell of burning bodies as he labored in his spare hours in the isolation camp all served to exhaust him. One evening he stumbled back to his tent and was sitting on his cot when his mate, Dr. Gardner, arrived back from the camp. The doctor wasted no words but announced that he had fallen victim to the pestilence himself and would soon die of cholera. But while he could still think rationally, he wished to make some last-minute arrangements. He dug into his tin trunk, brought out some papers and personal possessions, and began earnestly explaining to Marshall exactly how he wished them to be disposed of. As he talked on, the young lieutenant fell backward on his cot and was fast asleep.

"Next thing I knew, I woke up and it was morning," Marshall recalled. "I thought this was a dream. Then I realized it wasn't . . . and I was horrified that I should go to sleep while a man was telling me that he was getting the cholera and was going to die."

He got up and examined Dr. Gardner's cot and saw that it had been used but now was empty. He went to the celluloid window in the tent and looked out.

"He was coming across the plaza with some friends for breakfast," Marshall said. "He saw me and shook his fist and said, 'There's the damn fellow who went to sleep when I told him I was dying!'"

It was a considerably older and more worldly young man who arrived back in America in the summer of 1903, and George Marshall himself marveled that he had seen so much and was still not quite twenty-three years old. Photographs taken of him at this time show a tall, thin, handsome young man whose lean face seems etched with such serious lines that it would have taken a complete rearrangement of the structure to make him look cheerful. It was not a face made for smiling easily. He seemed habitually to wear the expression about which his elders must have nodded approvingly and said, "Now that looks like a serious young man." There must also have been many a young woman around who longed to make him relax and laugh, for though he was undoubtedly attractive, he also seemed self-conscious, introspective, and stiff.

He had much to be serious about, of course, for he had responsibilities. Immediately upon landing in San Francisco he was informed that he would be posted to Fort Reno in what was then still known as Oklahoma Territory, and he not unnaturally expected that Lily would accompany him there. But once he arrived in Lexington for his disembarkation leave, it was to be informed by his mother-in-law that her daughter's condition had not changed, and it was broadly indicated that Lily was certainly in no state to perform what were then known as "wifely duties." Emotionally, Lily was evidently overjoyed to be reunited with him, but physically she stayed as remote from him as ever. Moreover, as the weeks went by, it became apparent to the lovelorn young lieutenant that Lily had no intention of accompanying him when he left for Fort Reno. Both she and her mother (as well as the doctor) made it plain that her state of health was far too frail for her to endure such a rough posting. So when he left for Fort Reno—after an emotional farewell that must have been particularly painful for him, since he was still as much in love with his wife as ever—he left alone.

As if to rub salt in his wounds, he discovered upon reaching Oklahoma that he had financial problems. He had to keep himself, his wife, and (he now learned) his mother-in-law, on the salary of a second lieutenant, which was $116.67 a month. It was about this time that he began to realize that "there isn't anything much lower than a second lieutenant, and I was about the junior second lieutenant in the Army at this time."

Now that the United States was at peace and there were no wars around, the U.S. Army was hardly a popular institution among Americans. Congress grudged it money; and was not concerned whether it was starved for personnel, supplies, or even guns and ammunition. What did it need them for? The nation was at peace, wasn't it? If Marshall hadn't been so eager to see Lily again, he might have been pleased that she refused to join him at Fort Reno, for he would have had to pay for her moving expenses and her housing when she got there; the Army didn't foot the bill for the movement of wives and families. On his meager pay, an officer had to provide his own uniforms, his own food, his arms and equipment (saber, revolver, field glasses), as well as his bedding roll, mess kit, and any civilian clothes. It was a constant struggle to make ends meet, even in this remote posting.

Lily Marshall liked clothes, and so did her mother, and very smart and attractive they looked in them. But it was the young lieutenant who had to pay for them, and, as he ruefully recorded, "A spring hat was three dollars and fifty cents, and the spring suit was fourteen dollars. I can remember that quite well. I had to keep track down to the last dime. My struggle was to come out ahead. I really wasn't so much interested in whether it was a dollar fifty or ten fifty ahead for the month, but it was to be ahead and not get behind. I always struggled in those days to have a month's pay ahead and live on that."

In the meantime, there was no hope of promotion. The size of a peacetime army was such that officers and noncoms stayed in the same rank for decades and, in the meantime, lived and drilled by a set of rules which had hardly changed since the Civil War. As Marshall said later, "It wasn't as if brains didn't exist in the Army at that time, but it was just hazardous to use them. You followed the book."

He ran up against the Army's red tape in the spring of 1905, when a welcome break in the routine of barracks life at Fort Reno was presented by what he later described as "the hardest service I ever had in the Army." He was posted to 1st Cavalry headquarters at Fort Clark, Texas, and assigned to map 2,000 square miles of territory in the southwest of the state. Marshall's particular task was to survey an area between Comstock and Langtry, through a largely untraveled section of desert and scrub, where there was no water at all except for a small section near the Devils River. He was given a team consisting of a 1st Cavalry sergeant, a driver, a packer and his assistant, and a cook, two horses, an escort wagon, a four-line mule team, and a pack train of twenty mules and was told that the only place where he would get food and supplies for men and animals was at Langtry. He therefore put in a requisition to the quartermaster asking that rations and forage be shipped to various points along the railroad between Del Rio and Sanderson, Texas, so that they could come in and replenish whenever the need arose. The requisition was still being passed from post to post between Texas and Oklahoma when Marshall and his men were in the middle of the desert Southwest and was never executed. Luckily the lieutenant took the precaution of getting vouchers for buying forage en route.

The expedition set off in the summer of 1905 and had all the makings of a vintage western film. It was Marshall's first venture into Texan badlands, and he could hardly have picked a more colorful crew to go with him. His mule driver, Nat Cox of Brackettville, Texas, was a veteran of the Indian wars who had stood as a child at his father's knee and watched him shoot back at a Comanche raiding party trying to storm their cabin. His sergeant was a cavalryman with twenty years' service, proud of his luxurious drooping mustaches and capacity for hard liquor.

It was July, and the desert heat was fierce by the time the team started out from Comstock. They followed the railroad to begin with.

"The thermometer would go up to a hundred and thirty," Marshall recalled, "and I had to walk the track and count the sections of rails. That would give me an exact measurement which I needed as a sort of base line. I got my distances otherwise from the odometer on the wheel of the wagon and from the time scale on the walking of my horse."

Forage was not too difficult to come by, but food was another matter. The onions and potatoes that the group took with them were exhausted by the end of the first week. Thereafter they had to subsist on canned bacon and other meats, and Marshall did badly on it. Lacking fresh vegetables, his digestion suffered, and he was soon in great pain from heartburn, "and I could barely drink without gasping. As I recall, I went in there weighing about a hundred sixty-five to one seventy, and I came out weighing a hundred thirty-two pounds."

But lack of water was the greatest trial. The lieutenant made sure his animals were watered first and carefully rationed the rest among his men, but toward the end he denied himself any liquids at all. Nat Cox, claiming he was used to desert conditions, volunteered to abstain with him in order to sustain the rest. The young man and the old one (Cox was sixty) marched or rode the last fifty miles without any water and all but collapsed when they reached Langtry but were quickly revived by the hospitality of the citizenry.

Langtry, the old frontier town west of the Pecos, which had been named by its gun-toting judge after a famous English beauty, Lillie Langtry,* was a pretty wild town in 1905 and was prepared to give its visitors a hearty welcome, particularly if they had money. It so happened that there was mail awaiting the expedition in Langtry, and it included pay for the men. The sergeant promptly loaded up with liquor from the local store, found Langtry's principal bar and brothel, and moved in, threatening to shoot anyone who tried to interrupt him, declaring he was going to sit back and enjoy both drink and girls until such time as they, and his money, were used up. But if the girls were willing, the citizenry was not. They objected to having their source of entertainment and relaxation requisitioned by the U.S. Army and demonstrated before the entrance to the saloon, threatening to burn it down if the sergeant kept the padlocks on its doors. A panicky town committee roused Marshall from his well-merited slumbers to demand that he resolve the situation before all hell broke loose. He was taken down the street to the place where the riotous townsfolk were demonstrating and was interested to note that many of the protesters seemed to be "wives and other respectable-looking womenfolk." Having listened to their complaint, he went up to the door of the saloon, loudly demanded admittance, and was allowed in by one of the girls. He found his sergeant sleeping upstairs like a baby,

*Otherwise known as the Jersey Lily, after the capital of the Channel Isles, where she had actually been born. Langtry became the mistress of King Edward VII of England, subsequently went on the stage, and paid a visit to Langtry and embraced its founder, Judge Roy Bean, on a stopover during an American tour.

31

a blissful smile on his face, with one handlebar of his rich mustachios missing (he and the girls had been playfully shaving each other) and no one willing to wake him up since he still had his .45 revolver belted around his long johns. With his eyes averted from the girls, who were by no means bashful in welcoming this handsome young newcomer, the lieutenant took the sergeant in his arms, dunked him in a bathful of cold water, and then told the half-sobered and shaken veteran to share the place with the irate citizens. He agreed to do so, and Marshall went below to inform the crowd. But when the men swarmed inside, he was not among them. He went back to his quarters and gave no sign whatsoever that he had been tempted to stay.

It was three months later that the small unit of men and mules eventually limped back into Fort Clark, Texas, where Marshall and his sergeant reported to the officer of the day. The lieutenant looked by that time more like an Indian scout than an officer of the United States Army. His face and arms had been burned black by the sun. His old campaign hat, "which a mule had bitten the top out of," looked like a headgear for a scarecrow, and his uniform was in tatters. The captain was so embarrassed by his appearance that he "wouldn't look at me. He didn't think I could be an officer and talked entirely to my old sergeant," despite the fact that the noncom's facial adornment had not yet grown back in place.

But Marshall had a warmer reception when he reported with his findings to the chief army engineer, Southwest Division, who found his map "the best one received and the only complete one." In the office of the commanding general in San Antonio he was welcomed back by the military secretary, Captain George Van Horn Moseley. Marshall was near exhaustion, "feeling that I had had a pretty hard time, not only as a result of the climate and a harsh terrain," but because of the poor treatment he and his team had received at the hands of the Army quartermaster—"we darned near starved." But Moseley's sympathetic reception more than made up for it, and it was through his recommendation that the commanding general issued an immediate order granting Lieutenant George C. Marshall four months' leave.

He took the train at once for Virginia and a reunion with his beloved Lily. It was three and half years since their marriage, and she was still the bride he barely knew.

But now he had four months' leave to remedy that situation. Or so he may have hoped.

3

Fruitless Search

The trouble with Lily Marshall was that she looked so healthy and attractive. No one watching her deftly handling her pony and trap as she drove around the VMI campus or through the streets of Lexington could really credit the rumor that she was a semi-invalid. And soon everyone must have been wondering why she was taking so long to have children. In those days it didn't seem natural for a married couple to stay childless after the number of years she and George had been married, and even if they had been separated while he was away on military service, hadn't there been plenty of opportunities in between? The situation was the subject of arched eyebrows and whispered gossip in Lexington drawing rooms and even of some coarse and suggestive jokes in Army messes. True, the cognoscenti did realize that Mrs. Marshall was "delicate," but it was a time when the land was full of physically frail females who had produced families of four, eight, and even ten children, and no one seemed to be much concerned that they had wrecked their bodies and their nervous systems in the process. It was a woman's job, and George Marshall ought to see that Lily got on with it. Didn't he like children? Or was it, perhaps, all his fault?

His sister Marie married a doctor (J. J. Singer) in 1905 and his brother Stuart found a bride (Florence Heaton) in Virginia two years later. Stuart became father of a baby boy and was soon crowing about him wherever anyone would listen. It didn't decrease his oft-expressed contempt for his younger brother that after nine years of marriage "George hasn't even produced a daughter," as he delicately put it. In fact, Marshall would have given anything in the world to have a daughter because he was particularly fond of small children, girls in particular. But he was also deeply in love with his wife and knew that childbirth for her could almost certainly be fatal.

By this time he and Lily had had a chance to talk together and to the doctors about her condition. Marshall had been warned of the grave consequences of even attempting to start a family. Yet no one who watched Lily Marshall after her reunions with her husband and studied them while they were together had any doubt that she was now as much in love with him as he was with her. To the outside world she was still the haughty, self-confident, superior beauty, only too well aware of her attractiveness, background, and breeding, but with him she was gentle, eager to please, and adoring. But if it meant that for his sake and his need, she was willing to take the risk that becoming pregnant involved, she never confided the fact to anyone who passed it on. Certainly George Marshall would never have let her take the chance. But, of course, he did not talk about it. His private life was a closed book. All he ever said about Lily was in praise of her and to add, simply, "I was in love."

It must have been terribly frustrating for him and not simply because of his feelings for his wife. As one of his godchildren said later, "He loved and enjoyed children. He understood them. He had empathy for their shortcomings. He made allowances for their embryonic ethical values, and above all, he strove to resee through their wondering, inquisitive eyes, the forgotten enchantment of a child's world. All his life, long after I'd grown to the sober state of adulthood, wherever he lived, children were drawn to him and perennially frolicked in the sunshine of his extraordinary personality. . . . Colonel Marshall was born to be a father."

As the years went by, he still hoped that one day it would come to pass. The doctors advised him to be patient, to see what affection, sympathy, understanding, and propinquity could do. In 1910 he decided to see whether a second honeymoon—and a much more leisurely one this time—could bring about a miracle cure.

Despite the paucity of opportunities in the U.S. Army in the first decade of the century, Marshall was slowly making it up the military ladder. Somewhere someone must have been watching him and noting that here was not just a hard-slogging, trustworthy young officer, but someone with the knack of getting the best out of his men—and, it seemed, their wives. During his posting to Fort

Reno in 1903 in the Oklahoma Territory, he had transformed a sleazy and down-at-heels military slum into a barracks with the trimmest married quarters in the Army simply by persuading the women. They had come to him complaining of their unsanitary, ugly, bug-infested quarters, expecting to be told, as they always had been in the past, that there just wasn't any Army money around for refurbishing it, as there certainly wasn't at that time. But Marshall had been walking around the streets surrounding the married quarters, and he had been ashamed at what he saw. The poor conditions inside had bred a don't-care attitude among the wives, who left their yards untended, the streets unkempt, cans and litter everywhere. The quarter was known as Soapsuds Row, but soap was the last thing that was used around it.

"I came along one day," he recalled later, "and this wife waylaid me and asked me if I couldn't do something for her kitchen. I don't remember what the trouble was; but there was something very bad, and of course, the entire house was in a very sad state of repair. Her yard was of beaten-down clay, and there were tin cans and other trash things scattered around. An idea struck me, and I made a proposition to the lady. I told her, 'If you fix your yard up and make it look like something, I'll fix your house up. And I'll come back here in about two weeks. Meanwhile, I'll have this repair done at once about your kitchen sink.' So when I came back two weeks later, she had cleaned up her yard, she had made pots out of the tin cans which she had painted green, and she had really transformed the place and done a fine job."

The young second lieutenant congratulated her and then mentioned that scouring around the camp, he had found some paint of various colors, and he would now send someone over to do her house. She could choose her own color. The paint Marshall had discovered was of the powder type, usually diluted by about ten times the quantity with water.

"The painter came to me in some concern," Marshall said, "and said she wanted these things done in the original intensity of the powder, and it was going to be a terrific color. For instance, she wanted the living room red. Well, it is very hot down there in the summer, and this red was just like lighting a fire."

But the soldier's wife had kept her part of the bargain, and Marshall was going to keep his. He told the painter to give her what she wanted. "After he had finished it, he begged me to come over and see it. Well, actually when you opened up the front door, the living room almost knocked you down. It was an intense red, just a terrible red. And the kitchen was this vivid blue. She was just pleased to death. And all the other women were coming there to see this, to find out if they could have something like this too. . . . Anyway, all the way down the line, the women started fixing up their lawns."

It was this kind of elementary but instinctive psychology which seemed to win him the respect and approval of those serving under him, and the surprise is that it did not go unnoticed by his superiors either. The welfare of the serving soldier was not a first priority in the U.S. Army in those days, and that of soldiers' wives was hardly to be considered at all, and Marshall was therefore somewhat astonished when his efforts to improve conditions at Fort Reno were reported to his commanding officer and commended by him. Shortly afterward, he found his name on a list of officers posted to a course at Fort Leavenworth for those thought worthy of promotion. When he got there, toward the end of 1906, he discovered that he was the only second lieutenant among a group of captains and majors, and, as he remarked later, "it made it a little ticklish." From a one-year course, twenty-four officers would be chosen to go forward to advanced military studies, and the competition for the coveted places was intense.

"I know I was a little bit discouraged at the start," he recalled. "I hadn't any preparation. I found these other fellows had copies of all the problems of the previous years. I myself had never seen a tactical problem of that nature, and I had it all to do. And so I knew I would have to study harder than I had ever dreamed of studying before in my life. And I just worked night and day. My great trouble was going to sleep at night. And I remember I used to get up and shine my boots in order to wake up. So I had very shiny boots at that early period."

No one had an inkling of his deliberately sleepless nights, and no one guessed when they saw Lieutenant Marshall flashing his immaculate boots across the parade ground in the early-morning light that he had spent hours rubbing away at them. The captains competing with him did not sneer at his earnestness, but they certainly sniggered over those blindingly brilliant boots. It made him all the more determined to respond as he had done to his brother and wipe their nose. He did it by coming out number one in his class, first among the twenty-four chosen for the advanced class.* He was so elated at his triumph and so sure of his eventual apotheosis that he sent a message to Lily in Lexington, beseeching her to join him. She was the only person in the world with whom he felt he could celebrate his victory.

The message could not have come at a more fruitful moment. Lily was feeling better, and her doctors were encouraged. She wired back that she was willing to risk it and would be coming in shortly by train to join him at Leavenworth. Marshall scurried around and found accommodation in part of a former military quarters off the Old Parade, and when this was found to be damp and drafty as winter closed in, he transferred himself and his wife to the cramped bachelor quarters on the post itself. It was the best he could rate at that stage. Then promotion arrived, like a glorious gift from the Great White Chiefs in Washington. First Lieutenant George C. Marshall was a proud and happy man, paid enough to live reasonably on his military stipend, glad to have his wife at his side, for the first time feeling fulfilled in his military career and hopeful in his private life. The married quarters to which they now moved on Pope Avenue were spacious, dry, and so situated that "you could walk up on the mountain there; you could walk on the road towards town." Lily was so much better that she could join him in a stroll in the late-afternoon sun. And when the doctors saw her at her next examination, they were thoughtful. The change of scene seemed to have done wonders for Lily, soothing her nerves, lessening the strains in her body. Maybe if she got away from everything altogether, maybe if both of them were to relax completely in each other's company, the miracle cure might be possible, and they could begin a normal married life.

*Ahead of such future generals as Douglas MacArthur and Walter Krueger.

Marshall decided that what Lily needed was a second honeymoon—and why not in Europe, which both of them had often dreamed of visiting? He had read all about the spas in France, the therapeutic mud baths in Italy, the restorative hot springs in Bath, England, and Baden-Baden in Germany, all said to be good for female disorders. Whether Lily would be willing to try them—or whether they would be good for her heart condition—would remain to be seen, but meanwhile, he would give her a complete change of scene even if it meant a risk to his military career.

How Marshall managed it is one of the mysteries. True, he had several months of cumulative leave coming to him—four whole months, as it turned out—and not without some objections from his superiors, he persuaded the quartermaster's office to grant him two extra months on half pay. As he commented, to go to Europe with one's wife for half a year, even in 1910, "was quite a feat on a lieutenant's pay . . . we had to do it on a shoestring, but we managed to cover six countries." They sailed for Britain on a cattle boat (which also carried six passengers) in the spring of 1910 and spent several weeks each in England, France, Italy, and Germany as well as visited Greece and North Africa. They toured the French château country, tramped around Florence, stayed a month in Rome, and traveled through the English Home Counties, eventually sailing back to America from Trieste. Marshall made only one attempt to use his Army connections, and that was in London. He heard that the British army was about to go on maneuvers in southern England and went to the U.S. Embassy to ask if he could watch it with the military attaché. He was curtly rebuffed. So he rented a bicycle, and while Mrs. Marshall waited for him in a boardinghouse in Aldershot, he cycled through the narrow lanes and bypaths on Salisbury Plain, watching the exercises through his binoculars and carefully logging the behavior of men, horses, and guns as they made mock war across the rolling plain. The report he afterward wrote eventually found its way into the National Archives and is much more comprehensive than the one the U.S. military attaché subsequently delivered.

But if the experience had been mind-broadening for both of them, it did not do much to change the nature of their physical relationship. There is no record that Lily Marshall lolled in any warm springs, wallowed in any mud baths, or submitted herself to the therapeutic massages that were available to her during the European tour. She landed back in New York with her physical condition unchanged. No one would have guessed from his attitude that Marshall was disappointed, and he was, if anything, even more devoted to his wife. A stranger watching the two of them together would have been satisfied that their marriage was entirely self-sufficient and that no vital element was missing from it. There were, of course, those who knew better, as we shall see. One of them was his elder brother, Stuart, and as one might have guessed, he was not exactly sympathetic. Whenever Marshall met him these days, he had his new son proudly in tow. Marshall would not allow Stuart or his family into his home, for he had never forgiven him for his remarks about Lily, but he did often encounter him when he visited his mother. Mrs. Marshall, Sr., was now a widow, her husband having died from a stroke in 1909. Her two sons and daughter had agreed to sign over to her their share of their father's estate, and on this, plus her own legacy, she had enough to live in reasonable comfort. She began to spend extensive periods in Atlantic City, New Jersey, and it was there that her younger son journeyed to see her. He tried to visit her alone but was not always successful in dodging Stuart and his son.

The sight of his brother puffed up like a pouter pigeon as he strutted down the boardwalk with his son was bad enough. But Stuart also knew how to pierce the chink in his brother's armor.

"How's the belle of VMI?" he would ask. "Has she answered the call of duty yet? Ha-ha-ha!"

There were plenty of other things to worry George Marshall in that period of his life. He was thirty-four years old when World War I broke out in Europe in 1914. He had been an officer in the U.S. Army for twelve years, had served in fourteen different posts in the United States, twice in the Philippines, and twice with National Guard units, and everywhere, in every posting, he had been praised by his commanding officers. He not only had proved a good officer for the routine slogs of Army life—though he was patient and painstaking in those, too—but had also shown, time and again, that he was an excellent tactician on maneuvers and a resourceful, reliable, and rocklike linchpin in an emergency. Yet he was still only a first lieutenant. In 1916, his commanding officer, General Johnson Hagood, wrote in his efficiency report: "[Marshall] should be made a brigadier general in the regular Army, and every day this is postponed is a loss to the Army and the nation." The promotion board made him a captain, instead. He was in despair. He had written to the superintendent of VMI (General E. W. Nichols):

> The absolute stagnation in promotion in the infantry has caused me to make tentative plans for resigning as soon as business conditions improve. Even in the event of an increase as a result of [congressional] legislation next winter, the prospects of advancement in the Army are so restricted by law and by the accumulation of large numbers of men of nearly the same age all in a single grade, that I do not feel it right to waste all my best years in the vain struggle against insurmountable difficulties.

Nichols wrote back to advise him to "stick to it" and have patience, "and I am sure in time you will be among the highest ranking officers in the service." But Marshall was fed up and ready to throw in his hand. What finally restrained him was his conviction that the United States was soon going to become involved in war and that his services would be needed. Like many another U.S. service officer, he was not for the moment thinking of the conflict raging in Europe—between the so-called Allies (Britain, France, and Russia) and the Central Powers (Germany and the Austro-Hungarian Empire)—but one between the United States and Mexico.

The simmering crisis with Mexico was now coming to the boil. As early as 1913, after the murder of President Francisco Madero by military strongman General Victoriano Huerta's forces, U.S. troops (the 2nd Division) had been moved to the American-Mexican border and had been on a state of alert ever since. Then, in 1914, after a brawl outside a bar in Tampico, Mexico, a high-handed Huerta officer had ordered the arrest of the paymaster and some members of the crew of a visiting U.S. warship and locked them in the local jail overnight. They were released the next morning, without apologies, and it was a groveling apology that the United States wanted. President Woodrow Wilson went to Congress to ask it to support his demand for "unequivocal amends," and a haughty note was dispatched to Mexico City. While it was being studied by Huerta, Washington received the news that a German merchantman loaded with ammunition had arrived in Veracruz and was about to unload its cargo for use by Huerta's army. Wilson thereupon ordered the U.S. Navy to seize Veracruz. The marines took over and were reinforced by U.S. Army troops from Galveston under the command of Brigadier General Frederick Funston.

The Americans occupied the Mexican port for seven months, until the end of November 1914, finally forcing the humiliated Huerta to resign. His place was taken by President Venustiano Carranza.

But the situation between the two countries did not improve, and Congress, convinced that war with Mexico was coming, agreed to fund a recruiting program and to appropriate a quarter of a million dollars for airships and planes capable of operating along the frontier with Mexico. Despite the slaughter which was now taking place on the battlefields of the western front in France, political and military attention in the United States still continued to concentrate on the threat which, it was believed, was being made to U.S. security by Mexico. American anger surged anew in 1915 and 1916 over the behavior of its southern neighbor when Mexican guerrillas began making incursions into U.S. territory. Rebels under the command of Pancho Villa raided the border town of Santa Isabel and later rampaged through Columbus, New Mexico, attacking soldiers and killing some citizens. A week after this raid, Secretary of War Newton D. Baker authorized a punitive expedition by the U.S. Army into Mexican territory. The force was put under the command of Brigadier General John J. Pershing, and his orders were to capture Pancho Villa, the rebel chief, alive if possible and bring him back to the United States for punishment.

The punitive force never did succeed in capturing the Mexican guerrilla, who dodged the U.S. raiding parties with the skill and panache of a will-o'-the-wisp. It was hardly Pershing's fault. Under a tacit agreement with the Carranza government in Mexico City (which Wilson had recognized) the U.S. Army was instructed to avoid all populated areas in Mexico and to use roads and desert tracks rather than the railroad—which Villa and his bandits controlled anyway. The result was that U.S. Army resources were stretched to the limit, and by presidential decree the National Guard had to be called up for service.

By May 1916 not only were 140,000 national guardsmen on duty, most of them along the Mexican border, but the bulk of the Regular Army in the continental United States was on service with Pershing inside Mexico, in a vain endeavor to trap Pancho Villa. The tramp of U.S. Army boots on Mexican soil was heard so loudly throughout the country and was considered such an insult to the Mexicans, whose *amour propre* was already offended, that most thoughtful Americans expected Carranza to break any agreements he had made with Washington and declare war on the United States.

From Marshall's point of view, the situation was personally frustrating. While the Mexican crisis had been developing, he had been on a second posting in the Philippines, and this time the humid, hot climate had badly affected him. He began to suffer from insomnia and a painful form of "neurasthenia" which came at the end of a bout of overwork organizing Army maneuvers on the island of Luzon. His work was so effectively done, especially in his planning for an invasion of the neighboring island of Mindoro, that his commanding officer presented him to his fellow officers, saying: "This, gentlemen, is the greatest military genius since Stonewall Jackson."

But soon after he all but collapsed and was given two months' sick leave, which, on top of two months of regular leave, enabled him to pick up Lily in Tokyo and tour with her through Manchuria and Korea. The tour restored Marshall's health but had to be cut short by an attack of fever suffered by Lily. Back in the Philippines, Marshall was told by the doctor that his "neurasthenia" would disappear if only he would learn to relax and apportion his working hours, and it was at this time that he began taking regular morning exercise on horseback, riding out shortly after dawn, usually with two steady companions, Lieutenant H. H. "Hap" Arnold, who was to become commander of the U.S. Army Air Corps in World War II, and Lieutenant Courtney Hodges, who would command the U.S. First Army in that same conflict.

But it was hard to relax when the situation was developing in Mexico and he was thousands of miles away. The days and weeks of his Philippine tour slipped by as Pershing marched his men into Mexico. Marshall began ringing dates on his calendar and wrote to General Nichols at VMI that he feared he would be still stuck in the Far East when Pershing began to "advance on Mexico City" but that he still hoped to be home in time to take part in the U.S.-Mexican war.

By the time he reached San Francisco, however, the situation had cooled down again. The Mexicans had swallowed their humiliation and Pershing had withdrawn U.S. Army troops from Mexican territory. He was now back in Washington consulting with defense and political advisers on a very different crisis. At long last, American concern had turned from Mexico toward Europe, and Americans were facing up to the prospect of being involved in the European war. Clumsy German propaganda, sabotage, the sinking of Allied ships with U.S. passengers and cargo aboard all had combined to whip up feeling in favor of the Anglo-French cause, and it now seemed inevitable that the German government would commit an act of ultimate folly to provide President Wilson with the justification he was seeking to enter the war on the Allied side. That happened when the Germans announced the beginning of unrestricted submarine warfare in the North Atlantic, threatening U.S. as well as belligerent shipping. The British liner *Lusitania,* with hundreds of U.S. passengers aboard, was sunk by a U-boat off Ireland. The U.S. government promptly broke off relations with Berlin, and on April 6, 1917, America declared war on Germany. For Europeans, World War I was nearly three years old, but for the Americans a dreadful baptism of fire was just beginning.

Marshall arrived back in the United States in May 1916, eleven months before the declaration of war, and almost immediately was ordered to report to a promotion board. He was confirmed as a permanent captain in the U.S. Army—after fourteen years of service—and was posted to the Presidio in San Francisco as aide to General J. Franklin Bell. Bell was just back from Mexico, where he had marched with Pershing, and his main concern now was to beef up the strength of the armed forces and repair the weaknesses in the Army that had been shown up by the Mexican campaign. He had been put in charge of the military training program for civilian volunteers and was looking around for an experienced military assistant who could help him give it a shot in the arm.

The Citizen Military Training Program, as it was called, was entirely voluntary. Those who signed up for it paid their own expenses for uniforms, equipment, and keep, and volunteers were therefore, not unnaturally, confined to the better-heeled members of the community. Their ages ranged from nineteen to fifty, and they included doctors, lawyers, ministers, newsmen, playboys, and sportsmen, and there were 1,800 of them in the California section of the program. Their camp was set in the lush grounds of the Del Monte Hotel at Monterey, and it had become a popular summer preoccupation of local socialites, who liked spending hot days drilling in the grounds and their nights living it up in the hotel.

"They were all the hot bloods of San Francisco," General Bell recalled later. "I saw more Rolls-Royces and other fine cars around there than I have ever seen collected."

Bell ordered Marshall to bring some reality into the program by stiffening up the drill and conditions and taking off the gloves when it came to dealing with the volunteers. He warned his aide that it was a task not likely to help his career. The volunteers had plenty of powerful political friends and were, after all, paying their own way. They might not like it if they suddenly found themselves being treated like ordinary soldiers.

Marshall saw what he meant soon after reporting to the camp commandant, Brigadier General William L. Sibert. He was told to take one company out into the hills as part of an exercise and was astonished, when lunchtime came, to see cars beginning to arrive. They contained wives and girl friends of the volunteers,

45

and they had brought choice foods and champagne and wines with them; they proceeded to spread rugs under the trees and settle down to a choice picnic lunch. But when it was over, when the cars had departed, and a close-order drill began over the hills and along rough, winding paths, the behavior of the men was ragged and pathetic. Marshall waited until they were all but exhausted, still bleary from good food and drink, and stood them to attention and addressed them.

"You fellows came down here," he said, "because you were enthusiastic to do something in this time of emergency, and you are paying your own expenses. This morning you were in a maneuver and you hardly marched at all. You were in reserve, sitting around resting. Then your wives and girls all brought out good things and you had champagne, and it has been quite delightful to sit under the trees. Now you are so exhausted by this war service that you can't do a damn thing. I'm going to go out there and drill you again, and if you can't drill, I am going to march you in and report you as wholly ineffective."

He drilled them till they dropped—literally, in several cases. Then he drilled them until late that night and all through the next day and so exhausted them that their girl friends were soon grumbling that they were too tired to dance in the Del Monte Hotel ballroom and were falling asleep at the tables.

But no one complained to the politicians. And by the time the camp closed Marshall had turned at least five companies of volunteers into smart, well-drilled, promising soldiers. He earned himself a nickname from the volunteers. They called him Dynamite.

Once war began, General Bell was transferred as commanding general of the Eastern Department, with headquarters on Governors Island, New York. He took Marshall with him, and almost immediately, Bell came down with influenza and had to be hospitalized. Marshall found himself running the department and reporting to his commanding officer each day, "particularly to tell him of the displeasure of his senior staff officers with my actions." But Bell had developed great faith in his aide and gave him full powers to make decisions. As volunteers and trainees began to

46

swarm into Army camps all over the East, Marshall had the job of finding them tents, blankets, mattresses and also of getting the money to pay for them.

The United States was in turmoil. French and British delegations arrived in New York and urged the Army to send over an expeditionary force. There was no such force available. The Selective Service Act had only just been passed. Everything was lacking—men, uniforms, guns, ships to transport them.

Eventually, to appease America's allies, the President agreed that troops would be sent as soon as possible and that meanwhile, General John J. Pershing would lead a U.S. military delegation to France. Marshall tried desperately to get a post on Pershing's staff in order to go with him, but all his efforts were in vain.

But other factors were working in his favor. One of the Army's regular officers called to Washington to help form the expanding U.S. Army was William L. Sibert, now promoted to major general. He had been given the task of forming the 1st U.S. Division, and he was looking around for officers to put on his staff. The name of Captain George Catlett Marshall came up, and one colonel, asked if he would like to have him in his command, replied, "Yes, but I would prefer to serve *under his command.*"

Sibert wired General Bell in hospital and asked if he would release his aide as an officer "on my divisional staff and for immediate service abroad." Bell gave his permission and his blessing. From all over the United States, elements of the new 1st Division, including many men who had served in Mexico with Pershing, began to converge on New York, whence they would sail for the battlefields of France.

Marshall said good-bye to Lily and saw her off to Charlotte, North Carolina, where she would stay with her brother, Edmund, before returning to Lexington for the duration of the war. Then he went aboard the troopship *Tenadores* in New York Harbor to prepare it for the men of the 1st Division who would soon be coming aboard. He was impressed when he saw the gun crews drilling on deck and noted the polished cannons ready to go into action against the German raiders and U-boats which might soon be menacing their passage. But then he heard a petty officer complain that although there were guns aboard, there was no ammunition for them.

Marshall recalled thinking: "My God, even the naval part isn't organized, and we are starting off to Europe."

And to the bloodiest war in history.

The men of the 1st U.S. Army Division were the first American fighting troops to land in France during World War I, and Captain George C. Marshall was the second man ashore. He followed General Sibert down the gangplank of the troopship *Tenadores* when she docked at St. Nazaire on the morning of June 26, 1917.

Like many of his comrades in the division, Marshall was looking forward to getting into the war and was blissfully unaware of the horrors that lay ahead. Some of the veterans of the Mexican campaign seemed to imagine that this was going to be just a quick, cleaning-up operation and that the Germans, like Pancho Villa, would scamper for cover the moment they came on to the scene. Others were raw recruits who just wanted to "get into a good scrap" and then go back home and bask in the glory.

Marshall got his first inkling that maybe it wouldn't turn out as simply as that as the *Tenadores* tied up at the dockside. "A small crowd of the French inhabitants collected along the edge of the basin and at the end of the street to watch our arrival," he recalled later. "Most of the women were in mourning. Very few men were in evidence. There was not a cheer, and the general aspect was that of a funeral. Once we had tied up at the dock, General Sibert went down the gangway and I followed him."

The crowd stayed silent as a small group of French officials came forward to greet them. But all the time Marshall was conscious of the women. "Every one of them seemed to be on the verge of tears," he said.

He had been practicing French during the voyage and had made a secret vow that once he reached French soil, he would speak nothing but French whenever he encountered a Frenchman. The first morning after his arrival in St. Nazaire, he strolled through the town and passed an elderly man who nodded a greeting to him. The American stopped, saluted, and said, *"Je suis très beau aujourdhui!"*

The Frenchman gave him a peculiar look and hurried away. As for Marshall, he did a mental translation to himself of exactly what he had said ("I am very pretty today!") and made an entirely different vow. "During the ensuing twenty-six months," he said later, "I never spoke French again except when forced to."

There was no other language he could speak, however, when the division was eventually moved up toward the battlefront, for he was billeted with a French family at Gondrecourt, and the woman of the house, Madame Jouatte, was resolutely determined not to speak a word of any language but her own.

Marshall spent the next six months billeted in Madame Jouatte's house during what he later came to describe as "the most depressing, gloomy period of the war," commenting, "We often referred to it as the Winter of Valley Forge, and Madame Jouatte was in no small measure responsible for my being able to keep a stiff upper lip and wear an optimistic smile those days."

Slowly it was dawning on the Americans just what kind of war they had become part of, along with the realization that they were by no means trained, physically, technically, or emotionally, for its hardships and horrors. General Pershing had already arrived in France with his staff, ahead of the combat troops, and had made a tour of the battlefields. He had been appalled not simply by the carnage involved in the dreadful war of attrition in which both sides were now engaged, but by the knowledge that the Americans were entirely untrained for this type of combat. He was desperately anxious to keep them out of the trenches for as long as possible, until they learned how to survive. On the other hand, as Marshall soon realized, "The French were determined to commit us to the trenches at the earliest possible moment, since the morale of their soldiers was seriously depressed and it was felt that nothing but the actual presence of American soldiers fighting in the line would satisfy the 'poilus.' All subordinate French officials in any way connected with us undoubtedly had their instructions to push our training to rapid completion."

They appeared to believe that the 1st Infantry Division was a highly trained unit of the Regular Army of the United States and could not understand that most of the men were recruits. Once they did so, they set to work to persuade the Americans to allow them to take over the training, using French methods and routines entirely foreign to U.S. training manuals. It started the first of many quarrels over procedure with which the newly arrived Americans had to contend, and Marshall found himself increasingly involved in settling the squabbles—never, as he ruefully admitted, to the entire satisfaction of either party. And all the time the French pushed to get the American troops into the trenches.

One Sunday morning Georges "Tiger" Clemenceau appeared at the divisional headquarters. He was not yet prime minister but was an important member of the Cabinet, and he was looking for General Pershing. Having failed to find him, he had settled for a conference with General Sibert instead. The date was September 2, 1917. A member of the French General Staff, General Vicomte de Curières de Castelnau, who was accompanying Clemenceau stated, in his presence, that he expected to see the division go into the line by September 12.

"This was a 'facer,'" recalled Marshall. "General Sibert immediately explained that he was not empowered to make any such arrangement; that such decisions rested entirely with General Pershing.

"Up to this moment everything had gone smoothly, though I thought I noticed a very strained expression on General de Castelnau's face. Now, however, Clemenceau rose from his chair and walking back and forth in the little room, made an impassioned statement in English regarding the seriousness of the situation and the absolute necessity of the immediate appearance of American troops in the trenches. General Sibert had explained the status of the division as regards recruits and officers, and to this subject M. Clemenceau now addressed himself. He said it was not a question of our getting the division in perfect shape before committing it to the line. He said it was a question of losing the war; that the strength of the French soldier was exhausted; that his morale had reached its lowest point; that he had begun to doubt the good faith of the United States because months had passed and no American troops had ever been seen in the line. He said he had tried to see General Pershing and had not found him and the matter was so vital that he had come to General Sibert direct, because the Americans must enter the battle and make some sacrifice to prove to the French soldiers that they meant business and that they were there to fight to the finish."

Sibert was greatly embarrassed by this outburst. He tried to explain that it was not he who could give an order of this importance, that Pershing himself would have to be consulted, and then went on to point out, as gently but as firmly as he could, that to commit American troops to battle before they were sufficiently trained to meet the enemy on equal terms would be a very grave risk.

"For the reputed pick of our Regular Army," Marshall quoted Sibert as saying, "on its first appearance in the line, to suffer a serious or ignominious reverse would have a calamitous effect on the morale of the American soldier and on the Allies as well."

Clemenceau snorted, De Castelnau sniffed, and they bade the Americans a frigid good-bye. Marshall watched them depart with gloomy foreboding. The American entry into the line had been set for several months ahead, but after this incident he realized the pressure would really be on, and they would be in the trenches much sooner than they anticipated. It was a depressing prospect.

As he feared, on September 21, 1917, units of the 1st Division were ordered into the trenches in the Einville sector of the western front, side by side with a battalion of veteran French poilus. It was, in fact, some distance away from the main battles then raging in northern France, and as Marshall and the troops became aware, it "was not a cheerful or a busy front," just cold, muddy, and boring. Both sides seemed to prefer it that way. Only a grim muddy morass crisscrossed by deep bands of barbed wire separated the Americans and the French from the enemy, but they might have been a million miles apart for all the contact between them. True, the artillery on both sides sent over a daily quota of ranging shots, but as if by agreement, they were so directed as to avoid causing casualties on either side. These were men who were sick and tired of war and no longer eager to kill each other, and the exhausted French troops observed the arrival of these fresh-complexioned, keen-eyed doughboys from America with dull, unspoken fear.

What they did not know was that the doughboys had been instructed by the French high command to stay out of trouble as long as possible, and there was a strict prohibition against their making any forays out of their frontline trenches beyond the first barbed wire in no-man's-land. However, no one had remembered to give the same orders to the U.S. artillery, which now moved into the area, and the gunners, eager to make some kills, ringed their maps of the enemy terrain and opened fire with a mighty barrage which, as Marshall noted, "tended to break the calm and stirred the enemy to retaliatory measures." On the morning of November 3, Marshall called at French headquarters on his way to the American sector, and a member of the French staff, General Henri Bordeaux, rushed out, very excited, eyes shining. It was just twelve days since U.S. troops had moved into the line.

"Savez-vous?" he cried. *"Les premiers Américains ont été tués!"* ("Have you heard? The first Americans have been killed!")

With the general accompanying him, Marshall drove at once to the headquarters of the U.S. infantry brigade. There he learned that at about four o'clock in the morning an intense German artillery fire had been directed on the center of resistance of one of the U.S. groups, which had caused the death of three Americans and had wounded twelve or more others. While Marshall was learning these details the radio operator at the infantry brigade group intercepted the daily wireless communiqué sent out by the German government. In this was the statement that fourteen North Americans had been captured in a well-executed raid north of the Rhine-Marne Canal, which was the U.S. sector.

It was their first realization that this had been not simply an artillery barrage but an enemy operation against the Americans, and at Marshall's suggestion, he and the French general decided to go out and check exactly what had happened. They left their car at regimental headquarters and plunged through a complex of communicating trenches toward the American line. Soon, after scrambling through a jumble of collapsed trenches and shell holes (from the German artillery barrage), they reached a point in the barbed-wire entanglements where a hole had been blown by a Bangalore torpedo.* Leading back across no-man's-land was a tape to guide the German raiders home to their own trenches.

"Here was conclusive evidence of the German raid," Marshall noted, "and, in a dugout a short distance beyond, we found the bloody traces of a fight. The missing men had all been stationed in this particular trench.

"Another breach was located on the other side of the angle made by the frontline trench, and there were other traces of fighting. The bodies of the first three Americans who fell in the war—Corporal Gresham, Private Enright and Private Hay—were just being removed from the ground where they had fallen. One of the three had had his throat cut. . . ."

The sight of the bodies of the fallen U.S. soldiers, lying in the mud in their doughboy uniforms, was like an electric shock. It was as if General Bordeaux realized for the first time that the Americans were really here, fighting in France. His eyes were agleam. The young French lieutenant with him seemed so overcome that Marshall thought he was going to burst into tears. And as they scrambled back through the trenches to headquarters, Marshall realized that the whole situation vis-à-vis French-American relations had changed. General Bordeaux embraced him as they parted.

He announced that the French Army was going to take charge of the funeral of the three young Americans. On the afternoon of November 4, 1917, a service was held before an improvised altar in the village of Bathelémont, which had been decorated for the occasion. In addition to U.S. troops, there was a company of French infantry, a section of French artillery, a section of French engineers, and a detachment of French sailors. General Bordeaux and his staff led the procession, preceded by a French band playing a funeral march. After the farewell volley had been fired and taps sounded by a trumpeter, General Bordeaux, in dress uniform, made an impassioned speech which ended with these words:

*A metal tube filled with explosives used to destroy trench defenses.

"Men! These graves, the first to be dug in our national soil, at but a short distance from the enemy, are as a mark of the mighty hand of our Allies, firmly clinging to the common task, confirming the will of the people and Army of the United States to fight with us to a finish; ready to sacrifice as long as it will be necessary, until final victory for the noblest of causes—that of the liberty of nations, of the weak as well as the mighty.

"Thus the death of this humble corporal and these two private soldiers appears to us with extraordinary grandeur. We will therefore ask that the mortal remains of these young men be left here, be left to us forever. We will inscribe on their tombs: 'Here lie the first soldiers of the famous Republic of the United States to fall on the soil of France, for justice and liberty.' The passerby will stop and uncover his head. The travellers of France, of the allied countries, of America, the men of heart, who will come to visit our battlefield of Lorraine, will go out of the way to come here, to bring to these graves the tribute of their respect and their gratitude.

"Corporal Gresham, Private Enright, Private Hay, in the name of France I thank you. God receive your souls. Farewell!"

Marshall never forgot that incident. He learned a lesson from it about the behavior of allies in war. Nothing brought them closer together and ended their quarrels and suspicions more quickly than fighting shoulder to shoulder, danger shared. And for cementing relationships between them, there was nothing—alas!— quite so adhesive as blood.

4

Black Jack

So far as his official position was concerned, George Marshall was now a temporary lieutenant colonel on the staff of the 1st U.S. Infantry Division, and this gave rise to the belief later on—when he became a famous general—that he went through World War I without having taken part in a frontline battle. If that means he never actually went over the top with a rifle or bayoneted a German in hand-to-hand combat, that is true. But if it gives the impression that he spent most of his time in rear areas, safe from the dangers, rigors, and discomforts of trench warfare, it is the opposite of the truth. He saw more combat and dodged more gas, shot, and shell than many other Americans during World War I.

Marshall's job was to keep headquarters of 1st Div informed about the situation along the division's frontline position, to check on dispositions and supplies, and to keep an eye on the morale of the men. He took his role seriously, with the result that he was more often in the forward trenches than he was at headquarters. He went around the front on foot, always alone, carrying nothing but his gas mask, revolver, rations, and a heavy raincoat against the cold rain that swept continuously across the nightmarish land-scape. It was often foggy, and he welcomed that, since it meant he could climb out of the sinuous, quagmired, rat-infested trenches and slop through the mud of no-man's-land more directly from point to point, but without unduly exposing himself to the enemy. He grew used to shellfire and learned to keep going when his instinct was to throw himself in the mud each time he heard a missile whistling over head. Like every fighting soldier, he had one chief fear—that one of the bursting shells would rain poison gas down upon him.

It was hard to provide against the possibility of gas shelling. The exits to the dugouts were not so constructed as to protect the inmates against the effects of gas, particularly the new Yperine or mustard gas. Our men had not yet become so trained as to accurately detect the differences between a gas and an ordinary shell, which resulted in frequent false alarms. Walking back from the front line at dusk one winter's evening, I put on my gas mask to train myself to breathe freely while exercising. It was difficult to find one's way, as the windows of the mask quickly became fogged. At the celebrated "Dead Man's Curve" near Beaumont, I passed a column of escort wagons. One of the teamsters, observing me wearing the mask, emitted a blood-curdling yell. "My God, gas!" They all snatched at their masks, belabored their teams, and raced tumultously down the road.

Marshall never conquered his own fear of this "inhuman weapon of war" and was glad the U.S. Army never used it—though the British and French did in retaliation against German gas attacks. One of his most chastening experiences shortly after arriving in France happened during a visit to a unit of the French Foreign Legion. A raiding party had just come back to its forward lines and brought with it a batch of German prisoners. The raid had been preceded by an attack of French artillery during which a plentiful number of gas shells had been sent over. Several of the prisoners showed the effect of this and were coughing their lungs up.

Marshall asked if any of the prisoners spoke English, and a bare-headed little fellow in the rear managed to gasp out, "I do. I'm from Detroit."

Another one coughed and hoarsely whispered, "Me, too. I'm from Brooklyn. And will I be glad to get back there!"

They were German Americans who had volunteered to fight for the kaiser before the United States came into the war on the other side. One look at their gray, haggard faces and at the great gobs of blood and phlegm they were so painfully heaving up convinced Marshall that neither would ever see Detroit or Brooklyn again.

There was one soldier George Marshall came to admire more than any other during World War I, and that was General John J. "Black Jack" Pershing, Commander in Chief of the American Expeditionary Force in Europe. He had already put him in the top echelon of American military leaders from the moment U.S. troops landed in France, when Pershing made it clear to the French commanders, Henri Pétain and Ferdinand Foch, that the Americans had come as a separate and independent force. They were not, he emphasized, to be regarded simply as reinforcements for the weary and demoralized Allied troops already in the line, nor were they to be sacrificed as cannon fodder to make the French and the British feel better. It was true that Pershing agreed to put the 1st U.S. Infantry Division into the trenches before they were ready for it, but that would probably have happened whether the French had demanded it or not; the press, the public, and the Congress at home were longing impatiently to hear that the doughboys had had their first encounter with the by-now hated Hun. What Marshall and his fellow officers liked was Pershing's insistence that this was an *American* army, which was eager to fight side by side with the British and the French, but *never* under their orders. He had insisted on their U.S. entity, and Marshall was proud of him standing up for America's rights.

He was aware, of course, that Pershing was a very proud man himself, and touchy. He had become furiously angry when he had heard that his allies had sneered about the inexperience of the American troops and had vowed to make Pétain and Foch, French and Haig—the French and British commanders—eat their words by demonstrating that American troops were the best soldiers in the world, who, given the right leadership and opportunity, would gain signal victories on the very same battlefields where the weary Allies were experiencing nothing but stalemate or defeat. But to achieve such victories, he needed good officers, and word was out that anyone above the rank of major in the Expeditionary Force who showed exceptional talent and came under Pershing's eye was ripe for rapid, even spectacular promotion.

Marshall was well aware that both his name and those of a

number of other staff officers of 1st Div were on Pershing's short list. He was quietly confident that if only one officer were chosen, he would be the choice. He had always been a cool assessor of his own abilities, and he did not have to convince himself that he was better than his fellow lieutenant colonels. He wanted promotion badly. He had waited too long for it. He was well aware that the war was his opportunity and that once it was over, the U.S. Army would revert to its old habit of promoting by seniority, which would means years of waiting to step into old men's boots. So he had worked, studied, trained, and schemed to make himself first among his fellow colonels, and he did not need 1st Div's commanding officer, General William L. Sibert, to tell him that of all the colonels, he was the best of the bunch, though Sibert, who admired Marshall, made it clear that he so considered him.

The moment for which he had been waiting came when a signal arrived from Pershing's headquarters announcing that the Commander in Chief proposed to make a flying visit, and would 1st Div set up an exercise which he could witness? It so happened that when the signal came, both General Sibert and his chief of staff were absent and did not get back to their headquarters until just before Pershing's arrival. In the meantime, Marshall, as acting chief of staff, set up an exercise demonstrating a new method for storming an enemy trench. Marshall had worked it out himself, and neither Sibert nor his chief of staff had ever seen it before.

Nevertheless, the moment it was over, Pershing turned to Sibert and ordered him to conduct a critique of the exercise. Sibert flubbed badly, much to Pershing's evident annoyance. In Marshall's words, "he just gave everybody hell." Rounding on General Sibert, he curtly and woundingly criticized him in front of his junior officers, castigating him for being a poor commander in charge of an ill-trained division. Then, swinging around, he proceeded to question Sibert's chief of staff and ripped into him when he showed as much ignorance of the exercise as his chief had done.

Then, with an expression of deep disgust on his face, he dismissed the unfortunate chief of staff and made a move to go back to his staff car. For Marshall it was a moment of truth. He knew that Pershing was a prickly man who didn't like to be argued with. It was quite evident that he was tremendously angry. If Marshall intervened now, he could blow his chances of promotion to pieces for good and all. Yet he was angry at the injustice and unfairness of what had happened. He was only a junior officer, but he felt he had to intervene, had to try to explain, had to defend the integrity of his commanding officer, no matter what the consequences.

Taking a deep breath, he stepped forward and began to tell Pershing how and why things had gone wrong. The Commander in Chief stared at him for a moment in cold contempt but was evidently not listening, for he abruptly shrugged his shoulders and began walking away. Risking everything now, Marshall reached out and took Pershing's arm, forcing him to stop.

"General Pershing," he said, trying to keep the indignation out of his voice, "there's something to be said here, and I think I should say it because I've been here longest."

Pershing turned and stared at him now, and Marshall was well aware that the Commander in Chief was now taking in exactly who he was. A moment or two ago he had been any minor staff officer, but now Pershing would remember him, find out his name, and probably put a black mark against it in his little book.

"What have you got to say?" Pershing snapped coldly.

So far as Marshall remembered, it was just "a torrent of facts" which he poured out, while his fellow officers, frozen, stared at him and "were horrified." As for Pershing, he showed no expression at all as he listened to Marshall's explanation. When it was finished, he turned.

"You must appreciate the troubles we have," he said, an apparent reference to the headaches he and his staff had at headquarters running the whole Army. To which Marshall, who was now resigned to the fact that he had blown everything and had "gotten into it up to my neck," called after him, "Yes, General, but we have them every day, and they have to be solved before night."

The Commander in Chief's staff car and his entourage drove away, and General Sibert came over to thank Marshall for risking his promotion in defending him, but he seemed to share the opinion of the rest of the staff that for his temerity, he would soon be fired. Marshall was cast down by the prospect but stayed convinced that he could not have acted otherwise. The only comfort he got from the incident was the thought that if he did lose his staff job as a result of talking back to Pershing, at least that meant he would be sent to fight in the trenches—and that was really where he wanted to be.

Exactly the opposite happened, as it turned out.

For the moment, however, Pershing had bigger things on his mind than the fate of a lowly staff officer with 1st Div. In the spring of 1918 he did something which, in Marshall's eyes, elevated him in military stature above all the other commanders in chief fighting on the western front. The man who had made it crystal clear to both the French and the British that his was an American Army, taking orders from no one but Americans, demonstrated that when the situation was grim enough, he could reverse himself—and now Pershing proceeded to do so. As Marshall wrote later:

> Few Americans will ever realize the situation of the Allies at this particular period of the war. The Fifth British Army, virtually demolished, had been replaced by French reserves and these in turn were suffering severely. The enemy had made a penetration of sixty kilometers and had cut the principal railroad artery between the British and French. Amiens was under gunfire and with its fall rail communication between the two Allies would practically cease. During the onrush of the Germans there was one period of twenty-four hours when serious consideration was given to the plan of carrying the French line west to the coast and abandoning all efforts to keep in touch with the English.

All reports indicated that for the moment at least, the morale of the British infantrymen was at its lowest ebb, and both Haig and Foch doubted whether it could be relied upon any longer in the struggle.

It was in this critical situation that General Pershing, in Marshall's words, "rose to greatness." He who had fought so vigorously to maintain the separate identity and integrity of the American Army, now put it at the disposal of his desperate Allies as they faced disaster. Marshall wrote:

> Surrendering the direct control of his own troops, he released them to be scattered over four hundred miles of front. Temporarily jeopardizing his own and even American prestige, he laid all his cards on the table and directed every move toward the salvage of the Allied wreck. In the midst of a profound depression he radiated determination and the will to win.

He called all the officers of the 1st U.S. Division to meet him at his headquarters at Chaumont-en-Bassigny and informed them that they were about to take part in a gigantic combined Allied counteroffensive and that upon its result would depend the outcome of the war.

"Our people today are hanging expectant upon your deeds," Pershing told them. "The future is hanging upon your action in this conflict. . . . You are taking with you the sincerest wishes and the highest hopes of the President and all our people at home . . . with a feeling of certainty in our hearts that you are going to make a record of which your country will be proud."

Marshall was not exactly impressed by the words, but he was by the manner and expression behind them. He guessed how the Commander in Chief must be feeling. From the time Pershing had left the United States to set up the headquarters of the American Expeditionary Force in France, he had been dreaming of this moment. Though U.S. troops had been manning the trenches since the winter of 1917, and though they had had their casualties, so far they had done nothing more than stiffen the Allies, make raids, and fire guns at the enemy. Now they were about to launch the first great offensive of the war, one in which the bulk of the fighting men of the American armies would be taking part, and Pershing, who had worked so hard to bring it about and planned so meticulously to lead his men in an action that could turn the threat of defeat into the certainty of victory, would be there only in a subordinate role, taking orders from the French. It was hard medicine to swallow. In Marshall there was sown a respect for Pershing, a man big enough to make such a magnanimous gesture, that grew practically to hero worship in the weeks that followed. For in the late spring of 1918 the last desperate offensive of the German armies was turned back, and the stage set for an Allied victory. And Marshall recognized, long before the analysts and military strategists confirmed it, that the catalyst which changed the fortunes of war was Pershing's willingness to sacrifice personal pride and national prestige to the common cause.

For the next week or two America's attention was concentrated on a small town in a river valley called Château-Thierry, and a bloody baptism of fire it turned out to be for the doughboys from the United States. So far as Marshall and the 1st Infantry Division were concerned, though, the name that burned itself into their hearts and their brains was Cantigny. It was a small village held by the Germans which the Allies needed and 1st Div was ordered to take. The men finally flogged their way into it and were then told to hold on, and they did so under one of the most concentrated barrages of artillery fire that the Germans laid down during the final stages of World War I. Marshall wrote later:

> We held Cantigny. The Germans never afterwards reoccupied the village. The price paid was a heavy one but it demonstrated conclusively the fighting qualities and fortitude of the American soldier. Little has been heard or is known of this action. The enemy's rush on Château Thierry and the dramatic entrance of our troops at that point, at the psychological moment, naturally attracted the undivided attention of the public in America.

He added:

> It was not the ordeal of personal combat that seemed to prove the greatest strain in the last war. It was the endurance for days at a time of severe artillery bombardment by shells of heavy caliber, that proved the fortitude of troops. To be struck by these hideous impersonal agents without the power personally to strike back was the lot of the American soldier at Cantigny. On other fields later on, he overran the enemy, advanced deep into his positions, and suffered far heavier casualties. But the conditions were utterly different and the strain on the individual less severe.

Marshall almost missed the battle for Cantigny. Just before it began, his horse slipped in the mud while he was riding toward the trenches, threw him, and dragged him with his foot locked in the stirrup. His ankle was fractured. But he had it bound up and, in great pain, stayed on to see the military operation through to its successful conclusion. Cantigny would always be a benchmark in his development as a soldier and as a man.

> This little village marks a cycle in the history of America. Quitting the soil of Europe to escape oppression and the loss of personal liberty, the early settlers in America laid down the foundations of a government based on equality, personal liberty, and justice. Three hundred years later their descendants returned to Europe and on May 28, 1918, launched their first attack on the remaining forces of autocracy to secure these same principles for the peoples of the Old World.

He had no doubt in his mind that to the men of the American Expeditionary Force and, in large measure, to General John J. Pershing belonged the credit for turning the tide.

Once the Allied spring offensive was successfully launched, Marshall received news of two developments which banished permanently an apprehension which had been nagging him all through the battle for Cantigny: that Pershing's wrath would finally catch up with him for his interference during the Commander in Chief's visit to 1st Division and that he would be passed over for promotion. Far from it. General Sibert informed him that he had sent his name forward to Pershing's headquarters commending him for his work in 1st Division's forward areas during the operations, and as a result, he was being promoted on the field to the rank of temporary full colonel. There danced before him the happy prospect that very shortly now he would be given a battalion of his own and would be where he had always wanted to be—in the trenches, commanding men fighting in the front line.

But it was not to be. As it turned out, his temerity in buttonholing Pershing had done his career no damage at all. Just the opposite. It had drawn the Commander in Chief's attention to him and spurred him into making inquiries about his background and abilities. The result was that now an order came through that Colonel George Catlett Marshall be transferred at once to the General Staff of the AEF at its headquarters at Chaumont.

Marshall was truly distressed at this new posting, and the relief of his promotion did not assuage it. It had always been one of his lifetime ambitions to lead men into battle, and the casualties in 1st Division's battalion commanders now made it possible. But now he was denied the opportunity. Pershing was demanding his presence at Chaumont without delay. Marshall wrote later:

> Hurriedly packing my few effects and saying goodbye to my friends, I prepared to start by automobile at six o'clock the next morning. . . . It was hard to preserve one's composure to these men with whom I had been so intimately associated for over a year in France. We had been pioneers and our trials and tribulations had seemed to bind us very close to one another. I can see them now—gathered in the broad doorway of the chateau. The friendly jests and affectionate farewells, as I got into the Cadillac, made a deep impression on my mind, and I drove off hardly daring to wonder when and where would be our next meeting. Six days later they dashed into the great counterattack which precipitated the retreat of the German Army, and within seventy-two hours every field officer of the infantry, excepting three colonels, had fallen. Smith and all four of the lieutenant colonels were killed, and every battalion commander was a casualty, dead or wounded.

So perhaps it was just as well he never got that regimental command. He almost certainly would not have survived it.

Still, Chaumont was something of a shock. Pershing's headquarters was south of Paris, in château country untouched by war and remote from the mud, the blood, and the noise of battle on the western front. Marshall wrote later:

> I found myself in a strange atmosphere. These new associates had been working for a year on plans and organization for an army of several million men. Questions of ocean tonnage, ports of debarkation, constructions of docks and great depots in the SOS [Supply and Operations Sector]—these filled their mind every day. The methods of training divisions newly arrived in France, the problem

of securing French 75's [cannons] and British heavy guns, the manufacture of tanks, and our complicated relations with the French and the English were ordinary topics of conversation and discussion.

It was a different world from the one in which he had lived for the past year.

> In the First Division we had struggled with the concrete proposition of feeding, clothing, training, marching and fighting the men. Their health and morale was [*sic*] a daily issue; their dead and wounded a daily tragedy. For six months . . . we had been continuously in the line in immediate contact with the enemy. Our minds had been unconcerned with boats and ports and warehouses. Huge projects for the future made no appeal to us. We wanted trained replacements to fill the thinning ranks, more ammunition and horses; less frequent visits from critical staff officers in limousines would have met our approval. Each man was living in his own little world, ignorant to a surprising degree of all that occurred elsewhere.

Now he was part of that larger military world. Now he was one of those "critical staff officers in limousines," and he wasn't sure that he liked it at all. True, he was made welcome by Chaumont's top brass. General Fox Conner, chief of operations of the AEF, greeted him with the announcement that he would be sharing quarters with General LeRoy Eltinge, the AEF's deputy chief of staff, in Fox Conner's comfortably furnished château. Most of his colleagues in the Operations Section, where he would be working, were old friends or acquaintances with whom he had collaborated on Army posts throughout the world. He renewed acquaintance with Colonel Hugh Drum, who had just been appointed chief of staff of the U.S. First Army, and with a group of colonels—Upton Birnie, Walter Grant, Samuel Gleaves, John Murphy—most of whom were destined to rise to top rank in the U.S. Army after the end of the war.* The AEF mess served excellent French food and wines and entertained some distinguished

---

*And Marshall was forced to retire most of them when World War II came along.

guests, including French ministers, British generals, and visiting U.S. congressmen and ambassadors.

If Marshall had any feelings of guilt about the strange new world in which he was now moving, it could hardly have been assuaged by his first experience of what duties on the General Staff entailed. Within a few days of his arrival, Fox Conner informed him he had been coopted to an official board of inquiry. With a general and another colonel, he was dispatched to a U.S. unit in the trenches at the foot of the Vosges Mountains. A young captain had taken out a party of American troops on a raid against the German lines on the other side of the forest, and it had gone wrong. The men were ambushed by the enemy, came under heavy fire, and lost twenty of the party in killed and captured.

Marshall found the mission "most distasteful." He commented: "For the past year I had been in the position of resenting the frequent appearance of boards and inspectors from GHQ to examine into what we had done and discover what we might have failed to do. . . . Now I found myself in the role of an inspector or probably fault finder."

That night, as the board discussed the abortive raid over dinner, the other members of the board of inquiry, plainly bored with it all, informed Marshall that as junior member he would be expected to return to the unit the following morning and complete the "investigation," after which he would be expected to deliver his report to GHQ; they had other tasks to perform. Marshall demurred, saying he was unlikely to find any further evidence that would change the opinion he had already formed about the raid. His fellow members then asked him to tell them what his opinion was.

> [It] was to the effect that a telegram should be sent to the 77th Division commander by the Chief of Staff of the AEF congratulating him on the offensive spirit displayed in attempting this raid, and expressing the hope that the unfortunate result would not deter the division from undertaking further offensive operations.

To Marshall's surprise, and pleasure, the senior members of

the board said they entirely agreed with his opinion and that they, too, would recommend that a telegram should be sent along the lines he suggested.

He felt better. "Whether justified or not," he wrote later, "the outcome of this incident gave me personal satisfaction through a feeling that I was doing something to encourage those who were struggling to learn the intricacies of trench warfare."

But it did not entirely soothe his doubts about having left the infantry at such a crucial moment in the war. Nor did it help when he discovered what it was like to be on the receiving end of all the ridicule, criticism, antipathy, and contempt which many a serving officer in the field felt for members of the General Staff. Life in the operations room of Pershing's GHQ may not have been as physically dangerous as work at 1st Div, but Marshall found it exhausting and, when he had to make vital decisions about movements of troops and divisions, much more agonizing to the mind and spirit.

It was just about this time that Brigadier General Douglas MacArthur made an impact on his military life.

Marshall had run across Douglas MacArthur before, much earlier in his career, when they were both fellow lieutenants (though MacArthur was a first and Marshall a second lieutenant) at Fort Leavenworth. Not that their situation had brought them together in those days. MacArthur was already too cocky and self-confident a character to seek out a lowly "second loot" for companionship. He was already relying on his family connections—plus his undoubted military brilliance—to give him a leg up the military ladder. His father was the famous General Arthur MacArthur, hero of the Philippine insurrection. His mother, Mary Pinkney "Pinky" MacArthur, doted on her son and would go to any lengths to further his career. Her son had not taken it well that, even so, Marshall had topped his record at Leavenworth.

Now MacArthur was chief of staff of the 42nd U.S. Infantry Division (known as the Rainbow Division) and effectively its commander, since its actual commander, Major General Charles T. Menoher, was under MacArthur's thumb and was apt to turn any of his subordinate's suggestions into his own orders for the division. No one, least of all Marshall, denied MacArthur's military flair, and the Rainbow had done brilliantly as a result of his suggestions to his chief and his own conduct of the operations. But in the beginning it had been quite a struggle to keep the division in being. There were staff officers at Chaumont who resented the control MacArthur had over the Rainbow's official commander, and there was even a movement among some of them to have the division broken up and its troops and officers assigned to other divisions.

By complaining directly to Washington, where congressmen were suborned by telegrams from MacArthur and visits from Mrs. Pinky MacArthur, this plot was scotched, and the Rainbow stayed at the front as a fighting unit. But MacArthur never forgave GHQ at Chaumont for trying to sabotage him. He considered the assault on the Rainbow a personal affront and vowed vengeance. Meanwhile, he loudly asserted that it was the enmity and envy of the top brass at AEF headquarters at Chaumont which had so far denied him the medals, the promotions, and the acclaim he had earned on the battlefield.

In fact, few people doubted that Brigadier General MacArthur was one of the authentic American heroes of World War I. He had shown himself fearless in battle. He had fought side by side with his men, and for the danger and comradeship he had shared with them, he had earned their admiration and affection. He was undoubtedly a swaggerer and a boaster, but he boasted about his soldiers, too, and they loved him for it. He was a publicity hound, but what did they care if he posed and postured for the war correspondents, so long as he praised the quality of his men whenever he opened his mouth, drawing attention to them each time he shone the spotlight on himself?

If Marshall had any particular feelings about MacArthur when he joined the staff at Chaumont, they could have been only admiration for his soldierly skills and perhaps envy at the opportunities to lead men in battle which MacArthur had been given and he had been denied.

When he joined the staff at Chaumont, however, he discovered that some officers there positively cringed whenever another photograph of MacArthur appeared in the press. They were certainly antipathetic to his swashbuckling ways. But though it was true that there was, as MacArthur's biographer says, this "coterie of officers [at Chaumont] hostile to MacArthur," there is no evidence that they ever—as he subsequently claimed—denied him medals or promotions or tried to relieve him of his command. Not, at least, after he had turned the Rainbow Division into a magnificent fighting unit.

Nevertheless, MacArthur continued to direct dark accusations in Chaumont's direction, and any staff member became automatically his enemy. The only member of the AEF staff whom he exempted from his baleful attitude was the Commander in Chief, General John J. Pershing himself, with whom he stayed on good terms (publicly at least), and continually praised as "one of my father's most brilliant protégés."*

The fact that Marshall was now on the staff at Chaumont might never have drawn him to MacArthur's attention, however— for he was only a minor member of the hated group—had not an unfortunate incident put him on the enemy list which the Rainbow commander meticulously kept. As his biographer writes, "There were, [MacArthur] came to believe, people in the Army out to get him—deskbound men who envied and resented a fighting officer."

And in 1918, quite inadvertently, Marshall became one of them.

By November 4, 1918, the war was all but won. The German armies were falling back rapidly, and no troops were keeping up with them as doggedly, determinedly, and efficiently as the men of the AEF. Back in Chaumont, Marshall was manipulating the momentum of the advance by a series of complicated maneuvers, passing one well-supplied division through another which was running out of supplies, and leapfrogging forward, giving the enemy no respite. The left wing of the AEF had soon advanced far

---

*Pershing had served on Arther MacArthur's staff in the Philippines, as Mrs. Pinky MacArthur never failed to remind him when she wanted a favor.

beyond the progress point reached by the only other force in the running, that of France's Fourth Army.

"Our heavy guns had been in position from which they could fire on the sole line of rail communication which supplied all of the German Army from Picardy to Carignan, southeast of Sedan," he wrote.

He manipulated the red flags on his map and gave the go-ahead signal to MacArthur's Rainbow Division, which was topped up with ammunition and martial esprit, to pass through the 78th Division and strike forward, and he gave the advance another impetus by shoving his old 1st Infantry Division through the ranks of the 80th, which needed relieving.

There were rumors from back home that President Wilson was negotiating with the German government for an armistice, and the fear at Pershing's GHQ was that the enemy was "seeking to outmaneuver us diplomatically," to secure a temporary respite for its exhausted troops.

> If the fighting could be continued ten days longer, about a million German soldiers in front and to the West of us would either have to surrender to us or disperse as individuals. . . . We debated the question of whether or not the troops on the left wing of [our] army had enough punch left in them to be driven forward throughout the ensuing night. This portion of [our] line was headed direct on Sedan.

Sedan. Every general on the western front wanted to wrest Sedan from the Germans, and none more eagerly than the French commander, Maréchal Ferdinand Foch. It was Sedan's capture by the Germans which had particularly humiliated France during the war of 1870, and its reoccupation by the poilus would avenge the nation's bitterest defeat. But Foch's Fourth French Army had fallen badly behind the pell-mell pace of the American advance, and already U.S. gunners had brought their guns close enough to lob shells into the city across the Meuse River. Should they go ahead?

Consulting with his immediate chief, General Fox Conner, Marshall was told that the C in C had decided that waiting for the French would only lose precious time and that by force of circumstances Sedan had become a legitimate American target.

Accordingly, Marshall on November 5 issued an order to the U.S. commanding generals that was to prove one of the most controversial of World War I. It read as follows:

> 1. General Pershing desires that the honor of entering Sedan should fall to the First American Army. He has every confidence that troops of the 1st Corps, assisted on their right by the 5th Corps, will enable him to realize this desire.
> 2. In transmitting the foregoing message, your attention is invited to the favorable opportunity now existing for pressing our advantage through the night.

Marshall was only too well aware of the controversial nature of the order, for to carry it out, the U.S. armed forces would have to preempt one of the most oft-expressed aims of their French allies. He felt that he could not send the order out until both General Fox Connor and Pershing's chief of staff and spokesman, General Hugh A. Drum, had confirmed it, and it was not until six in the evening of November 5 that he was able to get hold of the latter.

Drum read through the order that his subordinate put before him and, as Marshall wrote later, "agreed immediately to the dispatch of the order." But before he did so, General Drum told Marshall to add a sentence on the end, and it was this that was to cause all the trouble. "*Boundaries will not be considered binding,*" the additional sentence read.

No doubt Drum considered the sentence necessary because the Americans, in order to get to Sedan, would have to cross the French line of advance and would therefore be poaching on their territory, and he was informing his commanders that they had his prior permission.

But it didn't quite work out that way.

The American commanders weren't worrying about the French, who were way behind. They were watching each other, and that final sentence in their orders gave them what they interpreted as permission to open up a race for Sedan.

"It did not authorize a free-for-all," Marshall said later, "although that is what happened."

Brigadier General MacArthur's Rainbow Division was within

three miles of Sedan, and its lookout posts could see into the city's streets, across the Meuse. MacArthur had laid his plans to cross the river and enter Sedan the following day. But meanwhile, General Charles P. Summerall of V Corps read the last sentence and phoned through an order to Brigadier General Frank Parker, now commanding the 1st Infantry Division, which told him to "march immediately on Sedan" and capture it.

Parker needed no further urging. He gave his men the signal, and they promptly swarmed straight through the lines of the Rainbow Division and the French 40th Division, to its rear on the left. Soon troops and transport were inextricably mixed, and the roads were jammed with trucks, guns, horse transports, and command cars.

Alarmed by the chaos and confusion, MacArthur went forward to find out what was happening. A young lieutenant from the 1st Division took one look at the angry man stalking toward him, dressed as usual in a flopping hat, a muffler round his neck, no regulation gas mask over his shoulder, and promptly mistook him for a German. He thereupon arrested him and disarmed him and would not release him in spite of MacArthur's violent protestations. It was not until an order came through from divisional headquarters that he was finally let go.

By that time GHQ had been informed of what had happened. Not only that, but the French Fourth Army had meanwhile become aware of unusual American activity in its area and became alarmed that it was going to be beaten into Sedan. Was France going to be humiliated twice over this symbolic town, first by the Boches, now by the Yanks? It must not be allowed to happen. Egged on by Foch, the French put on speed and closed in on the approaches to the town, only to find a jumble of quarreling Americans blocking their path to glory. An empurpled French general sent an urgent message to Frank Parker of the 1st Division, demanding that he get out of the way and further informing him, through clenched teeth no doubt, that even if the Americans did continue their rush into the town, he would still feel compelled to put down an artillery barrage on it. Yanks or Boches, they both were the enemy to the French so far as Sedan was concerned.

As it turned out, neither French nor Americans took Sedan.

The Germans held on to the town until the Armistice which ended the war was signed on November 11, 1918.

But though MacArthur subsequently professed to treat the whole incident as a big joke, he never really forgot it. He had seen the order that created all the confusion. He cannot fail to have noted that it was written by Staff Colonel George Catlett Marshall, who was therefore responsible for all the chaos that followed, his humiliating arrest, the sabotage of his carefully laid plan to capture Sedan. Moreover, had not Marshall formerly been on the staff of the 1st Infantry Division? And was it not his order which had loosed his buddies in the 1st Division upon his lines of communication in their eager rush to beat him into Sedan? Paranoid as he was about all members of the staff at Chaumont, MacArthur must have found plenty of reasons for suspecting Marshall of sinister motives in the way he had handled the whole operation. MacArthur was not a man to forgive insults or mistakes, whether intended or not, nor did he forget those who inflicted them upon him.

As for Marshall, he simply dismissed the mixup as "a typical American 'grandstand finish.' " But did he really regard it as nothing more? It is interesting to read the book he subsequently wrote on his World War I activities, for in it he mentions a long list of officers and men with whom he came in contact. He also makes several lengthy references to the famous Rainbow Division, but not once does he mention the name of its colorful acting commander, who was, of course, Douglas MacArthur. An oversight, perhaps, but it took on significance later.

The last picture we have of George Marshall in France in the aftermath of World War I is at a dinner party which the staff at Chaumont gave for the French notables of the region. For the colonel, it was altogether too formal. The truth was, Marshall liked parties, liked dancing, liked popular music, and was not as austere or serious as his appearance seemed to indicate, not, at least, when there was reason to relax. He wrote later:

> This was the first party these French people had enjoyed since the summer of 1914, and naturally they were not at their ease with

us. We attempted a little dancing after dinner but found the French ladies did not understand our steps and that we were unable to engage in the constant whirling of the French waltz.

When the army orchestra retired for its supper, Marshall, another colonel, and a couple of the younger Frenchwomen decided to organize an orchestra of their own:

> With the piano, trombone, saxophone and snare drum we mangled a few pieces, but awakened things a little. As the enthusiasm grew, we gained volunteers and finally we had an old French Count proudly manning the cymbals. From a stiff dinner party the dinner was rapidly transformed into a rather riotous celebration and our guests, instead of leaving at eleven, remained until 2 A.M.

Shortly afterward he was called to Paris to join General Pershing, and a round of victory celebrations began.

5

Anticlimax

One of the most popular and sociologically apposite songs of the 1920's was about the doughboys of the AEF, now sailing home to America from Europe. Its opening lines were:

> How're ya gonna keep 'em
> Down on the farm
> Now that they've seen Paree?

To no one could the words be more appropriately applied than to Colonel George C. Marshall. He did not sail back to the United States until September 1, 1919, ten months after the signing of the Armistice, and there is some suspicion that he may not have wanted to. What prospects had he to go back to? He was thirty-eight years old, good-looking, fighting fit, with a brilliant wartime record, and it was neither the oak leaves on his shoulder tabs nor his staff officer's patches that made men and women turn around to look at him when he came into the room. The war had given him an air of authority, and self-confidence shone out of him. Men liked him. Women found him devastatingly attractive. Wherever he went, doors opened to him, invitations poured in.

Marshall was still young enough to like the adulation, to appreciate being treated as a hero. He was also too cool a character not to suspect that things would be different when he got back to America and took off his uniform and went back to the grind of peacetime service in the U.S. Army. As for his personal life, he did not mention it to anyone, but he could hardly have contemplated a resumption of life with Lily as anything but a constant test of his patience and endurance. Her letters indicated that physically she had not changed at all and still regarded herself as an invalid, to be kept sacrosanct and inviolate. How would he react, after all he had seen and experienced, to the resumption of married life with a beautiful woman whom he loved as passionately as ever but whom he would still be forbidden to do more than touch? Would he be able to bear it? All that flirting and teasing in which Lily specialized would now be a thousand times more frustrating, filled with the direst temptations.

There is little doubt that had he wished to arrange it, Marshall could have gone back to the United States immediately after the Armistice, on furlough at least. That he did not do so is, one suspects, an indication of the lively apprehensions he felt about his future life and military career as well as his determination to see some more of Europe and have a little fun. There were cogent reasons, both personal and military, for postponing the return to reality. So he wrote to Lily to say that he had accepted service with the Army in the occupied territories of defeated Germany, where he was appointed chief of operations to the U.S. forces. Shortly afterward there was a message from General Pershing. Would he come back to Paris and become aide to his favorite general? "Black Jack" was about to set off on a series of official tours of Allied countries, where he and the U.S. Army would be hailed for their role in Germany's defeat. Marshall accepted with alacrity, setting his return date back even farther.

It was the beginning of six months in Europe that he would never forget, and worries about Lily and his career temporarily faded from his mind. Thereafter everything in his life and Army career was inevitably compared with those dazzling days, and the letdown when it was finally over cannot have been easy for the young colonel to bear.

For his first chore as Pershing's aide, Marshall rode behind the Commander in Chief in a great parade down the Champs Élysées, and in honor of the triumphant American Army the French government opened up the Arc de Triomphe for the doughboys to march under, the first foreigners to pass beneath the great arch since the Franco-Prussian War.*

But it was in London that Colonel Marshall tasted the headiest delight of being handsome, American, and a winner. The Brit-

*The Nazis did so again after France's defeat in 1940.

ish were already becoming disenchanted with their erstwhile allies the French, of whom one English statesman complained that they were "incomparable in defeat but insufferable in victory," and they were beginning to look across the Atlantic for new friends. The Americans, who had already had a few passages with the French themselves, found the warmth of the British welcome all but overwhelming, and seldom can they have been so hospitably received, and made such a fuss of, as they were in that halcyon summer of 1919.

Marshall kept a diary of his visit, and its entries are daily descriptions of grand parties filled with famous men and beautiful, beautiful women. The colonel was delighted to discover that some of the most gorgeous-looking of the ladies were Americans who had married into the British aristocracy but were thrilled to meet a charming officer from back home. At a Buckingham Palace garden party:

> I walked around for quite a while with Lady Curzon* who is supposed to be one of the beauties of London. . . . Later Lady Drogheda joined us. She is a very dashing sort of person and one of the champion golf and tennis players of England. I left with her by a little private gateway in the rear of the Garden and drove around to her house where we had some Scotch and talked for about an hour or more—then she drove me to the Carlton [Hotel]. . . . After dinner, a few of us went to a ball being given by Lady Ribblesdale, the former Mrs. John Jacob Astor. . . . I had a couple of dances with the Duchess of Sutherland, Lady Drogheda, Lady Ribblesdale, Lady Curzon—and several others whose names I do not remember. I left at about 2:30 A.M.

It was a ceaseless round of official ceremonies and less formal entertainments, and though he was impressed by the ceremonials, it was obviously the informal occasions that he relished the most. He and Frank Pershing (the general's son) drove out to Windsor while the general was having lunch with the king and queen at Buckingham Palace, and they were taken first for a tour of the

*Born Mary Leiter in Chicago.

castle and then for lunch at the old English pub The White Hart. Marshall noted:

> To add to the pleasure of the lunch, we invited the young women who drove the cars, they being members of the Women's Army Service Corps. We found that the English officers had very kindly arranged to have the most attractive chauffeurs for the cars. To our surprise, they were all of them very nice, and several of them were women of some position. After lunch we started back, and the girl driving the car that Frank Pershing and I had drawn was so very entertaining that we both sat in the front seat of the limousine with her. She took us back through Hampton Court and Richmond Park and made herself so generally entertaining that we were late in arriving for a reception at the House of Commons.

That evening, a glutton for all the hospitality on offer, he went on to Dudley House for a ball Lady Ward was giving in honor of General Pershing.

> Among the best known people [present] were the King and Queen of Portugal, the Prince of Wales and his two brothers, Princess Mary, the Princess Royal (daughter of Queen Alexandra) and a number of other minor members of the royal family. I had a fine time. . . . I danced more frequently with the Duchess of Sutherland and Lady Bingham than anybody else, but toward the latter part of the evening I met a Mrs. Ward, formerly Muriel Wilson, a famous beauty in London. She was a marvelous dancer. We had three on [sic] a stretch. I was principally impressed by the huge fans of ostrich feathers all the women carried, many of them in brilliant colors. Lady Ashburn's was scarlet, the Duchess of Sutherland's was emerald green, as was her dress. Their jewels and tiaras were so massive that they did not make much appeal to me as they looked like glass. Pearls were as common as beads.

All in all, it turned out to be the highlight of the visit so far as entertainment was concerned. He had been warned by some of the guests that the king of Portugal was "a pompous little squirt" and had this confirmed when he heard him expressing some sneering remarks about "loud mouthed Yankees," but he got his own back during the course of the evening. He wrote to Lily, on July 17, 1919:

> During the dance, I had the pleasure of stepping on the foot of the King of Portugal, who was sitting on the sidelines, and I think I about ruined his Royal Highness. He looked quite furious— but I had no apologies for that particular person. I had supper with Lady Bingham. About three-thirty in the morning, after a number had gone home, the party became very lively. The Princess Victoria was making her very first effort to learn American dances, and those she singled out for the honor of dancing with her had a deuce of a time. I received an intimation that I should ask her to dance— and immediately went home. General Pershing stepped on her foot and left a large black spot on her slipper. She told a lady-in-waiting she was going to keep it as a souvenir. I imagine her foot would make about as good a souvenir as the slipper after he got through walking on it.
>
> I finished up at this party with three straight dances with the Duchess of Sutherland. She is really beautiful, dances extremely well, and is quite delightful to talk to. She is at the head of the Queen's household, and occupies the first position in England after royalty.

Every day was the same: up at dawn to get ready for a ceremony in the City of London or Buckingham Palace or the House of Commons, afternoons in the country with one or other of the beauties he had met the night before, and then a dance until 2:00 or 3:00 A.M. It was all leading up to the great victory parade in which General Pershing would ride through London at the head of a regiment of American troops. Horses for the Americans were provided by the British army, and Marshall got himself a nice quiet mount; but just before the procession started off, it was discovered that one of the U.S. generals had picked himself an obstreperous animal, and Marshall volunteered to swap with him.

In a letter to Lily on July 19, 1919, he commented:

> For eight miles I had the ride of my life, and the worst phase of the trouble was that the horse tried to kick everything in reach. While I did not see it myself, I am told that he struck one little girl

in the chin, and I am afraid he must have hurt her very badly, if he did not kill her. . . . I eased him along for $7\frac{1}{2}$ miles, until we reached the Admiralty Arch, which forms the entry to the Mall from Trafalgar Square. In going through the small passageway of the Arch, I was forced to keep him straight, because women and children were jammed in close, and he would have killed a few if I had allowed him to turn sidewise. As a result of my straightening him out, he reared, and at the top of his pitch, lost his footing and went over backwards. However, I had been expecting this throughout the affair, and fell clear, landing on one foot, and then on my hand and hip. I was rolling before I struck and went over three times to keep out of his way. He was down so completely that I was able to get to him and get back in the saddle before he had gotten entirely up, and in that way was able to mount him.

He found later that he had broken a bone in his hand in the spill, but he hardly noticed it at the time:

> As it turned out, I entered the Arch on a horse, and came out of it on a horse—and did not even lose my place in the line-up, but I lost my temper for the rest of the ride. . . . I only had a brief period in which to straighten out before reaching the Royal Pavilion where the King and Queen reviewed the pageant.

More dances. ("All the Princes and Princesses were there. I had an unusually good time on this occasion, despite the fact that at three different times a Prince had my girl when my dance came. I had a laborious dance with Princess Mary. If she doesn't reign any better than she dances, they are in a hard way. . . . It was about 2 A.M. when I received another intimation from a lady-in-waiting of Princess Victoria that I should dance with her. That was the last seen of me at Lady Willoughby's.")

General Pershing and his entourage left England on July 23 to return to Paris, and there was a detailed tour of the French battlefields and an official visit to Italy before the Americans finally sailed back to New York aboard the USS *Leviathan,* on September 1, 1919. Brigadier General Douglas MacArthur and the soldiers of the Rainbow Division were also aboard the ship, and their commander was ostentatiously first down the gangplank when they docked in New York. But Marshall and MacArthur appeared to have kept out of each other's way during the voyage.

There was, of course, a great victory parade complete with ticker tape down Broadway to give New Yorkers a chance to welcome back the returning warriors, and later Pershing led a procession of 25,000 U.S. combat veterans down Pennsylvania Avenue to the White House, after which a grateful Congress voted him immediate promotion to permanent four-star general. But despite the crowds and the evident pleasure people took in greeting their victorious army, there was something a little anticlimactic about the return home. Already Congress was debating the future of the Army, and the mood was to get it off the backs of the American taxpayers. That meant reductions not only in armaments and men but in chances of promotion. From now on the men who had fought and won the war would be something of an embarrassment to have around. As Confucius might have said, gratitude is like fish; after a short time it goes bad.

It was not too long after arriving home that Marshall felt the first impact of being a Regular Army officer in peacetime again. He received official notification from the War Department that the temporary rank of colonel, which he had held until the end of the war, had now been taken from him. He was back to his substantive rank of captain again. It is true that shortly afterward he was informed that he had been promoted to the permanent rank of major. But after eighteen years as an officer in the U.S. Army, with war service included, that was hardly something to cheer about. Nor were his feelings in any way soothed by the name that caught his eye when he looked down the rest of the list of promotions.

Douglas MacArthur had been elevated, too. They were almost exactly the same age, they had entered the Army at the same time, and they had both served brilliantly in the same war. But Marshall had ended up as a major. Douglas MacArthur, he now saw, had been upped to the heady rank of permanent brigadier general, way above him among the top brass.

Pinky MacArthur had done it again. Where Army politics was concerned, MacArthur's mother had antennae as sensitive as a hummingbird moth, and she had soon discovered the way things were going in military circles in Washington. The Chief of Staff of the U.S. Army was General Peyton March, and one of the first things he had proposed when the future of the Army was discussed was its expansion into a permanent force of half a million men. But when General Pershing was called to testify before a congressional committee, he had come out against March's plan and proposed a much different permanent army backed by UMS (universal military service). That was bad enough. March comforted himself with the thought that though he and Pershing were both two-star generals, he (March) was senior to the former chief of the AEF. Then Congress awarded four stars to Black Jack Pershing, and he now outranked the Chief of Staff. March hated that.

But so long as March remained the Chief of Staff, while Pershing waited to be given a new job, it was he who had the power, and he knew how to use it. Pinky MacArthur sensed that. March, too, had once served under her husband's command and been favored by him; she did not fail to remind the Chief of Staff about it and renewed her efforts when she heard that he was looking around for a new superintendent for West Point. Obviously he was not going to appoint anyone connected too closely with Pershing (and that meant all former members of the AEF chief's staff were barred), but what about that young son of his former commander who had done so well with the Rainbow Division? Was it not true that he loathed the "Pershing gang," too? (Who could possibly have told him that?)

So Douglas MacArthur was given the job—and the brigadier generalship that went with it.

Marshall stayed on Pershing's peacetime staff—as a major.

Victorious generals can usually take their pick of postwar jobs in business or academia, and there was no lack of offers General Pershing received once he was home in the United States. He turned them all down because he wanted to become Chief of Staff of the U.S. Army, mainly, his associates soon came to suspect, because he despised the general who already held the post— Peyton March—and wished to demonstrate how much better he could perform in it. But that was the trouble. Peyton March was determined not to yield his position and prestige to his rival until the last possible minute, and he stuck to his office until he finally retired from the Army. In the meantime, the government had to find something for the bored hero to do, and it finally sent him on a series of tours around the country, talking about the war to the populace and getting an enthusiastic welcome at every whistle stop he made (he went by train).

There was only one period when Black Jack dithered about whether he really wanted the Chief of Staff's job, and that was when speculation began about who should be the presidential prospects in 1920, and talk began among the Republicans about drafting Pershing. Marshall was naïve enough to think his chief shared his own antipathy for politicians and believed along with him that soldiers should never get involved in politics. He learned otherwise when a delegation of Republicans from Tennessee came to see Pershing with a proposition that he should be their candidate in the forthcoming primaries. The general was away, so Marshall saw the Tennesseans instead, listened silently to what they had to say, and then curtly dismissed them with the comment that the last thing General Pershing would be interested in was fighting on the hustings for an elective position, even if it was that of President of the United States. He got a flea in his ear from Black Jack when he heard about it, and Marshall ruefully swallowed the fact that his hero was as vulnerable to flattery and temptation as the next man. In fact, Pershing was soon so bitten by the presidential bug that he hurried back to Washington from an out-of-town trip when he heard that the Republican Convention in Chicago was deadlocked. His aide was shocked when he realized that Pershing hoped and expected to receive an urgent summons to Chicago and was quite downcast when Warren Harding got the nomination instead.

Fortunately for Black Jack's *amour propre*, General Peyton March retired from the Army not long afterward, and he was appointed Chief of Staff in his place, in August 1921. Marshall moved to Washington with him as his chief aide and was promoted at last, though only one rung up the ladder. He became a lieutenant colonel and moved into married quarters at Fort Myer, near Washington, immediately asking Lily to join him. Except for a short holiday they had spent together in Atlantic City the year before—when they stayed with his mother—they had seen little of each other since his return from France, and Lily had remained in Lexington, Virginia. Now she and her husband were reunited at last. It was soon evident that even if the beautiful duchesses of London had momentarily turned his head, he was still as eagerly in love with Lily as ever. But if he cherished any hopes that their union might be fruitful at last (and his goddaughter maintains that he never gave up the dream), it was doomed to disappointment.

Lily Marshall had grown into a remarkably handsome woman. She was a living example of the deceptiveness of outward appearance, for no one could possibly have guessed from watching her move around that inside her body was a time bomb liable to go off at any moment. In public she never seemed to betray the nature of her fraught condition by a gesture or an expression. She presided at the small dinner parties and receptions which the Marshalls began giving at Fort Myer and was a charming and efficient hostess. True, she never rode a horse—though riding was Marshall's favorite hobby—but when she walked, her stride was purposeful, and her manner confident and serene. It was little wonder that some people speculated about the barrenness of the marriage and wondered whether it was really Lily's fault. But what none of them could possibly doubt was her husband's devotion, his obvious pleasure in being with her, dancing attendance upon her, looking after her every whim.

Marshall spent five years as aide to General Pershing, including service in Washington, and the remarkable thing is that he never lost his admiration for Black Jack's qualities as a man and a leader of men. In fact, as Lily sometimes complained, Black Jack was a selfish and unremitting taskmaster and often worked his aide to the point of exhaustion. He could be temperamental and petulant, inefficient, wayward, and ungrateful. Some of the Army wives whispered to Lily that he was "terrible" with women, and they were afraid to be alone with him. Marshall became angry when he heard such "slanders." Once he had given his loyalty to a man, his faith in him could not be shaken, and for five years he did most of Black Jack's job for him, writing (and sometimes making) his speeches, preparing his appearances before Congress, keeping his appointments, shaping his programs, correcting his most serious mistakes—and never complaining.

The pleasure he got from his home life with Lily seemed to be all the compensation he needed. He was later to look back on the two years he spent at Fort Myer as the happiest of his life, especially when, in 1922, the one element came into it which had been absent until then—the small daughter he had always yearned to have. She was not, however, *his* daughter or Lily's, for she belonged to an ex-Army family who lived nearby. But the Marshalls fell for her in a big way, and the feeling was mutual. The little girl was soon spending so much time with the Marshalls that she came to be regarded as a member of the family, and no one was surprised when her mother asked the colonel if he would become the girl's godfather. He accepted with alacrity and evident surprise and pleasure.

Her name was Rose Page, and she was a bright child five years old. Until Marshall made his appearance at Fort Myer, a father's affection and authority had been the only things missing from Rose's life, and as she recalled later, she knew instinctively that here was a man to fill the gap. His understanding and affection for children were obvious even to a small child, and he never seemed bored or impatient in her company. He taught her to ride, he bought her a pony, and every morning, before he went to the War Department and she to school, they cantered along the bridle paths together.

Whatever modern psychiatrists might have thought about this warm relationship between Marshall and his goddaughter, Rose Page was certainly never uncomfortable about it, and her memories of it, written much later in life, are warm with affection, admiration, respect, and filial love. She was also never in doubt about Marshall's feelings for his wife, and it was she, adoring her new surrogate father as she did, who was sometimes envious of the way in which he doted upon her. Rose recalled:

He showered Lily with a hundred little attentions. He fetched and carried. He planned little surprises. He was ever solicitous about her health and comfort. He relieved her of mundane financial budgeting and any like chores and decisions, and if he teased her, he paid her innumerable little compliments. When she performed some necessary or even quite simple extra service for him, he praised her as if she had suffered immeasurable inconvenience for his sake—in short, he gave her his unremitting consideration, smoothed the path before his queen and led her by the hand.

Watching Lily and George Marshall together, she was sometimes jealous of the solid union which these two had built in each other, and she might have resented it had not Lily demonstrated that she adored Rose as much as George did and wanted her to be part of their family. Rose decided later:

> He was a sucker for Lily, and [Lily] unquestionably enjoyed it, but she was never tempted to take undue advantage of him, and indeed often submitted to his attentiveness more to please him than to benefit herself. Once, when she asked me to run upstairs to fetch her embroidery scissors and I started to go, Colonel Marshall told me to sit down, he'd get them! After he left, Lily smiled and told me, "George just naturally has to look after me, it's his pleasure, bless his heart. You too," she added, "haven't you noticed how he absolutely has to take care of us fragile females?"

It was only gradually, as the years passed, that his goddaughter became aware of the essential element that was missing from his marriage and began to guess the reason why she was so much cherished by him. As the knowledge began to sink in, so did her awareness that even she did not entirely fill the void in his marriage. But she certainly helped. When he was away, he wrote her long letters. When he was at home and working on his papers, nothing was too important if she demanded amusement and attention. He wrote her verses, including this one, which she treasured:

> A little girl I strive to please
>   Is very shy but likes to tease
> And tell all sorts of funny jokes

About all kinds of curious folks.
   She likes to ride and dance and coast
      But, better still, to butter toast
And smear it deep with honey sweet
      And sit and eat and eat and eat.
I think some time along in spring
      She'll eat so much of everything
Her dress is sure to spread and split
      And open out to make a fit.
And then perhaps she'll look right thin
      With strips of dress and streaks of skin.
I think she'll look real odd like that
      With nothing whole except her hat!

He never lost his love for Rose even when she grew up and married. In fact, after she had been married for a year or two, he badgered her so much about when she was going to start a family—in the same way that Lily must have been badgered in her time—that Rose finally told him "to lay off," explaining that she had been consulting gynecologists for four years about her barren condition, but that "my insides were apparently lopsided. Probably due to all those thousands of miles you made me trot," she added jokingly.

"Colonel Marshall appeared to be so deeply concerned and unhappy about my possible sterility," she added, "that I had deliberately chosen to be flippant to conceal my own disappointment. Poor Colonel Marshall, who had always longed for a child of his own, was visibly disturbed by my news."

It was the thought of being separated from Rose which made both Lily and her husband reluctant to leave Washington, even when Pershing's term of office as Chief of Staff drew to a close in 1923, and Marshall was tempted when Black Jack was appointed head of the War Graves Commission and suggested he might like to stay on and run the Washington office. But if he was ever to go beyond his present rank—and he still hoped for a general's star one of these days—it was necessary for him to have his staff service supplemented by time spent with troops in the field. He applied for a post with the U.S. garrison in China and was informed that he had been assigned to the 15th Infantry, stationed in Tientsin, and ordered to report in the fall of 1924.

To his delight, Lily was pronounced fit to travel with him, and he was on good enough terms with his mother-in-law not to be too cast down when Lily insisted that she must accompany them. They sailed from New York in an Army transport in early July 1924, stopping at Colón, in the Panama Canal Zone, and San Francisco en route to the Far East. When they reached Tientsin, it was to find that the 15th Infantry had lost its commander, who had been posted back Stateside, and Lieutenant Colonel Marshall was delegated to take over pending the arrival of a replacement. It was the first time he had ever commanded a regiment of troops, and he found it an exhilarating and satisfying experience, especially since he was plunged into a crisis almost immediately after his arrival.

It was a most turbulent period in China, even more so than usual. The Nationalist party (then known as the Kuomintang) was still struggling for power, and a fight for leadership was going on within its ranks between an ambitious young soldier named Chiang Kai-shek and Russian-backed Communist forces within the party. Meanwhile, the land was being divided up between rival warlords, and battles for supremacy were going on between a Manchurian-based tyrant named Chang Tso-lin and his bitter enemy, Wu Pei-fu.

At the moment that Marshall, Lily, and his mother-in-law arrived in Tientsin, news reached the American garrison that Wu's forces had been driven out of that city and were retreating southward. It would not be long before Wu's men reached Tientsin, where they might well be tempted to seize the railroad, the depot and marshaling yards, and the valuable rolling stock. The 15th Infantry was ordered on alert, told to hold the railroad, and to defend itself from the rabble Chinese forces—but to do it without fighting, if possible. Like the other big powers—Britain, France, and Japan—the United States had seized concessions in China after the Boxer Rebellion and stationed its own troops there to protect the lives and property of its citizens, but they were not supposed to interfere in Chinese internal affairs or to clash with Chinese nationals.

As Marshall found, it wasn't easy to stand aloof. By November the undisciplined elements of an army 100,000 strong began to swarm into Tientsin. They came on hijacked trains, captured steamers, horses, mules, and foot. They were hungry and mean and, though without food, had plenty of arms and ammunition. How to keep these lost, angry, and ravenous men from looting and raping? Marshall raided his own commissaries and the food stores in the city for extra supplies and then sent his troops to Tientsin's outskirts to establish posts at every road junction, rail halt, and river landing. A corporal and five U.S. troops manned each post, with a team of Chinese to help them. Their instructions were to offer rice, boiled cabbage, and tea to the fleeing troops, but only in exchange for their arms.

"Make it plain to them," Marshall told his corporals. "You give arms, we give food. No guns—no rice."

It was bluff, of course. Had the retreating rabble decided to seize the food by force, no American troops could have stopped them. There were just too many Chinese soldiers and too few doughboys. But Marshall had instilled his men with a sense of pride in their uniforms and the might of their nation, and they exuded a self-confidence which they probably did not really feel but which certainly overawed the rabble.

"Sometimes they had guns and knives pointed at their stomachs," he said later, "but no one used them."

The massive army of retreating soldiers was disarmed, and not a single Chinese soldier entered Tientsin still in possession of his gun. Not only that, but the word spread through the countryside, amid the fleeing troops, that the U.S. Army was watching them, and they behaved themselves even in places where no doughboy uniforms were visible. The villagers around Tientsin were so grateful for this invisible but potent protection from the U.S. Army—thus saving their granaries from looting and their wives and daughters from rape—that they presented the garrison the following spring with a white marble memorial gate, which was erected at the entrance to the garrison.*

It had been an exciting baptism for the temporary commander of the 15th Infantry, and Marshall enjoyed every moment of it, particularly since his success was promptly recognized by his superiors.

"I snaffled a nice letter of commendation out of the affair," he wrote later, "which is worth my three years in China."

His triumph, however, was soon followed by a dismal anticlimax. Two and a half months after he took over, the replacement commander arrived in Tientsin, and Marshall dropped back to second-in-command. The new commander, Colonel William K. Naylor, quickly demonstrated that he was not pleased by stories he had heard of Marshall's achievements.

Jealous in the extreme of anyone who threatened his authority or prerogatives, Naylor proceeded to make life hell for Marshall by barring him from exercise of any command whatsoever, confining him to routine office work and other trivial occupations. After the heady moments during the recent crisis it was a chastening comedown.

Fortunately (at least for Marshall) it turned out that Naylor, in addition to a streak of black jealousy, had a weakness for the bottle. He spent days dead drunk in his quarters or stalking around the parade ground in a mad temper, bawling out anyone who got in his way. Morale in the 15th dropped like a stone. By the middle of 1925 the regiment, which had overawed an army of 100,000 men, now surpassed all other U.S. regiments in China in only one achievement: It was tops in the number of cases of VD among its personnel. As Naylor became increasingly sodden and incapable, Marshall quietly ventured to take over some essential duties. He was just beginning to assume discreet command in all but name when news reached U.S. headquarters in China of Naylor's alcoholism, and he was quietly removed.

So for another two happy months Marshall was reappointed

---

*It stayed there until 1938, when U.S. troops left China. It is now to be seen at Fort Benning, Georgia.

acting commander and got down to the job of whipping the 15th back into shape. He organized sports and social events and route marches to take the men's minds and energies away from the local brothels. He rounded up a herd of shaggy Mongolian ponies and put together a troop of mounted infantrymen as a makeshift cavalry unit. The 15th soon began to be known in Army circles as the Foot Hussars. The VD statistics went down, and the esprit de corps went up.

Marshall enjoyed command. The feeling it gave him confirmed every anticipation he had ever had about Army service. He felt immense pride in producing a fighting-fit and well-trained regiment, capable of coping with any kind of threat, and found particular satisfaction in the knowledge that the men felt a sense of achievement, too. There is no doubt that Army life on an overseas station suited him, even when a new colonel arrived and demoted him once more to second-in-command. He liked the rigorous conditions. He worked hard, and he played hard—a long ride every morning and two hours of squash every night—but still put on weight. And photographs taken of him at this time show that he even grew a small mustache and, for the first and last time in his life, looked like a dashing hussar, even in a swimsuit.

But when would he get a command of his own?

Lily Marshall enjoyed China, too. The crisp climate of Tientsin invigorated her, and with no household chores to bother her—she had ten servants to look after their quarters—she was able to devote her time to being a senior officer's wife, keeping the other wives occupied and happy, overseeing the welfare of the men. Her spare time was filled with trips to Peking or the seaside and shopping expeditions in the bazaars. She was almost sorry when Marshall's tour of duty came to an end, describing it in letters to relatives at home as one great big "three-years' shopping trip." But she was equally delighted when news came through, at the end of 1926, that her husband's next job would be lecturing at the Army War College. George Marshall was disappointed. He had hoped for an appointment as instructor at the Infantry School at Fort Benning and regarded the War College as very much second best. There was, however, the consolation that the college was in Washington, where his goddaughter was, and for Lily there was the added advantage that there was a house to go with the job.

"I'm radiant over the idea of a beautiful house at Washington Barracks," she wrote home, and she relished the prospect of filling its rooms with the rugs, screens, ornaments, and lacquer furniture she had picked up during her "three-years' shopping trip" in China.

She did not have much chance to enjoy it. Marshall, his wife, and his mother-in-law arrived back in Washington in June 1927 and moved into their new quarters the following month. It was all so exciting that Lily collapsed and had to be rushed to Walter Reed Hospital. There it was found that her heart condition had been complicated by a disease in her thyroid gland. She would need a long and difficult operation to right the situation and was sent home to build up her strength for the ordeal.

The operation took place on August 22. It seemed to be such a success that she was told she would probably be back in her own home at Washington Barracks by the end of September. Meantime, Marshall was spending every waking moment between his lectures at the college and watching over his wife, comforting and encouraging her, making sure she did not overtax herself with the slightest effort.

"George is *wonderful*," Lily wrote. "He puts heart and strength in me."

But not enough to defuse the time bomb that had been ticking away inside Lily Marshall's body for years. On the morning of September 16, 1927, it went off.

Classes had just begun at the War College and Lieutenant Colonel Marshall had started to speak when an orderly came in and called him to the telephone. There was an urgent message. He went into the adjacent office, sat down at the desk, and picked up the telephone. The orderly stood by.

"When Colonel Marshall answered the call," the orderly said later, "he spoke for a moment over the phone, then put his head on his arms on the desk in deep grief. I asked if there was anything

I could do for him, and he replied, 'No, Mr. Throckmorton, I just had word my wife, who was to join me here today, has just died.''

Lily had been told by her doctors to prepare to go home, and it was the excitement at the prospect which had lit the fuse.

Marshall wrote in reply to a letter of condolence from Pershing:

> Twenty-six years of most intimate companionship leaves me lost in my best effort to adjust myself to future prospects in life. If I had been given to club life or other intimacies with men outside, of athletic diversions, or if there was a campaign or other pressing duty demanding a concentrated effort, then I think I should do better. However, I will find a way.

He was forty-seven years old and the loneliest man in the U.S. Army.

6

New Deal—Raw Deal

The cult of public breastbeating was still two generations away, and Marshall gave no overt indication of his deep grief over Lily's death. But it was soon evident around the War College, at least, that he was taking the loss hard. There had always been cynics who had ascribed his punctilious devotion to his wife whenever they were out together as nothing more than window dressing, designed to camouflage the sterile and miserable existence his married life must have been in private. As evidence, they cited the obvious pleasure he took in the company of pretty women and other people's children.

Now that he was a widower, they expected him to go on the loose. As one of his fellow officers remarked later, "We imagined him saying, the moment his wife was lowered into the ground, 'Now just watch my smoke!' We'd heard all those stories about George's high jinks with the duchesses in London, and we waited for him to take off into society."

Instead, he quietly grieved. A few weeks after Lily died, he consulted the medical officer at Fort Myer about a facial tic that had recently developed. It tugged his mouth down at one corner and turned his rare smiles into something approximating an obscene leer. The doctor took the opportunity of giving him a general examination and found a thyroid condition, high blood pressure, an irregular pulse, and an alarming loss of weight. Compared with the fighting-fit officer who had come back from China, he looked like an undernourished waif; his bones were poking through his skin. He was warned that he faced a general breakdown if he didn't do something about himself, and the doctor added that in this small peacetime army, an officer who suffered a physical collapse could be invalided out of the service. He might have been equally concerned for Marshall's mental state had he visited his quarters, as his sister, Marie, did about this time. Though he had broken off relations with his brother, Stuart, Marshall had kept up with Marie, but only by correspondence. She was a doctor's wife living in Pennsylvania, and they had few opportunities—or excuses—for meeting. But now, as sisters do, she rushed to Washington the moment Lily's death was announced and began visiting him regularly thereafter. She was chastened when she walked around his house and noted that the drapes were drawn in every room and that there were large photographs of Lily all over the place, on the piano, on the mantelshelves, around his bed, and even in his bathroom. He lived with her presence every moment he was in the house.

Mournful and moody he might be, but he had no intention of being kicked out of the Army, and the doctor's warning jolted him into an awareness of his condition. He would probably have pulled himself together even had he remained at the War College, but as luck would have it, a new appointment came up about this time. He had always wanted to become an instructor at Fort Benning, the Army Infantry School, and now, thanks to his excellent teaching record at the college, he was offered the post of assistant commandant at Benning, with the opportunity to lecture as part of his duties. He accepted at once and moved out of Washington in November 1927.

Benning was the largest military school in the U.S. Army. Situated a few miles outside Columbus, Georgia, it comprised a reservation of 97,000 acres of land, including several old plantations, forests, streams, rolling hills. From the Army's point of view, it was ideal terrain over which to wage mock warfare. By the time Marshall got through reorganizing it the facility had its own tank units, smoke-laying planes, and artillery and the nearest approach to battlefield conditions a trainee soldier was likely to meet in peacetime.

Marshall was a first-class teacher, able to encapsulate difficult military problems into a few short sentences—he once summed up the causes of the Civil War in a five-minute lecture—and though most of his students discovered that he was a hard taskmaster, they also found him a stimulating and challenging stretcher of their mental and physical capacities. He challenged, encouraged, and inspired them. In the next five years young officers named Bradley, Stilwell, Bedell Smith, Collins, Ridgway, Hilldring, Deane and many others passed through his hands, and all of them credited Marshall for their subsequent apotheosis.

"It was astonishing, the way he remembered me from Benning," General Omar Bradley said when he was picked for a choice job in World War II.

It wasn't amazing at all, in fact. It was at Fort Benning that Marshall began something which was to prove invaluable when, later, he became Chief of Staff. He bought himself what he called "my little black book," and he began jotting in it the names of any young officers whose talents impressed him—"for future reference," as he put it. In those days at Benning he could hardly have guessed that he would one day be the top man in the U.S. Army and might have need of his "little black book." But it is an indication of the way his thoughts were turning.* He constantly referred to it later, when he came to pick the men to lead the armies in World War II.

A small house went with his job at Benning, and his sister, Marie, came down to help him furnish it. She quietly "lost" most of his photographs of Lily, except for one she placed on his piano (the piano with which Lily had first enticed him) and one for his bedroom. But she really need not have bothered. He had emerged from his slough of despond. From a brooding semirecluse in Washington he became the most visible officer on the post, at both work and play. In the classroom he drove everyone so hard that one officer, Major (later Major General) E. Forrest Harding, wrote a prayer for his fellow students which ended with the words:

Now into my bunk I creep
   To catch an hour or so of sleep
And dream about my monograph.
   Help me, O Lord, to stand the gaff.

*Marshall was once asked if he used his little black book to jot down the names of young officers who were the opposite of talented. "There wouldn't have been room," he said.

But he did not let anyone relax even after lessons were over. He was always organizing parades—not just simple parades and drills but marching spectacles often broken up by mock battles, cavalry charges, and cannon fire. He sponsored the Fort Benning Hunt with a pack of hounds and nearly 100 officers and wives were summoned weekly, in season, to follow them across the Georgia meadowlands and woods. He set up cross-country treasure hunts in which he enthusiastically participated—his sergeant laid the trails and the clues—and was once seen riding across a forest glade wearing a Japanese kimono and a Filipino hat and carrying a birdcage, all of which he had unearthed in his avid search for treasure.

He never seemed to stop, and if some of his students found it a wearing course and were sometimes heard to exclaim, "What on earth will Uncle George think up next?" it was certainly therapeutic as far as his own condition was concerned. He put on weight again, his bony cheeks filled out, and he was a different man. But still a very lonely one.

And then another woman came into his life.

In the summer of 1929 an attractive widow named Katherine Tupper Brown came to Columbus, Georgia, on a visit to a well-known resident of the city, Mrs. William Blanchard, who was the mother of an old college friend. She brought her daughter, Molly, with her, and one night she and Molly were asked out to dinner in town. It was a small party, but she was told that one of the other guests would be a certain colonel named Marshall who was on the staff at Fort Benning.

She didn't need to be told which one Colonel Marshall was when she came into the room.

"George had a way of looking straight through you," she recalled later. "He had such keen blue eyes."

She was introduced to this "very straight and very military"-looking man, and they were talking together when cocktails were brought around. She took one, but he did not, and she was intrigued. This was still the era of Prohibition; but that, if anything, had increased the consumption of alcoholic drinks, and it was a rare party which didn't serve them, a rare household which didn't have its own bootlegger, and a rare guest who refused a drink.

"Don't you drink anything?" she asked, and when he shook his head, she added, "You're the first military man I've ever met in my life who didn't drink."

He asked her how many she knew.

"Only two," she said. "They're in Baltimore. They usually have to carry them out of everything they go to. They used to be majors in the Army, but now, I think, they're out."

He laughed. "That's probably the reason they're out." He went on, as if to reassure her as she sipped her drink, "Oh, I drink. But I've had rather an unfortunate experience with Army men where alcohol's concerned.* I like a cocktail now and then. But," he added, "I don't break the laws of the United States."

Katherine Brown was attracted to him, and it was reciprocated. At the end of the evening Marshall came over and asked if he could take her home. She asked him if he knew where Mrs. Blanchard lived, and he replied that everybody in Columbus knew where Mrs. Blanchard lived. But when they got in the car, he just drove around and around, until finally, as her daughter, Molly, began to get restless, she said, "Colonel, you obviously don't know your way around Columbus very well at all."

"Mrs. Brown," he replied, "I know Columbus so well it's taken me all this time to keep away from the street where you're staying."

That was the beginning. The next day he sent his car and chauffeur over to bring her back to Fort Benning for a reception. She refused to go without her daughter, and when the chauffeur informed the colonel of this, he was dispatched to town to dig Molly Brown out of a lunch she was attending and drive her urgently over to Benning. There he kept mother and daughter in a corner of the reception, all by themselves, and introduced them to no one. When she protested, he said, "I haven't the slightest intention of introducing you to that lot. They just aren't worth your time."

---

*He was obviously thinking of Colonel Naylor in China.

From then on he monopolized her until her visit to Columbus ended and bombarded her with messages when she got back to Baltimore. Soon he persuaded Mrs. Blanchard to invite Katherine and her daughter back for a second visit, and this time he made it plain he wanted to marry her. "Provided my family approves of you," she said, and took him back to a summer home she maintained on Fire Island, New York, there to be looked over by her two young sons, Allen and Clifton (Molly had already given him the nod). They liked him. In some ways, it also seemed to help that both Katherine and Marshall missed their former spouses and both had sworn they would never marry again.

The wedding took place at the Emmanuel Episcopal Church in Baltimore on October 15, 1930, with General John J. Pershing as best man.

Katherine Marshall was a highly practical and worldly woman of forty-six and quite aware of what she was getting into when she married George Catlett Marshall. He was four years her senior and still only a lieutenant colonel in the United States Army, and there did not seem much likelihood that he would climb much higher in rank before retirement came. His nearest contemporary, Douglas MacArthur, was by this time an acting four-star general and Chief of Staff of the United States Army, but that very fact made the prospect of George's getting even a one-star generalcy now seem remote. The wrong people were in positions of influence, and even his great hero, Black Jack Pershing, no longer appeared to have much military clout. It was for his qualities as a man rather than his prospects as a soldier that she had thrown in her lot with George Marshall, and as she said later, "I never doubted from the start that I had found myself a wonderful man."

She was no mean bargain herself.

Katherine Marshall must have reminded her husband of some of the English peeresses he had met in London in the dazzling aftermath of WWI, for she had something of the same flair, panache, and sophistication. For all that, she was a country girl. Born in Harrodsburg, Kentucky, she was the daughter of a Baptist minister who turned his Sunday pulpit into a weekly drama about the wages of sin, with offstage fire and brimstone, and if Katherine was not quite inspired to become an evangelist herself, she did admire and envy her father's gift for histrionics. To the horror of her parents, she announced while still in college that she wanted to become an actress, took a course in drama in New York, and sailed for England while still only twenty to seek fame and fortune on the stage. Her father swore he would end her allowance and cut her out of his will the moment she made her first professional appearance in a public theater. She was not deterred. She had procured a letter of introduction to the famous actor-manager Sir Herbert Beerbohm Tree, who turned purple at the sound of her voice and thundered at her, "If you had the ability of Sarah Bernhardt, young lady, I couldn't take you with that dreadful American accent!"

"Sir Beerbohm," she replied, with youthful dignity, "how can you make such a charge? I have no accent. I come from the South."

She held back her tears until she reached the street, but she wept all the way down the Strand as she agonized over what she was going to do. But then she read in that day's newspaper that another well-known actor-manager happened to be in town. This was Mr. (later Sir) Frank Benson, who owned and operated a number of Shakespearean repertory companies. Unlike Beerbohm Tree, he was more than willing to turn a deaf ear to a transatlantic twang so long as it issued from the red lips of such an extremely attractive twenty-year-old. Katherine auditioned for him with an excerpt from *Camille* and, in her own words, "literally tore passion to tatters."

When she got through, Benson looked at her for a long time ("He had the kindest face," she recalled) and then said, "My goodness, what *would* a Yankee Portia sound like!"

But he took her into his company as a trainee, nevertheless, and when her father, true to his threat, cut her allowance, he waived the fee he normally charged. He assigned her to a veteran member of the company to teach her Shakespearean acting and polish some of the corners off her accent. Ironically enough, her tutor turned out to be a Frenchman named Monsieur Bertrand who had once been a member of the Comédie Française.

"Monsieur Bertrand was almost a case of Svengali," she said later. "He never left me and tried to own me body and soul. He worked me to death until three o'clock in the morning. He would do *Romeo* in the potion scene and the balcony scene and the death scene. He would take me through *Hamlet* in the mad scene and laboriously go over every intonation. I loathed Monsieur Bertrand to come near me. He had a way of walking into my dressing room, and this made me furious. But though he just worked me to death, I stuck with him."

The result was that the voice emerging from this extremely pretty and charming young American was melodious in the extreme, and Benson, for whom she cherished no antipathy at all, took her with his company on tours of Britain, Ireland, and Switzerland. He tried her out first as Hamlet's father's ghost, quavering in torment from offstage at the top of a ladder, and graduated her through *Twelfth Night* to her (and his) final triumph, the role of Portia in *The Merchant of Venice*. She was hailed by the critics as Benson's great discovery, "a Yankee Portia without a Yankee accent," and her reward was a seven-year contract with the company.

And that was where the trouble started.

"Frank Benson was one of the most wonderful men I have ever known," Katherine said later. Then she added, "But his wife was one of the meanest women."

Mrs. Benson was not at all partial to attractive young women, especially if her husband favored them. She proceeded to make life a misery for Benson's latest discovery, and it reached a climax when Katherine collapsed onstage in Glasgow and the curtain had to be rung down. Having been rushed to the hospital, she was diagnosed as suffering from "tuberculosis of the kidney" and told to go back to America for treatment. Benson probably surmised that her illness was nothing of the sort and more likely psychosomatic than physical, but he did not try to prevent her from leaving. He traveled with her to Southampton to see her off on the boat and told her she could come back and rejoin his company the moment she had recovered, but he must have guessed she never would.

She worked in the theater in the United States; but somehow it wasn't the same, and when a childhood swain named Clifton Brown came along and asked her to marry him, she accepted.

Brown was a successful lawyer in Baltimore, and there were three children from the marriage. The marriage was a success, especially when Katherine made it plain to her husband—who hated the theater—that she had renounced the stage forever. And then one day it all came to an end when Clifton Brown was murdered. An unbalanced client whose case he had won but who still refused to pay his fees waylaid him as he was entering his office and shot him in the back. He was dead by the time they got him to hospital.

"I thought life had stopped for me," Katherine said when she heard the news.

Instead, she went to Columbus, Georgia, and met Lieutenant Colonel George C. Marshall, and life started again—for both of them.

Shabbily at first, as it turned out.

Shortly after their marriage Marshall's tour at Fort Benning came to an end, and he got what he needed for promotion—service with troops—but at a camp which was widely referred to in the service as "the asshole of the Army." The name was Fort Screven, and its location was just outside Savannah, Georgia. The place was a dump which had been run down thanks to poor administration and lack of command.

"Fort Screven was a real backwash," Katherine Marshall recalled. "Believe me, when we got there, it was the worst I ever saw. . . . They'd had a colonel who was so disgusted at being on a small post where there wouldn't be any limelight that he and his wife didn't pay any attention, didn't try to add anything. They had no club building or anywhere to meet, and they were so apathetic no one would have gone if they'd had anything. It was just a mess."

The Marshalls cleared it up between them. Then they set out to establish some sort of relationship between the camp and the neighboring city of Savannah. The departing colonel had left a note behind saying, "I can't give you introductions to anyone in Savannah because I don't know anybody there. Nobody has ever come out to visit us from the city."

To Marshall the answer to that seemed simple. When Sunday came around, he and Katherine drove into Savannah and marched into the largest Episcopal church in time for morning service. Katherine remembered "the sort of hush as we walked down the aisle." But after the service was over, the mayor came up and welcomed them to the city; they were snowed under with invitations for a meal; and the following day the mayor came out on an official visit.

"Well, you ought to have seen that place by the time George got through with it," Katherine said. "We were there less than two years, and when we left, the City Council and all the businessmen of Savannah got together and gave us a farewell banquet. And they gave George a silver baton inscribed to 'The Marshall of Savannah.' "

By that time her husband had come up for promotion once more and had been recommended for the rank of full colonel. But this was the end of 1932, and the blight of the Depression had spread across America. There was a proposal in Congress to cut down the Army's establishment from 12,000 to 10,000 serving officers, and though General Douglas MacArthur was fighting tooth and nail to get the bill defeated, there weren't many jobs for full colonels around in the U.S. Army at that time. Marshall found himself shunted down to Fort Moultrie, near Charleston, South Carolina, a larger camp but still one that ranked a lieutenant colonelcy. Almost simultaneously the New Deal under President Roosevelt initiated, among its other emergency reforms, the establishment of the Civilian Conservation Corps (CCC) to cope with unemployment and malnutrition among the youth of the nation. In the grim winter of 1932–33, families all over the country were starving. The CCC program was designed to relieve some of them of the burden of their restless out-of-work sons and put them in camps where they could be trained in various skills or sent out to work on public projects. In return their families would receive an allowance of $20 a week, and the young men would get $5 a week plus their keep.

It was a desperate measure to take care of a threatening situation. Businesses were going bankrupt by the thousand. Every street corner had an able-bodied man on it begging for handouts because there was no work available for his hand or his brain. The food lines stretched for miles around the city blocks, the hills were full of rickety children, and the nation was becoming one big miserable soup kitchen.

General MacArthur, the Chief of Staff, was fighting a rear-guard action against attempts by Congress to reduce the strength of his Army, and he saw in the CCC an opportunity for preserving his manpower. He proposed that the armed forces should be given administrative control of the CCC camps. The President agreed so long as the youths, though under military control, would not be subjected to any form of military training. The Chief of Staff accepted and sent the word out to his regional commanders to expect a flood of civilians and to keep the drill sergeants off their backs.

At his new headquarters at Fort Moultrie, Marshall found himself no longer commander of an infantry division but the administrator of an enormous labor project involving 25,000 young men flooding into seventeen work camps all over the southern United States, from the Carolinas to Florida. Army economies had cut his staff to the bone, and he was desperate for manpower to help him cope. Katherine Marshall volunteered to take over some of the duties, and she was appalled by her first real confrontation with the results of the Depression and the havoc it was wreaking with America's youth. The youngsters were not just underfed. They had sores and skin rashes, and the condition of their teeth was appalling. They were so hungry that some of them would dump their food right on the tables, for fear that if they put it on a plate, someone might snatch it away. They fought and snarled at each other like packs of dogs, and half of them were illiterate.

She was not the only one who cringed when she saw them. Several of Marshall's officers were outraged.

"Some of the lieutenants thought these boys were beneath

them," she said later. "They thought they were the scum of the earth and why should they have to deal with them since it wasn't a military thing at all? Because of course, they wouldn't let them use these boys in the military, and you couldn't train them like you would a military man."

One major came in to see Marshall and stiffly announced that he was going to resign from the Army, and when asked why, he said, "I've put twelve years in the Army. I'm a graduate of West Point. I'm not going to come down here and deal with a whole lot of bums. Half-dead Southern crackers, that's what they are!"

Marshall never raised his voice when he was angry, and the only way you could tell was the way his complexion changed to a dull red flush. He said, evenly, "Major, I'm sorry you feel like that. But I'll tell you this—you can't resign quick enough to suit me. It suits me fine! Now get out of here!"

Katherine, who was working in the office when it happened, felt like cheering. She remembers giggling to herself when she saw the major's face.

"He looked so surprised," she said. "He knew we were desperate for staff, and he obviously thought George would beg him to stay."

Tucked away among the documents in the National Archives dealing with the trials and tribulations of the early 1930's some reports on the operations of the CCC camps can be found. Time and again the results achieved in the South by Lieutenant Colonel George C. Marshall are commended. He did well by the young men who came under his control. He brought in dentists and cleaned up the appalling condition of their teeth. He gave them food and taught them how to eat it for the best physical results. He gave the illiterate lessons in reading and writing. He had the boys build a seawall in South Carolina and then showed them how to fish from it. He organized clubhouses and game rooms for them. He went down to South Florida, where the great beach hotels were lying empty, and parlayed the managers into renting him rooms for next to nothing, then moved in his boys for courses in sailing and swimming.

"He thought of little things," Katherine said, "like on Sunday, when a boy went home to his family, he announced that his place could be taken by a guest. So the boys started a list and traded off with each other."

She added, "But most of all, he gave those boys back their self-respect. That was the first time those boys came to realize they weren't just nothing, that they were supposed to measure up to something. After they'd been there for a week or two, you would see them marching smartly along, smiling, because they'd got their teeth fixed. They were the finest set of boys I ever saw out of the Army. They came from good old American stock which had been run down to nothing—and George built them up again."

So brilliant was Marshall's achievement with the CCC that many in Washington expected him to be given—at last—the promotion that should have been his years earlier. It would be a belated tribute by the Army to one who had richly earned his star. He was not just loyal and reliable and unselfish but also, as report after report showed, a brilliant officer, adaptable, resourceful, quick-witted in a crisis, everything, in fact, that an army needed for its leadership. But these were grim days even for the most talented members of the regular forces of the United States. Military establishments had been cut so drastically that promotion simply could not be won by excellence of achievement. It was length of service *with troops* that counted, and to make brigadier general, Marshall needed one more troop command after leaving Fort Moultrie or two more years in the same post. Then he would be given his star for no other reason than seniority. Simply by his having stayed in the right jobs for long enough, advancement would be his by right. One more command, or just two more years at Moultrie, and he would be a general at last.

Was General Douglas MacArthur aware of this? And did he now deliberately set out to cheat Marshall of the promotion he had so worthily earned? There are grounds for suspecting that he did just that.

It will be remembered that General MacArthur was still Chief of Staff of the U.S. Army at this time, and he certainly had enough problems on his hands not to have time to spare to indulge in petty reprisals against contemporary officers, even those he might consider his rivals. The armed forces over which he commanded, though designed to protect what had now become one of the six most powerful nations in the world (counting Britain, France, Germany, Italy, and Japan as the others), numbered fewer men than those of the Greek and Belgian armies put together. Army camps were festering slums. Arms for the troops were so scarce and old-fashioned that *Fortune* magazine reported about this time that the image of the U.S. Army to Americans and foreigners alike was that of "a gaping-mouthed private carrying an obsolete rifle at an ungraceful angle." The Army was in disrepute, and no one— particularly in Congress—wished to vote it any money to improve its image or make it more modern and efficient. True, Douglas MacArthur himself had not exactly made the armed forces popular with the general public or the nation's governors. He had sent the U.S. Army into the streets during the march of the so-called Bonus Army on Washington in the last stages of the Hoover administration and ordered his men to open fire against starving, workless veterans who had once fought in their ranks. They had been beaten back by the troops on MacArthur's orders, their wives roughed up and their children tear-gassed.

Marshall considered himself lucky that he had had other duties to perform and had therefore not been ordered into the streets to superintend the dirty work involving the veterans and their families. Some of his old colleagues had been closely involved. A comrade from World War I, Major George S. Patton, for instance, had been put in command of tanks, infantry, and cavalry with orders to protect the Washington Monument "and break the back of the BEF."* In any event, it did not become necessary for Patton to order his troops to open fire and his tanks and cavalry to charge, but Marshall must have wondered what he would have done if he had been in Patton's place and the order had been given. Would he, for the first time in his life as a serving officer, have disobeyed an order—and refused to open fire on his fellow

---

*The letters stood for Bonus Expeditionary Force. The veterans were demanding a bonus from the government as a form of unemployment subsidy.

countrymen? Even Patton later confessed he had had his moments of doubt. So did one other regular officer who was serving with MacArthur at the time. Major Dwight D. Eisenhower was an assistant in the Chief of Staff's office, and he was so sure the clash with the bonus marchers was bad for the Army's image that he begged his chief not to go out and have a personal confrontation with the strikers. MacArthur ignored his advice and went out in full uniform, with all his medals on, to watch the tear-gassing of the marchers.

In the circumstances, the Chief of Staff surely had too many serious matters on his mind to bother about Marshall's promotion. So perhaps—to begin with—it was in pure ignorance of the circumstances that he wrote to Marshall at the end of 1933 first of all to congratulate him on the job he had done with the CCC boys at Moultrie and then to announce that he was transferring him to a new post. He was appointing him immediately to Chicago to take over command of the Illinois National Guard Division. It was a first-class and most important new job that Marshall was being given, the Chief of Staff pointed out. The situation in the Middle West was both tense and uncertain as a result of the Depression and the widespread unrest which it had caused. There was "incipient revolution" in the air, and a firm hand at the head of a strong and well-drilled force was needed to prevent the situation from going to pieces. He was relying upon Marshall to do the job well. And he added the welcome news that the new command carried with it a nice raise in pay.

Marshall was stunned when he read the letter.

National Guard units were not Regular Army troops, and service with them, even by a Regular Army officer, was not taken into consideration when it came to promotion. Was not MacArthur aware of this? Did it not occur to him what this appointment, at his age, could do to Marshall's chances of earning his star?

He was in such despair over this blow to his long-cherished hopes that he decided to do something about it. He wrote a letter to the Chief of Staff and actually asked him to change his mind about the posting, for the first time in his military career questioning the wisdom of an Army order. There is no copy of this letter in Marshall's papers, and there seems to be no record of it in MacArthur's documents either. But Katherine Marshall remembers the circumstances in which it was written even if she has forgotten the exact contents.

"He told General MacArthur that he had never made any request of the Army ever before," she said later. "He had always accepted what was given him. But, he pointed out, he had been a lieutenant colonel now for sixteen years. He was asking him [MacArthur] to leave him there with the troops [at Moultrie] because he had to have troops in training before he could get his eagle [a full colonelcy]. And furthermore, he couldn't get his generalcy without having been so many years with troops."

To bolster his plea, he got hold of his old chief, General Pershing, and asked him to add his weight to it. Pershing had good reason to be grateful to his aide by this time. Over the years Marshall had devoted much of his spare time to researching and helping Black Jack write his war memoirs, and, shortly after his marriage to Katherine, had even broken off his honeymoon to spend three days beavering away for the general. So Pershing, who certainly was in his debt, promised to do something about his dilemma. And he did. He picked up the telephone and spoke to MacArthur himself. He said he would consider it a personal favor if the Chief of Staff would promote Lieutenant Colonel Marshall at once to the rank of brigadier general.

The reaction was unforeseen. Nothing was more calculated to make MacArthur dig his heels in. In the beginning the posting of Marshall may well have been inadvertent, made without MacArthur's realizing its significance to the future rank of the lieutenant colonel. But Pershing's intervention reminded him forcibly that Marshall was Black Jack's man, a member of the hated Chaumont group, and the staff officer, moreover, whose order had caused him such chaos and humiliation in the last days of WWI. Like the Bourbons, he had learned nothing and forgotten nothing, except that the Chaumont group were his enemies, to be blocked or harried whenever they cropped up in the postwar Army. Pershing's published memoirs about WWI had, if anything, increased MacArthur's rancor toward anyone who had served on the General Staff, and the fact that Marshall's activities had received high praise in Black Jack's book increased rather than soothed his animosity. So he snubbed the general and, in reply to Marshall's letter, sent back the curt message "All requests refused." Marshall would go to Chicago and get the National Guard back in shape whether he liked it or not, and to hell with his chances of promotion.

Marshall never spoke out about the shabby treatment he received from General MacArthur in that black winter of 1933–34 and gave no sign that he resented what had been done to him. When the positions were reversed a few years later, and it was Marshall who was Chief of Staff and MacArthur was beholden to him, he behaved impeccably and bent over backward to be fair to the man who had caused him such grief. But though he kept silent in public, Katherine Marshall was acutely aware of how deeply he was hurt by MacArthur's action.

"When people ask me when I was proudest of him," she said later, after his fame had become worldwide, "I would say I was never so proud of him as when he was still a lieutenant colonel and he didn't think he was going any further because they wouldn't keep him with the troops, but sent him out there to Illinois. General MacArthur said it was because he was needed, that they were going to have a revolution out there . . . but I don't think it was that. George had been told that MacArthur said he was the only soldier he was afraid of. Without him in the running, MacArthur had it clear. His father was a general, he was a West Point man, he was very bright, a very good, in fact, a magnificent soldier, and he had his mother in back of him. She was a regular old —— But what her son did was make sure George didn't get his star. And he didn't even smile for three months. He saw all hopes of accomplishing all he had hoped to accomplish really gone."

The Marshalls took off for Chicago, with Katherine worried sick because her beloved husband had a "gray, drawn look which I had never seen before and have seldom seen since." It was the only sign he gave that he was unhappy at what had happened to him. Outwardly he appeared to accept that it was now too late to hope for more, that he would retire and die with no higher rank in the Army he loved than that of lieutenant colonel. It was a depressing thought, and if he seemed resigned to it, others did not. But not even Presidents seemed able to change what seemed to be his manifest destiny where the U.S. Army was concerned. Black Jack Pershing still continued to lobby on his behalf, and in 1935 he made a special point of speaking about his protégé both to President Roosevelt and to Secretary of War George Dern, stressing Marshall's soldierly qualities and superb service record. The President afterward sent a memorandum to Dern saying: "General Pershing asks very strongly that Colonel George C. Marshall (Infantry) be promoted to general. Can we put him on the next list of promotions?"

But so long as MacArthur stayed on as Chief of Staff, not even such a powerful recommendation had any effect. MacArthur's term of office had been due to end in 1934, but Congress would not let him go. It was he who had been given all the public credit for the success of the CCC camps, and despite strenuous opposition from Pershing, Congress had voted to continue him in office for another year. MacArthur was in his cockiest mood when Dern approached him with the President's suggestion that Marshall be given a star. He fobbed the secretary off by agreeing that Marshall was a first-class soldier but adding that what he deserved was not one star, but two. He therefore had it in mind to make Marshall the next Army chief of infantry as soon as the job became vacant, and it carried the rank of two-star major general. When Dern asked when the post would be free, MacArthur shrugged his shoulders.

"In a year or two," he said.

Any other man would have damned MacArthur for the hypocrite he was, but Marshall suffered in silence and wrote to Pershing: "I can but wait, grow older, and hope for a more favorable situation in Washington."

The favorable situation did not come until 1936. MacArthur resigned at last as Chief of Staff and departed for the Philippines, where he had accepted the position of Commander in Chief of the defense forces of the newly created commonwealth. With him out of the way, Dern put Marshall's name on the list of promotions. It was practically the last action he took as secretary of war; he was taken ill almost immediately afterward and forced to retire. But the promotion went through, and Brigadier General George C. Marshall was officially confirmed in his new rank on August 24, 1936. On the same day, it was announced that ex-Secretary Dern had died. Whether General Douglas MacArthur, in far-off Manila, got any satisfaction from either announcement is not on record.

Marshall was fifty-five years old when he received his promotion. He had nine years left to make his second star before he was compulsorily retired from the Army at the age of sixty-four. The way things had gone with his career so far, he was not optimistic. He was even less so four months later, when, shortly after taking a new command in Washington State, he collapsed and had to be rushed to hospital. The irregular pulse and faulty thyroid gland which had troubled him shortly after the death of Lily now acted up on him again, this time so seriously that an urgent operation was needed.

It looked as if Marshall would not even make retirement age, with one star or two. General MacArthur would certainly have been intrigued to hear about that—except that it was a deep, dark secret and not even Black Jack Pershing was told about it.

7

Apotheosis

"No soldier in the U.S. Army deserved it more," wrote Katherine Marshall after she heard that her husband's promotion had finally come through. "Quality and talent win out in the end."

In fact, neither had anything to do with it. But cronyism did.

MacArthur's successor as Chief of Staff of the Army was General Malin Craig, and that fact put a wholly different complexion on the face of Marshall's future. For Craig was a Pershing man* and, in marked contrast with his predecessor, was very much inclined to look with favor on any officer who had been with Black Jack at Chaumont. He strongly admired his old Commander in Chief, would do anything to please him, and was well aware that Marshall was one of his protégés. On that basis alone he was determined to see that the new brigadier general got all the preferment that was going from now on, and so much the better that his record made it plain that he deserved it.

Would it have made any difference, one wonders, if General Craig had realized that he and Marshall had had a meeting—if not exactly a face-to-face encounter—as long ago as thirty-three years? In 1903 Lieutenant Marshall had ridden into Fort Clark, Texas, to report the safe arrival of his survey party after a long and thirsty trek across the desert. The young captain to whom he had reported was Malin Craig. Craig did not remember because he had been so appalled by the lieutenant's sun-blackened skin and tattered uniform that he had refused to look at him. But Marshall had never forgotten the occasion, even if he deliberately did not bring it up now.

*It was Pershing who had made him chief of staff of the U.S. Third Army in WWI.

113

At the end of September 1936 Marshall got news of his first appointment as a brigadier general. He was told to clean up his office in Chicago and then proceed west to Washington State, where he was to command the 5th Brigade of the 3rd Infantry Division at Vancouver Barracks. He would also be in charge of the CCC camps which had been established in Oregon and parts of Washington.

Katherine Marshall, who had spent summer leave with her husband at a cottage she owned on Fire Island, New York, asked when he was expected to report to his new post. Told it would be toward the end of the year, she suggested that they drive to the West Coast from Chicago and take their time about it. She was worried. Shortly after the death of Lily, his first wife, he had been forced to consult a doctor about the malfunctioning of his thyroid gland. It manifested itself by an irregular pulse, and both in Chicago and on Fire Island, while he waited for news of his promotion, his pulse beat had begun acting up again, causing him acute discomfort. Katherine hoped that a leisurely journey across the country, with no worries, would clear things up. They took three weeks on the journey, visiting old battlefields, historic sites, Indian encampments, and arrived at Vancouver Barracks (accompanied by Katherine's daughter, Molly) in splendid form and spirits.

The new post was set in superb country, and they all were strongly taken with it. Marshall wrote to an Army friend:

> Vancouver Barracks is one of the old historic outposts of the Army. Established in 1849 on the site of a Hudson Bay Company station, the traces of whose lookout station are still discernible in a tall fir tree, for more than fifty years it was the center for the development of the Northwest. General Grant's log quarters are a part of the present post library building. Phil Sheridan left here a lieutenant to start his meteoric rise to fame. Pickett was a member of the garrison. My quarters were occupied by a succession of Civil War celebrities or Indian fighters. General Miles built the house, which was later occupied by Canby, Crook, Gibbon and Pope. . . . The Columbia River, bordering our aviation field (we have four planes) in extension of the parade, emerges from its famous

gorge a few miles above the post. In the distance the symmetrical cone of Mount Hood stands covered with snow, summer or winter.*

But almost immediately after he had reviewed his first parade of troops—who had been assembled to welcome him by an old comrade from the Philippines, Colonel Henry Hossfeld—he was troubled once more by his irregular pulse, so disturbingly and so continuously that Katherine persuaded him to see a doctor once more.

He was examined by the post medical officer, who suggested he should undergo tests at a hospital in Vancouver. He was then sent on to San Francisco, where he was almost immediately struck down by influenza, which was raging in the city. In a way, the flu was useful. It kept him bedded for a month, during which time he underwent examinations and a decision was made to operate on him.

The operation, for the removal of a diseased lobe of the thyroid gland, took place at the end of December 1936. But neither he nor members of his family mentioned it to anyone, and by the time he returned to Vancouver Barracks—where he was examined by a medical board and pronounced fit—everyone believed he had successfully recuperated from the flu. It was not until months later that the rumors about the true nature of his hospital sojourn began to circulate. General Pershing wrote to say he had heard that his protégé had become a semi-invalid and was "shocked." As for General Malin Craig, he was alarmed when he heard gossip in Washington that he had been "tricked into promoting a physical wreck." The story was that the moment George Marshall had pinned his brigadier general's star on his lapel he had collapsed and been carted off to the hospital. It was whispered that he would soon have to be invalided out of the Army—with a higher pension, of course, thanks to the promotion which Malin Craig had given him. Anxiously the Chief of Staff wired Marshall: "HOW'S YOUR CONDITION? ARE YOU FIT?"

*In a letter to Major General Roy D. Jeehn.

115

Back came the confident reply: "IN SPLENDID CONDITION. NEVER BEEN FITTER."

And it was true. Not only had the operation been successful, but Marshall had now begun a physical routine which toned him up to top condition. He had given up smoking and had taken up daily tennis and weekly golf, as well as his regular morning riding. In addition, he put in a considerably full working day and emerged with no trace of a flutter in his once-wayward pulse.

Malin Craig was relieved. He had plans for Marshall.

In the spring of 1938 Marshall heard from the Chief of Staff again. General Craig summoned him urgently to Washington for what looked like a melancholy but complicated duty. Black Jack Pershing, at the age of seventy-eight, had been struck down, and the Army doctors who had seen him believed that his illness might well prove fatal.

When a hero of Pershing's stature dies, the Army (and the nation) like to do him proud, and he had been consulted years beforehand to find out what kinds of personal touches he would like to see at his funeral. His reply had been to nominate George Marshall to take care of the arrangements. Now Craig instructed him to leave at once for Tucson, Arizona, where Black Jack was lying ill, so that he could spring into action the moment the nation's only four-star general breathed his last. He also informed Marshall that a special train, manned by Army engineers, was on its way from San Antonio to Tucson, ready to transport the dead hero back to Arlington Cemetery for the ceremonials, so he had better have an honor guard waiting in the wings.

Aside from the fact that he didn't want his old chief to die, Marshall did not look forward to the mission. The last time he had crossed the country in a funeral train was when President Warren Harding's dead body was brought back to Washington, and on that occasion Pershing himself had been in charge of the arrangements, with Marshall as his assistant. This would be a much more melancholy repeat of what had been a solemn and chastening journey.

116

Fortunately Black Jack decided that he was not yet ready for a hero's burial. The moment he heard that a funeral train was waiting for him in Tucson railroad depot, he began to rally, and by the time Marshall reached his bedside he was sitting up and taking notice. His ex-aide smiled with relief at the sight of him and said how glad he was to see him still alive and kicking.

Black Jack said, "George, they're not going to kill me off until I've seen that you've got your second star." He added, wistfully, "Why, one of these days you might end up with four stars, just like me."

"Never," Marshall reassured him, fervently. "I'd turn it down even if they were stupid enough to offer it me. There's only one American who has earned the right to four stars, and that's General Pershing. And there'll never be another!"

Marshall meant it, and Black Jack knew he did.

"Thank you, George," he said, tears in his eyes.

It had all been a great to-do over nothing, but it paid dividends as far as Marshall was concerned. General Craig, embarrassed over the fuss he had caused, decided to reward the brigadier general for all the trouble he had taken. Marshall came back from maneuvers in the Deep South to be handed orders to report to Washington, D.C. Reading them, he found he had been appointed chief of the Army War Plans Division. That was in the summer of 1938. He had barely moved himself, Katherine, and his stepdaughter, Molly, to Washington when Craig advanced him one more rung up the military ladder (though not in rank) to the post of Deputy Chief of Staff, U.S. Army.

The appointment came less than two weeks after the announcement that the two main bastions of democracy in Europe, Britain and France, had given in to pressure from their Nazi and Fascist rivals, Germany and Italy, and signed an agreement at Munich forcing Czechoslovakia to cede tracts of its territory to the Nazis. Neville Chamberlain and Édouard Daladier, the British and French prime ministers, respectively, believed that by putting Czechoslovakia at the mercy of Adolf Hitler, the German dictator, they had appeased Nazi appetites and avoided a disastrous war. But wiser and more cynical observers knew better and realized that a democratic ally had been sacrificed, and the war only postponed.

That September, as he settled into his new office in the War Department, Marshall found himself, for the first time since the end of World War I, worrying not so much about the welfare of his troops or the prospects of his career as about the safety of the United States. The news that the democracies had chosen to appease the Fascists at Munich stunned the American people, and a public opinion poll taken about that time revealed that 43 percent of them now believed that war was coming and that the United States was bound to be involved. To a further question whether that meant actually fighting in a war, a large majority answered yes.

But if so, what were they going to fight *with*? Marshall was acutely aware that the U.S. Navy was in reasonably good shape, but the Army was desperately short of manpower and equipment. The military budgets grudgingly granted each year by Congress were barely enough to keep the sewers open in Army cantonments throughout the nation and certainly not enough to paint the barracks or living quarters. With an annual grant of around $300 million, there was not enough money in the Army kitty to buy food, clothing, or ammunition for the small standing force of about 150,000 men, let alone find the equipment for new recruits. On maneuvers, bullets were issued by the handful, and big guns rationed to four rounds per day. A senator declared in a discussion of the military situation after the signing of the Munich agreement that the United States would now have to spend "millions of dollars for military purposes." Marshall sent a note to his chief, General Craig, saying, "It will have to be hundreds of millions of dollars."

While he had been in command of the 3rd Brigade at Vancouver Barracks, Marshall had shown his visitors around the airfield on the post and gestured to the four biplanes lined up there.

"This is our air force," he said proudly.

It was, in fact, the United States air defense force for that large segment of U.S. territory. Unique among the powerful nations in the world, the United States had not grasped the need to develop air power for the protection of its territory and its overseas interests. As early as 1925 a flying hero from World War I, Billy Mitchell, had campaigned for a separate U.S. air force and the need to develop a powerful bomber fleet. He had been court-martialed for daring to suggest—and then proving—that warships could be sunk by bombers. As war came nearer in Europe, and as Nazi bombers in the Spanish Civil War demonstrated the devastating menace of attack from the air, the United States still did not have a separate air force. The Germans had their Luftwaffe, the British had their Royal Air Force, and the Italians and the Japanese had their separately commanded fleets of fighters and bombers for use against enemy ships, planes, cities, and armies. But America continued to make air power an integral part of the Army, under its command, subject to the decisions and sometimes the whims, of ground commanders. It was an arm of the military, the U.S. *Army* Air Corps, and it did not become the U.S. Air Force until after the end of World War II.

It was true that Marshall was less blinkered than most Army generals about the possibilities of air power in war. One of his Army friends, right back from the early days in the Philippines, was a young officer named H. H. "Hap" Arnold, who had learned to fly and become a prophet of the efficacy of air power in war. He had shared his enthusiasm with Marshall and then gone on to take commands at Army air stations around the nation. Hap Arnold would rise by 1939 to become commander of the Army Air Corps. But he would still remain under the orders of the Army ground force commander, and he later considered himself fortunate that the commander turned out to be none other than George Marshall. But though Arnold knew he had convinced his friend of the efficacy of air power and the need for a strong air arm, he would never persuade him that U.S. air fleets needed a separate, independent command. In the years to come, Marshall would give his friend, as Air Corps chief, all the room to maneuver that he needed, but he still continued to keep him on the Army's leash.

So Marshall worried in the Fall of 1938 about the state of the nation's defenses. In his opinion, there was only one thing to do: There should be a crash program of rearmament, a drive to turn factories over to the building of thousands of guns and hundreds of planes, and a great recruiting campaign to fill up the yawning gaps in Army manpower. If that did not succeed, the only alternative was the institution of so-called selective service—or conscription of the nation's youth.

Unfortunately for Marshall the White House had other ideas. From the moment the European democracies had appeased the Nazi dictator at Munich, President Franklin D. Roosevelt saw as clearly as anyone that there would soon be a war. But he was also keenly aware that in spite of the polls, the bulk of the American people cringed at the thought of being involved in it and would support any developments which promised to keep them out of it.

There was already a strong isolationist movement in the United States, and the President had been bitterly attacked by its leading campaigners for appearing to support the democracies against the Nazis, thus threatening American neutrality in any future conflict. Roosevelt therefore took the politically more palatable attitude that Europe should be left to fight its own battles, and Britain and France encouraged to defeat the Germans by themselves when war came—thus making American participation unnecessary.

The big question was: Were they capable of defeating the Nazis by themselves? From the reports he was reading over the winter of 1938–39, the President was doubtful. His ambassadors and military experts in Europe's capitals were skeptical of democratic triumph if they had to fight a war with the weapons they had at the moment. They were so ill-equipped, they reported, that the better-armed Nazis would easily wipe them out. They needed guns. They needed planes. Only the great factories of the United States could supply them with the weapons they lacked.

On the other hand, it would be political suicide at the moment for the President to propose that his government plunge into the business of supplying planes and arms to the British and French alone. The isolationists would at once charge him with (a) selling them to one side only and thus breaching American neutrality, and (b) depriving the U.S. armed forces of weapons which they also vitally needed for American defense.

So on November 14, 1938, Roosevelt called a conference at the White House of members of his Cabinet and his military advisers at which he proposed a program for the building of 10,000 war planes. Ostensibly these planes would be used to bolster the strength of the U.S. Army Air Corps, and that was what Marshall and his chief, General Malin Craig, understood would be their purpose. In reality Roosevelt intended the planes, once they were built, to be shipped to Britain and France to strengthen their air arms. But he did not say that; he could not, since he would immediately have been attacked by isolationists in and out of Congress. He let it be assumed that they would be part of the U.S. air force.

Nor did anyone tell Marshall, who therefore was astounded when he heard the President's proposition. How could he possibly ask for new factories to be opened and 10,000 planes to be built and not at the same time also lay out a program for recruiting the pilots and crews and service personnel who would be needed to man those planes?

It was not the first time Marshall had met the President of the United States; but it was his first conference with Roosevelt, and he was shocked by the loose thinking he showed on this occasion. He was also astonished that no one took him up on it. Most of those present at the conference seemed to agree with everything he had said "and were very soothing," as he put it later.

Finally, after the President had finished, he came among his listeners and stopped in front of Marshall. To the annoyance of the Deputy Chief of Staff, he called him George, and no one did that with Marshall. He was never a first-name man. As he said later, "I don't think [the President] ever did that again. I wasn't very enthusiastic over such a misrepresentation of our intimacy."

The President said he thought he had made a good case for his program and added, "Don't you think so, George?"

Marshall looked at him stonily and replied, "I am sorry, Mr. President, but I don't agree with you at all."

A startled expression crossed Roosevelt's face. He seemed about to ask why and then thought better of it, and the meeting broke up. Afterward the others, who had been eyeing Marshall in silence, came up to him one by one to shake his hand.

"Well, it's been nice knowing you," said the secretary of the treasury, Henry Morgenthau.

Like the rest of them, he made it obvious he thought that Marshall had just ruined his career and that his tour in Washington was over.

In fact, it was not. There is no record that President Roosevelt ever referred to the incident again. Nor, on the other hand, did he display any resentment toward Marshall.

"Maybe he thought I would tell him the truth so far as I personally was concerned," Marshall said later, and added, "which I certainly tried to do in all our conversations."

But it was the beginning of a curiously cool relationship between the two men which would thaw slowly as the years went by and take a long time to grow warm. The President, who called everybody by his first name, never from that time on referred to Marshall as anything but General and always seemed wary in his company. Marshall's remarks continued to startle him. In his conversations with his advisers, for instance, the President—who was an old Navy man—continually made it plain that in an even argument he would be inclined to favor the Navy's case against that of the Army. This nettled Marshall, but he kept his mouth shut until one day Roosevelt's naval bias was so obvious that he blurted out, "At least, Mr. President, stop speaking of the Army as 'they' and the Navy as 'us.'"

Marshall stayed suspicious of him, less so, perhaps, than of other politicians as the years went by, but he was acutely aware that, by the very nature of his job and profession, the President had to be a devious man and that nothing he said or did could be taken at its face value.

"I never haggled with the President," he said later. "I swallowed the little things so that I could go to bat on the big ones. I never handled a matter apologetically, and I was never contentious. It took me a long time to get to him."

It also took Marshall a long time to accept the fact that Franklin D. Roosevelt was something more than an extremely agile politician. It wasn't until the United States had been plunged into the war, in fact, and the President immediately displayed the qualities of resource and leadership in crisis that Marshall eventually accepted him as a great man.

"I hadn't thought so before," he confessed later. "He wasn't always clear-cut in his decisions. He could be swayed."

For Marshall, the conference at which he had so incautiously blurted out his opinion was a sharp lesson in the way his career had changed. He came back home to tell Katherine that at the age of fifty-eight he would have to learn new tricks that were not taught in the military manuals or the battlefield. He was now a political soldier who would have to put his training in rapping out orders and making snap decisions on the back burner, and have to begin learning the arts of persuasion and guile, because he now appreciated what Roosevelt had been saying and what he was trying to do. He still didn't agree with him and continued to think that the priority for America at this time was to build up the U.S. Army and Air Corps and not sacrifice them to keep America's allies supplied with the arms they had failed to provide for themselves. But he realized that once it reached Washington, not even a straightforward request by the Army for more men, more guns, and more planes could be achieved without going through a whole rigamarole of lobbying, congressional hearings, deals, and quid pro quos. He would have to become expert in a whole new set of skills, and he was not sure he was going to like it. Was this what he had devoted his life to the Army for? "I'm just a simple soldier," he told his wife, disingenuously.

Katherine Marshall was well aware that a simple soldier was exactly what her husband was not, and he knew it. She had watched him turn the city of Savannah from a hostile no-man's-land into an enthusiastically pro-Army neighbor when they had been at Fort Screven. She had seen her husband deal with the young men in the CCC camps and give them back their will to grow up and succeed. She had admired the way he had won over her two sons and daughter, both before and after their marriage, and transformed them from suspicious stepchildren into loving members of the family. She was certain that her husband was as sharp a politician as some of the smartest men in Congress and would be outsmarting all of them once he had polished up his skills. Not that she told him that—he wouldn't have liked it. Instead, she assured him that nothing was likely to annoy him more about *his* new job than the one *she* was having to learn to live with again after years in the field: military protocol, Washington style.

"If we could have retired into our shell, life would have been far easier," she wrote later, "but as Deputy Chief of Staff, George's job placed him on the official list."

In the beginning, the burden had been placed on her:

> In official life your first duty was to leave cards at the White House. The wives of Cabinet members each had her day At Home, and you were expected to call at least once during the season—on those days only and the call must be no longer than fifteen minutes. This was also true of the wives of the Ambassadors and Justices of the Supreme Court. Any invitation from the White House was a command, always accepted, the reply being delivered by hand, not mailed. It was considered more courteous to answer Embassy, Cabinet and Supreme Court invitations in the same manner.

But George was caught up in the social life, too, whether he wanted to be or not, and almost immediately became conscious once more of his Army rank. Outside Washington a one-star general was quite important, but in the nation's capital he was a nobody, despite his high-sounding position of Deputy Chief of Staff. Katherine wrote:

> Of course, at any social or official affair other than a reception you waited for the first on the protocol line to leave first, and this was the most boring and exhausting part of the Social Code, especially for us. My husband was one of the busiest men in the Government and by evening he was really too tired to go out, yet in order not to give offense he had to accept certain invitations and

stay until extremely late, for there was nothing more lowly in Washington than a Brigadier General. Everyone, all the Senators, all the members of Congress, and their wives preceded the Army, and a Brigadier General was outranked by a Major General, a Lieutenant General and a General, and my husband was a junior brigadier at that. So it is quite easy to see where the Marshalls came in—and went out!

It was a wearisome round, and Marshall hated every moment of it. But once more he had hopes that things might be changing for him. In August 1939 General Malin Craig's term of office as Chief of Staff would be coming to an end, and there were rumors around that the choice of his successor was wide open. As far as the Army was concerned, no one thought that Marshall had a chance of getting the job. For one thing, the deputy chief rarely moved up to the senior position. For another, Marshall was out-ranked by twenty-one major generals and eleven brigadier generals and thus would have to leapfrog over thirty-two other officers to be picked.

But Marshall had been learning how to maneuver (and not in the military sense of the word) during his time in Washington, and as Katherine had surmised, he was becoming as smart as any politician in the art of getting the right kind of support. Early in 1939 he had a lucky break. One of his jobs as deputy chief had been to push the President's plane-building program and at the same time slog away at a campaign to get bigger appropriations for Army manpower and armaments. This interested Harry Hopkins, the secretary of commerce, who had charge of the building program, and he sent a message saying he would like to come down to the War Department and talk to the Deputy Chief of Staff. Marshall had already learned that nothing flatters a politician more than to visit him, rather than the other way around, and he replied at once telling Hopkins he would come see him. They had a long talk together, at the end of which Hopkins was so impressed with Marshall's facts, figures, and arguments that he promised to talk to the President about shifting appropriations the Army's way.

He was impressed by the caliber of the deputy chief, and Marshall could hardly have been unaware that he now had a friend at court. In the meantime, however, the lobbying had begun, and the big guns in the running for the Chief of Staff's job had been loading up their ammunition. The favorite was undoubtedly one of the Army's veteran generals, Hugh A. Drum, who had served under Pershing in France during World War I as a division and corps commander and, in the 1930's, had been given command of the most important and vital of America's overseas territories, the Hawaiian Department. But nothing meant more to Hugh Drum than the Chief of Staff's job, and he had been campaigning to get it for years. In 1930 his name had been submitted for the post to President Hoover, but he had been passed over in favor of Douglas MacArthur. In 1934, when MacArthur had been due to retire, Drum had made it known that he would like to take over, but thanks to MacArthur's influential friends in Congress and the heavy lobbying from his doting mother, Pinky, his tenure had been extended. Then MacArthur had departed for the Philippines, and Drum had hoped anew, only to be defeated for the post by Malin Craig, whom Pershing had preferred and recommended.

Now Drum was pulling out all the stops to secure the most important post in the U.S. Army as the final seal on his career. For the past two years any important visitor to his headquarters in Hawaii had been urged to write to Washington on his return to the mainland and recommend him when the job once more became vacant. One of his serving officers in Hawaii had been George Patton, and Drum now exhorted Patton to visit Pershing— who liked Patton—and persuade him to recommend him to the President.

There were three other generals, all senior to Marshall, who were candidates for the job, and all were campaigning to get it. One was General John L. DeWitt, who was president of the Army War College, a second was Major General Frank W. Rowell, and a third General Walter Krueger, who had also been on Pershing's staff during World War I and had only one drawback to his claims to the job: He had been born in Germany.

The friends of all these men were bombarding the White House with arguments in their favor. Marshall discovered he was not without his own friends eager to campaign for him. The secretary of war, Harry Woodring, made it clear he was for Marshall's appointment. A senator from Pennsylvania spoke up for him, mainly, as it turned out, because he knew his sister, Marie, socially and thought a Chief of Staff from Pennsylvania might earn him some praise from his constituents. The retiring Chief of Staff, General Malin Craig, told Marshall he would be prepared to recommend him as his successor.

Far from being pleased at this, Marshall was alarmed. He had sized up the situation and decided this was one occasion when lobbying might lose rather than gain him the President's favor. In any case, he thought the others were trying too hard. It was a time to keep quiet. If any of the big guns suspected that Marshall had a chance, they could easily wipe him out by citing his lowly seniority and rallying their forces in the government. Marshall wrote to an Atlanta newspaperman who had been urged by Woodring to write him up:

> Reference any publicity regarding me, or build-up, as it is called. I am now, in my particular position with low rank, on the spot in Army circles. The fact of my appointment as deputy while a brigadier general, junior to all generals of the General Staff, makes me conspicuous in the Army. Too conspicuous, as a matter of fact.

He added:

> My strength with the Army has rested on the well-known fact that I attended strictly to business and enlisted no influence of any sort at any time. That in Army circles has been my greatest strength in the matter of future appointment, especially as it is in contrast with other most energetic activities in organizing a campaign and in securing voluminous publicity.

So this was the moment for doing, he calculated, the opposite of what Washington expected of a candidate—nothing. All the other hopefuls were making such a noise about themselves, and so many big drums were being beaten on their behalf, that for once it was his silence that would make him most audible to the President.

He got an inkling of the way things were going on a Sunday afternoon in early April 1939, when he was summoned to the White House. Roosevelt wasted no words.

"General Marshall," he said, "I have it in mind to choose you as the next Chief of Staff of the United States Army. What do you think about that?"

"Nothing, Mr. President," Marshall replied, "except to remind you that I have the habit of saying exactly what I think. And that, as you know," he added, "can often be unpleasing. Is that all right?"

Roosevelt grinned.

"Yes," he said.

Marshall persisted. "Mr. President, you said yes pleasantly. But I have to remind you again, it may be unpleasant."

The President continued to grin.

"I know," he said. For a moment Marshall thought he was going to add "George." But he did not.

Marshall departed but said nothing to anyone, not even his wife. He did not quite know whether his bluntness had changed the President's mind or made it up.

The following Sunday Katherine Marshall went out to Green Spring Valley with the Malin Craigs to watch a point-to-point meeting. At one moment, to get a better vantage point, she scrambled onto the wall of an old cemetery, hitched up her skirt, and sat down. By the time she got back to Washington she had developed a raging case of poison ivy, and it was spreading all over her body. She called in the doctor and, knowing her husband was due to depart for a tour of the West Coast the following morning, gave orders that he was not to be told. Since he often slept in his separate bedroom when he was working late, she hoped she could conceal what had happened to her.

But nobody would have dared keep from him the fact that his wife was stricken, and the following morning the housekeeper whispered to him what had happened to Katherine. He was appalled and rushed in to see her. Watching her toss in agony, he desperately sought for some means of comforting her. Finally, he said, "I hate so to leave you like this. You look pathetic all bound up and lying there, so I am going to tell you some news. When the President sent for me last week, it was to tell me that he had chosen me as his Chief of Staff. It has now been confirmed. The newspapers will probably have it in a day or two—and now I must be off."

There was a telegram from the Malin Craigs: "AREN'T YOU ASHAMED OF YOURSELF? WHILE YOUR HUSBAND IS COVERED WITH GLORY YOU ARE COVERED WITH POISON IVY."

All Katherine Marshall could think of—beside her pain—was that a second star went with her husband's appointment, and henceforth they would no longer be the junior guests forced by protocol to stay on to the end of all the parties.

In the early hours of September 1, 1939, the telephone rang in the house on Wyoming Avenue, near Rock Creek Park, which the Marshalls had rented while in Washington. It was the War Department with the news that the German Army had crossed the Polish border a few hours earlier, and in accordance with the pledge they had made to the Polish government, Britain and France were bound to go to Poland's aid against Germany. It meant that World War II was about to begin.

Marshall had been working in his bedroom-cum-den when the call came. He went in to tell Katherine the news, but she was awake and had already heard it on the radio. They stayed talking together until the dawn came of a hot, sticky Washington day. September 1, 1939, had, in any case, been seen by both of them as a benchmark in their lives, for later in the day at a planned ceremony Marshall would officially become Chief of Staff of the U.S. Army. But now the ominous events in Europe added a new weight to the burden Marshall was about to shoulder.

The ceremonials were canceled, and instead, he went at once to the War Department. There, at nine o'clock, Brigadier General George Catlett Marshall stepped before the Adjutant General, raised his right hand, and solemnly took the oath as a newly confirmed permanent major general in the armed forces of the United States. A pause and a congratulatory handshake, and then he raised his hand again. This time he took the oath as a temporary four-star general and Chief of Staff of the U.S. Army. His voice was flat, firm, and emotionless as he pledged "To support and defend the Constitution of the United States against all enemies, both foreign and domestic."

Then he sped off to the White House to report to the President, his Commander in Chief, and preside at his first conference as senior member of America's high command.

Roosevelt was waiting for him, sweating slightly in the rising heat but looking cheerful, despite the grimness of the news. At a press conference he had held half an hour before, he had indicated his firm belief that despite the events in Europe, the United States could still stay out of the war.

So did Marshall. For the moment anyway.

II

Top Man

8

The Road to Pearl

No Americans were fighting and dying on the battlefields yet, but in their homes families were already at war with each other. In September 1939 the unity of the American people had shown signs of fraying at the seams, and a year later, when France fell and victorious Nazi troops marched into Paris, the United States became a torn, turbulent, and unhappy country. Fathers and sons, sisters and brothers, mothers and daughters, in-laws, workmates, friends, neighbors all squabbled over what policy the United States should pursue with regard to the war.

Very few Americans wanted the Nazis to win. On the other hand, even fewer wanted to get involved in the fight—unless they had to. But what would happen if they simply stood aside and allowed Britain, the last unconquered democratic nation in Europe, to be overrun by the Nazis? Wouldn't it mean that Germany and its totalitarian allies, Italy and Japan, would then turn on the United States, which would be forced to fight alone?

All over the land people were taking sides, and to be called an interventionist or an isolationist was either a dirty insult or a badge of sagacity, depending on which side pinned it on you. The interventionists supported a Committee to Aid the Allies Now led by a staunch patriot named William Allen White. The isolationists supported a well-heeled campaign to keep America out of war, led by a staunch patriot named Charles Lindbergh.*

One of the keenest interventionists was a Chicago lawyer named Adlai Stevenson, and on the day France fell he joined William Allen White's committee because he was convinced helping Britain was now the only way to stop the totalitarian powers from taking over the world. But Chicago was isolationist country.

*Whose mother-in-law was an ardent interventionist.

"Hysteria was so bad at this time," Stevenson said later, "that I recall a senior citizen, who shall be nameless, who came to the senior partner in my law firm and said, 'How can you tolerate having a man in your office who wants to kill my son?' He then withdrew his business."

In Washington the administration could be just as harsh with suspected isolationists. The White House discovered that a member of the War Department intelligence staff was a certain Colonel Truman Smith, who was a former military attaché in Berlin and an expert on the German Army. But he was also a close friend of Charles Lindbergh's and suspected of sharing his views.

The White House hinted that Truman Smith was a traitor and a spy and asked Marshall to throw him out. The Chief of Staff called in Brigadier General Sherman Miles, head of his intelligence staff, and asked him about Smith. Miles had heard the rumors.

"General," Miles replied, "no man here is so valuable if he worries you. Let me get rid of him."

"Is he a good man? Do you want him?" Marshall asked.

"He's very useful, I must say," Miles said. "But not with all these troubles around him."

"If you need him, that's the only thing that counts," the Chief of Staff said. "I'll tell the White House."

Next thing he heard was an accusation from a member of Roosevelt's Cabinet that Truman Smith had got drunk at a party and insulted the President. Confronted with the charge, the colonel proved that as a diabetic he didn't drink and never went to parties anyway. But he took the hint and, rather than be harassed further, retired from his job and the Army on the grounds of ill health.*

It was a difficult time for the Chief of Staff, and he bent over backward to avoid being tagged as a member of one camp or another. From the start he made it plain to the White House that though the President was *ipso facto* his Commander in Chief, he did not wish to be considered a member of Roosevelt's cozy family

---

*Marshall called him back after America entered the war.

circle of Cabinet members and advisers. Harry Hopkins was rebuffed when he tried to bring Marshall closer to the President. He approached a member of Marshall's staff, Major (later General) Walter Bedell Smith, and told him he "felt it was highly important that President Roosevelt and General Marshall become much more intimate." He said the President liked people to drop in after dinner and have a scotch in the library "and a quiet private discussion, and he knew the President would welcome that. . . . Hopkins asked me if I couldn't do something to bring them closer together."

But when Bedell Smith mentioned the conversation to his chief, Marshall said, "I'm at the President's disposal and he knows it, twenty-four hours of the day. But if I attempt to step out of character, then it would be artificial, and I just don't think that I can or should do it."

It did not prevent the isolationists from calling him a Roosevelt stooge each time he went before Congress and asked for more money and manpower for the Army. He found it hard to understand the thinking of Lindbergh and his fellow isolationists. If their policy succeeded, and America neither aided the democracies in Europe nor intervened on their side, then Germany would win the war and, with its fascist allies, become the most powerful and menacing force in the world. Wasn't that all the more reason to bolster America's defenses since, in any subsequent conflict, the United States would have to fight this monstrous coalition by itself? Otherwise, what did the isolationists intend to use to protect themselves: the Neutrality Act?

To get this point over to isolationists and other reluctant Congressmen, Marshall arranged with an old friend, Rep. James W. Wadsworth, to address a meeting at the Army and Navy Club in Washington to which some of the President's most diehard opponents in the Republican Party would be invited. He gave it to them good and strong, mixing facts and figures about the grim situation with appeals to the patriotism of the politicians. They listened in silence, and then one of them said frankly: "General, you put the case very well, but I will be damned if I am going along with Mr. Roosevelt."

Marshall said later that the man's statement "hit me like a blow in the face." Flushing, he said angrily: "You are going to let plain hatred of the personality dictate to you to do something that you realize is very harmful to the interest of the country."*

But he came away from the meeting with a feeling of failure, and he was right. Only ten or eleven of the forty-three Republicans present subsequently showed themselves willing to risk isolationist opposition and vote for Roosevelt's selective service measures.

And, in his opinion, selective service and its extension was going to be one of the vital keys to America's security in the months to come.

Right from the beginning of the war in Europe Marshall had devoted hours of his time trying to impress President, Congress, and the public with the fact that militarily speaking, the United States was in a bad way. Economically it was still the most thriving country in the world, richer than any other nation, but in the strength of its armed forces it was outranked by sixteen other countries, including Spain and Portugal.

Nothing but a crash program of expansion of the armed forces in both manpower and equipment could give the United States the defensive force it needed for the tricky months ahead. His experts calculated that the price for such a program would be $675 million. That would give him an army of 280,000 men and a reequipped National Guard of 250,000 men, the bare minimum needed for a nation still at peace but prepared for war.

To Marshall's dismay, he got little support for this modest program from any of the politicians, no matter what their partisan feelings. The isolationists called him a warmonger and a Roosevelt stooge for daring to ask for any expansion at all. Not only that, but the President and the pro-Allied groups in Congress backed off, too. Everybody was thinking about the elections coming up at the end of 1940 and frightened of scaring the American people by asking for the means of making them secure. "They'd rather lose a war than lose a vote," said one disgruntled member of Marshall's staff.

*Marshall's recollections in a tape made Jan. 22, 1957.

Marshall went up to the White House with Secretary of the Treasury Henry Morgenthau to ask the President for the necessary authorization and approval of the program and found him in one of his most flippant and cynical moods. These were early days in his relationship with the President, and he had not yet found a way of dealing with him.

"I might say here that early in my association with the President," he commented later, "I didn't understand that I must find a way to do the talking. Because he did all the talking and [we] just had to sit and listen to the President of the United States. . . . I was not sufficiently adept in dealing with a man who was as clever as Mr. Roosevelt was about holding the boards [stage] and putting over his ideas. In this situation he had all the pressures from the outside . . . and none at all of my issues. . . . It was a very trying, maddening situation and it was very difficult to keep one's temper."

Marshall was particularly annoyed at the casual way in which Roosevelt treated what was a grimly disturbing situation, and he wondered how he could seem so oblivious of the fact that the nation was in danger. He watched with slow-burning anger as the President gave Morgenthau's exposition of the Chief of Staff's program the most cursory attention and then seemed to fob it off with a sort of "smile and sneer." When Morgenthau asked for approval of the plan, he coolly replied that he couldn't possibly ask Congress to grant him such an appropriation at this time. It wasn't the moment. Morgenthau then suggested that perhaps Marshall himself, who was a good advocate, might go up to Congress and ask for approval of the program. The President glanced at his Chief of Staff almost with disdain and said, sharply, "Why do you want to go up on the Hill? Tell them to wait. I am going to have a message. Don't go up and tell them anything."

He waved a hand as if to dismiss them, causing Morgenthau, in desperation, to look across at the Chief of Staff and say, "Mr. President, will you hear General Marshall?"

"I know exactly what he would say," Roosevelt airily replied. "There is no necessity for me to hear him at all."

At this Marshall's neck and face began to flush brick red, a sure sign, his colleagues knew, that he was intensely angry. He walked in front of Morgenthau to the President's chair and said, quietly, "Mr. President, may I have three minutes?"

Roosevelt looked up in surprise and then, suddenly aware of the tension in the Chief of Staff's voice, registered a change of mood. Before he had been bantering and lightly contemptuous. Now his smile faded, and his face became serious.

"Of course," he said, adding, after a slight beat, "General Marshall."

There is no verbatim account of exactly what Marshall then said to the President, for the Chief of Staff never put it down on paper, and Morgenthau included only a summary in his diary. It began as a quiet exposition of the international situation and of America's inadequate means of dealing with the threat it constituted to American security. He spoke of the war in Europe and of the growing hostility and menace of Japan. He painted a graphic and detailed picture of the poor state, in mens, arms, equipment, and morale, of the nation's armed forces. Three minutes, five minutes, ten minutes passed, and his controlled sentences had taken on heat and passion. Did the President not understand the appalling danger in which America stood at this moment? Did he not realize that it was his hesitancy, his political timidity, which was putting his people in peril? He urged him to take instant action.

"If you don't do something, and do it right away," he ended, "I don't know what is going to happen to this country."

There was a long pause after he had finished, and then, with a nod of dismissal, the President said, "Thank you, General," and added, "Thank you, Henry."

He watched them go, and then, when Marshall reached the door, he called out, "Oh, General. Come back and see me tomorrow. And bring me a list in detail of your requirements."

When they got outside, Morgenthau was delighted. He congratulated Marshall on the way he had stood up to the President and said he was now convinced that the program—or most of it—would go through. The Chief of Staff was not so sure. He had still not quite got the measure of the President and did not know whether speaking out so roughly had saved the situation or ruined it.

He need not have worried. Two days later Roosevelt sent the program to Congress accompanied by the words "The developments of the past few weeks have made it clear to all our citizens that the possibility of attack on vital American zones [has made] it essential that we have the physical, the ready ability to meet these attacks and to prevent them from reaching their objective."

He asked for $900 million in appropriations, and he got them without too much trouble.

Marshall afterward regarded that as the turning point. The President and Congress had at last swallowed the unpalatable fact that there are some things more important than elections and that the United States, though still at peace, just had to get ready for war. Thereafter, he maintained, despite all the trials and tribulations that lay ahead, things would never be quite so desperate again.

One of the assistant secretaries on the General Staff was Colonel (later General) Paul M. Robinett, and he kept a diary of his impressions of life in Marshall's office during the early part of 1941. He wrote, on January 5, 1941:

> At the end of my first official week in the Secretary's office, I will jot down my impression of the chief, General Marshall. He is the most self-contained individual I have ever encountered. Apparently, he has no confidants. His aide-de-camp, Colonel Claud Adams, is used on personal affairs very little. . . . He is against yesmen and seems to dislike aides-de-camp though he has been one to General Pershing. He swears a good oath on occasion, does not smoke, and rides for exercise whenever he can. . . . He has a good memory and a keen political sense and what my old friend Brigadier General Guy H. Preston once described as a "golden streak of imagination."

He ascribed Marshall's fitness despite his "ever growing workload" to his "defense mechanism" which, he explained, worked in this way:

When he is through with his work at the office he jumps into his car and scurries to Fort Myer, where he occupies the house which has been the home of the Chief of Staff since the times of Leonard Wood, changes his clothes, and is soon off for a canter on his favorite mount [a sorrel named Prepared.]. He is generally alone or with some younger person [his stepdaughter, Molly, or his goddaughter, Rose Page] who cannot talk shop. He never rides with military people. He prefers jodhpurs and is never seen in boots. If he plays any game, I am not aware of it. If he smokes, I have never seen him do it. He swears . . . but does not do so by habit. He can tell anecdotes of his service in a charming way and has a fund of them to tell.

But though Robinett never saw him lose his composure during the winter of 1940–41, Marshall was, in fact, several times discomposed and once or twice disconcerted by the maneuvers of his Commander in Chief in the White House. By that time, of course, the fate of the British Isles was in the balance. London was reeling under the blitz. The new prime minister, Winston Churchill, had begun his regular transatlantic telephone conversations with Roosevelt, and what he was asking for was war matériel: ships to break the submarine blockade in the Atlantic, food to feed his people, guns and shells with which to fire back at the Nazi bombers, and planes with which to retaliate against them by raiding German cities.

Marshall was a practical soldier, and he saw the value to America of keeping Britain fighting as long as possible. To a question at a press conference, he went out on a limb by predicting that "England can win with our material aid," though he did not really believe it. He was in favor of giving Britain supplies for as long as it stayed in the battle, and when the British let it slip that they were running out of cash to pay for the matériel, he campaigned in favor of the lend-lease bill to give them the credit they needed.

But he thought he had made it clear to the President that no sacrifice to help the British was worth it if it was made at the expense of the American armed forces. The breathing space that British tenacity gave America was useless if it was made at the expense of the rearmament program. He was taken aback when he discovered that the President wanted to give the British everything they asked for, even matériel earmarked for the U.S. armed forces. He was summoned to the White House and told to make a fleet of B-17 Flying Fortress planes available to Britain. The British had originally put in an order for B-17's and then decided against them, and now Marshall pointed out that they had been immediately grabbed by the plane-hungry U.S. Army Air Corps. He was told to give them back to the British and replied that it wasn't possible. They now belonged officially to the U.S. armed forces, and Justice Department lawyers had ordained that such government property could be transferred only with congressional approval. He was well aware that the President was not likely to ask a suspicious, if not downright hostile, House for such a controversial decision. But just to make sure that the planes stayed where they were, he added that there were only forty-seven B-17's in the continental United States, and they all belonged to the Air Corps. The President swallowed that unpalatable news with a surprised grimace, and his "head went back as if someone had hit him in the chest."

On his way back from that particular encounter, Marshall was accompanied by the Secretary of War, Henry L. Stimson, who chuckled as he congratulated the Chief of Staff and remarked that the President had been given a short, sharp lesson in the facts of military life. They were met at the War Department by a smiling General Hap Arnold, chief of the Army Air Corps, who greeted Marshall with a huge grin and said, "You've just saved my Air Corps."

But they hadn't—or rather, not quite in the way they imagined they had. They reckoned without the ingenuity of their wily chief executive and his passionate determination to do anything to aid the British and keep them fighting.

"When it came to a battle of tactics, Congress couldn't touch him," Stimson said later. "They may have been experts at running rings around the people, but he was a master at outsmarting the experts—in Congress and over at Justice, too."

As the military historian Forrest Pogue has pointed out, months of dealing with a pesky and uncooperative legislature had given the President an instinct for finding loopholes in congressional legislation and Department of Justice advisements. Pogue wrote:

> If transferring B17s to the British served a good cause, then there must be a lawful way of accomplishing this end. He suggested to the Chief of Staff that the Air Corps send a limited number of bombers to Britain to be tested under combat conditions. Clearly no better laboratory could at the moment be found.

It was a trick, a "fine point of casuistry," and Marshall knew it, and it worried him. He spent several hours riding his horse along the bridle paths near Fort Myer and pondering whether or not to swallow the presidential stratagem. He was not the kind of man to ignore the spirit in favor of the letter of the law, and his conscience was troubled. He called in General Arnold and his second-in-command, General George H. Brett, and put the President's argument to them that here was a unique opportunity to test their aircraft in battle, and shouldn't it be seized upon? He discovered that all they were worried about was that they were going to lose aircraft, and he sympathized with them. On the other hand, what if he refused to go along with the President's ruse? Was it a matter of principle over which he should put his job on the line?

It was a moment when Robinett was writing in his diary:

> The shadow of the world situation seems to hang over us, yet no clear cut decisions relative to our role, except material aid to Britain and an unwillingness to yield anything at any place in the world, has been made. . . . Our military men do not have a say in matters with which they alone are qualified to give an opinion. If we only had a military man who could stand on his feet and talk with the best of them!

Finally, after wrestling with his doubts, the Chief of Staff went to the White House, told the President he would recommend the transfer, and immediately felt better about it.

"We turned over fifteen Flying Fortresses, I think it was," he said later, "to the British for experimental purposes. I was a little ashamed of this because I felt that I was straining at the subject in order to get around the resolution of Congress."

He added, "Actually when we got into it and did it, it soon became apparent that the important thing was exactly that—to let them have planes for experimental purposes. And we should have done it much earlier. Because we found difficulties with the planes the Air Corps had not perceived at all."

But though this was comforting, it did not still suspicions among some of his subordinates and among outside observers that he had made an important political concession. By giving way to the President and going along with his stratagem, he had taken a step into his camp, and it would have both practical and psychological consequences. Not long afterward, he discovered that the whole of the plane production of the United States over a four-week period had been used up in fulfilling orders from outside the country and that in one month 400 planes had been shipped abroad while the Army Air Corps, with large orders in the pipeline, had received no aircraft at all. But how could he complain? Had he not gone a long way toward the Rooseveltian point of view that the United States was already unofficially at war and Britain was its front line? On the other hand, how could he have acted otherwise and still remained Chief of Staff? Robinett wrote in his diary:

> In the light of what happened, I know that had he stuck his neck out it would have been cut off to the harm of the United States. He stuck to his job and did the best he could, playing politics along with the rest of them, and ultimately proved himself as good as the best. If he had been born with less self-control and tact, he would have become ineffective in his job and would have been replaced.

But General Marshall was not alone in taking his sympathies—as well as his doubts—into the Roosevelt camp that spring of 1941. Congress, if even more reluctantly, followed suit by passing the Lend-Lease Act, which, as Marshall remarked later, "plainly declared our relations with Great Britain and friendship with them. It didn't necessarily indicate we were going to war with them, but

143

it made it a probability rather than a possibility. I don't know what the result would have been if we had not had lend-lease. I think it would have been exceedingly difficult for the British [to have come through]."

Everybody swallowed a little harder, however, when the Nazi armies turned eastward that summer, and Russia became involved in the war. The British prime minister, Winston Churchill, immediately hailed the Communists as allies, saying he would welcome the devil himself so long as he declared himself an enemy of Hitler.

But was lend-lease to be extended to Russia, too? In the War Department most intelligence experts thought it was hardly worthwhile. Stalinian purges among the generals had lopped off the leadership of the Red Army, leaving little more than a mass of cannon fodder for the Germans to gulp down for breakfast. It would all be over by Christmas, and Hitler would soon be posturing in Red Square in Moscow as he had under the Arc de Triomphe in Paris the year before.

Marshall was not so sure. He expressed the view that if he were in command of the Red defenses, he would order a strategic retreat, seducing the Germans into the vasty depths of Russia in the same way the armies of the czars had once tempted Napoleon. He hoped the Reds would be "wise enough to withdraw and save their army, abandoning their people, if necessary," and advised them to do some efficient sabotaging of their oil production. They did just that, and survived.

On the other hand, the Chief of Staff was much more skeptical about the question of lend-lease. Keeping aid going to the British was difficult enough without entirely starving out the U.S. Army and Air Corps. But what would happen to his expansion plans if Russia were now included in the lend-lease program? He soon found out. The Russians had a good friend at court in the person of Roosevelt's confidential adviser, Harry Hopkins, and Hopkins was determined that the Soviet Union should get everything that was going. He persuaded the President to sign an agreement giving the Russians $1 billion worth of military aid in the next twelve months, and from that moment on it was grab, grab, grab.

"Hopkins had power in representing the Russians," Marshall ruefully recalled later. "His power could always override mine because of his closeness to the President. . . . Hopkins's job was to represent the Russian interest. My job was to represent the American interest and I was opposed to any what I called undue generosity which might endanger our security. I thought we gave too much at times, and Hopkins thought we gave too little, which would always be the case."

But it went much further than that. Hopkins dispatched to Moscow as his lend-lease representative a Russian-speaking Army officer, Colonel Philip R. Faymonville, who had a long record with Army intelligence for his pro-Soviet activities. He was upped to the rank of brigadier general by the President in the face of Marshall's opposition and, almost immediately on arriving in the USSR, began encouraging the Soviets to overload the U.S. with importunate demands for arms. He was backed up by the Russian ambassador Konstantin Sergei Oumansky, in Washington, who had a habit of stalking into the War Department, confronting the secretary of war, Henry L. Stimson, and accusing him of deliberately helping to murder Soviet citizens by denying them arms. In vain did Stimson explain that the U.S. armed forces had their demands, too, and at least some of them should be satisfied. What did the cowards in the American Army matter? asked Oumansky. They were just lying around getting drunk while the Russian soldiers did their dying for them. Wooden rifles were good enough for them.

Secretary Stimson reacted badly to the Soviet envoy's atrocious manners. He was seventy-five years old and well aware that his impeccable upbringing and love of old-world courtesies caused some people to refer to him snidely as "an English gentleman approaching senility." Senile he was not. But he was outraged at Russian insensitivity to American feelings, and whenever the ambassador departed at the end of a stormy session, he would rush into Marshall's office next door and inveigh against "that crook,

145

that slick, clever little beast" who had just left him. Marshall sympathized.

"I thought the administration dealt very generously with the Russian complaints," he said later. "The Russians demanded everything and criticized everybody. The point was that they were fighting to keep the enemy engaged as much as possible. But their complaints were continuous and always have been. No matter how much you gave them, they didn't hesitate at all to complain about the whole thing."

But he could live with that. What he could not live with was the movement which began to surface in the summer of 1941 and soon came to be regarded by Marshall as a grave threat not only to the future of the U.S. Army but to the safety of the United States. His whole concept of how the nation was to be defended seemed threatened. That summer the isolationists put on their strongest campaign to keep America out of war, with meetings all over the country, some highly successful rallies in the Middle West, and a concentrated lobbying campaign among members of Congress in Washington. They were well aware that they were losing the battle with the administration to stay out of the war. Each month seemed to bring the United States closer to involvement. Already the President and Winston Churchill had met at sea to discuss joint plans for meeting the Nazi U-boat threat in the Atlantic. American military chiefs, led by Marshall, had talked over secret plans with the British about coordinating strategy, and the isolationists suspected—quite rightly, as it turned out—that it had been tacitly accepted on both sides that the United States would soon be a belligerent. Meanwhile, U.S. ships were already engaged in a shooting war with the Nazis on the sea routes to Europe.

It was decided by the antiwar movement that a last-ditch struggle must be waged to halt the administration's plans, and after a number of strategy conferences they decided to concentrate on Marshall's plans for expanding the Army. The isolationists had failed the year before to prevent the passing of the Draft Act of 1940 whereby American males were called into service for twelve months. But now the year was up and the Army wanted to retain its conscripts as well as call up others, and the only way it could do so was by having Congress vote an extension. The antiwar movement set out to prevent this. They rallied isolationist congressmen and senators. They lobbied in Washington and started write-in campaigns from states where pro- and antiwar sentiment was divided. By far the most effective element in their campaign was what came to be known as the OHIO Movement, and that word *OHIO* soon became the most familiar piece of graffiti to be found scrawled on walls from White Plains to Peoria and Portland, Oregon, to Portland, Maine. It had nothing to do with the state of Ohio but was a call for draftees to desert when the renewal date came up. OHIO: "Over the Hill in October."

Despite the intensity and bitterness of the campaign, the administration won. But narrowly. Right until the last moment it was touch and go, until the motion for the extension of the Draft Act was passed at last. By one vote.

Before Marshall had time to draw in a deep breath of relief, however, another threat to his plans caught him off-balance. This time it came from a totally unexpected quarter, from America's fighting allies, no less.

The British and the Russians had grown alarmed at the prospect of what wholesale conscription in the United States could do to them since the arms and supplies they were getting under lend-lease would almost certainly have to be sacrificed if arms and equipment had to be found for a growing U.S. Army. American industry was not yet in top gear so far as armaments were concerned and was not yet capable of satisfying the urgent and ever-growing demands from both home and overseas. Undoubtedly the U.S. Army would insist on priority, and therefore, the British and the Soviets would suffer while domestic expansion was taking place.

Somehow American plans must be thwarted. Lobbyists began a campaign on the Hill, at the White House, and among the press to suggest that the Chief of Staff's plans for a grand army were not necessary at all. What America should do was continue lend-lease supplies to the allies and leave it to them, with the aid of the U.S. Navy and Air Corps, to do the fighting. Why go to the expense, trouble, and continuing embarrassment of building up a vast conscript army, when there were friendly foreign troops available, already fighting America's battles?

The movement caught on. Toward the end of September 1941 a remarkable article appeared in the New York *Herald Tribune*. It was written by one of the most influential columnists of the day, Walter Lippmann, and it was remarkable because it appeared at a critical moment in America's history, with the war going badly for the nation's allies in Europe, Africa, and Russia, with the Nazis sinking U.S. ships in the Atlantic and Japan's navy threatening American power in the Pacific. It was only sixty-eight days before the United States was, in fact, plunged into the maelstrom of war. Yet the title of Lippmann's article was headed "The Case for a Smaller Army" and included these words:

> All popular doubts, political confusions, all ambiguity would be removed by a clear decision to shrink the Army and concentrate our major effort upon the Navy, the air force and lend-lease. . . . Today the effort to raise such a large army is not merely unnecessary but undesirable. It interferes with our lend-lease and naval policy. It is, in fact, the basic cause of most of the discontent which exists in the Army, [is the] cancer which obstructs national unity, causes discontent which subversive elements exploit, and weakens the primary measures of our defense, which are the lend-lease policy and the naval policy. I think a surgical operation is indicated—an operation to shrink the Army which will at the same time increase its efficiency.

Marshall was appalled. The strength of his army at the moment was less than 900,000 men. He had plans to increase it to 1,700,000 by the end of the year and was pretty certain it would soon have to be very much greater than that.* To suggest that he should cut and slash instead of build seemed to him to be tantamount to sabotage. He blamed the British for it, believing that their lobbyists had used their influence on Lippmann, and he called them in and denounced them for their underhanded methods and their denigration of the quality and usefulness of the U.S. Army.

---

*It was 5,397,000 strong by the end of WWII.

He warned them that "if they didn't stop this business, I would have to come out and pillory them publicly."

Appropriately chastened, the British promised to behave in the future. But in the meantime, the damage had been done. On September 20, 1941, Marshall told his staff he had been summoned to the White House "to a conference in which would be discussed a proposal to reduce the strength of the Army in order to make available more material for other purposes." He demanded all the ammunition he could get to shoot down these treacherous propagandists among his allies. Two of the ablest assistants to the secretary of war, John J. McCloy and Robert A. Lovett, wrote him a long memorandum setting out the dangers of reducing the Army. It pointed out that the Allies, far from being in a position to fight America's battles, were losing their own. Russia was on the point of ceding Moscow. The British seemed about to lose the Middle East, the Suez Canal, and their lifeline of empire. And in the Pacific the Japanese were making belligerent noises everywhere. The free world would be dismayed if America now set out to reduce its army, and the government would be rightly accused of truckling to the totalitarian aggressor and seeking to make a deal.

"Abandonment of maximum effort in any form," the memorandum stated, "would be considered a step towards appeasement, for a negotiated peace is at the root of the Lippmann article—not a complete victory."

As it turned out, the President hardly read the paper Marshall handed to him. It seems likely that the British had reported back to Churchill in London about the box on the ears which Marshall had administered to them, and he had immediately telephoned the White House to make amends. At all events, the President was in his most conciliatory mood. He assured his Chief of Staff that ("contrary to what you may have heard") he had no intention whatever of interfering with plans to build up the Army and authorized him to have the secretary of war issue a statement to that effect.

But it had been a strenuous and worrying year so far, and Marshall suspected that there would be even bigger crises to be dealt with before the year was out. One of the things about Lippmann's article which had particularly incensed him was its implicit suggestion that the U.S. Army had grown too big. At the moment his article had appeared, despite a year of the Draft Act, the United States Army had only one infantry division ready for combat and only two bomber squadrons and three fighter groups ready to go into action as part of the U.S. Army Air Corps.

A crash program of expansion had been set going. But Marshall was only too well aware that even if it went through without a hitch, the United States would, by April 1942, have only three infantry divisions, an armored corps, seven bomber groups, and seven and a half fighter groups ready to go to war. The Nazis already had fifty times as strong a force deployed in its Russian campaign alone.

"We can't go to war because we aren't ready to go to war," Marshall told his planners.

But the isolationists didn't believe him, and on December 4, 1941, they told the nation why.

9

Bunglers

There was one thing General Marshall was acutely aware of during those tense last months of peace in 1941, and that was the deep antipathy some members of his staff felt toward the President and his pro-British attitude to the war. He was also conscious that they by no means approved of the way the Chief of Staff was now going along with presidential policies. That was all right with him. He knew there were isolationists as well as interventionists in the department, too, and realized that not all of them were willing to understand his point of view.

Since the outbreak of war in Europe two years earlier Marshall had endeavored to follow events with cold, hard military logic. Outwardly, at least, he had succeeded to such an extent that one of the department's most perfervid interventionist members, Walter Bedell Smith, burst out that he was "as cold as a fish" and added that "he had not the slightest personal loyalty to him and never had." In fact, as women and children knew, Marshall was a warm human being who, when pricked, bled like other men. But where the Army and the defense of the United States were concerned, he was brutally practical. If he had begun to go along with President Roosevelt's pro-British maneuvers, it was not because he had become emotionally involved with the struggle Great Britain was waging, but because he had reached the calculated conclusion that the United States would soon inevitably be involved in war, and the British were buying time for the American people.

The events which had forced him to accept the inevitability of war were threefold. First had come the so-called Pact of Steel, which the three totalitarian powers, Germany, Italy, and Japan, had signed at the end of 1940, pledging mutual aid to any signatory "attacked by a power at present not involved in the European war or in the Sino-Japanese conflict." This was an obvious reference to the United States, and though the aid would come only after a signatory had been "attacked," Marshall knew how seriously that could be taken. According to the Nazis, it was an "attack" by Poland on Germany which had started the war in 1939.

Secondly, the Japanese and the Soviet Union had signed a six-year nonaggression pact, which meant that the Russians would stay out of any conflict involving the Japanese in the Pacific. And thirdly, the Russians had been invaded by the Nazis in the summer of 1941. As their forces drew nearer to Moscow and the subjugation of the Soviet Union became more likely, with it grew the martial ambitions of the Japanese. They had already moved into Indochina. They were driving back the Kuomintang government in China. It would not be long before they had gained enough confidence to take on the United States.

So if, as the isolationists whispered, President Roosevelt was plotting to get America involved in the war, Marshall—while scoffing at the charge—went along with the President's thinking because he could not see how involvement was avoidable anyway, and all that concerned him was to keep the British in Europe and the Chinese in Asia fighting the totalitarians for as long as possible, while America got ready for the worst.

All he asked of those members of the department who did not agree with him was that they keep their arguments confined to military practicalities and stay out of politics. To begin with, there were three of his military advisers who had studied the German armies at close quarters and were enthusiastic admirers of their martial qualities. One of them was Colonel Truman Smith, the former U.S. military attaché in Berlin, who had got to know some high Nazi officials during his stay in Germany, but he, as a result of his friendship with Charles Lindbergh, the isolationist spokesman in the United States, had earned Roosevelt's enmity and, under pressure from the White House, had resigned his post. There was General Stanley D. Embick, a former Deputy Chief of Staff, who had close German connections. And there was Major Albert C. Wedemeyer, who had been to war college in Germany.

Marshall had objected to the activities and pronouncements of only one of this trio. When General Embick allowed himself to be quoted in the press as vaunting the valor of German soldiers and denigrating the qualities of their British counterparts, and when he followed this up by calling British Prime Minister Winston Churchill "a vainglorious fool" who ought to be thrown out of office for failing to make peace with the Nazis, Marshall called him in and rebuked him strongly for meddling in politics.

On the other hand, he had been furious with Roosevelt for provoking the departure of Truman Smith from the German section of the War Department because while it was true Smith was Lindbergh's friend and maybe shared his views, he had never brought isolationist politics into the office. On the other hand, he had often provided him with excellent information about the German Army and its leaders.

The same went for Wedemeyer. He was aware that Wedemeyer thought that German soldiers were the best in the world and that British and American troops were much inferior. But he never said so publicly. Marshall suspected that if it did come to war, Wedemeyer would probably have preferred to see Americans fighting on the same side as the German Army. But he never said so out loud. And Marshall was convinced that as a loyal American Wedemeyer would never do anything to sabotage the military strategy or the policies of the U.S. government, even if he disagreed with them. So he was unpleasantly surprised when, on the morning of December 4, 1941, John J. McCloy, the assistant secretary of war, stormed into his office and slammed a morning newspaper on his desk.

There was a flaring headline across the newspaper's front page: REVEAL FDR'S SECRET WAR PLANS! "Look what some bastard has done to us!" McCloy said.

Major (later General) Albert Coady Wedemeyer was forty-four years old in December 1941 and acknowledged by his colleagues to be the most fiercely ambitious officer on General Marshall's staff in Washington. He had quite a few things going for him.

A member of the German section of the War Plans department, Wedemeyer had already demonstrated that he had the talent, drive, and knowledge to make his mark in the U.S. Army. He had connections, too.

Although as a cadet at West Point he had coasted along and come out only midway in his class, he was a big-boned, handsome youngster who did well in sports and got along easily with people. One night at a West Point prom he had met and fallen in love with a girl named Elizabeth Embick, and it was only after he had proposed marriage to her, he claimed, that he discovered she was the daughter of the Deputy Chief of Staff of the U.S. Army, the aforementioned General Stanley D. Embick.

Embick was delighted with his new son-in-law and unabashedly pulled strings for him in the Army. It was he who arranged for Wedemeyer to be sent on a scholarship to the German war college in Berlin. He stayed there for two and a half years and had the good fortune to have as his instructor in war tactics an officer who was to become one of the most successful German soldiers in World War II, General Alfred Jodl.

Wedemeyer had arrived in Germany at the moment when Hitler ordered the German generals to beef up their forces in readiness for the war of conquest which he and the Nazis were planning, and the young American newcomer found the Wehrmacht in a fever of preparation and rehearsal for conflict. Sitting in on Jodl's lectures in mobile warfare, Wedemeyer was soon sufficiently in his instructor's confidence to be given permission to go into the field and train with German Army units. He thus became the first foreigner to see the Wehrmacht's new armored panzer regiments and antitank units on maneuvers, rehearsing the tactics that would shape the pattern of attack during the devastating blitzkrieg of 1940.

Young Wedemeyer was tremendously impressed by the strength, enterprise, and enthusiasm of the German armed forces and astonished at the brilliant new tactics they were trying out. He sat down and wrote a long report of what he had seen and urged the United States Army to emulate the Germans, to organize similar fast-moving armored units, and, in the meantime, to equip its troops with antitank weapons for stopping panzer forces. The United States Army had neither tank nor antitank regiments at that moment.

When Wedemeyer returned home in late 1938, his report was circulated in the War Department, where it fell with a dull thud. It was true that he talked to a number of senior officers, but they were put off by his too evident enthusiasm for the German Army. U.S. military opinion at that period was convinced that the best military units in the world belonged to the French. Wedemeyer's cocky insistence that the Germans would lick both the British and French armies together if they were stupid enough to go to war against the Nazis was something which grated on his listeners. Only one senior officer took him seriously, and that was Brigadier General George C. Marshall, who was then head of War Plans. He sent for Captain (as he then was) Wedemeyer three times and questioned him closely and repeatedly about his report. Finally, he invited him to join the War Plans department as a member of the section dealing with the German Army. It was the beginning of a long collaboration. Wedemeyer knew that Marshall had his eye upon him and that the prospects for his promotion were good, especially when his boss was made Chief of Staff. In fact, one of the first things that happened to him afterward was that he was promoted to major. And the future looked bright.

But then the waters around the War Department had begun to get distinctly choppy, at least for those members of the War Plans department who were known to be admirers of the German Army. First Wedemeyer's father-in-law, General Embick, had been rebuked for shooting off his mouth. Then had come the resignation of Colonel Truman Smith because of his friendship with Charles Lindbergh. Wedemeyer shared many of Lindbergh's sentiments, particularly his admiration for the German Army and his fears that in backing Britain and France, America was throwing in its lot with the losing side. But Marshall let it be known that he did not object to what Wedemeyer thought in private so long as he kept his ideas and opinions to himself and stayed away from isolationist and America First propaganda campaigns.

It so happened that one of the tasks Wedemeyer had been

given in the War Plans department was to draw up a campaign plan for exactly what actions the United States Army should take in the event of the nation's becoming involved in the war with Germany. It was called the Victory Plan. For years the War Department had drawn up contingency papers of this kind against any potential enemy of the United States, and the plan for dealing with Germany which Wedemeyer drew up was one of many.

But up and down the country controversy was raging, and Lindbergh and his isolationist supporters were hotly accusing President Roosevelt of deliberately plotting to get America into war with the Nazis. Two of the most perfervid supporters of the isolationists in the press, and also the bitterest enemies of Roosevelt, were the Washington *Times-Herald* in the nation's capital and the notoriously anti-British Chicago *Tribune*. All through the last days of November and the beginning of December 1941 both newspapers had been running a virulent campaign against Roosevelt, and on December 4 they brought it to a climax with an article by the *Tribune*'s Washington correspondent, revealing details of the Victory Plan and accusing the President of having drawn up "a blueprint for total war."

Who had leaked this highly secret document to Roosevelt's enemies? Suspicion inevitably, and not unnaturally, fell on the man who had drawn up the Victory Plan. As he said later, "Circumstantial evidence was very strong against me. All copies of the plan had been checked and registered. One had been sent to the secretary of war [Henry L. Stimson] by General Marshall and one to the President. I had retained one myself, and I kept it locked in my safe. Then, of course, there was the fact that I had a German name and that I had recently come back from Germany."

There were other circumstantially incriminating factors. Wedemeyer had actually met Charles Lindbergh when he had made his notorious tour of Germany in 1938 and been decorated by the Nazi air chief, Hermann Goering, and it was Wedemeyer who had acted as Lindbergh's interpreter when he had toured Nazi war plants and German Army posts. If he had kept his mouth shut in public, he had never concealed inside the War Department his belief that the United States should not get involved in a war against Germany. Moreover, when the FBI was called in to investigate the leak, it searched the desks, drawers, and safes of members of the War Plans department. Wedemeyer came in the morning after the scare story appeared to find his secretary weeping and Department of Justice agents standing before his open safe, a copy of the plan in their hands. Examining it, they discovered that exactly the same passages had been underlined in red ink—admittedly by Wedemeyer—as had been used in the newspaper stories. They also found that Wedemeyer had recently deposited money into an account in a downtown branch of Rigg's National Bank.*

It was easy to jump to damaging conclusions. Assistant Secretary of War John J. McCloy summoned Wedemeyer to his office, where, he remembered, McCloy, instead of asking him to sit down, as he usually did, kept him standing at attention and shouted at him, "There's blood on the hands of the man who did this!"

Secretary of War Stimson called a press conference at which he angrily declared, "What would you think of an American General Staff which, in the present condition of the world, did not investigate and study every conceivable type of emergency which might confront this country and every possible method of meeting that emergency?"

He added, "What do you think of the patriotism of a man or a newspaper which would take these confidential studies and make them public to the enemies of the country?"

McCloy was all for having the culprit court-martialed and drummed out of the Army for treachery—once he was discovered, of course. One man, however, who kept his head in a generally hysterical situation was General Marshall. He had an almost sublime faith in the loyalty of his staff and presumed that once he had appointed them to positions of trust, they would never let him down. Therefore, there was no point in suspecting any of

*Wedemeyer explained to the author that he had looked at his copy of the plan before the FBI's visit, compared it with the newspaper accounts, and underlined the passages quoted in both plan and newspapers. The money he had deposited in Rigg's Bank came from a windfall from a relative.

them. He informed the secretary of war that he proposed to make no changes in his entourage, institute no office inquiry, and carry on just as before.

Wedemeyer was immensely grateful for Marshall's trust both in him and in the other junior members of the staff. He carried on as usual. But he said later, "I would have died for him after that."

That was the way he felt in 1941, as World War II began. By the time it was over, and postwar problems raised their ugly heads, his sentiments had changed.

Not everyone was satisfied by Wedemeyer's oath and explanation. The Senate was anxious to know more about the Victory Plan and who had leaked it to the press. (They never found out.)* The Armed Forces Committee summoned the Chief of Staff and Major Wedemeyer to testify before them on the morning of Monday, December 8. But the confrontation never took place. Another military matter supervened.

On Sunday, December 7, 1941, Major (later General) John R. Deane was working in the War Department on some details of the Victory Plan which Marshall would need for his testimony the following morning. At one moment Deane looked up and saw a Navy enlisted man rushing into the room, waving a flimsy piece of paper. Deane could see some words in pencil scrawled across it.

Soon everybody knew what those words were: "PEARL HARBOR ATTACKED. THIS IS NO DRILL."

In the circumstances, nobody worried any longer about Wedemeyer or who had leaked the Victory Plan. World War II was upon them.

As in the case of the shooting of President Abraham Lincoln, the murder of the Lindbergh baby, the assassination of President John F. Kennedy, and the slaying of Martin Luther King, the American people are likely to go on speculating for generations

---

*One rumor in the War Department had it that the plan was leaked by an Air Force officer, upset over plans to send needed U.S. planes to Britain.

to come about the Pearl Harbor attack that plunged America into WWII. There were so many extraordinary elements connected with it.

How could the Japanese have gotten away with it? Why were the U.S. armed forces taken so disastrously by surprise? Was it really the Japanese who were responsible for the "day of infamy," as the President subsequently described it, or was Roosevelt himself involved in a deep, dark, diabolical plot to bring it about?

In the forty years since the Pearl Harbor debacle no fewer than four official inquiries have been held in an attempt to discover how the disaster was allowed to happen, and half the thirty-odd books which have been written about it charge or hint that it came about because of an outrageous conspiracy on the part of the American administration. The President of the United States was desperately anxious to get the United States involved as a belligerent in the war but feared that neither Congress nor the people would stand for it. So he deliberately sent the U.S. Pacific Fleet to Hawaii, where it was a sitting duck for the Japanese, and neglected to warn the island's defenders that the Japanese were getting ready to move and Pearl Harbor must be protected. The Japanese were tempted by the carrot the President waved in front of their noses, attacked—and the war was on. So the conspiracy theory goes.

Yet in spite of all the repeated testimonies at the inquiries, the continued cross-examination of witnesses, the release over the years of hitherto secret documents and monitored conversations, and for all the fevered accusations against this high officer and that elevated statesman, no one has so far proved that what happened on December 7, 1941, was anything more than a triumph of bold and unscrupulous enterprise on the part of the Japanese Navy—and colossal stupidity, inefficiency, ineptitude, and lack of elementary military precaution on the part of the U.S. Army and Navy. Nothing bubbles to the surface of the simmering caldron except the smell of a great American goof.

It had, of course, been common knowledge in military and political circles in Washington all through the last half of 1941 that the Japanese and U.S. governments were on a collision course over what was happening in Asia, and a clash between the two was becoming more and more likely as time went on. The war in Europe was regarded as a golden opportunity by the Japanese military to make easy conquests while the great powers were otherwise engaged. On the Chinese mainland, the Japanese Army was conducting a campaign of merciless sacking and killing, and the brutality and bloodshed with which their invasion of China was being carried out had aroused both revulsion and indignation among the American people. Those were the days when the United States regarded itself as the benevolent guardian of China and looked on its people as the simple, peace-loving peasants depicted in a favorite novel of the time, Pearl Buck's *The Good Earth,* needing protection from the bayonet-waving bullies from Japan. Their indignation over the massacre of a harmless people was compounded when, after France fell to the Nazis in Europe, that colonial power loosened its hold on Indochina, and the Japanese came into Saigon and Hanoi to take their place and commenced to use former French bases for their troops and ships and to harass and harry the Vietnamese. Where next? Obviously, now that the other colonial powers were preoccupied with the European war, Tokyo was looking around for other territories to snatch: Singapore and Malaya from the British; Batavia, Sumatra, and Bali from the Dutch.

How long would it be before they turned their greedy eyes on another tempting morsel: the U.S.-controlled Commonwealth of the Philippines? For were not the Americans also busily engaged, even if peripherally so far, with the war in Europe, and were not the Philippines thousands of miles nearer to Tokyo than they were to San Francisco?

To make it plain to the warmongers in Japan that at least the United States was not looking the other way, President Roosevelt made an ostentatious move. He took his most powerful deterrent, the U.S. Pacific Fleet, and ordered it to sail to its base at Pearl Harbor in Hawaii. There were only a few misgivings, even in the Navy, about this move at the time. Pearl Harbor was the best-defended base in all U.S. overseas territories, as impregnable as that other great power bastion in the Pacific, Britain's naval base at Singapore. Everyone was confident the U.S. armed forces in Hawaii could take care of themselves—and the fleet—in the event that the Japanese were foolish enough to try moving in. Meantime, the ships were there—as a threat and a warning.

At about the same time General Marshall made a gesture to demonstrate to the Japanese that the Philippines, America's most vulnerable overseas outpost, might not be such an easy picking either. General MacArthur was still under contract to the commonwealth and in charge of its armed forces. Marshall now brought him back into the U.S. Army and made him Commander in Chief of the combined U.S. and Philippine troops in the islands. At the same time he sent him $10 million to spend on beefing up Philippine defenses. No matter what he thought about MacArthur personally, he had no doubt at all that he was a splendid soldier, and he believed his appointment would both impress and deter the Japanese Army.

Not that any American really believed that such moves would cow or chasten the militants in Tokyo. Marshall thought they would gain time. Others were not even sure of that. And the President did not exactly help. That summer he instituted a boycott against the Japanese which would remain in being until such time as their armies moved out of China and Indochina. He banned their ships from the Panama Canal. He blocked shipments of petroleum, iron, steel, and other needed commodities. He froze Japanese assets in all U.S. territories. The Japanese regarded the boycott as a threat to their existence rather than as a reprisal for their aggressions and informed their Nazi allies in Berlin that it had created a situation that was "so horribly strained that we cannot endure it much longer. . . . [We] must take immediate steps to break asunder this ever strengthening chain of encirclement [by] the United States, acting like a cunning dragon seemingly asleep."

It was true that conversations were going on between two Japanese envoys in Washington, Ambassadors Kichisaburo Nomura and Saburo Kurusu, and the U.S. government. But the Americans had little faith in Japanese sincerity and believed the envoys were there only to lull them into a false sense of security. This was not just suspicion either. The Americans had long since broken the Japanese code by which the Foreign Ministry in Tokyo communicated with its diplomats overseas, and they were therefore aware of what the Japanese government was really up to behind its bland reassurances to Washington.

Two of the principal U.S. negotiators were the secretary of state, Cordell Hull, and the secretary of war, Henry L. Stimson. They both were liverish, feisty, and hawkish old men (Hull was seventy and Stimson was seventy-five) who grew increasingly irritated when they were stalled by the smooth Japanese go-betweens. They were particularly annoyed at Nomura, who put on an exceedingly sympathetic front and indicated that he agreed with U.S. complaints against the Japanese Army. Admiral Harold R. Stark, Chief of Staff of the U.S. Navy, known to all his friends as Betty, was particularly susceptible to Nomura's assurances, no doubt influenced by his distinguished naval background and by the fact that he had a very charming American wife. Stark told Marshall he thought the Japanese admiral was "quite sincere," and even the President, after a talk with Nomura, said to Stark, "You know, Betty, I think I could do business with that man."

But Nomura was only the front man for an increasingly belligerent and intransigent regime in Tokyo, and the settlement plan which it now ordered its ambassadors to submit to the Americans—who had, of course, already intercepted and decoded it—made only the vaguest promises to halt incursions into Southeast Asia and, at the same time, demanded in return an end to the U.S. boycott and a completely free hand for its army on the Chinese mainland. General Hideki Tojo, the new prowar premier in Tokyo, was quite aware that his conditions were certainly not going to be accepted by the Americans. But he wanted them submitted and negotiated, to give his armed forces, particularly the Navy, time to prepare for an attack.

Everybody in Washington was now sure that war with Japan was inevitable. Even Admiral Stark said as much in a warning which he had cabled to all commanders of U.S. Navy units in the Pacific on November 24, 1941:

There are very doubtful chances of a favorable outcome of negotiations with Japan. The situation coupled with statements of [the Japanese] Government and movements of their naval and military forces indicate in our opinion that a surprise aggressive movement in any direction . . . is a possibility. . . .

But he qualified the phrase "in any direction" by adding "including an attack on the Philippines or Guam." And nobody in military circles had much doubt that he was right when he suggested such was the target of Japanese intentions. In its secret cables to Japanese envoys abroad, Tokyo repeatedly referred to the Philippines as "a dagger pointing at Japan's heart," and Americans who read these messages after their cryptographers had decoded them became certain that this was where the aggressors would strike. In fact, General Marshall became so confident that he cabled General MacArthur in Manila and gave him an unprecedented order to put his forces on an immediate state of alert. But he did more than that. He told MacArthur to begin reconnaissance flights over Japanese possessions, inside Japanese airspace, to close-check Army and Navy movements in order not to be caught out if and when the Japanese forces moved toward him. Furthermore, if he came to the conclusion that Japanese intentions toward him were hostile, he was to strike back and not wait for a declaration of war.

Marshall gave no such order to his Army commander in Hawaii, Lieutenant General Walter C. Short. Nor did his Navy counterpart, Admiral Stark, send any similar instructions to his commander at Pearl Harbor, Rear Admiral Husband E. Kimmel. But why should they have done so, the way their minds were working? Unlike the Philippines, Hawaii was no dagger pointed at Japan's heart. It was the safe, solid, impregnable breastplate of America's defensive armor.

On the morning of November 27, 1941, General Marshall left Washington to attend the final days of a huge military exercise which was being carried out by the U.S. Army in North Carolina. It was a climax of a series of maneuvers which were the biggest and roughest ever undertaken by American forces in peacetime. A few weeks earlier the fighting units of the Army had divided up and fought mock battles all over Louisiana and Texas, and Marshall had been a keen observer, watching how troops and their commanders behaved under tough, if simulated, battle conditions. From those earlier exercises, he had learned some useful lessons and found at least two names of promising officers to jot down in his little black book.

Now he wanted to see whether the Army personnel in the field had read the reports he and his staff had written, profited from their earlier errors, and learned how to rectify the mistakes which, in real battle, could lose lives and make the difference between victory and defeat.

He would have been neglecting his duties as Chief of Staff had he not watched the maneuvers. All the same, to some it seemed a strange time to have left Washington and be out of minute-by-minute touch with what was going on both in Europe, where the Nazi armies were closing in on Moscow, and in the Pacific, where the Japanese forces were audibly revving up their war machine. However, Marshall had consulted with Admiral Stark before quitting the capital,* and between them they had worked up a message by which they planned to warn their commanders in the Pacific that the Japanese were on the brink of going to war.

No sooner had Marshall flown off than intercepted messages from the Japanese indicated that they were getting near to a breakpoint in their negotiations in Washington. Nomura had asked Tokyo for more time for his talks with the Americans. He had been told that he should, instead, begin to wind things up. Time had run out.

Stimson, the secretary of war, tried to get Marshall on the telephone to tell him this, but he was somewhere in the field and could not be reached. He consulted with Admiral Stark, instead, but found him "as usual, a little bit timid and cautious when it comes to a real crisis, and there was a tendency, not unnatural on his part and [Chief of War Plans Major General Leonard T.] Ger-

*Which was less than 500 miles away from North Carolina.

ow's to seek for more time." But Stimson did not believe there was any more time. He felt the commanders in the field, particularly MacArthur, should be warned that the pot was about to boil over. He therefore announced he wanted the message Marshall had left behind to be put on the wire.

It was sent out urgently on the afternoon of November 27 and read as follows:

> NEGOTIATIONS WITH JAPANESE APPEAR TO BE TERMINATED TO ALL PRACTICAL PURPOSES WITH ONLY THE BAREST POSSIBILITY THAT THE JAPANESE GOVERNMENT MIGHT COME BACK AND OFFER TO CONTINUE. JAPANESE FUTURE ACTION UNPREDICTABLE. BUT HOSTILE ACTION POSSIBLE AT ANY MOMENT. IF HOSTILITIES CANNOT REPEAT CANNOT BE AVOIDED THE UNITED STATES DESIRES THAT JAPAN COMMIT THE FIRST OVERT ACT. THIS POLICY SHOULD NOT REPEAT NOT BE CONSTRUED AS RESTRICTING YOU TO A COURSE OF ACTION THAT MIGHT JEOPARDIZE YOUR DEFENSE. PRIOR TO HOSTILE JAPANESE ACTION YOU ARE DIRECTED TO TAKE SUCH RECONNAISSANCE AND OTHER MEASURES AS YOU DEEM NECESSARY.

This is the message as it was sent to General MacArthur in the Philippines and was taken by him to be an instruction to put his forces on a war basis, as in fact, they already were.

But in the message as it was sent to General Short in Hawaii, and to the military commanders in the Canal Zone and at San Francisco, someone (almost certainly General Gerow) added some words to the last sentence which weakened its whole impact. The addition was these words: "BUT THESE MEASURES SHOULD BE CARRIED OUT SO AS NOT REPEAT NOT TO ALARM THE CIVILIAN POPULATION OR DISCLOSE INTENT."

General Short, the U.S. Army commander in Honolulu, did not believe that the Japanese were going to attack Hawaii. In fact, he was so sure about it that his antiaircraft guns were unarmed, the shells for them being in warehouses several miles away; he had ignored repeated requests from his air defense officer to bring the guns and ammunition together. But he did believe that the moment the Japanese attacked the Philippines—he agreed with the general thesis that that was where the enemy would strike—

Japanese civilians in Hawaii would begin to commit acts of sabotage.

In the meantime, Admiral Stark had at last decided that war was imminent, especially when his intelligence officers reported that a large Japanese force had sailed out into the Pacific. He plucked up his courage to send a strong danger signal to all U.S. Navy units in the Pacific which began with the fighting words "THIS IS A WAR WARNING."

But then he blew it. Never thinking that Hawaii or points nearer home could be the target, he added the words "AN AMPHIBIOUS [Japanese] EXPEDITION [moving] AGAINST EITHER THE PHILIPPINES, THAI OR KRA PENINSULA OR POSSIBLY BORNEO." He instructed all the commanders to show the message to their Army counterparts on the spot, but General Short subsequently said he never got a copy from Admiral Kimmel in Hawaii. In any case, as it turned out, Kimmel did not think the Japanese would be going to war yet, and therefore, there was no reason to get alarmed. He believed Tokyo was waiting until the Nazi armies had occupied Moscow before striking amid the general confusion that this disaster would cause in the West. Moscow had not fallen yet, so there was still time.* Therefore, he did not bother to alert Short about Stark's warning.

In any case, General Short had taken immediate action. But not the kind of action Washington had envisioned. Instead of callling out his troops, manning his guns (and calling up the shells needed to fire them), and putting the land forces on a war basis, he did something altogether different from what was expected of him. He took swift and efficient steps to prevent sabotage in Hawaii. He put a guard around the naval base at Pearl Harbor. He had the planes moved so that they could be protected from infiltrators trying to blow them up. Then he cabled Washington, no doubt proud of his speedy response: "HAVE ORDERED ALERT 'A'."

And this is where the bungling began and the disastrous foulup followed. It turned out that Marshall's chief of G2 (intelligence), General Sherman Miles, was particularly worried about

---

*See the report by Joseph Harsch of the *Christian Science Monitor* of his conversation with Admiral Kimmel published on December 5, 1941.

Hawaii, and he decided to send his own telegram to General Short in Honolulu. He wrote out a cable: "WAR IS IMMINENT. HOSTILITIES COULD BREAK OUT AT ANY TIME."

As an afterthought, he added these words: "LOOK OUT FOR SABOTAGE."

Unfortunately, the Army signalman who sent it out reversed the order of the message, and when General Short received it, the cable read: "LOOK OUT FOR SABOTAGE. WAR IS IMMINENT. HOSTILITIES COULD BREAK OUT AT ANY TIME."

So when Short's cable came back, it was completely misinterpreted in the department. "HAVE ORDERED ALERT 'A'." Splendid. General Short had responded by sounding the alarm, calling out the troops and guns, sending up the reconnaissance planes, and getting ready for war. The junior officers who read General Short's cable sighed with relief, happy that they could now stop worrying about Hawaii.

Only they couldn't. What they did not know, or had not remembered, was that a few days previously the Army command in Hawaii had altered the order of priorities. Until that time the top danger signals in both Hawaii and Washington were Alert A, Alert B, and Alert C in order of importance. Then Hawaii had switched them around. Alert A was now the lowest of the priorities, not the top, as the officers in the War Department presumed. As General Miles put it later, "I'd known about these war plans for many years, and I'm not quite sure I can get it straight; but I'm telling you as accurately as I can that Alert A, Alert B, and Alert C—A being the most important, B half alert, and C being alert just for sabotage—were, at the request of the Hawaiian Department, reversed just before Pearl Harbor. And therefore, Alert A became the lowest alert, B the next, and Alert C the big alert. And what Short reported was: 'I am on Alert "A."' The fellow who got it, one of Gerow's assistants, said he was still thinking it was the big alert. . . . And of course, they had been reversed. He thought A was the highest alert, and he [General Short] was reporting he was on the lowest alert."

General Marshall arrived back in Washington from the North Carolina maneuvers and was informed about the warning telegram which the War Department had sent out in his name to commanders overseas. He was also told that all the commanders—in the Philippines, the Canal Zone, San Francisco, and Hawaii—had responded by putting their forces on full alert. Then General Gerow showed him the added cable General Miles had sent to Short in Hawaii, together with Short's own cable: "HAVE ORDERED ALERT 'A' ."

Both men remembered that Hawaii had changed the priorities and that therefore, General Short's reference to Alert A meant only that he was taking precautions against sabotage. But for some reason, both of them assumed that this was an answer not to their own war warning but to the message from General Miles, with its reference to sabotage. It did not occur to either of them to wonder why, therefore, there was no other message from Short saying his forces were on a war alert.

As it happened, some doubts were beginning to burgeon in the War Department, but they never reached the Chief of Staff. Major (later General) Walter Bedell Smith, who was a member of the staff secretariat, had once served at Fort Benning with General Walter Short and did not have much of a favorable opinion about his capabilities. So he was interested in finding out what reaction the general had sent to the warning message. After he had read Short's reply, he turned to his boss, Colonel Orlando "Pink" Ward, and said, "For God's sake, do you suppose he means that he is only acting to prevent sabotage?"

"Why, certainly not," Ward replied. "He's putting that in there to indicate he's very much on the alert, but he's read the message."

"Well, Pink," Smith replied, "I'm sure you're right, and I hope you are; but from my contact with him, I sure do have misgivings."

But he was only a major, way down the list, and did not pass his misgivings on to anyone else.

So all the senior officers took it for granted that everything was all right.

"Why didn't I pick up the telephone during those ten days?" General Miles asked later. "I could have called up that fellow

[Short] and said, 'How are you doing?' and he would have said, 'We are doing all right. We have an alert against sabotage.' And I would have hit the ceiling." He added, "It never occurred to me that they weren't on a full alert by the minute."

Marshall believed that, too. "I feel that General Short was given a command instruction," he said later, "to put his command on the alert against possible hostile attack by the Japanese. The command was not so alerted."

He shared the sentiments of a senior U.S. officer who was asked, "General, what would you have done if you'd gotten that dispatch from the War Department sent out ten days before Pearl Harbor?"

"I wouldn't have done anything," he replied.

"You wouldn't have done *anything?*"

"No," he said, "why should I? All my troops would have been out two weeks before. I'd read the papers."

Evidently General Short didn't read the papers. The tragedy was that General Marshall, his Chief of Staff, didn't find some other way of making sure he knew what was going on.

10

A Day of Infamous Confusion

"The British sort of expect their generals to be stupid, and when disasters happen, they aren't really surprised. They don't look around so much for scapegoats as for miracles, the hand of God, to get them out of trouble with some sort of skin left. That is why they were so thankful about Dunkirk.

"On the other hand, the Americans expect their generals to be topnotch, never to be capable of making mistakes. So when disasters happen, they look for conspiracies and plots. It *couldn't* have been our generals or our fighting men. There must have been some dirty work somewhere. Who was the plotter? That is why everybody got so madly suspicious about Pearl Harbor."

So said General Sherman Miles later. No one came well out of the Pearl Harbor catastrophe, not even the Japanese. It was not quite the "day of infamy" that President Roosevelt dubbed it since even the enemy intended to play by the rules. Having read the Geneva Convention on the formalities for declaring war, the Japanese planned to present a legal note breaking off of diplomatic relations before they struck Pearl Harbor. They botched it because there had been a drunken party in the cipher room of the Japanese Embassy in Washington on Saturday night, December 6, and were all suffering from terrible hangovers by the time they came to decode the note from Tokyo on Sunday morning. Moreover, since it was a top secret note, only someone with security clearance could type it out, and the officials with clearance were terrible typists. The secretary chosen for the task was so bad he had to retype the message sixteen times and was still trying to produce a clean copy by the time the deadline for presenting the note came and went. That is the only reason why the Japanese were two hours late in presenting their ultimatum to the Americans on December 7, 1941.

As for the Americans, although there are no proofs whatsoever that the President of the United States deliberately sent the U.S. Pacific Fleet to Pearl Harbor and then goaded the Japanese into attacking it—as some of his wilder opponents subsequently charged—he was certainly not the unhappiest statesman in the world when they did so (until he read the casualty lists in men and ships, of course). And beyond all argument, the behavior of U.S. generals and admirals in both Washington and Hawaii in the last hours of peace was inept and incompetent to a degree rarely surpassed in military history.

However, as a result of the suspicious nature of U.S. reactions to the Pearl Harbor attack and to the shrill cries of "Conspiracy!" which arose from the isolationists in its wake, most Americans still do not realize how negligently their military leaders behaved. Four official inquiries probed for proof that there was a deliberate plot to get the United States into World War II and that it came to fruition at Pearl Harbor. Some scapegoats were found. But there still skulks in the dark corners of many American minds the suspicion that the real culprits got away with it. Including General George C. Marshall.

His naval opposite number, Admiral Harold R. Stark, was bluntly asked just before he died if he and General Marshall had been involved in a compact with the President to trick the Japanese into attacking the United States and if he and Marshall would have done anything Roosevelt ordered them to do.

"To my mind that is a terrible insult," he replied. "It is not true to say that because we were good soldiers, we would obey *any* orders. I crossed badly with Roosevelt once or twice. I had many uncomfortable situations with him with regard to the fifty destroyers.* The old Navy saying that you speak your piece and then when you get an order give a cheerful 'Aye, aye, sir!'—well, normally you do, and that is ingrained in us a good deal. But the time could come and does come—it did to me—when you absolutely refuse and won't go along, especially if it meant sacrificing our own forces and having them cut to pieces. To suggest that we would have acquiesced if the President had wanted that done is absolutely fantastic. That's all there is to it."

He added that never had the President asked him or General Marshall to withhold warnings from the Navy and Army commanders in Hawaii that a Japanese attack was imminent.

"No, on the contrary," he commented. "It might be of interest for you to know that when I wrote out the war warning message of November twenty-fifth and ordered it to be sent, I hadn't even told the President. That shows how free we really were. I did go over it very carefully with [Secretary of the Navy Frank] Knox, and I studied it pretty carefully myself. But it all came out of my own mind. I called up the President later because I thought: 'Here, I'd better tell the President what I've sent, the war warnings, etc.' I read them out, and he said, 'That's all right with me, Betty.' "

But what no one asked Admiral Stark before he died was why he allowed his "war warning message" to be treated so lightly by his naval commander in Pearl Harbor. And what no one ever asked Marshall was why he allowed his officers, both in the War Department and in Hawaii, to be so woefully unprepared for an emergency when the time came. Wasn't their readiness for war just as important as those of the U.S. armed forces whose maneuvers he had studied so keenly in North Carolina just a few days before the Japanese struck?

On Saturday afternoon, December 6, 1941, the Foreign Ministry in Tokyo transmitted a warning to the Japanese Embassy in Washington that an important message was on its way. It in-

---

*Which the President gave to the British, against U.S. Navy wishes.

formed the embassy staff that a fourteen-part telegram was being sent to the U.S. government and that the ambassador was to present it to the U.S. secretary of state, Cordell Hull, at a time to be designated later. The staff was urgently ordered to stand by.

U.S. cryptographers were standing by, too. As is by now generally known, the United States had cracked the top Japanese diplomatic code known as Purple, and these so-called Magic intercepts gave the government a priceless picture of Japanese thinking and intentions. The fact that Tokyo had sent a "pilot" message to alert its diplomats that a fourteen-part note was on its way obviously meant that something important was brewing, and the code breakers made haste to let the War Department know about it. Their alert was delivered on Saturday afternoon, and General Marshall was afterward to say he did not remember being shown it. Certainly the office copy does not bear his mark.* However, he cannot have been ignorant of the fact that this was likely to be a highly dramatic weekend. FBI agents watching the Japanese Embassy had noted that its staff was busy burning documents and showing all signs of getting ready to close down. That could only mean they thought diplomatic relations were about to break down—and war break out.

In the circumstances, Washington was uncannily calm. Nobody in Marshall's office called General Short in Hawaii to make sure he was on the alert or even General MacArthur in Manila to find out whether his aircraft reinforcements were arriving. Admiral Stark took it for granted that Rear Admiral Kimmel had ordered his ships at Pearl Harbor to stand by. He hadn't. Nor had Kimmel informed Stark that several Japanese aircraft carriers, usually meticulously tracked by Navy intelligence, had suddenly "vanished," though he did jokingly remark to his fleet intelligence officer, "Do you mean to say they could be rounding Diamond Head and you wouldn't know it?"

Early that evening the U.S. cryptographers began intercepting the fourteen-part message from Tokyo, and their task was made easier by reason of the fact that the Japanese had encoded it in

*He usually checked and initialed all documents he received.

173

English. But when the telegram reached Part 13, it came to a halt, and Tokyo informed the Japanese Embassy that Part 14, together with instructions on the exact time the complete message should be delivered to the Americans, would be passed to them in the early hours of the morning.

And this is where the Americans came unstuck.

No one reading the first thirteen parts of the Japanese message could have much doubt about what it was leading up to. The note dealt curtly and negatively with a message which Cordell Hull had sent to Tokyo earlier in the week demanding certain guarantees from the Japanese government. There could, therefore, be only one reason why the Japanese were holding back the ultimate paragraph. It did not need much imagination to guess that having rejected all the U.S. proposals, they had nothing else to say but something like: "We have therefore no alternative but to break off diplomatic relations. With the receipt of this message, we therefore declare war on the United States of America."*

Why did not the U.S. government and its armed forces take action accordingly? It was still early Saturday evening in Washington, and the Japanese did not plan to send over the vital Part 14 until the early hours of the following (Sunday) morning. That gave the Army and Navy Chiefs of Staff plenty of time to warn every U.S. military and naval base in the world.

The only trouble was, neither the Army Chief of Staff, General Marshall, nor the Navy Chief of Staff, Admiral Stark, as yet knew of the existence of the thirteen parts of the Japanese note. And nobody seems to have warned them about it.

Marshall was so untroubled by what was happening on that last Saturday night of peace that he afterward couldn't even remember what he was doing that evening. He *thought* he spent the evening at home.

"I can only account for [my movements] by sort of circumstantial evidence," he testified later. "The only definite thing I have is that I had no dinner engagement. I found our engagement book, or Mrs. Marshall's engagement book, and between the first of

---

*Though, as it turned out, they were much more mealymouthed.

December and the seventh of December I had one dinner engagement, that was the second of December.

"Also they checked on the [Fort Myer] post movie. It was about our only recourse for relaxation, and I had never seen the picture.* So I was not there.

"We were not calling. We were leading a rather monastic life. There was also in that record the affairs of the day for her [Mrs. Marshall], which involved, I think, an old-clothes sale, I think, all day long to raise money for one of these industries they had down there, so the probability is that she was tired and we stayed home."

If they did, no one telephoned him—not with any warning anyway.

This was the moment when the Japanese aircraft carriers were twelve hours away from their launching point, 650 miles to the north of Hawaii. Rear Admiral Kimmel was in downtown Honolulu, dining with a friend from the mainland. General Walter Short and his wife were guests at an Army charity dinner. At one point he was interrupted by his intelligence adviser, who told him that a Japanese dentist—all Japanese telephones in Honolulu were tapped by the Army—had just received a call from Tokyo urgently asking him what Navy ships were in the harbor. General Short shrugged his shoulders. Such Japanese spying was routine.

Back in Washington, Admiral Stark, his wife, his aide, and his aide's wife had gone into town to see a performance of *The Student Prince*. President and Mrs. Roosevelt were having a quiet dinner with friends at the White House. General Sherman Miles, Marshall's intelligence officer, was at dinner in Arlington with the Navy's intelligence chief, Admiral Theodore S. Wilkinson. And General Marshall, no doubt in his carpet slippers with his feet up, was relaxing at Fort Myer. Or he thought he was.

In the meantime, the first thirteen parts of the Japanese note intercepted by the American code breakers had been collected by Colonel Rufus Bratton, chief of the Far Eastern Section, War De-

*Meaning that the engagement book would have recorded the fact if he and Mrs. Marshall had gone to the movie.

partment, G2. It was his job and that of his assistant, Colonel Carlisle C. Dusenbury, to hand over the Magic intercepts to a selected list of recipients: General Marshall; his G2 chief, General Sherman Miles; his chief of war plans, General L. T. Gerow; Harvey Bundy, an assistant secretary of war; and the secretary of state, Cordell Hull. A naval officer, Captain Alwyn D. Kramer, had the responsibility of passing on the intercepts to the President; the secretary of the navy, Frank Knox; the Navy Chief of Staff, Admiral Stark; and other Navy officers.

Great precautions were taken about the security of these Magic intercepts. They were rightly considered such a treasure that only a few people were supposed to know of their existence, let alone what they said. None of the recipients was allowed to keep or make copies. They were to be read by the privileged few and then returned to the central files.

Normally, Bratton brought the Chief of Staff's copy down to General Marshall in a leather envelope with a lock on it, and took it in right away.

"If he was not there," said Major Walter Bedell Smith, "depending on the importance of the papers, they were put in a safe until he got back, or they were taken up to his house. . . . It was a question of the judgment of the man who had the envelope as to whether the contents were of sufficient importance. We did not, in the staff secretariat, know except by deduction. [Smith knew nothing at the time about the Magic intercepts.] I had come to my personal conclusion that they were either the reports of a spy—a paid spy—or that they were the product of some decoding system, but I didn't know what they were and never saw them."

It happened to be Smith who was working in the War Department about eight o'clock on Saturday evening, December 6, when Colonel Rufus Bratton hurried in with the leather envelope under his arm and asked for General Marshall.

"This is very important," Bratton said.

"The general's gone home," Smith told him. "Depending on the importance of the message you've got for him, either take it over to his house or lock it up. It's up to you to decide."

Bratton seemed uncertain what to do. He teetered around until finally he said, "Well, the message isn't all in yet. This is something that's being decoded, and it isn't all in yet. So I'll lock it up in the safe, and he can see it in the morning."

So the Chief of Staff never saw the incomplete Japanese note that night. Nor did General Gerow, his head of war plans. Neither had a chance to assess the importance of the thirteen parts and what they probably meant in terms of peace or war.*

Captain Kramer was meanwhile delivering his copies of the intercepts to his authorized list of recipients. President Roosevelt got his at the end of his Saturday night dinner and was in no doubt of the significance of the unfinished note.

"This means war," he said, after reading it.

He picked up the telephone to call Admiral Stark but, on finding he was at the theater, decided to wait to contact him in the morning. He seems to have made no attempt to telephone General Marshall, and this was no surprise to those who knew the relationship between the President and the Chief of Staff. Aware from what Harry Hopkins had told him that Marshall did not wish any after-hours relationships with his President, he would have been reluctant to call him up on a Saturday night and perhaps get a brush-off for his overconcern. In any case, it was known that the President was by this time fatalistic about war with Japan. He had done everything he could.† It was now up to his military chiefs to take steps to defend the nation. After all, he thought they knew more about the situation than he did.

Unfortunately he was wrong in that assumption. They did not know as much as he. It was now getting on to midnight in Washington, and no one had yet told the Chief of Staff that there was a time bomb ticking away in his safe.

Captain Kramer had, by this time, reached the home of Ad-

---

*Bratton subsequently testified that he *did* deliver the thirteen parts to Marshall and then abruptly changed his testimony. But the above from Walter Bedell Smith, not hitherto revealed, should end speculation about that.

†Including a last-minute appeal for peace to the emperor of Japan.

miral Wilkinson, director of naval intelligence, and there he found General Miles and one of the President's naval aides were guests in the house. They were not on his list, but because he knew they were cleared for reading the Magic intercepts, he allowed them to read the thirteen-part message so that all three could read it simultaneously. Miles asked him if General Marshall had been given a copy, and Kramer said he was sure Colonel Bratton had already handed one over. Miles did not bother to check and took full responsibility for that omission later. He attributed his negligence to the fact that he, his host, and the President's naval aide discussed the meaning of the incomplete note together and mutually decided there was nothing to get alarmed about. None of them felt action needed to be taken.

Yet the President of the United States, on reading it through, had been certain of its significance.

"This means war," he had said.

In the early hours of Sunday morning, December 7, a watchful cryptographer saw his warning light begin to blink and whispered to his colleagues, "Here it comes."

Part 14 was on its way from Tokyo. The Japanese fleet was drawing closer to Hawaii.

At the War Department Colonel Bratton, warned that the final paragraph of the note was being deciphered, waited in his office with no particular feeling that momentous tidings were on their way. He had dug the first thirteen parts of the Japanese note out of General Marshall's safe and was glancing idly through them, apparently unaware that they were the equivalent of the writing on the wall. Now the ultimate paragraph was placed before him, and he read it through: "14. The Japanese Government regrets to have to notify the American Government that, in view of the attitude of the American Government, it cannot but consider that it is impossible to reach agreement through further negotiations."

He was staring at it blankly when a messenger put another flimsy in front of him. It was an instruction from Tokyo to the Japanese ambassador to present the complete note to the Ameri-

178

can secretary of state at precisely 1:00 P.M. on December 7, this very day. Then he was to destroy his last code machine.

It was this message which finally galvanized Bratton into action. For 1:00 P.M. Washington time was 7:00 A.M. at Hawaii and just before dawn in the Philippines. By God, this was a declaration of war! It was 9:00 A.M. now. The deadline was only four hours away.

He shouted for his assistant, snatched up the telephone, and put through a call to General Marshall at Fort Myer. The Filipino orderly, Semanko, answered the call and said the general was out riding, Mrs. Marshall was sleeping and could not be disturbed, and could he take a message? Bratton could not mention Magic over the wire, so he simply asked Semanko to tell the general to drive himself down to the office as soon as he came back. In the meantime, Bratton put in a call to Marshall's driver-aide, Sergeant James W. Powder, who lived on the other side of town, and said there was an emergency. Instead of his coming in for the general's car and then picking him up at Fort Myer, it would save time if he drove straight to the office. The general would be driving himself in.

"I was called at nine o'clock and told to get down and have the car in front of the Munitions Building immediately," Powder said later. "In fact, I broke all the speed limits getting down because I didn't care whether a cop was after me or not. I figured he could catch me when I got to the garage. I parked in a no parking area at the garage and got the [official] car and went to the front of the Munitions Building."

He had been told he would be needed to ferry Marshall to the White House and other places during the morning, so he just waited there in front of the Munitions Building and did not check whether the general had already arrived.

He had not. He was still out riding. It was part of his Sunday routine ("I like to work up my kidneys," he said), and he would usually have the same horse, the sorrel named Prepared with a white star on his forehead, brought around from the Fort Myer stables. Then, calling his Dalmatian dog, Fleet, to follow, he would jog off down the bridle path leading from the fort to Arlington

Cemetery, pass through a gate, and jog and canter along the dirt road beside the Potomac River.

Still with no idea that the sands of peace were running out, he finally returned to Fort Myer and was informed that he was wanted at the War Department. He picked up the telephone and spoke to Bratton, who, by this time, was practically on the point of hysteria. The colonel still could not mention Magic over the telephone but pleaded with the general to come down at once. Marshall, who did not like exhibitions of emotion, reacted by responding with maddening slowness. He would take a shower. He would change his clothes. Then he would come down.

In fact, he was in the office by 10:30 A.M. to find Bratton waiting for him, "all of a tremble," as John Deane said later. Following the general into the office, he plonked down the Japanese note in front of him with shaking hands. Marshall carefully looked in one of his drawers for his reading glasses. (He would never have glasses made for him, preferring five-and-ten-cent-store glasses. Sergeant Powder would go down to Woolworth's and buy them, a half a dozen at a time, Number 18). Perching the metal frame on the middle of his nose, he began to read through the long screed.

"They didn't show me the last and important part first," Marshall said later, "but let me read all of it."

It took time. By now it was 11:00 A.M. in Washington and 5:00 A.M. in Honolulu. The deadline was two hours away. When he had finished, Bratton pointed to the instruction to the Japanese ambassador in Washington to hand over the note at 1:00 P.M.

"Don't you think that is significant?" he asked. "One P.M. in Washington is sunrise in Hawaii."

Marshall was only too well aware of it. At long last someone in the services had read the note and realized what it meant. He was still monumentally calm, but two of his senior generals, Miles and Gerow, who had meanwhile arrived in the office, sensed that he was deeply disturbed, and his concern was strong enough to communicate itself to them. Miles inwardly cursed himself for his neglect in not having telephoned his chief the night before.

Still, there was time. The deadline was an hour and forty

minutes away, and Marshall was writing out a message. It was addressed to all Army commands in the Pacific, and it read:

> THE JAPANESE ARE PRESENTING AT 1 P.M. EASTERN STANDARD TIME TODAY WHAT AMOUNTS TO AN ULTIMATUM. ALSO THEY ARE UNDER ORDERS TO DESTROY THEIR CODE MACHINE IMMEDIATELY.
> JUST WHAT SIGNIFICANCE THE HOUR SET MAY HAVE WE DO NOT KNOW BUT BE ON THE ALERT ACCORDINGLY.

Before sending it off, he called up Admiral Stark at the Navy Department. The Navy Chief of Staff had, by now, seen the Japanese note but had been as blank in his reaction to it as to all the others. It took him some time to understand Marshall's sense of urgency, and when asked whether he wanted the Navy to be included in the recipients of the warning message, he demurred. Hadn't they already sent out enough warnings? Wouldn't this be like crying "Wolf!" once too often? Finally, however, he agreed that Marshall should add "INFORM NAVY" to the end of his message.

Then, as an afterthought, he made an offer to Marshall. Would it be any help if he sent the telegram through Navy channels for him? No, no, replied Marshall, Army communications were quite efficient, and could handle it adequately, thank you.

Nobody was thinking particularly about Hawaii even now, though it was the only U.S. base anywhere in the world where dawn would just be breaking at the time the ultimatum was presented. In fact, at the moment Bratton was handed the telegram to put on the wire, Gerow was so sure the attack would come in a different place that he called out to him, "If there's any priority, let them send the message to the Philippines first."

And now came the biggest goof of all. Bratton took the telegram down the hall to Colonel Edward F. French in the War Department signals room and told French to have it sent off urgently to all bases in the Pacific. But French couldn't read Marshall's handwriting, and he and Bratton spent precious minutes deciphering some of the words. When that was done, Bratton came back to Marshall's office to report that the telegram would be on its way within thirty minutes.

The Chief of Staff was not satisfied. Something seemed to be nagging him. After a short lapse of time he ordered Bratton back to the signals room to check whether the telegram was really being dispatched. Bratton disappeared to consult and presently reappeared to assure Marshall that everything was in order.

But it wasn't. What he failed to reveal to his chief was that the Army signal service between Washington and Honolulu had broken down. Colonel French could not raise the Army in Hawaii. Instead, he had decided to use the ordinary commercial cable system. He did not even mark the message to Honolulu with a "priority" label.

The result, as everyone now knows, was that Pearl Harbor was attacked and the U.S. Pacific Fleet battered and burned into uselessness by the time the messenger boy from Western Union rode his motorbike up to Army headquarters with his all-important warning.

It added a touch of irony to the tragedy that the messenger boy might have arrived earlier—though still not in time—had he not been delayed several times en route by Army sentries manning hastily erected road barriers. They were highly suspicious of him—because he happened to be a Japanese.

"When the liquor's out, why clink the cannikin?" asked Robert Browning.

There have been enough postmortems on the Pearl Harbor disaster, and all they seem to have proved is that the U.S. armed forces had their fair share of stupid generals and admirals, too. In the end, it can hardly be said that the scapegoats had much to complain about. General Walter Short and Rear Admiral Husband E. Kimmel were afterward to protest that they were removed from their posts without being given a chance to defend themselves and that they should have been allowed a court-martial. In the circumstances, they were probably lucky that it never came to that. A truly impartial court would almost certainly have found them guilty of gross dereliction of duty, despite their complaints that they were not adequately briefed from Washington. They were the commanders of the best-defended base in the Pacific, yet

General Short did not even have shells ready to load into his guns or his planes on reconnaissance, and Admiral Kimmel had let half of his ships' crews go off on weekend leave. This on a weekend they must have known to be crucial.

Pearl Harbor was a sentry post, and the sentry was, indeed, caught sleeping.

Admiral Harold R. Stark was, perhaps, punished for less overt reasons. He was forced out of his position as Navy Chief of Staff and sent off to London to act as a liaison with the British, a post he held with great charm and efficiency. He took the blame, as the captain of the ship, for the disaster which struck his vessel and the failure of his staff to handle it without suffering grievous damage. He never complained afterward that he was unjustly disciplined.

But what of General Marshall? Except for the grilling he had to undergo at the various inquiries and a subsequent rebuke for the poor performance of his staff, he emerged from Pearl Harbor militarily unscathed. There was no question of his retiring as Chief of Staff and no objection to his assumption, from now on, of the central direction of U.S. participation in the war.

Yet if ever negligence was displayed by a senior officer, surely General Marshall showed it during the ten days before America's descent into World War II. From the beginning of the crisis to its climax, he was guilty of failure: failure to send a competent commander to Hawaii; failure to check that the islands' defenses were in order; failure to make sure that his warning messages had got through. What sort of picker of men was he that all along the line senior members of his staff let him down?

Many critics afterward wondered why Marshall, immediately after he read the Japanese note and realized its significance, did not pick up the telephone and warn his commanders that trouble was coming. His reply to that was he could not trust the telephone and that, even if he had used the instrument, he would have done so to call not Hawaii, but the Philippines. But why not call them both—and all the other bases—at the same time? Was there only one telephone in the War Department?

The truth was, of course, that he hated the telephone and

loathed having to use it. On the other hand, he had unbounded faith in the efficacy and speed of the Army Signal Corps. More's the pity he had not made sure a trustworthy officer was running it—one who would have had the courage to let him know when, at a critical moment, his vaunted signal service had broken down. It would not have saved the United States from war, but it would have saved the administration much humiliation and, perhaps, even spared some of the ships of the United States Pacific Fleet.

So there was general surprise in the armed services when the President failed to fire his Chief of Staff. His survival was particularly resented in the U.S. Navy, which felt his sins of omission had been just as disastrous as those of their own chief, and possibly more so. It was this sense of being discriminated against by the President which fueled subsequent Navy suspicions of conspiracy between Marshall and the White House. They could not seem to understand that President Roosevelt was being coldly and ruthlessly logical. Plunged suddenly into war as he was, he could hardly fire everyone in his armed services. But to appease the public, someone had to go.

And it was the Navy which, at Pearl Harbor, had so wantonly neglected to protect its fleet. It was, therefore, from the Navy that he chose the scapegoat.

It might be noted in passing that the Army Signal service also failed to deliver the warning telegram to General Douglas MacArthur in Manila. His arrived late, too, by commercial cable. But being a better soldier than General Walter Short in Hawaii, he already had his troops on the alert and his planes in the air. It didn't do him much good, as it turned out, but that was not his fault. With supplies and ammunition in short supply and the ships meant to guard the sea lanes burning in Pearl Harbor, he hadn't much of a fighting chance.

Nevertheless, he did make one gesture to General Marshall on that fatal morning. General Gerow called him up to tell him that Hawaii had been hit and that he would undoubtedly be next. Gerow found him in fighting form.

"Tell George not to worry," he said. "Everything is going to be all right here."

Of course, he didn't know just how badly the Navy had suffered.

"He asked me what the damage was and all that," Gerow said later. "We couldn't tell him that over the telephone. He said, 'You tell George,' as I recall now, 'that there have been some planes flying around for a few hours. We are watching them. You don't have to worry about us. We'll be all right.'"

They weren't. But at least they weren't sleeping.

There was one farcical footnote to the appalling confusion of the day, and it concerned the first official communiqué of the war. Because it was a Sunday, there were few civilians on duty in the War Department and only one woman stenographer. This was an extremely attractive young woman named Aileen Morgan.

"She had just come in there quite recently," recalled one of her colleagues, Major (later General) Maxwell Taylor, "and we were all joking that she couldn't be very good because she was so pretty."

Taylor got a buzz from the Chief of Staff, and when he went into the office, Marshall told him to send in a stenographer. He was about to make an official report about Pearl Harbor to the President, and he was in a hurry. Taylor told Miss Morgan to go in and take it down. She hurried through the door, clutching a stenographic machine, and presently he heard the general begin dictating in round, resonant tones.

"Miss Morgan came out after a while," Taylor recalled, "and sat down at her desk and started typing away. We didn't pay any attention to her. Then the chief buzzed, and I went into his office, and he said, 'Where's my dictation?' and I said, 'Miss Morgan's working on it, and I'll see how she's doing.' Well, I went over to Miss Morgan and said, 'How are you doing, Miss Morgan?' and she said, 'Oh, all right, Major.' I realized that the chief was getting impatient, and I sat and watched her, and I could see she was in trouble. I went over and asked her, 'Now, Miss Morgan, *really* how are you doing?' Well, she looked at me with those beautiful brown eyes filled with tears, and she said, 'Major, I didn't get a word of what the chief said.' "

Taylor had to go back in the office and tell Marshall. "At the end of the worst day of his life he had to dictate that all over again. That was the first dispatch of the war. I finally carried it over, a crumpled piece of paper, about eight o'clock that night to the White House."

Then he went home to change into Army uniform from the civilian clothes he (and all the others) had been wearing. His smelled of mothballs. The next day everybody was in uniform, and everybody smelled of mothballs.

11

Gearing Up

The trouble was, there weren't all that number of good officers around. It was one of the problems which had worried General Marshall from the moment he had taken over as Chief of Staff. Now that the United States was in the war, the scarcity became acute.

When he had started shaking up the military establishment shortly after his arrival in Washington, Marshall's first move had been to look over the records of his senior brass and mark down a large number of them for retirement. It wasn't that they were incompetent, but that so many of them were so old, veterans whose military thinking had been frozen by experiences in World War I and, in at least one case, by memories of the Spanish-American War. It was time to clear them out and bring in some younger, fresher minds.

He submitted to the President a list of generals whom he proposed to put on the retired list at once and, when that had been accepted, indicated that his own resignation would be offered as soon as he had finished cleaning out the stables. After all, he was a veteran, too, contemporary with most of those he was firing. He made it plain that at sixty-one it was time he gave way to a younger team better equipped to meet the challenges the United States was now to be facing.

Harry Hopkins came to him from the White House, grinning all over his face, and said the President refused even to think about Marshall's resignation. He just didn't believe he was serious. Only foolish politicians ever resigned, Hopkins pointed out, and the President didn't believe top brass did so either. Stung that Roosevelt thought he was angling for approval, the Chief of Staff firmly made it clear that he was serious, and he even suggested the name of an officer who would make a suitable replacement for him. He got an even firmer message back from the White House telling him to forget it; his resignation wasn't going to be accepted even if he continued to offer it.*

In the meantime, he needed vigorous, intelligent, and younger officers to fill the gaps in his ranks, and Army posts around the country were not exactly teeming with them. He had, however, still quite a few names inscribed in his little black book, and since the big prewar maneuvers in Louisiana, Texas, and the Carolinas he had put down some new ones. The one he had jotted down most frequently was that of a young colonel named Dwight D. Eisenhower, whose brilliant planning as chief of staff of the Third Army in the mock battles in Louisiana had knocked the stuffing out of his opponents. The Third Army's commander, General Walter Krueger, had also lauded Eisenhower's qualities, describing him as "a man possessing broad vision, progressive ideas, a thorough grasp of the magnitude of the problems involved in handling an Army, and lots of initiative and resourcefulness." He recommended Eisenhower for promotion as a result of his excellent showing in the exercises, and one of the actions Marshall took when he got back to Washington was to put Eisenhower's name forward for a brigadier general's star.

Another officer who had performed superbly well during the exercises was an old friend, and his name in Marshall's book had first been written there about the time he began to keep a list of talented officers. Major General George S. Patton had commanded the 2nd Armored Division during the maneuvers and done it with his usual effectiveness, ruthlessness, and panache. Marshall had first met him during World War I, when Patton had taken over the first tanks to be used by the Americans on the western front, and in temperament, attitude, and aggressiveness, he was the exact antithesis of Marshall. He was a peacock about his uniforms, he used language that made Marshall shudder, and he was forever

---

*It was just as well, he ruefully admitted later. His suggested replacement turned out to be one of the failures among wartime commanders—though he steadfastly refused to reveal who it had been.

reminding people that they were talking to the best soldier in the world. Yet Marshall liked him, even admired him, and he had written in his little black book after Patton's name: "George will take a unit through hell and high water."

Underneath that he had written: "But keep a tight rope round his neck."

And then: "Give him an armored corps when one becomes available."

Both Eisenhower and Patton soon benefited from the Chief of Staff's observations. Patton got his armored corps later in 1941. And as soon as he got back to Washington and forwarded his recommendation for Eisenhower's promotion, Marshall called in a member of his staff, Brigadier General Mark Wayne Clark, and asked him for a list of ten names of men to be considered for the vacant job of deputy chief of war plans in his office. Clark replied that if he had to write out ten names, all of them would begin with Dwight and end with Eisenhower. A summons was sent out to Third Army headquarters for Eisenhower to report to the War Department at once.

He poked his nose around the open door of Marshall's office about a week after Pearl Harbor and was irritably ordered to come in. (The chief hated people who hovered; he wanted them to stay out or walk right in, no matter what was going on, and wait until he could get to them.) Marshall knew that part of Eisenhower's service had been spent as aide to General Douglas MacArthur not only in Washington during the Bonus March but later in the Philippines, a salutary experience for all but the most sycophantic subordinate.* It was about the Philippines and MacArthur's presence there that Marshall now wanted an opinion from his new deputy chief of war plans. He rapidly brought Eisenhower up-to-date on the increasingly desperate situation in the islands, where the Japanese were now swarming ashore at a dozen different points, and asked him, "What should be our general line of action?"

---

*"Bootlickers" was the word Eisenhower used in his diary to describe the kind of officer MacArthur liked to have around him.

The newcomer asked for time to think it over and was told to return some hours later. When he came back, he was pessimistic. He told the Chief of Staff it would be a long time before reinforcements could reach the Americans, longer, he suspected, than the troops could hold out. Moreover, he had heard that the U.S. Navy, chastened by the losses at Pearl Harbor, was reluctant to risk its remaining ships in the Pacific in a rescue mission that would mean running the gauntlet of Japanese ships and shore guns. Without directly saying so, he implied that the Philippines should be written off.

"Our base should be in Australia," he said, "and we must start at once to expand it and improve communications with it."

What about MacArthur?

Eisenhower had no doubt about the answer to that one. Every commanding officer had to face it some time during a war. He recommended that MacArthur be instructed to stay with his troops and fight it out until the last soldier was overcome. In his diary later he wrote:

> [MacArthur] is doing a good job where he is, but I'm doubtful if he'd do so well in more complicated situations. Bataan is made to order for him. It's in the public eye; it has made him a public hero; it has all the essentials of drama; and he is the acknowledged king on the spot. If [he is] brought out, public opinion will force him into a position where his love of the limelight may ruin him.*

It was a sentiment which was echoed in some circles in the White House a few days after Eisenhower gave his opinion to Marshall.† The British prime minister, Winston Churchill, had arrived in Washington two days before Christmas, 1941, from the rubble of a London still smoking from the devastation of the Nazi blitz. He had come to seek reassurance from his friend and ally Franklin D. Roosevelt. Had the disasters in the Far East changed the President's attitude toward the strategy to be adopted in fight-

---

*February 23, 1942.

†Although the President's advisor, Major General Edwin "Pa" Watson, was all for getting him out. "He's worth five army corps," he said of MacArthur.

ing the war? Churchill had come to remind Roosevelt and his planners that the previous year, while Britain was still fighting the Axis powers alone, the President had secretly assured him that once the United States was involved in the war, America would join with the British in concentrating their efforts on defeating the Nazis in Europe first, before dealing with the Japanese in the Far East.

But now disaster had struck both the Allies in the Pacific. The U.S. fleet had been crippled at Pearl Harbor. Japanese planes had sent the two prize ships of the Royal Navy, *Repulse* and *Prince of Wales,* to the seabed off the coast of Malaya. Did these events mean the President's military advisers would now persuade him to change his mind? Would he renege on his promise, and instead of pumping planes, guns, and tanks across the Atlantic to Britain, would he now use them to try to salvage the desperate situation in the Pacific?

Churchill had been warned by the small coterie of experts he had brought with him* that Hitler would undoubtedly go all out to defeat Britain by the summer of 1942, before the armies of the United States could begin arriving to bolster the defense of the islands. It was therefore vital, in the prime minister's view, that America should continue supplying the British to enable them to hold the fort until reinforcements came.

At a private meeting at the White House at which the secretary of war, Henry L. Stimson, was present, the President assured Churchill that nothing had changed. The Philippines were being written off—unhappy fate though that might be for the troops fighting so gallantly there. The secretary of war nodded agreement. "There are times," he said, "when men have to die."

Roosevelt explained to the prime minister that he could hardly, of course, admit that he had given up on the Philippines either to the U.S. public or to General MacArthur and his troops. In fact,

---

*Field Marshal Sir John Dill, Admiral of the Fleet Sir Dudley Pound, Air Chief Marshal Sir Charles Portal, and Lord Beaverbrook, in charge of war supplies.

he had sent a telegram to the Far East commander assuring him help was on the way. The telegram was sent on his own initiative by the President, but MacArthur chose to believe it was a deception inspired by Marshall and connived at by his adviser, Eisenhower. He never forgave either—but particularly the Chief of Staff—for his "treachery."

In fact, when Eisenhower had suggested that MacArthur and his garrison were doomed and they should be left to fight it out to the bitter bloody end, Marshall had swallowed hard and then said, "Do your best to save them."

And between them, the Chief of Staff and his war plans adviser had done their damnedest. When the Navy refused to risk sending a convoy to the Philippines and diverted it to Australia, Marshall produced $10 million from his general Army funds—he'd been given $25 million by Congress without asking for it—and ordered it be spent on organizing ships and men to run the Japanese blockade. U.S. officers appeared in Southeast Asian and Australian ports, offering cash to skippers who would volunteer to carry supplies to the beleaguered American troops, and after it was all over, there were young lieutenants all over the Far East, still wandering around with anything up to half a million dollars in notes in their haversacks.

Marshall had also ordered his Air Corps chief, General H. H. "Hap" Arnold, to get pursuit planes somehow to the islands, to beat off repeated attacks by Japanese bombers. Crates of planes had been rushed to Australia, there to be assembled and flown on to the Philippines via the Dutch East Indies. But one of the vital elements in the mechanism of the wing guns of the planes, the solenoids (known to aircrews as "the hemorrhoids"), had been stuck to the sides of the crates, and they were discarded by the men racing to assemble the aircraft. The result was that when, after great risk and hazard, the planes eventually arrived in the Philippines, the guns would not fire.

Moreover, if Eisenhower was willing to see MacArthur die with his troops, Marshall was certainly not. Arrogant and unpleasant he might be, but he was too valuable a soldier to lose. For Christmas 1941, the Chief of Staff persuaded the President to promote MacArthur to the rank of four-star general, equal to himself and the only other U.S. soldier to be so distinguished, General John J. Pershing.* He now recommended award of the Medal of Honor to the Far East Commander and wrote the citation himself. He also strongly recommended to the President that MacArthur be ordered to leave his troops and be posted to Australia as Commander in Chief of the combined Allied forces in the battles to come.

Roosevelt, who had never been a fan of MacArthur's, had begun to accustom himself to the not unpleasant prospect of MacArthur as a martyr, a veritable American hero—but a dead one. He did not take kindly to the suggestion from his Chief of Staff that the Far East commander should be encouraged to live, fight, and strut another day. Why couldn't he be allowed to do what he wished and extinguish himself in a blaze of glory?

Marshall would not have it. If MacArthur refused to abandon his troops, he must be ordered to do so.

Not that Marshall lacked sympathy for the President's feelings. "I don't think I ever said an adverse word about General MacArthur in front of my staff," he said later, "though he was very difficult, very, very difficult, at times. I don't ever recall saying words in front of my staff, but I do recall suppressing them."

Roosevelt was in something of a difficulty because he had already discussed the future of the ground commander in future Allied operations in the Pacific with his British, Australian, and New Zealand allies. After some hesitation on their part they all had reluctantly agreed to the appointment of an American as commander of the combined forces. But not MacArthur. The Allies, too, had written him off.

---

*Typically MacArthur's reaction to the promotion was sour. Only a five-star award, putting him ahead of them all, would have satisfied him. He commented aloud to his staff the sarcastic remark of a WWI sergeant to him on a similar occasion: "At least, Captain, we're holding our own."

Now here he was, about to be sprung upon them, back from the dead, so to speak. The President didn't know what he was going to tell them and finally agreed to leave it to his Chief of Staff.

"I will tell you this now," Marshall said later. "The British, the New Zealanders, and the Australians knew nothing about his getting out of the Philippines, and we didn't dare to leak it, anyway, and it had to be a success before we could really decide upon it. . . . But when MacArthur landed in that desert country of central Australia* and we got the word—I got the word—confidentially, privately, before my breakfast, as I recall, I called up by telephone the prime minister of Australia and the prime minister of New Zealand . . . and explained why I had made this news release that he would be the Allied commander, because he would be our proposal for it and I wanted to release it instantly so that the Japanese couldn't say that he had deserted his command. And the same thing was in connection with the award of the Medal of Honor. I wanted to do anything I could to prevent them saying anything about his leaving Corregidor with his troops all out there in that perilous position."

But all of Marshall's efforts, though they appeased the Australians and New Zealanders, did not earn him a word of gratitude from MacArthur himself.

The news was generally welcomed in the Australian and New Zealand press and by the public of the two countries. Afraid they would soon be invaded in their turn by the Japanese, who had always cast covetous eyes on their vast, fertile, and largely unpopulated territories, they welcomed this sign of U.S. interest in their security. The fact that such a publicity-conscious general as MacArthur had been chosen to command the combined Allied forces in the area reassured them. At least so long as he was among them, there would be no lack of news about their situation in the

---

*He left Corregidor by PT boat with a party of seventeen, including his wife and son, on March 11, 1942, boarded a bomber on Mindanao, and flew to Australia, landing at Alice Springs on St. Patrick's Day.

United States, and they knew he would raise the dust in the U.S. press if ever Washington attempted to neglect them or leave them at the mercy of the Japanese.

MacArthur was given a huge and rousing reception when he arrived in Melbourne. But he gave no sign of being pleased at his new location.

"He thought we were selling him down the river," Marshall said later, "which we were not at all. It made it very, very difficult."

But at least the Chief of Staff could forget his peacock general for a little while and get on with war problems closer to home, of which, God knows, there were plenty. For the moment most of them had nothing to do with the enemy either. In addition to cleaning out the War Department of what one member of the staff called "deadwood and dead horseflesh," there were new offices to move into over at Arlington, where the Pentagon was now open, and relations to be settled with that imperious sister service, the Navy, and with the new Allies, the British and particularly the French. In the words of one of his departmental secretaries, Captain Frank McCarthy, who had worked in films before joining the Army, the situation could be encapsulated in the old joke about having a Hungarian as a friend: "In that case, you don't need an enemy." McCarthy discovered in that first spring of war that the War Department needed to keep its tactical antennae constantly weaving, not simply to detect hostile moves by the Axis powers but to avoid being outgunned by the Navy and outmaneuvered by its Allies.

Relations between Army and Navy had, in fact, been cordial and cooperative—in Washington, at least—up until the Pearl Harbor disaster. Though they had met for the first time only in 1939, when Marshall became Chief of Staff, his relationship with his naval opposite number, Admiral Harold R. Stark, had soon blossomed into a friendship of mutual admiration. Soon they were writing amiable notes to each other in which Marshall called Stark by his service nickname, Betty, and Stark replied by writing "Dear

George."* And they kept each other in touch with what each service was planning and how they were thinking.

But then Stark was forced to carry the can for the Navy's failure at Pearl Harbor, and though he stayed in Washington for some weeks after the attack, he was finally shipped to London in March 1942 to become chief Navy liaison officer with the Royal Navy. A much more formidable Navy type took his place. This was Admiral Ernest J. "Ernie" King. He was a seadog who, despite his age (he was sixty-three, two years older than Marshall), had teeth and knew how to use them. Ashamed of the Navy's errors in Hawaii, he stormed into his new office under full sail, having been appointed by the President not only as Navy Chief of Staff but also as Commander in Chief of U.S. Navy Operations. The acronym for that had previously been CINCUS, but it is indicative of King's frame of mind that he felt it sounded too much like "Sink Us," with its Pearl Harbor connotations, and therefore had it changed to COMINCH. By presidential decree, he became the most powerful sailor in the history of the U.S. Navy, able to make operational and policy decisions over the head of the secretary of Navy himself, Colonel Frank Knox.

In character, Ernie King was the direct antithesis of General George Marshall. It is true that they had in common a liking for attractive women, but while Marshall's mood lightened at the sight of a pretty face, King reached out at the approach of a seductive female rump. He was an inveterate bottom pincher, and the benchmarks of many a bright young officer's promotion in the Navy were the bruises on his wife's shapely posterior. King was very much married, with a family of six daughters and a son.†
His wife, Mattie, was one of those spouses who used to be referred

---

*Stark never did discover that Marshall had a nickname, too. As a schoolboy he had been called Flicker because of the way he dealt with a slick of hair which tumbled over his brow. It took a beautiful woman—Madame Chiang Kaishek—to discover that boyhood secret, and as will be seen, she used to write him letters beginning "Dear General Flicker."

†The story goes that a woman guest, having been told the size and sex of his family, asked what his son's name was. "Ernest Joseph King," he told her. "It should be Ernest Endeavor," she is said to have replied.

to as "long-suffering." She had known the time when her husband had been not only a dogged chaser of naval wives but a hard drinker, too, passed over for promotion on one crucial occasion for suspected alcoholism; but, typical of his strength of mind, he had taken the pledge to eschew hard liquor for the duration of the war and now sipped only an occasional sherry. He had taken no similar pledge to eschew the opposite sex, and Mattie King had learned to live with that, though she did occasionally retaliate by finding out which naval wife King happened to be visiting. She would then telephone and, refusing to speak to her husband, simply leave the message: "Tell him his wife called."

For all his human weaknesses, however, Admiral King was a magnificent sailor who excelled in all branches of seamanship. He had commanded a flotilla of destroyers in World War I with great skill and distinction. He was the hero of a between-wars catastrophe when a U.S. submarine—the *S51*—went down with all hands, and he and a team of divers had successfully raised it to the surface against all expert prognostications, though too late to save the crew. He was a pioneer of that new branch of the post–World War I Navy, the Air Division Command, had learned to fly a plane and land it on the deck of one of the first American aircraft carriers, which he had subsequently commanded.

He shared one other quality with Marshall: patience. Like the Army Chief of Staff, he had waited years for promotion, and though his elbow-bending propensities hadn't helped him, he had held in there, enduring and waiting. As he said later, when the top job finally arrived, "If one can only hold on for a little time longer, things will be eased up and in due time the trouble will iron out. That has been my own belief, not to say creed, but it works out for me."

He had a fighting philosophy, too. "No fighter ever won by covering up—by merely fending off the other fellow's blows," he once said. "The winner hits and keeps on hitting, even though he has to take some stiff blows in order to be able to keep on fighting."

He was certainly what the U.S. Navy needed in the black days of 1942, when morale was abysmally low. On the other hand, how was he going to get on with the Army? He was known to believe that it was under the thumb of the British, and the British were not exactly his favorite people. His experiences with them during WWI were rumored to have been unpleasant, though all he ever remarked afterward about it was: "The British were very nice to us. They allowed us to use the same sea."

Like most Navy men, he yearned to do something to restore the prestige of the service and dreamed of wiping out the humiliation of Pearl Harbor by taking the war to Japan, whereas, as he now began to learn, it was on Europe that the United States and its Allies were proposing to concentrate their efforts for the moment. Could Marshall persuade his opposite number to cooperate willingly and shift his priorities from visions of spectacular vengeance in the Pacific to the mundane convoy duties and U-boat hunts which were now desperately needed in the Atlantic and, at the same time, join him in the complicated planning that would now be needed to defeat the German, not the Japanese, enemy? The two chiefs needed to reach an understanding without delay.

Things did not start off well.

It was, in fact, Admiral King who made the opening gesture by doing something that was very unusual for him. He decided to go over to the War Department and introduce himself to Marshall and have an informal chat. Unfortunately he neglected to warn the Chief of Staff that he was coming, thinking that the moment he walked into Marshall's office, the aide would recognize who he was and have him announced at once. No one told him that though King ran a tight and highly disciplined ship in the Navy Department, the Army Chief of Staff did not operate in quite the same way.

"My reception room was across the hall from my office," Marshall said later. "It was presided over by a young woman. I very purposely didn't have a uniformed aide in it because I had to deal with such a large number of civilians . . . and with a great many congressmen coming in, I thought it wise not to have a very stern-looking military setup. . . . Now in this case Admiral King came to see me without my knowing he was coming and was received by this young woman in the reception room. Well, he was head of the Navy, and when you arrived on his side of the fence in his offices, a naval aide met you and you were escorted very formally into his presence. It was all done very formally and efficiently. Well, here was a young woman receiving the admiral of the Navy and his not getting to see me right away."

It so happened that the girl receptionist knew that her boss had a difficult visitor in his office and was scared to death of interrupting him. Marshall always professed to be surprised when his senior aides told him about it, but in fact, his manner often terrified junior officers who came to see him, and there was even a rumor around—which wasn't true—that a frightened lieutenant had collapsed and died of a heart attack when summoned into his presence. Quite often normally bright young men were turned into stuttering or tongue-tied idiots when confronted by the gaze from Marshall's cold blue eyes. Once one of them dropped his papers and fled from the room in a panic.

"What was the matter with him?" asked Marshall of his assistant General Tom Handy, who came in to rescue the papers.

"You scared the fella out of his wits," Handy said.

"Who, me?" said Marshall. "Why, I was trying to be friendly."

"That's what scared him," Handy said.

It was well known in the War Department that Marshall completely awed the receptionist who was on duty the day Admiral King called. When Marshall buzzed to summon her, she could be seen staring at the buzz box as if it were a rattlesnake. Often she bolted for the bathroom rather than answer it. The fact that on this particular day a highly gilded Navy officer was obviously in a hurry to see her awesome chief only increased her panic and froze her behind her desk.

Across the hall Marshall was talking to an irate Australian minister who had come to demand that the U.S. Army do more to protect his people from the threat of a Japanese invasion, and some acrimonious words had been exchanged. It took some time for the Chief of Staff to get rid of him, and when he came out at last and into the reception room, it was only to be told that Admiral King had been, waited, and then departed in a dudgeon.

Marshall did not hesitate. Grabbing his cap, he hurried across to King's office and was shown ("with full naval formality") into the admiral's presence. Without waiting to be greeted, Marshall launched into an explanation of why King had been kept waiting. Then he went on: "Admiral, I think this is very important. If you and I begin fighting at the very start of the war, what in the world will the public say about us? They just won't accept it for a minute. We just can't afford to fight. We just have to find a way to get along together."

King stared at him in sulky silence for a long time ("He was a very difficult individual because he was very short of temper and very sensitive," said Marshall later), and then he suddenly relaxed.

"You have been very magnanimous in coming over here the way you have," he said. "We will have a go at seeing if we can't get along." He paused again, and then added: "And I think we can."

But there were some "pretty mean fights" to come.

By the spring of 1942 Marshall had persuaded his Navy confrere to accept a Joint Chiefs of Staff committee at which matters concerning both the services could be discussed and operations projected. It had four members, including Marshall and King. Moreover, he had blunted the prospect of a future confrontation between him and Admiral King by bringing onto the committee two other officers neither of whom was likely to be an automatic ally of the Navy in any clash with the Army. It is true that the third member of the JCS whom he persuaded the President to elect was a Navy man himself, being Admiral William D. Leahy. But Leahy was just back from being ambassador to the Nazi-controlled puppet government of General Pétain, in Vichy, France. He was no friend of King, a firm friend of the administration, and a great admirer of Marshall. The fourth member of the committee was Marshall's own man, General Hap Arnold, head of the Army Air Corps. Since the Air Corps was part of the Army, and Arnold one of the Chief of Staff's subordinates, the Navy had objected to his elevation to a place and a vote on the JCS committee but had been finally overruled by the President.

Still, Marshall was aware that he might be able to close his eyes for a moment or two so far as the enemy was concerned, but he dare not even blink while Ernie King was around. The admiral made it plain that now he was in charge of the Navy, he was out for blood. Were Marshall and the Army out for blood, too? Were his allies? He indicated that he would be willing to go along with the strategic priority the United States and Britain had fixed between them—that of concentrating on defeating the Nazis first—but only on one condition. They must do something about securing that defeat fast. Otherwise, he would tell the Navy to go looking for blood in the Pacific, and to hell with priorities.

It was a constant threat to his military planning which Marshall had to keep in mind. It worried him not so much because he feared any procrastination in U.S. military circles but because he suspected there might be foot dragging on the part of his allies.

He had had a clear indication of British hesitations during the first wartime conference between the military leaders of the two countries in Washington, in December 1941. Discovering that several members of the British delegation had no invitations for Christmas—Churchill was dining at the White House with Roosevelt—he invited them to share his family celebration in his quarters at Fort Myer. The British ambassador and his wife (Lord and Lady Halifax), Lord Beaverbrook, Field Marshall Sir John Dill, Admiral Dudley Pound, and Air Chief Marshal Sir Charles Portal all accepted, and Katherine Marshall got down to preparing and cooking the turkey. During the course of the meal both Halifax and Beaverbrook were called to the telephone because Free French naval forces, on the orders of General Charles de Gaulle, had sailed in and occupied the Vichy French-held islands of St. Pierre and Miquelon, off the coast of Canada. This made everybody angry with De Gaulle: the Canadians because they had had their eyes on the islands themselves; the Americans because they were secretly negotiating with the Vichy French to neutralize other French-held islands in the hemisphere, such as Martinique and Guadeloupe, and feared they might not now be amenable; and the British—and this is what surprised and troubled Marshall—because they just seemed to be mad with De Gaulle. They considered him too pushy, too itchy for action, too eagerly looking around for opportunities to make trouble. He wondered about the British reaction. Why were they so disturbed? Didn't they want to make trouble, too?

In sounding out his guests, he discovered that what they feared about De Gaulle was the possibility that he might go on from adventures like St. Pierre and Miquelon and start agitating for action—or even initiating it—elsewhere. In Europe, for instance. And it was too soon. They were not ready. The Free French leader's overeagerness could make trouble, especially, they seemed to hint, if his feistiness affected the Americans and made them want to rush prematurely into France also.

So far as Marshall was concerned, the British reactions touched a nerve. He also had been bitten by the bug that was eating De Gaulle. To forestall any criticism from the office of Admiral King, he let it be known that the U.S. Army was looking for action—in Europe. By the spring of 1942 he began telling his British allies just what they did not want to hear: that he was planning for an early invasion of the Nazi-held continent.

With Harry Hopkins and Averell Harriman, he flew to London in April 1942 for conferences with the British about future war plans. Winston Churchill invited the Americans to Chequers and the new chief of the Imperial General Staff, Sir Alan Brooke, went with them.* It was Marshall's first encounter around the conference table with Brooke, and it was not exactly a meeting of minds. Those who did not know Marshall were apt to think of him as a cold man, but compared with the hard, distant, lofty Field Marshal Brooke, he was a ball of fire.

Brooke looked on with contemptuous amusement (which he recorded later in his diary) as Marshall came into contact with Winston Churchill's working habits. Usually Marshall endeavored to keep normal working hours and he had been known to remark that "no important decision was ever taken after four o'clock in the afternoon." Now, at Chequers, he found himself sitting down to dinner with the prime minister at nine o'clock in the evening

---

*Brooke had replaced Field Marshal Sir John Dill, who had been sent to Washington as chief British liaison officer with the U.S. Army.

and only beginning a discussion about war strategy after ten o'clock, when he was normally in bed. After a couple of hours, Churchill would break off and suggest they go in and see a film,* after which the discussions would continue until two or three in the morning.

To the supercilious Brooke, the expression on Marshall's face "was a study. He was evidently not used to being kept out of bed until the small hours of the morning and not enjoying it much." But Marshall considered it worthwhile because the prime minister seemed to be listening with sympathy and understanding to the American's contention that the Allies needed to go into action, and what he did not realize was that Churchill, while professing agreement, was filled with an inner determination to do everything he could to block what he considered the American's impetuousness and lack of military know-how.

Marshall believed him when, having listened to the Chief of Staff outline Operation Sledgehammer, a plan for an invasion of Europe in 1942, Churchill beamed at his guests, lifted his glass, and said "he had no hesitation in accepting the plan." He added, grandiloquently, that Briton and American would henceforth march together "in a noble brotherhood of arms."

It sounded marvelous, and Marshall was impressed. He sent signals back to Washington indicating that the Allies would be hitting back at the Germans in Europe this year and invading in earnest by 1943. He would have been chastened had he known what Field Marshal Brooke was writing in his diary after the conclusion of the meetings. One entry read:

> [Marshall] is, I think, a good general at raising armies and at providing the necessary link between the military and political worlds, but his strategical ability does not impress me at all. In fact, in many respects he is a very dangerous man whilst being a very charming one. He has found that [Admiral Ernest J.] King, the American Navy Chief of Staff, is proving more and more of a drain on his military resources, continually calling for land-forces to capture and hold bases in the Pacific. . . . To counter these moves Marshall has started the European offensive plan and is going one

*It was frequently Marlene Dietrich in *Destry Rides Again*.

203

hundred percent all out on it. It is a clever move that fits in with present political opinion and the desire to help Russia.

The British, in fact, were not really taking him seriously. In a way, they were right. Marshall should have known that at this stage in the game any cross-Channel invasion into German-occupied Europe would have had to be a mainly British operation. There just weren't enough trained American troops available yet to make up an invading force. Churchill did not say it out loud, but he was already beginning to have visions of an English Channel red with English blood as his armies were driven back into the sea by the better-armed, better-trained, better-motivated troops of the German Reich.

The disaster which had at one time all but blighted his political career was the one he had ordered against Turkey during World War I, when the British imperial armies had been destroyed at Gallipoli. He remembered that massacre with horror, as he did the bloodbaths in the trenches on the Somme in France. He had visions of a cross-Channel invasion turning into a similar horror. He hoped to avoid it and defeat Adolf Hitler's National Socialist regime by other means, but if that proved to be unavoidable, he was determined that the more fecund United States should provide the cannon fodder. And that meant postponing any cross-Channel operation until American troops were ready to make up the bulk of the invading force.

But meantime, he gave every sign of going along with Marshall's plans. The Chief of Staff was delighted at this evidence of British eagerness to get into action, and he and his party departed for home to plan a program for building landing craft and training crews in preparation for the great cross-Channel assault which he was confident would soon be coming.

The letdown was considerable when it came.

Marshall had got on well with Winston Churchill and, listening to the magniloquent phrases rolling off his well-oiled tongue, had made up his mind that here was a statesman he could not only admire but trust as well. He did not normally trust politicians, but he forgot that Churchill was a politician, too. By the time the Chief of Staff was back in Washington the prime minister had, in fact, begun to regret not so much his insincerity but the fact that Marshall appeared to have taken it literally. He had begun to realize that Marshall was one of those phenomena you rarely encountered at 10 Downing Street, a soldier who told you the truth when you asked him for it and expected to be told the truth in return. He had actually believed what the British had said to him.

Churchill's doubts were reinforced by bad news from the Middle East, which now came limping in. The British were doing badly in the Western Desert. The mobile Nazi armies under General Erwin Rommel had driven them out of the fortress of Tobruk and sent them reeling back into Egypt. Cairo and the Suez Canal were threatened. How could anyone contemplate an invasion across the Channel in the face of such setbacks?

The prime minister journeyed to Washington again in June 1942, ostensibly, as Marshall thought, to discuss landing craft programs and cross-Channel tactics. To his stupefaction, he found himself confronted by a British delegation which had turned its back on the whole idea. Both Churchill and the chief of the Imperial General Staff, General Sir Alan Brooke, were now all for an invasion of French North Africa instead. It was obvious that they were out to rescue the beleaguered British troops in the Middle East by coming in by the back door and had lost all interest in a cross-Channel operation.

Marshall was appalled. Later he would become much more sophisticated in his reaction to examples of political expediency, but on this occasion he was genuinely shocked by what he considered Mr. Churchill's casual perfidy, and he did something which was quite unusual for him. He hit back. To Admiral King's delight, he dug out a memorandum which his then-deputy director of war plans, General Dwight Eisenhower—whom he had now sent to London—had written. It made suggestions about what the United States should do if the British failed to agree on a cross-Channel invasion, and chief among those suggestions was one for the United States to turn its attention from the Atlantic to the

Pacific. Marshall now rewrote Eisenhower's memorandum, and encouraged by King and by his own minister for war, Henry L. Stimson, he sent the following message to the President on July 10, 1942:

> If the United States is to engage in any other operation than forceful, unswerving adherence to BOLERO plans [code name for the cross-Channel buildup], we are definitely of the opinion that we should turn to the Pacific and strike decisively against Japan; in other words, assume a defensive attitude against Germany, except for air operations; and use all available means in the Pacific.

This was just what Admiral King wanted to hear from Marshall, and welcoming him into the Pacific club, he insisted on cosigning the message to the White House. The President, however, was far from pleased. It was the last thing he wanted to read since he had an election coming up in the autumn and he had already told U.S. voters that Europe and the Middle East and Russia were the places where the war mattered.

Rightly suspecting that Marshall's volte-face was due to an unexpected bout of pique,* the President asked his Chief of Staff to provide him at once with a detailed plan for such a change of strategy. King called an emergency meeting of the Joint Chiefs and, aided by a bevy of assistants, got out a plan in a few hours. Marshall thought it a poor one, but King saw that it went to the President just the same. Roosevelt's reaction was sharp. He wrote back what amounted to a terse rebuke to both Marshall and King:

> I have carefully read your estimate of Sunday. My first impression is that it is exactly what Germany hoped the United States would do following Pearl Harbor. Secondly, it does not in fact provide use of American troops in fighting except in a lot of islands whose occupation will not affect the world situation this year or next. Third: it does not help Russia, or the Near East.
> Therefore it is disapproved as of the present.

---

*He was quite right. "In my case it was bluff," he said after the war, "but King wanted the alternative."

He signed it, with a flourish, "Roosevelt, C[ommander] in C[hief]."

The President did not conceal the fact that he was annoyed. He himself could sometimes be capricious, but he did not expect it of a grave and solid character like Marshall. Now he made it doubly plain that he wanted to see U.S. troops in action side by side with their British allies—and he wanted it by election day.

Marshall admitted later that he was relieved when his bluff was called. But he soon began to learn that not only could Allied politicians cause him trouble and rival services intrigue against him, but Allied commanders could give him the cold shoulder, too—or try to, through snubs to his subordinates.

That summer he sent Dwight Eisenhower and Mark Clark, two of the brightest young generals on his staff, to Britain to confer with the government about reception arrangements for the U.S. troops who would soon be arriving. The two officers happily reported back that Winston Churchill and the Cabinet were giving them everything they asked for. But from their British comrades-in-arms the reception was somewhat cooler.

One of their visits was to the headquarters in southern England of General Bernard L. Montgomery, commander of one of the main British army groups. Monty, as everyone called him, was not there when they arrived with their escort officer precisely at the time fixed for their rendezvous.

"We had never met him before," Clark said later. "He had that part of England which included the Channel. His job was to defend it against the Germans. Monty was somewhat irked that he had to come in from his recce [reconnaissance] just to meet two Americans. So Ike [Eisenhower] and I had to wait until he came into this little farmhouse. They had this wall with a big map on it, and Monty came in and we were introduced. He was very abrupt. There was also the brigadier with us who'd escorted us from town and some of his staff officers. He said, 'I have been directed to take time from my busy life to brief you gentlemen, so I will do so.'

"He got up with a pointer and proceeded to do so. While he was getting up, Ike got out a pack of cigarettes and offered me one. I said no. Then he lit one. In a minute Monty stopped, sniffed, and said, 'Who is smoking?'

"Ike looked around. There were five of us, but nobody else was smoking. So Ike said, 'I am, sir.'

" 'Stop it,' Monty snapped. 'I don't permit it.'

"So Ike stopped smoking."

Montgomery didn't even say good-bye to them when the briefing was over but rapidly walked out of the room, leaving the brigadier to apologize for the rough way they had been treated. The incident was never referred to by Eisenhower thereafter, but he never smoked in Montgomery's presence again, not even after he became the British general's commander in chief. "But it was hardly the start of a beautiful friendship," Clark said.

It was a French ally who gave Marshall the cold breath of his disdain, and the Chief of Staff came to the conclusion afterward that he had probably asked for it. He was in London that summer staying with members of his staff at Claridge's Hotel. One day he got word that General de Gaulle was expecting him. As head of the Free French, although not yet officially recognized as leader of the French government in exile, De Gaulle indicated that it was up to a mere chief of staff to pay his respects and not vice versa. But Marshall, who knew that both the President and Churchill were having trouble with the Frenchman, let it be known that if De Gaulle wanted to see him, it was he who would have to make the move.

De Gaulle sulked in his tent for some days but then finally swallowed his pride and asked for a rendezvous, and one was set up at Claridge's. Mark Clark was still in London and had been acting as liaison officer between the Americans and the Free French, and once the meeting was set up, he suggested that perhaps a bottle of champagne would be a useful lubricant for the occasion, to drink, perhaps, a toast to Franco-American friendship. Marshall, who had arranged several similar meetings as aide to Pershing in France, thought it was a good idea, and a magnum of Dom Pérignon was brought in.

"Then in comes General de Gaulle, stiff as a ramrod," Clark reported later. "He had one interpreter aide. He was introduced and sat down. It had been decided by the prime minister and the President that Mr. [*sic*] De Gaulle would not be let in on any of our plans for security reasons.* But De Gaulle had his wires out and he knew something was cooking. After the niceties, and I, being the junior there, had poured the champagne, he set it out on a little table. Marshall started talking to him about how beautiful the weather was and about everything except the war. De Gaulle listened for a minute, and then he said, 'General, I represent the Free French. I came to find out how I could help in the next Allied commitment to the war.'

"And Marshall couldn't tell him. It didn't take De Gaulle long to realize he was being given the runaround. When it became perfectly clear to all of us, and very embarrassing to all of us, he stood up and abruptly said, 'Messieurs, I bid you farewell.'

"And out he goes. Hadn't touched a drop of his champagne either."

Mark Clark let it be known that he thought it was a terrible mistake and they would pay for it later. Marshall made no comment at all. But he must have groaned over the difficulty of dealing fairly with America's allies while, at the same time, catering to the prejudices of his political masters.

De Gaulle was not, of course, the only Frenchman with whom the Americans had difficulties in the months to come. Marshall went back to Washington, having agreed that Eisenhower would command the combined forces after the invasion of French North Africa, and for the time being, Ike made Mark Clark his gofer, fixer, liaison officer in dealings with the French. For now other French senior officers were appearing on the scene, all of them determined to oust De Gaulle, and none of them any less arrogant and assertive than the Free French leader.

To facilitate easy communication between them, Clark and Ike made up a simple code, mostly of pseudonyms for the officers

---

*It was shortly before the landings in French North Africa.

and politicians with whom they would be dealing. Churchill was code-named Legree, Roosevelt became Bill, Marshall was Lex, and De Gaulle was Amour. At the end of the bibulous evening during which these code names and others were thought up, Mark Clark proposed that there ought to be at least one floating code name to apply to whoever caused them an unwonted amount of difficulty. He proposed, and Ike agreed, that such a person should be referred to as YBSOB, meaning "yellow-bellied son of a bitch." The messages between the two generals would, of course, have to be referred back to Marshall in Washington, and he (though neither Ike nor Clark realized it at the time) duly sent them on for perusal by the President. So they sent the Chief of Staff a copy of the code names, and he passed this on to the White House but omitted YBSOB since it did not as yet apply to any particular personage.

Then Mark Clark flew off from Gibraltar to Algiers to begin his negotiations with the French authorities there. Soon he ran up against his most difficult opponent, the local French commander, Admiral Jean F. Darlan. He asked Darlan to do two things when the Allied forces landed in North Africa: (1) order the French fleet to quit its base in Toulon, in mainland France, and sail to join the Anglo-Americans, and (2) order his troops to refrain from resisting the Allies in their advance across North Africa. Darlan refused to do either, and nothing Clark said could make him change his mind.

Soon the American was sending back irate messages in which there were now frequent references to YBSOB, meaning Darlan. Eisenhower knew who YBSOB was, and so did Marshall; but the White House did not. The President therefore asked the Chief of Staff to demand an explanation from Clark, since he believed YBSOB was a typographical error. Clark sent back a message explaining all, whereupon back came a cable from the War Department: "FROM MARSHALL TO CLARK. BILL [the President] INSTRUCTS FOLLOWING MESSAGE BE CONVEYED TO YOU: I THOROUGHLY UNDERSTAND YOUR POSITION. DON'T SEE THERE IS ANYTHING ELSE YOU COULD DO. I ONLY WISH I HAD ADOPTED YBSOB WHEN I CAME TO WASHINGTON. WE HAVE THEM HERE TOO."

12

Turning Pro

General Marshall had all of the professional soldier's lofty contempt for politicians, and in no sense did he set the President of the United States apart from the rest of the pack. His feeling that Roosevelt was just another elected manipulator was confirmed when he went to the White House to tell him that plans for the North African invasion were all ready. The President put his hands up in an attitude of prayer and said, "Please make it before election day."

Marshall could have made him the promise there and then. Instead, he austerely replied that he would do the best he could. Meanwhile, he pointed out, the British should be able to give the Democrats the fillip they needed. General Montgomery planned to attack the Nazis in the Egyptian desert at least three weeks before the elections. Roosevelt was alarmed rather than heartened by the news.

"Tell them to stop!" he cried. "The British always get licked!"

As it turned out, the British won a victory at El Alamein, but it had no effect whatsoever on the American elections. What the voters wanted to hear was that U.S. troops had gone into action against the Nazi enemy at last. But when they went to the polls on November 3, 1942, the war was still in the doldrums, and the Germans were still masters of the situation everywhere. The result was disastrous for the Democrats at the polls and dangerous for the manipulations of the Roosevelt administration. The party lost eighty-seven seats in the House and ten in the Senate.

Five days later, November 8, 1942, after the dismal results were all in, Marshall sent Frank McCarthy to the White House to tell Steve Early, the President's press secretary, that U.S. troops would be landing in North Africa the following day.

"You tell me that now, you son of a bitch?" exploded Early. "Why, oh, why couldn't you have done it a week ago?"

There is little doubt Marshall could have done just that. But the truth was, he still resented the North African invasion and had accepted it reluctantly right from the start. He regarded it as little more than a subterfuge adopted by the British both to avoid a cross-Channel invasion of France and to relieve pressure on beleaguered U.K. troops fighting the Germans in Egypt. The President had agreed to the operation simply because it was a quick way of involving American troops and getting vote-catching headlines in the newspapers. Why, therefore, should Marshall polish the image of either Churchill or Roosevelt when, between them, they had sabotaged any hope he had cherished of making a frontal attack against the Nazi-held fortress in Europe? Hitting the Germans on the other side of the English Channel was the only way of winning the war in Europe, he believed, and Operation Torch (as the North African campaign was code-named) had, by eating up landing craft and men, effectively postponed it for at least eighteen months.

"We failed to see that the leader in a democracy has to keep the people entertained," he said later. "The people demanded action. We couldn't wait to be completely ready."

But in regard to North Africa, that was not entirely accurate. It is true that some of the American troops were green so far as actual combat was concerned; but they had been trained on maneuvers, and they had to go into action some time. North Africa, where the Nazi troops were not exactly thick on the ground, was probably a better font for their baptism of fire than the mined, barb-wired and battlemented shores of northern France. Nevertheless, Marshall encouraged his planners to prolong the argument with the British as to exactly where and how the invasion should take place, and weeks were wasted on sterile squabbles during which, for once, the British were all for being bold and resolute and the Americans hesitated and held back. The British wanted to go through the Straits of Gibraltar into the Mediterranean and hit Nazi bases in Algeria and Tunisia. Marshall insisted the U.S. play safe and stay out of the Mediterranean, landing instead on the Atlantic coast of Morocco. It was true it would be easier to reembark troops from Morocco if things went wrong, but that was surely no mood in which to go into a campaign, and the Atlantic landing points were, in any case, a thousand miles away from the potential action.

The Allies split their differences in the end and landed at both places, but the prolonged discussions meant that the deadline of the American election was missed. It gave Marshall absolutely no qualms at all. How could you expect to go on playing politics as usual when there was a war on?

But if he never changed his mind about the North African invasion, that does not mean that Marshall allowed any skimping in preparations to make it a success. He told the British that the Americans would fight beside them with the best military brains, the best equipment, and the best troops the United States Army could muster. In turn, the British welcomed General Dwight D. Eisenhower as overall commander of the operation.

Marshall had long since decided that Eisenhower was the best field officer he had, and Winston Churchill, having met and conferred with him frequently in England over recent months, felt he was the ideal soldier-diplomat to command troops of both their countries without showing bias toward either.

The Chief of Staff called Eisenhower back to Washington to consult him about whom he would choose to lead his forces in the landings, and together they pored over Marshall's little black book for officers of talent worthy of being chosen for this first major operation of the U.S. Army in World War II. One of their first choices was General George Patton, who was picked to land a task force near Casablanca, and then they passed on to other names, some of them, like Generals Courtney Hodges, William H. Simpson, and John P. Lucas, being old classmen or staff members of Marshall's at Fort Benning, others, like Walter Bedell Smith and Mark Clark, being close buddies of Ike's. There were two officers in Marshall's book over whom Eisenhower hesitated. One was a swashbuckling old classmate of the Chief of Staff's named Major General Terry de la Mesa Allen, of whom it was said that "his fondness for fighting made enemies in peacetime but friends in battle." Unfortunately, as Ike well knew, Allen in peaceful moments was apt to get bored and become restless; at such times he often went out looking for a fight, not necessarily against the enemy. Ike accepted Allen reluctantly as one of his divisional commanders; he was told Allen would do proudly by him just so long as he gave him no leave but kept him constantly on the firing line, preferably with a stubborn enemy ahead of him. It worked out that way, and Allen scored some considerable successes. When not fighting Germans, however, Allen and his men took on the rear echelon's spit-and-polish regulations, and Allen had to be sent home.

Eisenhower had even less luck with another of Marshall's friends and favorites, Major General Lloyd R. Fredendall, who had a star against his name in his little black book. A barrel-shaped, belligerent infantry commander, Fredendall started off well in command of II Corps in North Africa. Eisenhower wrote back to the Chief of Staff: "I bless the day you urged Fredendall upon me and cheerfully acknowledge that my earlier doubts of him were completely unfounded."

Alas, they were not. There came a moment in the campaign when the capabilities of the U.S. forces were most severely tested, and that was during operations in the Kasserine Pass. Fredendall lost his nerve, and so did his men. There was a bloody disaster in which many troops were killed or captured and much equipment lost. Eisenhower had to fire Fredendall and send him back to the States, and General Patton was rushed in to save the day.

Finally, Marshall gave Eisenhower an officer who was soon to prove one of the most quietly effective leaders of men the U.S. military system ever produced. This was General Omar N. Bradley, who had been a classmate of Eisenhower's and a former member of Marshall's staff at Fort Benning. The Chief of Staff was so great an admirer of Bradley's qualities as a commander that he had determined to give him a corps to command when the U.S. Army launched a major campaign. It is a measure of his determination to give Eisenhower the best that he postponed that appointment in order to put Bradley on Ike's staff as his "eyes and ears." It was a brilliant choice, and it worked out perfectly, paving the way for a magnificent military collaboration later, when the major focus of World War II turned to France.

It was a rough and sometimes shocking baptism of fire for the U.S. Army in North Africa. Many things went stupidly and unnecessarily wrong.

"The decision having been made to go into Africa," Marshall said later, "a great effort was made to get what we needed. Some of the divisions were only partly trained and badly trained. The equipment was hard to get together. Eisenhower thought he had the necessary equipment in warehouses in the United Kingdom. It was scattered in small warehouses all over the country. When Eisenhower came to ship the stuff to Africa, he couldn't find it. The British didn't have our experience with large warehouses and improvised them. So we had to ship matériel to Africa from the United States when it was in the United Kingdom."

And aside from untrained troops, lost equipment, incompetent commanders, there was an absolute landslide of political troubles.

Marshall was always reluctant to admit that war and politics are inseparable, and it got him into real trouble once the landings in North Africa were accomplished and the German troops put on the run. For then the U.S. Army had to begin dealing with the local French authorities, both civil and military,* and politics became the order of the day. The Chief of Staff, who believed in leaving decisions to his officer on the spot, had given no specific instructions to General Dwight D. Eisenhower, the Allied military commander, except to make the best *ad hoc* deals possible once he had established himself in Algiers. The rest was chaos, confusion, and, in the end, bloodshed.

It was an exhibition of lack of foresight on the part of the Chief of Staff and, since he prided himself on being a meticulous

---

*Algeria was then still a department of France, and Morocco and Tunisia were French colonies.

planner, an indication of his apathy and antipathy to the whole North African operation.

He had, in truth, made his initial error in his dealings with the French months earlier when General de Gaulle had come to see him at Claridge's Hotel in London and offered his help and that of the Free French forces in forthcoming operations—even though De Gaulle could only guess, at the time, that those operations would take place in French North Africa. Why had Marshall not accepted the offer immediately? It was because, in this case, he had allowed himself to be swayed by politics. By the time he met De Gaulle he knew that President Roosevelt and Prime Minister Winston Churchill were beginning to loathe the Frenchman and actively resent his arrogant assertiveness. But it is surprising that General Marshall had accepted their orders to make no deal with the Free French leader. Normally he was extremely understanding with soldiers who were arrogant, boorish, or worse, so long as he was convinced that they were first-class soldiers. He had already demonstrated how tolerant he could be with his own generals when they ran off the rails. He knew one of them, General George Patton, to be a profane braggart, a bully, and a brute, and another, General Terry Allen, to be a riproaring drunk; but he nurtured both of them, covered up for them, protected them, because he knew they were splendid officers likely to prove brave, resourceful leaders of men on the battlefield.

So was De Gaulle. He was not only an expert on Nazi blitzkrieg techniques but also a genuine patriot, a dedicated anti-Nazi, and one of the few top French officers who had stuck his neck out and kept on fighting at the moment of France's defeat. For those qualities alone he might have been expected to win Marshall's respect and admiration. What better comrade-in-arms to have around in the forthcoming operation in French North Africa than a fighting leader of fighting Frenchmen, the symbol of French pride? It was a pity, therefore, that Marshall failed to protest to both the President and the prime minister when De Gaulle was barred from all or any share in the North African operation and allowed himself to take part in the shabby rebuff of a proud man when they met at Claridge's Hotel. For a soldier who professed to despise the sordid maneuvers of the politicians, it was a poor performance.*

Eisenhower had one civilian and one military adviser in North Africa in his dealings with the French. The civilian was a Washington politician named Robert D. Murphy, and the soldier was General Mark Clark, and both of them were as useful in solving the problems of the French in Algiers as goldfish in a pool of piranhas. While General de Gaulle was kept in fuming impotence in London, they proceeded to make deals with the very men against whom the Free French had struck out, the men responsible for France's shame and humiliation. General Mark Clark signaled back to Eisenhower that he had found a leader to take over both the civilian and military control of the French in Algiers and asked for his approval. Eisenhower consulted Marshall, who, true to his philosophy of trusting the man on the spot, agreed to abide by Eisenhower's decision. So General Henri H. Giraud was chosen by Clark to be the new French leader. It was a disastrous choice. Giraud had all of De Gaulle's peacock pride without his brilliance or, as Clark quickly discovered, his aura.

"We found out that the Arabs would shoot Giraud on sight," General Clark confessed later. "He wasn't the right guy at all. . . . We had to hide [him]. We kept him hidden [in Algiers] for weeks. The French feeling was, 'We just don't want him around.' "

But whom did they want? The officers' messes in Algiers, Bône, and Constantine were swarming with shopworn French generals, all of them soiled in the aftermath of France's defeat, who now saw an opportunity to rehabilitate themselves by persuading the Americans that despite the guilt marks around their collars, they were spotlessly clean patriots and good potential allies. They jockeyed and jostled to gain the ear of Mark Clark and Bob Murphy and Eisenhower, and from the shoddy crew one officer began to emerge. He was a certain Admiral Jean F. Darlan. General de Gaulle and any Free Frenchman could have told the Americans that Darlan was, politically speaking, one of the rot-

---

*"I was not proud of it," he said later, though he never learned to like De Gaulle.

tenest apples in the barrel, an unscrupulous and ambitious turn-coat who had collaborated enthusiastically with the Nazis after France's defeat and was not to be trusted even by his own coun-trymen.*

So far as the Americans in Algiers were concerned, however, Darlan was impressive because he was, in Clark's words, "issuing the orders . . . the boy everybody was obeying."

To the fury of the helpless Free French in London, Darlan was picked as the leader with whom the Allies would henceforth deal in North Africa—this in spite of the fact that he was shrill, unpleasant, pompous, and demanding and Clark was soon refer-ring to him in his cables, as we have heard, as YBSOB (or "yellow-bellied son of a bitch"). There could hardly have been a more unsavory choice for French leader or more convincing evidence among the French that the Americans were not really serious in their war aims; there was also a revulsion of feeling among press and public at home at the apparent willingness of the administra-tion to choose expediency over principle. It was this criticism which at last stirred some doubts in Washington, and Roosevelt ex-pressed the opinion to Marshall that maybe his front man in Al-giers had picked the wrong Frenchman. Marshall was much more anxious to bolster his commander's morale than to interfere with his political decisions, no matter how maladroit they were turning out to be, and he hesitated to criticize. Eisenhower was leading his troops in a battle with Axis troops in Tunisia and had dele-gated Mark Clark and Murphy to act for him in Algiers. So be it. He still refused to interfere, except to send Ike the kind of en-couraging words calculated to boost his self-confidence. He wrote on December 8, 1942:

> I want you to feel that you not only had my confidence but my deep sympathy in conducting a battle, organizing a fair slice of the continent, and at the same time being involved in probably the most complicated and highly supervised negotiations in history, considering the time element and other circumstances.

*"Not even," as one Frenchman quaintly put it, "with the key to his daughter's chastity belt."

218

He added, in a later message, "I intend to give you every support in this difficult situation." He meant by that: *I do not intend to intervene.*

But the President did. He had read the warning signs and had realized that "Darlan" was becoming a dirty word among the Americans and their allies. Its connotation was "collaboration"— with the enemy. Somehow, he told Marshall, Murphy, Eisenhower, and Mark Clark, they must now get rid of the tainted admiral. Clark cabled back that it might not be all that easy. YBSOB was beginning to like his new job of bossing the North African French. Maybe, *if* the Allies won the war, it could lead to even bigger things.

And then Clark had an idea.

"I'd arranged with Bob Murphy to have lunch with Darlan on Christmas Eve at Darlan's residence," he said later. "I asked him for it because I had a message from my government, to sound him out as to whether he would give up his position. The reason he was in North Africa at the time of our landing was that his son was there with infantile paralysis. . . . I asked the President if it might help if I arranged for the son to go to Warm Springs, Georgia, and back came an invitation with an authorization to use a plane with a doctor. And this message on Christmas Eve was to see the father, tell him about his son, and invite the father to take a tour of the United States and we'd take care of him and send him down to be with his son—just to get rid of him."

Darlan was quite aware of what was going on, and he listened quietly to Clark's proposition and then promised to "think about it." Both Clark and Murphy came away feeling that he had swallowed the bait. If he had done so, it was probably only because he was still not entirely sure that the Allies *would* win the war, and if they failed to do so, he and his son would probably be far safer in the United States.

As it turned out, he never had time to make up his mind. That night Murphy and Clark had a dinner date in Algiers, but just before the general was leaving for the rendezvous, "I heard Bob running down the hallway. He burst in and said, 'They've shot the little son of a bitch.'"

The two Americans rushed to the hospital where Darlan had been taken but arrived only in time to see him die from an assassin's bullets. They stood over his deathbed and looked at each other. What were they to do now? Rumors were already beginning to run through Algiers about the killing, and they were not exactly helpful to the Allies. Clark cabled to the President, Marshall, and Churchill: "THERE ARE BEGINNING TO BE RUMORS ABOUT DARLAN'S DEATH. I SHOULD PUT OUT A STATEMENT BLAMING IT ON SOMEBODY. THE FRENCH ARE BEGINNING TO CAST SUSPICIOUS GLANCES SAYING THE AMERICANS DID IT. I NEED SOME ADVICE IMMEDIATELY."

Back came an immediate reply from Churchill: "BLAME IT ON GERMAN AGENTS."

Since neither the President nor Marshall sent any answer at all, Clark took the prime minister's advice.

"So I put out a statement saying he'd been assassinated," Clark said later, "and there was every indication it was a German agent who did it. I was a hundred percent wrong. It was a Frenchman who did it. But we didn't find that out for a couple of days."*

He added, "So there we were without a French commander. Ike got the word and came right back, and we went into a huddle."

They cabled Marshall for advice. Whom should they appoint in place of Darlan? It was a golden opportunity for the Chief of Staff—and through him, the President and the administration—to repair the damage to public morale which the previous choice had made among the Allies. It was now plain to the most unpolitical of generals that both at home and in the armed forces themselves this was regarded as a war not just for freedom, not just against tyranny, but for principle and justice. Support for the war was shaken each time these precepts were abandoned in favor of cynical expediency.

It was a moment to restore public confidence by picking a leader of impeccable record and superlative soldierly qualities. To most ordinary people, even if not to Roosevelt or Churchill, that meant Charles de Gaulle, the only hero the French had left. In-

---

*He was shot in his office by a young French monarchist, Fernand Bonnier de la Chapelle.

stead, Marshall compounded his previous error by replacing the egregious Darlan by, of all people, the egregious Giraud. The peacock general was dug out of his retreat, his tail feathers dusted off, and paraded for the benefit of Allied correspondents in Algiers.

No one expected it to work out, of course—except, perhaps, the President, Marshall, and Eisenhower.

Roosevelt conceived an immediate liking for Giraud a couple of weeks later, when he met him for the first time at Casablanca. He came out of his first encounter with him beaming and exclaiming, "You know, I like Giraud." Cynics ascribed his enthusiasm to the fact that the general, who was not renowned as a good listener, had borne patiently with the President while he spoke to him in labored French.

Whether that was so or not, the President was so taken with Giraud's "easy manner," as he described it, that he decided that he would perform a miracle and persuade him and General de Gaulle to get together. As Mark Clark, who was present, remembered it later, "I brought General de Gaulle in. They shook hands. Then they went into a sparring match."

Churchill, who saw both of them later, said, "Oil and water came together and they did not mix."

Churchill's opinion of Giraud was: "He's a pipsqueak!" Then he hastily added: "But better than De Gaulle!"

Marshall and Eisenhower continued to believe that Giraud was an excellent soldier and therefore a first-class choice for the job of French leader in North Africa, and they never could understand later why they were vilified for it by their critics and regarded subsequently with such bitter resentment by De Gaulle. As Marshall naïvely said later, "We weren't interested in the politics of the thing. We were just looking for a good soldier and administrator."

They were genuinely distressed when Giraud was subsequently wounded* and had to give place, at long last, to General de Gaulle. It never occurred to them that much trouble would

---

*In another assassination attempt.

221

have been avoided, much public resentment and cynicism allayed, and maybe the shape of postwar politics radically altered, if they had fought for De Gaulle's selection in the first place.

But, as Mark Clark later remarked, "That's how screwed up things were."

His own disillusionment with Giraud did not come until later, during the Italian campaign, when the general came to visit some French troops who were under General Clark's command. Clark called a press conference for his benefit and assembled the war correspondents in the operations room at his headquarters, before maps of the front. Clark was a general who never took kindly to criticism, and he was both stupefied and annoyed when the first thing Giraud did was to go up to the maps, look them over, and then declare, in the hearing of the whole of the press, "Your headquarters are too far back."

There was a blackboard beside the maps, and Giraud now took up a piece of chalk and began to draw a diagram.

"In World War One I was a regimental commander," he said. He stabbed the blackboard. "Here was the front, and my headquarters were right up here. In World War Two I was a corps commander, and I kept my headquarters up at the front." He turned to the fuming American and added, with a smile, "I just want to give you the benefit of my experience, General. I think your headquarters are too far back."

Clark swallowed hard. "Is that all, General?" he asked.

Giraud nodded.

Clark kept his tones level.

"General Giraud," he said, "in World War One your headquarters were where you pointed to on the blackboard, and you got captured and spent a considerable time as a prisoner of war of the Germans. In World War Two, when your headquarters were up in the front line, you got captured again. In neither case were you able to exercise any influence over your troops from then on, being a prisoner of the Germans. Does that say anything to you?"

There was a heavy pause. Giraud's mustaches "positively bristled," according to Clark. Then, in silence, the two generals marched off toward a light plane that awaited them near head-quarters. General Clark's expression was, observers noted, "eloquent" as he watched the Frenchman climbing into the aircraft.

Maybe he was thinking that though Darlan was dead, YBSOB marched again.

The first big Allied conference since the end of the North African campaign was planned for January 1943 in Casablanca, Morocco, and not only would the heads of state be there—Roosevelt and his advisers, Churchill and his ministers—but so would the chiefs of staff of both British and American armed forces. To prepare for it, the U.S. Joint Chiefs worked daily all through December 1942 to thrash out a program with which to confront their allies from London. The Navy chief, Admiral Ernie King, argued for a buildup of naval forces in the Pacific and the movement of landing craft, used in the North African landings, to Asia for use against the Japanese.

General Hap Arnold, the Army Air Corps commander, produced a blueprint for a heavy-bomber offensive out of England against Germany and other areas of Nazi-occupied Europe. And General Marshall submitted a detailed plan for a cross-Channel invasion of France for the summer of 1943, which he had his new chief of war plans, General Al Wedemeyer, draw up for him.

The planners who worked for the JCS and tried to make practical sense of the ideas which the Joint Chiefs put up to them could have told the three service chiefs that there was little chance of their plans working out during 1943. Admiral King was unlikely to get his naval reinforcements in the Far East for the moment because the United States was not yet in a strong enough position to fight a global war. If the reinforcements King wanted were moved to Asia, the buildup in Europe for eventual use against Germany would have to be abandoned. The President, who still insisted that Europe should have priority, would never allow that.

As for a big U.S. bombing campaign, it was true that large numbers of new planes were now being turned out by U.S. factories. But there was still a desperate shortage of trained crews to man them, and until they were available, the brunt of the air war over Germany and Europe would still have to be borne by the RAF.

With regard to Marshall's hope for a 1943 invasion of Europe, General Wedemeyer had done his best to persuade him that even if possible, it could prove disastrous. He pointed out that U.S. ground troops, even if there were enough of them around, were still too raw to be pitted against the scarred veterans of the German Wehrmacht. During their first clash with Nazi troops in North Africa (during the Battle of the Kasserine Pass), the GI's had performed so poorly—admittedly thanks to poor leadership—that their British comrades had written a song about them which they called "How Green Was My Ally."* But Marshall had insisted that the lessons of North Africa had been learned. He sternly ordered Wedemeyer to go away and not come back until he had produced a detailed plan for a cross-Channel operation.

"And make it a good one," he said.

Wedemeyer had worked for seventy-two hours straight and had produced a first-class operational blueprint over which the Chief of Staff grunted with satisfaction when he read it through.

"This will produce a good impression when we surprise the British with it at Casablanca," he said.

Wedemeyer suggested that in that case, Marshall should be careful not to confide any details of the plan to anyone in case it came into "hostile" hands. When he used the word "hostile," he was not necessarily thinking of the enemy. He was well aware that the British were still as firmly opposed as ever to the idea of a cross-Channel operation, especially in 1943, and he feared that if they got hold of the plan in advance of the Casablanca Conference, they would have enough time to study it, find its weaknesses, and blow it out of the water.

On the last day of 1942 both JCS members and their planners rested from their labors and gathered in the War Department to celebrate General Marshall's sixty-second birthday. The party was hosted by Secretary of War Stimson, and for that reason, Admiral Ernie King was not present, though he was one of the Joint Chiefs.

---

*A reference to a popular novel of the period, *How Green Was My Valley.*

Stimson loathed him and once remarked that just being in the same room with him "makes me sick." One of the few outsiders present was the chief British liaison officer in Washington, Field Marshal Sir John Dill, of whom Stimson was extremely fond. But his affection did not in any way match the warmth felt for the Englishman by Marshall.

Sir John Dill had once been Chief of the Imperial General Staff in London but had lost the confidence of Prime Minister Churchill after Britain had suffered a series of military disasters. His quiet, almost supercilious manner had, in any case, grated on the more flamboyant premier, who always used to feel that Dill was sneering at him ("Dill's vinegar," he called it), and he had demanded his resignation and posted him to Washington, just to be rid of him. It turned out that quite inadvertently he had made a brilliant appointment.

Dill got on well with everyone in Washington, but with none more than Marshall. His easy calm, keen intelligence, and wide military and general knowledge impressed the Chief of Staff, and he soon made Dill one of his few friends and, probably, only confidant. Between them, as the war progressed, they were to build up an association so close and trusting that they would confide to each other the deepest (and sometimes the darkest) secrets of their own countries to each other, in the solid belief that this was good for Anglo-American cooperation in the war. This mutual trust had not yet come to full flower, however, by the beginning of 1943, and there were some people in the War Department who felt that Dill was getting more, much more from his friendship with Marshall than the other way around. Wedemeyer was one of those who resented the way the Englishman had "insinuated himself into Marshall's life" and watched him with a wary eye.

In Stimson's view, his Chief of Staff's birthday was a good day for a general as well as personal celebration, and when he raised his glass to drink a toast to the guest of honor, he also mentioned that the year's end marked a turning point in the fortunes of the Allies in the war.

There were certainly some gains to be recorded. The Japanese advance across the Pacific had been halted by the U.S. Navy during the battles of the Coral Sea and Midway. The Russian armies had turned the tide against the Nazis at Stalingrad. In the Western Desert of Egypt, that prim, nonsmoking martinet General Bernard L. Montgomery and his British Eighth Army had hurled back the German Afrika Korps under the Nazis' crack commander, Erwin Rommel. In the twelve months since the United States had become involved in the war, Marshall had raised the strength of the U.S. Army from just over 1,500,000 troops to 5,397,000 (73 active divisions and 167 air combat groups) at the end of the war. *And* at long last they had seen combat, fighting side by side with their British allies in North Africa, where they were now solidly established from Casablanca to Tunis.

But Marshall seemed—to some observers at least—almost to be a specter at the feast and in no mood for celebration. He appeared preoccupied, as if something were troubling him. His mood had not lightened ten days later, when members of the JCS took off by plane for Casablanca. The Chief of Staff, Hap Arnold, Field Marshal Sir John Dill, and General Wedemeyer went in one plane, and Admiral King and his staff took a plane of their own.* On the first leg of the journey Marshall's companions were astonished when he suddenly gave vent to a fit of prima donna temperament which seemed utterly untypical of the man they knew.

It so happened that Admiral King's plane was the first to arrive at the airfield in Puerto Rico, which was where they would refuel before flying on to Africa. When the Chief of Staff heard this, he flew into a temper and ordered his pilot to send a radio message at once to the Admiral's plane, forbidding it to land. As senior member of the Joint Chiefs, with precedence over King, he must be allowed to land first and receive the honors awaiting him on the ground. So while the Chief of Staff's companions studied their shoes in embarrassment, not daring to look at King's plane circling in the sky, they went down.

King was later to be heard complaining out loud about

---

*Admiral Leahy, the fourth member of the JCS, became ill en route and returned to Washington.

"wasting precious fuel in wartime just for a bit of blasted protocol." In private he was even more livid, asking his companions, "How dare that goddamned pillar of virtue pull rank on me?"

Everybody wondered what had suddenly got into Marshall. What had made him so petty-minded? Had something happened to disturb him?

It certainly had. When the British and the American chiefs sat down to discuss the future of the war a few days later, it turned out that someone had leaked to the British full details of the program the U.S. delegation planned to present, including Marshall's plan for a cross-Channel invasion in 1943. General Sir Alan Brooke, the Chief of the Imperial General Staff, Admiral Sir Dudley Pound, and Air Chief Marshal Sir Charles Portal all had had plenty of time to study it and solicit comments from their experts. They now proceeded to tear it to pieces, not least Marshall's pet plan for the invasion, which was ridiculed out of existence.

Who had passed on the U.S. program to the British? In this case, Wedemeyer had no doubt whatsoever about his identity. It had been the Englishman, Marshall's trusted friend and confidant, Field Marshal Sir John Dill.

"He got extremely close to Marshall," Wedemeyer said later, "and provided the British chiefs and the PM with information on Marshall's thinking which Marshall shouldn't have given him."

Wedemeyer was convinced that Dill had "sold Marshall short" and that Casablanca was a triumph for the British war planners because prior knowledge and better preparation enabled them to outmaneuver the Americans. He wrote an angry memorandum for the Chief of Staff about it afterward and urged him to make sure that it never happened again.

It never did. Marshall took the lesson to heart and never allowed the British to outfox him again. As for his friendship with Sir John Dill, it grew rather than diminished after Casablanca, but from then on, when the two soldiers exchanged national secrets, it was strictly on a basis of quid pro quo.

In the circumstances, it was hardly surprising that Marshall emerged from the Casablanca Conference well liked by the British, even if they did regard him as being, as one of them put it, "still a bit of an amateur when it comes to long-term strategy." It was Admiral King they came to loathe. He made it plain that he did not just mistrust them but disliked them, too. He was no respecter of persons, either, and did not just argue with his military opposite numbers—he all but got into a fistfight with General Brooke—but also showed his contempt for the prime minister, too. It was true that he had sworn off hard liquor for the duration of the war, but that did not prevent him from taking aboard an inordinate amount of wine, after which, speech slurred and mood belligerent, he lammed into Churchill and said exactly what he thought (which was not complimentary) about the French, the British, and the way the war was being run, and was too tanked up to listen to any of the arguments that came back at him. General Brooke primly commented that the prime minister "failed to appreciate fully the condition King was in. Most amusing to watch." King riposted that Brooke "talked so damned fast that it was hard to understand what he was saying."

But Churchill's chief military aide, General Sir Hastings "Pug" Ismay was fooled by neither the admiral's "thick voice" nor his "many gesticulations" and thought him a menace so far as British plans were concerned. He commented later:

> He was as tough as nails and carried himself as stiffly as a poker. He was blunt and standoffish almost to the point of rudeness. At the start, he was intolerant and suspicious of all things British, especially the Royal Navy, but he was almost equally intolerant and suspicious of the American Army.

He warned his colleagues not to treat King lightly. Ismay wrote later:

> War against Japan was the problem to which [King] had devoted the study of a lifetime, and he resented the idea of American resources being used for any other purpose than to destroy the Japanese. He mistrusted Churchill's powers of advocacy, and was apprehensive that he would wheedle President Roosevelt into neglecting the war in the Pacific.

228

Ismay counseled his colleagues to appease their contemptuous American colleague but never to turn their backs on him, for he was not to be trusted.* So, in contrast with their treatment of Marshall's proposals for action in France, they listened gravely to all of King's plans for the Pacific and solemnly promised to support them. They even accepted operations in Burma in which the British Army and Navy would be directly involved.

Not that they had any intention of carrying them out,† but Churchill and Ismay told Brooke to accept them anyway, just to get King in the right mood. It worked, too. The admiral began reluctantly to admit that perhaps he had misjudged the British and they were in fact ready to back him up in Asia and the Pacific. In return, Brooke got him to agree to support Allied plans in Europe, including an invasion of Sicily, a stepping up of the antisubmarine war in the Atlantic, an intensification of the bombing campaign against Germany from Britain, and beefed-up aid to the Soviet Union—everything, in fact, except support for Marshall's proposal for a 1943 cross-Channel invasion of France.

It was the last time Churchill and his war chiefs dominated an Allied conference, and as if suspecting the Americans would come better prepared the next time, they went all out for all the pickings and promises they could get.

"We must never allow them to catch us out this way again," wrote Wedemeyer in an angry memorandum to Marshall after the conference was over. The Chief of Staff never replied to it, but there is no doubt that he got the message.

He and Wedemeyer were supposed to fly on to Moscow after Casablanca to tell the Communist leader, Joseph Stalin, what had been decided at the conference. But all Stalin was waiting to hear was that the Allies would invade Europe and take the pressure off his armies fighting the Nazis in Russia. When he learned that

---

*"[King] always fought for American interests," Wedemeyer said later. "He tricked the British. They were quite right in thinking they had to watch him."

†They never did.

Marshall's plan had been shot down by the British, he curtly informed the Chief of Staff he would not be welcome. Doubly disappointed, Marshall flew back to Washington. Wedemeyer went on to see Chiang Kai-shek, the Chinese leader, in Chungking and General MacArthur in Brisbane, Australia, to brief them on what the Allies had decided.

Field Marshal Dill was traveling to India to visit his British colleague, General Sir Archibald Wavell, so the two men went as far as Delhi on the same plane. There Wedemeyer stopped off long enough to accept an invitation to go pigsticking with his British colleague and Wavell. Dill was unlucky. Tugged out of his saddle when he speared but did not kill a charging boar, he barely missed being gored by it, just managing to roll out of the way of the slashing tusks. But he twisted his back and ruptured himself in evading the wounded beast.

By the time the others got to him Dill was in great pain but bore it well. Everyone was impressed by his cheerful stoicism. But admiring him did not mean that Wedemeyer ever learned to trust the Englishman—not around Marshall anyway. And he was still jealous of his intimacy with his chief.

13

Great White Stepfather

No one doubted Marshall's deep devotion to his wife, Katherine, but there were moments when he must have tried her patience, particularly when his goddaughter, Rose Page Wilson, came round to visit them at Fort Myer. Rose was associated in his mind with his first wife, Lily, and while she was in the house, that is the name by which he would address his wife. One day Rose couldn't stand it any longer.

"Colonel,"* she said, "you're a great officer, but you're a real dope when it comes to women. Will you *please* stop calling Katherine *Lily*?"

Marshall looked astonished. Then he smiled and remarked that Katherine was not the sort of person to be bothered by a little thing like that. He was sure she understood.

"Maybe," said Rose, "but I don't hear her calling you Clifton or Cliff or whatever else it was she used to call her first husband. Of course she understands. But that doesn't mean she likes it."

He solemnly promised to remember in future, but he never did.

There is no evidence that Katherine Marshall ever mentioned it to her husband. It was all part and parcel of being married to a man who was not just Chief of Staff of the United States Army but someone who now concentrated his whole mind, twenty-four hours of the day, on the business of running the armed forces and winning the war, and that took priority over everything else, including her, her feelings, and her family. There were those who envied Marshall because he worked in Washington and, more often than not, could come home at night to his wife, whereas millions of young Americans had now been wrenched away from home and family to serve in the Army. Katherine, on the other

---

*Colonel was always his "family" name.

231

hand, was only too conscious of the fact that her husband envied *them* and that he was waiting impatiently for the moment when he could leave her to go overseas and take part in the fighting. He did not conceal it from her. She knew that the moment the inevitable invasion of Europe came along, he was determined to be there. As Commander in Chief.

Meanwhile, she was aware there was one thing she never dared do with him, and that was to ask him to use his influence as Chief of Staff on her behalf or that of her children. By this time, of course, he had given up hope of ever having any children of his own, but Katherine's two sons, Clifton and Allen, and daughter, Molly, were a happy compensation. He had become extremely fond of all three, particularly the younger boy, Allen, but Katherine knew better than to ask for any favors on their behalf. Though he was married and had a baby son, Allen volunteered for the Armored Corps and was sent as a private to the training school at Fort Knox. When he came to see them on leave, an old Army sergeant who worked around the house came into the breakfast room in some embarrassment and asked Katherine how he should address her son now he was in the armed forces. She replied that he should go on as always and call him "Mr. Allen."

"Oh, no, you won't," broke in Marshall. "He's in the Army now. You call him Private, and make sure he calls you Sergeant. And don't forget," he added, "it's you who will be giving the orders now."

Allen did well at the Armored Forces Center in Fort Knox, Kentucky, and when he won his commission, the camp commandant wrote to ask whether his stepfather would be interested in attending the young man's graduation ceremony. He was rebuffed. Marshall wrote:

> The fact of the matter is I had very much hoped that Allen could get through the school without his identity being disclosed, and I ask you now to see that his graduation bears no comment on his connection with me. The fact that it is known that he is my stepson denied him a good bit of the credit for earning his own way and I am disturbed that it has become public.

But when Allen became a second lieutenant in the Armored Corps and was due to be shipped to North Africa, Marshall did arrange a quiet farewell party for him and his family and brought together to toast his departure his sister, Molly, and her husband, Major James J. Winn, and his brother, Clifton, a lieutenant in an antiaircraft unit. On the other hand, once the young lieutenant was in the combat area, the Chief of Staff let it be known to the few who realized his relationship with him that he was to receive no favors and that any senior officer recommending him for promotion would have his own credentials closely examined.

Katherine complained that it was unfair to her son—"At least don't penalize him because he is a relative," she pleaded—and Marshall admitted that this was so but maintained that there was a more important principle involved than her son's career in the Army. It must never be suggested that the Chief of Staff was favoring his stepsons. Better that Allen should suffer than the rumor go around that General Marshall was susceptible to petticoat influence.

The result was that Lieutenant Allen Brown saw rather more of the rough side of war than most other equivalent officers in a similar space of time. He fought in North Africa and Sicily and was then transferred to a New Zealand outfit and was engaged with them in the bitter fighting on the slopes of Monte Cassino, in Italy. But he never complained.

"I personally don't give a damn who I fight with," he wrote his stepfather, "just so I can be part of the 'show' as these 'blokes' call it."

Marshall wrote back to him, on the eve of attending a dinner in Washington: "I wish you could join us and spread yourself in the warmth of a heated room and with the beautiful food I assume will be at hand. You could do much better by it than I shall be able to do, and with better results too."

He ended: "Still, you are young. I had rather be young and in the mud than at my age and in an office chair, though it seems to me I spend a great deal of my time in the air not to mention slogging over considerable muddy terrain. All good luck to you and may the good Lord watch over you."

He did so until the end of May 1944, when he moved with his tank unit north toward Rome, probing forward to make contact with troops breaking out of the Anzio bridgehead. On May 29, in the lead tank, he reached the outskirts of a small village called Vellettri, in the Alban Hills. Pausing to survey the situation ahead, he raised the turret of his tank and rose with his binoculars to his eyes to spy out the land. A German sniper hidden in a nearby building put a bullet through his head and killed him instantly.

Katherine bitterly mourned her younger son. Marshall was doubly shattered at the death of his favorite stepson and, at the memorial service in Washington, came as near to breaking down as he ever did in his lifetime when he came face-to-face with Allen's young widow, Madge, and her son.

In the circumstances, he might have been tempted to pull a few strings on behalf of Katherine's older son, Clifton, when he too became restless over his position in the Army. And he did indeed do him one favor. Clifton suffered from bad feet and had already undergone several operations on them. Nevertheless, he, too, had volunteered for service and, after scraping by several medical boards, had finally been sent to training camp and officer candidate school, and then given a commission in an antiaircraft regiment, but for service in the mainland United States only.

After a few months in camp in Virginia, Clifton found the service irksome and frustrating. He longed to see action overseas, and his boredom and discontent were hardly helped by the letters which Allen was writing home from abroad. Why should it be his younger brother and not he who was finding out what the war was all about? He began to bombard his mother with letters and calls pleading with her to use her influence on the "Colonel" and persuade him to allow his stepson to be posted to a war zone abroad.

Katherine Marshall informed her son that she could not possibly interfere. She had a strict understanding with her husband that never under any circumstances would she try to influence him about military affairs, particularly where her family was concerned.

Then maybe, her son suggested, she could use her own clout as the Chief of Staff's wife and mention her son's name to someone in the Adjutant General's office and get him a posting that way, without telling her husband anything about it.

No, replied Katherine, even more firmly than before.

She did not tell her son that she had already had a painful experience as a result of being pressed into using her status as Marshall's wife. It had not even been on behalf of her family, either, but because of her husband's dog. It may be remembered that George Marshall had a pet Dalmatian named Fleet which always accompanied him when he was out riding and of which he was extremely fond.* Unfortunately Fleet had a habit of wandering and getting lost. Katherine had to go out and find and bring him in, knowing her husband would be greatly distressed if Fleet were not there to greet him when he came home.

But while Marshall was away on one trip, Fleet disappeared and could not be found anywhere, though Katherine searched the streets and offered rewards. She was frantic. What would he say when he got home and discovered she had lost his beloved Dalmatian? She had reached the depths of despair when the telephone rang. It was a night caretaker in the Navy Department to tell her that he had found her dog, complete with the name and number on the collar. Katherine was overjoyed. She would come right over—and bring the reward. What sort of reward? Money.

The man hesitated and then asked if she was *the* Mrs. George Marshall, wife of the general. She said she was. In that case, the man said, instead of money, he would like her to use her influence to get him a better job in the Navy Department. When she demurred and said she couldn't possibly do that, his voice changed, and he asked her whether she wanted her dog back or not. He could always push it through a back window and let it wander off again.

Desperate, knowing that George was due in a few hours' time, anxious only to get Fleet back home, she finally said she would write the man a letter of recommendation and sent it around to him by messenger. He would get the sealed envelope the moment he handed over Fleet.

---

*"His strong affection for that silly animal was the only stupid thing I ever knew about George," Katherine said later.

That night the daffy Dalmatian was waiting on the mat, all
ready to fawn and whine with pleasure when Marshall walked in.
It was only later, after dinner, that Katherine confessed what she
had done. Marshall was furious. She should never have done it.
It was outrageous for her to have used the power of his office, as
his wife, in this way, even if she had been blackmailed into it.
Better for him to have lost his dog.

He was so angry that Katherine began to cry. He softened
then and came over to comfort her. But presently, after she had
dried her tears, he came back to the subject again and still seemed
angry. What sort of letter had she written? What sort of job could
the man now be expecting to get in the Navy?

"I thought you might ask that," said Katherine. "I kept a
copy."

She went to the bureau and took out a piece of paper and
handed it to him. He read the message on it:

> To Whom it May Concern in the United States Navy:
>   The bearer of this note is a good dog-catcher.
> [signed] Katherine T. Marshall (Mrs. George C.)

Marshall was silent for a moment, and then he began to
laugh.

All the same, it was something Katherine Marshall was not
willing to repeat, even on behalf of her son. She told Clifton he
would have to work things out for himself. He would probably
have stayed with his AA unit indefinitely had it not been for a
chance meeting in Richmond, Virginia, with Marshall's assistant
Frank McCarthy, to whom he poured out his tale of woe. Mc-
Carthy saw no reason at all why Clifton should not serve overseas
and went back to Washington and mentioned it to his boss. He
was told by Marshall that if he could arrange something, the Chief
of Staff would not stand in his stepson's way.

McCarthy fixed it for Captain Clifton Brown to be posted
to an antiaircraft unit in North Africa under General Eisenhower's
command, and he sailed on a slow convoy for Oran, Algeria, in
September 1943, arriving in Algiers a month later. McCarthy had
specifically asked that no one except Eisenhower's headquar-

ters should know who he was, nor should Clifton be informed what action had been taken on his behalf. But Marshall was hypersensitive about him, and when he heard that his stepson had been posted to an antiaircraft battalion at supreme headquarters in Algiers, he cabled personally to Ike's chief of staff, General Walter Bedell Smith: "I DO NOT WANT MY STEPSON SETTLED ON A SUPREME HEADQUARTERS. ALSO I HAVE TRIED THROUGH MCCARTHY BY EVERY HOOK OR CROOK TO AVOID EMBARRASSING PEOPLE BY DISCLOSING HIS CONNECTION WITH ME."

Smith replied:

> PLEASE INFORM GENERAL MARSHALL THAT CAPTAIN BROWN'S CONNECTION IS KNOWN IN THIS HEADQUARTERS ONLY TO MYSELF AND THE SECRETARY, GENERAL STAFF. BROWN'S ASSIGNMENT WAS MADE BY THE ADJUTANT GENERAL AS A ROUTINE MATTER TO FILL A VACANCY AND IT IS BECAUSE I DID NOT WISH TO ORDER A DEPARTURE FROM NORMAL PROCEDURE THAT HE WAS PLACED WHERE THE VACANCY EXISTED RATHER THAN IN THE ARTILLERY BRIGADE HQ WHICH IS LOCATED HERE. HOWEVER I WILL CARRY OUT THE GENERAL'S INSTRUCTIONS.

Clifton was posted to a brigade headquarters nearer the action in Tunisia and gave a good account of himself in the air bombardments in which he was later involved.

But then things went wrong—at least in Marshall's view. The war moved away to Italy, and Clifton attempted to go with it. Unfortunately his feet went bad on him, and yet another operation upon them was called for. He wrote a long letter to his stepfather, in which he said in part:

> ... There is another matter I would like to ask you about. Both General Stayer and a certain Colonel Churchill [both Army medical specialists] have looked at my one remaining bad foot and told me another operation and grafting job will be necessary, and I will be laid up for two and a half to three months. From all appearances this HQ will fold up within the next few weeks. Our work here at the antiaircraft section is already finished and we do nothing now except sit around.
>
> In all probability I will be sent to the replacement pool when this happens. The usual procedure in replacement pools over here is to let the officers sit on their fannys [*sic*] anywhere from three

months to a year. If possible when we do fold up here I would like to get back to the States and get the operation over with instead of waiting around over here for months doing nothing and then go home and have to lay around in the hospital for three more months. All I need is your okay to go ahead on this. I can handle all the details myself, and you need not be envolved [*sic*].

If, after my operation is over, the war in the Pacific is still going on, I will try and get out there with an AA unit. . . .

Marshall was furious when he read the letter. It seemed to him to confirm his worst fears that his stepson was pulling strings to get himself out of North Africa, and fond though he was of him, he was determined he was not going to get away with it. He wrote two letters. The first was to General M. C. Stayer, deputy surgeon general at Allied force headquarters in Algiers. He summed up the contents of Clifton's letter and went on:

I am much embarrassed over this business; specifically with regard to the last sentence, "I can handle all the details myself, and you need not be involved," because it would appear to me that he would either be in the process of being sent home now if you surgeons thought it necessary or he is depending on the fact that a request from him carries something of my influence.

Clifton got out to the Mediterranean through my having an exception made to limited service in his case. He was very anxious to go and has been there less than a year. . . .

I do not want anything to be done that would not be done for Tom Dick or Harry, and as he has consulted you in this matter I am taking the liberty of writing you direct to make my position clear. There are thousands of officers who have been overseas longer than two years, some of whom have had several bouts of malaria, all anxious to get home and in some instances developing very heavy pressures in this country to get them home. I must not be put in the position of backing favorites in my own family.

Will you please radio me your views on this matter. . . .

He waited until he had received General Stayer's reply, and then he wrote to Clifton:

I am answering your letter regarding your returning home for an operation. You stated that if I had no objection you can make arrangements over there. This of necessity creates a most embarrassing situation for me because if an operation were plainly indicated they would send you home without regard to you or me either. The fact that they have not ordered you to the United States for an operation means that the necessity for one is not clearly established.

However, to make certain no injustice was done you I communicated directly with General Stayer who stated to me in a radio [radiogram]

> PROVIDED MINOR LONG STANDING LIMITING DISABILITY DOES NOT INCREASE NO REASON EXISTS FOR EVACUATION THROUGH MEDICAL CHANNELS OR OTHER PREFERENTIAL MANNER.

You must understand that where countless thousands are endeavoring to be returned home, for one reason or another, most of whom have been overseas for two years or longer, it is not to be supposed that you would be returned on your own recommendation except by reason of your relationship to me. You mentioned this matter in a previous letter or two and also in one to your Mother. I have not commented up to the present because it is an embarrassing issue that you have raised.

You went to the Mediterranean on your own urging with the necessity of our arranging to avoid your limited service status interfering, and you have been out there less than a year. . . . I should prefer that you make no mention of this to General Stayer as it is embarrassing to him as well as to me. If your foot develops badly then take it to the doctor and let him decide.

So Clifton was stuck. Had he been an ordinary, run-of-the-mill officer with no top-brass connection, he would probably have managed to wangle himself a trip home. But his stepfather's rebuke inhibited him, and he did not even dare use his own contacts and initiative to work a passage for himself, in case it should anger the Chief of Staff and distress his mother. It was not until the war in Europe was over that Clifton finally managed to get himself shipped back home to the United States and into a Stateside hospital for his operation.

Where service in the armed forces was concerned, it certainly did not pay to be related to General Marshall.

On the other hand, no one could accuse the Chief of Staff
of singling out his stepsons for especially rigorous treatment. He
expected the same impeccable standards to be observed by his
staff and by the Army's top brass, too, and woe betide any of
them who tried to pull strings—for themselves or anyone else.

President Ronald Reagan probably does not realize how closely
he came to being refused a commission in the U.S. Army Air Corps
as a result of a letter written to him during WWII by Frank
McCarthy, then still a major in the War Department. McCarthy,
as has been mentioned earlier, had worked in prewar Hollywood
and still kept up with news of the film world after he joined
Marshall's team. In April 1942 he read an item about Reagan and
at once sent him a letter, in care of Warner Brothers studios in
Hollywood:

> Dear Ronnie:
>
> I have just read in the newspaper that you are going into the
> Army on April 19th, and I wonder whether you will enter as a
> Reserve Officer or as an enlisted man.
>
> Although I have not seen you since the summer of 1938, when
> I was in Hollywood as technical adviser on BROTHER RAT, I
> have not forgotten the pleasant association with you at that time.
> It occurs to me that if you are going in as an enlisted man, you
> will certainly make every effort to secure appointment after the
> first three months to an officer candidate school. In such an event,
> I do hope you will not hesitate to use me as a reference if you think
> it would be worthwhile. I don't know anybody I could say a better
> word for.
>
> Please give my love to Jane [Wyman], who I still think is the
> most attractive girl in Hollywood, and remember me to Wayne
> Morris, Jeff Lynn, John Payne, Bob Lord and Carol Sax if you
> happen to see any of them.
>
> > Sincerely,
> > Frank McCarthy,
> > Major, General Staff,
> > Asst. Sec. General Staff

Marshall saw the letter while glancing through the files and
went into one of his formidable tempers. Roundly berating
McCarthy for daring to use his office to nurture and promote his

Hollywood friends, he seemed tempted to contact Reagan's training post and warn his commanding officer to keep him out of officer candidate school no matter how suitable he might be. McCarthy managed to persuade his chief that it would be grossly unfair to Reagan, who had in no way solicited the letter. The future President of the United States went on to get his commission in the Air Corps, little knowing how close he had come to sweating out the war in the ranks.

But Marshall could be really tough with his generals when they transgressed the rules. He was an austere character, but no prude, and he did not expect the commanders of U.S. troops to be puritans. He knew that in their spare moments they often drank too much or wenched too much, and all he asked of them was that they be discreet about it and not cause gossip or scandal. When they did, he let them know exactly what he thought.

When word reached him, for instance, from Cairo that the U.S. Middle East Air Forces Commander, General Lewis H. Brereton, was ostentatiously bending the rules, he called in a courier and dispatched him to the Middle East with a message marked "Personal and Confidential." It was incisive to the point of bluntness:

> Dear Brereton:
>
> Information, official and otherwise, reached me indicating that your relations with your secretary have given rise to facetious and derogatory gossip in India and Egypt. Ordinarily I have little interest in an officer's personal affairs that are not related to the performance of his military duty. However, your conspicuous position of command in a foreign theater of war makes it imperative that your personal affairs do not give rise to comment detrimental to the prestige of the American Army. I wish to make it clear that anything short of this would destroy my confidence in the effectiveness of your leadership.
>
> I wish you to release your secretary and if practicable see that she returns to her permanent residence. You will not permit members of your command to have their women secretaries accompany them on their official trips. Please advise me personally and confidentially as soon as you have carried out these instructions.

General Brereton made haste to ship his secretary back to

the United States and faithfully promised to behave himself in future. Less than a year later Marshall was praising him publicly for his command of Middle East air operations instead of chiding him in private for his sexual peccadilloes.

But sometimes it could not be done quite so simply and straightforwardly, as he discovered when the case of General Dwight D. Eisenhower came up.

Marshall was meticulous about the morale of American servicemen overseas, and he sent a series of roving military ambassadors permanently circling the world, visiting Army and Air Corps stations in every place where U.S. troops were fighting or serving with no other mission than to listen for gripes and recommend how to remedy them. It was as a result of one of these reports that the Army's post exchange service was completely reorganized, and no base PX was supposed to open until similar facilities were available for troops up in the front line. A GI could come out of the fighting to find a bottle of Coke, a pack of Luckies, and a Hershey bar waiting for him right there amid the shot and shell, and if it didn't make the place any less dangerous, it certainly made it easier to bear.*

When the Chief of Staff himself arrived at a station, he would dispense with the commanding officer, set off for a tour with only his driver, and then proceed to keep his ears open for complaints. It was thus that he learned the truth about a Southeast Asian air station where morale had slumped to the depths. The pilots were becoming edgy, the commanding officer reported. They were flying constant missions against the Japanese and coming back with their nerves shot to hell. They needed leave.

But what Marshall discovered was that it was not the pilots but the enlisted men servicing the USAAC planes who needed leave. The air station was stinking hot, humid, and alive with mosquitoes. All the enlisted men had come down with malaria and were now so pumped up with Atabrine they were punch-drunk, so weak from fever and so groggy from the drug that they could barely see what they were doing as they worked on the

---

*That was Marshall's aim, at least. It didn't always work out—but he tried.

242

aircraft. Most of their work was done at night, in fetidly hot conditions under cover and under lights, with mosquitoes swarming all over their sweat-frothed bodies.

The pilots were afraid not of the Japanese but of their planes and what the enlisted men were doing—or not doing—to them.

Marshall went back to order emergency shipments of camouflage nets and new fan units to cool the repair sheds, and he put in a series of rotation leaves for the enlisted men. The pilots lost out on that one, but as Marshall later remarked, "All they really wanted was girls—and there wasn't really much we could do about that. And anyway, they felt much better once they knew the mechanics were back on the ball, and they could rely on their planes again."

But it wasn't always the enlisted men who got Marshall's especial attention. He looked after the top brass, too. Whenever he visited a U.S. war front (and he was constantly on trips to Europe, Africa, the Middle East, and Asia), he would have McCarthy visit and talk to every commanding officer in the area and jot down notes about him, and he himself would see and talk with all the top officers.

Back in Washington, he would then write a personal note to the wife, mother, or nearest relative of every senior officer he and McCarthy had met, passing on messages, commenting on their condition. It was one of his most appreciated gestures, and the Marshall archives are full of grateful notes from wives, daughters, and parents. Many of the wives, of course, he knew, for he had served in prewar days with many of the wartime generals and got to know their families well. He kept up a regular correspondence with the wives of old colleagues like Mark Clark, Walter Bedell Smith, George Patton, and with Eisenhower's wife, Mamie, acting as a conduit between the spouses and making the separation less hard to bear. It goes without saying that he never snitched on his generals, particularly to their wives, but somehow the word got around to them that in an avuncular way Marshall was keeping an eye on their husbands, and not just as soldiers, and would see that they did not go off the rails when they were away from the battle.

Just before the beginning of the invasion of North Africa,

while General Eisenhower was still in London, information reached the Chief of Staff that Ike had got himself a new driver. The branch of the U.S. Army that became the Women's Army Corps (the WAC) had not yet shipped volunteers for service overseas, and a number of British volunteer services had begun providing chauffeuses and secretaries to the American military (and to top British ministers and civil servants, too). Ike's driver belonged to one of these. Her name was Kay Summersby, and by the time she was brought to Marshall's attention she had begun to do things for the general in addition to driving a car "above and beyond the call of duty," as the report put it.

This did not particularly disturb Marshall. After all, he had learned at first hand himself, at the end of WWI, how devastatingly charming Englishwomen could be. No harm would come even if Eisenhower lost his heart so long as he kept his head.

But then his staff received a report which gave him quite a jolt when he read it and made him wonder whether Ike had not only lost his head but also taken leave of his senses. Among the list of decorations which arrived from U.S. headquarters in North Africa was one for a certain Miss Kay Summersby, recommending she be awarded the Legion of Merit.

It was no moment for the Chief of Staff to send off a peremptory cable asking if Ike had lost his marbles; he was too deeply involved in the campaign. But it was certainly necessary to give him some shock of a kind calculated to restore his sense of proportion. Accordingly Marshall had his staff prepare a memorandum, which read as follows:

January 5, 1943

Memorandum for Major Bell
Subject: Legion of Merit for Kay Summersby

This is to advise you that it has been decided not to decorate Miss Kay Summersby at this time. She is not qualified for the Legion of Merit by virtue of not being in the Military Service. Also, her services are not believed to be such as to qualify her for the Medal of Merit. In view of these facts, I suggest that the medal and certificate be re-

turned to Colonel Gardner with instructions to destroy
them or file them without action.
> B. W. Davenport,
> Major, General Staff,
> Asst. Secretary, General Staff

There, that should do it. If the general was finding comfort
and solace by enjoying the companionship of a beautiful and
charming Englishwoman, no one, least of all Marshall, was going
to deny them to him, and so long as he remained discreet about
his liaison, no word of it need ever get back to Mamie Eisenhower.
Everyone hoped that he had taken the hint, and as the weeks went
by, it seemed as if he had done so. True, Miss Summersby had
changed her tailor-made British volunteer uniform for one closely
resembling the service dress of the WAC. But no one read anything
particularly significant into that fact. Not for the moment anyway.

Then, one morning in the summer of 1944, Frank McCarthy
walked into Marshall's office and announced that Eisenhower had
sent a message to the Assistant Chief of Staff, Major General
M. G. White. He had particularly asked that General Marshall
not be bothered with it, but in view of the nature of Ike's message,
both he and McCarthy thought the Chief of Staff should be told
about it. As Marshall looked up from his desk and waited,
McCarthy went on to inform him that General Eisenhower had
asked that Miss Summersby, who had now become his secretary
as well as his driver, should be given a commission in the U.S.
Women's Army Corps.

What were they going to do about that?

They did not panic. Neither Marshall nor any member of his
staff considered sending a harsh message or an ultimatum to General Eisenhower at Supreme Headquarters Allied Expeditionary
Force (SHAEF) in Europe. For the moment he was far too vitally
involved in the outcome of the struggle with Germany to do that.

On the other hand, everyone in the War Department was
determined to prevent Ike's girl friend from becoming an officer

in the WAC. It seemed far too dangerous. If it leaked out, it could cause quite a scandal in the press and considerable embarrassment to Mamie Eisenhower.

McCarthy sent a memorandum to General White on July 7, 1944, in which he wrote:

> I talked to General Marshall further about commissioning General Eisenhower's driver and confidential secretary in the WAC. He concurs with me that the best course of action is to have you write General Eisenhower the official reason, as strongly as possible, why this should not be done. I will take up the personal side in a conversation with Colonel Lee, General Eisenhower's aide, who will be here in a few days.
>
> Will you let me have your letter to General Eisenhower as soon as possible? It will be carried to the U.K. by Lee.
>
> [signed] Frank McCarthy

It had been announced that Colonel Ernest R. "Tex" Lee, Ike's aide, would be flying into Washington by special plane on an urgent visit, and McCarthy was assigned to go out and meet him at the airfield. It was not until he got there that he realized that Lee had brought another passenger with him. Emerging from the plane was the elegant figure of Miss Kay Summersby herself. She had come to Washington to be personally sworn in as an officer in the WAC.

Now Marshall's staff did begin to show signs of nervousness. McCarthy rushed to the telephone to apprize his chief and General White of the advent of the beautiful but unwelcome visitor. White had only one piece of advice: Get rid of her. Send her on a tour, but at all costs, get her out of Washington while tactics were discussed.

Putting on an extra load of his considerable charm, McCarthy welcomed the two visitors to Washington and then explained that things were happening in Washington and no one was available in the War Department at the moment. How would it be if they took a few days off? Colonel Lee jumped at the chance of visiting his family in Indiana. Kay Summersby, who had never been to the United States before, was extremely happy to be sent off on an inspection of Army leave centers in Florida, where, McCarthy figured, she would win enough wolf whistles from the GI's to gladden a girl's heart.

He found them transport and then hastened back to the War Department and more conferences with General White. On July 9, McCarthy sent a note through to Eisenhower:

> Sec. Gen. Staff 3542. To Supreme Headquarters Allied Expeditionary Force London WAR62711
> For General Eisenhower personally from McCarthy.
> LEE IS IN INDIANAPOLIS SUMMERSBY IN FLORIDA BUT BOTH OF THEM WILL RETURN HERE IN TIME TO TAKE OFF AS PLANNED. IN THEIR ABSENCE I HAVE BEEN HANDLING THE COMMISSION PROPOSITION WITH THE WAC PEOPLE AND GENERAL WHITE, G1. THERE ARE SOME COMPLICATIONS AS A RESULT OF WHICH GENERAL WHITE THINKS IT BEST TO BRING YOU A PERSONAL MEMORANDUM FROM HIM. I WILL GIVE THIS TO LEE UPON DEPARTURE.

Meanwhile, he sent Marshall a copy of White's note along with this memorandum:

> The attached memorandum from General White to General Eisenhower explains the official reasons why General Eisenhower's driver and confidential secretary should not be commissioned in the WAC. General Eisenhower specifically told his aide that you were not to be troubled with this, so I think you should be left out of it altogether.
> On reflection over the *personal* aspects of the appointment, I believe it better not to mention these at all unless this memorandum fails to hit the mark. I believe the memorandum itself will accomplish the purpose and we will hear no more about it.
> Frank McCarthy

General White's memorandum was dated July 8, 1944, and was delivered to General Eisenhower in London two days later. It was slightly amended by the Chief of Staff before being sent off and is a good example of Marshall's method of dealing with his top general.

8 July 1944

WDGAP210 1WAC
Memorandum for General Eisenhower

Colonel Lee has indicated to us your desire to have Mrs. Summersby appointed a first lieutenant in the Women's Army Corps. Our first reaction to any request of this nature from you is to approve it without hesitation. But in this particular case the proposed action will put us in such a difficult position that I feel obliged to lay the facts before you before any final decision is reached.

The statute establishing the Women's Army Corps as a part of the Army limits enlistment to citizens of the United States. Thus we cannot take a noncitizen as an enlisted WAC and put her through the WAC OCS [officer candidate school] in the normal manner. Strangely enough, by a peculiar twist of language in the law, we can, relying on a rather hair-splitting legal technicality, appoint a noncitizen as a commissioned officer in the Women's Army Corps and actually this has been done in two very special cases. As a matter of principle, however, I do feel that we are somewhat bound by the law to restrict the Women's Army Corps to citizens only.

The officer situation within the Women's Army Corps is such that we have now cut the Officer Candidate School to a total of fifty in each class, which means that the opportunity to acquire commissioned grade is practically closed to the vast majority of enlisted women who have worked their way up and would otherwise merit consideration for promotion. We have, since the Corps was organized, adhered rigidly to the principle of requiring graduation from the OCS as a preliminary to officer appointments. By this method we have avoided any charge of favoritism or partiality (which is, unfortunately, more likely to be made when we are dealing with the opposite sex than in the normal case of the enlisted man) and we have maintained a fairly high officer standard in the Corps. In adhering to this policy we have refused many requests, both from high commanders inside the Army and from influential persons outside the Army, to appoint civilian women directly as officers and to appoint enlisted women as officers without sending them to the School.

Now came the punch lines:

If we now make the appointment you desire, we will be in the position of giving a noncitizen, not a member of the Corps, treatment that we have steadfastly refused to equally deserving women in the Corps. There are many hundred WACs there in England to whom this appointment would immediately become known. They would know that although they are denied appointment and denied opportunity to go to Officer Candidate School, a British woman, not a member of the Corps, could become a first lieutenant overnight. They would not understand the reasons for the appointment, nor would it be possible to explain to them the justification for the appointment. I need not elaborate on the inevitable reaction nor to explain that we would have had to go to Congressmen and others here in the States, and to commanders in the Army whose recommendations for the direct appointment of enlisted women have been disapproved.

So far as [this department] is concerned, we have attempted to approve every request from you which could conceivably be granted, and I am not at all sure that General Marshall would support me in even hesitating to grant this seemingly small request. Yet it could prove so embarrassing, not only to me, but to the Chief of Staff and to you, that I am reluctant to take any action without giving you the whole picture. If, in spite of these considerations, you feel that the matter is of such importance that we should ignore them all, I will, without further hesitation, recommend that the appointment be made.

[signed] M. G. White,
Major General, Asst. Chief of Staff

The memorandum was delivered to General Eisenhower in London on July 11, 1944, and there was some apprehension, at least in General White's department, as they waited for Ike's reaction. Five days passed. Then, on July 16 the reply came:

From SHAEF in London England. To War Department No. SVC4768 16 July 1944

For General Stoner Signed Eisenhower: Please pass following to General White in G1 Division:

HAVE READ YOUR MEMORANDUM TO ME OF JULY 8 ON SUBJECT OF WAC COMMISSION. NOW UNDERSTAND DIFFICULTIES AND POSSI-

BLE EMBARRASSMENT WHICH I FORMERLY DID NOT REALIZE. PLEASE
DROP THE MATTER. THANK YOU SINCERELY FOR YOUR CONSIDER-
ATION AND TROUBLE. [signed] EISENHOWER.

General White breathed a sigh of relief. That little problem
had been nicely and quietly dealt with.

But General Marshall wasn't quite as confident. From what
Frank McCarthy had told him about her, Kay Summersby was
not only a very beautiful but also an extremely determined young
woman. McCarthy passed over to him a letter which had just
come in by courier. It read:

> Dear Colonel McCarthy,
>
> I just want to express to you again my deep appreciation for
> the courtesy you extended to me during my stay in the U.S. I had
> a most enjoyable visit and was greatly impressed with everything
> I saw. Many thanks again.
>
> Sincerely,
> Kay Summersby

It was not exactly the missive of a woman who had just had
the door slammed in her face. Both Marshall and his assistant had
the feeling that they would be hearing from her again.

14

Thwarted

It was 1943. The tide of war had at last begun running against the Axis powers. In Russia the Red armies had smashed German resistance at Stalingrad and forced the surrender of the Nazi garrison there. The whole of Africa had been cleared of the enemy by the combined Anglo-American forces, and that formidable German general Erwin Rommel, whose Afrika Korps had been leaning against the gates of Cairo at the beginning of the year, was now back in Germany, explaining his defeat to Hitler, while his vaunted Nazi troopers languished in Allied prison cages.

The Allies had already got a toehold in Nazi-occupied Europe by landing in Italy and pushing up the peninsula toward Rome. But when the Allied planners and the general public thought about getting back into Europe, they were thinking not of the Mediterranean, but of France, the Low Countries of Holland and Belgium, and Germany itself. Not until the Anglo-American armies crossed the English Channel and stepped on the shores of Nazi-occupied France would the counterattack and the drive for final victory really have begun.

Once Marshall had hoped it would take place in 1942, and then he planned for a landing in the summer of 1943. Simple logistics had prevented the first, and the apprehensions of the British had sabotaged the second. But now this was the eve of 1944—and in 1944, Marshall and his planners were determined, the Channel would be crossed, the great struggle with the enemy begun, and the campaign to drive the Nazis out of Europe forever finally engaged.

General Marshall was not alone in presuming that he would be the Supreme Commander of the Allied armies when their combined forces at last invaded the Nazis' European stronghold. It

251

had been generally accepted by Americans and British alike that he was the only man for the job.

It is true that there had been a time when the British, though continuing to shudder at the bloody prospect, had assumed that once the invasion became inevitable, it would be one of their own generals who would be chosen to lead the troops into the inevitable slaughter. They envisioned General Bernard Montgomery—the victor of Alamein—or Field Marshal Sir Alan Brooke—the Chief of the Imperial General Staff—as the leader who would command the liberators of occupied Europe. And if the operation had taken place in 1942 or even 1943, as Marshall had planned, that might have been so; the British would have had the majority of trained troops available for the operation and could therefore have insisted that to them belonged the privilege of commanding the invading armies.

Thanks to Marshall's organizational genius, however, a vast force of trained men had been turned out by the Americans, and men and matériel had been crossing the Atlantic from the United States to the United Kingdom as regularly as ferry boats to Staten Island, despite the packs of Nazi U-boats harrying them during their passage. Britain was now practically sinking beneath the weight of GI's waiting to take part in the invasion of Europe. In the circumstances, Churchill had no option but to agree with Roosevelt that no one but an American general would be appropriate to command such a preponderantly American force. He accepted that fact with good grace and assured the President that the British would be proud to serve under an American general.

Provided, that is, the name of that general was George C. Marshall, for whom the British now had solid affection and in whom they had more faith than many of their own military leaders.

Word had got around in Britain that General Marshall, though a loyal American, was prepared to make sacrifices for an ally when the emergency was dire enough. He had proved it the year before when one of the main British bastions in the Middle East, Tobruk, had fallen to the Nazis. Britain's hold over Egypt and the Suez Canal were threatened, and matériel was desperately needed. But these were early days for the Americans, too, and their divisions were only just gearing up for action. Churchill, in Washington to confer with Roosevelt, pleaded with him for armaments to save the situation, and the President summoned Marshall. He told him the Allies were in trouble and desperately needed some Sherman tanks. Marshall said, "Mr. President, those tanks have just been issued to the First Armored Division, and it is a terrible thing to take a weapon out of a soldier's hands. But if the British need is so great that they must have them, then they shall have a hundred—right away."

It helped stem the next German attack and saved Egypt, and the British had not forgotten.

They were not the only ones who now trusted Marshall. By the autumn of 1943 not even the President himself was more admired by the American people, in the forces and out of them. U.S. troops and airmen were now seeing action on six different fronts throughout the world, and the canvas on which the war was being painted was huge; yet chaos, confusion, and, often, disaster were avoided because Marshall back in Washington was in firm control, a master of the needs and priorities of every force under his command.

There was a move in the country, and some backing in Congress, to have him nominated for the Democratic ticket in the 1944 presidential election since Roosevelt had not by that time intimated that he would be running for an unprecedented fourth term. Marshall quickly scotched that, insisting that he was not and never would be a political soldier. Thereupon a movement began in the House to have him named to the highest rank ever awarded in the U.S. Army, that of field marshal. Roosevelt indicated his approval, and a bill was introduced into Congress. But Marshall discouraged that one, too, on the publicly stated grounds that it would sound silly if he were henceforward known as Field Marshal Marshall. In private, however, he confided he was really against it because it would make him higher in rank than the man he considered really America's greatest soldier, General John J. Pershing, still alive though bedridden in the Walter Reed Hospital. He did not want the old man's standing damaged or feelings hurt.

In one of his popular radio broadcasts, Eric Sevareid applauded the decision to abandon the bill. "The organization, training and equipment of this great force of freedom," he declared, "with the fact that it is the healthiest, best clothed, best fed and best paid army in the world is [*sic*] not the result of chance. It stands as a monument to the genius, indomitable energy, almost superhuman foresight and leadership of George Marshall. This soldier needs no field marshal's baton."

But Marshall did want the supreme command when the invasion of Europe was launched, and he was delighted when the Allied leaders, meeting at a conference in Quebec in the fall of 1943, mutually agreed that he would be their choice. The President made no immediate announcement. Instead, when he came back from Quebec, he announced that Marshall's appointment as Chief of Staff, which was due to expire on September 1, 1943, would be indefinitely prolonged. But word soon leaked out that General Dwight D. Eisenhower would soon be coming back to Washington to take over as Chief of Staff, and Marshall would be leaving for London to prepare for the invasion.

There was general approval, except in one surprising quarter. Black Jack Pershing, no less, objected to the appointment and wrote to the President to tell him so. His letter from Walter Reed, dated September 16, 1943, read in part:

> I am so deeply disturbed by the repeated newspaper reports that General Marshall is to be transferred to a tactical command in England, that I am writing to express my fervent hope that these reports are unfounded.
>
> We are engaged in a global war of which the end is still far distant, and for the wise strategical guidance of which we need our most accomplished officer as Chief of Staff. I voice the consensus of informed military opinion in saying that officer is General Marshall. To transfer him to a tactical command in a limited area, no matter how seemingly important, is to deprive ourselves of the benefit of his outstanding strategical ability and experience. I know of no one at all comparable to replace him as Chief of Staff.
>
> I have written this, Mr. President, because of my deep con-

viction that the suggested transfer of General Marshall would be a fundamental and very grave error in our military policy.

Roosevelt had a great admiration for Pershing and put tremendous store in his military wisdom, and the letter alarmed him. After some thought he wrote back on September 20:

> You are absolutely right about George Marshall—and yet, I think, you are wrong too! He is, as you say, far and away the most valuable man as Chief of Staff. But, as you know, the operations for which we are considering him are the biggest that we will conduct in this war. And when the time comes it will not be a mere limited area proposition, but I think the command will include the whole European theater—and, in addition to that, the British want him to sit with their own Joint Staff in all matters that do not pertain to purely British island affairs. More than that, I think it is only fair to give George a chance in the field—and because of the nature of the job we shall still have the benefit of his strategical ability.
>
> The best way I can express it is to tell you that I want George to be the Pershing of the Second World War—and he cannot be that if we keep him here. I know you will understand.
>
> As ever yours,
> Franklin D. Roosevelt

Pershing did not reply to the President's letter. Nor did he tell Marshall about what he had written, and the Chief of Staff learned about it later.

One senior member of the government who was particularly delighted to know Marshall would be commanding Overlord (code name for the invasion) when the time came was the secretary of war, Henry L. Stimson. He even feared there would be no invasion at all unless Marshall handled it. He had had several talks with Churchill recently, in Washington, London, and Quebec, and had come to the conclusion that the British leader was still doing his damnedest to avoid a cross-Channel operation, preferring to switch the main thrust of the Allied attack into the Mediterranean and what he called "the soft underbelly of Europe." As he told General Tom Handy, Marshall's chief of operations, Churchill would "slide from under" if he could find the right excuse.

"Churchill was against it all the time," Handy said later. "Mr. Stimson told us after one of his trips over there that Churchill talked an awful lot about WW One and the British losses. You couldn't blame him or any Englishman because England had really lost their [*sic*] seed corn. All this about the end of the British Empire started right there. And the losses were just god-awful. And Churchill had gone through that. He painted this horrible picture to Mr. Stimson about a Channel full of corpses and the beaches flowing with blood. That sort of thing. Well, old man Stimson told him, 'Now look, you and I are getting to be old men. We've been up against a lot of propositions, some of them very difficult. You and I know that if you really intend to do a thing, dammit, you don't talk about beaches running with blood or a Channel full of corpses. There are gonna be plenty of corpses and plenty of blood, but you don't talk about it if you intend to do it. And you know it's going to happen, and I know it.'

"Churchill was always bucking about it. But of course, we realized his position. If we in the United States had had losses in WW One comparable to those of the French in comparison to our population, we would have lost more men than we had in the whole of our army. We weren't in it all that long. Whether we would have taken it as well as the French did, as well as the British did, I don't know. Of course, it was in their backyard, not ours. But when you think of it on that basis, you can realize the reason for Churchill's deep-seated feelings."

Handy added, "Of course, Churchill, on the other hand, when he wanted to do something, he could be the most optimistic guy in the world."

Stimson believed that Marshall would instill in him that feeling of optimism. He was certain he was the only possible choice.

But Admiral Ernest King wasn't by any means as sure. His relationship with General Marshall was as frosty as ever, and it hadn't been helped by a contretemps during the summer over an Army leak of an invaluable Navy secret. The Navy had shot down a Japanese plane carrying Admiral Isoroku Yamamoto, commander of the Imperial Japanese Navy, thanks to U.S. ability to intercept and read the enemy code giving the time and destination of the flight. When the news of Yamamoto's death was announced in Tokyo, rumors that it was not just a lucky chance—that we were reading the enemy's codes—had somehow spread around Washington.

Ernie King had hit the ceiling when he learned that the Japanese, alerted by U.S. newspaper articles, had changed their naval codes and that the person believed to be responsible for the leak was no less than Major General Alexander M. Patch, just in from the Pacific. It seemed that Patch had been the guest of a Washington luncheon party given by *National Geographic* magazine at the time when news of Yamamoto's death came in. According to a fellow guest, "Patch's face immediately brightened, and he said he had been waiting anxiously for this announcement. He then stated that it was he who had issued the order which resulted in Yamamoto's death" and went on to reveal that the United States had had prior notice that a Japanese "bigwig" would be on a plane following a certain route on a certain date. The fellow guest had indignantly telephoned the Navy Department to complain about such dangerous tattling.

The result was a frigid note from King to Marshall in which he stated:

FROM ADMIRAL KING by messenger.
Memo for General Marshall
1. The Japanese have recently changed one of their naval codes which we had broken. The code in question has been most useful to us, and the loss of the information we have been getting from it is a very serious matter.
2. We obtained our knowledge of the Yamamoto affair from this code. As you know, rumors about that incident have leaked out. I am concerned lest there would be some connection between the rumors and the change of code.
3. In the course of investigating the source of the leakage, the statement attached [about the luncheon party conversation] was obtained. I have hesitated to do anything about it since it involved

an officer of high rank who has well earned the admiration of the Navy as well as the Army, but I have come to the conclusion that the security of radio intelligence is of such overwhelming importance that I would be derelict in my duty if I failed to bring the matter to your attention. Some additional aspects of the leakage of information about this code have been brought to the attention of General [Sir Kenneth] Strong [British intelligence chief] in connection with security control activities.

4. I am taking drastic steps to tighten up security in the Navy with respect of radio intelligence. If the Japanese become aware of what we are doing, they can adopt codes that will completely baffle us. I am sure you will agree that we cannot afford to let this happen.

5. In view of the specially secret nature of this matter, I am not retaining copies of this correspondence.

(Signed)

E. J. King*

Marshall was alarmed over the leak and considerably embarrassed that one of his generals should be blamed for it. Patch was an old colleague and friend, and he admired him both as a man and as a first-class soldier. Clearly Admiral King wanted some action taken and was rumored to be telling his subordinates he was waiting for the arrest and court-martial of "that Army loudmouth."

Meantime, Patch, perhaps from shock, had collapsed and been rushed with pneumonia to Fort Lewis Hospital, where he was seriously ill and forbidden visitors. What should the Chief of Staff do about him? After forty-eight hours of deep cogitation he decided that he was damned if he was going to lose a good officer just because Admiral King was demanding his head. As for a court-martial, he noted: "Disciplinary action in this case in a corps commander inevitably involves publicity which would make matters worse. Without publicity the deterrent effect on others, which is desired, would be lacking."

In the end he decided that Patch had been punished enough and had undoubtedly learned his lesson. He informed King that instead of being court-martialed, Patch would be reprimanded as

*June 23, 1943.

soon as he came out of the hospital and then posted immediately to a combat command in Europe.*

King was angry when he heard that Patch was getting off "scotch free," [sic] and he sulked over Marshall's softhearted approach to his military colleagues. But he was a realist, and he knew a good Chief of Staff when he saw one at work, and he knew that if Marshall became Supreme Commander in Europe, his replacement might be even more difficult to deal with. At least he knew that Marshall was a straightforward and honest man.

He had already expressed doubts about moving Marshall out of Washington when the question came up during the Quebec Conference earlier in the year. In November 1943, when the Americans set off for Cairo and Teheran for more conferences—with the British, Chinese, and the Russians this time—his objections solidified, and he made up his mind to do everything in his power to prevent Marshall from getting the Supreme Commander's job.

It had taken months of careful diplomacy, but Joseph Stalin, the Russian leader, had finally agreed to meet his American and British opposite numbers for a planning session for what everyone hoped would be the final campaigns of the war in Europe and subsequent strategy for defeating Japan. It had been a difficult task persuading Stalin to leave Soviet territory. He had refused to meet in Greece, in the Bering Strait, in Basra, Iraq, but had finally agreed to come to Teheran, capital of Iran, where he felt he could be adequately protected. Both before and after talking with him, the Anglo-Americans had decided to talk in Cairo, and Roosevelt had also invited the Chinese leader, Chiang Kai-shek, to be present at one of the sessions.

President Roosevelt was in no physical condition to fly, so he and the Joint Chiefs sailed out of Hampton Roads aboard the battleship *Iowa* and crossed the Atlantic, passed through the Strait of Gibraltar, and landed at Mers-el-Kebir, in Algeria. There they

*He commanded the U.S. Seventh Army in the invasion of Southern France.

were met by General Eisenhower and Admiral of the Fleet Sir Andrew Cunningham, the British naval chief, who flew with them to Tunis. Eisenhower had arranged for Marshall and King to stay together at a seaside house at La Marsa, near Carthage, and assigned to them his car and its uniformed driver, a willowy young Englishwoman called Mrs. Summersby. Stopping by the house that evening, Eisenhower heard for certain what had until then only been a rumor—that Marshall would be named Supreme Commander when the invasion of Europe, Overlord, took place. It was King who informed him, adding, to Marshall's embarrassment, that he thought the appointment was a mistake, since changing the Chief of Staff at this moment in the war could have serious consequences. As if to mollify both his listeners, King added that Eisenhower was probably the only soldier in the U.S. Army who might be able to take Marshall's place; but all the same, he and the other Joint Chiefs thought it all wrong, and he hadn't given up the idea of persuading the President to change his mind.

Later that evening the President also broached the subject with Eisenhower. He said he was fearful of what could happen to global operations if Marshall was replaced, that he dreaded losing him, but that he thought he owed it to him to give a chance in the field.

"Ike," Roosevelt said, "you and I know who was Chief of Staff during the last years of the Civil War,* but practically no one else knows, although the names of the field generals—Grant, of course, and Lee, and Jackson, Sherman, Sheridan, and others— every schoolboy knows them. I hate to think that fifty years from now practically nobody will know who George Marshall was. That is one of the reasons why I want George to have the big command—he is entitled to establish his place in history as a great general."

Eisenhower, who knew that it was he who would lose out if Marshall were picked, said nothing. The President and Joint Chiefs left two days later for Cairo, and when Eisenhower saluted Marshall as he climbed aboard his plane, he imagined he was saying

*Henry W. Halleck.

good-bye to his own hopes and acknowledging the future Supreme
Commander in Europe.

So did Marshall.

The British and the Americans had some gritty encounters
during World War II, but none more abrasive than their meeting
at Cairo in November 1943. It was an American general in WWI,
Fox Conner, who once said, "If you want to have a decent war,
first thing you do is get rid of your allies." There were soldiers
and statesmen, both British and American, who echoed his words
as they clashed over plans during their meetings in the Mena House,
a hotel outside the Egyptian capital. Through the hotel windows
they could see the brooding shapes of the Pyramids of Giza and
catch an occasional glimpse of the enigmatic expression on the
face of the Sphinx, but nothing soothed their sense of frustration
and irritation with each other.

General Joseph W. Stilwell, who commanded Sino-American
troops in the Chinese theater, had flown into Cairo with the
Kuomintang leader, Chiang Kai-shek, and his slim, beautiful wife,
Mei-Ling. Stilwell was a rabid hater of the British and became
angry with the way they deliberately diminished the importance
of the Chinese effort.

"It was wonderful the way we slapped the limeys down," he
said afterward. "Brooke got nasty, and King got good and sore.
King almost climbed over the table at Brooke. God, he was mad.
I wished he had socked him."

Marshall was mad, too, at Brooke, because of the supercilious way in which he tried to denigrate the Chinese side of the
war and shy away from any suggestion that British troops should
help. King had proposed that the British should launch an operation out of Burma code-named Buccaneer to aid the Chinese and
purpled at Brooke's cold rejection of it. Marshall also became
frigidly angry at the curt British reaction, and observers wondered
why. He must have known that it was strategically impossible for
the British to carry it out and at the same time fulfill their military
obligations in Europe. Had he, perhaps, been influenced by the
perfervid support of the proposal by the Chinese leader's wife,

Madame Chiang Kai-shek? At one meeting with the Chinese delegation at Mena House, he had happened to remark that he hoped "we will all be able to get together on this matter." The ravishing Mei Ling had thereupon leaned forward, put a slim hand on Marshall's knee, looking directly into his eyes, and said, "General, you and I can get together anytime."

He was a sucker for beautiful and intelligent women, and Madame Chiang could do no wrong from that time on. He resented it when the British treated her, and the Chinese, lightly.

But undoubtedly what caused him most unease was British antipathy toward Overlord and their preference for Mediterranean operations. Marshall admired Winston Churchill more than most men in the world, but at Cairo he had his first stand-up row with him. While the Americans itched to hit the German armies in northwestern Europe, the prime minister still dreamed of a two-way push into the Balkans, one through Italy, where Allied troops were now fighting, and the other through Greece and Turkey. He did not spell it out since he no doubt thought Marshall would be unsympathetic, but implied was his fear of their mutual Soviet ally; he still hoped that Anglo-American troops would be in Rumania, Hungary, and Austria before the Russian armies got there, and it was beginning to loom larger in his mind than a cross-Channel defeat of the Germans.

An invaluable stepping-stone into the Balkans, Churchill believed, would be the Greek island of Rhodes, close to the Turkish mainland, now occupied by Nazi troops and their air force. He would like to see a combined Anglo-American operation launched against it, and when the Chief of Staff demurred, he deliberately egged on his service chiefs to approve it and urge Marshall to go along.

"All the British were against me," Marshall recalled later. "It got hotter and hotter. Finally, Churchill grabbed his lapels, his spit curls hung down, and he said, 'His Majesty's government can't have its troops standing idle. Muskets must flame,' and more rhetoric like that. I said, 'God forbid if I should try to dictate but . . . not one American soldier is going to die on [that] goddamned beach.'"

The British officers looked horrified that anyone could speak so harshly to their leader, and Churchill himself seemed hurt and sullen for the rest of the evening. But it was the last the Chief of Staff heard about Rhodes.

The Cairo talks adjourned while the Anglo-Americans moved on to Teheran, the Iranian capital, where meetings had been scheduled with Joseph Stalin and the Soviet Army chiefs. It was the moment when British dominance over the Americans during these wartime discussions was finally ended and was never really felt again. J. Edgar Hoover, head of the FBI, claimed to have heard that German spies were active in Teheran, some of them dressed in American uniforms, and that a Nazi commando raid, also by troops in U.S. uniforms, had been threatened. As a result, security regulations were strict. The U.S. Embassy was out of the inner city, and Roosevelt was urged to stay with Winston Churchill in the walled British Embassy. Instead, he moved into the even more thickly walled and more heavily guarded Soviet Embassy, down the road, where Churchill could not get at him for those late-night talks which had previously so significantly affected war strategy.

The result was that the Americans drifted away from the British viewpoint and closer to that of Joseph Stalin. Marshall met the Russian leader for the first time and liked him, thinking of him as a rather lovable, if dangerous, bear. Stalin responded by making it plain he admired Marshall as a soldier and was convinced he should command the Allied forces when the second front was opened in northwestern Europe. He was all for Overlord's happening as soon as possible in 1944 and also for another proposal which the Americans had put forward, a simultaneous landing by Allied troops in southern France. To this the British were adamantly opposed since it would take away landing craft and men and matériel from the Italian front and end any possibility of operations in the Balkans—which was, of course, why Stalin was all for it.

"I found the generalissimo a very astute negotiator," Marshall said later. "He had a dry wit. He was agreeable, and in regard to me he made a sort of semiaffectionate gesture. When we were in opposition, he would stand with his hands on my shoulders. He was arguing for an immediate second front. . . . He recognized the great effort then was to get us to do these things."

The President and Marshall were all in favor, and they had no qualms whatsoever when Stalin and his Soviet advisers ridiculed British timidity over the second front and firmly blocked any suggestions they made for operations elsewhere, particularly in the Balkans. The President, in fact, took a certain masochistic pleasure in seeing Churchill mocked and harried by the Soviet dictator.

"[Stalin] was turning the hose on Churchill all the time," Marshall said later, "and Mr. Roosevelt, in a sense, was helping him. He used to take a little delight in [watching Stalin] embarrassing Churchill. . . . Stalin was very free in probing Churchill but did not follow this course at all with Mr. Roosevelt."

So it seemed all fixed. The Anglo-Americans moved back to Cairo, and General Marshall told his assistant Frank McCarthy to be ready to fly directly from Egypt to England because it looked as if they would be starting Overlord preparations at once.

But then suddenly Roosevelt changed his mind. There is little doubt that if the Chief of Staff had gone to him directly and asked him for the appointment as Supreme Commander, Roosevelt would have given it to him. He knew quite well it was the job Marshall wanted above all others, the fulfillment of his career, and he would not have been able to deny it to him. On the other hand, he was beginning to realize what Washington would be like without Marshall there to exercise his magical influence on Congress and the committees and what the global war would be like without his cool, calm, rocklike figure to lean on when the big military crises came up, as they inevitably would.

Moreover, he had just received shocking news from his aide Harry Hopkins. Until now he had presumed that if Marshall did go to Europe, General Eisenhower would take his place, and though he might not be up to Marshall's standard, he had proved himself a reliable military leader and administrator. But now Ike's chief of staff, General Walter Bedell Smith, was in the nation's capital and broadly hinting to Hopkins that Eisenhower did not want all the hassle of the Chief of Staff's job but would rather be given an army group and stay and fight in Europe under Marshall's command.

Whom else could the President get to replace Marshall? All the rest were hopeless.

So he was not prepared to give Marshall what he wanted unless he asked. And that Marshall was too proud to do.

"I was determined that I should not embarrass the President one way or the other," he said later, "that he must be able to deal in this matter with a perfectly free hand in whatever he felt was [our] best interests. . . . I was utterly sincere in the desire to avoid what had happened so much in other wars—the consideration of the feelings of the individual rather than the good of the country."

Toward the end of the resumed Cairo meeting, he was called to the President's villa at Mena House to "finalize" the choice of the Supreme Commander.

"After a good deal of beating about the bush," he said later, "[Mr. Roosevelt] asked me just what I wanted to do. Evidently it was left up to me."

It was the moment when Marshall realized that he could have the job of Supreme Commander for the asking. The President was making it plain that he was leaving it up to him. And never in the history of U.S. military politics had a President taken a more calculated risk. It was a supreme example of Roosevelt's masterly skill as both a politician and a President, knowing full well that if Marshall was tempted by his attitude and prepared to take on the European job, he had a crisis on his hands. For who could possibly take Marshall's place as head of America's global military effort and conduct it so well?

But of course, Roosevelt knew the quality of the man he was tempting. *I know what this means to you,* he was indicating to his Chief of Staff. *This is what you have always dreamed about, the apotheosis of your career, the command that will write your name in the halls of fame as the most famous soldier of them all. Take it. You only have to ask.*

The two men were alone. No one heard the silent words, noted the pauses and hesitations, or glimpsed the expressions on the faces of President and Chief of Staff as the decision was made.

All we have are Marshall's own words of description of how it went.

"I just repeated again," he said later, "in as convincing language as I could that I wanted him [the President] to feel free to act in whatever he felt was the best interest of the country and to his satisfaction and not in any way to consider my feelings. I would cheerfully go whatever way he wanted me to go, and I didn't express any desire one way or the other."

Did he realize that with those words he had played directly into the President's hands and that Roosevelt's calculated risk had succeeded? Probably. Time and again in his career, Marshall had been aware that a little flattery here, a little bootlicking there might have eased his path to the top, but so far as his own personal promotion was concerned, he had never used his influence. Pride and principle always held him back. As Chief of Staff, on behalf of the United States Army and his country, he had often wheeled and dealt with Congress, with senators, with the President himself. But on his own behalf, he had never cut a corner and he never would. It would have offended his own pride in himself, his *amour propre*.

So though he was almost certainly aware of Roosevelt's subterfuge in making him ask for the Supreme Commander's job, well knowing he would refuse to do so, Marshall was not about to complain. He would never beg a favor of anyone, not even the President of the United States—not for himself anyway.

Therefore the dream of his lifetime never came to pass, and the job passed to Dwight Eisenhower instead. And all he said afterward was: "Then [the President] evidently assumed that concluded the affair and I would not command in Europe."

And, breathing a sigh of relief, Roosevelt added, "Well, I didn't feel I could sleep at ease if you were out of Washington."

What does a man do when his lifelong ambition is shattered? In Marshall's case, he took it on the chin. The next morning, at the end of a Chiefs of Staff meeting, he wrote out a telegram for Joseph Stalin in Moscow and took it to the President for a signature. It read: "THE IMMEDIATE APPOINTMENT OF GENERAL EISEN-HOWER TO COMMAND OF OVERLORD OPERATION HAS BEEN DECIDED ON."

After the cable was sent off, the Chief of Staff retrieved the original and wrote a message on it, in pencil, to the new Supreme Commander: "Dear Eisenhower: I thought you might like to have this as a memento. It was written very hurriedly by me as the final meeting broke up yesterday, the President signing it immediately. G.C.M."

Then, and only then, did he give any sign of pique. Without saying a word to the President, he disappeared from Cairo and vanished into limbo. It was not until several hours later, after he had asked for him several times and been fobbed off with excuses, that FDR was told that his Chief of Staff, accompanied by General Tom Handy and Colonel Frank McCarthy, had taken off in an Air Force plane and was flying back to Washington by way of Ceylon, Australia, and the Pacific.

The President never commented on Marshall's sudden decision. Nor did Marshall. His companions were his two closest collaborators, but never once did he mention to either of them how he felt about not being chosen as Supremo. In fact, the subject did not come up at all. But Frank McCarthy sensed his chief's deep and abiding disappointment and guessed the extent of the anguish he must be feeling from the fact that he had decided to take this sudden trip around the world.

He knew that originally Marshall had intended to go home by way of Italy, stopping off there to visit his favorite stepson, Allen, who was fighting in the muddy olive groves north of Naples. His abrupt change of plans meant that he was never to see Allen alive again. His trip to Italy did not take place until the following year, when he went to see the exact place where his stepson had in the meantime been killed.

15

Perfidious Allies

General Marshall came back to Washington from his around-the-world trip to find the newsstands plastered with his photograph. He was on the cover of *Time* magazine for January 3, 1944, as its Man of the Year and hailed by it as "trustee for the nation" and "the indispensable man."

"In general's uniform," *Time* wrote of him, "he stood for the civilian substance of this democratic society. *Civis Americanus,* he had gained the world's undivided respect. In the name of the soldiers who had died, General George Catlett Marshall was entitled to accept his own nation's gratitude."

It was easy for anyone visiting the Pentagon to understand why the President had decided he couldn't do without General Marshall. It was unlikely that any other man could have handled all the demands which the Chief of Staff's office now made upon its holder. In size, in complexity, in the gravity and complication of its daily problems, it had grown astonishingly since Marshall had first taken over in 1939. There were 3,000 officers and men now working directly for him, keeping him in hourly touch with how the war was going, how the Allies were feeling, what the enemy was planning, what the President was thinking, how Congress would vote.

Marshall had always been a dedicated delegator of duties, who believed in picking the best man or woman for a job and then letting him or her get on with it. If those subordinates were good, he occasionally rewarded them with a grunt of appreciation. If they failed, he would throw them out without a moment's hesitation. But the astounding thing was that he kept in touch with every operation his delegates were overseeing. He made it his daily duty to know everything they knew—hence his dictum that anyone on his staff, but *anyone*, could walk right into his office if he had anything to tell him.

He suffered fools badly and couldn't stand people who came before him and stuttered or postured and didn't get to the point. But he listened. He listened to everything that was told him, and his sure control of all the activities reported to his department— from an obscure raid on an island outpost in the Marianas to the latest report from the Ultra intercepts—enabled him to keep a heavy, palpitating, often frenetically busy organization under smooth, efficient control.

"Marshall never had a clique or gang," said his Deputy Chief of Staff, General Tom Handy. "One could work and argue with him. As long as you did your job, everything was all right. He could be rough when he wanted to be. He could raise hell, and he could freeze you. But he could listen for long periods when he was being briefed, and it was astounding how much he could remember, even the little things. He once came back from a session before a congressional committee on the Hill, when he had been asked some prickly and meticulous questions on minor but complicated matters. He had reeled off the answers with ease and authority. I asked him how on earth he had remembered all the details. 'I picked them up over a number of weeks from the briefing officers,' he said."

He hated people who didn't want a precise account to be kept of exactly what had been said, and this was where President Roosevelt annoyed him. As a military man he wanted an accurate record kept of exactly what was said each time he went to report, or attend a conference, at the White House.

"It was very difficult to deal with the President under these conditions," Marshall said later. "Mr. Roosevelt didn't want things on the record. He didn't want a recorder. I brought up [General John R.] Deane once to keep some notes. He brought along a big notebook, and the President blew up. Next time Deane brought along a book so little he couldn't use it."

From 1943 onward, after his early aides like Eisenhower, Mark Clark, Walter Bedell Smith and John R. Deane had gone off to foreign battlefields, Marshall staffed his office with reserve officers or officers who had been wounded in action. General Tom Handy, who was a rock of Gibraltar in an emergency, was his right-hand man, but he relied upon two younger officers to keep his machine running smoothly. One was the ex-film man and newsman named Colonel Frank McCarthy, and the other, his assistant, Major H. Merrill Pasco. It so happened that both were Virginians and both graduates of VMI, although Marshall had not known that at the time. To a certain extent, they acted as talent scouts for the Chief of Staff's office, picking out bright and promising young officers to come in and work in the organization for a year or two years, before being sent on to the battlefronts. They were to expect no favors because they had been on Marshall's staff. When he released one of them for service in Italy, he sent a typical letter to the commander to whom the ex-aide was being attached, General Jacob "Jake" Devers:

> I want him attached to a United States division in the line in Italy, not as a liaison or observer but a member on duty with artillery. What I want is to give him the experience in fighting as a final step to offset his long service to me here in this office. Thereafter he is on his own. You can keep him or we will assign him to a division training in the United States.

It was these bright young men who organized the briefing sessions at Marshall's headquarters which became his pride and joy and the envy of American and Allied commanders at headquarters throughout the world. Every morning authorized personnel could walk into Marshall's conference room and get a graphic—yet accurate—picture of exactly what was happening in every operational zone in which the United States was involved. It began promptly at 9:00 A.M.

"We had gradually," Marshall recalled later, "gotten to a point where the presentation of the world picture was of great importance to me and the principal staff—because we had so many different theaters operating at once and along with that the stormy time with things at home. We had available artists of some talent and plenty of them, so we gradually formed the morning show on the basis of presentation by young men who were chosen for their ability to speak in an attractive manner. They got up at four o'clock in the morning and worked on the cables of the night before—and were ready for the presentation at nine o'clock."

The charts had been set up five minutes before, the team bustling around Marshall's desk no matter how hard he was working or whom he was seeing.

"It just went off like a theatrical thing," he said. "They became very expert at it, and it was really a thrilling presentation. You saw the whole war up to the last minute—done in such a way that it was easy, in a sense, to comprehend."

When, later on, Marshall went to a briefing at Eisenhower's headquarters in London, he was appalled at the ham-handed way in which it was handled and ordered General Walter Bedell Smith, who was in charge, back to Washington "to see how it really should be done."

Marshall's greatest triumph with his daily briefing technique came when General MacArthur, who was asking the impossible from Washington as usual, sent back one of his staff, Colonel Philip La Follette,* to demand more supplies. Halfway through his message the briefing team came in, set up their charts, and presently began. La Follette was invited to stay and sat popeyed, listening to the world survey.

When it was over, instead of continuing with his master's peremptory message, he saluted the Chief of Staff and departed, a thoughtful look on his face. Marshall did not hear from him again until he met him after the war.

"And he asked me," Marshall recalled, " 'Did you keep me back there purposely to see that [briefing]?' Because he changed his whole state of mind the moment he saw the enormity of what was going on and what our [global] requirements were. . . . He began to see the picture in the light of real circumstances. . . . If those fellows could see what the [world situation] was like, they would understand more the impossibility of many things they were talking about."

*Later governor of Wisconsin.

Considering the burdens of his day, Marshall kept extraordinarily fit and unruffled. Except when he was traveling, he never went late to bed, and he saw his wife, Katherine, at least for an evening meal, which she had waiting for him when he got home.

His day began at 6:00 A.M. when he went down to feed the chickens which he raised in the run behind Quarters One at Fort Myer—they provided eggs for the house—after which he rode along the Potomac bridle path and through Arlington Cemetery, sometimes accompanied by his stepdaughter, Molly Winn, or by his goddaughter, Rose Page, if either happened to be staying in the house. Then he came back to a breakfast cooked by Staff Sergeant William Farr, who had once worked in the kitchens of a hotel in Savannah, Georgia. During this time he glanced through the first of the nine newspapers he read every morning.

At one time he had been driven around by a single orderly, Sergeant James W. Powder, but when the Army began to recruit women for the services, he added a WAC driver, Sergeant Marjorie Payne, the pretty blond daughter of a Michigan truck driver, who had once worked as a cosmetician and never looked ruffled. She delivered him to the office by seven forty-five each morning and brought him home at five-thirty each afternoon.

In between, he read reports, wrote memorandums, heard briefings, received visitors, testified before Congress, went to see the President, and made the big decisions that affected the direction of the war. He was constantly scribbling comments or instructions in pencil on the edge of office memorandums. He wrote in his own hand most of the papers which the President subsequently read to Congress about the progress of the war. He had three competent women secretaries to screen the visitors who streamed into his office, and control the flow of paper across his desk, and see to it that not a note or a letter was left to be answered at the end of the day.

"He had a fetish for a clean desk," said one of them, Mona Nason. "He liked it cleared up by five every afternoon."

The only time he stayed late and kept the secretaries waiting for him was, in fact, during the Cairo Conference, when he came out of a long day of strategical discussions to find a note for him from Washington about the exemption from the draft of a famous athlete. He was a baseball catcher who had been put on limited duty because he had broken two fingers in the course of his career. Marshall, his face flushed with rage, kept his assistants on duty while he found out from the States who else had been exempted. He was appalled when he got the list and cabled an urgent memorandum to his office:

> I fear a serious scandal in this matter if this action was taken by Army doctors. It is ridiculous from my point of view to place on limited service a man who can catch, with his broken fingers, a fast ball. If he can't handle a machine gun, I am no soldier. What I have in mind is to check up on these particular cases, having the Inspector General go into the matter with the doctors concerned, to see if we are guilty of a serious dereliction. If the rejections were carried out by local boards, that is another matter, but if an Army officer on active duty is a participant, then we are responsible and I don't want any damn nonsense about this thing. I have seen dozens of men with half a dozen serious complaints in addition to their years passed by their Army doctors—and now to find great athletes, football and baseball, exempted is not to be tolerated.

It hardly seemed a matter that the Chief of Staff of the United States Army should have been worrying about when he was in the middle of discussing the future course of the war. But to him it was just as important as military strategy since, when the news got around, it would demonstrate to the fighting troops that no one got favored, neither the Chief of Staff's own stepsons nor the pampered heroes of sport.

The friendship and working relationship between General Marshall and Sir John Dill, the British liaison officer in Washington, had become so close by 1944 that they no longer had any secrets from each other. Marshall had given Dill a copy of his own private code for use in communicating with him when he was out of town or out of the country. He had also put Dill's name on the highly restricted list (there were no more than a dozen names) of those who were allowed to read the daily Magic intercepts of secret Japanese code messages. Dill, in return, turned over to Marshall all the confidential summaries of decisions made in London by the Imperial General Staff, an invaluable insight into the ways in which British military minds were going.

If either man had been indiscreet, they could have shattered Anglo-American relations—and some private ones, too. But they had become adept at handling each other's hot potatoes and took care to see that neither they nor anyone else got burned.

So far as Marshall was concerned, one of Dill's most useful functions was his ability to let him have information not only about British military thinking but also of the way in which President Roosevelt's mind was working.

"I hate to say it," General Tom Handy remarked later, "but I think it is true that our military people were at a marked disadvantage compared with the British. You see, Mr. Churchill was not only the prime minister, but also he was minister of defense, and, as you know, he was in intimate touch with his staff officers at all hours of the day and night. And he was vitally interested. But the prime minister of England is not the same as the President of the United States. You don't just casually see the President—it isn't that kind of thing. The British knew what was on Churchill's mind. We didn't know what was on the President's. So at times the only way we could find out what the prime minister and the President were up to was through Sir John."

There was another way in which Dill helped Marshall, and that was in letting him know whenever the British staff chiefs were trying to deceive him over some operation or military project and when they were serious.

"The British chiefs were the tops of their services," Handy said, "and if they felt a certain way or believed a certain thing, you paid a hell of a lot of attention to it. You might not accept it, but you gave it a lot of weight. But what our people were up against was whether what the British were telling us really represented their best military opinion or whether it was something they'd been dragged into by the prime minister. That was where Sir John was just wonderful. Of course, everybody liked him, and the British chiefs paid a lot of attention to him. Because he also reported on us, of course. He opposed certain things we favored.

But he also opposed certain things the British favored. And boy, when we got an opinion from Sir John, we knew it was Sir John's and not the prime minister's."

It was through Dill that a particularly nasty little Anglo-American crisis which might otherwise have led to Marshall's resignation was solved in the summer of 1943. It concerned the appointment of a supreme commander for the so-called South East Asia Command, the headquarters of which were in Kandy, Ceylon, and the operational area of which included India, Burma, Indochina, and the frontiers of China itself. It had been accepted among the Allies that this was a British bailiwick since it included large tracts of the Indian Empire and was manned by mainly British, Indian, and Burmese troops—though there were American and Chinese troops there, too—and that thus, its commander should be a Briton. Churchill wanted a prestigious figure who was not a soldier but would symbolize the all-service nature of the command, and he therefore nominated one of the heroes of the air battles over Britain in 1940, Air Marshal Sir Sholto Douglas. Dill sent a confidential note to Marshall about it before the official announcement was made.

From the Chief of Staff's point of view, a more unsuitable name could not have been chosen. In his private file he had a dossier on Sholto Douglas, and fine airman he might be, but as a human being he was a loudmouthed anti-American entirely unsuitable for the position of command over mixed troops. He picked up the telephone and expressed his strong objections to the appointment to Dill and suggested that London should choose someone else. Dill dutifully reported that Marshall had "somehow" heard about Sholto's appointment and was all against it, and couldn't they change their minds? London replied that Sholto was a particular favorite of the prime minister's and that he had already sent on the name to the President. Anyway, what did it matter if Sholto was anti-American?

"If we can stomach Stilwell, surely they can stomach Sholto Douglas," retorted the British, stiffly.

Simultaneously there was a message from the White House that Roosevelt had accepted Sholto Douglas's appointment. At that point Marshall really hit the roof. He sent a message in their private code to Dill, who was in San Francisco, and let him know that he was ready to resign if Douglas got the job. He *would not*—repeat *would not*—have a man so virulently anti-American in command of American troops, and he was going to take a stand on it.

Dill thereupon demonstrated how closely the two men could work together in an emergency. Instead of alerting his own office in Washington, he telephoned Marshall directly and dictated to him the telegram he proposed sending to his chiefs in London. After securing Marshall's approval of it, he then asked the Chief of Staff if he would telephone it through to the British liaison office and instruct the officer in charge to dispatch it to London. This the Chief of Staff did. The telegram read as follows:

> HAVE HAD TALK WITH MARSHALL REFERENCE YOUR TELEGRAM OF JULY 10 FOR MY EYE ONLY REGARDING SHOLTO DOUGLAS. REGARDING STILWELL THE POINT IS THAT HE IS NOT REQUIRED OR EXPECTED TO COMMAND OTHER THAN U.S. AND CHINESE TROOPS WHEREAS SHOLTO DOUGLAS IS PROPOSED TO COMMAND U.S. AND CHINESE TROOPS AS WELL AS BRITISH TROOPS.
>
> MARSHALL STATED THAT THE ISSUE ON THIS SIDE IS NOT THE MILITARY QUALIFICATION OF DOUGLAS BUT RATHER HIS CAPACITY FOR SUCCESSFUL COMMAND OF AMERICAN UNITS. MARSHALL STATED THAT ON MORE THAN ONE OCCASION DOUGLAS HAD SPOKEN IN DEROGATORY TERMS OF U.S. UNITS AND OPERATIONS. SOME OF THESE REMARKS, ON AT LEAST ONE OCCASION, ALMOST LED TO A PHYSICAL ENCOUNTER. THE MORE MARSHALL LOOKS INTO THE MATTER THE LESS HE LIKES THE PROPOSAL. IS IT NOT POSSIBLE THAT IN VIEW OF THIS PERSONAL PHASE OF THE MATTER REGARDING WHICH FEELING HERE IS VERY STRONG SOME OTHER NAME, [Air Chief Marshal Sir Arthur] TEDDER'S FOR EXAMPLE, SHOULD BE PROPOSED?

Dill did not mention the fact that Marshall was prepared to resign on the issue to his military chiefs in London, but he did drop the news among friends at the White House. The President urgently telephoned Churchill. The prime minister, who considered one Marshall in Washington worth a hundred Sholto Douglases in Southeast Asia, immediately canceled his nomination of the xenophobic airman from his list and substituted a name he was sure would be welcomed by the U.S. Chief of Staff.

That name was not Tedder, but Admiral Lord Louis Mountbatten, who was known to be so pro-American that U.S. Ambassador John Winant, asked to an early-morning meeting in London, had once been lectured by his host on the pioneer virtues of Little Orphan Annie while being served breakfast food. No GI was ever going to be insulted by him.

But Churchill had a blind eye so far as Dill's diplomatic virtues were concerned, and he never truly appreciated the field marshal's services on behalf of Britain in wartime Washington. In fact, at one period in 1944, the prime minister thought it was about time Dill was brought back to Britain and someone more persuasive was substituted for him. When Marshall heard this, he was alarmed. It was almost as disastrous, in his view, as alerting the Japanese that the Americans were reading their codes. If Dill was replaced, his conduit into the labyrinthine corridors of the Churchillian mind would be cut off, and he would be forced to start all over again. Desperate to save Dill, and not just because he was his friend, he sought for means of preventing his recall and finally hit on a solution. Through academic subordinates in his office, he canvassed first Harvard and then Yale to give Dill an honorary degree. Yale agreed and penciled in a ceremony for February 16, 1944, when the field marshal would be given a doctorate.

For one of the few times in his life Marshall actively sought publicity. He brought a host of dignitaries, including the secretary of war, to New Haven for the ceremony, accompanied by a flock of reporters and photographers, and willingly posed for pictures with the field marshal. He made sure that British correspondents were invited, too, to listen to the encomiums of praise poured on the blushing head of "this great Englishman, this architect of Anglo-American understanding," Sir John Dill.

It worked, too. When Churchill read the stories and saw the pictures, he murmured to his staff that "Dill really seems to have hit it off with the Americans"—and confirmed him in his job. Marshall had hated every moment of it, because he genuinely disliked being in the limelight, but concluded that it had all been worthwhile. His pipeline to 10 Downing Street had been saved. His close collaboration with the field marshal continued, and their friendship became warmer than ever.

There was, unfortunately, no Dill to come between the White House and General de Gaulle, and relations between the President and the Free French leader had become malodorously bad by the time the invasion of France loomed in 1944.

No one, not even Marshall, had discovered a way of dealing with the haughty and ultrasensitive Frenchman. Tact and infinite patience were needed, and neither the Chief of Staff nor the President felt they had the time; constant needling from De Gaulle's minions had thickened their skins, and they now could be downright blunt and insulting in the way they treated the Free French leader. For instance, it was on Marshall's instructions that Eisenhower, while still in North Africa, had told the local French military authorities that they would be denied arms, equipment, and money if they continued to agitate for recognition of De Gaulle as their commander. Marshall learned no lesson from the fact that a large number of officers and men nevertheless refused to succumb to such pressure and went on supporting him. Churchill had his "Frog File," in which he kept all the bad news about De Gaulle; Marshall and Roosevelt referred to him as "our prima donna"; and all three believed that if they just kept making it plain that they considered him an upstart and a boor, he would finally go away, and a more polished Frenchman who knew his status in the world—which was that of a poor relation—would eventually take his place.

President Roosevelt had no intention whatsoever of allowing De Gaulle to take any part in the Overlord operation when it was finally launched across the English Channel. Nor did he intend to tell him or the Free French anything about it in advance. He was convinced that they could not be trusted with Allied secrets. He knew that both the Americans and the British were reading the Free French code and presumed the Germans probably were doing so, too, and he was certainly not proposing to warn De Gaulle about this since he would immediately have the code changed and thus prevent his allies from finding out what he was up to.

In any case, he did not believe that Gaullism or the Free French had any real support in metropolitan France and shuddered at the prospect of their starting political quarrels and impeding Eisenhower's progress once the Allied push into France began. On the other hand, Marshall reminded the President that De Gaulle had solid support among the American and British public, and it was therefore vital that he should not be publicly rebuffed. What policy was Eisenhower to adopt toward the Free French once the landings were consolidated? How was he to deal with the different factions?

The question came up when Ike flew into the United States at the beginning of the year on Marshall's orders. The Chief of Staff wanted him to have a good rest before he began the countdown to the invasion and was particularly anxious to reunite him with his wife and family since the first rumors were beginning to reach him about Ike's entanglement with his English driver, Kay Summersby. It would be a good opportunity to mend some domestic fences and build some political ones at the same time.

In a memorandum to the President, Marshall said:

> I had brought him home, over his strenuous objections, to force him to take a brief rest before he undertakes his heavy obligations in England. He was to have left Washington the evening of the day he arrived, but bad weather intervened and he was delayed until the next evening when he went up to see his son at West Point. He goes on to see his mother. He will then take a few days with Mrs. Eisenhower in a cottage at the White Sulphur Springs Hospital,* after which he is to come back to Washington.
>
> As you have been confined to your room [with flu] and it was desired to get General Eisenhower out of town as quickly as possible, to avoid publicity, I did not bring up the matter of seeing you. On his return to the city, I should like to have you give him an appointment. . . .

---

*It had been requisitioned by the Army and was, and is, better known as the Greenbrier Hotel.

Ike and Marshall were smuggled into the White House ten days later, and a general discussion took place about both military and political affairs connected with Overlord. It appears that Eisenhower came away convinced that in no circumstances was he to have anything to do with the Free French, not even after the Allied armies had firmly established themselves in France and some sort of civilian authority had been set up to run the country. In a memorandum which he subsequently sent back to Marshall about civil government in France, he seemed to take it for granted that the President would not accept De Gaulle or a Free French regime under any circumstances and that the Frenchman was anathema to him. Marshall passed the memorandum on to the White House without comment.

On June 2, 1944, Marshall got ready to fly to Britain. D-Day for the invasion was seventy-two hours away* and he wanted to be there. Just before he left, a note arrived for him from the White House. The President wrote:

> When you get over there, tell General Eisenhower that I have read his memorandum to you but that I still think he does not quite get the point. He evidently believes the fool newspaper stories that I am anti-de Gaulle, even the kind of story that says that I hate him, etc. etc. All this, of course, is utter nonsense. I am perfectly willing to have de Gaulle made President, or Emperor, or King or anything else so long as the action comes in an untrammeled and unforced way from the French people themselves.
>
> But it is possible in an election so to influence it, so to restrict the vote, so even to count the vote, that the people in power can swing it overwhelmingly their way. . . .
>
> I want Eisenhower to do what we have done in Italy—i.e., have a British and American representative go to the community and talk with a number of leading citizens, such as the curé, the doctor, the avocat, the leading merchants, some leading farmers and see who should be installed, if any. . . .

Roosevelt maintained that most of the officials in Vichy France

*D-Day was originally slated for June 5, 1944. Owing to bad weather, it was postponed to the following day.

were not pro-Vichy at all and had kept their noses out of politics. The President went on:

> I do not agree when Ike says that there are only two major groups in France today—the Vichy gang, and the other character-ized by unreasoning admiration for de Gaulle. I wonder how he knows this because nobody else knows anything really about the international situation in France. Most of the people who get out come out with the help of the [Free] French National Committee, and they are rightly grateful. Tell Ike that it is my thought, based on talks with many people who have come out of France recently, that he has overlooked the biggest group of all—bigger than the Vichy group and bigger than the de Gaulle group. It consists of the people who do not know what it is all about. . . . Probably most of them like the symbol of de Gaulle and his early actions in 1940, but they have not made up their minds as to whether they want de Gaulle and his Committee as their rulers.

He then came to the crux of his message:

> It is awfully easy to be for de Gaulle and to cheer the thought of recognizing that Committee as the provisional government of France, but I have a moral duty that transcends "the easy way." It is to see to it that the people of France have nothing foisted on them by outside powers. It must be a French choice—and that means as far as possible forty million people. Self-determination is not a word of expediency. It carries with it a very deep principle in human affairs.
>
> As a matter of practical fact, Ike has plenty of time because for some time every square kilometer under his control will be part of a military zone. I count on his good judgment in case Germany collapses or in case he can move his armies towards Germany at the rate of ten miles a day.
>
> Good luck to him. We shall be thinking much of him and his problems.
>
> F.D.R.

Winston Churchill grinned when he read the message.

"Well put," he said. "Let the voice of democracy be heard—even in France!" And then he added, sotto voce, "And pray heaven it doesn't speak for De Gaulle!"

If Marshall had cherished any doubts about the snubbing of De Gaulle during Overlord, they were laid to rest by an incident which occurred shortly after the invasion began, in June 1944. When the Free French leader heard about the landings in Normandy and realized that the Free French would not be recognized as an official part of them, he did his damnedest to be as obstructive as possible. He sabotaged the transfer of a number of specially trained French liaison officers. He sent secret messages to France warning the people not to accept the money the Allied troops brought ashore, but to treat it as counterfeit. And when, at last, the Allies invited him to send a senior officer across to France, he demanded that his representative should be taken over in a battleship, no less, and accorded the full honors of an acting head of government. When the envoy, who happened to be the governor-general of New Caledonia and a strong Free French supporter, presented the demands to Marshall, the Chief of Staff displayed considerable irritation.

"It was the way he *demanded* these things," said General Tom Handy. "I always thought General de Gaulle was a pain in the neck and this guy was a pain in the neck, too. He *demanded* we furnish him with a capital ship to go to France in. Well, General Marshall was said never to lose control of himself, and I don't think he did; but believe me, he could open up and shoot with both barrels. And he did to this guy. He shot the paint off the walls. But he didn't get his ship. He went in a landing craft, like the rest of us."

It was not the only display of temper from Marshall during the Overlord operation. A few nights later, while dining at Chequers with the prime minister and Anthony Eden, the British foreign secretary, he discovered that General de Gaulle and the Free French had at least one friend in the British Cabinet. Eden hotly defended them and argued vehemently that they should be recognized at once as the legitimate government of France. Churchill was all against it but could not seem to make any headway against his colleague's passionate arguments. Marshall listened with growing anger, for he had just come back from Normandy and had seen for himself how De Gaulle's obstructive tactics were making dif-

ficulties for the troops. He had already been on the telephone to
Secretary Stimson in Washington to complain that De Gaulle was
playing with fire and that "as soon as the American people learned
that the cause which their boys were dying for was being ob-
structed by the French, there would be a tremendous explosive
reaction against the French themselves."

Normally he would never have interfered in a political argument between a British premier and one of his ministers, but
now he could not contain himself. As Secretary Stimson later recounted the incident, "Marshall broke loose. He said he couldn't
talk politics, but he said he knew more about the Army and he
knew more about the people of the United States than Eden did
and that if Eden went on in this way and the things that had
happened from De Gaulle's course came out in the press in full,
how he had attacked our money and how he had refused to send
over men who had been trained for the very purpose of helping
us in the invasion, it would make a wave of indignation in the
United States which would swamp the whole damn British Foreign
Office."

In tone and in content it was a most unusual outburst to
come from Marshall, who was normally the most respectful of
men with politicians. For once, in a way, he had failed to do his
homework and did not realize what position Anthony Eden played
in British public life, that he was not just foreign secretary (which
was important enough), but the logical successor to Churchill if
anything happened to him, as well as leader of the House of Commons and one of the most popular figures in Britain. He was also
extremely sensitive and was shattered by rudeness—and Marshall
had been downright rude. Leaping to his feet, Eden swept out of
the room, leaving Marshall looking after him in stupefaction and
Churchill with an expression on his face of fond concern. Eden
did not come back.

Later Marshall regretted his outspokenness. "I am ashamed
to say that I was ignorant of his leadership in Parliament," he
said. "I didn't appreciate him at his full value. We had some
difficult scenes, especially over De Gaulle."

But it never did occur to him that if he (and, of course, his political bosses) had paid more attention to Eden, the future of Franco-American relations might have been considerably less stormy, and postwar Europe much more secure. Tom Handy remarked later that he simply regarded De Gaulle as "an ungrateful son of a bitch," since, to quote Handy, "we gave him everything, including a pillow on which to lay his head." He added that Marshall always believed De Gaulle acted in the way he did because he resented the fact that he and the French owed so much to the Allies.

"If you want a man to be for you," the Chief of Staff had once told Handy, "never let him feel he is dependent on you. Because he is then not going to like you at all. If you really want the guy to be for you, find some way to make him feel you are in some way dependent on him."

But of course, in De Gaulle's case, both he and the President were far too proud to do that.

Pride, national pride, was soon affecting Anglo-American relations, too.

In spite of the Free French blocking tactics, the D-Day invasion was successful and the Allied troops swarmed ashore in Normandy and secured solid bridgeheads all the way from the Cherbourg peninsula to the old cathedral city of Caen. But back home in the United States, President Roosevelt was far from satisfied with the political results of the invasion. He had a presidential election coming up in the autumn of 1944, when he would be running for a fourth term, and so far neither he nor the Americans were getting their fair share of the credit for the success of the cross-Channel operations. For security reasons, details of which troops had landed where had been deleted by the censors, and the only name to make its way into the headlines was that of the Allied commander on the spot.

This was General Bernard L. Montgomery, and he was, of course, British. Soon the dispatches from the battlefront began to give the distinct impression that this was a largely British operation. One operation in which no British troops were involved at all was headlined MONTGOMERY'S FORCES DRIVE ON CHERBOURG.

Soon people all over the United States began asking where the American Army was and, particularly, what had happened to Ike.

Eisenhower, in fact, was still operating out of his main headquarters in England, where his lines of communication were and where he could keep control over all phases of the battle, on land, on sea, and in the air. He planned to stay there, too, until the Allied armies pushed well inland and established themselves. And that might have been all right if Montgomery had not turned out to be such a publicity hound. Even when General Omar Bradley arrived in France to take over command of U.S. forces, the censors concealed this fact, and Monty's name continued to make the headlines, causing the Washington *Times-Herald* to make the caustic comment "It is generally recognized in congressional circles and common gossip in military circles that General Eisenhower is merely a figurehead, and the actual command of the invasion is in the hands of the British General Staff and the British dominate the American War Department and Army."

This came at a moment when the casualty lists were coming in, showing that out of 21,000 dead in the first six weeks of the campaign, 14,000 were American. The President began complaining to Marshall that Montgomery was hogging all the credit and that the sooner Ike moved across the Channel and took over personal command, the better for public (and Anglo-American) relations. Marshall cabled SHAEF and told Ike to get moving. Ike protested it wasn't possible yet, that the lines of communication just weren't there. But then, as if to rub American noses in the Normandy dust, Churchill announced that General Montgomery would be rewarded for the superb military qualities which had now made him "a household word." As of September 1, 1944, he would be promoted to field marshal, making him superior in rank to all other officers, British or American—including Ike.*

"Tell Ike to get over there," came the message to Marshall from the White House, and the Chief of Staff reluctantly sent the necessary instructions.

"We felt it was important for General Eisenhower to appear

---

*And, incidentally, General Marshall.

in closer control of the troops," he said later, "because of the buildup in the press and otherwise in this country—and, apparently, as I recall, in Great Britain—that General Eisenhower wasn't in the show and Montgomery was the sole, dominant figure. So we thought for political reasons it was important that General Eisenhower should get himself established in Normandy."

Tactically it was a disastrous move. The telephone lines just weren't there. For three whole days Eisenhower and his staff milled around in confusion, trying to keep up with the battles, attempting to control the huge amount of supplies coming across the Channel, and endeavoring to coordinate the activities of the Allied bomber fleets operating along the front but out of England. During one forty-eight hour period, they were completely out of touch, leaving Monty more completely in control of the situation—and the publicity—than ever.

Then his minions got a grip on themselves and got their headquarters functioning, and Eisenhower took over at last.

It was now more than two years since Eisenhower and Montgomery had had their first, prickly encounter in England, and their positions on the military ladder had changed considerably in that time. On the occasion when Ike had been sharply told to put out his cigarette by a prim and angry Monty, he had been a lowly brigadier and the Briton had been two steps above him in rank. Today he was a five-star general, and although Montgomery flaunted a field marshal's baton, it was the American who gave the orders now.

It cannot be said that the two men had learned to love or respect each other in the interim. It is true that Ike had been impressed by Monty's considerable victory over Rommel's Afrika Korps at the Battle of El Alamein, and he had saluted the British Eighth Army's operations in Cyrenaica with genuine admiration. But thereafter his faith in the Briton's military genius had considerably diminished, from the moment, in fact, that Montgomery had come under his command. He found him slow, overcautious, and selfish. He "dawdled" on the Sicilian plain and missed a golden opportunity to gain a foothold in Italy by refusing to cross the Strait of Messina.

"Damn you, Monty," Ike had said, staring at the toe of Italy through his glasses. "There isn't a thing there. You can go over any time."

"Oh, no," said Montgomery, "we've got to be all prepared."

Eisenhower reported back to Marshall that in the opinion of his tacticians, Montgomery's procrastination had added weeks to the length of the Italian operation and cost the Allies thousands of lives. He now showed every evidence of doing the same in the battles in northwestern Europe.

Two of his principal objectives in the first wave of the invasion were the old cathedral city of Caen, which was a rail center, and the so-called Falaise Gap, strongly held by the Germans but, once captured, a gateway into northern France, the Low Countries—and Germany. He failed to get them both.

"He had to get Falaise instantly," said Eisenhower later, "because the high ground on the South was good for landing grounds. But he just couldn't take them. He never really did get them until we had broken out on the western flank and surrounded them. Yet do you know that that man tried to say the attack on Falaise went exactly as planned! He's one of those fellows who wants to make sure the world knows he's the greatest soldier that ever lived, and he never made a mistake."*

He added, "He was slow. He never did anything as quickly as anyone else did. And he was always bellyaching that he was being denied opportunities I was giving to other generals. . . . He's just obsessed with the idea of his own brilliance."

It was Marshall's job to keep relations running smoothly with America's allies, and he kept reminding Eisenhower that all generals were apt to be "a bunch of prima donnas" and never to forget that "Montgomery is about the only hero the British have

---

*Eisenhower could have added that Montgomery knew exactly what troops were in front of him because Ultra intercepts were giving him the exact dispositions and movements of the Germans in the Falaise pocket.

got." Therefore, don't knock him. Ike kept his temper until that disastrous moment, in the winter of 1944, when the Nazi armies started their desperate last attack against the Allies in the Ardennes in what became known as the Battle of the Bulge. American troops in the area were in danger of being split in two, thus threatening to separate the commanding officer from his fighting units; panic was liable to break out if someone did not take over quickly. With Marshall's approval, Eisenhower asked Montgomery to assume command of a combined Anglo-American forces for the first time since the early days of the invasion. Everyone crossed his fingers and prayed Monty would handle the job and do it without too much public crowing. It was too much to hope.

"I accepted [the appointment] as a very natural reaction on General Eisenhower's part," Marshall said later. "Afterwards I came to regret it because I didn't think Montgomery played at all square on the deal. He made use of it politically and through the press to General Eisenhower's . . . disadvantage."

Montgomery often refused to attend military conferences at Ike's headquarters to discuss the military situation but, instead, gave briefings on his own to war correspondents,* at which he posed as the sole general left who could handle the military situation, broadly hinting it was about time Eisenhower gave way and put a real soldier in supreme command.

"In this situation," said Marshall, "he allowed to build up—maybe assisted in building up, I don't know—a feeling that he was being put in charge there in the north because of his superior abilities. That was not so at all. It was a matter of communications."

He also became quite peremptory in his demands on Ike's headquarters, couching his requests for men and matériel in either-or terms which made the Supreme Commander first smolder and then burst into flames. In the wake of the crisis Montgomery's chief aide, a well-liked British general called Freddy de Guingand, arrived at SHAEF with a note from Monty which was even ruder

---

*Including the author.

in tone than usual. Ike read it, turned puce with anger, and said, "All right, Monty, this does it."

Eisenhower later described himself as being "just madder than hell." He reached for a scratch pad and began to scribble a message. To De Guingand, standing in front of him, nervously fingering his mustache, he said, "Freddy, this is a telegram I'm sending to Monty. I've had just about enough. He's going to do what I order from now on, or by God, the Chiefs of Staff are going to throw one of us out—and I don't think it will be me."

De Guingand said, "Ike, please! Don't send that telegram tonight. Keep it until tomorrow morning—give me time to get back to Monty so I can talk some sense into him."

The Supreme Commander finally promised to hold the message back until the following morning, and De Guingand scurried out of headquarters and off to the airfield, to report back to his master. It was a wild, snowy night in the bitter midwinter of 1944. All planes had been grounded, and all roads back to Brussels were blocked by ice and snow. In despair that he would not make it back in time, Monty's aide wandered around the airport messes, asking for volunteers. Finally, a young USAAF pilot took pity on him, and offered to fly him in his decrepit cargo-carrying DC-3.

"How in hell he got there I don't know to this day," Ike said later. "But he got there by two-thirty to three in the morning and went in at once to see his boss. I was awakened in the morning by a code message, one of those one-time pads, and it was the most abject apology from this guy you ever saw. 'I'm with you one hundred percent,' he [Monty] said. 'Just tell me what you want and I'll do it.' I tell you, the man was obsessed with proving himself before the British army and the world. And then he had the sauce later to say I was rough on him."

The crisis was over—for the moment anyway. De Guingand had given Montgomery the fright of his life by convincing him his military future had really been on the line in the Supremo's office the night before. But it was not long before Monty tried to wriggle into Eisenhower's shoes again.

Meanwhile, the chaos and confusion in the snow-clad hills of the Ardennes were finally sorted out, thanks to some first-class Anglo-American cooperation. The U.S. forces came back under their own commanders again,* and Monty went back to command his Twenty-first Army Group. The spotlight of the war switched away from the British in the direction of two U.S. generals, Omar Bradley and George Patton, as they drove into Germany in the final stages of the war against the Nazis.

While Eisenhower and Montgomery had been arguing, the willowy Mrs. Kay Summersby had been winning a battle of her own with the U.S. Army. Several months had passed since Ike's application for a commission in the WAC for his driver-secretary had been not so subtly rejected, and other matters, such as the war with Germany, had tended to put the matter out of his mind. But Mrs. Summersby had not forgotten. Nor had she lost her determination to get what she wanted, which, for the moment, was a first lieutenant's bars in the WAC. In the autumn of 1944 the senior WAC officer in the Chief of Staff's office, Lieutenant Colonel Florence T. Newsome, arrived in newly liberated Paris for a visit, accompanied by a delegation of U.S. congressmen. Ike delegated Mrs. Summersby to look after them, and she did a good job. It was not entirely coincidental that during the visit the Supremo's desire to see his driver-secretary get a commission came up, and neither Colonel Newsome nor the politicians could see any reason why she would not be an asset to the corps.

They took back a strong recommendation to Washington. In the circumstances, Marshall could have denied it, but chose not to.

On December 21, 1944, a letter arrived for Colonel Frank McCarthy from Supreme Headquarters, Allied Expeditionary Force, Office of the Supreme Commander, and it said:

> Dear Colonel McCarthy,
>   This is literally the first opportunity I have had to write and

---

*With the exception of the Ninth Army.

thank you for your trouble in securing me a commission in the WAC. I am most grateful. It was a real disappointment to me to give up driving, but my secretarial work has become so heavy that it takes up every moment of my time.

If you think it appropriate, I should like to ask you to give an expression of my thanks to General Marshall.

My best wishes for Christmas and the New Year.

Sincerely,

Kay Summersby

P.S. We were all very much taken with Colonel Newsome when she was here with the Congressional party.

She did not add "1st Lieutenant, WAC," to the end of her signature. But then, in this case, she did not need to.

16

The Bitter End

Tom Handy suspected there were moments when Roosevelt actively resented his Chief of Staff because he had more influence over certain people and got greater respect from them than the President.

"It's no use saying General Marshall was an easy man, because he wasn't," Handy said. "He could be extremely rigid. And his manner terrified young people. Some female members of his staff were scared to death of him. But he had terrific influence and power, especially over the British and the Congress. I think FDR envied him this. I think that the basis was that they knew, in Marshall's case, there was no underhanded or selfish motive. The British knew that he was not out to make American points or British points, but trying to win the war the best way. The Congress knew he was talking to them straight, with no politics involved."

At one point in the war Congress granted the Chief of Staff an allocation of $100 million to use for any purpose he wished, without having to account for it in detail to the House. It was, in fact, to be the initial financing of the plant for the building of the atomic bomb, which was still a highly secret project, but no one demanded that he be specific about it.

"In fact," said Handy, "he used the first million from that fund for an entirely different purpose. There was a French village which was wrongly bombed by us during the D-Day operations, and it was badly damaged, people killed. 'Just tell them you're sorry it happened,' Marshall told me, 'and give them a million dollars.' As it happened, the State Department refunded us that million later, but we just handed it over, and no questions asked. People had great confidence in him. The President didn't like it at all."

Eisenhower believed Marshall's success with both Congress and the people was, like his own, due to his resolute determination to eschew any part in political decisions. At one stage in the battles in Europe, Winston Churchill asked both the Chief of Staff and Ike not to go through with the plan to reinforce the Allied armies by landings in the south of France, which he considered unnecessary. Ike wanted to capture Marseilles as a supply port. Churchill preferred to use the troops and matériel to bolster the Allied armies in Italy and push northward through the Ljubljana Gap toward Vienna, arriving there before the Russian armies. But why? Why was he so frightened of the Russians? Eisenhower told the prime minister, "Winston, look, I know full well you fight wars for political purposes. If you can get the order through the Chief of Staff, then I can do this. But I am allowed to talk and think only in military terms. My directive is to defeat the German armies in the best way I can. I will not give up this. . . ." Eisenhower added, "We had a seven-hour argument."

To Marshall he wrote:

> I had a long conference with the Prime Minister and I must say his obvious reactions to latest decisions in the Mediterranean disturb me greatly. He seems to feel that the United States is taking the attitude of a big, strong and dominating partner rather than attempting to understand the viewpoint that he represents. His real distress comes about from our seeming indifference towards the Italian campaign, in which he feels there are tremendous potentialities . . . he still has strong hopes of reaching Trieste before Fall. So far as I can determine he attaches so much importance to the matter that failure in achieving this objective would represent a practical failure on his whole administration. I am not quite able to figure out why he attaches so much importance to this particular movement, but one thing is certain—I have never seen him so obviously stirred, upset, and even despondent. . . .

In fact, he understood quite well why the prime minister was distressed, but as he said later, "my job was not to make political policies." In later years he confessed that it was Marshall who had drilled him in the need to stay neutral. In the early days of the war, when he was still working in Washington, a Red Army emissary arrived and "began throwing his weight around." He demanded to be shown certain new weapons and restricted documents, and when Ike asked him why he wanted to see them, the Russian replied, "I don't think that is any of your business. We want them and that is that."

Ike had stormed into Marshall's office, told him what had happened, and said, "I recommend we throw the guy out. The hell with him."

The Chief of Staff had disagreed. "Our bosses believe that we've just got to keep Russia in the war," he said, "and therefore, we've got to handle them with kid gloves—or they'll do a France on us.* So treat with them. Do your best to get along with them."

Ike had been staying out of politics ever since and adhering strictly to the directive Marshall had given him: *Defeat the German armies.* True, his concentration on purely military affairs was now beginning to have some unfortunate consequences. Large numbers of Russian prisoners and slave laborers were, for instance, being liberated by the Anglo-American armies, and the orders from the politicians were that they should be sent back to Russia. But it seemed that thousands of them feared to go home. What should they do about that?

"I mean, we were supposed to send them back by force," Eisenhower said. In normal circumstances, he would have been outraged and, as a good American believing in freedom of choice, refused to abide by such an authoritarian edict. But he was traumatized by the knowledge that Russia was an ally, and Russia wanted the Russians back. "We didn't even think about it," he said, adding, "I forget how many suicides we had one night."

Marshall just did not want to get into politics, and he kept warning Eisenhower to stay away from them. Politics was the business of the arbiter in the White House. Leave it to him. The only way in which it impinged on his duties as Chief of Staff was in its effect upon the outcome of military operations, and so far as he was concerned, these were entering their most complicated

---

*He obviously feared they might make a separate peace with the Nazis, as the French had done.

phase. The drive to defeat the Nazis in Europe was going well, thanks not just to Anglo-American military efforts but to the magnificent achievements of the Red armies. But what was to happen once victory was achieved? Technically the Russians could then declare that it was all over as far as they were concerned. The enemy had been overcome. The victory had been won.

But for the Anglo-Americans, it was far from over. There was still Japan. They must then turn their efforts eastward and face the bloody struggles and losses in life involved in gouging the Japanese out of Malaya, Indonesia, the Philippines, and China, before defeating them in the Japanese islands. The Russians were under no obligation to help them in that gargantuan task. They were not at war with Japan. They could easily stand to one side and stanch their wounds while they watched the Anglo-Americans bleed and die in the Pacific.

It was important—or so everyone thought at the time—to persuade them that the comrades-in-arms who had fought against the Nazis in Europe should fight on ("shoulder to shoulder," as Roosevelt put it) against the Japanese in the Far East.

How could the Russians be persuaded unless, in Europe, the unity of Allied command was preserved and the needs and demands of the Soviets were observed and respected—even if, as in the case of the Russian prisoners of war, it meant the crushing of individual human rights? Anyway, it would all be straightened out at the forthcoming Allied conference in Yalta. Meanwhile, the Chief of Staff could remind himself and his commanders around the world that people were the concern of the politicians. It was the behavior of their allies in battle that soldiers needed to worry about.

It was not that Marshall was ever naive about his Russian allies. In fact, in the last stages of the war, he was well aware of the way in which their minds were working, though like many other Americans, he thought that Churchill was getting far too worked up about them. Shortly after the USSR and the United States had become involved in the war, he had sent one of his brightest young staff officers to Moscow to supplement Ambassador Averell Harriman's military advisers and also to act as head of the military liaison committee with the Soviets. The officer was Major General John R. Deane, and his job was to monitor the needs of the Red Army and, at the same time, keep Marshall in touch with Soviet plans and strategies. He had done a first-class job, ingratiating himself with the Red Army generals and securing some measure of confidence and trust of the Kremlin despite initial suspicion and stubborn opposition.

In the winter of 1944, when it seemed all but certain that the Germans were being defeated, and when plans for the Yalta Conference were being drawn up, Deane wrote to Marshall to give his boss a situation report on the political climate in Moscow. It is worth quoting at some length.

Moscow, 2 December, 1944

Dear General Marshall:

Now that I have been in Russia for some time and am qualified as an "expert," I think it might be of some interest to you to know my general reactions. They may be of value since I have served under you long enough to enable you to evaluate them. A report is always more useful if you know the reporter.

Everyone will agree on the importance of collaboration with Russia—now and in the future. It won't be worth a hoot, however, unless it is based on mutual respect and made to work both ways. I have sat at innumerable Russian banquets and become gradually nauseated by Russian food, vodka and protestations of friendship. Each person high in public life proposes a toast a little sweeter than the preceding one in Soviet-British-American friendship. It is amazing that these toasts go down past the tongues in the cheeks. After the banquets we send the Soviets another thousand airplanes, and they approve a visa that has been hanging fire for months. We then scratch our heads to see what other gifts we can send, and they scratch their heads to see what else they can ask for.

This picture may be overdrawn, but not much. When the Red Army was back on its heels, it was right for us to give them all possible assistance and no questions asked. It was right to bolster their morale in every way we could. However, they are no longer back on their heels; and, if there is one thing they have plenty of, it is self-confidence. The situation has changed but our policy has not. We still meet their requests to the limit of our ability, and they limit ours to the minimum that will keep us sweet.

The trouble with the Russians, Deane went on, was that they were just not interested in cooperation and wished to have as little to do with foreigners ("even Americans") as possible.

> We never make a request or proposal to the Soviets that is not viewed with suspicion. They simply cannot understand giving without taking, and as a result even our giving is viewed with suspicion. Gratitude cannot be banked in the Soviet Union. Each transaction is complete in itself without regard to past favors. The party of the second part is either a shrewd trader to be admired or a sucker to be despised. . . .
>
> Some will say the Red Army has won the war for us. I can swallow all of this but the last two words. In our dealings with the Soviet authorities, the U.S. Military Mission has made every approach that has been made. Our files are bulging with letters to the Soviets and devoid of letters from them. In short, we are in the position of being at the same time the givers and the supplicants. This is neither dignified nor healthy for U.S. prestige.
>
> The picture is not all bad. The individual Russian is a likeable person. Their racial characteristics are similar to ours. Individually I think they would be friendly if they dared to be—however, I have yet to see the inside of a Russian home. Officials dare not become too friendly to us, and others are persecuted for this offense. The Russians have done an amazing job for their own people—both in the war and in the prewar period. One cannot help but admire their war effort and the spirit with which it has been accomplished. We have few conflicting interests, and there is little reason why we should not be friendly, now and in the foreseeable future.

He believed it was necessary to revise the American attitude towards the Russians and felt it should be done on the following lines:

> 1. Continue to assist the Soviet Union, providing [*sic*] they request such assistance and we are satisfied that it contributes to winning the war.

2. Insist that they justify their needs for assistance in all cases where the need is not apparent to us. If they fail to do so, we should, in such cases, refuse assistance.

3. In all cases where our assistance does not contribute to the winning of the war, we should insist on a quid pro quo.

4. We should present proposals for collaboration that would be mutually beneficial, and then leave the next move to them.

5. When our proposals for collaboration are unanswered after a reasonable time, we should act as we think best and inform them of our action.

6. We should stop pushing ourselves on them and make the Soviet authorities come to us. We should be friendly and cooperative when they do so.

I think there is something here worth fighting for, and it is simply a question of the tactics to be employed. If the procedure I suggest above were to be followed, there would be a period in which our interests would suffer. However, I feel certain that we must be tougher if we are to gain their respect and be able to work with them in future.

Sincerely yours,
Deane

Marshall read the letter through with great interest and approbation and then passed it over to the secretary of war, Henry L. Stimson, who was most approving of its contents and urged the Chief of Staff to let the President see a copy of it without delay. It was shortly after Roosevelt's reelection for a fourth term, and he was known to be in a strange mood: mentally quirky, physically febrile. The last time Marshall had seen him, he came away worried at the change in Roosevelt's attitude toward his allies. The almost nightly telephone conversations with Winston Churchill in London no longer took place, and he had ceased to regard the British prime minister as his oracle. He made odd remarks, in a slightly sneering tone, about the British being interested only in the preservation of their empire and implied that only the Americans and the Russians were now fighting this war for the preservation of freedom.

How would he react to Deane's letter? After some thought

Marshall sent a memorandum back to Stimson on December 21, 1944:

> Before receiving your note suggesting that it might be a good thing to send Deane's letter to the President I had already considered this, and had in mind speaking to you about it after you had read the letter. Since receiving your note I have had Handy and [Lieutenant General John E.] Hull consider the matter and they both recommend against sending it to the President for the reason that they feel it might prejudice him against Deane, and also that it might irritate Mr. Harriman to find Deane's views were going direct to the President instead of through him.
>
> I agree with them, though I am sorry we can't send the letter to the President because his ideas are very well expressed and I agree with them in toto.
>
> GC Marshall

After he had sent this memorandum to the secretary, Marshall brooded over Deane's note. The more he studied it, the more he thought the President should see it. He spent Christmas Day with Katherine, his daughter-in-law, and his grandchildren at Dodona Manor, in Virginia, but he might just as well have not been there. He was preoccupied with military problems which were surfacing in all parts of the world, and in particular, the letter from Deane nagged at him. Back in the office, he sent a letter by special courier to Moscow (dated January 2, 1945) to ask Deane whether the ambassador had seen his missive and whether it would embarrass him if he sent it on to the President.

Deane cabled back the following day:

> The ambassador has seen my letter to you of 2 December. . . . He concurs fully in the thoughts and recommendations contained in the letter and believes that they apply with equal force to political matters. We both concur in the suggestion that the letter be shown to the President and the State Department. . . .

Good. Marshall sent it off at once to the White House. That was the last he heard of it.

"War in a democracy is no bed of roses," Marshall complained to Eisenhower in the spring of 1945.

He might have added that for a global chief of staff like himself, it got harder to handle the nearer it came to victory. Everywhere squabbles were breaking out, between the services, between the generals, between the public and the Army, and, most particularly, between the Allies. Marshall was afterward to say that the past year was the most strenuous and difficult time of his life, and there were times when his staff feared that the problems confronting him were so formidable that he would break in health before he solved them. When Eisenhower turned down the Chief of Staff's job in 1943 because of "all that hassle," he can have had little idea of how massively complicated the position had become.

In the Pacific, in China, in the Mediterranean, and in northwestern Europe, daily decisions, any one of which would normally need the whole of a working day to deal with, had to be made. MacArthur, fighting his way back toward the Philippines, bombarded the Chief of Staff with strident demands for more men and more matériel. Before sending them to him, Marshall had to persuade the Joint Chiefs that the Philippines was a legitimate military objective, since the U.S. Navy, which hated MacArthur, was determined to cheat him out of it. "I shall return," MacArthur had vowed to the Filipinos, but Admiral Ernie King had added, "Not until we're good and ready—after we've taken Tokyo." Moreover, even when the Navy was reluctantly brought around, there was a manpower shortage standing in the way of MacArthur's demand for extra troops. There were now more than 8 million young Americans serving in the armed forces, and the U.S. Senate, convinced that war was practically over, thought that was quite enough. In a play for the votes of doting mothers, they were opposing the drafting of seventeen-year-olds.

In the China theater, Marshall had been forced to sack his commanding officer, General Joseph W. Stilwell, not because he lacked brilliance as a soldier but because he was a xenophobic Yankee who despised foreigners and could not keep his mouth shut about them. He called his overall commander, Chiang Kai-shek, who was president of China, "a lily-livered Chink" and a "slant-eyed snake." The fact that the descriptions were not wholly inaccurate did not lessen the nature of his offense. Moreover, he quarreled with the British in Southeast Asia, too, referring to Lord Louis Mountbatten as "a limey mountebank" and "sometimes as dumb as that thick-headed cousin of his, the King." Marshall had done his best to intercede with both men to point out that Stilwell was a brilliant soldier when he was not putting his foot in his mouth. It was not just the fact that he liked Vinegar Joe (his nickname) personally that made him fight to keep him in his job; he earnestly believed that Stilwell was good for China and good for the war. He spent hours thinking up ways of saving him from his own folly, cabling him, in the case of his differences with Mountbatten:

> I SHOULD LIKE YOU TO SEEK AN IMMEDIATE PERSONAL INTER-
> VIEW WITH ADMIRAL MOUNTBATTEN AND TALK OVER THE WHOLE
> MATTER FRANKLY AND AT LENGTH REPEAT AT LENGTH AND SEE IF
> YOU CAN REACH A WORKING ACCORD WHICH IS ESSENTIAL BETWEEN
> TWO OFFICIALS IN THE POSITION YOU AND HE OCCUPY. THIS IS A
> MATTER OF GREAT IMPORTANCE NOT MERELY TO YOUR THEATER
> BUT IN ITS EFFECT ON COMBINED OPERATIONS ALL OVER THE WORLD
> WHICH DEPEND ON OUR RELATIONSHIP WITH THE BRITISH. I AM NOT
> CONSIDERING WHETHER HE AND YOU AGREE OR DISAGREE ON A CER-
> TAIN COURSE OF ACTION. ALL OF US DISAGREE WITH EACH OTHER
> FROM TIME TO TIME AND THERE ARE FEW DECISIONS WHICH ARE IN
> COMPLETE ACCORD WITH THE VARIOUS HIGH OFFICIALS' OPINIONS. I
> AM REFERRING TO A WORKING BASIS THAT IS NOT COMPLICATED BY
> SUSPICIONS AND A STIFFNESS THAT MAKES ALLIED PROCEDURE UN-
> WORKABLE.

But it was no use. News of Stilwell's undiplomatic behavior leaked into the press, and Marshall, who was implacably determined to maintain good relations with America's allies, felt he had no option but to bring him home. He replaced him with General Al Wedemeyer, who was no admirer of Chiang Kai-shek or the British himself but had learned the art of diplomacy with the passage of the years.

In every theater now there were troubles brewing, crises to be solved, differences to be smoothed over. There was, however, one element in which Marshall did not expect to find it necessary to involve himself, and that was in the presidential election of 1944. It had seemed to him from the start that Franklin D. Roosevelt was bound to be reelected, despite the fact that this would be his fourth term and he was really in no physical or psychological state to continue in office. But how were the people to know how frail he really was when his condition was concealed from them by the censor and by general agreement in the press—on the grounds that it would be detrimental to the Allied cause? No one really thought that the Republican candidate, Governor Thomas E. Dewey of New York, had a chance, with the possible exception of Dewey himself. But then his backers thought up a ploy calculated to damage Roosevelt where they believed he was also vulnerable, and that was over the disaster which had got them into the war in the first place, Pearl Harbor. A new report had just been written by a House investigating committee but not yet issued to the press, again on the ground that it might cause public despondency and undermine confidence in the direction of the war. Dewey was egged on by his advisers to take the questions raised by the report to the public and charge the President with dereliction of duty or worse on the eve of war.

Marshall was alerted and became alarmed at what secrets—particularly about codes—might become public property if the Pearl Harbor controversy were revived. But how could he shut Dewey's mouth without being accused of involving himself in domestic politics? He wrote later:

> It was decided that the only way this could be done was by some method which avoided any political implications, and that method appeared to be a communication direct from me to Governor Dewey with a frank statement of the situation and assurances that the President and the Cabinet were unaware of my action. To guard against the accidental disclosure of the information given Governor Dewey by letter, he was requested not to read the letter unless he would bind himself to secrecy.

The Chief of Staff sent a copy of the letter across to Ernie King with a memorandum which read:

September 25, 1944

MEMORANDUM FOR ADMIRAL KING:

Attached is the draft of a letter which I feel it advisable to send to Governor Dewey. It may be that you do not care to be involved in the matter and, if so, I can strike out the reference to you. In any event, I would like your opinion.

A recent speech in Congress had deadly indications and I now understand much more is to be said, possibly by Governor Dewey himself. This letter of course puts him on the spot, and I hate to do it but see no other way of avoiding what might well be a catastrophe to us.

Just what he can do in the matter without giving reasons I do not know, but at least he will understand what a deadly affair it really is. I had in the back of my mind the possibility, without telling him, that if he responds favorably I would secretly, here in my office, tell Republican Floor Leader [Joseph] Martin the dangers of the business so that he, on the Washington side of the fence, would understand something of Governor Dewey's attitude, without being informed that Governor Dewey had the same facts in his possession that I was giving Martin.

The whole thing is loaded with dynamite but I very much feel that something has to be done or the fat will be in the fire to our great loss in the Pacific, and possibly also in Europe.

GC Marshall
Chief of Staff

Admiral King, well aware that it would be the U.S. Navy's ships which would suffer most if the Japanese discovered their codes had been broken, hastened to back Marshall's plan to the hilt. Marshall thereupon called in a trusted messenger,* told him to don civilian clothes, and gain access to Dewey, who had a speaking date in Tulsa, Oklahoma. When the Republican candidate read the opening paragraph asking him to be bound to secrecy before reading the rest, he refused to proceed. Clarke came back, and Marshall wrote out another version of the letter and

---

*A Colonel Clarke in cryptographic intelligence.

instructed him to carry this one to Dewey at the Governor's Mansion in Albany, New York. It opened with these paragraphs:

My dear Governor:

Colonel Clarke, my messenger to you of yesterday, September 26 [1944], has reported the result of his delivery of my letter dated September 25th. As I understand him you (a) were unwilling to commit yourself to any agreement regarding "not communicating its contents to any other person" in view of the fact that you felt you already knew certain of the things probably referred to in the letter, as suggested to you by seeing the word "cryptograph," and (b) you would not feel that such a letter as this to a presidential candidate could have been addressed to you by an officer in my position without the knowledge of the President.

As to (a) above I am quite willing to have you read what comes hereafter with the understanding that you are bound not to communicate to any other person any portions on which you do not now have or later receive factual knowledge from some other source than myself. As to (b) above you have my word that neither the Secretary of War nor the President has any intimation *whatsoever* that such a letter has been addressed to you or that the preparation or sending of such a communication was being considered. I assure you that the only persons who saw or know of the existence of either this letter or my letter to you dated September 25th are Admiral King, seven key officers responsible for security of military communications, and my secretary who typed these letters. I am trying my best to make it plain to you that this letter is being addressed to you solely on my initiative, Admiral King having been consulted only after the letter was drafted, and I am persisting in the matter because the military hazards involved are so serious that I feel some action is necessary to protect the interests of our armed forces. . . .

He explained that he would have preferred to speak to Dewey personally but had failed to devise a method of avoiding press leaks and speculations over the reasons for such an encounter. Then he got down to the basic dilemma:

The vital element in the Pearl Harbor matter consists of our intercepts of the Japanese *diplomatic* communications. Over a period of years our cryptograph people analyzed the character of the machine the Japanese were using for encoding their *diplomatic* messages. Based on this a correspondent machine was built by us which deciphers their messages. Therefore, we possessed a wealth of information regarding their moves in the Pacific, which in turn was furnished the State Department—rather than as is popularly supposed, the State Department providing us with the information—but which unfortunately made no reference whatever to intentions towards Hawaii until the last message before December 7th, which did not reach our hands until the following day, December 8th.

He went on to point out that cracking the Japanese diplomatic code had enabled U.S. cryptographers to get hold of other codes, too, both Japanese and German, but though these were the codes involved in the Pearl Harbor events, they were still being used by the enemy. Reading them had helped put U.S. ships in the right place for the Battle of the Coral Sea, had enabled the Navy to block the Japanese advance on Midway, the landings in Attu and Kiska in the Aleutians. U.S. submarine actions largely resulted from the fact that the codes told the Americans the sailing dates and routes of Japanese convoys. He went on:

> The current raids by Admiral Halsey's carrier force on Japanese shipping in Manila Bay and elsewhere were largely based in timing on the known movements of Japanese convoys, two of which were caught, as anticipated, in his destructive attacks.
>
> You will understand from the foregoing the utterly tragic consequences if the present political debates regarding Pearl Harbor disclose to the enemy, German or Jap, any suspicion of the vital sources of information we possess. . . .
>
> I am presenting this matter to you in the hope that you will see your way clear to avoid the tragic results with which we are now threatened in the present political campaign. . . .

After reading the letter, Dewey picked up the telephone and called Marshall in Washington. He said that as the Republican party representative in the campaign he could not consider himself an individual and that he felt he had to let at least one of his trusted advisers read the letter. Marshall agreed. Dewey also refused to accede to a request from the Chief of Staff to return the letter after reading it, and insisted on retaining the copy for his files for "protection."

"I agreed to this," Marshall wrote later. "So far as I was concerned this closed the incident, Governor Dewey reading and keeping the letter. There was no further mention of Pearl Harbor, as I recall, during the campaign."

And of course, President Roosevelt romped home an easy winner over Dewey. But the Chief of Staff resented the time he had had to waste over "politics" in the midst of his intense military preoccupations, and he was irritated rather than amused when members of the White House staff, having heard rumors, subsequently chided him for dallying with the Republicans during the campaign.

In fact, his principal concern during the presidential elections had been not the fate of the candidates, but the physical condition of his British friend and collaborator, Field Marshal Sir John Dill. Dill had been taken ill a couple of times during the year, and following one of his bouts, Marshall had provided an airplane and they had flown together for a few days' rest in Bermuda as guests of the governor and his wife, Lord and Lady Burghley. The Chief of Staff had found it a particularly pleasant and invigorating break, especially since it introduced him to yet another beautiful, charming, and talented woman, Mary Burghley, of whom he was to become extremely fond. But if Marshall returned refreshed, Dill was not improved at all.

That summer the Chief of Staff sent his friend for treatment at the Army hospital at White Sulphur Springs, West Virginia, providing him with a cottage for himself and his wife, separate accommodation for his aide-de-camp, and posting his own trusted aide-cum-driver, Sergeant James W. Powder, to the hospital for use as a liaison. Dill continued to function from his hospital bed. Ironically, one of his last communications to Marshall was news of some secret successful experiments the British had concluded in biological warfare, including the invention of a substance for the destruction of crops and "a good deal of data which can be passed over straight away."* He envisioned it as being possibly effective against the Japanese.

Dill's condition continued to deteriorate, and he was brought back to Washington, where Marshall saw and spoke to him for the last time. He died a few hours later, on November 2, 1944. The next day Marshall issued an official announcement:

> The fact that Allied forces stand poised at the gates of Germany is due in no small measure to the breadth of vision and the selfless devotion of Field Marshal Sir John Dill to our common cause.
>
> I know of no man who has made a greater contribution to that most vital requirement of an Allied victory: complete military cooperation between the British and American forces. His death signals a loss of no less magnitude to the United States than for his own country. The direction of his matchless efforts towards combined victory gave him strength to lay aside all other considerations.
>
> I speak for all ranks of the Army in mourning a great soldier and military statesman one to whom both nations could look for wisdom and guidance through difficult days. I speak for myself in mourning the loss of a dear friend.

No one paid much attention in America to Dill's death, since November 3 was election day. But Marshall was deeply affected by it. It was the man and the friend he was going to miss most.† But he was also acutely conscious that he had lost his pipeline into the counsels of the British Chiefs of Staff and the secret thoughts of the man in 10 Downing Street. And that was going to cause a rift in Allied unity in the tricky days to come.

Franklin D. Roosevelt was inaugurated for his fourth term

---

*It was the same substance which was subsequently used for defoliation of crops in Vietnam.

†In his determination to make Americans realize the extent of Dill's contribution toward winning WWII, Marshall arranged to have his friend buried in Arlington Cemetery, the first non-American to be interred in the American Valhalla, and later raised the money to have an equestrian statue of Dill sculpted and erected over the tomb.

as President of the United States on January 20, 1945, in a quiet ceremony on the south portico of the White House. Normally there was a big show in front of the Capital, but not this time; the discreet nature of the ceremonials was ascribed to the fact that there was a war on, but most insiders were only too well aware that they had been scaled down because the President was ill. Ernie King, who thought Roosevelt was not now up to the job, would rather not have been present and said afterward he was there only because "we were told to attend the inauguration."

Almost immediately afterward Roosevelt and his staff boarded the cruiser *Quincy* to sail to the Black Sea for a conference with the Allies at Yalta. He was too frail to fly, so Marshall and King preceded him in separate planes. The Chief of Staff stopped off in Marseilles for a conference with Eisenhower, who apprized him of the fact that he was having trouble again with Montgomery. The British commander wanted to push straight ahead to Berlin, but as Ike had told him, "Monty, this is nuts. You can't start any thrust until you get across the Rhine, and only when you get across the Rhine and establish a bridgehead will I support you."

But, Ike added, he had gone behind his back to complain to the British Chiefs of Staff and the prime minister. The Supreme Commander warned his chief that Monty was stirring up trouble for them all, adding, "Somebody just ought to smack him down."

Marshall flew on to Malta, the British-controlled island in the central Mediterranean, where the members of the Imperial General Staff, led by Lord Alanbrooke,* were waiting for him. The general idea was that the Americans and British should coordinate their strategies, particularly about Japan, before confronting the Russians at the Yalta Conference. Unfortunately the British made it clear they wanted to settle matters about Germany first. They complained that Eisenhower was too cautious and was not moving fast enough in his operation to "close on the Rhine." They maintained that control of the battle for Germany should now be switched to Montgomery, who should be encouraged to

*Formerly Sir Alan Brooke, he had now been made a peer by Winston Churchill.

make a thrust for Berlin and capture as much German territory as possible before the Russians arrived. Meanwhile, they felt it important to get Eisenhower out from under the influence (they didn't call it "pernicious" influence but implied it) of Generals Bradley and Patton, whom they quite plainly despised.

Ike had primed Marshall's mood, which was feisty, and he reacted with unexpected combativeness to Alanbrooke's supercilious remarks. What was all this rhetoric about "closing on the Rhine" anyway? Walter Bedell Smith, who was there to watch out for Ike's interests, explained that it was a British phrase which Churchill had used. Marshall brushed it aside.

"It was a sort of Gettysburg Address stuff," he said later, "not a simple statement of what was wanted."

Marshall's temper rose when Alanbrooke twice mentioned the influence of Bradley and Patton on Ike, with its implication that they were all Americans ganging up on the British. He retorted, "Well, Brooke, you're not nearly as much worried as the American chiefs are worried about the immediate pressures and influence of Mr. Churchill on General Eisenhower. The President practically never sees General Eisenhower and never writes to him—that is on my advice—because he is an *Allied* commander. But we are deeply concerned by the pressures of the prime minister. I think your worries are on the wrong foot."

It was, he said afterward, "a terrible meeting." The British would not give way in their pressure to get the German campaign switched to Montgomery's favor, based on a single powerful thrust to Berlin, with all available gasoline and matériel taken away from Patton and Bradley and transferred to the combined British and American forces, under Monty's command, in the north.

But Marshall would not yield either. He refused absolutely to give any orders whatsoever to Ike, insisting that a commander on the spot must make his own decisions and that he had full confidence in the Supreme Commander's judgment.

"We were in a situation," said Admiral King later, "where neither would give an inch, so that matter had to be carried over until FDR arrived in Malta."

Churchill had come to the meeting in his own cruiser, the

Orion, and he was on her deck in Valletta Harbor as the *Quincy* steamed in. He wrote later:

> As the American cruiser steamed slowly past us towards her berth alongside the quay wall, I could see the figure of the President seated on the bridge, and we waved to each other. With the escort of Spitfires [fighter planes] overhead, the salutes and the bands of the ships' companies in the harbour playing "The Star-spangled Banner," it was a splendid scene.

That same evening the President, the prime minister, and the Joint Chiefs of Staff gathered in the wardroom of the *Quincy.* Marshall and King had drawn up between them what they regarded as a binding contract for Anglo-American agreement as to how they should jointly face up to combined operations against the Nazis and the Japanese. So far as the Germans were concerned, it moved not an inch toward the British point of view. There would be no switch in either tactical or strategical policies, and Montgomery, Bradley, and Patton would continue to be supported on an equal basis, as and when the military situation demanded. There would be no unilateral thrust by Monty for Berlin.

Everyone noticed that Churchill was brimming with energy, but that Roosevelt did little to influence, in any way, what was going on.

"Churchill did most of the talking that night," King said later. "Roosevelt seemed to understand what was said, but he didn't say much, using nods rather than speaking."

But King notwithstanding, he had already made it plain, both to Marshall and to the prime minister, that he backed the Marshall-King contract to the hilt, especially over plans for Germany. In the circumstances, the British chiefs had little option but to agree.

"I noted that Brooke was rather glum," said King later, "after Roosevelt and Churchill agreed to what Eisenhower wanted done."

But Marshall did not feel glum at all; justified, rather, by the firm stand he had taken. He was normally sympathetic and understanding toward the British point of view, but on this occasion his allies grated on him. He kept remembering Alanbrooke's lofty attitude toward two of his favorite generals in the American Army, Omar Bradley and George Patton, and the overall standpoint of the British staff chiefs had struck him as being altogether too cynical and "political," far too much interested in scoring off the Russians and stealing a march on their advancing armies than in the task of defeating the Nazi forces in Germany.

Had Field Marshal Dill been along, as he usually was at these conferences, to argue and explain the British point of view, Marshall might have gained a more sympathetic understanding of their fundamental motives. But Dill was dead. All the Chief of Staff could think about was Eisenhower's resentment at the way Montgomery had been intriguing behind his back and of the fact that the insufferable British commander was once more trying to hog all the credit for himself in the war against the Nazis.

The delegations moved on to Yalta for the last big conference between the Allies before the end of the war in Europe.

17

Berlin to the Bomb

Sergeant James W. Powder accompanied General Marshall to Marseilles, Malta, and Yalta. He went with the Chief of Staff everywhere and was the only member of his entourage whom he considered indispensable.

Powder was the nearest any member of the U.S. Army ever came to being Marshall's military aide. He had picked him out in the beginning because he had once been General Pershing's orderly-cum-driver, and he had come to admire his smartness, his efficiency, and the soldierly looks of him. He was six feet four and three-quarters of an inch tall, built like an oak tree, and still, when he could, wore a Stetson campaign hat tilted just to the point of rakishness on the side of his huge head.

It had, of course, often been pointed out to Marshall that his aide ought to be an officer, but in the early days, when he had first rated one, the idea of some snooty lieutenant sitting in the front seat of his car while he went on his rounds was too much to swallow.

"I don't want to be looking at someone who needs a haircut at the back of his neck," he said.

But when he became Chief of Staff, he was reminded that he really did need an officer, and if he was so fond of Powder, why didn't he just give him a commission? The trouble was, Powder didn't want a commission. He refused an offer from his boss on four different occasions, and finally, Marshall enlisted the help of his wife, Katherine. One day, while being driven by Powder, she said, "Sergeant, why don't you take a commission? Is it because you've only been offered a captaincy? Would you like to be a major?"

Powder firmly shook his head. "No, ma'am, it's just that I

don't have the education. I didn't even get out of high school. I left home when I was twelve years old."

"Well," said Katherine, "if you don't want it, we certainly aren't going to make you take it. But I think it would be awfully nice."

When General Malin Craig, of the commissions board, heard about it, he stormed in to see Powder. "What the hell is the matter with you?" he roared. "Are you too damned big to be a commissioned officer?"

"No, General," said Powder. "I don't feel that way. I just don't feel I'm qualified to be an officer."

"Why not?" rapped Craig. "We've got shoe clerks who are colonels these days."

But Powder was adamant. And so was Marshall in keeping him. If his aide preferred to stay in the ranks, so be it. But he certainly wasn't going to exchange him for any officer in the Army. By the time the war in Europe had reached its climax Powder had become valet, chauffeur, trusted confidant, and adviser, all rolled into one. He looked after Marshall's uniforms, his baggage, his secret papers, and, when they were away on trips, his engagements. He was constantly available, day and night.

He always made sure Marshall had a pair of glasses handy to read the documents handed to him. As has been mentioned, Powder bought them by the dozen in the five-and-ten-cent store and always carried a spare pair with him, so that when the chief said, "Powder, I don't have any glasses," he could reply, "I have a pair right here," and pull one from his pocket.

What troubled Katherine and Powder alike was the tremendous burden of responsibility Marshall carried around with him. Only too often his problems kept him awake at nights.

"When we were away that was one of the things I did for him," Powder said later. "I always had a massage vibrator, and he would lie there and read and try to fall asleep. We used to carry around those paperback books the Army used to issue, a box of them, and he would say, 'Sergeant, I just can't sleep,' and I would say, 'General, don't worry about it.' And I would come

into his room, and before I got the vibrator, I would massage him
with my hands and would start the massage at his neck and go
all the way down to his waist and then go down and rub his legs
for him. By the time I got down there he would be asleep, and I
would turn out the light and sneak out on him. It would relax
him; his muscles would relax. But two or three hours later I would
wake up in the night, and his light would be on and he would be
reading."

One sure way for an officer to get the Chief of Staff angry
was to treat Sergeant Powder like an ordinary enlisted man. A
billeting officer in Marseilles sent Powder up to the attic with the
other orderlies, instead of putting him in a room next to the general. When Marshall found out, he had the major brought before
him and quietly pointed out that Sergeant Powder was different.
Then he waited while the billeting officer personally lugged the
sergeant's baggage down from the attic, turned a colonel out of
the room next to him, and installed his aide there instead. Then
he said, "Son, I've been looking for you all afternoon. Come
on in."

For the Yalta Conference, Powder flew in a separate plane
to Sochi, 180 miles away from the site of the meeting. The Chief
of Staff had already landed and gone ahead, and the sergeant
needed to get there fast. He had the baggage of Generals Marshall,
Arnold, and Bull, as well as all their secret papers, and he went
at once to the transport officer and asked for a truck.

"He assigned a truck to me that was full of mud," Powder
said later, "and I said, 'I can't put all these bags in that truck.' I
had all the official papers for the meeting, and this was one of
those Lend-Lease trucks with a Russian driver. The major said,
'If you don't want to put them in there, you can wash it out.' I
said, 'I'm not going to wash it out, and I'm not going to put those
bags in there.' He said, 'Then you don't have to. You can just sit
there.' I said, 'I don't want to sit here either. I haven't got the
time.' He said, 'You've got all kinds of time because you're not
going to leave here until Stalin arrives.' I said, 'When is Stalin
going to arrive?' and he said, 'I don't know. Nobody knows. But
you will wait here until he arrives, before you leave.' "

Fortunately for all concerned, Powder then caught sight of an officer he knew, General Laurence S. Kuter, and explained his predicament to him. Kuter went up to the major and said, "My God, Major, don't you know who this is? See how goddamn fast you can find him a truck and get those things into it and let him go."

"He can't go," the major said. "I haven't got an interpreter for him."

"Major," said General Kuter, "that guy is Sergeant Powder. He don't need no interpreter. He can do anything. Get him out of here."

Kuter was right, too. The Red Army driver of the truck turned out to be a Lithuanian, and Powder, though of mixed Irish and French ancestry, had been brought up in a Lithuanian neighborhood in Rockville, Illinois. He remembered quite a few of the words, and he got along fine with the driver and had absolutely no trouble guiding him over the mountains to Yalta.

He found Marshall pacing the floor, waiting for him to turn up, and in a bad mood. He was not too pleased at having been asked to share quarters with Admiral King. They had been put in the czarina's palace, and although that implied spacious and luxurious quarters, in fact, the rooms had been stripped practically bare and even the beds were Soviet Army issue.

"The general had this room here, and Admiral King was in the other over there," said Powder later. "His was supposed to be the czarina's boudoir, and the general teased him about it."

Powder had the little room, practically a closet, in between, with drawers for storing the uniforms of both guests. He could hear the general and the admiral shouting at each other from either side and was surprised that King called Marshall George, and the Chief of Staff was equally familiar.

"Hey, George," he heard King shout that first evening, "what the hell would you do if Rasputin suddenly came through that window?"

"Hell, Ernie," Marshall replied, "I'd call Powder."

"General," called Powder, "if Rasputin comes through that window, I'm going out through that door."

The czarina's quarters had one facility which proved both an advantage and a disadvantage. It had the only functioning flush lavatory in the area. But as Powder and Marshall learned to their sorrow, Ernie King was an inveterate reader-on-the-toilet and refused to come out of the closet even when the Chief of Staff thundered on the door and demanded entry by right of seniority. Moreover, all the other members of the U.S. delegation demanded squatters' rights, too, and what Colonel Frank McCarthy later termed a time-and-motion system had to be instituted. The Soviet government poured out hospitality for the delegates, and there were running banquets, replete with vodka, caviar, and Black Sea turbot, bass, shrimp, squid, and crayfish, and gallons of flat, oversweet Crimean champagne, but the Soviet plumbing system proved inadequate to cope with it.

For Marshall it was a gastronomic nightmare. He could handle vodka but did not like fish and was positively allergic to shrimp and other shellfish, which made him sick. Fortunately Powder had brought along a big store of chocolate and saw that there were jumbo bars of it on the chief's bedside table when he retired every night.

"Yalta is the place where he lived on Hershey bars," he said later.

He wasn't the only one. Powder had stocked up at the PX in Marseilles in preparation for the Russians and came loaded down with everything from Camel cigarettes to Kodak film.

"I sweetened all the Russians, even the MVD," he said. "The servants didn't care a damn about us when we arrived, but I soon changed all that. Every time they saw the general they brought him a glass of tea and a little something else. By the time I left I could have walked up to Stalin himself and said, 'Hiya, Joe,' I was so popular. In fact, I did get Stalin's signature on a short snorter,* to go alongside those of Winston Churchill and Chiang Kai-shek, but lost it when I gave it to a steward to get the President's signature on the way home."

---

*A dollar bill signed by other air travelers, signifying the owner had made a transoceanic flight—still a rarity in those days.

Yalta turned out to be a political conference in which the Joint Chiefs of Staff played hardly any role at all. In Germany the enemy was all but defeated, and so were Britain's ideas on how the enemy's territory should be parceled up among the Allies. They had lost out at Malta and finally agreed that General Eisenhower, the military man on the spot, should make all future decisions about that. As if they knew he would keep away from anything smelling of "politics"—the occupation of Berlin, for instance— the Russians had no objection to such an arrangement. It was the British high command they mistrusted.

What President Roosevelt and his political advisers wanted from the Soviet government was a declaration of war against Japan, and they were well aware that for that they would have to pay. But what? Marshall was not consulted. "I did not talk to the President about the need of making concessions to Russia in order to get help against Japan. Stalin had been very specific as to what he could do if we gave him time in which to do it. He discussed with me how long it would take to move the troops they would have to move through Siberia to get ready for an attack in co-operation with us."

He was quite well aware, however, that the Soviets would exact a price. His colleague, Admiral King, agreed with him but felt that the alternatives were too horrendous to contemplate.

"It was the belief of the Navy," he said later, "that Japan could and should be defeated without an invasion of the home islands. Our contention was that blockade and bombardment could bring about Japanese capitulation and that in connection with this course of action, engagement of the Japanese armies in Manchuria by the Soviets would hasten that capitulation."

No one seemed to be putting any faith in the power of the atomic bomb, not even General Marshall, who was about the only man around at Yalta who had even an inkling of its potential. It had not yet been successfully tested, and no one was even certain that it would work. Paul Nitze, who had been helping make a report in Europe for the Strategic Bombing Survey, remembers getting a message about this time telling him to get back to Washington fast in order to discuss strategy against Japan. On his way home from Frankfurt his plane stopped in Prestwick, Scotland, to pick up a couple of generals and George Ball. General H. H. "Hap" Arnold, chief of the U.S. Army Air Forces, was waiting to meet them at the airport. He had opted out of Yalta at the last moment because of a mild heart attack but had been in constant touch with his boss, General Marshall. He told the three men that he wanted them to embark on a project at once and think up an Air Force plan for attacking Japan, in the light of what USAAF had been able to do in Europe. They were then taken to a briefing by General Alexander Surles, his deputy, who told them there were already five plans for defeating the Japs floating around.

Surles said the Army believed it could win by invading the islands and capturing Tokyo. The Army Air Forces thought it could win by demolishing all the main Japanese cities. The Navy believed it could win by blockading Japan. The State Department was convinced the only way to win was to induce Russia to come in. And then there were the scientists. They had this damned Manhattan Project—some sort of bomb.

"I've been all through that one," said Surles, "and we're sure it won't work. So I want you three to go away and study those five plans and come back with just one—one that the Air Force can back but which the Army, the Navy and the State Department, even if not the scientists, can agree on."

No matter what plan the task force came up with, it was hardly likely to affect what the statesmen were agreeing to at Yalta. While their military staffs watched from the sidelines, the Americans and the British dug into their pockets and got ready to pay Russia's admission fee to the Far East war. Averell Harriman, the U.S. ambassador, had warned them what the cost of the Soviet ticket would be: "[He] stated that Stalin would likely wish to raise the question of what the Russians could get out of the Pacific War, and observed that they would want the Kuriles and the southern half of Sakhalin."*

President Roosevelt was more than willing to pay. It is true

*The Kuriles were Japanese islands north of Hokkaido. Sakhalin was divided between Russia and Japan in the peace settlement of 1905.

that he was now in no condition to resist any pressure because he was a very sick man indeed, but the truth was that pressure was not needed. He and his advisers were convinced that Russia's aid was essential in defeating Japan and were quite ready to ante up, especially with gifts of enemy territory. If Winston Churchill, who did not share the President's enthusiasm for his Russian allies, was more skeptical, he did not voice his objections at the time. He had learned from the Teheran Conference that the Americans rather liked the idea, which negotiations with Stalin had suggested to them, of bossing the postwar world in a big brother partnership with the Soviets, and he had learned from the painful quarrels at Malta that a little brother like Britain was now very small fry indeed.

"At Yalta we were ready to give," was the rueful way he described the situation later, adding, "But five weeks later things changed."

By which he meant that Roosevelt died, and the bomb was born.

On the evening of April 12, 1945, General Marshall and Katherine were relaxing on the porch of their quarters at Fort Myer when Colonel Frank McCarthy drove up. He had just got the news from Warm Springs, Georgia.

"The President is dead," he said.

Marshall had had a long, busy, if heartening, day at the War Department—the dispatches from both Europe and the Pacific had been good—but he rose at once and drove to the White House, where he condoled with Mrs. Roosevelt. She asked him to look after the funeral arrangements, and as he had done before in the cases of President Harding and General Pershing, he swung into action to prepare the ceremonials a nation demands when a great man dies. A special train and 2,000 men were ordered to Warm Springs, honor guards were organized along the route the funeral train would take northward, and troops were mobilized to line the road from Union Station to the White House.

The following day, while the train was on its solemn way, Marshall and other members of the Joint Chiefs of Staff, accompanied by Secretary of War Stimson and Secretary of the Navy James V. Forrestal, went for their first conference with their new President and Commander in Chief, Harry S. Truman. Marshall had known him during his years in the Senate, where the dapper little man from Missouri had chaired a committee on the conduct of the war, and knew him as a shrewd and bouncy politician, not a man you could fool or lie to. On this occasion he seemed deflated, the resilience squeezed out of him, with a look on his face as if he had been slightly stunned. It was unlikely to be because he was mourning Roosevelt's death—for the President had always treated him coolly—and was more probably due to the burdens suddenly placed upon his shoulders. For most of his time as Vice President Roosevelt had deliberately kept him in ignorance of all the more important secrets of the war, and it was only an hour earlier, for example, that he had learned for the first time—in a briefing from Stimson—that the United States was in process of making and planning to explode an atomic bomb. He still did not know the nature of the agreements the dead President had made with the Russians at Yalta.

In the circumstances, he could have been forgiven if he had looked around for an expert to hold his hand until he had found his presidential balance. At Stimson's suggestion, the two senior service chiefs gave him a summary of the war news as it stood as of that moment. Ernie King was a monstrously bad speaker, found it difficult to put his thoughts together, and wasn't particularly pleased to be around anyway. He had never liked Roosevelt and refused to look sad at his death; he thought Truman was nothing more than "a pipsqueak haberdasher," as he put it later, and thought him beneath the Navy's dignity.* On the other hand, Marshall suspected that Truman was a man of spunk and principle, and though he told Stimson later that day that they wouldn't really know what Truman was like "until the pressure really begins to be felt," he went out of his way to brief him to the best

---

*He changed his mind about that later, assigned a Navy deputy to brief the President, and carefully rehearsed him beforehand to be sure he made the right impression.

of his ability. Marshall was a clear, cogent, and effective speaker, and the new President signified by his manner that he was grateful to the Chief of Staff for having gone to such trouble to inform him. He thanked him warmly. Stimson got the impression that Truman had found the steadying hand he needed to grasp, and it was the one at the end of General Marshall's arm. Meanwhile, he thanked them all for coming to see him and told them he was planning no changes at all in the direction of the war and was relying upon them to serve him as they had his predecessor.

"He hasn't got much option," said Admiral King, dryly, and hurried out.

The funeral procession, with Sergeant Powder marching behind the flag-draped, horse-drawn caisson, made its way through silent streets to the White House, where 300 mourners gathered before the coffin in the East Room to hear Bishop Angus Dunn conduct a simple service. The next day it was on to Hyde Park for the burial, with Sergeant Powder once more watching over the coffin.

"General Marshall had told me to pick the pallbearers for the funeral," he said later, "so I went up to the White House to select the most uniform group of military men I could find from the selection that paraded before me. The marines had simply sent along two buck sergeants and an officer, and they were little short, tubby fellas. I said, 'Even a general officer would have a master sergeant as pallbearer. We have the President of the United States here, and we can't have buck sergeants. If you don't have master sergeants here by this afternoon, the Marine Corps will not be represented. These are the orders of General Marshall.' The officer was furious. He called the chief's office, and the office verified that whatever Sergeant Powder said was the way it would be. And by gosh, he had eight master sergeants to select from by the afternoon, and I selected one from [the Battle of] Tarawa and one from England, both of whom had been wounded and shipped home. When we got to Hyde Park and they lined up and shouldered the casket to carry it to the grave, one of the marines just about gave out. He had been shot up pretty bad, and he began complaining he was slipping, that the casket was slipping out of his hand. I watched him as they neared the grave, and he was getting weaker all the time.

"Then the colonel in command of the detail moved in and tried to get ahold of the casket. So did I. It was a really terribly heavy casket, and when we got to the grave, we found the opening was extremely wide, you had to lean out. The marine kept whispering, 'I'm slipping,' and I whispered back, 'If the casket slips in, go in with it, don't stand there.' I leaned over to help while I whispered, and I had my hand on his back to steady him. I'm not kidding you, it was very wide and the casket was so heavy, and you had to lean way out to set it on its way."

They managed to get the interment over without mishap, and no one seemed to notice except Mrs. Roosevelt.

"She sent an awfully nice letter to the general," Powder said, "and he sent me the original."

The Chief of Staff flew back to Washington to find there was a crisis brewing in Germany—over the Russians and Berlin. Trouble with Moscow had started in the last days of Roosevelt's life, when Stalin had sent him an urgent message complaining that the Anglo-Americans were trying to make a separate peace with the Nazi armies in Italy and accusing the President's advisers of going behind his back.* Roosevelt, in turn, wanted to know what Marshall had been up to.

Angered by Stalin's suggestions, Marshall had insisted on a hot reply's being sent back to Moscow expressing "bitter resentment" at such "vile misrepresentations of my actions or those of my trusted subordinates."

He added, "It would be one of the great tragedies of history if at the very moment of the victory, now within our grasp, such distrust, such lack of faith should prejudice the entire undertaking after the colossal losses of life, material and treasure involved."

Marshall drafted the message for Roosevelt, and it was one

---

*Stalin was referring to private negotiations which Allen Dulles, the Office of Strategic Services chief in Switzerland, had been conducting with the Nazis in Italy.

of the last he signed and dispatched to the Soviet dictator. It went off on April 4.

Stalin, jolted, perhaps realizing he had gone too far, came as near to apologizing as he ever did in his life and assured the President that "I had and have no intention of offending anyone." When the message was read by the new President, Harry Truman, he had to have its significance explained to him by Marshall.

But everyone knew already that the Russians were very touchy and suspicious and that Stalin regarded Berlin as an exclusively Soviet prize. Winston Churchill did not agree with this and thought it would be splendid for British prestige if Montgomery's forces reached the German capital first. So did Montgomery. On the other hand, Eisenhower considered it much more important for U.S. troops under Bradley, Hodges, and Patton to gain Nazi-held territory, defeat the German armies, and link up with the Red armies to the east. To Churchill's intense irritation—but with Marshall's approval—Eisenhower even began communicating with Stalin directly, to assure him that no Allied troops from the West would encroach on "his" territory. He did not mention Berlin, but he did make it plain that his line of advance would be along the Erfurt-Leipzig-Dresden line, around the German capital. This was the direction in which Bradley's armies were pointing, and if they continued that way—and Eisenhower was determined they should—they would effectively block the British Twenty-first Army Group under Field Marshal Sir Bernard Montgomery in the north from pushing on to Berlin. Montgomery was furious and complained to the British Chiefs of Staff, who in turn complained to Churchill. But when these protests reached Washington, it was Marshall who assured Eisenhower he would back him in whatever decisions he made on the spot. When Montgomery (on April 6) persisted in talking about Berlin and asked for ten American divisions to aid him in a thrust on the capital, Ike slapped him down in no uncertain terms. He could forget about it.

"You must not lose sight of the fact," he told the British commander, "that during [Bradley's] advance to Leipzig you have the role of protecting [his] northern flank. It is not his role to protect your southern flank. My directive is quite clear on this point."

He added, "As regards Berlin I am quite ready to admit that it has political and psychological significance, but of far greater importance will be the location of the remaining German forces in relation to Berlin. It is on them that I am going to concentrate my attention. Naturally, if I get an opportunity to capture Berlin cheaply, I will take it."

But he made it plain that if that opportunity came, it would be Bradley's American troops, not a British army group, that would be allowed to seize the opportunity. Unwittingly, however, in his rebuke to Montgomery, he did include in his message a sentence which, when read by one of the Allied army commanders, was seized upon as an excuse to drive forward and maybe circumvent Eisenhower's desire to leave Berlin to the Russians. The sentence read: "Naturally, if Bradley is delayed, and you feel strong enough to push out ahead of him in the advance to the Elbe, this will be all to the good."

On April 12, the day Roosevelt died, rumors began to circulate around Eisenhower's headquarters that elements of the British Twenty-first Army Group had reached the Elbe River and put two bridgeheads across it, the closer of them fifty-three miles from Berlin. Shortly afterward, the commander signaled that although one bridgehead had been thrown back, the other was firmly held and patrols were probing along the road eastward without opposition. Could he have permission to start an advance and occupy Berlin before the Russians got there?

To the correspondents who heard the rumors, it sounded very much as if that mountebank Montgomery couldn't take no for an order and was making mischief once again—this time, no doubt, egged on by Winston Churchill, who was known to be more eager than ever to "beat the Bolsheviks into Berlin."

As it happened, the Allied troops who had thrown their bridgeheads over the Elbe were not English at all, but American, and their identification with Montgomery's Twenty-first Army Group was all a misunderstanding. They belonged to the U.S.

Ninth Army and were veterans of a series of often bitter and sometimes costly campaigns which had taken them all the way across Europe from Brest, in Brittany, to the heart of Germany. The reason for the confusion was the fact that until a few weeks before, the Ninth Army had indeed been part of Field Marshal Montgomery's British army group but had come to feel that they had been so churlishly treated by their overall British commander, and assigned such menial and trivial military tasks, that they had asked to be transferred to General Bradley's U.S. Army group. The change had taken place just before the advance across the Rhine began, and lots of observers still imagined they were part of the British group. But they were not. They were part of an American force once more and extremely happy about it—so happy, in fact, that they had mown down all German resistance confronting them in their drive to the east. Now here they were, sitting firmly astride the road to Berlin, less than fifty-five miles away, and eager to push ahead and grab their biggest trophy of the war, the capital of the German Reich.

Their commander shared that ambition. He didn't agree at all with Eisenhower's idea of letting Berlin be taken by the Russians. His name was Lieutenant General William H. Simpson, and he was one of the most attractive and fascinating characters in the U.S. Army. General Marshall had once warned parents of drafted soldiers to beware when their sons wrote home to say how much they liked and admired their commanding officer because it usually meant he was too soft with them, and that could mean slackness—and death—when it came to going into battle with him.

Marshall made an exception for Bill Simpson. He was almost universally admired by his men, not because he mollycoddled them, but because he handled them with fairness, understanding, and good humor. He was once called upon to whip into shape a battalion of troops who were undisciplined, sullen, rebellious, resentful, and downright sloppy. They had a reputation for wrecking every new officer they got. Simpson lined them up, shook his head over their unkempt appearance, and told them, "The first thing every officer and man in this regiment is going to get is a haircut.

I want to see you trim and tidy—and I'll give you an example of how trim and tidy I mean."

With that he swept off his campaign hat and revealed that he was as bald as a coot, not a hair growing on his egg-shaped head. There were hoots of laughter and cries of "Baldy!" but he had made his point, done it with humor, and the men shaped up.

In the Ninth Army men knew Simpson had a rule which he stuck to in every battle and drilled into his subordinate officers: "Never send an infantryman in to do a job that an artillery shell can do for him."

It did not mean that his men were never given sticky operations to carry out, but they knew that when he gave an order to go in and fight, there was just no other way.

Simpson had already heard rumors that Berlin was a prime Russian target and that the territory in front of him might subsequently be ceded to the Soviet zone of occupation. As a soldier he had no particular views on that; in his book, an army took what it could capture and hold. But when his troops reached the Elbe and he went to look over the situation, he discovered that the enemy forces in front of him were crumbling. Groups of German soldiers had begun scrambling across the river to give themselves up. Berlin lay straight ahead. The more the Ninth Army commander thought about it, the more it beckoned to him. On the other side of the German capital, it was true, the Russian armies were only thirty-five miles away. But Simpson knew from interrogations of Nazi prisoners that the Russians were engaged in a desperate, last-ditch battle with the Germans, who were determined to hold them back, whereas his own troops were now solidly established across the Elbe, and there was every indication that the Germans were increasingly inclined to let them through.*

*He was afterward to say that Eisenhower did not seem to understand how firmly they had established their bridgehead or how feeble was the Nazi opposition to their advance. The Supreme Commander cabled Marshall on April 15: "While true that we have seized a small bridgehead over the Elbe, it must be remembered that only our spearheads are up to that river; our center of gravity is well back of there."

Would it not be good soldierly tactics to go forward and exploit the situation?

It seemed to Simpson that the opportunity now presented itself to "capture Berlin cheaply" in exactly the way Eisenhower had casually mentioned it to Montgomery in his message to him of April 6. Only circumstances had so worked out that it was the Ninth U.S. Army, not Montgomery, which was in a position to exploit the unexpected opportunity, and Simpson would not have been human if he had not savored the irony of the situation.

He called in his chief of staff, General James E. Moore, and on April 16 sent a message through to Bradley's headquarters saying he proposed to exploit the military situation in front of him and push on to Berlin. He ended his message with the words "CONFIDENT CAN BE THERE IN TWENTY-FOUR HOURS."

Later on that day, however, there was an urgent telephone call from Bradley. "He said he wanted to see me right away," Simpson said later, "and to get in my plane and come and report to him at once. So I got in my plane and flew to this town—I've forgotten the name of it now—and arrived there half an hour later. He was waiting for me as the plane came in, and as soon as I got out, he said, 'I've got orders for you to stop at the Elbe River and not go into Berlin.' "

Simpson was stunned. "But why? How has that happened?" he asked.

"It comes from Eisenhower," Bradley said.

Simpson gave a rapid résumé of the military situation, pointing out that the roads were open, the Russians held up, and he could reach Berlin without too much trouble by the following morning. He pleaded with Bradley to call Ike and "please try and change his mind."

They went into Bradley's office and put through a call to the Supreme Commander, SHAEF, and Simpson stood by while Bradley explained the situation. Bradley obviously shared the Ninth Army commander's eagerness and was at his most persuasive, but it was soon apparent that he was getting nowhere. Finally he said, "Well, I'll tell Bill."

He put down the telephone and turned to Simpson.

"Ike says no way," he told him. "You can't do it."

Remembering that moment thirty-five years later, Simpson was still deflated.

He never did get an explanation of why he had been halted.

And that was that. It was more than a week later that elements of the Red Army appeared at last on the Elbe, and the commanders exchanged visits.

"One of [the generals] appeared at my headquarters with about nine members of his staff," Simpson said later, "and we had lunch together. We exchanged toast after toast in vodka. Finally, we got pretty drunk and the Red Army commander said something to his people, and they grabbed me and put me on my back and threw me up to the ceiling, about ten times. Nearly scared the tar out of me."

When he was at last allowed back on his feet, it was explained to him that this was a Cossack custom, a signal honor, and their way of thanking him.

"It wasn't me they should have thanked," Simpson said. "I wasn't the one who let them be first into Berlin."

Later there were inquests on why American troops were not allowed to take Berlin. One military historian, Colonel S. L. A. Marshall, calculated that Simpson would have run into much more enemy opposition than he had estimated, and Bradley hazarded a guess that going on to Berlin could have cost U.S. forces 100,000 casualties.*

"Ridiculous," Simpson said. "We really had no opposition at all. Anybody who suggests otherwise doesn't know what he is talking about. There was practically nothing ahead of us except German troops pleading to be made prisoner."

His chief of staff, General Moore, agreed with him. He cited the fact that among the Germans who retreated into Ninth Army's lines was a senior Nazi officer, General Walther Wenck, chief of staff of the German panzer corps straddling the road between the

*Though he later backtracked on this.

Elbe and Berlin. Wenck was taken into his presence, and the first thing the German said to him was: "General, we Germans have been fighting the Bolsheviks for four years. You Americans are going to have to fight them next. Don't you think it would be better if we joined forces and fought them together right now?"

Moore curtly replied that the German was talking about America's "noble ally" and that he was not prepared to listen to such language from an enemy officer. What sort of proposition did the general have to make about his own position and the fate of his men? Wenck answered that he wished to surrender the whole of his forces to the Americans and that if he were allowed to go back to his headquarters, he would order his panzer group to abandon its positions and his men to give themselves up. He could deliver 100,000 troops.

"I told him the river was the boundary," Moore said later, "and that if he wanted to surrender his forces, he could do so— to the Russians on his side of the Elbe. Or, I added, he could go back and tell his men to lay down their arms, and under the rules of land warfare we had to accept them. Soon they were streaming in by the thousand."

Shortly after this, the Russian command approached General Simpson again, this time in a rather less exuberant frame of mind. The Russians demanded that the Americans return at once to the custody of the Red Army the 100,000 German troops who had come across the river to surrender to them. Fortunately for the fate of the Germans, the Americans had already shipped most of them to the rear.*

All through the operation itself Marshall backed Eisenhower to the hilt and resisted protests from Churchill and the British that a great propaganda victory had been thrown away for the West

---

*On May 14, 1980, General Wenck wrote to Simpson from Germany to extend his greetings and respects to the U.S. general. "It is due to you," he wrote, "that my then very young soldiers—there were well over 100,000—were rescued and saved for the rebuilding of their country because of the crossing of the Elbe to the West . . . I have never forgotten this chivalrous, and, as I would say today, comradely act of yours."

by the abandonment of Berlin. For him it had been a purely military decision. It was a decision, moreover, which had to be made in the hours immediately following the death of President Roosevelt and while President Truman was still trying to get his bearings, still being briefed about the basic secrets of the war. Therefore, there was just no one around able to make military-political decisions of such importance. All Marshall could do was think like a soldier and back Eisenhower in what he considered soldierly thinking. Both of them bore constantly in mind the fact that Russia was still the ally of the West.

"No, I do not think we should have gone into Berlin at that time," Marshall said later, after years of reflection. "[I]t must be remembered that all this time we were trying to do business with the Russians. We had been fighting with them. They were part of the armed forces—a very decided part. They had played a great part in the fighting, the wearing down of the German strength, and we had to take all that into careful record. At that time, toward the close of the struggle, they were exceedingly sensitive, looking all the time for something that would indicate that the British and the Americans were preparing to go off alone and settle the thing. . . . So we were very careful about this, the Americans more so than the British, because Mr. Churchill was quite positive in the matter, and events have rather proved that he was possibly more nearly right than the American position."

But Churchill was a non-American politician, and to have consulted him, or agreed with his viewpoint, at that time would have meant going over President Truman's head. As U.S. Chief of Staff Marshall did not think he could have done that. All he could do in the circumstances was leave it to the Allied commander on the spot, General Dwight D. Eisenhower, and remind him that his directive remained as it always had been so far as the conflict in Europe was concerned: *Defeat the Germans, win the war, and stay on good terms with your allies.*

What had the question of who should capture Berlin to do with that?

It was certainly a military point of view. But the time was approaching when General Marshall would have to begin learning to think beyond soldierly terms—and sooner than he imagined.

George Catlett Marshall, Sr., the general's father, and his mother, Laura Bradford Marshall (circa 1905).

The three Marshall children in Uniontown, PA (no date). Left to right, Marie Louise, Stuart Bradford (older brother and sister), and George Catlett Marshall. Below: Marshall, age 17, in Uniontown (August 1897).

Marshall at VMI reunion (class of 1901) seen in second row, third from right.

His wedding day, February 11, 1902. Seen left to right, Marie, the bride, Elizabeth (Lily) Coles, and her new husband, Stuart, Mrs. and Mr. George Marshall Sr., and Mrs. Elizabeth Coles (the bride's mother).

World War I. The C-in-C of the AEF, Gen. John J. Pershing, seen on the Western Front with his chief aide, Col. G.C. Marshall. Marshall stayed on as Pershing's aide after the war. He is seen below, left, at Fort Meyer, Washington, D.C., in 1923. Below, right: his wife, Lily, accompanied him when he was posted to China in 1926 as assistant commandant of the U.S. garrison there. She is seen here at Tientsin railroad station.

Marshall picnics on a North China beach with fellow officers and their wives in 1926.

Left: A cook-out on the shore with his second wife, Katherine, at Fire Island, N.Y., 1939.

Below: Marshall, just before he was made a general.

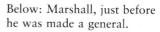

Marshall's second wife, Katherine Tupper Brown, 1934. She had two sons and a daughter from a former marriage. Below: Marshall dines with his wife, stepdaughter Molly (standing), and stepsons, Clifton S. Brown, Jr., and Allen Brown.

Gen. Marshall confers with the Secretary of War, Henry L. Stimson, in the War Department, Washington, D.C., about World War II strategy.

Anglo-U.S. conference at Quebec (Quadrant) decided the date of D-Day invasion of Europe. This picture was taken on August 18, 1943. Front row: Mackenzie King, Canadian prime minister; President F.D. Roosevelt; Winston S. Churchill, British prime minister. Back row: General H.A.P. (Hap) Arnold, Commanding General, U.S. Air Corps; Air Chief Marshal Sir Charles Portal, Chief of British Air Staff; General Sir Alan Brooke, Chief of the Imperial General Staff; Admiral Ernest J. King, Chief of Naval Operations USN; Field Marshal Sir John Dill, British liaison chief in the U.S.; General G.C. Marshall, U.S. Chief of Staff; Admiral of the Fleet Sir Dudley Pound, First British Sea Lord; and Admiral William D. Leahy, presidential adviser.

Marshall and his close friend, Field Marshal Sir John Dill.

British prime minister Winston Churchill visited allied troops in North Africa in 1943 and General Marshall flew out to confer with him about the forthcoming invasion of Sicily. General Sir Bernard L. Montgomery, who commanded British troops in that operation, was also at the conference (right).

Marshall found Free French leader, General Charles de Gaulle, a prickly personality but always tried to give him a patient hearing. Here they are seen together in Washington, D.C. in July 1944, after the invasion of France—in which De Gaulle was not allowed to take part.

In December 1943 Marshall learned that President Roosevelt did not want him to command the Allied invasion of Europe, and he gave way to Eisenhower. Piqued and disappointed, he flew around the world, stopping off in Australia to confer with General MacArthur, seen with him at right.

Marshall learned the bad news during the Cairo Conference. Seen here at this meeting on Thanksgiving, 1943, are (seated) President Chiang Kai-shek of China, President Franklin D. Roosevelt, and Prime Minister Winston Churchill. Marshall is standing second from the left in the foreground.

The three men whose leadership resulted in victory for the Allies in World War II are seen here together in Normandy after the successful invasion of France began in June 1944. Left to right, Admiral Ernest J. King, Chief of Naval Operations, USN; General George Catlett Marshall, Chief of Staff; and General Dwight Eisenhower, commander of the combined Allied forces.

Marshall's most trusted aide was Brigadier General Frank McCarthy, who later became a well-known Hollywood producer (he won the Oscar for *Patton*). They are seen here together on a tour of Germany during World War II.

At the Yalta Conference, the lines were drawn for the shape of postwar Europe, on February 4–12, 1945. Seated: Churchill, Roosevelt, and Stalin. Behind: Admiral Sir Andrew Cunningham (1st Sea Lord); Air Chief Marshal Sir Charles Portal, Chief of British Air Staff; Admiral Leahy, presidential adviser; and, behind him, Marshall.

The round table at Yalta on the first day of the conference, February 4, 1945. Top left (seated): Joseph Stalin. Top right: President Roosevelt with Admiral Leahy and Marshall beside him. Foreground: Winston Churchill sporting a cigar. The scene is the Livasia Palace, Yalta.

Above: Secretary of State Marshall confers with Soviet Foreign Minister Vyocheslov Molotov at a postwar London meeting, December 1947. Right: Mme. Chiang Kai-shek, wife of the Chinese Nationalist President, with whom Marshall established a warm friendship, in 1958. Below: On Marshall's mission to China, 1946–47, he almost brought the warring sections together. Here he is conferring with Nationalist representative Chang Chun (left) and Communist leader Chou En Lai in his head-quarters in Chungking in 1946.

Above: Prime Minister Clement Attlee of Britain flew to Washington for urgent talks with President Truman during the Korean war crisis. Standing behind them are Secretary of State Dean Acheson and Secretary of Defense George C. Marshall.

Below: Queen Frederika of Greece was a warm admirer of Marshall and carried on a correspondence with him through the CIA. She is shown here on a state visit to the U.S. in 1958.

Marshall and his wife, Katherine, in retirement at their home in Virginia.

Bill Mauldin, famous wartime cartoonist, invented two GI characters to comment on the events of World War II as they affected the drafted civilian soldiers of the U.S. Army overseas. In a comment without words, he published this cartoon of their reactions to news of General Marshall's death on October 16, 1959.

18

New Direction

No one was more aware than George Marshall that by the end of 1945 he would be sixty-five years old. All through the war he had watched his physical condition like a hawk, keeping regular hours, rarely staying late at the office, taking plenty of exercise, and, as Frank McCarthy once put it, "eating like a bird—a cup of soup, and three grapes for dessert."

But if he was in fair condition bodily, mentally he was exhausted. The war had begun to squeeze him dry. Every day since 1941 he had had to make daily decisions which he knew must affect the lives of men and the fate of nations. The global responsibility had grown with the expansion of the war, and so had its nagging worries and time-consuming irritations. As Chief of Staff he had never allowed himself the luxury of showing doubt or uncertainty. Everyone, from the President, the Congress, and the Allies to the people and the Army, needed to be convinced that amid chaos and confusion, he at least knew what he was doing and was ready to make a decision or promulgate an order. He had been the rock to which everyone had clung in the blacker and stormier moments of the war, convinced that if they stuck to him, he would see them through the crises. As Lady Mary Burghley, wife of the British governor of Bermuda, wrote to him in the spring of 1945:

> When we dined with you that evening when you passed through Bermuda on your way to Europe, I remember thinking that you would hasten our victory and felt so confident that all would be well. You must be receiving many other letters about it but may I also add my congratulations to you on the magnificent achievements of your splendid Army and say how greatly we admire the man who inspired them and who *made* that Army, and how much we feel that this longed-for victory is due to *him*. There is a whole

lot more I would *like* to say about you but I haven't quite the courage so will refrain and just say how proud I feel to know you as a friend.

Now the war in Europe was truly won. Hitler was dead. The Nazi armies had surrendered. All he longed for now was release from the burdens of office. As if to remind him of the relaxations to come, he was at the Potsdam Conference (settling future strategy with the Russians and the British) when a courier arrived for him with a basket of tomatoes, lettuces, carrots, beans, and cabbages. They had come from the kitchen garden at Dodona Manor, his home in Virginia, and were a not-too-subtle hint from Katherine Marshall that it was time he came back and started growing them himself.

But there was still the war with Japan to be finished and lots of old and new problems with America's allies still kicking around. For instance, the worst row of the whole war with the Free French had just blown up, and President Truman had made an anguished plea to Marshall to solve it for him. In this case, he picked the wrong man in the wrong mood. The Chief of Staff had, by war's end, had about enough of General de Gaulle, and his resentful attitude toward him was in no way changed by the fact that he was now head of the provisional government of France. In the last days of the campaign elements of the Free French Army, under direct orders from De Gaulle, had occupied the German city of Stuttgart and refused to evacuate it despite an urgent plea from General Eisenhower that it was needed as a base for U.S. combat troops. Ike had swallowed the rebuff and allowed the Free French to stay, a decision with which Marshall had strongly disagreed.

But now the French had done something he considered even more unforgivable. Free French troops had marched into the Italian province of Cuneo, claiming it was a legitimate part of the Alpes Maritimes and therefore belonged to France, and added that their "honor and security" would be involved if anyone tried to throw them out. In a message to General Willis D. Crittenberger, commanding U.S. troops in northwestern Italy, the local French general had warned him not to try to interfere and informed Crittenberger:

> I have been ordered by the provisional government of the French Republic to administer this territory. This mission being incompatible with the installation of an Allied military agent in the same region, I find myself obliged to oppose it. Any insistence in this direction would assume a clearly unfriendly character, even a hostile character, and could have grave consequences.

When Crittenberger had objected to this barely disguised ultimatum, the local French commander had sent another, this time even curter:

> General de Gaulle has instructed me to make as clear as possible to the Allied High Command that I have received the order to prevent the setting up of Allied Military Government in territories occupied by our troops and administered by us by all necessary means without exception.

Marshall was outraged when copies of these messages were put before him. President Truman was at San Francisco, attending the inaugural meeting of the new United Nations, and the Chief of Staff told him the gist of the messages over the scrambler phone, insisting that the time had come when De Gaulle had to be taught a short, sharp, salutary lesson. An official protest had already been sent to the provisional French government, but something personal was also needed—from one head of state to another.

"You write it for me, General," the President said, "and make it as strong as you like. I'll sign anything you tell me to."

On June 6, 1945, a telegram marked "No stencil, no distribution" was sent to the U.S. Embassy in Paris with instructions that it should be delivered personally to General de Gaulle by the ambassador, Jefferson Caffery. It was signed by President Harry S. Truman. It began:

> My dear General:
> You have by this time no doubt seen the message from this Government which was communicated to your Foreign Ministry

today. I wish to appeal directly to you in this matter and to notify
you with what great concern and how seriously I view the action
of the First French Army in the province of Cuneo in Northwest
Italy. This Army, under the command of General Eisenhower, the
Supreme Allied Commander on the Western Front, ignored orders
issued to it to withdraw to the frontier in keeping with the arrangements for the occupation and organization of Allied Military Government in Italy under Field Marshal Alexander, the Allied
Commander in Italy. More recently the following events have taken
place. . . .

The President here set out the partial text of the two messages
which the local French commander had sent to General Crittenberger. He went on:

This [the second message] constitutes a very blunt statement
of the intention of the French Government to maintain its forces
contrary to the order of the Allied Supreme Commander and is in
direct contravention of the principles which I accept, and I know
you will agree, as representing the best interests of all Allied government in preserving a hard-won peace, namely the avoidance of
military action to accomplish political ends.

The messages above referred to also contain the almost unbelievable threat that French soldiers bearing American arms will
combat American and Allied soldiers whose efforts and sacrifices
have so recently and successfully contributed to the liberation of
France itself.

Indeed, this action comes at the time of the very anniversary
of our landings in Normandy which set in motion the forces which
resulted in that liberation. The people of this country have only
the friendliest motives and feelings towards France and its people,
but I am sure they would be profoundly shocked if they were made
aware of the nature of the action which your military officers,
presumably with your personal approval, have threatened to take.
Before I acquaint the people of the United States with this situation,
I beg of you to reconsider the matter and withdraw your troops
from the area, and await an orderly and rational determination of
whatever ultimate claims your Government feels impelled to make.
Such action cannot fail to advance rather than reduce the prestige

of France and at the same time operate to the immediate advantage and welfare of the French people.

Then came the sting in the tail. The presidential message concluded:

> While this threat by the French Government is outstanding against American soldiers, I regret that I have no alternative but to issue instructions that no further issue of military equipment or munitions can be made to French troops. Rations will continue to be supplied.
>
> Truman.

It took forty-eight hours for De Gaulle to make up his mind, but the moment it became evident that the embargo on supplies to the French forces included gasoline, thus immobilizing his armies, he instructed his foreign minister, Georges Bidault, to inform the Americans that French troops would begin withdrawing into France at once—provided, of course, the U.S. military gave them the necessary fuel.

No such strong-arm tactics were, of course, possible against the Russians, and in any case, Joseph Stalin did not have the same abrasive effect on Marshall's temper as General de Gaulle did. It was surprising what insults and deceptions he would accept from the Soviet leader that he would have found outrageous and inexcusable if they had come from the Frenchman. Once, when having lunch with Winston Churchill at 10 Downing Street, he listened while the British statesman inveighed against Stalin for sending him a note that was very rude and tough.

"And Mr. Churchill showed it to me—quite furious," Marshall said later. "And he said he didn't see how he as political head of his country could accept such a thing—the political head of the British Empire—such a message as that from Stalin. I was very new at the business then, but it seemed to me quite clear that Stalin was in a desperate situation—we all knew that—he was in desperate need of these things which we couldn't furnish him. He saw only his side of it, which is not unnatural—we have that all the time—and he was a rough character . . . facing possible defeat or destruction, and in tremendous need of these things he wanted. And he was to be forgiven if he wrote very much in character. And I thought the prime minister should consider that . . . it was Stalin *au naturel.*"

Not all of the U.S. delegation members were as tolerant of Russian behavior, and there were some unquiet thoughts when it became known through intelligence sources that the Japanese had sent a delegation to Moscow to ask the Soviet government (still at peace with Japan) to act as an intermediary in peace negotiations with the Allies. The overtures came from Emperor Hirohito, who had become convinced that Japan had lost the war and wished to bring it to an end. What disturbed some of the Americans was that the Soviets had not only refused to help the Japanese envoys but had dismissed them without informing the United States of their approach. The Soviet government was, of course, by no means anxious to see the Japanese surrender before it had had a chance to declare war, thus earning its share of the victors' spoils, as it had been promised by President Roosevelt at Yalta.

All the same, some of the delegation felt the Russians might at least have mentioned the fact that the emperor was ready to negotiate, even if they didn't believe his efforts would work. On the other hand, there were a number of delegates who took comfort from this revelation of Soviet deceitfulness because it justified their own reticence over a much more promising solution to the war: the atomic bomb.

Postwar critics of the steep price the Allies paid for Russia's brief participation in the war with Japan tend to ignore the fact that even as late as the Potsdam Conference, and long after Yalta, no one was absolutely sure that the atomic bomb would work. Harvey Bundy, assistant to the secretary of war, pointed out that even Admiral William D. Leahy, fourth member of the Joint Chiefs of Staff, did not believe in the bomb's efficacy right up to the last minute. He arrived at Potsdam "ridiculing the idea" to his colleagues. "He said this was a bunch of woolly-headed scientists and it was all the biggest bunk in the world," Bundy said.

But then one morning Secretary Stimson and Marshall were

having breakfast together when they were handed a confidential message. The atomic bomb had been successfully tested at Alamogordo.

Neither was in any doubt of the significance of the news. It was Marshall, with Stimson's backing, who had maneuvered Congress into granting first $100 million and then a further $500 million to finance a project of the exact nature of which it was never informed. Now the two men realized that all the time, expense, and secrecy had been justified. It did not occur to either of them to mourn the fact that in the circumstances, Soviet participation in the Japanese war was no longer necessary and that they had therefore paid too high a price for it. At the time it had been necessary. Did one regret paying an insurance premium for a disaster that never happens?

What the two men did discuss that morning was where the bomb should now be dropped: not *whether* but *where*.

"Because, of course, the secretary [Stimson] was absolutely convinced about dropping the bomb once we had it," Bundy said. "This was the kind of demonstration which could bring the war to an end. And we couldn't fail to use it. He never could see the difference between killing a hundred thousand people and ending the war at once, and sending in five hundred air raids and killing a thousand people an air raid. He couldn't see any difference. When you are in a battle, you end the battle."

Marshall was in no doubt either. "We regarded the matter of dropping the bomb as exceedingly important," he said later. "We had just gone through a bitter experience at Okinawa. This had been preceded by a number of similar experiences in other Pacific islands, north of Australia. The Japanese had demonstrated in each case they would not surrender and they would fight to the death. . . . It was expected that the resistance in Japan, with their home ties, would be even more severe. We had had the one hundred thousand people killed in Tokyo in one night of [ordinary] bombs, and it had had seemingly no effect whatsoever. It destroyed the Japanese cities, yes, but their morale was not affected as far as we could tell, not at all. So it seemed quite necessary, if we could, to shock them into action."

He knew, of course, even if the Russians were trying to keep it secret, that the Japanese had sent a peace mission to Moscow. He didn't know the details of what the Japanese were offering as their terms for surrender, but he did know, from reading messages to Japan's ambassadors in Europe, that the Japanese prime minister was having difficulty controlling the military. He doubted whether the premier or even the emperor himself could stop the war if the Army wanted to go on fighting. But Marshall was determined to try anything to jolt them into giving up.

"We had to end the war; we had to save American lives; we had to halt this terrific expenditure of money which was reaching a stupendous total," he said. "And there was no way to economize on it until we stopped the war. The bomb stopped the war. Therefore, it was justifiable. . . . The Army was dominant in these matters, and they could only apparently be slugged into submission. And we slugged them."

That morning, with the news from Alamogordo in their hands, Marshall and Stimson discussed the place in Japan where the bomb could most effectively be dropped. They went through a list of Japanese cities.

"[Stimson] did veto the dropping of the bomb on Kyoto," said Harvey Bundy, because of its shrines and ancient monuments. They eventually plumped for Hiroshima instead, and Stimson went to see Truman to get his consent. Between them, he and Marshall convinced the President that though they couldn't guarantee the result of their gamble, they believed this single bomb would end the war with Japan. It was dropped on Hiroshima on August 6, 1945.

What Marshall did not reveal until years afterward was that he and Stimson, in the next forty-eight hours, believed that their gamble had failed and that they would therefore be forced to proceed with what the Chief of Staff had dreaded—a landing in Japan.

He had already agreed on an invasion plan with the Joint Chiefs of Staff, and more atomic bombs were supposed to play an integral part in it.

"There were supposed to be nine more bombs completed in a certain time," he said later. "And they would be largely in time for the first landings in the southern tip of Japan. There were three corps to come in there, as I recall. They didn't know about it at the time, but I had gone very carefully into the examination out in New Mexico as to the aftereffects of the bomb because we were having in mind exploding one or two bombs before these landings and then having the landing take place—and then reserving the other bomb or bombs for later movements of any Japanese reinforcements that might happen to come up. And it was decided then that the casualties from the actual fighting would be very much greater than might occur from the aftereffects of the bomb action. So there were to be three bombs for each corps that was landing. One or two, but probably one, as a preliminary, then this landing, then another further inland against the immediate supports, and then the third against any troops that might try to come through the mountains from up on the Inland Sea. And that was the rough idea in our minds."

In the light of what we now know about atomic explosions, it was a horrendous plan with consequences far beyond the terrible havoc created at Hiroshima and Nagasaki.

And it seemed that Marshall would be forced to give the signal that would implement it because it appeared that, far from shocking the Japanese into surrender, slugged into defeat, the first atomic bomb on Hiroshima had done nothing to change Japanese determination to fight on. No word, no appeal for mercy came from them.

"What we did not take into account, as nearly as I recall," Marshall said later, "was that the destruction would be so complete, that it would be an appreciable time before the actual facts of the case would get to Tokyo. The destruction of Hiroshima was so complete that there was no communication at least for a day, I think, and maybe longer."

Marshall was still desperately anxious, if he could, to avoid having to give the invasion signal, and in one last effort to convince the Japanese he agreed to the dropping of a second bomb, on Nagasaki this time. It was the only other one the United States possessed for the time being, and since it used a different system, the Americans didn't even know if it would work, but he hoped the Japanese would not guess that. "It was not until the second destruction took place at Nagasaki that the Japanese were really aware of what had happened in the earlier explosion," he said. "Quite evidently they were shocked into action. . . . The fact that we had no more bombs completed at the time was unknown to the Japanese, and they could imagine Tokyo being wiped out next. And they were shocked into immediate action which otherwise we would not have gotten out of them—and saved a terribly bitter and frightfully expensive price in lives and treasure."

The Japanese sued for peace twenty-four hours after the dropping of the Nagasaki bomb, on August 10, 1945.

Now, at long last, World War II was definitely over.

It had taken a long time, and there were already murmurs from some that the Allied terms for "unconditional surrender" had made it longer, more costly on both sides in lives, in property, in suffering.

"I think there was quite a possibility," Marshall said later, "that the Germans and Japanese might have conceded the war a little earlier if it had not been for the unconditional surrender formula. However, I think it had a great psychological effect on our people, on the British people, and on Allied people generally . . . that we were going through with this thing to the finish."

What gave him the greatest satisfaction, now that the Allies had won, was the knowledge that, in a war between totalitarianism and democracy, it was democracy which had triumphed and which had done so without losing or abandoning its political philosophy.

"A democracy has a very hard time in a war," he said, "particularly at the start of a war. They can never get ready in advance. The conditions are such that they are susceptible to surprise action, and an arbitrary government like the Hitler government has every advantage in those respects. They are just bound to win at the start unless they are very, very stupid. Of course, in the end, if the democracy is a firm democracy, it builds up a power which outlasts the other and the dictatorship bogs down."

He did not add that even democracies in wartime need firm and clearheaded direction and that without it even the stoutest democracy can perish. Those who had watched the dramatic course of WWII had no doubt that George Marshall had given the democratic armies the firm direction they would otherwise have lacked. It was no turn of phrase when Winston Churchill hailed him as "the organizer of victory."

Now that it was all over, Churchill followed it with another message that summer:

> It has not fallen to your lot to command the great armies. You have had to create them, organize them, and inspire them. Under your guiding hand, the mighty and valiant formations which have swept across France and Germany were brought into being and perfected in an amazingly short space of time. Not only were the fighting troops and their complicated ancillaries created but, to an extent that seems almost incredible to me, the supply of commanders capable of manoeuvring the vast organisms of modern armies and groups of armies, and of moving them with unsurpassed celerity, were also found wherever they were needed. . . .
>
> There has grown in my breast through all these years of mental exertion a respect and admiration for your courage and massive strength which has been a real comfort to your fellow-toilers, of whom I hope it will always be recorded that I was one.

But "organizer of victory" was all the tribute Marshall asked for. He instructed his staff not to release to the public the British leader's encomium on the ground that "while very complimentary," it would be "embarrassing to him in relation to his Chief of Staff associates." The last thing he wanted to do was hog any of the credit.

On August 20, 1945, he sat down and wrote a letter to President Truman:

> My dear Mr. President:
> Now that hostilities have terminated, the demobilization of

the Army is actively under way, the major military decisions regarding the cut-back of war production have been taken and the
postwar military planning is in an advanced state, I feel free to
propose my relief as Chief of Staff.

I have been on duty in the War Department continuously for
more than seven years, six as Chief of Staff. Aware of the wear
and tear of the job, I am certain that it would be advantageous to
make a change.

If I may be permitted to propose a successor, I suggest that
General Eisenhower is unusually well qualified for the duties of
Chief of Staff at this particular time. . . .

There. It was done. The long, exhausting chore was over.
Dodona Manor, and the kitchen garden, beckoned at last.

The British Chiefs of Staff who had served with him throughout the war, not always equably, were well aware of what caliber
of a man they were losing. They cabled him:

On your retirement after six years as Chief of Staff of the
United States Army, we, your British colleagues in the Combined
Chiefs of Staff, send you this message of farewell.

We regret that Field Marshal Sir John Dill and Admiral of
the Fleet Sir Dudley Pound, two of your greatest friends and admirers, are not alive today to add their names to ours.

As architect and builder of the finest and most powerful Army
in American history, your name will be honoured among those of
the greatest soldiers of our own or any other country.

Throughout your association with us in the higher direction
of the Armed Forces of America and Britain, your unfailing wisdom, high principles and breadth of view have commanded the
deepest respect and admiration of us all. Always you have honoured us by your frankness, charmed us by your courtesy and
inspired us by your singleness of purpose and your selfless devotion
to our common cause.

Above all would we record our thankfulness to you for the
leading part which you have always taken in forging and strengthening the bond of mutual trust and co-operation between the armed
forces of our two countries which has contributed so much to final
victory and will, we believe, endure to the benefit of civilization in
the years to come.

In bidding farewell to you who have earned our personal affection no less than our professional respect, we would address to you a tribute written more than 200 years ago:

> . . ., Friend to truth; of soul sincere,
>   In action faithful, and in honour clear;
> Who broke no promise, serv'd no private end,
>   Who gain'd no title, and who lost no friend. . . .*

> [signed] Alanbrooke of Brookeborough,
> Portal of Hungerford,
> Cunningham of Hyndhope

Marshall had hoped he would be able to go some time before the end of the summer, but when Truman wrote back to accept his resignation, he asked him to stay until November 1945, the earliest time Eisenhower could hope to get back from Europe. So, as it turned out, it was Secretary of War Stimson, who resigned after Marshall, who was able to get out of Washington first.

One of the Chief of Staff's last official duties was to give the secretary an official sendoff when he left Andrews Air Force Base that September. Marshall summoned the top brass of the U.S. Army to say good-bye to him and lined them up in the hot fall sunshine beside the plane that would carry the secretary off to retirement.

It so happened that Stimson had to attend one last Cabinet meeting at the White House on the day of his departure, and it lasted much longer than usual. Harvey Bundy, the secretary's assistant, was waiting with the distinguished guard of honor, and, as the minutes ticked by, he watched them visibly wilting.

"It was the hottest damn day you ever saw," Bundy said later. "And here were these fellas, sweating and sweltering, and he was held up at the White House. Everybody was just lined up and standing there, all those generals!"

Finally, he couldn't stand it any longer. Marshall was waiting

---

*The lines were by Alexander Pope and were written to Joseph Addison in memory of his friend, James Craggs, Esquire, onetime secretary of state. The British had left out two words at the beginning of the poem which might well have been included. They were "Statesman, yet. . ."

at the near side of the plane, and Bundy said to him, "General, don't you think it's only fair to let the officers stand at ease and come in a little from the sun?"

The Chief of Staff grinned and shook his head.

"Bundy," he said, "those officers have kept more GI's waiting in the sun than you and I can count, and it's about time they found out what it's like. By golly, let them wait."

And wait they did until Stimson at last appeared and Marshall snapped them to attention.

It was not until November 26, 1945, that his own release from Washington finally came, and he locked up his office in the War Department for the last time and departed for Dodona Manor.

Where, of course, ten days later, the telephone rang and it was the President on the line.

"General," said Truman, "will you go to China for me?"

III

The Statesman

19

Mission Impossible

The war was won but the sour smell of suspicion about the way in which the United States had become involved in it still hung over Washington. Doubts about Pearl Harbor persisted, and Congress was gearing up for a new inquiry into the origins of the disaster. Marshall had to face the fact that he would inevitably be one of the principal witnesses.

Just about the same time that he penned his note of resignation to the President, his old friend Admiral Harold R. "Betty" Stark arrived back from his wartime service in London. He had been fired as Navy Chief of Staff after the Pearl Harbor debacle and sent across the Atlantic to be liaison officer with the Royal Navy, a job he had carried out with his usual quiet effectiveness.

But now he was in disgrace again. A recommendation had been forwarded to the secretary of the Navy, James V. Forrestal, that he be awarded a Distinguished Service Medal for his work in London, and Admiral King had personally written the citation: "His performance of his manifold duties was distinguished by such exceptional tact, intelligence, judgment, devotion to duty and professional skill as to reflect great credit upon himself, the naval service and his country."

Forrestal had torn it up. He wanted Stark's head. A Navy board of inquiry had produced a report in 1944 censuring both Stark and Admiral Kimmel, the Navy commander in Hawaii, for dereliction of duty. It had been suppressed at the time because of the war. Now Forrestal wanted it implemented. Kimmel had retired and was out of his reach, but the Navy secretary—who did not, in fact, really like admirals and rarely slapped one on the back without a dagger in his hand—was determined to get Stark.

Instead of being brought back home to plaudits and a medal, Stark was officially informed that he was being relieved of his duties and relegated to a position "in which [his] lack of superior strategic judgment may not result in future errors."*

Marshall was cast down when he heard of the obloquy heaped upon his friend and colleague and wrote to commiserate with him. They resolved that when the Pearl Harbor inquiry did begin in Congress, they would work together for mutual protection.

In the meantime, the Chief of Staff worked hard to clear the decks for the time when Eisenhower would be brought back from Europe to take over his job. With no inkling yet that the President had a mission lined up for him, he pressed on with nothing more tantalizing in his mind than the thought of retirement. He wrote to Stark:

> As a matter of fact, I have never been busier or more closely engaged. The affairs of demobilization, hearings on the Army Appropriations Bill—I was before the Committee from 10 A.M. to 5 P.M. on Wednesday—military government matters etc., have been very pressing.
>
> I hope to get away some time today, Saturday, for the weekend, coming back from Leesburg tomorrow night.
> Hastily and affectionately,
George

Marshall had never allowed his relationship with Eisenhower to get on such first-name terms, but he had come to admire the ability of his Supreme Commander in Europe and had confided to his trusted subordinates the hope that Ike would not mess up his peacetime prospects by prolonging his wartime liaison with his attractive English secretary. His anxiety on that score had hardly been allayed when, in April 1945, Lieutenant Kay Summersby wrote to his assistant, Brigadier General Frank McCarthy, and asked him to sponsor her application for U.S. citizenship.

Did that mean the relationship would continue once Ike moved back home? And how would Mamie Eisenhower and his family

---

*The relegation was expunged and the DSM awarded him three years later, after Forrestal's departure.

react to that? It was hardly a background against which to recommend him to the President as the next Chief of Staff.

Then, on June 4, 1945, he received a letter from Eisenhower in Germany which greatly relieved his mind:

> I want to discuss with you one subject on which I must confess that my own conviction is somewhat colored by personal desire. It involves the possibility of enunciating some policy whereby certain personnel in the Occupation forces could bring their wives to this country. . . . So far as my own personal case is concerned, I will admit that the last six weeks have been my hardest of the war. I presume that aside from the disappointment in being unable to solve in clear-cut fashion some of the nagging problems that seem to be always with us, part of my trouble is that I just plain miss my family.
>
> My youngster is with the 1st Division and I can get to see him about once a month but it is not the same thing as being able to reestablish, after three years, something of a home. Moreover, the strain of the past three years has also been very considerable so far as my wife is concerned, and because of the fact that she has had trouble with her general nervous system for many years, I would feel far more comfortable about her if she could be with me.
>
> In the event that no policy of any kind could be approved by the War Department at this time, the personal question would become whether this whole Command or public opinion would resent my arranging to bring my own wife here. This is something that, of course, I cannot fully determine, but my real feeling is that most people would feel that after three years' continued separation at my age, with no opportunity to engage, except on extraordinary occasions, in normal social activities, they would be sympathetic about the matter.
>
> I should like very much to have your frank reaction because while I am perfectly willing to carry on in this assignment so long as the War Department may decide I should do so, I really would like to make it a bit easier on myself from the personal viewpoint. . . .

It was hardly the sort of letter one would expect from a

general who was supposed to be entangled in a tempestuous affair with a long-legged English beauty. If he was so badly missing his wife, could that mean he had shown the door at last to his driver/secretary?

There were ways of finding out about that. Several times during the war Marshall had had to put discreet inquiries in train when one or another of his commanders was involved in a scandal. There was the general who had got himself mixed up in a contested British divorce suit, and when a relative of the officer named in the suit had written to declare that it couldn't possibly have happened, that the general had been "framed," Marshall had replied:

> I have looked into the matter we talked about—I shall mention no names. I am sorry to tell you that the report appears quite conclusive, with no evidence of framing whatsoever. On the contrary, the principal testimony is from the managing director and the floor maid of the hotel in which the apartment was located. As many as eight nights in a period of about three weeks, the evidence is virtually conclusive that his friend spent the night until 11 A.M. or thereabouts the following morning. He would leave at 7.15 A.M. and she would remain behind a bolted door until about 11 A.M.
>
> The incident of the clothing coupons was a minor bit of contributing evidence but one in which the offense, under the British law, was a one hundred pound fine and six months of hard labor.
>
> I must ask you to destroy this letter. . . .

Now Marshall's staff went to work to find out what was happening between Ike and his British girl friend. The answers they got back indicated that so far as the general was concerned, the couple had reached the parting of the ways—though Lieutenant Summersby might not yet be convinced of that fact.

Eisenhower flew back to the United States that summer for a triumphal tour of a nation eager to hail the victor of the war in Europe. It was a hero's welcome, and Mamie Eisenhower, who accompanied her husband, happily shared in it. Marshall was delighted. When he saw them in Washington, he informed Ike of his intention to resign as Chief of Staff and to nominate the Supreme Commander as his successor. He had feared domestic complications and a possible public scandal, and that was the last thing he would have wished upon the highest office in the U.S. Army. But now the sight of the Eisenhowers together convinced him that the decision was right, and there would be no scandal involved. Like the war, the Kay Summersby affair was over and done with.

Not quite, as it turned out.

One afternoon, shortly after Eisenhower had taken over as Chief of Staff, Mrs. Summersby walked into the War Department and asked to see "the boss."

Cora Thomas, who was the Chief of Staff's secretary, stared at her popeyed as she sank onto a sofa in the office, crossed one shapely leg over the other, and proceeded to pet the Scottie dog she was carrying under her arm. He was called Felix, and he had gained her admission to the War Department since he still wore the collar Ike had given her at the same time as the dog and she had shown it to the guards. "Felix. This dog belongs to Kay and Ike," a plaque on the collar said.*

Kay Summersby could hardly have chosen a worse moment to visit. It was the day Field Marshal Montgomery was arriving from England on an official visit. Mamie Eisenhower was due in the War Department at any moment to pick up her husband and travel to the airfield to meet the British commander.

"Get her out of here!" said Ike's aides when they were apprized of her presence.

She was taken into a back room and kept there until Ike and Mamie left the building.

"She sat there for hours with her Scottie," said Cora Thomas later. "I'll never forget how panic-stricken Ike's aides were at the thought that Mamie might see her. 'Get her out of here!' they kept hissing."

She never did see "the boss" again. She waited in the office

---

*The dog became famous at Ike's headquarters during the Battle of the Bulge, when, during an urgent war conference, he peed on the campaign map, eliminating all marks of Nazi penetration. A joke later became current around HQ. "Where's the enemy?" "Pissed off!"

for him to come back; but that afternoon Ike's mother died, and he returned instead to his quarters at Fort Myer. Kay Summersby, still clutching Felix to her admirable bosom, stayed in the War Department until the place began to close up and it became manifest that Ike was not coming back. She then left with one of the girls she knew and took a cab back to her hotel. Everyone was relieved. She had gotten the message without its having to be spelled out. The next day she left Washington and got out of Eisenhower's life.*

The incident might have disturbed Marshall had he heard about it, but by that time, fortunately for his peace of mind, he was in China and he was not told about it until later.

"I'm afraid I played an awful trick on Eisenhower, getting out so fast," he said later. "He inherited all the headaches."

But Mrs. Summersby was not the kind of headache he was thinking about.

Later there were plenty of people who declared that General Marshall should never have undertaken the mission to China, that he must have known it was an unsolvable problem, and that he had accepted it because he believed he was the only man in the world who could find a solution to it. His success in the war had made him overconfident, convinced him that nothing now was beyond his capabilities, that he possessed a magic touch. In other words, it was hubris which had motivated him in taking it on.

It was a total misreading of his character. Not only was hubris foreign to his nature, but if he had ever had a trace of arrogance in him, events during the past few weeks would certainly have driven it out. By the winter of 1945, in fact, he must have been feeling abysmally low in spirits. For a man who had given all he had for his country and done so much for America and its allies, he was being given remarkably shabby treatment by his countrymen.

Even after his appointment as the President's special envoy

---

*A little later she went for a visit to California, leaving Felix behind with a friend. She never saw the dog again. Someone came and collected it while she was away.

to China and right up until his departure on his mission, Marshall had continued to testify before the joint congressional committee once more inquiring into the Pearl Harbor attack. He had imagined when he had first been called before a committee consisting of five senators and five representatives (presided over by Senator Alben W. Barkley) that he would be questioned chiefly on the quality of military judgment he had shown during the period leading up to the Pearl Harbor disaster. To his stupefaction, he discovered that the questions were loaded with attacks on the motives of the late President Roosevelt and that the statements he made about his own actions, which he was ready to defend on military grounds, were, in fact, examined for what he called "sinister political implications."

Two senators in particular, Homer Ferguson and Owen Brewster, bore down on him harshly in their attempts to tie him in with a plot to plunge the United States into a war which they could otherwise have avoided. All his questioners repeatedly made the point that they were not being hostile to him personally.

"The investigation was intended to crucify Roosevelt," Marshall said later, "not to get me."

But though he made it constantly clear that neither he nor the War Department had anything to hide, it was a long, wearying, and humiliating ordeal. By the time it was over Marshall was a chastened man who might have been forgiven for feeling embittered at the rough treatment he had received from a body of men he had served so well. He was too experienced in the way these things went to expect gratitude. But he was exhausted, and most of his admirers would have understood and sympathized if he had walked away from the congressional inquiry and called up President Truman to say the hell with it, he had had enough. If all service to one's country earned for you was such treatment, then he was damned if he was going to undertake another difficult mission—especially one to China.

His devotion to duty was still so ingrained that he did not do that. But in the circumstances, it can hardly be said that he prepared for his new and complicated task with the thoroughness he normally expended on a big new project. Had he done so, and had he had the time, he might have seen the difficulties ahead in achieving the miraculous solution to the China problem that President Truman quite evidently expected of him.

For the situation in China in 1945 was a mess.

Militarily speaking, conditions were worse than they had been even during the grimmer periods of World War II, when the armies of Japan had occupied most of China's main cities, all of its ports, and large tracts of the mainland. The myth had spread abroad during the war that it was the valiant efforts of the Chinese government which had prevented the armies of the Rising Sun from taking over the whole of China. In fact, had it not been for China's allies, the Japanese would have triumphed everywhere.

It was the United States which had poured in vast supplies of guns, planes, and ammunition. It was the United States which had helped raise and equip Chinese armies and stiffened their resistance to Japanese invasion by bringing in U.S. troops and advisers to encourage it. A volunteer air force, largely composed of U.S. pilots and aircrews, had been organized and soon won worldwide fame as the Flying Tigers (under the command of General Claire Lee Chennault), and it was this force, flying in all weathers under appalling conditions, which had held the Japanese bomber fleets at bay. And on China's periphery, in the steamy Burmese jungles, an Anglo-American force under British command had constantly jabbed at the flanks of the Japanese invaders in China.

Now the war was over—with Japan at least. The vast armies of the Rising Sun had been captured, rounded up, and were slowly being shipped back to the shattered homeland. But far from bringing peace back to China, the defeat of the enemy had only served to provoke an even more painful conflict, one that threatened to tear the country apart. It was a bloody civil war between the official government armies of the Nationalist (Kuomintang) regime, the leader of which was President Chiang Kai-shek, and the so-called People's Army of the Chinese Communists (Chicoms), under their leader, Mao Tse-tung.

Judged on purely theoretical military terms, it should have

been an easy war for the government side to win and therefore an unwise one for the Communists to provoke. It had been to the Nationalists that the United States and its allies had given their support in arms and money during the war. As Truman was to say later, "They were just loaded down with guns." Moreover, the Nationalists had in the field several different armies numbering between 4 and 5 million well-equipped men, whereas the Chicoms had a fighting strength estimated at not more than 300,000.

And yet it seemed certain that unless a persuasive and influential mediator arrived in time to separate David from Goliath, it would be David (in other words, the Communists) who would win the bloody struggle now going on. The common belief among U.S. advisers in China was that Chiang Kai-shek had told Nationalist Army commanders to fight as little as possible against the Japanese during the war, in order to conserve the matériel the Americans had given him for use against the Chicoms once the official war was over. But these same experts were convinced that while the Nationalists had, indeed, evaded clashes with the Japanese, they had failed to keep in training; by the time the war was over they had developed fat instead of muscle, had lost their appetite for any kind of fighting at all, and replaced their martial spirit with an insatiable appetite for corruption. Whereas, with little money and scant armaments, the Communists had harried the Japanese all through the war, and now that only the effete Nationalists stood between them and the control of China, they were lean, fit, feisty, and ready to do battle in order to wrest control from the degenerate regime of Chiang Kai-shek.

To State Department experts on China, it seemed that there were only two alternatives if the Nationalists—who were, after all, still their allies—were to be saved from the consequences of their own folly, and China from horrendous civil war. They could decide that the Communists were as much an enemy as the Japanese, send in U.S. generals to take over military control, stiffen the Nationalist armies with U.S. troops, pump in more matériel, money, and know-how—and then wipe the Chicoms out. Or, on the other hand, they could try a less cold-blooded approach and persuade the two sides to sit around a table and talk accommodation, resolve their political and ideological differences, and form a coalition regime which would rule China until such time as the postwar ferment had simmered down. Meanwhile, Nationalists and Communists would jointly run the country under the benevolent eye and guidance of the United States.

But in fact, the first alternative was not possible. In the social and political climate of the United States in 1945, with the nation still convalescent from the draining ordeal of war, there were few voters (and, more important, few congressmen) willing to contemplate the expenditure of more lives and more money to restore the status quo in faraway China. Some sort of peaceful solution to Chiang Kai-shek's difficulties had to be found without risking any more American lives. But how?

So long as the ambassador to China had been the loquacious Irishman Pat Hurley, there had never been much chance of bringing the two opposing Chinese factions to the meeting place. Neither side trusted him. He had neither balance nor clout. His colleagues thought he talked too much and had no discretion. Chiang regarded him with a mildly irritated contempt, and the Communists treated him as a lightweight, not to be taken seriously. But he had been appointed to his job by the late President Roosevelt, who liked him, and he still had powerful political friends. Truman had hesitated to remove him until his uncontrollable tendency to run off at the mouth had given the President the excuse to fire him and there was someone prestigious (even if he wasn't waiting in the wings) to replace him.

General Marshall had all the clout in the world, and Truman never doubted that he was just the man for the job. Time and again in World War II he had reconciled the irreconcilables. Even the bitterest rivals had shaken hands and promised to behave when Marshall had told them to do so. He had smoothed the feathers of such martial peacocks as George Patton, Douglas MacArthur, Ernest King, Bernard Montgomery, and Charles de Gaulle. When Harry Truman closed his eyes, he saw a picture in his mind: of Chiang Kai-shek and Mao Tse-tung fondly embracing, while, behind them, an avuncularly smiling General Marshall looked benevolently on and the sky glowed with the dawn of a new day in China.

The President was certain Marshall could do it. The mess in China was as good as cleaned up. There was nothing this great and good man could not achieve.

Except perform miracles unfortunately.

20

Showdown in Shanghai

December 20, 1945, was a damp and miserable day in Shang-hai. It was spitting with rain, and a chill wind was knifing down from the northern plains of China, stirring foam caps on the oily waves of the East China Sea. The big USAAF transport plane came out of a thick, low cloud cover, circled once over the ravaged rooftops of this once-thriving but now devastated port, and then lumbered down to a heavy landing on the bomb-holed airfield. Marshall was first out of the plane and led the way across the field to a line of U.S. and Chinese troops drawn up in the lee of a wrecked hangar. He came to attention and took the salute as a marine band played him a welcome with a slightly hangdog ver-sion of "Yankee Doodle." Then he climbed into a U.S. military command car and drove through the shabby Shanghai streets, staring blankly at the cringing figures of Chinese coolies huddled in the doorways of shuttered shops, shivering in their thin cotton clothes. His two companions in the back of the car watched him warily, no doubt wondering whether the vacant expression on his lean face signified numbness, weariness—or what? Finally, the tall military figure on his right, General Albert C. Wedemeyer, ven-tured to speak, though his words were hardly of earthshaking significance.

"Welcome to China, General," he said.

The other man in the car was Walter Robertson, charge d'af-faires at the U.S. Embassy in Chungking* and, until this moment, America's senior diplomat in China. He cleared his throat and hesitantly chuckled. "You'd never guess it was the Christmas sea-son, would you?" he remarked.

---

*Still, for the time being, the seat of the Nationalist government, as it had been throughout World War II.

Marshall still said nothing. He continued to gaze in silence as the car bumped and splashed its way through the muddy streets toward the waterfront. He seemed wrapped in thought, and Wedemeyer, who remembered Marshall's silences from the past, guessed his thoughts were probably miles away from China at the moment. His appearances in Congress had gone on until the last moment; he had hardly had time to say good-bye to his wife before boarding the plane. How could he possibly have had time to adjust?

The command car came at last on to the Shanghai Bund and cruised along the waterfront before pulling up outside the grand façade of the Cathay Hotel. There was a large U.S. flag flying outside the canopied entrance. This was the hotel where, in lush prewar days, the rich Chinese and their ladies, the taipans from Hong Kong, the arms dealers and the warlords used to gather for tea dances in the lounge and more esoteric pleasures in the private rooms. The well-known British millionaire Sir Philip Sassoon had always kept two suites of rooms permanently rented in the hotel for the occasions on which he arrived from London or Paris to inspect his multifarious textile and other enterprises in China. The suites were the most expensive and luxurious that Shanghai (and probably all China) could offer, and Sir Philip had added some exotic personal touches to the furnishings. Each suite had large panoramic windows and balconies looking down on the normally teeming streets of the Bund and the usually busy sea-lanes beyond. There were exquisitely brocaded chaises longues, thick Persian carpets, soft, broad beds, silken Chinese screens on the walls, and coyly seductive Mogul prints and Mysore carvings. In these opulent surroundings many a Chinese warlord, many a Japanese general, many a European and an American wheeler-dealer, many a White Russian or slinky Asian tart had sipped Dom Pérignon, nibbled the best Beluga, and then made a deal of one kind or another (for vast quantities of money, of course) with Sassoon or his friends. But now General Al Wedemeyer, as U.S. Commander in Chief of the China Theater, had requisitioned the suites for his own military purposes, and though some of the furnishings were still there, he had opened the windows and driven out the scent of exotic perfumes, the delicious odors of corruption, which had clung to the walls, the fabrics, and the bed sheets.

Now he informed General Marshall that the suite upstairs had been assigned to him for the duration of his stay in Shanghai, and for the first time the special envoy's manner briskened. In that case, Marshall said, it would be a good idea to repair there at once. Wedemeyer could help him unpack, and it would give them a chance to talk.

Chargé d'Affaires Walter Robertson watched the two men go upstairs with the feeling a civilian often gets when two old military comrades are reunited—that of being not so subtly excluded from the club. In this case it was understandable, of course. He knew that Wedemeyer had once been a junior officer on Marshall's staff in Washington and that the bond between them was close—so close, it was rumored, that in the last days of peace, in 1941, when the FBI was breathing down Wedemeyer's neck and threatening him with possible arrest and court-martial, it was Marshall who had stood by his subordinate, declared his unswerving faith in him, and helped save him from public disgrace and the wreck of his military career.

All the same Robertson could not help feeling shut out. He was, after all, the most senior accredited U.S. diplomat in China. He had a vested interest in what Marshall had to say; he was deeply involved in the thrust and significance of this new mission to China; and in addition, he had some personal problems he was particularly anxious to talk over with the general.

But in the circumstances, what else could he do but wait for the two men to finish their private consultation?

In later years General Marshall never wrote or said anything about what passed between him and Al Wedemeyer at the Cathay Hotel that afternoon of December 20, 1945. It is true that, toward the end of his life, when he did finally agree to make a series of tape recordings about the major events in his long career, Dr. Forrest Pogue, the military historian, submitted a long list of questions to him. A number of those questions referred to General Wedemeyer; the general kept postponing his answers to them, insisting that he would get around to them later. He died before doing so. He did not seem to wish to talk about Wedemeyer at all.

This is unfortunate because the only other version of the encounter necessarily comes from Wedemeyer himself, and it would have been fascinating to compare it with Marshall's account, especially since the hour the two men spent together in the Sassoon suite in the Cathay Hotel on December 20, 1945, was a disastrous encounter. It smashed the close bonds of friendship which had long existed between the two men, and that was sad for both of them. As Walter Robertson said later, "They went away as trusted colleagues, and they came back deeply suspicious of each other. Things were never the same between them again."

But worse than that, the encounter had a profound effect on the outcome of the China mission, and that was unfortunate for the United States.

What went wrong between the two men?

As far as promotion in the Army was concerned, Albert Coady Wedemeyer had not done too badly during World War II. From a humble captain in 1940 and a mere major just before Pearl Harbor precipitated America into the war in 1941, he had risen to the rank of lieutenant general in 1945 and the title of Commander in Chief of an important theater of war. Yet he was a frustrated man, and if you had asked him point-blank, he would probably have told you that nothing had gone right for him since the accusing fingers had pointed at him in the War Department after the leak of the Victory Plan to the Chicago *Tribune* in December 1941.

It was true that his chief, General Marshall, had stood by him after suspicion had fallen upon him. Marshall had made it manifest to everyone, including the White House, that he trusted Wedemeyer and had no doubts about his loyalty. He had taken him with him to many of the big Allied conferences and eventually appointed him his chief of war plans. He had sent him around the world on special missions.

But there was one thing he had never been able to give Al

Wedemeyer. That was any sort of command in the European theater of operations. It will be remembered that Wedemeyer was probably the greatest expert the U.S. Army possessed about the tactics, the thinking, and the personnel of the German officer corps. In view of his encyclopedic knowledge of the Wehrmacht, nothing would have been more logical than to post him to a battlefield where he could utilize his expertise in fighting Germans. For instance, Generals Juergen von Arnim and Erwin Rommel had made their appearance in North Africa during Anglo-American operations in Egypt and Tunisia. Wedemeyer had known both of them in Germany, was as familiar as they were with the military theories on which they had been weaned, and could have guessed which stratagems of field warfare they were likely to pursue. His old military college professor, General Alfred Jodl, had later appeared in Russia and was subsequently responsible for the defense of Berlin. There was nothing Wedemeyer did not know about Jodl. More than any other American officer, he knew how all the top Nazi generals worked, played, thought, and fought. He did not fail to point out to Marshall that sent to Europe and given command of a division, a corps, or, better still, an army, he could have outfoxed, outwitted, and outfought them.

He was never given a chance. The White House had seen to that. In President Roosevelt's mind, Wedemeyer was mixed up with those isolationists like Charles Lindbergh and pro-Germans like Truman Smith who had opposed him before World War II. With Marshall standing behind his subordinate, the President could hardly have asked for Wedemeyer's head after the scandal over the Victory Plan leakage—how could he when there was no proof of Wedemeyer's guilt? But he did let it be known that he would not be pleased if Wedemeyer had anything to do with fighting Germans.

He indicated that Marshall could assign him anywhere in the world—except to those war theaters where there were Nazis fighting, the enemy he knew best.

So that was why Al Wedemeyer had spent the bulk of World War II in Asia and why he was still there when Marshall arrived in Shanghai on his mission for President Truman.

In one way, of course, he had been lucky. Had it not been for Marshall's staunch support, he would most likely have been banished to the military wilderness and spent the war eating his heart out as some embittered colonel in a remote training unit, watching less able and intelligent men leapfrog him for promotion. On the other hand, it had not been easy for him to sit in Ceylon and India and finally China and read reports from Europe about the final campaigns against the Nazis because time and again the name of his old German mentor had come up—General Jodl masterminding the Battle of the Bulge in the winter of 1944, General Jodl commanding the last-ditch battles against the Red Army in Prussia. How he had yearned to match his skills against him in those last dramatic engagements of the European war.

Instead, he had been not so much fighting battles as keeping himself uneasily afloat in the scummy waters of Chinese politics. In that tricky specialty, however, he had done well. His military-cum-diplomatic activities, exercised with a great deal of tact, had done much to restore good relations between the Chinese and U.S. administrations, both of which had suffered from the xenophobic blunders of previous American commanders.

By the end of the war, General Wedemeyer had made himself an expert on Sino-American affairs and had won admiration in Chungking and Washington alike. Long before Truman fired Patrick Hurley, Wedemeyer had quietly let it be known in his reports (mainly to Marshall, who was then still Chief of Staff) that the ambassador was a bungler and a loudmouth and was doing no good whatsoever to American policy in China. Realizing that Hurley's days were numbered, he had also indicated that, in contrast, his own standing was high with the Chinese. He wrote Marshall:

> The Generalissimo [Chiang Kai-shek] often asks advice concerning political matters involving other countries as well as China's internal affairs. I have emphasized tactfully to him that advice under such circumstances is given no official cognizance. At times his trust and dependence are almost childlike.

If and when Hurley was recalled, Wedemeyer was obviously hoping that the President would pick him to take the Irishman's place and that if he did succeed in being considered as a candidate for the job, then Marshall would give him his backing and blessing. He had already informed Marshall that Chiang Kai-shek was so impressed with his capabilities that he had offered him a job at a fabulous salary, asking him to stay in China for five years as head of the Military Advisory Commission. He had turned it down, he said, on the ground that his mother in America was "eighty years of age and I wanted to spend some time with her, and therefore couldn't possibly accept." It was such an obviously transparent excuse that it was evident he wished Marshall to understand he was open to a different kind of offer. But it did not come. Instead, he heard from Washington that the new envoy would be none other than Marshall himself. It must have been difficult for him to conceal his frustration and stupefaction. Why, what could George Marshall possibly know about the complicated problems that faced China now that the war with Japan was over? It was thirty years since he had even been in the country, and then only as a lowly officer in an isolated foreign garrison. How could he possibly, even with all his great wartime prestige, avoid making a fool of himself?

There was only one way. Al Wedemeyer would help him and put every last shred of knowledge he possessed about China at Marshall's disposal. With Marshall's reputation and Wedemeyer's know-how, they would make a success of the task together. It would be Wedemeyer's chance to show his loyalty and his gratitude to his chief, who had stood by him so faithfully in the stormy days at the beginning of the war.

Because of the many hours he had been forced to spend on the congressional inquiry into Pearl Harbor and the necessity of going over all the documents once again, General Marshall simply did not have the time to do much work on the brief which was drawn up for him for his mission to China. That was unavoidable, but ominous. He would certainly never have allowed that to happen when he was Chief of Staff. As Dean Acheson (then a junior official in the State Department) said later, "A number of people in the War Department and State worked on it. General Marshall was terribly busy with the Pearl Harbor inquiry, and he had little time to work on the directive. He did sit in with the War Department planners and undoubtedly agreed with the views of the people there. But he was too busy to have worked on the draft. State made the draft. Then the Army made a counterdraft. Then we made another, and the final directive had some of it all."

There was a significant tendency in the State Department at the time to believe that the only real obstacle to the establishment of lasting peace in China was the arrogant stubbornness of one man: the Nationalist leader, Chiang Kai-shek. Among some of the so-called China experts, he was thought of as a kind of Asian General de Gaulle, full of the same touchiness and overweening vanity. They felt the time had come to give him the same treatment ("the bum's rush," as Harry Hopkins had called it) as Roosevelt and Churchill between them had administered to De Gaulle. Only they needed someone of stature to do it for them. Their attitude (as Acheson described it) was: "We think Chiang Kai-shek is a fine fellow, but if he doesn't behave, kick him up the ass."

In other words, they were convinced that the rival political factions in China were on the brink of tearing the country apart not because they espoused irreconcilable ideologies, but because one man alone refused to compromise with his rivals: Chiang Kai-shek. He had the power, and he was determined to cling to it. But now that the war with Japan was over, the time had come to do something about him. With him out of the way, the problems would solve themselves. The Nationalists and the Communists (who, in the view of these experts at State, were more agrarian reformers than Reds in tooth and claw) would then come to a mutual arrangement for sharing power, and from the rapprochement would come stable government.

It was this rapprochement which General Marshall was directed by the President to bring about. His brief counseled him to begin with an immediate cease-fire between the Nationalist armies and the Communist guerrillas, meld the two martial groups into a unified force, and then get the political leaders around the table and persuade them to agree to a coalition. Out of the whole exercise would come what China had needed since the days of the Manchu dynasty: one army and one government to run the country. With his prestige, State was convinced that Marshall could pull it off. There were some who believed that, with his international reputation for impartiality, wisdom, and fair play, he could even persuade Chiang Kai-shek to go along. It *could* happen. But if it didn't . . . .

When the directive was finished, Marshall asked that it be condensed on one sheet of paper—as he had in the case of all his wartime directives—and it was with this 400-word brief in his baggage that he flew into Shanghai on December 20, 1945. As he and General Wedemeyer unpacked his case in the Cathay Hotel that afternoon, Marshall handed over the directive to his companion. "Wedemeyer, I want you to read this," he said, "and tell me what you think."

Al Wedemeyer knew that one of Marshall's most engaging characteristics was his detestation of yes-men. He could not stand, and would not tolerate, people who failed to give honest opinions when asked for them. Once, during the Casablanca Conference, Wedemeyer had been asked his opinion of the Allies' decision to demand unconditional surrender from the Germans, and he had got into a heated argument with Winston Churchill about it.

Afterward, he had apologized to Marshall for having talked back to such a distinguished statesman. He ought to have kept his mouth shut or chosen his words with more care. Marshall had stopped him in his tracks. "Wedemeyer," he had said, "don't you *ever* fail to give me the benefit of your thinking and your knowledge and experience."

"I would have jumped into Niagara Falls after that for General Marshall," Wedemeyer said. "That's the way I felt about him."

Now, in Shanghai, as the general's sergeant-aide put his last shirts away in the drawer, Wedemeyer read through the one-page directive his old chief had given him to read. As far as he remembered it later, the directive could be summed up as YOUR MISSION IS TO BRING ABOUT THE CONCILIATION AND AMALGAMATION OF ALL THE OPPOSING FORCES IN CHINA, THE NATIONALISTS, THE COMMUNISTS, AND THE INTELLECTUALS. YOU WILL PERSUADE THEM TO

COMBINE INTO A SINGLE INSTRUMENT OF GOVERNMENT FOR THE FU-
TURE CONTROL OF CHINA AND THE CHINESE PEOPLE.

"Well?" asked Marshall.

"General Marshall," said Wedemeyer, "you can never do this. It just won't work."

Marshall looked startled. "Why not?"

"Sir," Wedemeyer said, "the Nationalists, the Kuomintang, have all the power here, and I can assure you they are not going to relinquish one iota. And the Communists are determined to get all the power here, and they have an alien supporter—Moscow. There isn't the remotest chance you can bring them together. I know these people. I know Chiang Kai-shek, and you can work with him and his entourage as long as you remember this is a manorial country. I know the Communist leaders. They have stayed at my house. We've talked about Karl Marx and the dialectics of communism. But I have to be perfectly honest and tell you that they'll never mix. It just won't work."

He drew himself up, and then looked Marshall in the eye. "You have come here on an impossible mission," he said.

Wedemeyer maintains that normally Marshall would have taken this comment, unpalatable though it may have been, calmly and in silence. But to his astonishment, this time there was a totally different reaction. As he remembers it, the general's eyes "flashed" and his face went "red with anger." His voice rose as he rasped, "Wedemeyer, it *is* going to work! I *am* going to do it! And what's more," he added, "*you* are going to help me do it!"

The tone of his voice was like nothing Wedemeyer had ever heard from Marshall before.

"God," he said later, "you could have stuck a stiletto in my spleen, and it wouldn't have hurt more."

At first he was flummoxed at what to say. Finally, he said, "Well, sir, all I can say is every facility I have in hand and every-thing I can do to help, I want you to know it is yours."

Marshall continued to glower at him. When they came back into the other suite, where Walter Robertson was waiting for them, the diplomat sensed at once that all was not well between the two men. Marshall had a high flush, and his eyes were hard. Wede-meyer, whose manner was normally quite arrogant, almost im-perious, for once looked diminished and subdued.

They went down to the hotel restaurant for dinner and for the next few hours talked solidly about China's problems. Wed-emeyer briefed Marshall on the military situation, and Robertson on the political situation. Both of them strongly maintained that in their judgment there was absolutely no basis either politically or militarily for a coalition with the Communists. Wedemeyer pointed out that the Kuomintang and the Communists were two diametrically opposed power groups, one trying to stay in power and the other striving to get their hands on it. How could they get together when they distrusted each other so much? They wanted different things for China, and there was no room for compro-mise.

Both Wedemeyer and Robertson got the impression that Marshall listened carefully to everything they had to say, even though he made absolutely no comment. Save for the air of tension between the two old military comrades, Robertson had no feeling that there had been a rift between them and that from now on they would regard themselves as adversaries. He would have been astounded if he had known that when Wedemeyer climbed into bed that night, he was still feeling wounded because of Marshall's attitude toward him.

"It hurt me, you know," Wedemeyer said later. "In bed my thoughts ran through my mind like this. I loved and respected this guy. And I was loyal to him. I said to myself: 'He's old; he's been through a terrible war; he's drained, emotionally drained. He's old now. He came across the Pacific Ocean.' At that time we weren't allowed to go over nine thousand feet. You get awful turbulence. 'He might have been ill.' I was trying to find all kinds of excuses for him, you see. You do that for someone you love. You forgive them. Also there are few people who are truly humble, and he was one of them. He'd been called the greatest man in the world, the greatest American, by Truman, and the accolades and awards had been heaped on him. And now, unwittingly, I had penetrated his armor."

A few days later Marshall penetrated Wedemeyer's armor. Having already snubbed his old subordinate so painfully that it had felt like "a stiletto in my spleen," he now proceeded to twist the dagger in the wound.

On the following morning (December 21), Marshall informed his staff they would be leaving at once for Chungking, the Nationalist capital, and that Walter Robertson would be going with them. Pointedly he did not ask Wedemeyer to come along.

Though his official job in China was chargé d'affaires of the U.S. Mission, Robertson was actually running under false colors, for he was not a professional diplomat at all. He had been dug out of industry in 1941 because he had lived and worked in China and had been sent to Chungking to fill a wartime gap. Before taking on the job, he had extracted a promise from the State Department that he would be allowed to return to his wife, family and business (in Richmond, Virginia) the moment the war was over. He had been pleading and threatening (in vain) ever since the defeat of Japan to be brought home.

Like Wedemeyer, he had built up friendly relations with the Chinese. He knew how to deal with evasive Oriental officials. As a result, it did not take him long, once Marshall and his party reached Chungking, to arrange a series of meetings with Chiang Kai-shek, Madame Chiang Kai-shek, some of the more important members of the Kuomintang hierarchy, and a number of local leaders of the Communists. Contacts with the Communist chiefs, Chou En-lai and Mao Tse-tung, would follow later.

It was not until after these series of meetings and the preparation of initial reports and memorandums that Robertson managed to get some time alone with Marshall. Unlike Wedemeyer, he did not get the impression that the general was ill, tired, emotionally drained, or even old, but he did sense that he was under a certain pressure and wanted to get something achieved quickly. In the circumstances, he hesitated to talk about his own problems but eventually found the courage to do so.

He explained that he was not a career diplomat, that he had already tried to resign twice from his post, and that he was pulling every string he knew in Washington in order to get home to his wife and family. While the war was on, he had heeded every call to service and had done his duty like a good American. But now the war was over—and he wanted to go home.

Marshall said nothing. He simply gazed across the room (they were in his quarters in Chungking) above his glasses, not saying a word or making a gesture. It was a well-known Marshall ploy. Robertson, who was a stranger to it, felt he had to fill the silence somehow and rushed on, saying that his wife was unhappy, his children neglected, and all he could think of, day and night, was that they were there and he was here, and it wasn't good enough. He repeated again and again that he wanted to go home.

At last Marshall spoke.

"I want to go home, too," he said.

Then, very quietly, he began to explain how his presence in China had come about. He explained how he had retired as Chief of Staff and driven out to Leesburg with Katherine to their new home, Dodona Manor, and as they went into their new bedroom, the telephone was ringing. It was the President asking him to go to China.

His reply had been: "Yes, Mr. President."

He hadn't unpacked his bags. He didn't even tell Katherine until she heard it on the radio in the bedroom. He had simply got into the car the next morning and driven to the White House and said to the President, "Here I am."

There was a heavy silence until Robertson, glumly, said he was still worried about his family situation, and what was he going to do about his family situation? He couldn't go on like this for much longer.

"Bring them out here," said Marshall.

He put his hand in his pocket and pulled out an envelope, on which he scribbled rapidly, then passed it over. It was a message to Secretary of State James Byrnes in Washington, and it said, "I've talked to Walter Robertson. He's agreed to stay on. Send the family out by next plane."

And all might have been well if they both had then made

their adieux. Instead, Marshall fixed Robertson with his blue eyes and said, "Tell me, Robertson, how do you like Wedemeyer?"

Robertson was about to explain that Wedemeyer was his cousin, they had known each other from boyhood, and that therefore, he might be biased. But unfortunately Marshall intervened to add, "I think he is getting too big for his breeches."

If Walter Robertson had been a professional diplomat, maybe he would have kept that comment to himself. Alas, he could not resist mentioning it to his cousin when he met him again a few days later.

"And that hurt me. It hurt me deeply," Wedemeyer said later. "It confirmed to me, you see, the feeling of the meeting at the Cathay Hotel a few days earlier. And I was hurt because of his attitude towards me. He obviously didn't care for me any longer. And I decided from then on that I didn't give a damn about him either."

It was an attitude that would come back to haunt him later.

21

"Don't Look Back"

At first everything seemed to go terribly well. Marshall wrote a note to Admiral Stark in Washington to tell him that his wife, Kay Stark, was probably responsible for the initial success of his mission. She had found a four-leaf clover in a field in Pennsylvania and insisted her husband send it on to the general for luck. It had seemed to work. He had received promises of cooperation from Chiang Kai-shek *and* the Communists. His contact with the Chinese Nationalist leader had, of course, been made pleasant by a renewed encounter with Chiang's beautiful American-educated wife, Mei-Ling, known as Madame. To everyone else she was a high-powered female of fearsome personality, compared by some Americans to the Dragon Lady in "Terry and the Pirates," but in Marshall's presence she seemed to melt into an adoring deb. They had not met since the Allied conference in Cairo, and now she went out of her way to make him feel welcome, sending him gifts of candy, urging him to go out and "get some color in your cheeks." When he came down with a bout of flu, undoubtedly caught from Chiang's entourage, for they all were suffering from it, she dispatched couriers with gifts and encouragement.

"I hope this basket of fruit will prove enjoyable," she wrote. "I am taking the doctor's advice and staying in bed until the coughing stops. I have definitely caught flu from attending our cold Assembly meetings. I hope to be up for your birthday. MLS."*

Her influence on her husband was great, and she gave every sign of being willing to use it on Marshall's behalf to persuade the Nationalists to fall in with his plans.

In a totally different way, Marshall had also made something of a hit with the Communist representative Chou En-lai, with

---

*Mei-Ling Soong. Soong was her maiden name.

372

whom he had conferences in Chungking. The two men had something of the same straightforward, uncompromising outlook on things and appeared to speak the same unequivocal language. During these conferences Marshall had been accompanied by a China expert, Henry A. "Hank" Byroade,* who was delighted at Chou En-lai's reactions to the U.S. proposals.

According to Byroade, Marshall was convinced he would have no chance of success with his mission unless he could get rid of the Communist Army. Byroade pointed out to him that the Red Chinese were both a political and a military force at the same time, but the interesting fact was that whenever Chou En-lai or his leader, Mao Tse-tung, talked about Chinese military affairs, they always referred to Generalissimo Chiang Kai-shek as "Commander in Chief of all Chinese forces in China."

Did this give them an opening? Byroade thought it did. He persuaded Marshall to approach the Communists with a very simple proposition. He should convince them that it would make things easier if they announced their acceptance of the generalissimo as their Commander in Chief as well as that of the Nationalist forces. Once they did so, Marshall would explain, the different armies throughout China could be split up in such a way that they would become a "digestible force," with local commanders of different political complexions but accepting overall control from the generalissimo.

Naturally Marshall would have to promise the Communists something in return for this concession.

He would propose that they be given membership in the Nationalist government. Of course, they would move into posts where they would have no chance at all of having veto power over government actions—though this aspect was not stressed. But if they did accept his proposition and were persuaded that the Nationalists would institute a number of badly needed reforms, then there was a good chance that a coalition could be forged, and a start made in combined government in China, and an end to the civil war.

*Later U.S. ambassador to Egypt.

For nights on end Byroade joined with Marshall working out the details of the proposal. Though he himself had initially proposed it, Byroade grew increasingly skeptical of the plan's chances as the hours passed. On the other hand, Marshall was optimistic. To an old China hand, it seemed impossible that the Communists would ever consent to split up their armies as they were suggesting. But Marshall had met and talked with Chou En-lai and believed he was a man of honesty and goodwill and ready to make a deal.

He was right, too. To Byroade's amazement and Marshall's evident pleasure, Chou En-lai read through the plan, nodded his head at the special envoy, smiled—*and initialed the proposal*. What, no miracles? This was February 1946, and in less than two months since his arrival in China, Marshall seemed indeed to be achieving the impossible. He was making Nationalist oil mix with Communist water and bringing the irreconcilables together. It is true, as Byroade noted, that Marshall was a little surprised himself at how easy it was proving. But he had great faith not only in his own integrity but in that of the government behind him, the United States of America, ready to get behind and guarantee any settlement which was made, and he exuded from every pore a belief in the rightness of his cause and his interest in the future and the fruitful welfare of the Chinese people. It was touching. Even the most cynical Nationalists and the most diehard Communists seemed to put their trust in him.

This was, of course, only a first stage in the progress toward a settlement, but it was an enormously significant one just the same. The Communists did not initial any documents lightly, and in Nationalist circles there was a stunned surprise when the news became known. It was announced from Marshall's office that the plan would now go to Chiang Kai-shek for him to initial, too. Then would come a formal meeting of the two sides and their signatures to the official document.

Even General Wedemeyer's gloomy prognostications seemed to have been confounded, and he generously admitted it. He made haste to congratulate Marshall on his success, mincing no words in expressing his surprise and pleasure. In return, Marshall, by now in a most benevolent mood, reacted as if never a moment of unpleasantness had ever marred their friendship. Their differences seemed to have been forgotten.

When news reached Washington, President Truman at once cabled his congratulations and summoned his envoy back to the United States to report personally on the next stage. And suddenly every American in China was in an optimistic mood, as if, after a long dark journey, they had rounded a bend in the tunnel and felt the sunlight beckoning them. They found it hard to conceal their astonishment at the sudden change in the political and military climate. They were awed by the power and influence wrought by Marshall's great prestige. There was nothing he could not achieve.

It was an ambience in which Marshall himself could hardly fail to be affected, and it was noticeable that this tired sixty-five-year-old man, who had come into China only weeks ago burdened down by the problems of the world, now seemed happier, bouncier, younger. So convinced did he seem that his mission was all but achieved that he took Wedemeyer to one side and sounded him out on whether he would be willing to take over as ambassador to China once the agreement between the two factions was signed, sealed, and delivered. Wedemeyer asked time to think it over, but of course, it was what he had always wanted. He wrote from Shantung on February 17, 1946:

> I would be lacking in candor if I did not state that I feel happy in your expression of confidence in my ability to fill the difficult post of ambassador to China. Naturally I have qualms about succeeding a man of your ability, particularly after your signal success in handling the delicate situation in this area.

But of course, he accepted, and Marshall told him they would discuss the details when he got back from his trip to the United States. On his departure, Chiang Kai-shek and Madame personally came to see him off, and he told them he would be back in April and this time would be bringing his wife with him. They wished him a safe return.

Three days after his departure, officials gathered in Chung-king for the signing ceremony. Gold pens and decorated scrolls had been prepared for the great event.

But then Chou En-lai arrived. He was sorry, he said, but he had received new instructions. He could not sign.

What had gone wrong?

Those were the days when the Chinese Communists and the Russians were still allies, and Byroade at first suspected that Moscow had been consulted and had advised against it. The Russians were hardly likely to welcome an arrangement which merged the only Red Army outside the Soviet Union into the forces of the anti-Communist Chiang Kai-shek.

But then he and his fellow experts doubted whether even in those days the Chinese Communists took orders from Moscow. They finally decided they had made up their own minds about this one, and it was almost certainly Mao Tse-tung who had turned thumbs down and told Chou En-lai to reverse himself.

"The longer I looked at it," Byroade said later, "the more I was inclined to put it down to the fundamental differences between the two sides, between Mao, who had spent years in caves, and the Nationalists, who had been living it up on other people's money. Mao just couldn't see himself going along with the other side, and in the end he refused to support Chou En-lai in going ahead with trying the plan."

He took the setback philosophically.

"Looking back," he said, "I wonder how it could possibly have worked. I'm doubtful that it could. We Americans looked at China and we would say, 'There's China, it's a nation, and the generalissimo is president. He can arrange things.' It wasn't true, really. The generalissimo did not have the power to do the necessary—the power and the means to have made our plan work. After all, he was balancing warlord against warlord. There were limits to what he could do and the resources he could do it with."

When the news that things had gone wrong was cabled to Marshall in Washington, there were those among his staff who hoped he would not come back. He had brought the negotiations to the brink of success, and it was not his fault if, at the last moment, one of the parties had backed out of the agreement.

Unfortunately, as Byroade remarked later, Marshall was "not a type that could accept defeat. It was foreign to his nature."

He sent a message to Chungking to let them know he would be returning with Katherine, on schedule. And Byroade remembers thinking: "What a terrible position to put him in! It was his last role. [He] is used to a life in which there is always an answer—so let's get it!"

Only in the case of China, there wasn't one. Not the sort of answer, at least, that would satisfy General Marshall. It would be failure and disillusionment from now on.

On his initial arrival Marshall had been hailed by the Chinese people as the possible savior of their nation, and he was cheered wherever he went. But now he saw the other side. Chiang Kai-shek was still as deferential to him as ever, and Madame quite obviously continued to adore him; but there were elements in Chiang's entourage who suspected that Marshall had come back determined to "reform" them and curb their greedy appetites for bribes. The rumor that he would insist on a purge of corrupt elements, to demonstrate to the Communists that the Nationalists were worthy partners in running the country together, spread in Nationalist circles. Rather than lose their jobs and lucrative perks, they set out to denigrate the character of the American who threatened them.

On June 11, 1946, Marshall wrote to General Eisenhower, the Chief of Staff, in Washington:

> I gave Mrs. Marshall your message of concern regarding her reported illness. The facts are these, amusing and a commentary on the virulence of the present propaganda warfare: she merely made a weekend trip to Shanghai with Madame Chiang, but some of the diehard Government political boys, in their assaults on me, to weaken my influence and clear the way for a war of extermination [against the Communists], which they are incapable of carrying through without our assistance, built up a press attack that Katherine and I had fallen out and she had left Nanking in a huff.

Then I had gone to Shanghai to bring her back, but she immediately went into the hospital. They left her there, I returning empty-handed. She was never sick, never saw a hospital, and returned here with me and Madame Chiang. The part which greatly amused us but outraged Katherine was a description: "Mrs. Marshall, though over 60, still demands her diversions. Throughout the war, General Marshall had to take her to the movies and other diversions. Since he came to China, he has been too busy, so she left him, etc. etc."

He had begun what would soon be an exhausting routine of traveling between Communist headquarters in northern China, for long conferences with Mao and Chou, and Chiang's offices, which were either nowadays in Nanking or up in the mountains at Ku-ling. He had tried to make things easier for himself by inviting Chou to Nanking but had not repeated that experiment after the Nationalists, angry over a pro-Communist demonstration which greeted Chou's appearance, had sent in police and brutally beaten up the crowd.

He had enjoyed his Army service in China as a young man, and to begin with, this return visit had excited and enlivened him. He was genuinely fond of the Chinese people. But now his enthusiasm was souring. It was beginning to look like a thankless job, and he felt sorry not for himself, but for the Americans in the field who were devoting so much time to China's problems and getting so little thanks or recognition in return. He told Eisenhower:

> Life is pretty hard on all our officers in the field because of the scarcity and danger of the food and bad water, especially with no beer or wine or soft drinks to resort to. Tea is the only "out" though not always safe. Sleeping accommodations are terrible in these war-torn communities, with germs thick and no doctors, troops or facilities to help them get established. It is a pretty rough and thankless business. Two have had interpreters killed alongside of them. . . .

He added, "I am now in the midst of continuous conferences usually all day long—very tiring and trying. But the issue is vital. My people here in the office in my house are simply swamped with work and back to the old-time 10–14 hour war day."

Admiral Stark's four-leaf clover had long since crumbled into powder, and with it the expectations of his staff that anything would come of his efforts. But Marshall had not given up hope.

"He was a man who didn't like to be put in a position where there wasn't an answer," said Hank Byroade later. "In foreign affairs there are some problems that can't be solved just like that. You have to wait them out. But he couldn't see that. It was his form, his whole life, to find an answer."

Backstopping his mission in Washington was an assistant in the State Department named Dean Acheson, who would later become one of George Marshall's greatest admirers. But now he thought that the general was the wrong man sent on the wrong mission at the wrong time. He believed he should be brought home and suggested it to the President. Truman replied Marshall was his own master and would come home when he was good and ready. Acheson was disappointed because he believed Marshall did not possess the kind of mind to understand the Chinese.

"On the military side in China I thought the general was remarkable," he said later. "It was amazing how he got the [Reds and the Nationalists] to go along. He may have been helped by the fact that each side, feeling it didn't intend to keep its word, willingly agreed to what he suggested. But the military was something he thoroughly understood.

"But on the political side, matters took on a complexity, an Oriental complexity, which was foreign to the general's thinking. Things tended to escape from his control. He got lost in the trees. He didn't know where he was going. It was a geometric progression of confusion and complexity. One side would make a proposal and the other side would say, 'We won't say no, but here are three amendments.' And the other side would say, 'I have six amendments to that,' and the other side would say, 'And I have ten more.' After a while one had not the faintest idea where he was."

In Acheson's view, what America needed was someone in China who knew the Far East, understood the Communist mentality, and could deal with Chiang Kai-shek, "who was always breaking his promises, kept overextending himself, and kept getting licked by the Reds." He added, "My impression is that from April 1946 [when Marshall returned from Washington] until the end of his mission, things were out of control. The general didn't have the same sureness and deftness he had on so many other things. It needed someone who might have said to him, 'We aren't getting anywhere. Let's reappraise all this and see where we are.' "

Only no one had the nerve to tell Marshall this. The President was too much in awe of him. Acheson was too much his junior. What it needed was someone to make it possible for him to back out gracefully, without losing too much face, and leave what had obviously become the same old unsolvable problem to the old China hands, who were used to the hopelessness of it. Acheson thought that perhaps Marshall was actually paving the way for his own retreat when he cabled home about this time and told the President he was nominating General Wedemeyer as permanent ambassador to China.

"Truman called me in," Acheson said, "and said, 'We promised him we would give him who he wants, and it's Wedemeyer.' He called Wedemeyer in and said it was all right with him. He would be the ambassador."

Wedemeyer had come back to the United States for a sinus operation, and he was plainly delighted at the news of his appointment, even though it would mean temporarily resigning from the Army. He went to New York and embarked on a shopping spree at Brooks Brothers, buying up evening clothes, cutaways, and other ambassadorial trimmings. What added zest to the prospect of his job was the rumor circulating in Washington that Marshall would be coming home as soon as he arrived in China, leaving him to face the China problem alone, and he was already working out the method he would use to solve it.

Then a new cable arrived from Marshall. "PLEASE DELAY UNTIL FURTHER RECEIPT OR NOTICE FROM ME WEDEMEYER'S NOMINATION," it said. It was signed Marshall.

Shortly afterward he nominated someone entirely different.

"He's changed his mind," said Truman to Acheson. "Tell Wedemeyer the deal is off."

"I thought you were the Commander in Chief," Acheson said, not relishing the prospect. "But I notice you're having me do this."

"You go ahead," the President said.

So Acheson called in Wedemeyer and told him the bad news. He had no explanations or excuses to give. He didn't have any.

Wedemeyer must have found Marshall's action both capricious and confusing as well as highly inconvenient; for one thing, he had already informed the Army that he was temporarily leaving the service. But Acheson was impressed with his sangfroid. On the surface, all Wedemeyer seemed to be worried about was what he was going to do with all those civilian suits he had bought from Brooks Brothers. The undersecretary reassured him. The State Department had a secret fund which wasn't audited, and if he would send the bills in, the department would pay them. Then Wedemeyer asked what he was going to do with the clothes themselves.

"Keep them," Acheson said. "They won't fit anyone else."

He added that altogether Wedemeyer was "very fine about it," but Acheson felt that it must have been a bitter blow. What he did not know was that Marshall's action—taken so abruptly and without explanation—finally broke the bonds of loyalty that had bound Wedemeyer to his old chief.

Even today Wedemeyer still cannot explain why Marshall so abruptly turned against him. Could it have been because of a letter which he wrote to China about this time, which may well have confirmed Marshall in his feeling that Wedemeyer was indeed, as he had once put it, "getting too big for his breeches"?

Wedemeyer, still in the United States after his sinus operation, was eager to return to China and could not understand why Marshall had not summoned him back. On May 29, 1946, he wrote to his chief (in part):

> With reference to my own status, I hope you will not construe my previous radios on the subject as ill-considered or tempestuous.

Believe me, it is only because of my desire to help you in your difficult task that I have repeatedly expressed my conviction that I should return to China as early as practicable.

He went on:

There have been rumblings and rumors around Washington to the effect that you have been taken in by the Chinese Communists and there are suggestions carefully veiled to the effect that your decisions have placed the Generalissimo and the Central Government in an embarrassing position. I have been striving to obtain something tangible and pin down the persons responsible. . . . I talked to Congressman [Walter] Judd. I do not know him well but he impressed me as a very intense individual capable of illogical conclusions that might prove dangerous. He also expressed great admiration for you but emphasized the fact that the American people should know that apparently US policy as now implemented would accord recognition of the Communist elements in the Far East.

Wedemeyer always wrote long letters to Marshall, and they always made fascinating reading. But coming in the midst of Marshall's complicated negotiations in China, this one may have struck a wrong note. It not only suggested he was pursuing a dangerous line in his dealings with the Communists but went on to make heavily sarcastic references to Marshall's advisers in the State Department, calling one of its chief experts, for instance, "John Carter Vincent of milkweed tendencies" and referring to "the lack of moral courage in our leaders. Apparently we have few men in positions of responsibility who will think a problem through to logical conclusion and then adhere to same."

Did he not realize that Marshall was in a sensitive mood, that the negotiations were particularly tricky at this time, and that he would interpret Wedemeyer's strictures as criticisms of himself? At all events, the result was the message to the State Department indicating he did not want Wedemeyer back in China.

The letter he got back from his erstwhile subordinate admirably concealed his disappointment, while at the same time expressing his regrets that "I will not be associated with you in the effort to bring about stabilization in that complex area" and hoping that "you will not jeopardize your health in your present task." But Wedemeyer did give a hint of how he interpreted Marshall's sudden decision to cancel his appointment:

> When you suggested in March that I should accept the post vacated by Pat Hurley, I told you that I did not think I would be acceptable to the Communists who would feel that I could not be non-partisan after serving two years as the Generalissimo's Chief of Staff. You did not seem to feel that this would militate against my employment so I agreed to accept the post. . . . It will not be easy to explain my failure to return. . . .

Then he added that instead of going back to the Army, he and his wife were retiring to a farm thirty miles outside Washington, where he proposed to write a book:

> I have received several offers from publishers to write a book and am considering them. . . . I sometimes feel duty bound to present the facts as I understand and interpret them. If I could do this anonymously I would prefer, for I dislike publicity. Publishers inform me however that anonymity is usually interpreted unfavorably and it would be better to admit authorship. . . . The best of luck to you in your important negotiations.

It was the signal that a friendship had come to an end.

It was not the end of Marshall's mission, but that was in sight. And so was failure. That summer renewed and bitter fighting broke out between the Red Army and the Nationalists, in which, despite their numerical inferiority, Mao Tse-tung's forces made considerable gains. There were strong rumors that the Communists were being egged on by the Russians, and the Red Army became hostile to U.S. troops trying to keep the two contending forces apart. In one instance, U.S. marines at Anping were attacked and badly mauled by the Communists, and Admiral Charles M. Cooke, commander of the U.S. Seventh Fleet, angrily cabled Marshall demanding he take action to protest the clash and secure an apology from the Chicoms.

Marshall hesitated.

"I have felt I would sacrifice too much in other directions by doing this," he informed the President, "though I may be forced to such action within a few days. The tragedy is that it will virtually terminate executive headquarters and result in a general military conflagration."

He went on to say that he had notified Chou En-lai he would not tolerate any further delays from the Chicoms in bringing about a cease-fire and added that "a small group in the Kuomintang party" was blocking his efforts to persuade the Nationalists to stop fighting, too.

Even the President now began to suspect Marshall was staying in China too long, and the more he lingered, the more his international reputation could be damaged. That he was anxious to avoid, for he had another job in mind for his favorite general. Finally, he summoned Dwight Eisenhower and told him to fly to Nanking and say the President wanted Marshall to become the next secretary of state, and would he be interested in accepting? If so, could he be back by the beginning of July—this being June? Marshall wrote later:

> My reply, via Eisenhower, was yes, *but* I could not—to be fair—leave China before September, 1946, because it appeared that an agreement was about to be reached between Government and Communists and if effected I must remain a few months to see it well under way. I suggested I be nominated and confirmed but that I be permitted to delay acceptance until September.

In the circumstances, there was little else the President could do but agree. But of course, there was no agreement in China; both factions were still mouthing promises they had no intention of keeping. September came, and still Marshall stayed on, with Truman growing more and more impatient.

"He stayed too long," Byroade said later. "But day after day what we would call good Chinese came to his door, put their arms around him, the elders, and said, 'Please don't leave. You're our only hope.' "

He and Ike had arranged a simple code between them, in which the name "Pinehurst" stood for secretary of state, and

"Owner" stood for President, and every week or so Ike would cable: "PLEASE COME HOME. OWNER NEEDS YOU AT PINEHURST."

But somehow Marshall did not seem to be able to pry himself loose.

"My battle out here is never-ending," he wrote to Ike, "with both ends playing against the middle—which is me—and every world complication adding to the problem. All I dream of is coming home and raising chickens."

But when?

Byroade finally decided to make him accept defeat. He came down from Peking to see the general, convinced that they were faced with certain failure. He said to the general that he thought the important thing was to tell America in the best possible way why we had failed. "If a man of Marshall's stature had really tried to do this and it didn't work," he decided, "then we had to put the picture to America and make them [sic] understand the position better—that nobody could do it."

He persuaded Marshall that they should bring in two well-known newsmen, Art Steele of the Chicago *Daily News* and Tilman Durdin of the *New York Times,* and have them write a white paper on the tribulations of the Marshall mission. Their newspapers agreed to give them leave of absence, and they settled down in Nanking to write the paper.

About two weeks later Byroade came back to Nanking from a trip and found Steele and Durdin sitting on the porch of their bungalow, feet up on the coffee table, doing nothing. He asked why they weren't working.

"The general doesn't want us to," Durdin said.

Byroade went to see Marshall and asked him why.

"Well," he said, "there's a number of things. First, if I get in your state of mind, then we certainly have a failure, and I'm not yet ready to accept that. Until I do that, I am not going to start looking backwards. Those two fellas can't write the paper without me spending a lot of time with them, and I'm not willing. Because I don't believe in looking back. During the war many people thought I should keep a diary. I could have. I could have done it fifteen minutes every morning. But the decisions we have to make in wartime are so great and so difficult that there is only one way to do it—you make the best decision you can, and at the end of the day you don't look back. I'm not looking back now."

Byroade hadn't the heart to tell him that he wasn't looking forward either, and the day was fast approaching when he would have to. But an adequate white paper never got written, and Marshall never did attempt to explain what had gone wrong. Instead, back in the United States, General Al Wedemeyer was writing a white paper of his own, and it was not flattering to his onetime chief, friend and protector.

On November 7, 1946, President Truman quietly informed Marshall's liaison men in Washington that he had seen a rough copy of Wedemeyer's report, and he didn't feel it was going to do General Marshall any good when it was circulated. It criticized him and the State Department for neglecting the Nationalists and laying China open to a takeover by the Reds. When the State Department got hold of a copy of its own, they claimed that the report contained several inaccuracies. A cable was sent to Marshall suggesting he should contact his erstwhile subordinate and ask him to correct and otherwise alter his statements.

Wedemeyer maintains that the general subsequently did so. "When he came to me later," he said, "and asked me to change the report I had written on China, I was forced to refuse him. I told him I couldn't do it. I had already written my report, and I had written it for my country."

There is, however, no record in Marshall's files that he ever approached General Wedemeyer and requested him either to alter or to suppress anything he had written. All that is confirmed is that the President was distressed when he heard about Wedemeyer's criticism, and he hastened to let General Marshall know that he retained the strongest faith in him. He sent a message via Marshall's liaison officer:

> The President asked that you convey to General Marshall the following remarks from him, which are quoted as nearly verbatim as I can remember them:

The President stated that he was continually and deeply grateful for General Marshall's patience and perseverance in China. He wanted General Marshall to be told, as he has so often told him before, that the President has the most complete and unwavering confidence in General Marshall's activities. He wanted General Marshall to know that he relied entirely and only on General Marshall's judgment in the China problem and that he would continue to do so "at least as long as I am President."

What the President did not put in his message were the words "And now, for God's sake, come home!"

But even Marshall realized that that was what he meant. He sent a cable to Eisenhower saying, "PLEASE TELL OWNER AM COMING BACK TO PINEHURST."

22

Initiation

It had been common knowledge for some time in Washington that the President didn't get along with his secretary of state, James F. Byrnes. He had an irritating habit of making off-the-cuff statements about foreign policy with which Truman strongly disagreed and would often adopt political stances at international conferences without first checking with the White House.

Truman reacted to this insubordination by calling Byrnes to the White House and "skinning him alive," to use one of Truman's favorite phrases, but the President's rebukes rolled like water off the secretary's back and never stopped him from repeating the offense. He felt quite safe in his job anyway. He kept a bottle of I. W. Harper in his bathroom at the State Department, and he would bring it out at the end of the day and invite his chief assistants to join him. It so happened that the trio concerned were among the best and the brightest rising stars in government in those days, all of them considerably superior in intelligence and foreign expertise to their boss. They were Dean Acheson, Charles "Chip" Bohlen, and Benjamin "Ben" Cohen, and all of them would go far.

After a few drinks Byrnes would remind his assistants that he suffered from a heart murmur and wanted to get out of his job. He pointed out that he had several times offered his resignation to the President, but it had always been refused. He added, in maudlin tones, "What else can Truman do? Who could he get to replace me? There's no one around they could appoint."

Acheson was often tempted to reply, "How about George Marshall?"

However, he kept his mouth shut and did not realize that the President had been thinking along the same lines until Truman mentioned to Acheson that he had sent Eisenhower to China to sound out Marshall, who had promised to become secretary whenever Truman asked him to take over the job. That put Acheson in an awkward position. He knew something about his boss that his boss didn't know—that the President was planning to replace him. He was also intrigued about how and when it would be done. Harry Truman was a feisty little guy who was willing to stand up and fight anyone, but he was quite a coward when it came to giving someone the sack. How was he going to summon up the courage to tell Byrnes his resignation had been accepted?

Then, in January 1947, there was a diplomatic reception at the White House, and as is usual on these occasions, a lot of gossip was being passed around. Acheson met Byrnes near the stairs, and it was evident that his boss had heard rumors. The secretary said, "This Marshall thing worries me. I talked to Pat Carter,* and I think he knows more than he's saying."

Byrnes added that he didn't think Marshall was really in line for a big Cabinet job—not after his failure in China. Because of age and tiredness, he had dropped the ball toward the end.

Acheson replied that he thought the figure of speech was wrong. "There was no ball to drop in China," he said. "Of course, he might have covered his retreat a little better."

Acheson was afraid that the next thing Byrnes was going to ask him was what *he* knew about Marshall's next job, and he hated the thought of having to tell him the brutal truth. Luckily he was saved from his embarrassment by the arrival of another guest, who swept up to Byrnes and said, "Congratulations, Mr. Secretary. I hear you are going to lay your burdens down."

The speaker then added he thought it was wonderful that the President had chosen General Marshall to succeed him.

"So," said Acheson, "[Byrnes] got the word at the White House—but not from the President. I must say, he put on a good show and acted as if he had known it all the time. In fact, Mr. Truman said only one or two curt sentences to him, and no one could tell there was anything unusual."

---

*Who had taken over as Marshall's assistant after the departure of Brigadier General Frank McCarthy.

But although Marshall was there that night, and Byrnes could see him across the room, he took his time in going across to congratulate the new secretary of state.

In the state of the world as it was in 1947, the President's choice was reassuring—and adroit. To the general public the name of Marshall meant sober, steady control of events, no matter how earthshaking. He was approved of by government officials as an outsider who listened to professional advice. He was trusted by the politicians—though not, of course, by all of them.

The feeling of everyone was, perhaps, best summed up in a letter he got from his old chief, ex-Secretary of War Henry L. Stimson, who wrote to him on January 10, 1947: "Your appointment as Secretary of State has filled me with a great sense of security so far as our country is concerned. Mr. Truman made a very wise as well as a very shrewd appointment."

Stimson, who had once also been secretary of state himself, warned Marshall that in taking on the job he was abandoning the heel-clicking, highly disciplined, conscientious barracks of the military establishment for a very different, and much sloppier, organization:

> You will not find it an easy task. You will miss the support of an organized and loyal staff which is always behind the leaders of the War Department and the spirit of whose influence runs far down into the lower echelons. To a certain extent that lack of organization is necessarily inherent in the kind of work which the State Department is called upon to do, and it would be a great mistake to think that by the imposition of a strict discipline you can remedy its deficiencies. In the State Department you will feel yourself far more often standing alone than you did as head of the General Staff. . . .
>
> Surprise bombshells from the outside world will drop upon you with much greater frequency than in the War Department even in time of war. Philander Knox used to say that nothing surprising could happen in any part of the world without news of it coming across his desk within four hours . . . and the variety and unpre-

dictability of these bombshells are greater than anything we experienced during the war in the War Department.

After cautioning Marshall to be ultracareful in his dealings with the press (which, he forecast, would be made up of a lot of "young spot reporters" each anxious to "worm out" of him "some kind of story regardless of its importance or danger"), he asked forgiveness for his long disquisition:

> I am so fond of you and so anxious that you shall be spared from unnecessary annoyance after your long hard service during the past six years that I have yielded to the temptation of giving you the result of some of my own experiences in the State Department in the hope that it may help you. I send you my deepest and most heartfelt good wishes for your success. I hope that your health will continue to carry the strain. You have to an extraordinary extent the confidence of your countrymen throughout the United States and it is very fortunate for all of us that that is so.

General Marshall took the oath of office as secretary of state on January 21, 1947, three weeks after arriving back from his abortive mission to China. There could hardly have been a more unpropitious time for anyone to take charge of the foreign affairs of the nation because the world was going to pieces.

A letter from Moscow which arrived on Marshall's desk just before the swearing-in ceremony accurately summed up the task he faced. It came from General Walter Bedell Smith, Ike's old chief of staff, who was now U.S. ambassador to the USSR. Smith wrote to Marshall:

> Herewith both my sincere congratulations and my sympathy. It is good to be serving directly under you again, but they certainly passed the baton to you in the final lap of the race. The conferences which have been held so far are only the curtain-raisers for the coming all-important session [in Moscow], and unless I miss my guess badly you will need all your great patience and self control before it is over.

But difficult conferences, particularly with the Russians, were by no means the worst problems that Marshall would have to tackle in his new position. In Europe the miseries of the people, still stunned and bomb-shocked in the aftermath of the war, were compounded in 1947 by one of the bitterest winters in living memory. Food was scarce even among the victorious nations, and in the defeated territories of Germany and Austria people were dying in the streets of starvation. Industry had ground to a standstill owing to a lack of raw materials and the destruction of railroads, highways, and ports. Money was running out, and currencies were becoming worthless. Black markets and the crime that went with them flourished like stinkweed in all the big cities. Added to that was the fact that the one ally upon whom the United States had hoped to rely for help in maintaining democracy and civil order in the postwar world seemed on the brink of collapse. Britain had been hardest hit by Europe's dreadful winter. Factories had been forced to close down owing to electricity blackouts; 6 million workers were out of jobs; there was no fuel for heating and little food to eat. Rations were even lower than the meager allowances maintained all through the war, and Britons, for the first time in their lives, were queuing for bread.

What worried the Americans was the possibility that Britain would be obliged, from sheer poverty, to opt out of the pledge it had given to maintain peace in Eastern Europe and the eastern Mediterranean. Churchill's worst wartime fears had come true, and the Soviet occupation forces in the Balkans were now threatening to take over the two countries in the region which still maintained friendly relations with the Western democracies. In Greece, military intervention by the Royal Army, with reluctant help from the U.S. Navy,* had temporarily succeeded in crushing a brutal civil war fomented and supplied by the Soviets in Bulgaria, Yugoslavia, and Hungary. In Turkey, British aid had kept the authorities immune to alternating Soviet threats and blandishments.

---

*Admiral Ernest King had tried to deny tank landing craft to the British for the operation, on the ground that it was "political."

But three weeks after Marshall took office, the United States was faced by the bad news from London that the British were pulling out. Soviet-backed guerrillas were swarming into Greece. Greek children were being driven in herds into Bulgaria and Hungary for "reeducation." The local currency was collapsing, and the government had lost its grip. But the British had reached the end of their tether. They had no more money to spare, and at the end of another six weeks they would be forced to get out.

It was Marshall's first big crisis, and he was poorly briefed on it. All through the last stages of the war he had been bombarded by Prime Minister Churchill with pleas to allow him to send troops into the Balkans, to forestall the Russians there, to make sure of postwar stability in the region; and in the belief that the Russians, as allies, had to be trusted and that Churchill was pushing his program purely for reasons of British prestige, Marshall had resisted it and sabotaged Churchill's ambitions. He was still not convinced that the Russians were the greedy exploiters of disaster that their enemies made them out to be and far from certain that Greece and Turkey wanted or needed to be saved from Moscow.

Dean Acheson, who had stayed on as undersecretary of state, had no doubt at all of the extent of the disaster the Western democracies would suffer if Greece and Turkey were lost to the Soviet camp. So he was astonished when he listened to Marshall addressing a meeting of congressional leaders to ask them to back aid to Greece and Turkey in order to fill the vacuum the departing British would leave behind them. Normally the general was a persuasive speaker before congressional committees and usually had no difficulty persuading members to give him what he asked for. But this time, as Acheson put it later, "my distinguished chief, most unusually and unhappily, flubbed his opening statement." The President had come along to hear him and looked disappointed. One glance at the stony, unreceptive faces of the congressional leaders convinced the undersecretary that the situation was desperate. He urgently whispered to Marshall to be allowed to speak and was given permission. Acheson wrote later:

Never have I spoken under such a pressing sense that the issue was up to me alone. No time was left for measured appraisal. In the past eighteen months, I said, Soviet pressure on the Straits [Dardanelles], on Iran and on Northern Greece had brought the Balkans to the point where a highly possible Soviet breakthrough might open three continents to Soviet penetration. Like apples in a barrel infected by one rotten one, the corruption of Greece would affect Iran and all to the east. It would also carry infection to Africa through Asia Minor and Egypt, and to Europe through Italy and France, already threatened by the strongest domestic Communist parties in Western Europe. The Soviet Union was playing one of the greatest gambles in history at minimal cost. It did not need to win all the possibilities. Even one or two offered immense gains. We and we alone were in a position to break up the play. These were the stakes that British withdrawal from the eastern Mediterranean offered to an eager and ruthless opponent.

There was a long silence after Acheson sat down. Then Senator Arthur Vandenberg rose and, addressing the President, said that if he would go out and repeat those words to the American public, he and his colleagues would support him in a program for aid to Greece and Turkey.

As for Marshall, he congratulated his assistant and looked at him with a new respect. But Acheson got the feeling that so far as the menace of the Soviets were concerned, he was still by no means convinced.

That, of course, was before the new secretary left for Moscow for a conference with the Russians a few weeks later.

The speech the President subsequently made before Congress (in March 1947) became known as the Truman Doctrine, and it won $400 million in aid not only for Greece but for all "free peoples who are resisting attempted subjugation by armed minorities or by outside pressures." Marshall was not there to hear it. He was leading the U.S. delegation to a meeting in Moscow to discuss with the Soviets plans for the occupation of Germany and the terms of a peace treaty with Austria.

It was his first conference with the Soviet government as a

statesman rather than as a soldier and his first hint of what post-war Soviet attitudes toward collaboration were going to be like. He began with great optimism, and it was only gradually that his hopes wound down.

The U.S. delegation consisted of some of the country's top military and political advisers, several of them with a well-marinated record of dealing with the Soviets. Among the soldiers were General Lucius Clay, military governor of the U.S.-occupied zone in Germany; General Mark Clark, an old and trusted wartime subordinate of Marshall's and now U.S. military governor of Austria; General Walter Bedell Smith, Eisenhower's former chief of staff and now U.S. ambassador to Russia; Robert D. Murphy, a lawyer and politician; Chip Bohlen, an expert on German and Russian affairs; Ben Cohen, a State Department adviser on Russia; and John Foster Dulles, a New York lawyer who had been nominated by the Republican party to attend as a bipartisan observer.

The soldiers, all of whom had had practical experience in dealing with the Russians both during and since the war, were in favor of taking a tough line with them in settling postwar policies toward the defeated powers. The State Department line, as enunciated by Ben Cohen, was to fall in as much as possible with Soviet wishes, in view of the part the Russians had played in winning the war. Dulles, to everybody's surprise, since as a Republican they had expected him to be strongly anti-Communist, was inclined to go along with Cohen and appease the Soviets whenever possible.

Marshall told his advisers he would try to hold the balance. For the moment his old friend Mark Clark suspected that he was, if anything, leaning toward the Soviets. But as the conference dragged on, and Soviet intransigence began to manifest itself, his attitude began to change. It soon became apparent to most members of the Western delegations that what Russia wanted was not so much a settlement in Europe as revenge against Germany and Austria for the losses the Soviet people had suffered in the war. The Russians demanded the stripping of all portable assets in the defeated countries and their transfer to the USSR as some compensation. Against the instincts of General Clay, the U.S. delegation was inclined to go along with that so far as Germany was concerned. After all, the Nazis had pillaged Russia. Why should Germany not be pillaged in return?

But when it came to Austria, General Mark Clark dug in his heels. He described how the Russians had already carted away millions of dollars in Austrian assets and then left them to rust away on railroad sidings on the frontiers of the Soviet Union. He pleaded for the right of the Austrian people to be allowed to get their factories working again without having them pillaged by the Soviets the moment they had repaired them.

Clark's attitude toward the Russians was not improved when U.S. experts discovered Soviet bugs hidden in the rooms of the U.S. Embassy, planted there to eavesdrop on American policy meetings. As a reprisal, Clark and his staff worked up a plot. Among the Russians attending the Austrian discussions was a Soviet general from Vienna whom they all loathed because, after several meetings with the U.S. occupation forces, he had gone back on his promises and double-crossed them.

Clark and his staff decided to go after him. They gathered around a table in one of the bugged rooms and expressed surprise at what they had heard at that day's meeting of the foreign ministers.

"The Russkis did exactly what Rudi said they would," Clark remarked. "The information he slipped us was absolutely correct." After two or three days of dropped remarks of that kind, Clark said, "this guy [didn't] come to any more meetings."

But what Clark was most worried about was State Department appeasement, its willingness to make concessions in order to get some sort of agreement, anything as long as they all signed a paper.

"Finally, we got to this reparation thing," Clark said, meaning what the Russians demanded they should be allowed to take out of Austria. "It was the gist of the whole thing. If we ever settled that, everything else would fall into place. But I was pretty sure the Russians were not going to be reasonable and give in on that."

On the morning of the session on Austria there was a policy

meeting of the U.S. delegation, and General Clark announced he had drawn up a position paper and had persuaded the British and French delegations to sign it. He handed it over.

"This, General Marshall," he said, "is the final agreed position on reparations, which is coming up today. This is how far we can go. We can't go any further than this."

Marshall passed the paper over to Ben Cohen and asked him what he thought of it. He read it through and said, "The Russians won't agree."

Everybody laughed. Clark said, "I'm sure they won't."

Marshall was still looking at Cohen. He asked him what he would do, what he would recommend.

"I recommend," said Cohen, "that we use the same language we've already agreed to in the satellite treaties—you know, with Rumania, Bulgaria, et cetera."

Clark burst out that the language in those treaties was double talk, subject to such misinterpretations by one side or the other that the Soviets were bound to twist the meaning.

"It just won't do," he said. "We do that, and we'll be letting Austria go down the Danube just as we're letting the others."

Marshall looked at John Foster Dulles, indicating he would like his opinion.

"I'm inclined to agree with Mr. Cohen," the Republican said, much to everyone's surprise.

General Clark was so shocked that he interjected, "General Marshall, may I say what I think?"

"We know what you think," Marshall said sharply.

"Then let me say it again," Clark said. "I didn't want to come here. I've been working with these devils in Vienna for two years, and you can no more give in and do what Mr. Cohen suggests than the man in the moon. If you do, you will sacrifice all we've been fighting for, what thousands of men have died for."

Marshall rose to his feet. "I'll make a decision later," he said.

"You've got to make up your mind now," insisted Clark. "You've got to decide now because we go to this meeting at two o'clock, and I've got to prepare exactly what your position is going to be, and that's going to take some time. It has to be carefully worded because it's going to be the end. What you say is going to break up the conference."

Everybody was looking at Marshall. He was looking at Clark. "Clark," he said, "you prepare it exactly as you think it should be prepared, and you bring it to my room."

So when the afternoon meeting took place, Marshall had Clark's position paper with him.

"It [the meeting] was more vitriolic than ever," Clark said later. "While [Soviet Foreign Minister V. M.] Molotov was speaking, I kept slipping Marshall messages, and Cohen was slipping him messages, and Dulles was slipping him messages. It was getting on for seven in the evening. Molotov was getting meaner and meaner."

Clark sensed the weariness and frustration creeping over his chief and scribbled a last message: "Don't you think it time to read over that American position paper? It will probably break up the meeting."

The secretary of state fumbled among his papers, pulled out Clark's memorandum, and began to read it. After a few moments Molotov rose to his feet and, in cold, clipped tones, moved that the conference be adjourned. It was the last meeting between the Americans and the Russians for fifteen years. But it saved Austria.

"If we'd given in to what the Russians demanded," said Clark, "it would have been the end of Austria utterly and completely. It would have given them carte blanche to destroy the country, take it to pieces, move it out. But Marshall was so disappointed."

As they drove back together to the U.S. Embassy through the icy Moscow streets, the secretary broke a long silence. "Clark," he said, "I think you are a fine general, but I've come to the conclusion that as a diplomat you're not so hot."

When they got back to the embassy, he invited his subordinate into his room for a drink, and they drank a couple of large scotches together, lamenting the acrid end of the conference but getting good and mellow at the thought that tomorrow they could go home.

Then a messenger knocked on the door. Would the secretary and General Clark please come to the Kremlin and have dinner with Generalissimo Stalin? Wearily they climbed into their uniforms and set off for a long night of what Clark called "hollow toasts, dead fish, and caviar."

So far as the American public was concerned, however, the Russians were still the gallant allies of World War II, and no word of criticism of their hardening attitude passed the lips of President Truman or his secretary of state. Marshall kept quiet about the way in which the U.S. delegation had been treated in Moscow.

Not so Mark Clark. Technically, though a general in the U.S. Army, he came under State Department jurisdiction as military governor of Austria, and he should have cleared with Marshall or his subordinates in the department any statements he planned to make about Soviet actions. Asked to give a talk over NBC, he failed to inform anyone, but instead let rip with some choice descriptions of Russian rape and pillage in Austria, double dealings with their allies, and intransigence at postwar conferences. The next morning the telephone rang, and it was General Tom Handy, now working for Eisenhower, the Chief of Staff, but still in close touch with Marshall.

"Welcome home, Wayne [Clark's middle name used by intimates]," said Handy. "We all heard you last night. If you'd rolled a skunk right down the middle of the Pentagon, you couldn't have created more of a furor. Marshall wants to see you. The White House is calling everybody and screaming blue murder."

"My God," said Clark, "are they planning to shoot me or what? I'm ready to retire anytime."

"Well," said Handy, "come around and see Ike first and then Marshall."

The first thing Ike said was: "This is a hell of a homecoming, Wayne. Everybody's mad at you."

"Ike, what do you expect me to get up and do?" asked Clark. "D'you expect me to tell falsehoods about the Commies?"

"It's the State Department," said Ike. "You know how the State Department feels about this. And you're under the State Department." He added, with a grin, "You'll be under me when they relieve you of your job later today."

Marshall shook him by the hand when he came into his office and said, "Clark, by God you really got us into a jam with that talk of yours last night. I know it's tragic what the Russians are doing, but we can't say it." He paused and then said, "Well, forget about it. What are your plans—after I relieve you from your State Department job, that is?"

Clark said he was going home on leave and then Ike had appointed him to command the Sixth Army.

"Any more speeches?" asked the secretary.

Clark explained he was due the following day to address the National Press Club in Washington. Marshall grimaced.

"Well, pull your punches," he said. "Don't do that same talk over again."

"All right, General," Clark said, "I'll obey right to the letter what you say. But what's going to happen when I do that? When I get up and make a speech that's quite conciliatory, quite different, they're going to put questions. What do I say when they ask me, 'Who throttled you?' Do I answer, 'General Marshall'?"

"Don't be a damn fool, Clark," the secretary said.

But he was thoughtful. After a long silence he said, "Well, go ahead. Make your speech."

Then he added, "But soft-pedal on the epithets. Just stop calling the Soviets sons of bitches."

It was six months before the two men saw each other again. General Marshall was due to address the Commonwealth Club in San Francisco, and General Clark invited him to stay with him at his Army quarters in the Presidio. That night, over dinner, Clark said to the secretary, "Do you remember the bawling out you gave me at the State Department—over the terrible things I said about the Russians?"

"I do," replied Marshall. "But I take it all back now."

23

Marshalling Europe

Everyone was aware in those first few months that Marshall was feeling his way into the job and that occasionally he fumbled, out of sheer ignorance of the ways of diplomacy and misplaced trust in the promises of statesmen and politicians. He got criticized for it, but as someone remarked later, "He appeared to be untroubled by the fact that the slings and arrows were going to hit him. He didn't seem to let that sort of thing ever bother him."

Harry Truman brushed aside any derogatory or patronizing remarks that some of the politicians made about his new secretary.

"He was the most important military man in the Second World War," he said, "and he will become the most important secretary of state in the next decade. He has qualities that cannot be beaten. He is good at organization and as a judge of men. He is not an overbearing man. He gets along with people. And people trust him."

He added, later, "People not only thought he was telling them the truth, he did tell them the truth. He always told me the truth when I was President of the United States."

To Truman they were unmatchable qualities, and he put his faith in George Marshall as in few other men. "General," he once said to him, "if you feel that something has to be done, and needs to be done in a hurry, do it. Don't wait for me or for Congress. I'll settle it with them later."

That was why the President was as surprised as the rest of the world when, in the summer of 1947, the Marshall Plan was born.

In one of his first conversations with Dean Acheson the new secretary had urged his assistant always to be candid and outspoken with him and brutally frank if he thought it necessary. He needn't worry about hurting his feelings, he said. He had no feelings, "except," he added, "those I reserve for Mrs. Marshall."

This wasn't true, of course. Marshall tried never to show his feelings and did not usually give way to emotions except when he did it deliberately, to achieve an effect. But underneath the mask he was a very humane, sympathetic, and understanding man. Acheson, watching him closely during his first year in office, was soon aware that the reports from Europe were affecting him deeply. News poured in of starvation and suffering in the war-torn cities of Britain, France, the Low Countries, Germany, and Eastern Europe. He had seen enough ruined buildings and wrecked people in the USSR to know how badly the Russians had bled and died. And each telegram from U.S. diplomats on the spot warned that the end of the war had somehow made conditions worse because despair and hopelessness had been added to the suffering. Unless something could be done, and done quickly, a disaster too dreadful to contemplate threatened this devastated corner of the civilized world.

On April 28, 1947, Marshall arrived back in Washington from Moscow in a somber mood, downcast by the hostile attitude of the Soviet leaders, worried about the dire prospects in Europe, convinced that only some radical action on the part of the United States—the only belligerent nation to have emerged comparatively unscathed from the war—could restore the situation. He came back to a pile of chastening documents which, together with what Acheson called "his own cargo of bad news," persuaded him to go on national radio and speak of "the suffering people of Europe, who are crying for help, for coal, for food and for the necessities of life." He warned the American people that "the patient is sinking while the doctors deliberate."

Acheson had been down to Mississippi while the secretary was away to make a speech along similar lines, appealing to the nation to galvanize itself and spring to the help of Europe. Now Marshall galvanized his own department into coming up with some sort of plan. In the middle of doing so, Acheson was alarmed when a delegation of Democrats came down from Congress to tell him they had heard rumors that the administration was cooking up a plan and told him to warn the secretary and the President that if Truman tried to present them with a *fait accompli,* they would refuse to vote grants or credits.

So how was Marshall to rally the nation without embarrassing Truman with the Congress? There was only one way. Keep the President in ignorance of what he was planning. Spring it on him as well as on the people and Congress.

It so happened that for some time Harvard University had been trying to give General Marshall an honorary degree, and he had finally agreed to a date: June 5, 1947. He summoned Acheson. Would this be a good platform on which to launch a plan for aiding Europe? His assistant shook his head. Nobody ever listened to speeches at graduation ceremonies. Marshall said nothing but asked Acheson to let him have the draft his staff had been working on. Told it was still unfinished, he said he would like to look it over anyway.

The honorary degree was due to be bestowed on Marshall on the afternoon of June 5, and an announcement from Harvard said that as was usual on these occasions, the secretary would be making a speech afterward. A few hours before the event the Associated Press telephoned the State Department and asked for a copy of Marshall's reply.

It was then discovered that he had failed to leave a copy of the speech with the department. Acheson was consulted and he thereupon telephoned the secretary's aide, Marshall Carter, in Cambridge and asked him to dictate what his chief was planning to say. Carter replied that he couldn't do that since the general was writing his own speech and hadn't finished it yet. He promised to phone back when he had a definite text.

"It will," wrote Acheson, "surprise many that the Secretary of State went off to deliver so momentous a speech with so incomplete a text and never informed the Department of its final form. I had to pry it out of Colonel Marshall Carter at almost the last moment over the telephone."

403

Acheson seemed to believe that Marshall had, however, discussed his speech with the President. But he hadn't. He had said nothing to anyone.

The ceremonials were over. Marshall had received his honorary degree and had been lauded as "the soldier and statesman whose ability and character brought only one comparison in the history of this nation."* He rose to speak and rapidly described to his audience the devastation and despair which was plaguing Europe and of the need for the United States to address itself to its solution. As if to rebut the confrontational aspects of the Truman Doctrine—with whose anti-Communist tone he did not agree—he proceeded to declare:

> Our policy is directed not against any country or doctrine but against hunger, poverty, desperation and chaos. Its purpose should be the revival of a working economy in the world so as to permit the emergence of political and social conditions in which free institutions can exist.
>
> Such assistance, I am convinced, must not be on a piecemeal basis as various crises develop. Any assistance that this Government may render in the future should provide a cure rather than a mere palliative.
>
> Any government that is willing to assist in the task of recovery will find full cooperation, I am sure, on the part of the United States Government. Any government which maneuvers to block the recovery of other countries cannot expect help from us. Furthermore, governments, political parties, or groups which seek to perpetuate human misery in order to profit therefrom politically or otherwise will encounter the opposition of the United States.

Then he came to the nub of his plan for alleviating the sufferings in Europe and did not waste any words in its exposition. It was in the best tradition of his lifelong philosophy: that God helps those who help themselves, God, in this case, being the United States. He declared:

> It is already evident that, before the United States can proceed

*A Harvard man wrote to his alma mater to ask to whom it had compared Marshall in its citation and got back the reply: George Washington.

much further in its efforts to alleviate the situation and help start the European world on its way to recovery, there must be some agreement among the countries of Europe as to the requirements of the situation and the part those countries themselves will take in order to give proper effect to whatever action might be undertaken by this Government.

It would be neither fitting nor efficacious for this Government to undertake to draw up unilaterally a program designed to place Europe on its feet economically.

This is the business of the Europeans.

The initiative, I think, must come from Europe.

The program should be a joint one, agreed to by a number of, if not all, European nations.

The role of this country should consist of friendly aid and in the drafting of a European program and of later support of such a program so far as may be practical for us to do so.

And that was it. Such was the Marshall Plan. No more and no less. A slightly stunned audience rose to give the secretary a great ovation, but more for the man he was, the soldier he had been, than for the words he had just spoken to them. They were not quite sure of what he meant or the significance of what he had said.

But Dean Acheson was quite clear about what was in his master's mind. He had read the short speech through as soon as Marshall Carter had read it to him over the telephone and silently praised Marshall's genius for the way he had set it out.

"Surely no sensible man could object," he wrote later, "to a suggestion that if the Europeans, all or some of them, could get together on a plan of what was needed to get them out of the dreadful situation depicted . . . we would take a look at their plan and see what aid we might practically give."

What it needed was someone with imagination in Europe to stimulate them into action, and Acheson thought he knew just the man.

At the same time as he sent out the last-minute copy of Marshall's speech to the press, he called three influential British correspondents he knew in Washington: Malcolm Muggeridge of the

Daily Telegraph, Leonard Miall of the British Broadcasting Corporation, and René McColl of the *Daily Express.* He stressed to them the importance and seriousness of the speech and urged them to send over the text in full and also ask their editors to send on a copy to Ernest Bevin, then foreign secretary in the Labor government.

Bevin caught on at once, according to Acheson, who later wrote:

> Some years later Bevin told me that after reading the speech, William Strang, then Permanent Under Secretary at the Foreign Office, suggested inquiring through the British Embassy in Washington what specifically the Secretary of State had in mind. Mr. Bevin vetoed the suggestion. He would not, he said, pry into what General Marshall was thinking about; what he had said was good enough for Bevin.

The British foreign secretary telephoned the French foreign minister, Georges Bidault, and they made a rendezvous with Molotov, the Soviet foreign minister, to discuss drawing up a European recovery plan. At first the Russians seemed willing to play ball, and the first of the Eastern European protégés, Czechoslovakia, agreed to collaborate. But then Molotov suddenly changed his mind.

"It seems that Molotov has a bump on his forehead which swells up when he is under emotional strain," said Bevin later. "The matter was being debated, and Molotov had raised relatively minor questions or objections at various points when a telegram was handed to him. He turned pale, and the bump on his forehead swelled. After that his attitude changed, and he became much more harsh."

It was an order from Stalin to have nothing to do with the Marshall Plan. Bevin suspected that Molotov thought the instruction was stupid. Bevin, on the other hand, was relieved since "the withdrawal of the Russians made operations much more simple."

On July 3, 1947, Bevin and Bidault issued an invitation to twenty-two European nations to send delegates to Paris to draw up a recovery plan. Only one country, Czechoslovakia, subsequently withdrew its acceptance—on orders from Moscow. The rest made preparations to discuss a blueprint for recovery, and the Marshall Plan was on its way.

By the time the secretary got back to the State Department it was already apparent that Bevin had taken the ball he had thrown and was running with it. But now came the most difficult part. Congress had to be persuaded to produce the money to finance any schemes the Europeans came up with. And that was not going to be easy. It was true that the nation was by this time in the mood to help, but was a dollar-conscious Congress ready to go along?

"I think there was a readiness in this country," said Lucius D. Battle.* "It was partly the euphoria of victory in World War II; it was belief in the United Nations; it was belief in a new postwar world; it was belief in a whole series of things—and this was the first major obligation we would be called upon to fulfill. Marshall's conception was big. It was grasping for a huge star. And we, the American people, were going to measure up. And I honestly don't think that the professionals, the politicians and the diplomats, quite saw how big the response would be or the excitement it would produce. I mean, everyone was just enchanted with it. But neither the Hill nor the State Department was quite prepared for the way people responded."

But if there was such euphoria around, Marshall was still wary so far as Congress was concerned. He was too old a hand with congressional committees to be fooled into thinking that nationwide moods automatically made them reach out to loosen their purse strings. As he had so often done in the past as Chief of Staff, he knew he would have to go before the committees to argue, wheedle, and persuade them to give him the money, and he knew that it was not going to be easy. The man who had had to plead for a U.S. Army just before World War II and had eventually won the appropriation by just one vote, knew that he would have to be more persuasive than ever to get money for hungry

*Later Dean Acheson's aide when he became secretary of state.

mouths in faraway Europe, and he must plan his strategy accordingly.

"One day Secretary Marshall received word," said Paul Nitze, who was an adviser in the State Department at the time, "that [Senator Patrick A.] McCarran, chairman of the Appropriations Committee, was going to hold hearings on the European Recovery Plan the following Monday morning at ten o'clock. Secretary Marshall was summoned to appear to explain why the appropriations were necessary. On the Thursday before, Marshall called in [Chip] Bohlen and me and told us about the Monday appearance and asked us to write a statement for him which he would submit to the committee. Chip was to do the political part of it, and I was to do the economics part."

The two experts went home early and worked together all that night and all the next day on a statement about the Marshall Plan. They dug out all the facts. They made all the necessary pleas. They gave persuasive arguments, backed by a luxury of authoritative details, as to why the plan could save Europe from disaster and at the same time benefit the future of the United States. Then, not unpleased with the result of their labors, they went back to Marshall and handed him the paper they had written.

He read it through, and then, for a time, he didn't say anything. Finally, leaning back in his chair, he said, "I don't think I'll use this."

"Of course, Chip was horrified, and so was I," said Nitze later, "because we had worked hard, really hard."

As if he realized what they were thinking, Marshall said, "Don't misunderstand me. I think it's a good statement. But when you think about it, what does McCarran want? What he wants to know is what I, General Marshall, understand about this plan. It's not whether you two understand it. And if I go there and read this statement, they'll know you wrote it. And then they'll start asking me questions. I think it would be much better if I go there with no statement at all. I'm there at their request. I don't have to make a statement. What's more, you may have noticed that one of my old generals just died, and his funeral is on Monday. I think I'll go to his funeral, and only after that will I appear at

McCarran's committee. Everybody will be waiting for me, and they'll expect a statement from me, and I'll say, 'Mr. Chairman, you've asked me to appear, and I'm ready to answer your questions.' And then they'll ask me questions, and no matter what the questions are, I will have studied this memorandum over the weekend, and I can introduce every point you've made in answering their questions. And this will satisfy them because what that committee really wants to know is whether *I* understand this plan."

As Nitze said later, "It worked like a dream. He got what he wanted. The Marshall Plan appropriations went through in full."

He added, "It gave me a different slant on Marshall, this revelation of his sense of tactics and strategy. By and large, his reputation is that of being a direct and candid character, but he also had this cunning facility for getting people to do what he wanted them to do."

That autumn Katherine Marshall produced a pleasantly gossipy book about her husband's wartime service, and it was well received in the press. Winston Churchill wrote from London to convey his congratulations and also to commend Marshall on his plan: "It gives me confidence in these days of anxiety, in some ways more painful than wartime ordeals, to know that you are at the helm of the most powerful of nations, and to feel myself in such complete accord with what you say and do."

Shortly afterward Marshall flew into London for a foreign ministers' conference and caught up with many of his wartime colleagues at a dinner at Churchill's country home in Kent. He also managed to get over to Paris for a reunion with his wartime assistant Frank McCarthy, who was now back in the film world, acting as European representative of the U.S. Motion Picture Producers Association. McCarthy's principal task was to get American films showing again in Europe and also to find a way of unfreezing the millions of dollars in motion-picture rentals which had been blocked by wartime and postwar currency restrictions in the belligerent countries. So long as the money could not be exported, McCarthy was able to draw on it as he wished, and he had a wonderful time. He had a large suite in the Meurice Hotel in Paris, he gave large and lavish dinner parties, and his expense accounts were never queried in Hollywood. Why should they be since he was living on money which earned no dividends and Hollywood was unable to touch?

Then came the Marshall Plan. Among its many other and more important effects, it unfroze all the blocked accounts owed to Hollywood. McCarthy found he could transfer the money to the United States.

"My first remittance from Paris was for the sum of thirteen million seven hundred fifty thousand dollars," he said. "The American movie companies were ecstatic."

But it had a sobering effect on McCarthy's sybaritic life. From now on, his expense accounts would be watched by the hawklike eyes of accountants in Hollywood since he would be spending *real* money. It may have been a coincidence, but shortly afterward he decided it was time to go home.*

Marshall was guest of honor in Paris at a dinner given at the U.S. Embassy by the ambassador, Jefferson Caffery, and McCarthy was among those invited. The two old colleagues went off to talk, and during their conversation McCarthy mentioned his feelings at sending such a large check to Hollywood. "General," he said, "you'll never know what the Marshall Plan has done for me. I'm the hero of the whole American motion-picture industry."

"I'm delighted to hear it, Frank," Marshall replied, "but I have to be honest and say it wasn't exactly being helpful to you that I had in mind when I made my speech at Harvard."

He was even fonder of another old friend with whom he renewed acquaintance when he reached London. On several occasions during the war he had stopped off for his plane to refuel in Bermuda when on trips to Europe, and he had on each occasion

---

*He returned to Hollywood to become chief aide to Darryl Zanuck at Twentieth Century-Fox, and later went into film producing himself. Among his subsequent productions was *Patton*, which won him an Oscar.

been the guest of the governor-general and his wife, Lord and Lady Burghley. He had conceived a great affection for Mary Burghley and her two young daughters, and he had been quite shocked at a letter he had received from her earlier in the year. It congratulated him on his appointment as secretary and then added, "David [Burghley] is now married again to a lady who has been a complete obsession with him for the last twelve years. It is all a great tragedy and a thing I have always done everything in my power to avoid, so it's a bitter blow to have failed. . . ."

What shocked him was not so much the news of the divorce as the fact that this so outwardly serene, charming, and attractive person had been enduring such unhappiness for so long. He wrote back (on February 17, 1947):

> My dear Lady Burghley:
> I was tempted to start this letter "My dear Mary" but I thought that would be rather a liberty.
> I was gratified to receive your congratulations and to know that you still had me in mind and chose honoring me with your confidence. I've often thought about you and actually with great frequency since those days at Bermuda. . . . I read in China the tragic news of your divorce. It's hard for me to comprehend such action, knowing you and your children. Frankly, it is impossible for me to understand any such state of mind. . . .
> With affectionate regards,
> GCM

The London Conference was, as he described it later, "difficult and unprofitable and rather wearing," and a reunion with Mary Burghley more than made up for it. Considering the number of his official engagements, which included banquets given by the Labor government and by his old wartime colleagues Churchill, Alanbrooke, and Portal, he saw quite a lot of her—no fewer than two dinners and two lunches. He wrote to Frank McCarthy later:

> I had dinner with Lady Burghley, her sister and the Duke of Gloucester one night at St. James's Palace, and Queen Mary indicated her desire to come and came with the Princess Royal. She

was congenial, interesting and by far my most appreciative audience, particularly of any stories I had to tell of our lives at Leesburg, etc.

The next night he dined with Mary Burghley and her brother, the Duke of Buccleuch, and wrote her next day:

> I received your note regarding Wednesday, and told Mr. Hummelsine [his appointments secretary] to accept it when your message came through. I will keep the date open in the hopes of seeing you. . . . I was rather astonished at what you had to say about Queen Mary, though I did feel that she was not only gracious but was most congenial in her bearing. Judging by her facial expressions, she appreciated my stories more than you did. Possibly you had heard most of them before. . . .

He had by now begun to address her as Mary and sign himself George and would continue to do so from now on. As for Mary Burghley, she made no bones about her admiration for and trust in this quiet American and now kept no secrets from him. She wrote to him a few months later:

> With regard to a "certain individual" who I wished you to single out at a dinner one night, I am indeed *glad* you were not able to do so, for he turned out to be very different from what I thought. As I value your opinion more than that of anyone in the world, I would have hated you to think poorly of my taste. . . .

There was no doubt that he liked English society women, and they were certainly mad about him. In their presence, he obviously felt at ease, relaxed, and rejuvenated, probably because their company revived heady memories of those exhilarating days with Pershing in London after World War I. In addition, of course, they were such a relief from the bickering of all those (exclusively male) politicians to whom he had to listen nowadays.

It was in London the following spring that he had one other memorable encounter, also with a woman—though she was not English and certainly did not belong to London society.

One night, after an official banquet, he was invited back to

Claridge's Hotel and taken up to the penthouse suite. Standing in front of the fire was a sunburned young woman in evening dress, and she made what Marshall subsequently described as "an unforgettable impression on me." Not just because she was extremely attractive but because of what she was saying. She was talking about Europe and the way in which its postwar problems should be tackled and solved, and while she was speaking, the secretary indicated she should not be interrupted for him to be introduced. Only when she had finished did he allow himself to be presented to the twenty-nine-year-old Queen Frederika of Greece.

He told her gravely that she had talked more sense in a few minutes than he had heard from any statesman or politician since taking office as secretary of state. She blushed and thanked him and said there was no one in the world from whom she would rather have received such a compliment.* She wrote later:

> Do you remember when you came to see me the first time in London? I was very upset thinking only a Queen looking as royal as Queen Mary would be taken seriously by you! Well, many years have passed, and we met only once or twice since then, yet I feel as if we knew each other all our life.

It was the beginning of a remarkable friendship and collaboration between the sixty-eight-year-old American and this European queen, great-granddaughter of Victoria of England, granddaughter of Kaiser Wilhelm of Germany, forty years his junior. As Marshall had shown shortly after taking office, Greece and its problems had not until this moment made much of an impact on his feelings. But that night Frederika brought to life for him the nature of the struggle her country was waging against Communist subversion. In vivid language, she described how she and her husband, King Paul, had ridden by muleback into the bitter mountains of Greece to see for themselves the depredations of the Communist-backed guerrillas. She told of rescuing a group of starving children who had been kidnapped, and then abandoned,

---

*She was not, in any case, used to compliments from Western statesmen. As a girl in Germany she had belonged to a Nazi organization and had not been forgiven for it.

by infiltrators from Bulgaria. She pleaded for American aid in food, money, and arms, to bolster her army, and for U.S. technical advice and direction in winning the battle for Greek independence.

Marshall was stirred and impressed. He wrote her that same night a "Personal and Confidential" letter which he sent around to Claridge's by hand:

> Your Majesty:
>
> As one result of our conversation at Claridges this evening, before your return to Athens I arranged to have Lieutenant General James A. Van Fleet sent to Greece as Senior American Official. This action was taken to give the Greek Government, and particularly the Greek Army, the benefit of the advice of probably the most aggressive and hard-driving Army Corps Commander developed by us during the War. His success from the hour of his landing on the Normandy beach as a regimental commander until the final weeks of fighting east of the Rhine as the commander of 200,000 men was phenomenal. And yet, withal, he remains a rather modest and retiring type. I think he can be a great help in the campaign against the guerrilla forces.*
>
> I would appreciate your considering this personal note to you as a confidential matter, particularly as I am hopeful behind the scenes that your personal interest in Van Fleet may be helpful.
>
> Faithfully yours,
George C. Marshall.

From that time on a clandestine correspondence—routed through the CIA—began between the two and continued until the day of Marshall's death.

---

*The choice of General Van Fleet had its ironic side. For years while Chief of Staff Marshall had confused him with another regular officer with a very similar name who had a reputation for being both a poor soldier and a drunk. For years he had consistently rejected Van Fleet each time he had come up for promotion until one of his staff had realized what had happened and pointed out his error. Thereafter Van Fleet had received his just rewards for good soldiering and went on to become a distinguished Army commander in Korea. But no one ever told him why he had been allowed to twist in the wind for so many years.

24

Light in the Refrigerator

Like the approach of winter, General Marshall had always known that one of these days the question of recognizing an independent Jewish state in Palestine would have to be faced, but he had never guessed when the prospect first loomed that it would be he who would have to decide what to do about it.

As early as 1944, while he was still Chief of Staff, the war was still on, and Roosevelt was still President, he received a memorandum on the subject from his assistant, Frank McCarthy:

> February 5, 1944
> The Secretary of State [Cordell Hull] telephoned you late this afternoon to say that he was deeply concerned about resolutions introduced in both houses of Congress advocating the establishment of an independent Jewish state in Palestine. They will probably reach a vote on Tuesday. Mr. Hull's principal fear relates to the effect which adoptions of these resolutions may have on the Arabs and he foresees the possibility that such action may "play hell with" our oil interests in Saudi Arabia, not to mention our present friendly association with the Arabs throughout all areas in which we are in contact with them. There may be "a very damaging clash extending through the entire military area."
> Today one of Mr. Hull's assistants went over to the Hill to see Senators Barkley, [Thomas] Connally, [Walter F.] George, [Arthur] Vandenberg and [Robert] La Follette, all of the Senate Foreign Relations Committee. The assistant explained that the State Dept. had constantly taken the position of "not supporting, while not opposing" a free Jewish state in Palestine, but that, confidentially, the danger might be very serious if the resolutions were passed. . . .
> Mr. Hull said that, if you feel as strongly as he does on this subject, you may wish to write a confidential note to Senator Connally, Chairman of the Senate Committee, and possibly also to the

chairman of the House Committee [Sol Bloom], stating that passage of the resolution would involve great military risks and hazards which cannot be discussed publicly at the moment, and urging the defeat of the resolutions. He also feels that you may wish to speak to the President about it.

McCarthy

Marshall had no particular views at the time about the Palestine question and was anxious only to prevent anything which might interfere with the winning of the war. He drafted a note to Hull on February 7:

> With reference to the Wagner-Taft Resolution No. 247, I share your views that its passage at this time might definitely interfere with the most effective prosecution of the war. Any conflict between Jews and Arabs would require the retention of troops in the affected areas and thus reduce the total forces that could otherwise be placed in combat against Germany. The consequent unrest would keep United Nations resources away from the combat zone and would probably interfere seriously with the arrangements now being made to procure Arabian oil for the use of our combat forces.
>
> The Secretary of War [Henry L. Stimson] is not here, but the Assistant Secretary, Mr. [John] McCloy, is in agreement with the foregoing.
>
> GC Marshall

Before the note could be sent off, however, Stimson came back from an out-of-town trip, and Marshall sent McCarthy to see him and tell him about Hull's message. Later that day there was another memorandum from McCarthy:

> I went with Mr. McCloy to see the Secretary of War about the Palestine matter. Mr. Stimson felt he should telephone Mr. Bloom and Senator Connally asking them to postpone any action to include public hearings on the Palestine resolutions. He is now in process of doing this, and will also sign notes to Bloom and Connally. I am holding your memo to Mr. Hull until I can attach it to the copies of Mr. Stimson's notes. All will reach Mr. Hull this afternoon.

Four years had passed, and now it was 1948, with the British mandate over Palestine about to come to an end, British troops preparing to get out, and the Jews and Arabs left confronting each other. What should the attitude of the United States be in the circumstances? As secretary of state General Marshall would have to make the policy this time.

So far as the department was concerned, he had already discovered that opinion had not changed at all. To State experts the formation of a separate Jewish state in Palestine now would cause even more upheaval and bloodshed than it would have done in wartime. Led by Dean Rusk, who was chief adviser on Near Eastern affairs, and Robert A. Lovett, assistant secretary of state and close adviser to Marshall, the Department's experts believed there was only one solution to the problem: the formation of a federal Palestinian state equally shared by Jews and Arabs. They both were vehemently against a proposal to partition Palestine and divide it into Jewish and Arab entities. That would mean war, and in that war the Jews, outnumbered and outgunned by the Arabs, would be annihilated.

Did they persuade Marshall to accept this viewpoint? The received opinion, especially in some Jewish accounts of this period, is that Marshall was against the Israeli state and threatened to resign if President Truman recognized it. Certainly he wrote to Mrs. Eleanor Roosevelt, a passionate supporter of the Jewish state, on May 9, 1948, six days before the British were due to abandon their mandate: ". . . I am grateful for your activities in England and for your vigorous support of the European Recovery Program. At the same time, I understand your disagreement with our handling of the Palestine problem."

A few days later she was even more dissatisfied. On May 14 the Republic of Israel was unilaterally proclaimed by the Jews in Palestine. The new state was immediately recognized by the United States in a proclamation from President Truman from the White House. But at the same time the U.S. delegate to the United Nations in New York was simultaneously introducing a proposal for a U.N. trusteeship over Palestine as a whole, to protect the interests of both Jews and Arabs. Mrs. Roosevelt rushed another letter over to Marshall at the State Department asking him what was going on. He replied:

May 18, 1948

Dear Mrs. Roosevelt:

I have just read your note of May 16 regarding the recognition of Palestine [he meant Israel]. All I can say in reply is that in relation to the United Nations, Ambassador [Warren] Austin was advised shortly before the recognition was to be made public, but unfortunately he was not present with the Delegation at the time the public announcement became known, and Mr. [Francis] Sayre [who was introducing the trustee motion] had not been advised of the situation by Mr. Austin.

We were aware here of the unfortunate effect on our situation with the United Nations, which is much to be regretted. More than this, I am not free to say.

With my thanks for your letter.

GC Marshall

What he was not free to say at the time, nor has it been made clear since, was that he was fully aware of Jewish intentions to declare an independent state two days before it happened, and the only thing he was not aware of was what the state would be called because the Jews hadn't yet decided on the name of Israel. On May 12 Moshe Sharett, head of the Jewish Agency in Palestine, who was leading the Jewish delegation to the United Nations in New York (his assistant was Abba Eban), telephoned Marshall and asked for an interview. He was invited down to Washington.

There he informed the secretary of state that an independent Jewish state would be declared on May 14, twenty-four hours before the British mandate officially expired, and that Jewish forces would be mobilized and ready to fight for their new homeland. What would be the U.S. reaction?

Sharett is now dead, but he gave a full account of the meeting to Eban, who said later, "First of all, the way Sharett's impression came to me was that Marshall was very tough, very rigorous, very skeptical about the whole adventure—but with a very surprising twist. His people like Lovett and Rusk were in New York, trying to persuade us to postpone any military operations in the desert by all sorts of pressures. The picture of Marshall with Sharett was that he took the empirical point of view—that we couldn't make it, that they were more numerous, they had more arms, they were stronger. His approach was pragmatic, not moralistic. He advised us not to do it because the result would be one of two distressing alternatives: Either we would go ahead and just kill ourselves, get ourselves massacred, or, more likely, because of this possibility, the United States would be in a ferment and public opinion would compel them to intervene, which they would do with the utmost resentment. And we would be dragging them into a military adventure which had no logic in terms of their foreign policy."

Marshall went on to tell Sharett that he couldn't even guarantee that they *would* intervene, except in a purely humanitarian and evangelical capacity, just to get the Jews out of their desperate situation.

"That was his basic position," said Eban. "The twist was that on that twelfth day of May (and this is something which is not very well represented in the literature of the period) he said in his conversation with Sharett, 'I advise you not to go ahead. Your military people feel they can make it. My advice is don't take military advice. But fundamentally, it is your decision. If you make the decision to go ahead, and succeed, then good luck to you. You will probably be recognized by us. But we are not going to take any responsibility for the decision itself.'

"In other words, America's attitude depended on results. Which wasn't too bad: 'If you get your head knocked off, it's too bad. If you come through, and your head is still on your shoulders, then we'll look at you again.' "

From Sharett's point of view and that of the Jewish Agency, Marshall's attitude was encouraging. There wasn't anything punitive about it. It was quite different from the line Rusk was taking, which was to threaten to stop funds to the Jews and put on all kinds of pressures if they went ahead.

"Admittedly, it wasn't very heroic," said Eban, "to stand on one side and back the winner. . . . Marshall was rather like a blue cold light in a refrigerator, pragmatic, unsentimental, empirical: *If you survive, you survive; if you don't, it's not my business.* He

showed not a sign of passion or emotion over what was a very
dramatic moment for us. You did feel a sort of chill."

All the same, Eban does not feel that Marshall was against
recognition of Israel when it came. "Truman told me later," he
said, "that it was not true that Marshall had been against, and
that he came round only later. According to Truman, there was
a certain stage, quite a crucial stage, when Marshall said, 'Okay,
go ahead.' I say this because of the conventional portrayal of the
situation in which Marshall was overruled by Truman and even
said he would resign if the President took a step which was dictated by purely domestic considerations."

Eban said Truman insisted later that Marshall at the time
was not against his intention to recognize Israel.

"And one proof of it," said Eban, "was that at that period
in 1948 Truman didn't go in for all that number of foreign policy
decisions against Marshall's viewpoint. I think that with his election at the end of 1948 he became a little independent of State
Department advice and wrote his remarks about 'striped pants
State Department boys' who led him astray, but that was later."

But then something happened that radically changed Marshall's attitude toward Israeli independence.

The summer of 1948 was a dangerous one, fraught with all
manner of dire possibilities. It was not simply in the Middle East
that trouble was brewing.

Despite all of Marshall's efforts to conserve some semblance
of the wartime unity among the Allies, cooperation was breaking
down. The Soviet Union now seemed determined to divide Europe
into hostile camps. A Russian-backed putsch had toppled the
moderate, left-wing coalition government in Czechoslovakia and
replaced it with a rigid, authoritarian Communist regime, thus
adding the Czechs to the USSR's other satellites in Eastern Europe.
Soviet delegates had ostentatiously marched out of the Allied Control Commission in Berlin and begun a campaign of harassment
against Allied movements in and out of the city, which was supposed to be under Four Power control. The Soviet blockade of
Berlin was about to begin, and East Germans were about to be

cut off from all commerce with their brothers and sisters in the West.

Nor had Communist threats to the stability of Greece in any measure lost their menacing tone in the months since the British had withdrawn their aid and the Americans reluctantly taken over. Bands of guerrillas were still swarming in from Bulgaria and other Red satellites in the Balkans, and there were fierce battles going on between the Greek Army and Albanian troops in the mountainous border regions between the two countries. The Greeks were now armed with U.S. weapons and the Albanians carried Soviet arms, and there were many pessimists who now believed that here the seeds of World War III were being sown. If that were so, Queen Frederika of Greece took care to let her new friend, General Marshall, know that neither she nor her people would be found wanting if a new war came.

The correspondence between the two was now flowing regularly, by courier, with Marshall's aide appending a note to each of his missives to say, "The Secretary desires that you personally deliver this letter into the hands of Her Majesty. The Secretary also desires that this matter should be handled on a personal and confidential basis directly between you and me. I would appreciate confirmation of delivery."

On April 8, 1948, the queen wrote to say that General Van Fleet was now in Athens as chief U.S. military adviser to the Greek Army and that he had made a favorable impression with everyone. But she went on to say that the situation was grim along the Greek frontiers with the Soviet Balkan satellites and that there were now 800,000 Greek refugees from guerrilla incursions. She said the Greek Army was fighting well. She went on:

> God give them the strength to face a foreign invasion. Should that happen, we shall fight again. My husband [King Paul] feels strongly that talks between our staff and the American and British staffs might facilitate preparations against any future complications. Let us better be ready for all eventualities. Our present organization is not in a position to face a major war. It is debatable whether aid from our friends will arrive in time. To save us from the Blitz action of our neighbours, my husband considers it now

421

already necessary that a study be made between the staffs for a plan of common action for such an emergency, for us not to be caught unaware. We want to be convinced that not only can we rely in our hour of need on our friends, but also the aid of our friends can reach us in time.

She added:

I shall now finish this long letter by expressing to you once more, as I did in London, our gratitude and admiration for all the courageous leadership you are giving to all of us in these troubled times. The signing by the President of the Marshall Plan filled us all with enthusiasm. May your own people continue to appreciate this leadership, as shown by yourself and Mr. Truman, as much as it is appreciated by us in Europe. May God help us to play our part well, so as to live up to it and make it a success. To know you fills me with confidence. This is one reason why I have written as openly as I have done, knowing that you will consider all I have said as purely personal and unofficial. . . . Hoping that you will visit us one day here in Greece and with best wishes, your very good friend,

Frederika R.

It was undoubtedly flattering to be addressed in such terms by such a dashing and powerful young queen, but Marshall, though personally susceptible, was too professional both as a soldier and as a statesman to fall for royal blandishments on such tricky subjects as "staff talks." He delayed his reply to Frederika's letter for a whole three months and brushed off the queen's suggestion by saying, "I felt it necessary to proceed with much caution because of my confidence in General Van Fleet and especially because of my distance from the scene of action." He added, as if in mollification, "With reference to a continuation of our correspondence, so long as it can be 'absolutely private and confidential' I will be glad to exchange views with you whenever you feel this will be helpful."

Queen Frederika needed no encouragement. She needed a sounding board for her views on Greece, the world political situation, and the Communists, and in Marshall she knew she had found a receptive one.

The crisis did not ease in Europe. On June 24, 1948, the Soviet government ordered a full blockade of Berlin, and the immediate reaction of the U.S. commander in Germany, General Lucius D. Clay, was to test it.

"This was done," he said later, "by sending a train through which got quite ignominiously sidetracked where it couldn't move. Well, my next reaction was to go in with a convoy—an armed convoy I set up under General [Arthur G.] Trudeau. They took a complete combat team for this purpose. I then almost concurrently started an airlift to do what we could."

It was only then that Clay cabled to Washington for permission "to send an armed convoy into Berlin."

"I felt I had to ask permission," Clay said, "because if it were stopped and had to shoot its way in, we would start the shooting war and not the other side."

He added, "I was turned down. Or rather, let me put it another way. I was advised that I could send a column in unarmed, and I decided that that would mean that we could be stopped by a Russian presence, and that if we had to retire under those situations or stop, the resulting loss of prestige would just be too much for us to take."

Clay believed that the Russians would not have dared oppose the passage of a U.S. armed convoy and that such a show of strength at the time might well have prevented other military crises later, including the Korean War. He felt that President Truman was quite ready to take the risk. But Marshall and the U.S. Joint Chiefs of Staff turned him down.

"The decision was basically a military decision," Clay said. "[Marshall and the Joint Chiefs] all recommended against it on the grounds that if it did mean war, we did not have the troops on the ground in Europe or elsewhere to fight a war. We weren't ready."

An airlift was substituted, and supplies were flown into the beleaguered city across East Germany, with, as it turned out, no opposition from either East Germans or the Soviets.

But for a time the atmosphere was tense. One clash in the air over Berlin could precipitate WWIII. Just when the tension was reaching its height, Marshall called an old friend, Bernard Baruch, and asked if he could fly in to his home in South Carolina and talk to him. Baruch was one of America's most respected elder statesmen, friend, confidant, and emissary between Roosevelt and Churchill. The secretary walked into Baruch's office and said, "I'm very much disturbed by the movements of Russian troops on the front up there, between Russia and Poland and Germany. I don't know what it portends."

He seemed to feel that it might signal that the Russians were getting ready to advance westward, take over Berlin, and prepare to begin WWIII. How were they going to be dissuaded from such a suicidal step?

"You know," he said, "we have the power to destroy Russia from the Baltic to the Black Sea."

He added, "I have the say on whether to use the bomb or not."

Baruch was surprised to hear him say that, for it meant that the President had passed on to Marshall the decision on whether to begin an atomic war. But he had no doubt that the secretary was telling him the truth. If so, what was he proposing to do—start a preventive war?

"I told him he'd better get all the facts first," Baruch said later. "I said it would be a terrible thing for us, just because the Russians have an inferiority complex, because they move fast and don't believe anybody, don't trust their own judgment or anybody else."

Marshall said he was, of course, getting all the information together and bearing all the consequences in mind. Then he departed. It seemed to Baruch that he had just come down merely to unload some of his anxieties on one who would understand.

But shortly afterward, Baruch was asked to attend a meeting of what he called "great minds" in Washington—he refused to name those involved—who were worried about the international situation, and they wanted to talk about whether a preventive war was not the way out of the West's present worries. Before the Russians acquired atomic weapons themselves and used them to communize the world, would it not be best to use the bomb and pound Moscow into submission?

"They wanted someone to make a decision about this," Baruch said, insisting that they were quite serious. "It was certainly a tough decision."

Finally, Baruch went to see Marshall and told him there was a movement, backed by powerful influences in the country, to persuade the administration to start a preventive war against Russia, and what was his reaction to it? What did he think of preventive war?

"Well, I'll tell you, Baruch," Marshall said. "This reminds me of a story about an Eastern potentate."

There was this caliph, the secretary said, who had a reputation for being ruthless with troublemakers at his court, and when two of them were brought before him for judgment, he sent the first one away at once to be executed. But when he came to the second, this one fell on his knees and said, "Please, Your Majesty, don't cut off my head. If you'll give me just one year, I can teach your favorite stallion to fly."

The caliph was not impressed and told the guards to take the man away and decapitate him. But the man insisted, pleaded, promising faithfully to teach the ruler's favorite stallion to fly if he was given just one more year of life. Finally, the caliph relented.

"But I warn you," the ruler said to the fellow, "if you fail to deliver, if you don't teach my stallion to fly in the next twelve months, it will be the worse for you. There'll be the most terrible torture you'll have to endure before you die."

Well, said Marshall, they finally let the man go and dispatched him to the royal stables. On his way there he passed the prison and came across the first troublemaker, awaiting execution the following morning. The condemned man sneered at him.

"You've won a year's reprieve," he said, "but think how

much worse it's going to be for you when your time is up. How could you make a promise like that? You know as well as I do you can't ever teach the caliph's stallion to fly."

"Maybe not," said the reprieved man, "but just think. I am free for a whole year. In that year the caliph may die, I might die, the stallion might die—and, who can tell, I may even teach the stallion to fly!"

Marshall grinned at Baruch, and they never discussed the idea of preventive war again.

In the autumn of 1948 the United Nations met at the Palais de Chaillot in Paris to take up the Palestine question again. A Swedish envoy had been sent by the UN to report on the situation there and decide how best the land could be divided between the Jews and the Arabs. The envoy, Count Folke Bernadotte, had strongly recommended the partition of Palestine along the frontier lines drawn up the previous year, giving the bulk of the Palestine territory to the Arabs.

But much had happened since those lines had been drawn. Not only had the Israelis declared their independence, but they had repelled fierce attacks against them by four Arab armies and captured territory well beyond the demarcation lines. This they proposed to hold onto. They also proposed to apply to the United Nations for membership as a new and independent state, and this was a question upon which UN members would be asked to vote at the autumn session.

Marshall's UN delegation consisted of Dean Rusk and Robert A. Lovett, both of whom were known to be strongly pro-Arabist, like many other members of the State Department; Ben Cohen and Eleanor Roosevelt, who were known to favor the Israeli cause; and John Foster Dulles, once more sent by the Republican party as a bipartisan observer of Democratic negotiations of U.S. foreign policy. Dulles was by no means pro-Jewish, but on the other hand, he was a deeply religious man, a firm believer in the Bible, and strongly convinced that Israel belonged to the area, and the world should acknowledge that fact and admit the state of Israel to the comity of nations.

Dulles was surprised to discover that Marshall was much more cautious. The secretary was inclined to accept the State Department's point of view that Israel, having won acceptance by the United States, should play it cool from now on and neither insist on world recognition through the UN nor hold onto the territories the young state had captured from the Arabs. He announced at a policy meeting of the U.S. delegation in Paris that in accordance with the advice of the department's experts, the Bernadotte plan for Palestine partition would be accepted, and the delegation would, for the time being, vote against Israel's admission to the UN.

Dulles was so disgusted by this decision that he walked out of the meeting and did not come back. However, Dulles was an inveterate leaker, and he did not fail to let it be known in Paris how the U.S. delegation was leaning and urged the Israelis to do something about it. Chaim Weizmann, the Jewish leader, charged the two Israeli delegates in Paris, Moshe Sharett and Abba Eban, to contact Marshall at once and do their best to change his attitude.

"Marshall had come out in support of the Bernadotte plan," Eban said later, "and I was a little apprehensive of him. If I could portray him in the Israeli-Jewish pantheon, it would definitely be on the negative side. It was not that he was fanatically against us. Not like [British Foreign Minister Ernest] Bevin, who wanted us thrown out of the territories we had taken and threatened to do it with British troops. But he didn't seem to be uplifted by our enterprise and, unlike Dulles, had no sort of religious feeling for us, no biblical, historical curiosity about us. He was, as I say, negative."

Then, in the middle of Israeli lobbying, in which they were joined by Eleanor Roosevelt and Ben Cohen, news arrived from Palestine that Count Folke Bernadotte, the UN envoy, had been assassinated, almost certainly by Israeli terrorists. Marshall became more distant toward the Israeli delegates than ever, almost as if he blamed them for the UN envoy's murder. Things would have gone hard for them, and certainly the U.S. delegation would have been given specific instructions to register an anti-Israeli vote, had not Ernest Bevin ruffled Marshall's temper. He evidently decided that Marshall was being pressured by President Truman to vote for the Israelis and was determined to scotch it. He made several insulting remarks to Marshall about Truman's political integrity and declared on one occasion that the President would "lick any Jewish arse that promised him a hundred votes."

"I do remember some very definite irascibilities about Bevin," said Eban. "[Marshall] remarked that Bevin was obstinate, mulish, that he didn't seem to realize Britain didn't represent any sort of power anymore, and that he was trying to call the tune without the responsibility. He spoke to Sharett and myself very resentfully about Bevin's disrespectful remarks about Truman. 'Who does he think he is?' he asked angrily. This created a bond with us which had a sort of psychological effect."

The net result of all this was that he failed to give specific voting instructions to the U.S. delegation right up until the eve of the vote. He would make up his mind on the day, he said.

And then he took sick. For some days Katherine, who had accompanied him to Paris, had been distressed to find him clutching himself in the bathroom of their hotel suite, obviously in great pain. Sometimes he was in such agony that he vomited. She urged him to see a doctor, and when he did so, he was told he had kidney trouble and would need an operation. Not immediately, perhaps, but certainly soon. In the meantime, he was strongly advised to eschew all strain, mental and physical.

It is a measure of his condition that he let the President know and was immediately told to take himself out of the U.S. delegation at once and get some rest. It is an indication of his ambivalence over the forthcoming UN vote that he immediately did so—allowing John Foster Dulles to take his place.

Marshall cabled Athens to tell Queen Frederika of Greece that he and his wife were taking up one of her many invitations and were coming for a visit. They were in Greece when the United Nations voted to admit Israel as a member nation, principally as a result of intensive lobbying behind the scenes by John Foster Dulles and, on his orders, by the U.S. delegation. Despite efforts by the Swedes, who attended the meeting in mourning dress to symbolize their disapprobation of the Israelis, the Bernadotte plan drawn up by their murdered compatriot was defeated.

It is interesting to speculate how the Americans would have voted on the resolution had Marshall still been in charge of the U.S. delegation and what effect it would have had on the future of Israel and the Middle East.

Or, for that matter, on Truman's chances of staying on as President for another four years.

Undoubtedly the President was happy to see his secretary leave Paris and place U.S. decisions on Israel in other hands. He was in the middle of a tricky election campaign, and there were few political experts in the United States who believed he would make it. The betting men and the pollsters were backing the Republican candidate, Thomas E. Dewey, and it was because everyone was so certain he would win that John Foster Dulles, a Republican most people believed would be Dewey's secretary of state, had been allowed to take Marshall's place in Paris.

As it turned out, the experts were wrong, and Truman easily defeated his rival. But for the moment he needed every vote he could get, including the Jewish ones, and must have been desperately afraid that an anti-Israeli vote from Marshall would turn them against his administration. It says much for Truman's guts and for the faith and trust he put in his secretary of state that he sent no instructions and no pleas to Marshall during the crucial period leading up to the vote, but he must certainly have breathed a sigh of relief when illness forced him out. It would now be left up to Dulles. If the United States voted against Israel, he could blame the Republicans for sabotaging him. If Dulles voted for Israel, the administration could claim the credit.

So there must have been a certain political cynicism attached to the genuine good wishes he sent to his secretary as he departed for Greece. Not surprisingly, Queen Frederika was delighted to know that he was coming and hastened to write him in her own hand (on October 15, 1948):

> This is just a short note to tell you how glad we are to receive

you and your wife in Greece. My husband and I being on an unofficial tour that has lasted already two weeks, will break our journey for twenty-four hours and fly to Athens so as to have the
pleasure of seeing you. We shall be in Athens all Sunday and leave
again to continue our trip on Monday.

My husband would like to see you very much on Sunday
morning for a long talk. In the evening we hope that you and your
wife will have an intimate dinner with us at home. It will all be
quite unofficial and just the four of us. Unofficially one can sometimes talk so much better than officially. We hope nothing will
prevent you from accepting our invitation. I am saying this because
I am sure you will be threatened with all sorts of official dinners
and receptions. Please don't accept them. Keep Sunday morning
for my husband and the evening for both of us, and for your wife
who I shall be able and delighted to meet. We would have also
loved to take you and your wife in the afternoon to our country
place to meet the children, but that is up to you, if you can spare
the time.

Once more let me tell you that we are delighted to know you
in Greece. We owe you a lot and are very conscious of it.

My best regards,
Frederika R.

He must have known before setting out for Greece that once
he got there, not just Frederika and King Paul but everybody else,
too, would bend his ear with political gossip and exhortation. He
was also aware that nothing that was said to him or what he said
in return would remain a secret for long since Frederika, in one
of her letters, had warned him that "no secret service can work
either in Japan or in Greece, because in Japan nobody talks and
in Greece everybody talks!" His most secret remarks (or what
purported to be them) were quoted in all the newspapers, but so
was news which made him highly popular with the Greek conscript army. As a result of his conversation with King Paul, he
agreed to provide personnel from the United States "to make possible the immediate establishment of a trained replacement system,
to refresh the Greek Army and also to permit soldiers to enjoy the
reassuring and stimulating effect of visiting their families." He had

brought R&R and an army welfare system to the Greeks, and he became a hero in every encampment in the country from then on.

Despite the impassionate interviews with all the politicians, he enjoyed his trip to Greece, and as always in the presence of active and intelligent women, he was stimulated and rejuvenated by the attentions of the bronzed young queen and delighted to meet her children. He had read all the Greek legends as a boy, and now, as Katherine and he traveled around the country, the ancient stories came alive for him. But he lamented the political situation and wrote to King Paul: "The more I ponder about the Mediterranean, the more I deplore the failure of man on his part to measure up to the beauties and bounties of nature in this respect."

He stopped off in London on his way back to America and took the opportunity of introducing Katherine to Mary Burghley. Katherine's enthusiasm for his distinguished and adoring female admirers was always restrained, and later she tartly commented that they soon gave up writing to her the moment her husband was no longer around; but he never guessed her feelings on this score and never noticed the occasional old-fashioned expression on her face when he was waxing enthusiastic about them.

But he found Mary Burghley was distressed on this occasion, and there was little he could do to comfort her or a number of British statesmen who were also worried. The rumor that he was considering giving up his job as secretary was current in Britain at the time of his visit, and the British statesmen were aware that they and Britain would be losing a good and powerful friend in high places. Mary Burghley wrote to him:

> What a *peculiar* world it is at the moment. Don't take your finger off its pulse just yet, PLEASE. *Someone* has got to keep it steady and going round the right way. As far as I can see, *You* are the only one who keeps any control over it at all. Your nom-de-plume should be "Atlas."

He was back in Paris when the returns came in of the presidential election, and he was delighted when it became evident that Harry Truman had confounded the pollsters and romped home the winner. His assistant, Robert A. Lovett, who had flown back to Washington for the occasion, wrote him:

> The President returned to Washington Friday to receive one of the most genuinely enthusiastic receptions I've ever seen. The crowd lined the streets solidly from the station to the White House. . . . The police estimated there were about 750,000 people. The welcome given the President and Senator Barkley [now Vice President-elect] was a humbling thing to see. There was even a large banner over the office building of the Washington POST.* They had a painting of a very large black crow lying on its back with its feet in the air, dead as a doornail. The sign read: "Welcome home, Mr. President, from the Crow Eaters."

In the middle of the celebration at the White House the President called Lovett over and spoke to him about rumors he had heard from Paris that Marshall wanted to resign. He appeared to think the secretary's decision might have had something to do with the way the Israeli vote had gone at the United Nations and said he hoped Marshall would suspend judgment until the President had had a chance to talk with him. He then thanked Lovett for "carrying the ball" while he had been out campaigning and said he hoped press rumors that Lovett was also thinking of resigning were false. He urged him to ignore press reports that he was thinking of replacing him and said he never paid any attention to the newspapers, the "damn politicians," or the Palestine pressure groups, and Lovett shouldn't do so either. His message to both Marshall and his aide were to "sit tight and say nothing."

There was nothing Marshall was longing for more than to get back to private life, however. In a letter to the film star Walter Huston, with whom he had occasionally played tennis in the Adirondacks, he had written earlier in the year: "It will be a great treat, beyond anything you can imagine, for me to be relieved of responsibility and be free to pursue my own desires and family life."

*Which had predicted Truman's defeat.

432

But what would he say if the President pleaded with him to stay on, using the same argument as before—that the country had need of him?

The question was answered for him shortly after he got back to America at the beginning of December. He collapsed suddenly with a dreadful pain and was rushed to Walter Reed Hospital. There he was told he had a badly diseased kidney, and it would have to come out.

He would be sixty-eight years old on December 31, 1948. If he survived the operation, that is.

No Respite

December 12, 1948
Through the U.S. Embassy in Athens
Please have the following message delivered to Their Majesties the
King and Queen:

> YOUR MAJESTIES' GRACIOUS MESSAGE TO MY HUSBAND AND THE
> SWEET MESSAGE FROM THE CHILDREN TOUCHED HIM DEEPLY.
> HIS RECOVERY IS PROGRESSING SATISFACTORILY. HE WISHES ME
> TO EXPRESS TO YOU BOTH HIS GREAT APPRECIATION AND
> THANKS FOR YOUR THOUGHTS FOR HIM.
>
> [signed] KATHERINE MARSHALL

It was almost embarrassing how the world responded to General Marshall's illness. From all points of the globe, messages flowed in, from characters as disparate as Winston Churchill and General Charles de Gaulle, Joseph Stalin, Marshal Tito, Chaim Weizmann, Chou En-lai, Mao Tse-tung, Chiang Kai-shek, General Dwight Eisenhower, and Field Marshal Bernard L. Montgomery. There were get-well cards from scores of senators and congressmen, including those Republicans who were not exactly enamored by the Democratic policies of his President. And thousands of letters from ordinary people poured in.

It was a big operation, but he took it well, and Dean Acheson was able to write him on December 14, 1948:

> I listened with great pleasure to a good report of you from one of your most recent visitors. It is good news to hear you are past the worst period, that all is going very well indeed. You have all the most earnest best wishes of a great company of which Alice and I are enlisted. I heard both the Vandenbergs' message to you and—to employ the Vandenberg style—I say Amen. . . .

It was noticed by some members of Marshall's staff that the

message from Chiang Kai-shek was not signed by his wife, who was definitely the member of that family from whom the general would prefer to have heard. Could that be because she blamed the general for the deteriorating situation of the Nationalists in China or the fact that their armies were being pushed into the sea by the victorious Reds? There were already whispers in the House and Senate in Washington that Marshall's failure to advocate U.S. military aid had helped bring about the disaster. Did Madame share this view?

Swiftly it became apparent that such was far from being the case. So far as Chiang Kai-shek and his wife were concerned, Marshall was still the best American friend Nationalist China possessed. As if to prove it, Madame flew into Washington and, on hearing that Marshall was in Walter Reed, tore around at once to visit him. She found Katherine at his bedside, and they left together. Katherine invited her to come and stay with her at Dodona Manor, the Marshall home in Leesburg, Virginia, and was genuinely delighted when she accepted, for in Madame's case, she had no reluctance in sharing her affection for her husband. They spent the next few days working in the kitchen garden of Dodona Manor and the next few evenings talking about General Marshall. Katherine confided many a domestic secret about him, including the fact that, as a boy, he had once been nicknamed Flicker because of the way he wore a lick of hair on his forehead.

Just before she left to fly back to her husband, Madame Chiang Kai-shek wrote a message to General Marshall at Walter Reed. It was probably the most unusual get-well letter he (or anyone else, for that matter) had ever received and was a good example of the affection in which he was held by China's imperious First Lady.

It was couched in the form of a military report and marked:

TOP SECRET. FOR YOUR EYES ONLY.
REPORT FOR GENERAL FLICKER.

It consisted of a comic commentary on the garden labors in which she had been engaged at Dodona Manor while the general had been "lolling in silken sheets" at the hospital and described her prodigious efforts planting "giant-caliber daffodils of the Holland type" and "raking leaves to keep off enemy frost" and, after these "back-breaking efforts," spending "harrowing hours" in the kitchen, "peeling spuds, boiling bully beef, and inventing wonderful new salad which tastes like mud—but sure to faze the enemy in close contact in combat" because of its garlicky base.

She ended her report:

> Repeated requests to Deputy Commander [Katherine] for pay have fallen on deaf ears, who countercharges that since billeting in the present bivouac the undersigned has browner cheeks, better color, and there is a noticeable increase in girth. Any claims of a financial nature are therefore invalid and illegal.
>
> Undersigned, however, feels that such a reply is undemocratic, unfair and discriminatory, since the better color may be tubercular flush, and increased rotundity may be due to oedema or an unhealthy obesity known to the world as Bay Window, which will need attention. Is there no justice?

She ended her message:

> Hence this SOS to the Commanding General to get out of them silken sheets! Home sweet home was never like this!!! Undersigned calls upon high heavens to witness this unChinalike treatment. My good friend the house thermostat registers riotous indignation, for it turns hot and it turns cold.
>
> I am awaiting prompt and immediate Congressional attention a la Connally, due to one who is on the soil of the Pilgrim Mothers—down with slave labor.
>
> Respectfully submitted,
Mei-ling Soong

It was hardly the letter from someone, as his enemies later charged, who considered General Marshall the man responsible for the downfall of her husband and Nationalist China.

Nor did it seem a characteristic epistle of the woman who was widely believed by her critics to be the most imperious and arrogant of all Chinese. After reading it through, Marshall roared with laughter and wrote to tell her he would never show it to another soul, for fear of damaging her reputation as the dragon empress of China.

Slowly he recovered from his operation, but the more he contemplated the prospect of returning to the State Department, with all the work and travel it would involve, the more he flinched at the thought of carrying on as secretary. On the day after his sixty-eighth birthday he told Katherine he had decided to resign. She informed him that it was the best news she had heard for years and began preparations for a convalescent holiday which they planned to take in Puerto Rico. He sent his official resignation to the White House on January 3, 1949.

The President wrote back to him four days later:

My dear General Marshall:

Your letter of January third emphasizes to me that considerations of health compel your decision to return to private life which I had hoped in your country's interest could be long deferred.

Those of us who have had extensive experience in public affairs know full well that there are very few indispensable men. Happily for the continuity of government, there appears from time to time a man of outstanding ability whose service in one post of responsibility gives him exceptional qualification to discharge other duties of equal moment in a quite different field of activity. You are the exemplification of the type of public servant I have in mind.

As Chief of Staff of the United States Army you were the guide and counselor of two Commanders in Chief. You brought to the performance of your task abilities and qualifications which inspired the armies of the Democratic nations to victory in a war unparalleled in magnitude and in the vastness of the issues involved.

When the great office of Secretary of State became vacant it seemed to me fortunate that you were available for the position, although you had richly earned retirement. As it turned out, your previous training and experience were a preparation for the onerous duties which befell you in directing our foreign affairs—particularly in the formulation and execution of the Marshall Plan.

I had hoped that with medical treatment and rest and recuperation you could continue in office. I am, however, unwilling to assume the responsibility of further jeopardizing your health. I accept, therefore, effective on January 20, 1949, your resignation as Secretary of State. In taking this action reluctantly and with deep regret, I heartily reciprocate your sentiments of affection and respect.

> Very sincerely yours,
> Harry Truman

It was done. His professional life was over at last—or so he thought. Extremely sore in body ("I am still considerably swollen up around the waist—about six inches and still quite tender"), but well content in mind, he penned a note for his assistant, Robert A. Lovett, to read out to members of the State Department thanking them and saying farewell. Lovett wrote back to say it had been done and added:

> If you ever feel that I can ever be of any conceivable help, in anything, it would be a great favor if you would let me lend a hand. This open-ended request, which comes from deep inside me, has only two reservations. I have neither the stamina nor the courage to join you in putting dead fish-heads under your tomato plants, and I might have to think twice before joining you on a Zionist mission to Tel Aviv. Otherwise, the sky is the limit. I send you my very dear love and affection,
>
> Yours ever,
> Robert A. Lovett

The next three months were the laziest he had spent since his boyhood. He lolled in the sun in Puerto Rico and Florida. He took Katherine to New Orleans for the Mardi Gras, and they ordered themselves a fabulous dinner at Antoine's. Now that he was up and about again, invitations poured in on him, to lecture and speak, to open buildings, to hand out prizes. But each time he contemplated "getting back in harness," as Eisenhower termed it in one of his letters, a stab of pain in his middle reminded him to proceed with caution. Even Queen Frederika of Greece urged him to put aside any regrets he might have at no longer being in power and henceforth conserve his strength and use his influence from the sidelines. She wrote to him after his resignation:

> I think that today no matter if in power or out of power, you are one of the most clear-minded, far-sighted and at the same time human-minded statesmen in the world. Your example is felt everywhere we go, consciously by some people and unconsciously by most. It is this influence which is so far more important than all the material help which your country has so generously produced.
>
> You must smile when you hear such words coming from Greece, because as far as political leadership goes, so far we have not exactly followed your example!!

But he still could not resist a call to duty, and when Dean Acheson, the new secretary of state, asked him to testify on the North Atlantic pact before the Senate Foreign Relations Committee (in April 1949) he consented. But he did add: "My clothes are an irritation after a few hours, and getting up and sitting down, which seems to be my principal occupation at any gathering, is an uncomfortable business."

He mentioned that he had not been able to refuse an invitation to come to Washington when it was announced that Winston Churchill, on an official visit, had particularly asked to see him, but he confessed that the trip "was an expensive business for me, as I was pretty well knocked out for several days." But yes, he told Acheson, he would testify, adding, "Frankly, what I most dread but cannot avoid is that one appearance will immediately result in calls [to testify] on ECA, China, and numerous other questions. I need a month or more to get firmly on my feet. I hope you can understand this résumé of my situation."

Acheson hastened to assure him that, in the circumstances, his actual presence would not be necessary, and would he write out a statement to be read out instead?

The word spread around Washington (and through U.S. Army camps around the world) that General George Catlett Marshall was *hors de combat* at last.

Not so long as Harry Truman was President, he wasn't.

IV

Recall

26

Eminence Grise

Dean Acheson was well aware that it was General Marshall who was really responsible for his appointment as the new secretary of state. He was fifty-six years old and had waited long years to get the job, yet the President had let him know that he would never have been chosen over Marshall's disapproval. He was not only grateful but flattered, too, and he wrote at once to say so. The letter he sent to Marshall on January 10, 1949, is a good illustration of the relationship which had built up between the two men while they had worked together at the State Department:

> To contemplate taking up your burdens is more than I am able to do. I am comforted by the remark of an old lady in Vermont who was asked how she stood the winters there. "Well," she said, "the thing is that they only come one day at a time." Even this is small comfort.
>
> Another comfort will be something which it is hard to say but which I cannot leave unsaid. It will come from the eighteen months during which I was privileged to work with you. To say what makes greatness in a man is very difficult, but when one is close to it, one knows. Twice in my life that has happened to me—once with Justice [Oliver Wendell] Holmes and once with you. Greatness is a quality of character and is not the result of circumstances. It has to do with grandeur and with completeness of character. Other men have had very great qualities, but there has been some crevice where some weakness lurked.
>
> Those eighteen months were a great honor. I hope also they have been a great lesson. I shall try to profit by them, and shall take comfort in thinking from time to time that if what I am doing is what you would have done, then it meets the highest and surest test that I know.

These words are not easy to write. I hope you will forgive me.

Of course, it was obvious that the moment he was up and about again, he would not be left alone. It was only for a few weeks that he was allowed to work in the garden at Dodona Manor and putter happily around the house. Then he made the mistake of seeing an emissary from the American Red Cross and found himself, shortly afterward, the new head of that organization. He had accepted in the naïve belief that it would be a part-time job but soon discovered that, what with all the misery going on in the world, the Red Cross was working as hard now as it had done during WWII.

One advantage was that he could now take Katherine with him and was often lent the President's plane, the *Sacred Cow,* for his trips, and that would have been fine had it not been for the fact that she hated flying. He wrote to Madame Chiang Kai-shek in the spring of 1950 that they had been out on a Red Cross mission together to Hawaii.

> [Katherine] stood the trip around and back to San Francisco in fine shape, but flying East from there in a plane like the "Sacred Cow"—which, as you know, has no pressure cabin—she suffered from altitude sickness because they had to fly rather high and she did not tell anyone she was feeling badly and did not take oxygen in time.

Katherine was now suffering from an affliction which she shared with Madame, a kind of shingles which, in her case, affected her eyelids and made reading difficult. Madame had a similar disease which caused maddening itching in her fingers that no ointments and unguents seemed to cure or soothe. They commiserated with each other and corresponded about possible remedies and ruefully decided that most were no more than anodynes and suffering must be endured.

Life had suddenly become as busy as ever for Marshall, if hardly fraught with the same political consequences. All the same, at a time when travel by air was by no means as comfortable even for VIP's as it is now, he was flying as much as 25,000 miles in a year, going from one Red Cross meeting to another.

Queen Frederika of Greece was extremely happy when she heard about his new job. "I'm delighted to know you are so well again you can travel thousands of miles on very strenuous Red Cross work," she wrote. "The Greek Red Cross has made me their President, so you see we have become 'brother and sister in arms'!"

She went on: "But it is not on Red Cross work that I want to write to you but once again on the Greek situation. . . ."

Though he was no longer secretary of state, he was still the queen's political sounding board. In addition, Madame Chiang Kai-shek continued to write him long screeds about the situation in Asia. He read each carefully through and replied to them, though—like a young man running two girl friends—he never told the one that he was hearing from the other. He was quite obviously flattered that two such vital and beautiful women considered him worthy of their confidences, and he was enormously pleased to have such spectacular female admirers. And of course, he kept the State Department informed of what they were reporting about their respective political situations. Acheson wrote him on March 6, 1950:

> Thank you for sending over Queen Frederica's [*sic*] letter, which I read with interest and return herewith. In spite of the difficulties which may lie ahead in Greece, I am heartened by the progress already realized there, cognizant, in this respect, of the contribution made by King Paul and Queen Frederica in promoting the welfare and morale of their people.

He added:

> The Queen is a remarkable personality, but it seems to us that she displays a tendency to overlook the danger of compromising the Crown by excessive involvement in the operation of parliamentary democracy in her country. It would be unfortunate for Greece if such involvement were to inflame an issue which has plagued that country for many years.

That summer *Time* magazine saluted Marshall with his picture on the cover and commended him for his efforts through the U.S. Red Cross to save Greek children from being involved in the East-West conflict.

"Bravo!" cried Frederika in one of her letters. She was growing increasingly combative, both against the socialist influences in her own government ("they're simply disguised Communists") and the Red menace over the borders. Then came the incidents in Korea which were soon to precipitate the United States (and the United Nations) into the Korean War. As the fighting began, Marshall hastened on July 10, 1950, to assure the queen that she must not be apprehensive over the initial setbacks U.S. forces had suffered at the hands of the Korean Communists:

> Of course the present incident in Korea has tremendous possibilities for good or for bad and this Government will act with determination, I am sure, which I think is essential if we are to get a good result. The present fighting, of course, involves the usual disadvantage of democracy which cannot engage in secret mobilizations and arbitrary decisions for violent action. It will be some time before the United States forces and other United Nations contingents have concentrated the necessary strength in Korea, but the process is under way at top speed, though the difficulties are tremendous and the distances are very great. The most heartening phase of the entire matter is the apparent united attitude not only of the people of this country but of the democratic world.

That was not good enough for Frederika. To her way of thinking, the United States was reacting altogether too tamely to what was a worldwide Communist menace which happened, at the moment, to be confined to Korea. She wrote back on July 20, 1950:

> When you have to defend yourself on one front would it not be a good idea then to immediately go into attack on another front? Greece should be that front. It should be built up for the use of United States forces from now on. All war materials needed for whatever amount of troops necessary in waging an attack should be built up and distributed in different parts of the country. Then

it would only need the fly-in and landing the troops in a very short time. The heavy equipment they would find on the spot.

She went on:

> It may be argued that something like this could never be done without the Russians knowing about it. Our feeling is that they should know about it. Why should our side be so tactful all the time? It is not necessary any more.
>
> If this is considered unwise, then the stuff could be sent in under cover of assistance to the Greek Army. It may be thought that my husband and I are suggesting such an idea since we wish to save our own skin, and that of our people. This is wrong. We know very well that our skins will not easily be saved anyhow. We will fight, anyhow, to the last man, fully aware that there might be no salvation.

She ended by hoping that her idea would receive serious consideration in Washington. She didn't wish to see the struggle with communism drag on endlessly. There was need for a "dynamic, aggressive plan." She concluded:

> I repeat once more, to call on Greece would never be for a purely rearguard action, but would be developed as a springboard. . . . Instead of withdrawing to Africa, and be there for a year or two until we retake Europe, one would have a bridgehead in Europe for good. The best place is Greece. You may smile about my unorthodox reasoning, but we live in unorthodox times.

Marshall laughed out loud at this fighting letter from his beautiful Greek queen and sent it over at once to Dean Acheson at the State Department, who took one glance at it and passed it on to his Middle East and Mediterranean expert, Dean Rusk. Dean Rusk, who was not the boldest of men, quailed before this example of royal female belligerency.

"My God!" he whispered. "She's actually inviting us to join her over there in World War Three! She'd welcome it!"

"What a woman!" agreed Acheson.

But what he wanted to know was how were they going to advise Marshall in answering it.

447

"For heaven's sake, tell him not to encourage her!" Rusk said.

Acheson, who had already begun to refer to Frederika as "George Marshall's friend, Boadicea," accordingly sat down and wrote a memo to his old chief:

> Dean Rusk feels that you could say that you are glad to have her views, and that you assume that recent events have considerably changed the situation she describes, and pretty much let it go at that. Rusk feels we could not get involved in our long-range future here. . . . He feels that her letter just requires a pleasant acknowledgment.

How do you write a "pleasant acknowledgment" to a call for all-out war with the Soviet Union? Fortunately for Marshall, he did not have to find the answer to that question. While he was still thinking about what to say to Frederika, another matter supervened. The President called him on the telephone once more, and shortly afterward he was a member of his Cabinet again.

One of the characteristics of the Truman Cabinet after the 1948 election was that it contained almost no political deadheads. So few people had expected him to win that few of the big-money men had contributed to his campaign funds, and he had no obligations to pay off in political preferments. As a result, he was able to build what became to some extent a bipartisan Cabinet, with Republicans like Dulles and, later, William D. Pawley, filling important positions in the State Department, and with most of the major diplomatic jobs overseas going, for the first time, almost completely to career men from the Foreign Service. The Foreign Service, in fact, came into its own. With practically no political debts to pay, Truman could allow his secretary of state to pick the skilled man for the key post, and whereas, in most administrations, ambassadorial appointments and career appointments were divided about fifty-fifty between the pols and the pros, under Truman the career men got most of the pickings.

There was an exception. One determined and assiduous fund raiser had been a fervid Democratic and Truman supporter named

Louis Johnson, and the President felt obliged to give him a job as his reward. He made him his secretary of defense. Even Truman suspected very soon afterward that he had made a mistake but was not about to do anything about it. Others, particularly in the State Department, considered him a great disaster.

"Louis Johnson was just unbelievable," said Lucius "Luke" Battle, Secretary Acheson's aide. "He made a terrible secretary of defense. He was perfidious. He was devious. He was everything that was bad. He undercut Acheson, and most of the policies Johnson represented were contrary to the tenor of the times."

It was a period in American history when the nation had taken on the mantle of global protector of the free world, and it was expensive. There was the Marshall Plan, there was the Military Assistance Program, there were aid schemes in Greece and Turkey—and they needed money and appropriations to keep them going. Louis Johnson, who was a dedicated member of the "let's cut the budget" club, wanted them either slashed or abandoned entirely, and Acheson maintained that if he got his way, U.S. foreign policy would be irreparably damaged.

But how to get rid of him?

Acheson's undersecretary of state, James E. Webb, set himself the task of persuading the President to dismiss Louis Johnson.

"You know, Louis Johnson's got to go," he said to Battle. "But we mustn't let Dean get involved in it."

"So he played a major role in it, and without letting Dean know anything about it," Battle said later. "[Webb] was close to President Truman. He'd been the President's budget director, and they'd worked together, and Truman liked him, he was one of his favorite officials. And that helped enormously in getting rid of Louis Johnson."

When he got around at last to firing Johnson, the President found himself involved in a storm of vituperation, from the press, the Senate, and the Democrats, among whom the ex-secretary had powerfully vocal friends. He desperately needed a replacement who would take the heat off him and deflect public attention away from the controversial firing. What about George Marshall? He was obviously quite well recovered from his operation since he was whizzing around the world in behalf of the Red Cross. His name still spelled "trust" to the nation and to the civilized world. The President picked up the telephone and asked the operator to get Marshall on the line.

When a President of the United States wants to speak to someone, the operators at the White House pride themselves on finding him or her, no matter where or what time of the day or night. Marshall was eventually found at a hunting camp in the Michigan woods where he had gone to seek relaxation fishing for bass and trout. What the President did not know was that the nearest telephone was fifteen miles away, in the middle of a village store, and that when the general finally answered his call, there were half a dozen customers who had recognized him and were hanging on his every word.

"General," said Truman, "I want you to be my secretary of defense."

"All right," said Marshall, and abruptly hung up.

"The place was full of people with their ears open," he explained to the President later, "and I didn't want them to know what you and I were talking about, and that's the reason I said I would do it."

By that time it was too late to back out because the canny President had made the appointment public, and Marshall was back at Truman's side, where, the President considered, he belonged.

Acheson was delighted, too. He wrote later:

> No change could have been more welcome to me. It brought only one embarrassment. The General insisted, overruling every protest of mine, in meticulously observing the protocol involved in my being the senior Cabinet officer. Never would he go through a door before me, or walk anywhere but on my left; he would go around an automobile to enter it after me and sit on the left; in meetings he would insist on my speaking before him. To be treated so by a revered and beloved former chief was a harrowing experience.

But the results of the appointment brought enormous strength to the Cabinet and bolstered it just when the Republicans were girding themselves to tear it to pieces. Acheson wrote:

> [T]he result in government was, I think, unique in the history of the Republic. For the first time and, perhaps, though I am not sure, the last, the Secretaries of State and Defense, with their top advisers, met with the Chiefs of Staff in their map room and discussed common problems together.

The new Chief of Staff of the U.S. Army was General J. Lawton Collins, and the Chairman of the Joint Chiefs was General Omar Bradley. Collins and Bradley were, of course, Marshall's appointees and old friends, and the whole nature of these conferences therefore changed from now on. Neither Acheson nor Johnson was a military man, and they had sometimes received dusty answers from the soldiers when they had sought enlightenment. Now conditions were such that, Acheson observed later, he and Bradley were able to make a compact: "The phrases 'from a military point of view' and 'from a political point of view' were excluded from our talks. No such dichotomy existed. Each of us had our tactical and strategical problems, but they were interconnected, not separate."

In some important ways, Marshall's arrival could hardly have been more timely. The invasion of South Korea by its ideological enemies in North Korea had demonstrated for the first time the willingness of the Communists to use force to achieve their objectives and the pattern the Russians would henceforth use—attack through satellites. To prevent anything similar from happening in Europe, it was necessary to unite America's allies into some sort of defensive military organization, and the North Atlantic Treaty Organization had been proposed. But the French balked at the idea when it was suggested that included in the NATO forces should be troops from their late and still-hated enemy, Germany. The French defense minister, Jules Moch, was particularly opposed to any such plan, and he had personal as well as patriotic reasons for doing so. His son had been taken prisoner by the Germans in the war while fighting with the French Resistance, tortured, and finally choked to death by the Gestapo; he had no desire to see his countrymen fighting beside such thugs, even in the defense of Europe.

Marshall's first appearance as secretary of defense was at the United Nations in New York when the NATO question was being thrashed out. He had come practically straight from his swearing-in ceremony, only superficially briefed, and not fully cognizant of Allied feelings on the problems involved. But he quickly became aware that some brusque words had been thrown around and that feelings had been hurt. Acheson wrote later:

> To me General Marshall brought immense help in two ways. His great prestige and calm, compelling exposition left no doubt in any mind, including the French minds, that without Germany the defense of Europe was not possible. He also became convinced himself, and was able to persuade the Pentagon.

Marshall knew Moch from previous meetings, and the two men liked each other. With great patience and sympathy, he talked over with the Frenchman the need to swallow his pain and the necessity of adjusting to the realities of the new world. He finally won him around, and he, in turn, convinced his prime minister, Robert Schuman, to whom a military alliance with Germany was also anathema. It was quite a triumph.

"Everybody was delighted to see him [at the UN]," said Luke Battle. "They welcomed his appointment as secretary of defense. And his appearance seemed to heal the breach. It was not that he did anything brilliant at that meeting, but his mere presence was rather a healing one. He had this charisma—it was rather hard to understand."

He would need all the charisma he possessed, and more, to deal with the problems which faced him when he got back to Washington. There was China. There was Korea. There was the question of his confirmation—which would involve his patriotism. And there was General Douglas MacArthur.

27

Front Man

A five-star general in the United States Army can never officially retire from the service, and there was, therefore, no question of Marshall's giving up his rank when President Truman appointed him secretary of defense.

But the job did rightly belong to a civilian, and in order to enable Marshall to take it, a bill had to be introduced into Congress for him to officiate while remaining on active service with the Army. No one anticipated that there would be any objections. After all, wasn't Marshall the most respected and admired soldier in the nation? And in such fraught times, who was more fitted to be secretary of defense?

The U.S. Senate in 1950, however, was a nest containing vipers. One of them, Senator Joseph R. McCarthy, had already begun the evil and sordid maneuvers which, in future years, would add his name to the dictionary beside that of Justice Lynch and of Captain Boycott. Another was a less flashy opportunist but no less mean-minded man named Senator William E. Jenner, a Republican from Indiana, who believed that the way to win victory for his party at the polls in the next election was by riding what a shocked fellow Republican* called "the Four Horsemen of Calumny—fear, ignorance, bigotry and smear." He had already hurled some wild charges at both Truman and Acheson, accusing them of having lost China, brought about the Korean War, and encouraged Communist subversion. Both men were used to the rough-and-tumble of the American political process, and even when it

*Margaret Chase Smith.

453

got excessively abusive, they were well able to take care of themselves.*

But what about Marshall? He was not the kind of man to have his probity called in question. As Truman said of him later, "[He] was an honorable man, a truthful man, a man of ability. Honor had no modifying adjectives. A man has it or he hasn't."

His close associates had noticed that during the congressional inquiries into the Pearl Harbor disaster he had had to swallow hard over some of the pointed questions about his role in it and had accepted them only because, in the end, no one had doubted his motives, only his watchfulness. But now how would he react? Because Senator Jenner rose to call his honor into question. Stating flatly that he opposed the confirmation of the general in his new post, the man from Indiana declared, "George Marshall is not only willing, he is eager to play the role of a front man for traitors."

He then launched into a virulent attack on Marshall's record since the end of World War II, citing the loss of China, calling him "not a living legend but a living lie," who was now going to attach himself "as an errand boy, a front man, a stooge or co-conspirator for this administration's crazy assortment of collectivist cutthroat crackpots and Communist fellow-traveling appeasers."

He ended: "How can the Senate confirm the appointment of General Marshall, and thus turn Dean Acheson into a Siamese twin, in control of two of the most important Cabinet posts in the executive branch of the Government? This is what we are asked to do. It is tragic, Mr. President, that General Marshall is not enough of a patriot to tell the American people the truth of what has happened, and the terrifying story of what lies in store for us, instead of joining hands once more with this criminal crowd

---

*Although Acheson, when asked how the charges affected him, did say he was reminded of a victim of the Indian wars who was brought into hospital one day in bad shape, scalped, bleeding, an arrow sticking out of his chest. As the surgeon was about to operate to remove the arrow, he asked his patient, "Does it hurt?" "Only when I laugh," the fellow replied.

of traitors and Communist appeasers who, under the continuing influence and direction of Mr. Truman and Mr. Acheson, are still selling America down the river."

The leader of the Republicans might have been expected to rise to deplore the fact that a member of his party could stoop to such libels. But Senator Robert A. Taft, the leader in question, was already beginning to envision himself as the next President of the United States and was being tempted to believe that such McCarthyite tactics would help him achieve his goal.* He sat tight, and not even a flicker of disgust or disapproval passed over his face. The Senate had indeed become, as Acheson remarked later, "a place of easy standards."

The President, outraged by the attack, worried that his new secretary might take umbrage and resign rather than be subject to such insults, called him up. "General," he said, "when I get my hands on that skunk from Indiana, I'm going to skin him alive."

"Did he stop my confirmation?" Marshall asked.

"Oh, no," said Truman. "You got your confirmation, all right."

"Then I suggest you keep your hands away from him, Mr. President," the new secretary said. "The stench from that sort of animal is difficult to wash off."

Truman laughed with relief. "Welcome to the club, General," he said.

But if Marshall was reluctant to see anyone wrestle with skunks over his own reputation, he would fight with polecats to protect members of his staff.

One of his most controversial appointments after he became secretary of defense was the choice of a woman to be his assistant secretary. There had been women in the Defense Department before, but mainly to look after the interests of the female elements in the wartime forces. Marshall had not picked Anna Rosenberg to superintend the welfare of the WAC or the WAVES. She had been chosen because he had seen her operate under the late Pres-

---

*He lost the nomination to Dwight D. Eisenhower.

ident Roosevelt and knew she was good at running big departments; so far as he was concerned, it was strictly her general
ability and not her sex that mattered.*

All the same, he was never unaware of the fact that she was
a fascinating young woman—and he liked young women. She
never got the same rough treatment that he sometimes gave the
male members of his staff. Rosenberg to this day still tells the
story of how she was waiting nervously for news that the Senate
had confirmed her appointment and had been told by Marshall
to come into his office at once and tell him when the news came
through.

Finally, the confirmation was announced. Rosenberg rushed
into the secretary's office to find him presiding over a full-dress
meeting of the Joint Chiefs of Staff. They were all dressed up
because they were just about to go on for a conference at the
White House. Marshall looked up as she burst in.

"I was all choked up," she said later.

She could hardly get the words out that she had been confirmed.

"Well, that's good," said Marshall. "Now go home and get
a facial. You look like hell."

The Joint Chiefs looked quite shocked—"not because of me,"
she said, "but because the secretary knew about facials."

The next morning he came into her office, stared at her fixedly
behind her desk for a few minutes, and then summoned an aide.
"George," he said to the aide, "get her a chair that will fit her.
Her feet don't touch the floor."

He had remarked when he first made the appointment that
it would either prove "my biggest boner or will be recognized as
a stroke of genius," and he set out to help her make it a success.

"He carefully educated me to the job," she said later. Marshall would casually mention to her some military subject and
would expound on his experience in those areas. Subsequently she
would find herself in front of a hostile committee from the Joint

*As an active trade union leader she had been an early supporter of Roo-
sevelt's New Deal.

Chiefs who would start shooting questions at her, and she would find that they were all concerned with what the chief had briefed her on the previous day.

He sent her on tours of Army camps. He had her flown out to Korea and was pleased when she cabled back reports from the forward combat lines.

But then she ran into trouble with McCarthy.

One of the reports she brought back from Korea was about the use of black troops. The U.S. Army was still, even in 1950, to a large extent a segregated army, and "colored troops," as they were then called, were not generally used in combat. Rosenberg wanted that changed, for both reasons of social justice and those of simple defense.

"We have to use them out there," she told Marshall. "We have lots of casualties out there. We need those colored troops. They should have been used in battle long ago."

Marshall had old-fashioned conventional army ideas about the use of black troops in combat. He didn't believe they were much good. He had once read an adverse report about the behavior of black troops during nighttime operations in North Africa and flippantly commented, "The only place these colored troops are likely to prove useful is, perhaps, in summer operations in Iceland."

"He was opposed to integration," Rosenberg said. "But when I argued with him and accused him of being a stick-in-the-mud conservative, he said sharply that he had no political philosophy, that he belonged where it was right and didn't care whether it was conservative or liberal, and that he was ready to change his mind on any subject so long as he was given information to convince him. Well, I convinced him."

He finally agreed to order integration and the use of black troops in Korea.

"Not everyone agreed with him," said Rosenberg. "He had an off-the-record row with Eisenhower about it because he was against [it]."

There was a "great hue and cry" when the news of Anna Rosenberg's appointment came out and the McCarthyites zoomed in on her for special attention. Summoned before the House Un-American Activities Committee, she was accused of being a card-holding member of the Communist party. This she denied. But what good would that do? She had been smeared and had no way of clearing herself. She told Marshall there was only one thing to do, and that was resign.

"It was the only time I saw him get mad," she said later. "He said, 'I told you this would happen. They're not after you, they're after me. We will stick this out.'"

He rang up the FBI and spoke to J. Edgar Hoover and dis-covered that there was a special file on a certain Anna Rosenberg, a Communist cleaning woman from California, and also a sepa-rate one on Anna Rosenberg, the assistant secretary, giving her a clean bill, but that the bureau was not ready to release either file. The assistant secretary later said, "He called me and said, 'I'm on the way to the White House to ask the President to show the House committee your file.' I said, 'Don't ask him. He's trying to uphold the right to withhold executive files from HUAC. President Truman has the principle to uphold and I'd rather resign than have him break it.' Then he said sharply, 'There's something more important than principle, and that is that administration people don't suffer.' So he insisted the President show the file to the committee, and they found nothing, and we were in the clear. Mr. Truman would do *anything* for the general."

Soon she was able to bring him proof that black troops were splendid fighters, in daylight or darkness; all they had needed was the time, the place, and the esprit de corps. He thanked her for providing much-needed enlightenment.

In theory the job of secretary of defense was two stages re-moved from direct contact with the U.S. armed forces, and as a member of the administration's civilian Cabinet Marshall was ex-pected to go through his service chiefs when he wanted anything done about Army, Navy, or Air Force dispositions. General Brad-ley, as the new Chairman of the Joint Chiefs of Staff, handled overall matters concerning the activities of the combined services, and General Collins, as Chief of Staff, was responsible for the Army. But since Marshall knew more about their jobs than either of his subordinates, he must often have been tempted to go over their heads or disagree with their decisions. He did his best, however, to follow his own rule of delegating authority and then trusting his delegate to do the job well. He had been tempted once in Europe to overrule General Eisenhower's plan for the D-Day invasion of Normandy* and several times to countermand MacArthur's tactics in the Pacific, but he had always limited himself to advice and never given orders, preferring to leave it to the commander on the spot. There were those who said that the war might have been over sooner, and casualties fewer, if he had insisted, but he deprecated any speculation of that kind.

The Korean War had already begun by the time he took on the job as secretary, and he considered it no part of his duties to tell his staff chiefs how to run it. In any case, they had, in turn, already delegated that responsibility to a commander whose peacock pride made him incapable of accepting advice, orders, or even the mildest of suggestions on how he should conduct his operations. General of the Army Douglas MacArthur, Marshall's old Army rival from the misty past of World War I, had taken charge of the Korean battle and, after some initial setbacks, was handling it well. By a particularly brilliant maneuver he had made a landing and driven the enemy out of a strategically important center at Inchon. Marshall, who believed that even peacocks should be praised for a successful display, sent him a telegram:

FROM SECRETARY OF DEFENSE   9/30/50
PLEASE ACCEPT MY PERSONAL TRIBUTE TO THE COURAGEOUS CAM-
PAIGN YOU DIRECTED IN KOREA AND THE DARING AND PERFECT
STRATEGICAL OPERATION WHICH VIRTUALLY TERMINATED THE
STRUGGLE. GC MARSHALL

MacArthur replied:

FROM DAI ICHI† TOKYO   1 OCTOBER 1950
THANKS, GEORGE, FOR YOUR FINE MESSAGE. IT BRINGS BACK VIVIDLY

*He wanted a simultaneous airborne landing closer to Paris, which Ike and his advisers rejected.
†"Number one."

THE MEMORIES OF PAST WARS AND THE COMPLETE COORDINATION
AND PERFECT UNITY OF COOPERATION WHICH HAS ALWAYS EXISTED
IN OUR MUTUAL RELATIONSHIPS AND MARTIAL ENDEAVORS. AGAIN
MY DEEPEST APPRECIATION FOR YOUR MESSAGE AND FOR YOUR UN-
FAILING SUPPORT. MACARTHUR

If the secretary found the use of his first name overfamiliar—
he would *never* have thought of addressing MacArthur in a cable
as Douglas—and the tone of the message on the treacly side as
well, he did not say so, although the President grumbled, when
he was shown it, that *he* never got any cables like that from "that
fella."

For once Truman may well have found his favorite adviser
lacking in sympathy when he lashed out, as he had a frequent
habit of doing, about the arrogant and imperious ways of
MacArthur and his lack of respect for his President. For the moment, however, Marshall was as near to feeling a rapport for
General MacArthur as a human being as he ever came in his
lifetime, mainly because of a letter he had recently received from
one of his favorite women, Madame Chiang Kai-shek.

Chiang Kai-shek and the Chinese Nationalists had, by this
time, been driven out of mainland China by the Communists and
had retreated with the remnants of the Kuomintang armies to
Taiwan (formerly Formosa), where they had set up headquarters
and established protective outposts on strategic islands in the South
China Sea, Quemoy, Matsu, and the Pescadores. With the approval of the Joint Chiefs (but before Marshall assumed the post
of secretary of defense), MacArthur had announced that he was
leaving for Taiwan to inspect Chiang's position for himself and
talk over future plans.

He subsequently sent back to Washington a far less comprehensive report of what had taken place than Marshall received in
a chatty private missive from Madame. She not only filled him in
on the personal details, giving him piquant pictures of Mac-
Arthur's staff lolling in sulfur baths between sessions, but also
described the exact nature of the military discussions, which were
to prove invaluable to him when he did take on his new office.

But there was one paragraph in Madame's letter which both intrigued and alarmed him:

> The Generalissimo also told General MacArthur that from various quarters, including the guerrillas [in China], there have come requests and suggestions that I head the guerrilla movement on the mainland. He asked the General what he thought of the matter. The General replied that as far as the effectiveness of the work is concerned, he thought it would be fine. The person heading the movement should be someone the enemy would not suspect and certainly I would be the last one the enemy would suspect.

Marshall must have gulped at the thought of MacArthur's actually approving of a hare-brained plan to throw the delicate and fragile Madame Chiang Kai-shek into the guerrilla struggle against the Reds. Then he read on:

> But [the General] thought that the sacrifice on my part would be tremendous because whoever heads the movement would be fraught with danger and subject to torture and death if caught. He said that Cardinal Mindszenty was a case in point. The enemy did not subject him to mediaeval torture but by hypnotism and injections they were able to make use of him by taking away his will and making him do their bidding. The enemy could certainly find no one better to serve their purpose if they capture me, and therefore the sacrifice would be too great on my part. His last words as we left the car at the [air]field to me were: "I would not like to see you in such danger."

Nor would Marshall. He hastened to write back and say:

> Naturally I was much interested in what you had to tell me about General MacArthur's visit, but my special interest focused on the possibility of your being utilized to head up the guerrilla movement on the mainland. I think this would be a terrible responsibility not only from the viewpoint of danger but also, considering your uncertain state of health, you would be bound to suffer heavily from the hard living running such an enterprise.

He was glad to know that MacArthur had discouraged her, and for a time, at least, some warmth came into their relationship.

However, though they never did get around to calling each other George and Ike, his rapport with General Dwight D. Eisenhower would always be much more cordial, and even when Ike left the Chief of Staff's office to take over as president of Columbia University, he continued to consult him. One of his principal concerns upon taking on the Defense job was a problem with which he had been wrestling most of his military life: how to find manpower for the U.S. armed forces. Demobilization after the end of WWII had been so precipitate that America had found itself inheriting responsibility for world security without anything like the armed forces to provide the necessary muscle. One of the reasons for the initial success of the Soviet-backed attacks by the North Koreans had been the paucity of U.S. troops for stemming their advance.

Ike had recommended the immediate introduction of universal conscription. Marshall, who was much shrewder than Eisenhower in sizing up the feelings of Congress and the nation, was convinced that they would never get away with it. They started a lively exchange of letters over other ways of achieving it by less drastic means. Marshall wrote, on October 23, 1950:

> I am convinced judging from my own experience, which has been rather terrific along these lines of changing public opinion, that unless we get into some system which does not involve so many men in uniform for prolonged service, we will find ourselves flat on our faces again as appropriations vanish. I have been through this too often—1921–1924, especially the summer of 1941, and finally the late summer and early fall of 1945—to feel that the American public has learned its lesson. Taxes, the political importance of the budget, the reaction of restless young Americans and the tremendous influence of the family, would combine to wreck us again, however keenly we feel at the moment the necessity for taking drastic action.

He told Eisenhower he was working up a scheme to use the National Guard, plus some form of universal military training, to get the men the armed forces needed—to "be really a great force in the world and yet not on the daily payroll." But he counseled Ike to keep it confidential "because I have not yet come forward with a complete statement of my views here" and "Bradley and Collins know my general feelings only."

Their close, if unofficial, collaboration led him to agree with America's allies that once the new North Atlantic Treaty Organization (NATO), began to operate, there was only one man who could head it and keep the disparate armed forces of the associate members working together. He strongly backed Truman's choice of Eisenhower and, on December 21, 1950, wrote to Ike:

> I repeat again what I told you the other day that I think your attitude in the matter and the sacrifice you are making is [*sic*] a very great offering to your country, and I am certain you will acquit yourself with the highest honor, which is so greatly to the national interest and the interest of the world generally.

He added a tribute the openly expressed warmth of which was quite unusual for him:

> There are a great many men of wisdom and of courage, men of reputation in the world, but your combination of these qualities together with a rare ability to work harmoniously with other people and control their efforts, capped by an outstanding quality in the high degree of integrity which has characterized your every action, makes you rather [*sic*] unique in the world.

The next presidential election was not due until 1952, more than a year away, but it was noticed in Washington that Senator Robert A. Taft was already running for the Republican nomination and, in the process, moving politically closer to the idiot fringe represented by McCarthy and Jenner. If Republican delegates and national support were to be gained by pinning Communist labels on members of the Truman administration, Taft was ready to begin the process early. His remarks these days, especially those made within the privileged walls of the Congress, were apt to be laced with dark charges against "certain members of this administration" who were prepared "to put loyalty to their President before loyalty to their country." He also referred to the "untold story of the Pearl Harbor betrayal" and of "the misguided men who lost China for America." There were plenty of people who got the distinct feeling that if Taft was not yet pointing a finger at General Marshall, he was certainly casting baleful looks in his direction.

It so happened that Marshall had an admirer who was also a staunch Republican and quite close to Taft and other leaders of the party. His name was William D. Pawley, and he was one of the most knowledgeable experts on China in the country. A flier and airplane designer and builder, he had been responsible for the formation of the famous Flying Tigers which—with U.S. volunteer pilots—had fought the Japanese in China long before the United States came into the war. Marshall had met, conferred with him, and finally made him his assistant during his China mission and knew him to be a shrewd expert on that country, even if his opinions did take the opposite line to that advocated by the State Department's tame advisers. He did not, for instance, believe in the policy some experts in the department were peddling—that the Chinese Communists were not really Reds at all but socialist-minded agrarian revolutionaries and, therefore, no danger to the United States at all. On the contrary, Pawley considered them a menace to U.S. security. He believed it would be a serious error if America recognized the Chicoms as the legitimate government of China and thus abandoned the Nationalist Chinese on Taiwan, and on this Marshall agreed with him.

Marshall admired Pawley's expertise, respected his opinions, and recommended him to the President as an additional adviser on China. He would help keep the administration's policy on an even keel and demonstrate the bipartisan quality of his thinking on China. Truman turned him down on the ground that taking Pawley under his wing might be regarded as a criticism of Dean Acheson, but he did see the wisdom of Marshall's recommendation and sent instructions to the State Department that Pawley should be given a job as a bipartisan expert on Chinese affairs. The department did so, with the utmost reluctance.

When Pawley arrived for his first day at the State Department, he was whisked off to lunch by Assistant Secretary James Webb, who wasted no time in apprizing him of the situation.

"Bill," he said, "I don't want you to feel badly about this.

There was a meeting in the secretary's office today and it was decided you are to see no paper dealing with the Far East, you are to attend no meetings dealing with the Far East; in fact, the secretary has requested you must not discuss the question of the Far East while you are here."

Pawley looked astonished.

"What's the matter, Jim?" he asked. "Am I considered subversive?"

"Of course not," Webb replied, "but your views on what ought to be done about China and the views of the State Department are diametrically opposed, and therefore, the secretary doesn't want any difficulties."

Pawley said, "Is the secretary trying to get me to resign? Is that the purpose of this move?"

Webb: "I don't know. I don't think so."

Pawley: "You can tell the secretary that I shan't resign, and he cannot, in my judgment, prevent me from participating in discussions on a matter with which I'm somewhat familiar." He paused and then went on: "Jim, have you ever been to the Far East?"

"No," said Webb.

"Has the secretary of state?"

"No," said Webb.

"Then why am I being eliminated as a devil's advocate on a subject I'm very familiar with?"

"Because your views do not coincide with those held by the State Department," Webb said.

Pawley: "Does that mean the views held by the State Department are infallible?"

Webb: "Bill, I think it's useless for us to discuss it."

He changed the subject at that point and began to talk about other ways in which he thought Pawley might make himself useful, and they seemed to be so ridiculous that his companion gave them no attention whatsoever. Instead, the moment lunch was over, he walked over to the Defense Department in a cold fury and told General Marshall what had happened.

"Why, that's ridiculous," said the secretary of defense. "What's the use of your being there? Would you like me to drive over and discuss this with the President?"

Pawley shook his head. He said the last thing he wanted to do was involve Marshall in his troubles. If he went to the President, it could well create a breach between himself and Dean Acheson, and Pawley didn't want that.

"Yes, I recognize that," Marshall said. "But this is very wrong. This should not happen." He thought for a moment and then went on: "All policy papers dealing with the Far East pass over my desk. And I think I know of no one whose judgment I value more. You've been my assistant [in China] in evaluating such documents. You will see them here in future."

So from that time on Pawley went across to Marshall's office to read the documents on China that were being held back from him at the State Department.

"And I must say," he said later, "that at least on two occasions we together were able to prevent policy papers from being adopted that might otherwise have gone through."

So Pawley not only admired Marshall but had reason to be grateful to him, and it was he who became alarmed at some of the moves in Taft's camp to saddle the secretary of defense with America's past failures. He was not comforted when he learned that General Al Wedemeyer, who had been one of Senator McCarthy's original supporters, had now become one of Taft's advisers on Far Eastern affairs, for that boded no good for Marshall. Wedemeyer was known to cherish some dark thoughts about Pearl Harbor and the part played in it by his bête noire, President Roosevelt. "Was Marshall doing his duty when he said he didn't know where he was on the morning of Pearl Harbor?" he had once sepulchrally asked. "Was it in order to protect the President? Was he hiding out?"

Pawley, acutely aware of the breach which had opened between Marshall and Wedemeyer during the China mission, was only too conscious of the fact that it was no loyal friend of the general's who had now joined the camp of the Republican contender. While Wedemeyer could hardly accuse Marshall of having taken the Communist side in China, he could easily suggest that he had too slavishly followed the State Department line and thus become a Communist dupe. And what had he told McCarthy about Pearl Harbor?*

"My experience with George Marshall [in China] indicated that he was not sympathetic," Pawley said, "to any policy that would weaken the U.S. where communism was concerned. This is important. I'm just positive of that because he took a very strong position. Anyone who tries to associate him with any policies or recommendations that would have been helpful to the Communists does not know George Marshall."

Or wanted to do him harm.

Pawley worried. And it did not help his peace of mind when he saw that General Marshall did not appear to be worried at all.

---

*Wedemeyer later explained that he had initially supported McCarthy because he thought he was doing important work in rooting out secret Communist sympathizers. "I always said I would never support him if he was doing all this for aggrandizement. I always felt he was a dedicated man." Then a man "high in the Republican Committee" told him that McCarthy "personally was a rotter," and he joined Taft instead. "If Taft was an isolationist, he was my kind of isolationist. He wanted what we did abroad to be in our interest." He added that he was "strong for Taft" and became head of Citizens for Taft in the 1952 election.

28

Clash

"Jittery" was the word President Truman used to describe the world situation in the last days of 1950.

"I have worked for peace for five years and six months," he wrote on December 9, "and it looks like World War Three is near. I hope not—but we must meet whatever comes and we will."

It was the conflict in Korea which was causing all the worry. Suddenly everything had started to go wrong. After his initial success at Inchon, about which Marshall had sent him that congratulatory telegram, General Douglas MacArthur had decided on a general offensive against the North Koreans and ordered the United Nations forces to attack and annihilate the Communist armies of North Korea.

There was some hesitation in Washington when the news that he was doing so came in, and the State Department queried General Marshall and the Defense Department. Marshall passed on the question to the Joint Chiefs of Staff, who pointed out that it seemed foolish to interfere with an Army commander who was winning a war, a sentiment with which he was inclined to agree. In any case, as General Collins, the Army Chief of Staff, who had just come back from a visit to MacArthur, pointed out, "The success of Inchon was so great, and the subsequent prestige of General MacArthur was so overpowering, that the Chiefs hesitated thereafter to question later plans and decisions of the general which should have been."

But as the victorious UN forces advanced northward, provoking chaos, panic, and retreat among the North Korean armies, new doubts began to be expressed about the wisdom of this headlong advance, particularly from America's allies. Not far away was the Yalu River, separating North Korea from China. How would the Red Chinese of Mao Tse-tung, newly and triumphantly established as overlords of China, but not yet recognized by the United States, react to this seemingly belligerent approach to their frontiers?

General MacArthur seems to have felt confident that there was nothing to worry about and appears to have assured the President when they consulted together on Wake Island on October 15 that they would stand aloof, having neither the muscle nor the willingness to interfere. If this is so,* neither MacArthur nor Truman can have been reading his newspapers. There had been repeated reports from Peking, and several messages transmitted through the Indian ambassador, to the effect that China was extremely concerned by UN incursions into North Korea and would not stand idly by if its frontiers and its security were threatened.

Nevertheless, when the question of MacArthur's plans was brought up before a meeting of the National Security Council, at which both Acheson and Marshall were present, the main point of discussion was not whether the UN armies should pursue the North Koreans but how far.

The Joint Chiefs of Staff, led by their Chairman, General Omar Bradley, and backed by General Collins, the Army Chief of Staff, were supportive of MacArthur in his declared intention not merely to drive the Communists out of Korea and into China but to destroy them in the process—which could mean possible incursions into China itself. The prospect did not seem to alarm the JCS.

"Only by doing so," wrote Collins, "could international peace and security in Korea be restored, as required by the UN resolution of June 27."

What had begun as a war to repel the invasion of South Korea by the Communist North had now become a campaign to liberate the whole of the Korean peninsula from the Reds, and no one seemed to smell any danger in it—not, at least, among the Americans. It is true that Marshall began to have some second thoughts and, with the approval of the President, prevailed on the

---

*There is no impartial account of the Wake Island conversations.

JCS to send MacArthur some instructions which allowed him rather less leeway. He confirmed that the UN commander's objective was still to destroy the North Korean forces but added, "UNDER NO CIRCUMSTANCES WILL YOUR FORCES CROSS THE MANCHURIAN OR USSR BORDERS OF KOREA AND, AS A MATTER OF POLICY, NO NON-KOREAN GROUND FORCES WILL BE USED IN THE NORTHEAST PROVINCES BORDERING THE SOVIET UNION OR IN THE AREA ALONG THE MANCHURIAN BORDER [with China]."

This was, unfortunately, a secret telegram for MacArthur's eyes only, and it did not become known until later. In the meantime, there were repeatedly belligerent statements from the bloodthirsty old man who was head of the South Korean government, a firebrand named Syngman Rhee, who angrily declared that "the war cannot stop at the Yalu River" but would continue into China. At the same time, a powerful Republican backer of MacArthur's, Senator William F. Knowland, began calling for an advance into China proper by U.S. forces and the establishment of a "neutral zone ten miles north of the Yalu River." The name of Yalu began to ring like a call to war among the U.S. supporters of preventive action, like an alarm bell among America's allies, and like a tocsin to the Chicoms in Peking.

The Republicans and their right-wing friends began to agitate for the activation of the Nationalist Chinese armies in Taiwan. The British warned the United States to be more prudent. But it was the Communists who took action. First in the guise of Chinese-based North Korean "volunteers" and then more openly as Red Army irregulars, they began infiltrating troops across the Yalu to ambush and entrap the unwary UN forces.

MacArthur was, as usual, directing the war from Tokyo and did not seem to appreciate the quicksands into which his forces in Korea were so confidently marching. In reply to some tentative inquiries from the JCS, he expressed doubts that the Chinese Communists were directly involved or had plans seriously to impede him. But although he was even farther away and not directly involved with the military assessments and decisions that were being made, Marshall in Washington smelled something menacing in the air. He was not comforted when his old assistant and Ike's former chief of staff, General Walter Bedell Smith, telephoned him with some disturbing information. Bedell Smith was back from his post as U.S. ambassador to Moscow and had been put in charge of the new intelligence organization, the CIA, which President Truman had somewhat reluctantly allowed to be established.

On direct orders from the Dai Ichi in Tokyo, the CIA was forbidden to engage in intelligence-gathering activities in the Far East since MacArthur insisted on retaining those operations as a special perquisite of his own espionage services. But because the Dai Ichi was extremely selective in what items of information he passed on to Washington, and quite often "edited" the items to fit in with his own assessments of given situations, Bedell Smith had decided to achieve surreptitiously what he was not allowed to do officially and gather information on a doubly clandestine basis. He called in his director of operations, Frank Wisner, and asked him to get reports the best way he could about Far Eastern affairs.* Wisner may well have sent operatives to Peking, New Delhi, and Jakarta but probably found all he needed in the files of the Dai Ichi in Tokyo.

Now Bedell Smith telephoned Marshall to warn him that MacArthur was not telling the JCS the whole story about the Korean situation. In the first place, not only were the Chinese Communist armies planning a full-scale attack against the UN forces in North Korea, but MacArthur had been informed of this by his own intelligence services and for the time being was deliberately holding the fact back from the JCS. In the second place, MacArthur's planning staff in Tokyo was in the process of producing a plan for all-out war in the Far East, including the blockading of China by the U.S. Navy, the naval and air bombardment of China's industrial centers by U.S. forces, and the use of Chinese Nationalist forces against the Chicoms both in Korea and on the Chinese mainland. And in the third place, Bedell Smith added, the CIA had been given to understand by informants in direct contact

---

*Later the task was turned over to Allen Dulles, who joined the agency about this time and had a special interest in Korea. His son was in the Army and was subsequently shot in the head by a sniper during the campaign.

with Communist sources that if these plans were accepted by the United States or the United Nations—or forced upon them by military commanders supposedly acting on their behalf—a full-scale global war could result which would involve the Soviet Union and would not be confined to the Far East.*

Almost simultaneously with Walter Bedell Smith's disquieting message, a cable arrived for the Chief of Staff from MacArthur in Tokyo to tell him that Chicom attacks on the UN forces were increasing in intensity and that Chicom reinforcements were pouring across the Yalu River. Accordingly, he said, he had ordered his air commander in Korea, General George E. Stratemeyer, to send a fleet of bombers to the Yalu to "take out" the bridges over the river.

When news of this development reached Collins, he immediately telephoned his chief, Omar Bradley, who in turn called the JCS together and informed Marshall. It was agreed that to allow such a raid to take place on the Chinese border without carefully considering the international consequences could be disastrous. The air strikes were due to take place on the morning of November 6, 1950, and it was November 6 in Washington; but luckily Korea was on the other side of the international date line, and they had some hours in hand. The order "POSTPONE ALL BOMBING OF TARGETS WITHIN FIVE MILES OF THE MANCHURIAN BORDER" was sent to MacArthur in Tokyo and reached the pilots of Stratemeyer's B-17's just as they were beginning to load their bombs.

MacArthur reacted angrily. He was later to call the order "the most indefensible and ill-conceived decision ever forced on a field commander in our nation's history." In the meantime, he snapped back a message to point out that bombing the bridges was the only way to prevent hordes of Chinese troops from pouring over the Yalu into Korea. No longer trying to conceal from

---

*This warning was probably passed on by the British double agent Kim Philby, who was in Washington at the time in his cover role of chief liaison officer between the CIA and the British SIS (Special Intelligence Service). Wisner (and Dulles) already suspected Philby of working for the Soviets. Wisner and Philby met frequently, and a day rarely passed without their meeting for a drink, in either Wisner's office or the bar of the Mayflower Hotel.

Washington that he was now facing a full-scale attack by the Chicom armies, he insisted he could save his troops and those of his allies from heavy casualties only if he could take urgent countermeasures. He confirmed to the JCS that he had called off the projected air strike but added:

> I cannot overemphasize the disastrous effect, both physical and psychological, that will result from the restrictions which you are imposing. I trust that the matter will be immediately brought to the attention of the President as I believe your instructions may well result in a calamity of major proportions for which I cannot accept the responsibility without his personal and direct understanding of the situation.

Truman was quite well aware by this time that General MacArthur respected him and his opinions even less than those of the JCS and that he was being brought into the quarrel only as a political ploy and as a stick with which to browbeat the opposition. As he did on all such military matters, he called in Marshall to ask his opinion. The secretary of defense was worried. All the dire forebodings contained in Walter Bedell Smith's warning through the CIA were coming true. In the space of forty-eight hours MacArthur had repainted the whole picture of the Korean situation, changing it from a purely local war to one with all the potentials for a global conflict. As a soldier, Marshall's instinct was to leave it to the commander on the spot and allow MacArthur— in whose military ability, at least, he had great confidence—to take the measures he considered necessary. As the President's political adviser on military affairs, however, he felt the need to temper his instincts with some civilian prudence. Accordingly, he advised the President to allow MacArthur a limited franchise, but to make it plain that Washington was aware that he had not been giving them the whole picture of the situation. The JCS cabled Tokyo:

> THE SITUATION DEPICTED IN YOUR MESSAGE [of November 6] IS CONSIDERABLY CHANGED FROM THAT REPORTED IN LAST SENTENCE OF YOUR MESSAGE [of November 4] WHICH WAS OUR LAST REPORT FROM YOU. WE AGREE THAT THE DESTRUCTION OF THE YALU

BRIDGES WOULD CONTRIBUTE MATERIALLY TO THE SECURITY OF THE FORCES UNDER YOUR COMMAND UNLESS THIS ACTION RESULTED IN INCREASED CHINESE COMMUNIST EFFORT AND EVEN SOVIET CONTRIBUTION IN RESPONSE TO WHAT THEY MIGHT WELL CONSTRUE AS AN ATTACK ON MANCHURIA.

The message ended:

HOWEVER . . . YOU ARE AUTHORIZED TO GO AHEAD WITH YOUR PLANNED BOMBING IN KOREA NEAR THE FRONTIER INCLUDING TARGETS AT SINUIJU AND KOREAN END OF YALU BRIDGES PROVIDED THAT AT TIME OF RECEIPT OF THIS MESSAGE YOU STILL FIND SUCH ACTION ESSENTIAL TO SAFETY OF YOUR FORCES. THE ABOVE DOES NOT AUTHORIZE THE BOMBING OF ANY DAMS OR POWER PLANTS ON THE YALU RIVER.

MacArthur's reaction to the order to stay on the Korean side of the river was to exclaim to his subordinates, "How the devil can you bomb half a bridge?"

A day later he cabled the JCS to report that UN troops were being repeatedly attacked by Chinese and Russian bombers which promptly, when the USAF responded, took refuge in "sanctuaries" on the Manchurian and Soviet sides of the Yalu. He demanded the right for Stratemeyer's fighters to engage in "hot pursuit" and hit the enemy bombers in airspace where they felt safe.

This request worried Marshall most of all. As Adlai Stevenson, who was seeing him socially as well as professionally during this period,* said later, "His great dilemma was during the Korean War over the 'hot pursuit' doctrine, chasing Chinese and Russian aircraft over the Yalu. He knew how dangerous it was."

And on this decision, particularly. There was a great deal of agitation going on now, in Congress and among the public, over what they considered MacArthur's "tied hands" in Korea, and both Acheson and Truman himself were inclined to bow to the pressure and let MacArthur have his way. Marshall reluctantly agreed. Then the cautious Dean Rusk cantered to the rescue by

---

*Stevenson's sister and brother-in-law were neighbors at the Marshalls' at their winter home in Pinehurst, North Carolina.

reminding them all that any such decision would need the approval of America's UN allies. Their reply was a decisive no, none louder than that delivered by Ernie Bevin, the British foreign minister, who was promptly charged by MacArthur as being a craven heir to the Munich tradition.

But then the mood suddenly changed in Tokyo. MacArthur exultantly reported that no more infiltrations were coming over the Yalu and that the Chicom armies had disappeared. Things were so quiet that Stratemeyer's planes could no longer find targets. The Reds had evidently been frightened off, and MacArthur therefore proposed to proceed with the cleaning up of the campaign by marching his forces to the Yalu, giving the UN complete control over the Korean peninsula. He flew to Seoul and went to the front to assume personal command.

"If successful," he proclaimed, "this should for all practical purposes end the war, restore peace and unity to Korea, enable the prompt withdrawal of the United Nations military forces, and permit the complete assumption by the Korean people and nation of full sovereignty and international equality."

It would just be a cleaning-up process. Newsmen promptly dubbed it the "Home for Christmas Drive."

That was on November 17, 1950. On November 26 disaster, in the shape of General Lin Piao's Chinese Communist Fourth Army, struck.

The reason for the quiet in North Korea during the middle weeks of November was that 200,000 Chinese troops had been secretly filtering through the hills from Manchuria and poising to pounce on MacArthur's unwary forces. When they struck, they dealt the UN forces a devastating blow that sent panic waves all the way back to Tokyo. General Bradley rushed to the telephone and called the White House.

"A terrible message has come in from General MacArthur," he said.

The message was that U.S. and UN troops were reeling back all along the line, and the great retreat south had begun. Fifteen days earlier MacArthur had talked of the conquest of the whole of Korea. By November 30 he was considering the total evacuation of the same vast territory. The situation, he reported, was totally "fluid," an assessment, the President commented dryly, which was "a public relation man's way of saying he can't figure out what's going on." He turned for guidance to Marshall and asked for his military assessment.

"Marshall refused to give a military judgment," said Acheson later. "He insisted on sitting on the civilian side of the table with me and would say, 'No military judgment from me. What can we do? We are seventeen thousand miles away from the battle. We don't know the terrain except that it is bad. There are only two things we *can* do. One is the way we've operated since the Spanish-American War, which is to trust the commander in the field, say to him, "Go to it, brother." You don't say, "Send this division here, or use these supplies and movements there." Churchill tried to do that and got everything bollixed up. The second way is to relieve him—and who wants to do that?' "

All the same, Acheson wished that Churchill had been sitting in on the emergency discussions. "At least he would have done something with assertiveness," he said. "He was always so confident about damn near everything. He was wrong about half the time, but at least he was confident."

For the moment no one sitting around with the President and discussing Korea seemed to be confident at all. It appeared to many of them that MacArthur was worrying not so much about the military situation in Korea as about the damage to his reputation as the Chicoms hardened their attacks. He began giving interviews to his favorite newsmen designed to draw the blame for the disaster away from him and to place it on the shoulders of the JCS and the President, who had created an "enormous handicap" for him by forcing him to put a *cordon sanitaire* along the Yalu River. He broadly hinted that the retreat now going on would never have happened had he not been so hamstrung by fearful men in Washington and by the craven anxieties of America's allies.

Marshall promptly sent out a sharp note, countersigned by Acheson, forbidding "military commanders and diplomatic representatives" to communicate with the media directly on military or political affairs. It was not addressed to MacArthur personally, but everyone guessed it had been written for his benefit.

It was, however, not only MacArthur who could not keep his mouth shut. Truman lost control of his tongue, too. At a press conference he was asked whether he would be prepared to use the atomic bomb in Korea to restore the situation and sent the winds of panic skittering around the world by insisting that he would refuse to exclude the use of any weapon in the U.S. arsenal. That brought Prime Minister Clement Attlee hurrying across the Atlantic, declaring to anyone with a notebook in his or her hand that Britain would never agree to the use of atomic weapons. He was assured that it had simply been a *lapsus linguae,* and to reinforce this explanation, the President issued a public statement:

> The President wants to make it certain that there is no misinterpretation of his answers to questions . . . about the use of the atom bomb. Naturally, there has been consideration of this subject since the outbreak of hostilities in Korea [but] it should be emphasized that, by law, only the President can authorize the use of the atom bomb, and no such authorization has been given.

Truman did not mention to Attlee that he had, in fact, already passed control of the bomb over to his trusted secretary George Marshall, who had revealed that fact to his friend Bernard Baruch. (By a curious coincidence, Baruch just about this time called in the assistant secretary of defense Robert Lovett and asked him to pass the message on to Marshall that in Baruch's view, "the American people increasingly favored the use of atomic weapons in Korea." Lovett dropped this nugget of information into the ear of Dean Acheson, who counseled him to let it go no further.)

Meanwhile, the ignominious retreat in Korea continued, with much loss of life and many prisoners taken by the victorious Chinese. There were such reports of chaos, confusion, and panic that Marshall told General Collins, the Chief of Staff, to get out to Korea and report back on the way it was going. Collins was favorably impressed and considered that in the circumstances, MacArthur and his chief lieutenant, General Walton H. Walker, were handling the withdrawal from the North with stiff-lipped efficiency. But that did not allay the panic felt in Washington. So sure were some Cassandras that World War III was almost here that wild rumors spread around the capital when the U.S. early-warning radar system picked up formations of flying objects, presumably planes, heading toward Washington and calculated to arrive there in about two hours. Marshall was alerted and authorized the interception and defense forces to get ready for action; meanwhile, he hastened to the White House to be with the President if and when the button needed to be pushed to set atom bomb reprisals in action.

Dean Acheson was warned to "inform but not advise" Mr. Attlee. He called him up at the British Embassy to tell him that "Pentagon telephones would be closed for all but emergency defense purposes" and that he would not be able to call back. The British premier sounded so calm when he got the news that Acheson "asked whether he believed that the objects picked up were Russian bombers. He said that he did not."

Among those who had heard the rumors in the State Department, however, it was well and truly believed.

"One of our senior officials burst into the room," reported Acheson later. "How he had picked up the rumor I do not know, perhaps from the Pentagon. He wanted to telephone his wife to get out of town and to have important files moved to the basement. I refused to permit him to do either and gave him the choice of a word-of-honor commitment not to mention the matter to anyone or being put under security detention. He wisely cooled off and chose the former."

Acheson walked over to the White House to join Secretary Marshall and the President, his sense of the dramatic heightened by the thought that, very shortly now, he would be dying in a most distinguished Valhalla. He was met in the corridor by a sweaty Robert Lovett, wearing a rueful smile. He reported that the mysterious flying objects had disappeared from the early-warning screen. It was thought they had probably been geese.

It was while his American hosts were in a suitably chastened mood, depressed by the defeat in Korea, prey to panicky fears in Washington, that Prime Minister Attlee pushed home the British view that it was time to seek an armistice in Korea. At successive meetings with the President, with Acheson and Marshall, and with the JCS, he and his military adviser, Field Marshal Sir William Slim, pointed out that the danger to world peace was much greater in Europe than in Asia. He characterized the Korean campaign as nothing more than a Communist ploy to involve the resources of the allies in the wrong place at the wrong time, in order to trap them when the real attack struck home—in Europe. He made it plain that the British and their UN allies were scared of what General MacArthur might get them into if he was allowed to continue his activities on the Asian mainland.

Marshall and Acheson had a hard time concealing their agreement with such strictures but pointed out that MacArthur was a great general, that a commander in battle must be trusted, and that Asia could not be abandoned just because the British did not consider it as important as Europe. The President rather more sharply interrupted to say that America proposed to stay in Korea and fight, even if its allies abandoned it. At that point Attlee looked across at Slim, shrugged his shoulders, and wisely decided to take the argument no further.

But in fact, the meek-looking British leader, who had once been described by Winston Churchill as "a sheep in sheep's clothing," had taken the measure of the meeting and rightly suspected that his American allies wanted to get out. Not out of Korea, if they could avoid it, but certainly out of the Korean War. Their unspoken resolve to do so was reinforced when MacArthur's commander in the field, General Walton Walker, was killed in a jeep accident while directing the retreat of the Eighth Army. The War Department's chief of military operations, General Matthew B. Ridgway, was rushed out to Korea to take his place.

Ridgway, who had followed the battle on his wall map in Washington and come to some depressing conclusions, stopped in Tokyo to confer with MacArthur and found him in a gloomy frame of mind. He was not the greatest admirer in the U.S. Army of the Far East C in C, mainly because, in Korea, he had committed the fault Ridgway found unforgivable in a commanding officer. Ridgway's motto, which he pinned on the wall behind his desk, was: "The only inexcusable offense in a commanding officer is to be surprised." Surprised was what MacArthur had certainly been in Korea, and Ridgway secretly thought he should have been fired for it. As a result of his blunder, all the hopes of victory in Korea, of liberating the peninsula from the Communists, had vanished in the smoke of Chinese shot and shell. And Ridgway had been given the unpalatable job of holding the fort until the ultimate disaster struck—or an armistice could be obtained.

It was not a pleasant assignment, and if he shared MacArthur's gloom, he did not waste any sympathy over him.

Marshall had hoped that he and Katherine would get a few days over Christmas 1950 to celebrate at Pinehurst; but the President had declared a state of emergency over the Korean situation, and no one was allowed to leave Washington. On the day after Christmas, Truman called a meeting at Blair House at which the secretary of defense, the secretary of state, the secretary of the treasury (John Snyder), and the Chairman of the JCS, General Bradley, were present. They had gathered to write a new directive for General MacArthur on how he should conduct himself in the Far East from now on. It was predicated on the belief among the President and his advisers that the danger of WWIII loomed ahead but that Korea was not the place in which to fight it.

The four-point directive which was subsequently cabled to the Commander in Chief in the Far East stated:

1. Additional forces would not be committed to the Korean campaign because of the "increased threat of a general war," which would not be fought in Korea.

2. If, with present UN strength, the United States could resist the Chicom armies and deflate their apparent military and political prestige, it would be of great psychological importance and boost our national interests.

3. "Your directive is to defend in successive positions, subject

to safety of your troops as your primary consideration, inflicting as much damage to hostile forces as possible."

4. If evacuation was inevitable, the decision should be reported well ahead to give the JCS time for an orderly evacuation. General MacArthur's views were particularly requested on the conditions which would determine the need to evacuate.

This was a very different message from the one MacArthur had been expecting from the Joint Chiefs. His own pessimistic messages had been mainly aimed at causing some sort of panic in Washington and bolstering the demand he simultaneously sent for reinforcements. He had urgently asked for at least four divisions, the minimum he believed were required to keep the United Nations in Korea. Now he heard he would get no reinforcements at all.

Angered by this, he sent back by way of a riposte a new four-part plan which, he grandiosely claimed, would completely eliminate the Communist threat not just from Korea but from the whole of the Far East. The plan arrived on Marshall's desk on December 30, the eve of his seventieth birthday, and when he looked through it, he saw it was the same plan which Walter Bedell Smith had leaked to him some weeks earlier.*

Unless something like this plan was adopted, MacArthur declared, then disaster threatened. Korea would have to be evacuated.

His pessimistic forecast was jolted by a report which now came in from the new Eighth Army commander in Korea, General Ridgway. It flatly contradicted MacArthur's bleak assessment of the local situation. Ridgway had arrived at Eighth Army headquarters expecting to take over a defeated and demoralized force; he found that all it lacked was leadership and the incentive to get up and go. His report back to Tokyo exuded a tingling sense of confidence and hope.

And what irked MacArthur was Ridgway's assertion that he

---

*To blockade China, bombard its industrial cities, use Chinese Nationalist troops in Korea, and activate Taiwan as a base for a mainland campaign.

was confident he could handle any new assaults General Lin Piao sent against him, and could do it, moreover, without any re-inforcements at all. The Eighth Army had all the men, guns, and guts he needed.

News began coming back from Korea that Ridgway's optimism was catching and that it had begun coursing through the UN troops like a zephyr breeze in winter, melting doubt and disillusionment. It fired up the GI's of the Eighth into a defiant, dogged, and determined body of men, who now began punching hard at the Chicom armies, driving them slowly and relentlessly back to the North.

Naturally it was an achievement which did not please General MacArthur and the prophets of doom in Tokyo. But then he quickly adapted himself to the new situation and calmly assumed credit for his field commander's successes. As Ridgway began driving northward and the Chicoms fell back, the old warrior's ambitions began to stir again. If the Eighth Army went on like this, why, they could sweep up the peninsula and reach the Yalu. And this time, why hesitate? Why not just go on into the strongholds of the Communists across the river?

It was just about this time that news reached the Dai Ichi from MacArthur's Republican friends in Washington that the Truman administration had no intention of approving such a plan. It was not even thinking of an incursion into North Korea. It was looking for a way to "weasel out," as his Republican friends put it, of the whole war. Egged on by his craven allies, the President was looking for an escape route and was ready to settle for two Koreas—in other words, the *status quo ante,* the same situation as had existed before the war began.

MacArthur was appalled. What, had it all been in vain? Had 54,000 Americans died for nothing?

From Tokyo he hastened to let the President know that as far as he was concerned, the war was certainly not over. He was not satisfied to see half of Korea liberated. The Communists must be driven out of North Korea as well. And this time, if the Chicoms tried to interfere, he must be allowed a free hand.

On February 11, 1951, he cabled the details of a new victory plan, which, he asserted, would effectively clear the Korean peninsula of the enemy. It would be done in three phases:

1. Massive air attacks upon the enemy's rear areas all the way across North Korea, to create utter chaos and confusion and wipe out road and rail systems;

2. Effective countermeasures against any reinforcements sent across the Yalu River. If the bombing of the Yalu and beyond was still forbidden, then the creation of a field of radioactive waste across major enemy lines of supply, cutting off North Korea from Manchuria;

3. Simultaneous amphibious and airborne landings at the upper ends of both coasts of North Korea, to close a gigantic trap around the enemy. They would then have to starve or surrender. "It would be something like Inchon," he added, "but on a much larger scale."

And, in his opinion, it would finally and definitely win the war.

The reply to these proposals from the Joint Chiefs was curt to the point of rudeness. The gist of the message: FORGET IT. THE PRESIDENT WANTS OUT.

But General MacArthur was not willing to accept that. And there was now probably only one man in the world able to save him from his own folly.

29

Crossing the Rubicon

Because Douglas MacArthur disliked, mistrusted, and resented George Marshall it should not be thought that his prejudices were reciprocated. They were not, and maybe that was the trouble.

For almost the whole of these two men's lives and professional careers, they had shared the same vocation, served in the same Army, fought in the same wars. Wherever in the world GI boots had stamped to attention, they both had taken the salute, watched a regimental march-past, celebrated a soldierly anniversary. There was no battlefield where U.S. troops had fought and died on which they had not ducked the same shellfire, dodged the same bullets, faced the same setbacks, savored the same victories.

It was true that fate had ordained that it was MacArthur who commanded the vast armies in the field and Marshall who stayed behind to manipulate the martial pieces on the global chessboard. But if any envy had been engendered as a result, surely it should have been on Marshall's part. Like the director who masterminds the movements of crew, cameras, and cast, it was Marshall, the "organizer of victory," as Churchill called him, who might have been expected to show resentment when the limelight was focused elsewhere.

By no word or gesture had he ever done so.

Yet from World War I onward it had always been MacArthur who had complained about Marshall, and as his biographer has remarked:

> This was the beginning of his paranoia, which was to bring so much anguish to him and to others in the years ahead. . . . In France the antagonism between the two men would grow, with grave consequences for the country both served so well in other ways.

484

In fact, however, the "antagonism" was entirely one-sided, and never once did Marshall harm MacArthur either as a man or as a soldier. On the other hand, MacArthur seemed to take pleasure in damaging Marshall's career. It was he, while Chief of Staff during the interwar years, who had deliberately blocked Marshall's advancement. It was he who had sneered at his appointment as Chief of Staff when WWII began. It was Marshall he blamed for starving him of supplies during the Pacific campaigns, sneered at him as a chairborne soldier, a Roosevelt stooge. Then he would add, "And no friend of mine."

Marshall must have known all about these snide remarks on MacArthur's part. Not only did he ignore them, but he never once allowed them to influence the respect in which he held the Far East commander or to deflect him from giving him all the support and protection of which he had need. Twice during WWII he saved him from what, for MacArthur, would have been a fate worse than death—obscurity.

The U.S. Navy hated MacArthur, really hated him. Early in the Pacific War it began agitating for an overall command in the area, the idea being to get MacArthur and his troops under its control. Believing Marshall to share their antipathy, the Navy enlisted his support and was delighted when he appeared to give it.

"But on one condition," he said. "If we're going to have an overall commander in the Pacific, there isn't any question about it, you will have to pick MacArthur—on the basis of pure competence alone."

The Navy abruptly abandoned the idea.

Later, when the Navy wished to bypass the liberation of the Philippines in favor of operations against Formosa, it was Marshall who again intervened to insist MacArthur be allowed to fulfill his pledge to the Philippine people, to whom he had vowed, "I shall return." He was given the go-ahead to do so and, of course, was hailed as the greatest hero of the Pacific war.

"I supported MacArthur through thick and thin through most of the questions and opposition to his policies," said Marshall toward the end of his life, adding, mildly, "He had a great many prejudices and intense feelings. . . . I was fighting his battles from start to finish."

Now, in 1951, Marshall was still doing it and, as usual, getting neither recognition nor thanks for his efforts. The support was even more crucial this time than it had been during WWII because Marshall's struggle now was not to bolster MacArthur's fame or boost his ego but to save his neck.

> Doubtless the General's champions on Capitol Hill [wrote William Manchester] encouraged him to believe he was untouchable. Even without them he might have been convinced of it. After all, in World War II the Joint Chiefs had given him more latitude than any other commander. They had deferred to him again in Korea, remaining submissive when, ignoring their instructions, he had sent GIs right up to the Yalu.

So far as Marshall was concerned, this was a misreading of the prevailing situation. It was true that the Joint Chiefs hesitated to discipline him or force him to toe a line they had drawn. The Chairman of the JCS, General Omar Bradley, had been a splendid battle commander in World War II, but he was not woven from the stuff of which supreme commanders and great military administrators are made; he was not a man prepared to stand up to overweening arrogance, as he had proved several times in the war when confronted by the rampaging egos of a Montgomery or a Patton. His instinct had been to get out of their way and plug his ears until their noise had stopped. MacArthur simply overawed him. As for Army Chief of Staff General Lawton Collins, he had no desire at all to tether the Far East commander. He approved of MacArthur's methods (he himself had not been called Lightnin' Joe for nothing)* and believed in winning battles, and be damned to the political consequences.

Marshall's attitude was not similar at all. It was unlikely that there was any man in the world who had ever overawed him— even Winston Churchill, whom he admired above most men, turned out on closer acquaintance to have the weaknesses of every poli-

---

*Though he got his nickname from having commanded the "Tropic Lightning" Division in the Pacific.

tician—and his attitude toward Douglas MacArthur as a human being was that of indifference. It was as a soldier that he approved of him: his high quality as a commander in battle; the self-confidence of his military leadership; the smooth efficiency of his administration.

Marshall had never been afraid of busting an officer, no matter how high his rank, when he had failed on the battlefield. Eisenhower once sent home a well-known general for grave military incompetence and apologized, knowing that he was one of Marshall's old friends and colleagues. Marshall had immediately reduced him in rank to a colonel and cabled Ike: "IF I'D BEEN IN YOUR PLACE, I WOULD HAVE DONE IT SOONER." On the other hand, he would forgive a commander all kinds of personal transgressions so long as he did well the job for which he had been picked. He kept George Patton in his command after he had slapped a soldier and talked out of turn because he won battles in the field and helped bring victory closer. He ignored Montgomery's prim expressions of anti-American contempt so long as he beat back the Nazis.

His creed was: Pick the right man for the command, and then let him get on with the job. In the case of General MacArthur, he sympathized with him, understood what he was trying to do, and did his best to shield him from the interference of Monday morning quarterbacks and meddling politicians. He had been ordered to resist the attack by the Communists in North Korea, had he not? He had done it. He had done it so well that he had then been encouraged to drive them out of the peninsula and make sure they never repeated their aggression. Was it his fault that at this point the Chinese had intervened and the politicians had panicked? Could he be blamed because America's allies had suddenly lost their nerve?

Faced by President Truman's increasing anger at what he called MacArthur's "sassy contempt" and by Acheson's obvious loathing for the Far East commander, Marshall sensed that a showdown was coming. As he had done so often during World War II, his reflex action was to put himself between his commander in the field and his critics at home and try to take the brunt of the slings and arrows. For a time it was successful. The President was even persuaded to write MacArthur a personal letter praising him for "splendid leadership" and "superb performance" and gently seeking his cooperation in the political purposes of the war. It is a measure of Truman's trust in Marshall and faith in his counsel that he wrote the letter at all because by this time he abhorred MacArthur and wanted desperately to be rid of him.

Unfortunately it secured only a temporary truce between the Far East commander and his President. Soon MacArthur was bombarding Washington with telegrams again, harping on the old theme song: that his hands were being tied, that he ought to be hitting the Chinese where it would hurt most—on the Yalu—and that Ridgway and the Eighth Army should be allowed to march north of the thirty-eighth parallel and unify the whole of Korea.

The danger was that he might be tempted—as he had been in the past—to disobey orders and carry out these "military priorities," and in Truman's present mood, that would be fatal. He had been heard to exclaim, "I ought to fire him. That man's after my job. He wants to be President!"

The crisis was rapidly turning into a head-on clash between the two men, and if news of it became public, there could be just one outcome. How could it be averted?

There was really only one way, and Marshall knew it. He was the only man left in the world who could sit down with MacArthur, talk out the situation as one old soldier to another, and make him see reason. He must therefore make the gesture and fly to Tokyo and there, one seventy-year-old veteran to another, produce all the eloquence of which he was capable to persuade his defiant colleague to behave—or take the consequences.

It might have worked, but we will never know. At the end of February 1951 Katherine Marshall came down with a bad case of flu, an epidemic of which was sweeping through Washington. The apartment was small, and there was no escaping the germs, and soon Marshall was bedded with the virus, too. He rose from his sick bed once to testify before the Senate Armed Forces Committee on defense appropriations, but he looked so frail and feverish that the chairman cut short the session and sent him home.

Still weak, unable to get rid of the germs, he staggered back to his office on March 6, and told his staff to start setting up a Far East trip for him toward the end of the month, when he calculated he would be fully recovered.

But that turned out to be too late. The following day, March 7, MacArthur returned to Tokyo from a visit to the Korean battlefront and called a press conference. The word around the Dai Ichi was that he had decided on a showdown.

As it happened, the March 7 conference was used by MacArthur to fire a ranging shot, and if it alerted Washington, it was not regarded as worthy of retaliation. The Far East commander complained that the situation in Korea, now that the front had been stabilized, was in danger of settling down into a stalemate. Unless reinforcements of troops were sent in the immediate future, the enemy would start counterattacking again, and there could be savage slaughter. Decisions needed to be taken "on the highest international level."

He waited for Washington's reaction, and when none came, he fired his second shot. On March 15 he summoned Hugh Baillie, president of the United Press, to see him and gave him an exclusive interview in the course of which he criticized the orders he had been given to halt the Eighth Army on the thirty-eighth parallel. This fell far short of the UN's military mission, he complained, which was to bring about unification of all Korea—a mission which, in fact, had long since been abandoned by the United States and its allies.

Both these public statements were in direct contravention of the order Marshall had sent out the previous December forbidding military commanders to communicate directly with the press. The administration, however, chose to ignore this in favor of acquainting the Far East commander with its plans for achieving something far different from what he seemed to have in mind. He wanted to extend the war. Truman wanted to end it. Accordingly, a message was sent to him by the JCS which read, in part:

> State [Department] planning a Presidential announcement shortly that with clearing of bulk of South Korea, feeling exists

that further diplomatic efforts toward settlement should be made before any advance with major forces north of the 38th Parallel. Time will be required to determine diplomatic reactions and permit new negotiations that may develop.

MacArthur was appalled at the pusillanimity of his President, his advisers, and the allies, and he made up his mind that they were not going to get away with it. The Yalu River was a long way away now, but on March 24, 1951, he decided that the time had come to cross the Rubicon. He ordered out his big guns and opened up a thunderous psychological barrage. It had a two-fold target: to shatter U.S. and UN hopes of obtaining an armistice—by making it impossible for the Red Chinese to accept one.

Cleverly designing his campaign to insult the Chicoms where they would be most humiliated, he hailed the achievement of the UN forces in regaining the initiative in Korea and then went on:

> Of even greater significance than our tactical success has been the clear revelation that this new enemy, Red China, of such exaggerated and vaunted military power, lacks the industrial capacity to provide adequately many critical items essential to the conduct of modern war. . . . Formerly his great numerical superiority might well have filled this gap, but with the existing methods of mass destruction, numbers alone do not offset vulnerability inherent in such deficiencies. . . .
>
> These military weaknesses have been clearly and definitely revealed since Red China entered upon its undeclared war in Korea.

Then he came to the crux of his message:

> Even under inhibitions which now restrict activity of the United Nations forces and the corresponding military advantages which accrue to Red China, it has been shown its complete inability to accomplish by force of arms its conquest of Korea.
>
> The enemy therefore must now be painfully aware that a decision of the United Nations to depart from its tolerant effort to contain the war to the area of Korea through expansion of our military operations to his coastal areas and interior bases would doom Red China to the risk of imminent collapse. . . .
>
> Within the area of my authority as military commander, how-

ever, it should be needless to say I stand ready at any time to confer in the field with the commander in chief of the enemy forces in an earnest effort to find any military means whereby the realization of the political objectives of the United Nations in Korea, to which no nation may justly take exception, might be accomplished without further bloodshed.

In other words, MacArthur was saying to the Chicoms: Forget about Washington and the UN, and come in and talk peace with me. And when you come in, *crawl.* It was an ultimatum, and he must have known the Chinese would never accept it.

Marshall was at home and in bed on the evening of March 23, 1951, when the telephone rang and Robert Lovett, his assistant secretary, read him out MacArthur's statement.* Without waiting for his chief to respond, Lovett said, "This time he's really gone too far. We'll have to fire him."

"There's only one man who can do that," Marshall said. "His Commander in Chief."

He had an out-of-town engagement for the following day, and it would have caused too much publicity had he canceled it, so he sent Lovett along to the White House the following day for a conference with the President, Dean Acheson, and Dean Rusk. Truman appeared to be "perfectly calm," although in "a state of mind that combined disbelief with controlled fury." The other three men ought to have guessed what thoughts were running through his mind when he mentioned that it seemed to be the fate of presidents to have trouble with their generals and that Lincoln was the only man who knew how to handle them.† He had obviously been talking to someone, and Lovett guessed he had been consulting Marshall. If so, it was probably Marshall who had

---

*Because of the international date line, March 24 was a day earlier in Washington.

†"[Lincoln] had to fire five generals before he was successful in finding one who could handle troops in the field," Truman said later. "But the man with whom he had most trouble was George B. McClellan; he was the most egotistical man who ever walked and he thought he was the smartest man in the world. Lincoln had to fire him twice before he got rid of him."

persuaded him to wait for the time being before firing Mac-Arthur—which, as Truman said later, he had now decided to do—and to give him a short, sharp jolt instead. The President now directed Lovett to send a cable in the name of the Joint Chiefs (written by Marshall?) which peremptorily informed MacArthur:

> The President has directed that your attention be called to his order as transmitted on December 6, 1950. In view of the information given you on March 20, 1951 [that the UN had decided to seek a Korean armistice] any further statements by you must be coordinated as prescribed in the order of 6 December.
>
> The President has also directed that in the event Communist military leaders request an armistice in the field, you immediately report that fact to the JCS for instructions.

The December 6 order was the one forbidding direct communication by military leaders to the press, notifying MacArthur that the JCS was aware he had disobeyed it—a court-martial offense. But though this warning was calculated to pull MacArthur up sharply before he crashed over the brink (as Marshall, as one soldier to another, surmised that it would), it was a move unfortunately taken too late to avert the crisis. By one of those accidents of fate, MacArthur had written a letter outlining his views on the Far East situation. It was penned four days *before* he issued his March 24 statement. It was sent to Joseph W. Martin, Republican leader in Congress. Congressman Martin held onto it for some days, not being quite sure whether it was a confidential communication or not. It was not until April 5 that he resolved that it was not and decided to read it into the *Congressional Record*. In the critical situation which had now developed in Washington, MacArthur's statement could hardly have been more inflammatory:

> It seems strangely difficult for some to realize that here in Asia is where the Communist conspirators have elected to make their play for global conquest, and that we have joined the issue thus raised on the battlefield; that here we fight Europe's war with arms, while the diplomats there still fight it with words; that if we lose this war to Communism in Asia the fall of Europe is inevitable;

win it and Europe most probably would avoid war and yet preserve freedom. As you pointed out, we must win. There is no substitute for victory.

It could not have been more cunningly contrived to sabotage everything that the President and his UN allies were trying to do. The prospects of peace were wrecked. Stung by his harsh words about them, the Chinese rejected any suggestion that there should be an armistice. As his Eighth Army commander, General Ridgway, remarked, MacArthur had "cut the ground from under the President, enraged our allies, and put the Chinese in the position of suffering a severe loss of face if they so much as accepted a bid to negotiate."

Marshall said, more soberly, "It created a very serious situation with our allies, along the line of their uncertainty as to just how we were proceeding; the President bringing something to their attention, and gauging their action to find agreement with him, and before that can be accomplished, the leader in the field comes forward to handle the matter. It created, I think, specifically, a loss of confidence in the leadership of the government."

And yet, even now, General Marshall did not favor MacArthur's dismissal. Was it because he found the Far East commander's arguments persuasive, even if his methods of expressing them were unscrupulous? That we shall never know, since he resolutely refused to discuss this period in the tapes he made toward the end of his life.

The fact remains, however, that when he met with the President the following morning, April 6, following a Cabinet meeting, and Truman asked him point-blank what he should do about MacArthur's defiance of him, Marshall temporized. He said he would have to consult with General Bradley, and they would need to confer with the Joint Chiefs. Plainly, and much to the President's annoyance, he was in no mood to hurry. Truman, whose dander was now really up, had already made up his mind that MacArthur would have to go, and it irritated him to have his favorite and most trusted general talk about "not taking precipitate action." The President sharply reminded him and all those others present—Acheson, Bradley, and Averell Harriman—that they were discussing "General MacArthur's disobedience of orders in getting in touch with people with whom he had no business getting in touch, and that as a member of the armed forces he seemed to forget that the President is the Commander in Chief of the armed forces."

Bradley then spoke up and said that in the circumstances, he did think MacArthur should be dismissed at once. But still Marshall didn't agree. How about calling him back from Tokyo to Washington for consultation?

"Good God, no!" said Acheson and Truman almost simultaneously.

There had undoubtedly come into both their minds an image of a triumphant MacArthur riding down Pennsylvania Avenue to address a joint session of Congress, rousing both elected and electors to a fever of enthusiasm for the belligerent cause he was advocating in the Far East.

Finally, with a touch of exasperation, the President suggested that Marshall go back to his office at the Defense Department and read through the files. There he would find repeated evidence that MacArthur had consistently disobeyed the orders of successive presidents, his commanders in chief, and had now committed the most flagrant act of disobedience of all. He would wait until he had done this and then ask his opinion again.

The next morning Marshall reappeared. He did not waste any words. He told the President "he had gone over all those telegrams and communications between General MacArthur and the President of the United States over the past two or three years, and he had come to the conclusion that the general should have been relieved two years ago."

"Thank you, General Marshall," said Truman quietly. "Now will you write me the order relieving General MacArthur of his command, and I will have him brought home?"

In the circumstances, there was little else he could do. He went back to the Defense Department and, with Lovett's help, wrote out a message which was short, sharp, and brutal:

YOU ARE HEREBY RELIEVED OF YOUR POSTS AS SUPREME COM-
MANDER ALLIED POWERS (SCAP), UN COMMANDER AND COM-
MANDER-IN-CHIEF FAR EAST. YOU WILL TURN OVER YOUR COMMANDS,
EFFECTIVE AT ONCE, TO LIEUTENANT GENERAL MATTHEW B. RIDG-
WAY. YOU ARE AUTHORIZED TO HAVE ISSUED SUCH ORDERS AS ARE
NECESSARY TO COMPLETE DESIRED TRAVEL TO SUCH PLACE AS YOU
SELECT. MY REASONS FOR YOUR REPLACEMENT WILL BE MADE PUB-
LIC CONCURRENTLY WITH THE DELIVERY TO YOU OF THE FOREGOING
MESSAGE.

He took it back to the White House for the President's signature, and the message of doom was sent winging on its way to
Tokyo.*

But though it was Truman who signed the curt dismissal note
and did it with a triumphant presidential flourish, there was no
doubt at all whom MacArthur blamed for his removal from office.
The old paranoia still lurked in the dark crevices of his canted
mind, and he was convinced that his ancient enemy, after years
of patient waiting, had seen his hated adversary momentarily uncovered and struck at last. So far as he was concerned, this was
the last low blow from the "Chaumont gang," who, ever since
1918, had been waiting in the wings for their revenge. It had fallen
to their only survivor, George Marshall, to deliver the fatal, the
treacherous final message. To the surprise of his acolytes in Tokyo,
MacArthur did not blame the President, who was beneath his
contempt, or even the members of the Joint Chiefs. He was just
not interested, he told them, in "who had been on the firing squad."
All he had to do was read his orders and know instinctively who
had been the real executioner.

"George Marshall pulled the trigger," he declared.

Nobody ever did tell him that in fact, right until the last
moment it was George Marshall who had maneuvered and manipulated to gain him a reprieve. He would never have believed

---

*Not very efficiently, as it turned out. Someone leaked the news before it
was delivered.

it anyway. Nor did Marshall himself ever attempt to explain the role he had played in the drama. He was not a man for looking back, particularly on the distasteful moments in his career. And in his opinion, this had been one of the most distasteful.

It was left to Dean Acheson to pronounce the final words on the whole sorry incident:

> I don't take the slightest pride in the MacArthur deal. Not one person, I, George Marshall, the Joint Chiefs, had the faintest belief that he was doing what he ought to do. But what *could* we do? You may say we were grave failures, and I would say you could make out a good case. I don't think any of us did very well. All of us were staying in our proper spheres—decision, law, good teamwork, call it what you will—except MacArthur. It gave him the same power as the USSR has in the world when everyone is subject to restrictions except them. . . . We either had to relieve him, or leave it up to him.

30

Chinese Laundry

When the Truman Cabinet met for the first time on the morrow of MacArthur's dismissal, the President asked Dean Acheson what his reactions to the crisis were. The secretary of state replied that he was reminded of the story about the married couple with a very beautiful seventeen-year-old daughter who lived on the edge of a U.S. Army camp. The wife worried and continually harassed her husband over the dangers to which the proximity of all those soldiers exposed their daughter. One day the husband came home to find his wife weeping bitterly. She announced that the worst had happened and their daughter was pregnant. Her husband thereupon breathed a sigh of relief and said, "Thank God that's over!"

But of course, in the case of MacArthur, far from being over, it had only just begun.

Everyone in the administration had hoped MacArthur would take the long way home, pausing to say his proconsular farewells to the Japanese, the Filipinos, even perhaps the Australians and New Zealanders, before returning to the United States, thus giving time for the Democrats to cool off the heat engendered by his dismissal. But neither MacArthur nor the Republicans were about to let that happen. One of MacArthur's favorite historical characters was the British statesman Lord Curzon, who had resigned as viceroy of India after a blazing row and came back to England, hoping to be acclaimed as an unjustly traduced hero; only he had taken his time on the way home, and he arrived in England to find the public had forgotten him, the government had changed, and he was greeted by a deafening silence. It was a mistake MacArthur was not going to repeat. Nor were the Republicans, who sensed in the public's indignation and dismay over his dismissal the cause which could win them the presidential election in 1952.

General MacArthur returned to a ticker-tape parade up Broadway and was waving to the multitudes from the Capitol steps on April 19, after which he went inside to address both houses of the Congress with a fighting speech on lost opportunities in Asia. He was thereupon called as a principal witness before a joint House inquiry. The U.S. Congress likes nothing better than to conduct an inquest on government mishandling of a situation, and the more dirty linen it can arrange to have washed in public, the more attention it is likely to get from TV, newspapers, and the world. This one was labeled an "Inquiry into the Military Situation in the Far East and the Facts Surrounding the Relief of General Douglas MacArthur from His Assignments in That Area." From the moment it opened the Capitol was transformed into a Chinese laundry at which the sweaty socks, the soiled shirts, and the bloodstained underwear of the Truman administration were wheeled into view. There were some protests, notably from Generals Marshall and Bradley, that some of the more intimately revealing lingerie ought to be held back, on the ground that the sight of a rip here, a fray there together with some telltale stains might show America's neighbors more than they needed to know. But the committee wanted everything displayed, down to the last shift. As an official report put it later, "To serious students, and, presumably, to foreign governments and intelligence services, the debate had special interest because it led to the release of quantities of normally sacrosanct information about American political and strategic thinking."

But, as the report added, "to the nation as a whole, its principal value may have been more like that of a safety valve or a lightning conductor—a device which permitted the relief of terrific tension."

It had been noted that General MacArthur, in his address to the joint House, had made no mention whatsoever of the United Nations, of whose armies he had, after all, been in command in Korea. He was asked about this when he became first witness at the inquiry but almost contemptuously waved it aside. He did not see why the administration had paid so much attention to the views of its UN allies. When it came to the crunch, the great majority of them would have fallen in with what he had decided to do.

"I still believe the interest of the United States being the predominant one in Korea," he declared, "would require our action."

"Alone?"

"Alone, if necessary. If the other nations of the world haven't got enough sense to see where appeasement lies . . . why then we had better protect ourselves and go it alone."

At one moment he was asked point-blank how, if his calculations in Korea and Asia generally had turned out to be wrong and all-out war had resulted, he would have arranged the defense of the American nation.

"That doesn't happen to be my responsibility, Senator," he replied, and it caused the first frisson of doubt about what he stood for to ripple through the chamber.

But he was an effective witness, and as if to patch this small rent in his credibility, he hastened to make it clear that it was not he who had weakened America's defenses, abandoned its allies, allowed the Communists to take over; it was the Truman presidency.

As if on cue, a Republican senator asked a question about the administration's China policy and the meaning of the mission General Marshall had undertaken to China in 1946. What did he think about it? It was as if MacArthur had been waiting for the opportunity to comment on just this subject from the start. It was the mishandling of China which had started the rot, lost us a faithful ally, let the Communists take over, and from this all the other disasters flowed. Why had we abandoned Chiang Kai-shek? Why had we allowed the Chicoms to drive him out? He could have saved us 50,000 American lives. He could have saved us from disaster in Korea. As for Marshall's mission to China, "It was the greatest political mistake we made in a hundred years," MacArthur declared. "We will pay for it for generations—for a century."

Reporters besieged the Defense Department for the secretary's comment on what the newspapers called "this below-the-belt thrust at an old comrade," but Marshall was not to be drawn. He was the next witness to be called before the committee after MacArthur stepped down, and he refused to be goaded into a quarrel over China. It was MacArthur's recall he was interested in, and why it had been done. It had been done, he said simply, to preserve world peace—and was not everybody interested in that? He pointed out that the Joint Chiefs had already, through their chairman, General Bradley, characterized the MacArthur strategy as involving the United States "in the wrong war, at the wrong place, at the wrong time and with the wrong enemy," and then Marshall added, "General MacArthur would have us accept the risk of involvement not only in an extension of the war with Red China, but in an all-out war with the Soviet Union. He would have us do this even at the expense of losing our allies and wrecking the coalition of free peoples throughout the world. He would have us do this even though the effect of such action might expose Western Europe to attack by the millions of Soviet troops poised in Middle and Eastern Europe."

By not one word, gesture, or facial expression did he make any criticism of MacArthur as a soldier or a man, but he went out of his way to praise him for the lifetime of "brilliant contributions" he had made to the security of the United States. None of the senators tried to stir anything up by suggesting a rivalry or an antipathy between the two men, and it is unlikely that they would have got anywhere had they done so. It was plain from his attitude that Marshall actually admired MacArthur and thought him an outstanding military genius, if not always an easy one to control.

Even more than MacArthur, he was a persuasive witness, and as he went out of the committee room one of the Republican senators, Wayne Morse, said loudly, "I know which of those generals I trust."

At which a fellow Republican, Richard M. Nixon, retorted, "And I know which one of them is going to win us the next election!"

In any event, even that didn't turn out to be true. It was

another Army general entirely who became the next President of the United States, and Dwight Eisenhower made it clear from the start that he wanted absolutely no help at all from General Douglas MacArthur.

Nor, as it turned out, did he solicit the aid of General George Marshall either, and that was more surprising because to him Eisenhower really owed everything.

Korea and China were by no means, of course, the only problems troubling the United States in 1951. It was a turbulent year. There was concern over the increasing frigidity of relations with the Soviet Union and the fretful realization that this was an adversary that could no longer be threatened or cowed by the atom bomb since the USSR now had atomic weapons of its own. There were new NATO crises in Europe and splintering squabbles between the former Allies over how to treat vanquished Germany. There were worries about whether it was right, wise, or politic to help these same Allies hold onto their former colonies. France was fighting desperately to cling to its control of Indochina. Britain was finding it increasingly difficult to preserve its oil interests in Persia and its hegemony over Egypt and the Suez Canal. The British Empire was crumbling away, and the red spots on the global map, marking the places where the British had maintained bases and outposts, were being rubbed out by native militants seeking freedom and independence.

If America was not willing to risk all-out war to maintain its own bases in Asia, it was hardly likely to assume Britain's colonial burdens or provide the troops and supplies to shield it against the processes of imperial decay. In the circumstances, what could a secretary of defense offer America's partners but lip service to the alliance (necessarily hypocritical) and a willingness to *discuss* military aid without making anything but vague promises?

It was no role for an honest man, and Marshall found it both exhausting and demeaning. As a soldier he was used to being taken at his word. His wife, Katherine, said, "He had authority, and when he spoke, people listened," and he could not stomach the thought that mixing with politicians, acquiring their loose habits, would make people lose confidence in his judgments and pronouncements. That was one of the troubles with his boss, the President. He had grown fond of Harry Truman, but as he remarked to Katherine, "He makes his decisions too quick."

Either that, or he relied entirely too much on Marshall's judgment, even in political spheres where the general knew next to nothing.

"He told me," Katherine said later, "that President Truman left the decisions up to him, and it used to frighten him. He said, 'I realize there are things I don't know all about. All I know is about military things.' That was one of the nice things about him. He didn't think he was wisdom's egg bag. He said, '[Truman] frightens me; he just accepts everything I say.' "

But this had had the effect of doing something entirely contrary to his nature, and that was forcing him to think politically. He didn't like it. He was all for seeing a situation as it was, facing up to it, and making the decision which he thought was the right one, without considering the politics involved in it. Now, with elections looming up, there was hardly a situation about which a man could make a soldierly, honest decision without thinking of the politics of it first, about how it would affect the administration, whether it would make the President vulnerable to the Republicans. Repeatedly he told Katherine that he was getting too old to learn the kinds of tricks professional pols imbibed with their mothers' milk and that since they involved prevarication, procrastination, deceitfulness, and evasiveness, they were skills he despised anyway. Katherine, who knew he was feeling old and suspected that he was also ill, told him that if he felt that way, there was only one thing for him to do.

In September 1951 he did it. He told President Truman he was resigning his job and getting out before all the fuss began over the 1952 election. The President may have made him feel better by confiding that when the time came, he was getting out, too. If a professional pol like Harry Truman was no longer able to stand the heat of the kitchen, maybe he need not feel guilty about quitting.

This time Marshall's departure from office was quieter and

did not cause the same dismay, the worldwide fuss, that his resignation as secretary of state had stirred up. But the administration missed him—badly. Especially to the young, up-and-coming aides in the departments of Defense and State, he had long been looked up to as something special.

"By that time he had risen above everything and everybody," said Luke Battle. "He was on a plane of his own. And the great joke around the building was, whenever a new problem or a new project came up, someone would say, 'We need someone like General Marshall for this.' And then everyone would say, 'But there *is* no one like General Marshall.' "

Battle said this became a kind of cliché around government offices in Washington for years afterward, even after the government had changed. "Every time you wanted a distinguished global figure for some special job, you automatically said, 'We need someone like General Marshall'; only there wasn't someone like General Marshall around any longer."

The original model was retired to private life in Virginia, safely puttering among his vegetables in the kitchen garden of Dodona Manor, out of the public eye at last.

Or so he thought.

In the summer of 1952 it was confirmed that Dwight David Eisenhower would be the Republican candidate for the U.S. presidency, and since Ike had been handpicked by Marshall and nurtured for leadership from before the beginning of World War II, he felt a personal pleasure in his selection. He wrote to tell him so. The candidate wrote back:

> Brown's Hotel
> Denver 2, Colorado
> 17 July, 1952

Dear General:

My very deep appreciation for your fine note. I often wonder how I got into my present situation—I venture a guess that if I had suggested at the time you and I were working so hard in the early spring of 1942, that one day I would be scratching my head over the political and economic problems of the country, with a view to leading a great political party to victory, you would have had me locked up as a dangerous character.

The events of recent years have reminded me more and more of the truth of the old aphorism: "You never know what is over the brow of the hill." You must frequently have had such thoughts following upon that day in December 1945, when you thought you had retired from active service for good.

In any event here I am, and I shall, of course, fight as hard as I can with a single limit on my efforts defined by honor, fairness and decency. I am firm in my belief that our government cannot stand the excesses that come about through one party domination for too long a time. Many of our present ills stem from this single fact. But on top of this I am, of course, in disagreement with the present administration on many vital points of policy. Consequently I am buoyed up by the belief that I am performing a real service and I am doing my duty.

But the whole atmosphere is so different from that to which soldiers of long service become accustomed that I sometimes find it difficult indeed to adjust myself. Since you are well aware of this, through your own experience, I will not belabor the point.

Mamie and I send you and Mrs. Marshall our affectionate greetings and hope you both are enjoying every good thing of life.
Sincerely,
Eisenhower

In the circumstances, everybody expected that if the election battle turned out to be hot, hard, and heavy, at least it would be clean. How could it not be with the hero of World War II holding aloft the Republican banner? And had he not promised Marshall that he would fight with "honor, fairness and decency"?

But those who reasoned this way forgot about Senators McCarthy and Jenner. The witch-hunt against Communist sympathizers was still in full cry in the United States, and in McCarthyite eyes, the Truman administration hid the most dangerous Reds of all. McCarthy and his aides looked around for the target most likely to produce the gasps of surprise and the big newspaper headlines on which their appetites fed and moved in on General Marshall. It was the simplest thing in the world to gain publicity that way. All that was necessary was to choose the man the public admired above all others and then to prove he had feet of clay. Even Katherine Marshall was taken by surprise.

"I was so amazed when the attack on General Marshall came from McCarthy," she said later.

At first no one took much notice because it seemed so ridiculous. General Marshall was a traitor, McCarthy said. He had conspired with President Roosevelt to provoke Pearl Harbor and get the United States into World War II. He had deliberately lost China to the Reds by abandoning Chiang Kai-shek. He had personally fired General MacArthur and lost us the Korean War. When no one listened to these charges, he repeated them: *Traitor—Marshall is a traitor. He tricked us into war. He lost us China and Korea.*

At that point everyone waited for the riposte. Not from Marshall, of course, because the press and the public knew the general too well to expect him to answer such outrageous attacks. No, it was from McCarthy's fellow Republicans that everyone waited for the repudiation. And as the days passed and McCarthy's vituperations got more poisonous, so anticipation grew that the putdown, when it came, would be all the more devastating. For who else now could deal with such monstrous accusations but Marshall's old friend and protégé, the most important Republican of them all, Dwight D. Eisenhower?

At last came the announcement that Eisenhower would be appearing at a big Republican rally in Milwaukee, Wisconsin, and since that was McCarthy's home state, everyone assumed that this would be the day. Ike would have with him on the same platform the governor of Wisconsin and also Senator William Jenner, making the occasion even more piquant, since Jenner was McCarthy's fellow demagogue who had accused Marshall of treachery in the House in 1951.

The newspapers, the wire services, and the broadcast media alerted their top correspondents and sent them winging to Wisconsin, and for days the speculation built up not so much about whether Ike would rebut the scurrilous attacks on his old chief's reputation as about how choice would be the words he would use in his denunciation of the slandermongers.

An hour before the meeting was due to begin, a copy of Eisenhower's speech was circulated among the press, who thumbed through it rapidly—and there, tacked on the end, was the pregnant passage. Ike, like the sheriff in the western film, was finally riding in to the rescue of his friend and soon would be reaching for his gun. All they needed now was to hear the actual words and cheer as McCarthy bit the dust.

Senator Jenner rose and launched into his usual scathing attack on the Democrats, then sat down. The governor rose and announced the main speaker of the day, and Ike rose to deliver his long-awaited denunciation.

Only he didn't deliver it. At the last moment he lost his nerve—and cut out from his prepared manuscript the words he had intended to use in defense of General Marshall. To the newsmen it was an astonishing anticlimax.

Why? What stopped him at the last moment? It was not until twelve years later that he attempted any explanation at all. In a conversation on June 4, 1964, after his retirement from the presidency, Eisenhower was asked why he had failed to stand up for Marshall.

"You know the story of that, don't you?" he replied. "It was that damned McCarthy gang and some of the newspaper people who played that up. I had made a strong statement in [Marshall's] defense at Denver a short time before. Then I put it in my speech for Wisconsin. When the governor saw it, he said it was dragging it in by the tail and would be regarded as something dragged in. So I said, 'Well, I will take it out, since I have already made clear my feelings about General Marshall.' "*

There is only one thing wrong with that explanation. General Eisenhower had not made "a strong statement in [Marshall's] defense at Denver a short time before." He did not speak in support of Marshall at Denver until after it was all over.

"The thing that I really fell out with [Ike] about," said former President Truman later, "was that he sat on the platform in Milwaukee, Wisconsin, while that good-for-nothing senator from In-

*In a telephone conversation with Forrest Pogue.

diana stood there and called General Marshall a traitor. And the President didn't interfere with him, didn't take the part of General Marshall at all. I was in Colorado at that time making a speech in the campaign. And when I found out . . . I skinned him from his head to his heels."

Katherine Marshall was mad, too. She was infuriated with her husband when he shrugged his shoulders over what had happened, merely muttering that it was all politics. She knew that deep inside him he was hurt, and she decided that she would never forgive Eisenhower for his cowardice for as long as she lived.

On the other hand, Marshall bore no grudge. When the result of the election was announced, and Eisenhower was the President-elect of the United States, he wrote him (November 7, 1952):

Dear Eisenhower:
Congratulations on your triumph seem rather futile in view of the immensity of your victory.

I pray for you in the tremendous years you are facing. I pray especially for you in the choice of those to be near you. That choice, more than anything else, will determine the problems of the years and the record of history. Make them measure up to your standards.

I hope the severity of the campaign did not wear you down seriously, or Mrs. Eisenhower. I thought she did a wonderful job for you.

Faithfully yours,
GC Marshall

The following year, after the inauguration was over—Katherine refused to attend it—the White House announced that Winston Churchill, newly reelected as British prime minister, was coming to the United States on an official visit. The Marshalls were invited to attend a banquet at the White House in Winston's honor.

"Never," said Katherine emphatically.

Marshall pleaded with her. He thought they should go—not for Eisenhower's sake, perhaps, but for Winston's. Katherine knew that despite everything, Marshall wanted to see and talk with Ike again, and this annoyed her, that he could be so forgiving. But when he finally said, "Please, will you go for my sake?" she knew she would have to give in.

"I finally agreed," she said later. "Eisenhower was very gracious. Churchill drank to the President. The company drank to the Queen."

Then President Eisenhower rose, turned to the man sitting beside Clementine Churchill, and said, "And now I want to drink to General Marshall."

The distinguished company rose and toasted the shyly smiling man to whom they all, in one way or another, owed their presence there that night.

31

Final Chores

King George VI of England had died at the beginning of 1952, and there was general pleasure and approval in Britain when it was announced that General George Marshall would head the U.S. delegation the following summer to the coronation of his daughter, Queen Elizabeth II.* It was typical of Marshall that when he walked to his place in the front stalls of Westminster Abbey, he noticed that the throng of richly clad and bejeweled princes and princesses, lords and ladies, and envoys from all over the world rose to their feet as if to pay homage to someone among them, and he whispered to his fellow delegate General Bradley, "Who are they rising for?"

"You," said Bradley.

Katherine was too frail to face the long ordeal of the crowning in the abbey, so one of the royal gentlemen-in-waiting sat with her in the crowd that watched the Queen drive by from Buckingham Palace. After that she needed to go back to her hotel. But how to manage that in the maelstrom of milling crowds, marching troops, blaring military bands? Finally, her escort found a taxi, which drove slowly through the streets until halted by a phalanx of Royal Marine bandsmen playing in front of the palace. The gentleman-in-waiting managed to reach their conductor and asked him to let him through with the wife of the head of the U.S. delegation.

The conductor was firm. It was not possible. Even for a gentleman-in-waiting in full dress the streets would remain closed to all vehicles until nightfall. Then he glanced at Katherine, cowering, pale, and exhausted, in the back of the cab and asked who

*The other delegates were General and Mrs. Omar Bradley and Fleur Cowles.

she was anyway. He was told she was the wife of General George Marshall. The expression on the Marine captain's face changed. In that case . . . He stepped forward to consult with his leading bandsman. Suddenly the musicians were on their feet and forming up around the taxicab. The conductor's baton swung into action, and slowly the cab moved off, with the band marching on either side, playing "Black-Eyed Susan Brown" for Katherine all the way to Hyde Park Corner.

That night the throng around the Dorchester Hotel, where the Americans were staying, was so thick that they could not reach the cars lined up to take them to the Queen's first banquet at Buckingham Palace. At long last the gentleman-in-waiting, crying, "Make way, make way!" got them into the reception hall, where, to his horror, for it was a gross breach of etiquette on such an august occasion, the Queen and her consort, Prince Philip, had already arrived. But the Queen was all smiles when she sighted General Marshall.

"Now," she said regally, "we can begin."

She gave a nod to the band, which struck up the strains of "God Save the Queen."

To his chagrin and self-disgust, he no sooner returned from his European trip than the dreaded flu virus, to which he had seemed particularly vulnerable since his kidney operation, sneaked up on him again, and try as he might to ignore its fevers, inflammations, and weakening effects, he could not shake it off. As he wrote in one of his regular letters to Madame Chiang Kai-shek, he was particularly anxious "to rid my system of the bug" because "I had a date to come up to Washington on the 30th October" which he was desperately anxious not to miss. His favorite queen, Frederika of Greece, was coming to the United States on a state visit with her husband, King Paul, and had asked him to be "my private guest of honor (for, of course, the President will be the official one)" at a banquet the royal family would be giving on that date at the Greek Embassy in Washington.

Alas, it was not to be. He took to his bed in a determined effort to get fit in time, but no amount of devoted nursing by

Katherine seemed to do anything to help him get rid of the virus. Finally, his doctors decided he should be moved to Walter Reed Hospital for closer care and attention, and President Eisenhower ("who now seems ready to do anything to make it up to George," Katherine remarked wryly) ordered a special plane. He was installed in the President's suite at Walter Reed, but unfortunately he was still there when the date of Frederika's banquet came and went. It was a deep disappointment. She really was someone he admired above most other human beings, and he missed the magic sparkle of her presence.

And then, a few days later, she burst into his room at Walter Reed like sunshine breaking through his clouds of melancholy. She had been about to go off to a reception with her husband in New York when the thought struck her that she would be leaving in forty-eight hours to return to Greece without having had a glimpse of her beloved General Marshall.

"So I dropped everything, canceled all my engagements, and just flew down here," she explained to the delighted Marshall.

It was a golden afternoon. Bouncing with vigor and good health, fragrant with her favorite Joy perfume, talking ten to the dozen (but very sagely) about the political problems of the Mediterranean, the stupidities of the politicians, the villainies of the Soviets, she transformed the sickroom into a royal parlor full of high-quality conversation and most entertaining indiscretions. They were interrupted only when Katherine came in for her daily visit, and Frederika, declaring that she must get back to (with a roguish smile) "resoom my skedule," kissed a blushing Marshall on the brow and swept out, leaving a glow behind that lasted for the rest of the day.

He was so delighted that he broke custom in his next letter to Madame Chiang and mentioned one of his favorite women to the other.

"[Frederika] skipped a reception to make the trip," he wrote. "She is a very beautiful and most interesting woman and you might consider her 'working' royalty, as she certainly devotes all her time and energy to her people."

Then he added, ruefully, "After she left, I had a very interesting thought. It seems whenever I receive women of this stature, I am a patient in the hospital."

If he was not already aware that he was growing frailer, Marshall was sharply reminded of it that winter of 1953. While he was still in Walter Reed, news came through that he had been awarded the Nobel Prize for Peace, in recognition of his valiant postwar efforts as secretary of state and his creation of the Marshall Plan. The President telephoned him to convey his congratulations, and Marshall wrote back on November 2 to thank him for his concern:

> I have had no official word on the arrangements incident to the presentation [of the prize] but understand that the ceremony will be held in Stockholm in December. I plan to go by ship and have decided on the Southern route to avoid heavy weather. Needless to say, I was very much surprised by the announcement, and in accepting this recognition I do so on behalf of the American people, for it was they who made it possible.

The ceremonies in Sweden could hardly have been held at a more inclement time of the year, and certainly not a period for traveling for a man of seventy-three just risen from a sickbed. It was a horrendous journey, despite the so-called southern route that Marshall took on the Italian liner *Andrea Doria* (via Gibraltar, the Mediterranean, and Italy). It was so rough that it was impossible for him to work, as he had hoped, on his acceptance speech, and he was still weak and unsteady when he staggered ashore at Genoa. Fortunately his old aide General Tom Handy had arranged for a plane to take him straight to Heidelberg, where Handy was now commanding the U.S. occupation forces in Germany, and saw to it that he got some rest on terra firma. Handy's daughter, who was there, fussed over him, helped him with his notes, and insisted he spend four or five days with them before proceeding north.

But he was not really well even when he reached Scandinavia, and the speech he made at the acceptance ceremonies was not one of the more notable examples of his eloquence.

"I think that transatlantic journey really punished him," Tom Handy said later. "I don't think he ever got over it."

He was still making his way home when his seventy-third birthday came around on December 31, 1953, and it was not until he reached Pinehurst and immediately took to his bed that he found best wishes to "my dear General Flicker" from his "affectionate" Madame Chiang. She had written:

> Your birthday will soon be here, and on that day particularly I shall be thinking of you and wishing you long life and happiness. . . . Please tell Mrs. Marshall that the Chinese character embroidered on the evening bag [I sent her] means "long life." According to Chinese custom, when we wish either the husband or the wife "long life," it means wishing long life to both of them.

If the good wishes of his women admirers could give him a long life, he would certainly have it. To Queen Frederika of Greece, for example, it didn't matter a whit that he was out of office and no longer influential in the government; she still poured torrents of words at him, asking his advice about how to cope with the worsening situation in Greece. He wrote her on December 16, 1955:

> I was surprised and much complimented to receive your lengthy personal discussion of the situation in Greece, Cyprus and Turkey and the serious reactions resulting. . . . Since receiving your letter, I have been scratching my head trying to decide just how I can be of help without violating your confidence, and also without inflaming [Secretary of State John Foster] Dulles who you tell me has not been so friendly on his part.

She was not alone in that, he confided. Dulles had rebuffed him, too. He had never said a word to any of his former colleagues or associates about how much he had been hurt by the attacks on his record by McCarthy and the lackluster defense of his reputation by President Eisenhower, and he had managed to convince most people that he was impervious to the shabby way in which he had been treated. But to Frederika, and to her alone, he dropped his defences and revealed the depth of his hurt. Warning her that his influence in the government was by no means as strong as it once had been, he went on:

> Important groups of the Republican Party are extremely hostile to me in their pre-election endeavor [this was in March 1956] to tear down everything the Democratic Administration did, and are now attacking foreign relief assistance. . . . You may not be aware of the fact that I have been more viciously attacked than any other public figure in this generation.
>
> In view of these conditions, I fear that my assistance . . . would concentrate a bitter and hostile press attack.

She wrote that nevertheless, she would love to see him, talk to him, have him help her coordinate a campaign to gain U.S. understanding of how best to help Greece survive the crisis the nation and the regime were now facing. Could she come over quietly and be a guest of the Marshalls at their home at Dodona Manor, so they could talk and plan together?

In normal circumstances, he would have been touched and pleased, and he hastened to reply that both he and Katherine were "vastly complimented and charmed by your suggestion." But it was impossible. In any case, they were at their winter cottage at Pinehurst, North Carolina, where Katherine was tending a mortally sick older sister. It was embarrassing to have to refuse her because she was "the one person in this world who we would most love to have in our home . . . and that person, a great Queen, and her Country facing a desperate crisis."

But then he came to the real reasons why he thought she could only harm her cause by coming, especially to see him:

> It could not be done secretly, as you apparently thought possible, and the hostile reaction would be immediate and probably bitter.
>
> Strange to say, if you were less of a person, had less charm and beauty, the opposition would be less to your efforts.

He added:

As to me personally, I must admit that there was also una-
nimity [among my advisers] that I personally would stir up a storm
of political opposition by the virulent group in the opposition. They
count all the billions my policies have already cost the American
tax payer and, in this pre-election demagogic scramble, they want
no more of my influence or interference....

In all of this I have been completely frank and I trust to your
goodness to understand me. All of this has been very difficult for
me to write, but it is directed by my heart as well as my head. With
increased admiration and devotion,

GC Marshall

It was a painful letter to write because he sensed that in dissuading
Queen Frederika from coming to America, he had probably made
sure that he would never see her again.

There is nothing more saddening than to watch a great man
receding into old age, frailty, helplessness, and death. The decline
of George Marshall was slow and physically painful, but it did
not, thankfully, turn him into the childish or babbling idiot into
which some giant figures regress in the final stages of their life.
He kept command of his cool, clear, sharp mind until the last and
neither wept over past defeats nor slavered over remembered victories. He stayed the remembered George Marshall right until the
end. But it wasn't easy, and it wasn't short.

"The last time I saw General Marshall," said General Tom
Handy, "was when he was in [Walter Reed] hospital [for the last
time]. As a matter of fact, he was in terrible shape for quite a long
time. Some of those other doctors in some of those other places
said he wouldn't have lived as long as he did if it hadn't been for
Walter Reed. I remember Winston Churchill came over, and together he and Ike went to see the old boy. Ike said afterwards,
'I'd hate to hell to be in the shape General Marshall's in.'"

And he knew it. As he had never flinched at facing up to a
grim situation in war and peace, he did not fear looking square-
eyed at his own.

One day his old aide, Sergeant James W. Powder, stopped
by to say hello. He had long since retired from the Army to live

in Florida, and each time he came to Washington he never failed to pay his salutations to his old chief and Mrs. Marshall. Now he walked into Walter Reed and asked to see the general.

"So this major came down and said the general would see me in about fifteen minutes, and would I go up," said Powder later. "Colonel [C. J.] George [his aide] was in there, and he had been dictating, and I said, 'General, if you're dictating, I'll come back later,' and he said, 'No, you'll sit right down.' I asked about Mrs. Marshall and Mrs. Winn [his stepdaughter], and then I sensed the conversation was running down, and he said, 'Are you in a hurry? Have you got someone waiting for you out there?' and I said, 'No, sir, I don't want to tire you.'

"He said, 'I slipped and broke a couple of ribs, and I don't want Mrs. Marshall to know. I don't want to tell her.' I said, 'I ain't going to tell her.' He said, 'I just wanted to warn you. I know you wouldn't, but it might come out.'

"So I started to get up to go, and he said, 'Powder, are you in a hurry to get out of here? Are you tired of looking at me?' And I said, 'No, sir, I don't want to tire you. Besides, there are others out there waiting to see you.' He said, 'Those are people who come and go. They don't have anything in common, like you and I have.'" Powder waited until he fell asleep and then stole away.

He dictated a lot in those final phases of his life, and he hated the idea of not being able to write himself, especially to those he liked or admired. To Queen Frederika he sent a special message through Colonel George. George wrote to say that the general had been feeling badly for quite a long time and had been unable to write longhand for several months. He had purposely delayed writing, hoping he could handle this matter personally, but he felt that word had been too long delayed. The general wanted to explain that he had been so delinquent in writing because he hated to confess that he was reduced in physical activity and unable to do more than walk with a cane or with Mrs. Marshall's help. Fortunately, he was merely lacking in strength and appetite and had lost too much weight.

He asked her not to bother replying.

But that was not likely to deter Frederika from putting pen to paper at once, even though she herself was sick in bed. As if she sensed that her good friend was fighting his final battle, she was full of sentiment and nostalgia. From Grünau Castle in Austria* she wrote:

> I received your message here in my Austrian property, where my husband and I are staying for a few weeks with my brothers. Whenever I am here I always think of you, especially as thanks to your kind intervention this property was saved for me and my family. I myself as well as the Greek people owe a great deal to you that never can be repaid, but I believe that friendship means more than any material sign of gratitude; knowing that you feel like this too I am quite satisfied in my mind that our friendship needs no other sign nor explanation.

She then harked back to the first time they had met in London, when "I was very upset thinking that only a Queen looking as royal as Queen Mary would be taken seriously by you!" She reminded him that it was Field Marshal Smuts, the South Africa soldier and statesman, who had first praised Marshall to her. She went on:

> What a great human he was. It was he and you who made this world into a better place. It actually seems to many people, no matter how many rockets, satellites or God knows what technical devices may boast of man's greatness, the quality of the individual human spirit will always remain the measure of what is truly great and what is not. You and General Smuts are the forerunners and examples of a new epoch where the values of the spirit which you represent will come to be fought for and achieved. . . .
>
> I seem to be philosophizing. You must excuse it, but I am writing from my bed having just passed a violent attack of what the world calls Asian flu. I look out of the window and see the most beautiful high mountains. I have climbed the highest one when I was a young girl. I wish you were here and could also look at them. Great beauty is healing not only to the body but also to

*She had inherited it from Kaiser Wilhelm of Germany, her grandfather.

the spirit, and that is all that matters. I expect being ill, one's mind becomes more reflective and introspective. I look at the mountains. They seem so real. Yet science tells me that matter as such does not really exist, my body is not really me. (What a pleasant thought!) The mountains and me being made out of atoms and all atoms divided and split into energy waves, I and the mountains are made up of the stuff which is energy or waves. . . .

You see, in this letter I did not bother you with politics but with philosophy. You must blame it on the high fever, the Russian satellite [which had just been flown] and the beautiful view!

I am quite happy if your aide will let me know about your progress. As long as you can write yourself, I shall write regularly to you. It gives me pleasure to do so.

So, on January 11, 1958, he struggled to send her a letter written in his own hand, in which he said, "I never see your photograph—I am referring now to that on your Christmas card—without recalling the first time I saw you standing by the fire of a little sitting room at Claridge's, and made an unforgettable impression on me."

He had struggled to keep in touch with world affairs, he went on, but had finally given up.

"People are always questioning me on the subject of Europe and the Middle East," he wrote. "They will never believe me when I assure them I know no more than I see in the papers or hear on television, and Mrs. Marshall is better informed that way than I am."

Colonel George, his aide, noticed that he paused for a long time after writing that sentence and went into one of his long silences during which he was thinking about—what? One could only guess. All the dramatic events of his lifetime? The state of the world? The way President Eisenhower was handling the multiple problems of his administration: Laos, Vietnam, the rise of Nasser in Egypt, the significance of the Soviet sputnik, the threat of Fidel Castro?

Then Marshall roused himself, took up his pen, and began writing again, and what he scribbled indicated that he had been thinking of something quite different. Once upon a time he had dreamed of having a daughter, but neither his beloved Elizabeth nor his devoted Katherine had given him one. Now he peered fondly at Frederika's card and wrote: "Judging from your card, your oldest girl is an exact replica of you as you must have been as a younger woman."

He paused again and then hastily added, "The youngest lady is charming looking, too, she has her father's serious aspect."

He went into one of his long, introspective silences again.

The rumor spread around Washington during the spring of 1959 that Marshall was dying at last, and since the long illness of a national hero can be something of an anticlimax, everyone hoped that the end was in sight. A famous man, for posterity's sake, should not stay around too long after he has disappeared from the limelight.

When the news reached Athens, the queen sent an urgent telegram: "ALL MY THOUGHTS AND BEST WISHES ARE WITH YOU CONSTANTLY. A VERY SPEEDY RECOVERY. FREDERIKA R."

"She can't mean it," Dean Acheson said when he heard. "She should know the longer he lingers on, the less people will remember what he stood for. And they *need* to remember." He added, with one of his cool smiles, "Wait till she becomes an ex-queen. She'll find out."

Maybe Marshall was clinging on to life so as not to die in the shadow of another secretary of state—still actually serving, in fact—who was also lying mortally ill in Walter Reed at the time. John Foster Dulles had been brought in with terminal cancer and had also had a visit paid to him by President Eisenhower and Winston Churchill.* Marshall and Dulles had seldom agreed on foreign affairs, and Dulles stood for tactics—from brinkmanship to the big stick—which Marshall had eschewed and abhorred. He was too decent a man to resent Dulles's presence in the same hospital and sympathized with him in his last hours of pain. But

---

*Who had once called him "the only bull I've ever met who carries his own china shop with him."

he must definitely have had no wish to share the obituary columns with him.

So he held on.

John Foster Dulles died at the end of May 1959 and was buried in Washington by the Republicans with great pomp and ceremony, causing Dean Acheson to remark, as he came away from the funeral, "You know, the greatest mistake I made was not to die in office."

In July Colonel George wrote to Marshall's former aide, General Marshall Carter, to say he was not too happy with events at Walter Reed. In a period of ten days, General Marshall had lost five pounds and at that moment weighed only 136, a clear indication of how he looked.

"The Old Man," as George called him, had so many different problems that, in attempting to cure one, another was aggravated. For instance, he needed the equivalent of 2,000 calories a day, and it was straining the ability of his one kidney. He had a spell of hiccups, but to attempt to stop them completely might have affected the brain. Yet, astonishingly enough, he still had brief periods of brightness and was mentally alert and talkative.

George added that Mrs. Marshall continued to watch over him and, since March, had not been away from the hospital over a half dozen times.

It was too long, and it was not until the fall of the year that he finally stopped living and breathing. He died in bed at Walter Reed on October 16, 1959. As was only to be expected in such a man, he went quietly and without fuss. One moment he was there, and the next he wasn't.

Dean Acheson was wrong about one thing.

Though it was long since he had held office or been in the public eye, General Marshall did not die unmourned or unsung. Among many millions of people throughout the country and the world, a great sadness spread when the news was known that he was dead.

Winston Churchill in London summed up the feeling. "He was the last great American," he said.

Harry Truman added, "He was the greatest of the great in our time. I sincerely hope that when it comes to my time to cross the great river, Marshall will place me on his staff, so that I may try to do for him what he did for me."

And his country.

Taps

Among his other qualifications, Marshall was an expert at arranging state funerals. Over the years he had learned how to bury a nation's heroes, its presidents and statesmen with all the pomp and ceremonials their service to their country had earned for them. As aide to General Pershing he had manned and scheduled the funeral train which brought President Harding's body back from the West Coast to Washington way back in 1923. He had handled all the arrangements for the funeral procession through the nation's capital, the lying-in-state at the White House, and the burial at Hyde Park of President Franklin D. Roosevelt in 1945, and had been warmly thanked for the touching splendor of it by the President's widow, Eleanor Roosevelt.

He had fought Congress to be allowed to bury his good friend, Field Marshal Sir John Dill, in Arlington National Cemetery in 1943—until that time barred to all but U.S. soldiers—and had seen to it that the Englishman was interred in his honored resting place with memorable ceremony. And five years later, in the same hallowed soil, he had interred the mortal remains of the man he had always considered America's greatest soldier, his model and mentor, John J. Pershing. He was placed in the nation's Valhalla in a veritable blaze of glory.

So it was perhaps natural that he be consulted about his own funeral. He would, of course, be buried in Arlington. But what ceremonials should the President, the Congress, and the Army ordain for the interment of such a great man? General Tom Handy, his old Deputy Chief of Staff, came to see him and, with some diffidence, broached the subject. At once Marshall shook his head.

"You don't have to worry about it," he said. "I've left all the necessary instructions."

He had indeed, and they were short and to the point and in keeping with his nature.

When the news reached the White House of the death of George Catlett Marshall, President Eisenhower proclaimed a day of mourning, and those who knew the true value of what he had done for the nation and the world sighed regretfully and saluted the departure of such a truly great man.

His body lay in its coffin over the weekend of October 17 in the Bethlehem Chapel of the National Cathedral in Washington, and a steady file of young and old, rich and poor, soldiers, sailors, airmen, and old war workers filed past for a last look at his very ordinary American face.

From then on, Marshall's own instructions were followed to the letter, and they were: "Bury me simply, like any ordinary officer of the U.S. Army who has served his country honorably. No fuss. No elaborate ceremonials. Keep the service short, confine the guest-list to the family. And above everything, do it quietly."

Since they considered themselves his friends, the President and a former President insisted on being invited to the short ceremony in the small Bethlehem Chapel. Eisenhower and Truman sat uneasily side by side in the front pew, chatting together about the only subject on which they were ever likely to agree: the qualities of George Marshall. Beside them, on one side, were Katherine Marshall and her family and, on the other, a number of the general's wartime aides and subordinates, among them a couple whom nobody outside the inner circle recognized. One was Marshall's old Filipino orderly, Semanko, and the other his old wartime barber, Nicholas J. Totalo, who had cut the general's hair in Cairo, Teheran, Potsdam, and the Pentagon and learned to like every hair on his head.

On Marshall's orders, nobody had written a funeral peroration, and all Canon Luther D. Miller did was thank God for the memories which the dead man had left behind him.

After which everybody except the family went home. There was no flag-draped caisson to take the body to Arlington. It was sped there in an undertaker's limousine. A soldier did sound Taps as the body was lowered into the earth, and some of Marshall's old aides who had infiltrated the cemetery came to attention and felt the tears running down their faces.

Then it was over. All done quietly, simply, without fuss, as effectively as any other operation General George Catlett Marshall had planned in his lifetime.

Source Notes

First let me say that the indispensable guide for historians, biographers, or general readers alike wishing to make the journey across the landscape of George Catlett Marshall's life is the one provided by his official biographer, Forrest C. Pogue. Pogue has already written three volumes* of a projected four- (and possible five-) volume life, and his detailed account of Marshall's experiences and achievements as both a private person and a military leader is so carefully plotted that no subsequent account of his hero's career—at least up until the victory in Europe during World War II—can hope to achieve accuracy or balance without keeping in sight the track of his firmly outlined footprints.

It is probably true to say that if it had not been for Pogue, the documentation on the major and minor events in Marshall's life would never have come together in one place. He played a principal role in gathering them in, and instead of being scattered around the world in various archives, anterooms, back attics, and the dark corners of his colleagues' memories, many of the original documents have ended up in Lexington, Virginia, at the George C. Marshall Research Foundation.

The Marshall Foundation came into being in 1953, after General Marshall had repeatedly turned down lavish offers from magazines and book publishers and had firmly indicated that he would never write his war memoirs. Instead, President Harry Truman persuaded him to donate his letters, reports, and papers† to a research library which would be built in his name on the grounds of his alma mater, the Virginia Military Institute, at Lexington. President Truman authorized the copying for the library of all Marshalliana from the National Archives, the Library of Congress, and other government repositories, as did Presidents Eisenhower and Kennedy later. It was decided that a necessary function of the Marshall Foundation would be the production of an authorized biography of the general, and Forrest Pogue was chosen for this task. Pogue was well suited to the job. He had been a combat historian in

*1. *Education of a General, 1880–1939* (New York: Viking, 1963).
2. *Ordeal and Hope, 1939–1942* (New York: Viking, 1966).
3. *Organizer of Victory, 1943–1945* (New York: Viking, 1973).
†But not a World War II war diary, which he destroyed.

World War II and later joined the Office of the Chief of Military History, Department of the Army, and General Marshall, satisfied with his credentials, agreed to cooperate with him in providing the raw material for his official life, with the proviso that it would be made available to other scholars. Pogue began his researches in 1956 with a series of tape-recorded interviews with the general, some forty hours in all, plus about fifteen hours of more informal talks subsequently recorded by a stenographer. At least half of these interviews were face-to-face encounters between General Marshall and Pogue; but in 1957 Marshall's physical condition deteriorated, and he found it less tiring to have questions read to him by his orderly, Sergeant William Heffner. No follow-ups were, therefore, possible during these sessions. Even this method of interrogation became too much of an ordeal toward the end of 1957, and so General Marshall never did get around to answering questions about some of his more controversial experiences both during World War II and afterward, when he became first secretary of state and then secretary of defense.

Nevertheless, the tapes make fascinating listening. They give a unique glimpse of the way in which Marshall's mind worked. I must thank the Marshall Library for allowing me to listen to them and record his words, and they have kindly made copies for me.

With Marshall's blessing and approval, Pogue was also able to talk to most of the officers, government officials, and ex-secretaries with whom he had had dealings during his career. In addition, he was able to question two former Presidents, Truman and Eisenhower, about their associations with them. I have made full use of these invaluable oral histories, which Marshall insisted should be made available to historians and scholars. Most of the originals are now deposited in the Marshall Library archives, together with copies of many hundreds of letters, telegrams, memorandums, and military orders which Marshall and his staff exchanged with Army commanders and heads of state during different phases of his career.*

To supplement this fascinating trove of comparatively untouched documentation, I have been able to call upon some research resources of my own. Since at least four of my previous histories or biographies

---

*Copies are also to be found in the Eisenhower and Truman Libraries, the National Archives, the Library of Congress, the F. D. Roosevelt Library, U.S. Navy Department files, Naval Institute Oral History Collection, and the Army Library at Carlisle Barracks, PA.

have covered periods in which General Marshall was active,* it was possible to consult my own library for letters, documents, and interviews concerning Marshall which were gathered in the course of my researches but not necessarily used in the books concerned. Where these resources have been used will be indicated in the detailed notes below.

Another rich source of military material which I have used is that to be found at the Military History Institute, Carlisle Barracks, Pennsylvania, and I must thank Dr. Richard Sommers, the archivist there, for so willingly guiding me and my fellow researcher to some hitherto uncovered Marshall documents as well as to fascinating oral histories from several of the general's commanders in the field.

I have, too, followed my usual method and have sought out, both in this country and in other parts of the world, those ex-officers and former statesmen who had close dealings with Marshall during the crises of his career, to ask for their memories of what was happening at the time and how they view today the decisions which he made, the actions he took, and their part in them. These interviews produced some particularly interesting comments from the late General William Simpson, with whom I talked in San Antonio, Texas, six weeks before he died, and from Mr. Abba Eban, former foreign minister of Israel, whom I saw in Herzlia, Israel. The names of others whom I interviewed in such widely spaced places as Beverly Hills, California, Pittsburgh, Pennsylvania, Washington, D.C., Egypt, England, France, and Germany are given elsewhere in this book. Details of sources, chapter by chapter, follow below.

Prologue

Marshall's letter of resignation to President Truman is to be found both in the archives of the Marshall Foundation (MF) and the Truman Library (TL) at Independence, Missouri. Winston Churchill's letter is in the Churchill Papers and in the British Library (BL) in London. Admiral

---

*1. *On Borrowed Time: How World War II Began* (Random House, 1969).

2. *Hirohito: Emperor of Japan* (Prentice-Hall, 1966).

3. *Dulles: Eleanor, Allen, and John Foster Dulles and Their Family Network* (Dial Press, 1978).

4. *Lindbergh: A Biography* (Doubleday, 1976).

Stark's note is in MF. Truman's panegyric to Marshall is in both MF and TL, and his remark to his Chief of Staff after the decoration ceremony is mentioned by the President in his oral history in MF and TL. So is his account of his call to the Marshalls at Dodona Manor. Katherine Marshall's rebuke to her husband ("Oh, George, how *could* you?") comes from Marshall's own tapes.

Chapter 1: A Disgrace to the Family?

The account of Marshall's boyhood and days at VMI is largely taken from Marshall's own tape-recorded conversations. His voice on most of these tapes is matter-of-fact but takes on an emotional note when he remembers the incident with the dog Trip. These recordings also describe the mischievous tricks he played on his sister, Marie, and his rivalry with his brother, Stuart, which stimulated his determination to succeed at VMI. The description of what life was like at VMI at this time comes from records at the institute, papers in MF, and memories passed down by VMI alumni and their parents. The bayonet incident figures both in Marshall's tapes and in the institute medical records.

Chapter 2: Shavetail

In his tape recordings, made in the twilight of his life, Marshall makes many references to Elizabeth "Lily" Coles Carter, his first wife, and from both his words and the timbre of his voice it is obvious that his warm affection for her never dimmed. He was not the type to use the word "love" casually, and there is therefore a special quality to one's reaction when one hears him saying, simply, of Lily, "I loved her." The description of how he risked expulsion from VMI in order to see and court her comes from Pogue (*Education of a General*, op. cit.).

About her illness: Marshall mentions Lily's mitral insufficiency in his tapes but, it goes without saying, does not complain in any way about the burden her semi-invalid status put upon his marriage. His yearning for a child and his fondness for children—especially little girls—are implicit in many of his letters. His goddaughter, Rose Page Wilson, says she was constantly aware of it and stresses what a gap in his life was created by the absence of a family of his own. The quotations from Mrs. Wilson are taken from her book, *General Marshall Remembered: The Recollections of a Forty-Year Friendship with a Great Soldier-Statesman* (Englewood Cliffs: Prentice-Hall, 1968). I have discussed the difficulties Lily's illness may have caused to the marriage, emotionally and physically, with medical experts, and they are generally agreed that in Marshall's day it could only have been dealt with by fortitude, forbearance, and abstinence.

Marshall's comments on his brother, Stuart, and about Lily at home come from Wilson (op. cit.).

The posting to the Philippines and the conditions Marshall encountered there are taken from Marshall's own account in his tapes, in which he described the stormy voyage to Mindoro, his first encounter with obstreperous U.S. troops, and the great cholera outbreak. The reminiscences of General Krueger are to be found both in MF and in the Carlisle Barracks archives (CB). The anecdote about Lily's slimming regime is mentioned in Marshall's tapes and by Krueger and other officers in their oral histories in MF. The description of the survey trip across the Texas badlands is to be found in the Marshall tapes, supplemented by a "Statement on Mapping Trip, Fort Clark," dictated but not signed by Marshall, in MF. There are also references to the trek in the letters and reports of Major General Van Horn Moseley, in MF.

Marshall's description of life back on the mainland for a junior officer comes from the tapes.

Chapter 3: Fruitless Search

More details of Marshall's life with Lily and of his relations with his brother and sister come from letters, diaries, and documents in MF from former classmates of Marshall's at Leavenworth, including Generals Krueger, C. D. Herron, and Royden Beebe. The period is also dealt with at some length in the tapes, including a description of the "second honeymoon" in Europe. The comment on Marshall's military capabilities in 1916 ("should be made a brigadier general") by General Johnson Hagood is in MF, as is the letter of despair sent to General Nichols of VMI. The short account of U.S.-Mexican relations at this period and of the depredations of Pancho Villa in the American Southwest comes from a study of contemporary documents.

Marshall's taped memories are quite detailed about World War I.

The experience obviously left a deeper impression upon him of what life was like for the ordinary soldier and officer in the line. The poignant account of the silent Frenchwomen greeting the arrival of the U.S. 1st Division at St. Nazaire in 1917, his struggles with the French language, and his first impressions of the western front come from the tapes. It was also about World War I that he wrote his only book, *Memories of My Services in the World War 1917–18* (Boston: Houghton Mifflin, 1976). It was written, in fact, after he returned from Europe in 1919 and finished some four years later, by which time U.S. publishers were finding there was no market for wartime reminiscences, so it remained among his papers until rescued by his stepdaughter, Mrs. Molly Winn, who found a publisher for it.

Chapter 4: Black Jack

The portrait of General John J. Pershing in this chapter is an amalgam of impressions gained from Marshall's own tapes, his written memories of World War I (op. cit.), and many contemporary books and records. Marshall's descriptions of the western front conditions and of the meetings with Clemenceau and the French generals are to be found in his written reports in 1st Division archives and in his book about the war. The account of Brigadier General Douglas MacArthur's quarrels with Pershing's GHQ at Chaumont and his "paranoia" toward the General Staff is based on contemporary records in the National Archives, in MF, and on William Manchester's biography of MacArthur, *American Caesar* (Boston: Little, Brown, 1978). The narrative of the chaotic confusion during the attack upon Sedan comes from official reports in the National Archives, Marshall's own reports, his tapes, and his war book.

The account of the farewell party to the French at Chaumont in 1918 comes from Marshall's war diary and taped memoirs in MF.

Chapter 5: Anticlimax

The account of Marshall's state of mind and the circumstances which persuaded him to stay in Europe for ten months after the end of World War I is based on a close study of his postwar diary, his letters to Lily, and Pershing's own account, *My Experiences in the World War*

(New York: Frederick Stokes, 1931, two vols.). It is particularly interesting to note the difference in tone—and in detail—between his accounts in his diary and those in his letters to Lily of his outings and adventures in London. All the descriptions of the London visit are taken from these diaries and letters.

The military situation and the state of the armed forces in the United States after the end of World War I have been dealt with in many books, and the apathy is referred to frequently by Marshall in his tapes. Manchester's biography of MacArthur also approaches the theme from another angle. Descriptions of Marshall's personal life during this period are based on his tapes and on the impressions from Wilson (op. cit.). The quotations about Lily and the verse to his goddaughter are to be found in Wilson.

The China interlude is based on Marshall's reports from Tientsin to be found in the Pershing Papers in the Library of Congress, on his tapes, in several oral histories, including one by General Lawton Collins in MF, and in material on the period at Carlisle.

Marshall's reaction to Lily's death is based on a letter he wrote in reply to condolences from Pershing (Pershing Papers).

Chapter 6: New Deal—Raw Deal

Marshall's life at Fort Benning in the wake of Lily's death has been reconstructed from several oral histories in MF, notably from Generals Omar Bradley, Lawton Collins, Courtney Hodges, Matthew Ridgway, Charles Bolté, and Truman Smith. The description of his first meeting and courtship of Mrs. Katherine Tupper Brown, who subsequently became the second Mrs. Marshall, comes from various accounts, including two oral histories by Mrs. Marshall herself in MF, Marshall's own tapes, and *Together: Annals of an Army Wife* by Katherine Marshall (Atlanta: Tupper and Love, 1946). Mrs. Marshall's oral histories also give details of her early life as an actress, the murder of her first husband, and her life with her second husband at Forts Screven and Moultrie. It is in these interviews that she also mentions her interrupted honeymoon with Marshall, so that he could answer Pershing's summons to help him write his memoirs.

The general picture of life in the CCC camps during the Depression years comes from contemporary documents, and details of Marshall's work in the camps from documents in the National Archives. It is in Katherine Marshall's oral history that she describes her husband's attempts to solicit aid from General MacArthur over posting and Marshall's feelings of despair at this time. Pershing's efforts to get Marshall a promotion are in the Pershing Papers, as are Marshall's expressions of hopelessness.

Chapter 7: Apotheosis

The opening quotation is from Katherine Marshall's oral history in MF.

Details of Marshall's illness at Vancouver Barracks and of his hospitalization are to be found in MF and also in the Pershing Papers, where there are letters to and from Marshall about his own illness and Pershing's much more serious collapse. Marshall's remark to Pershing that there would never be another four-star general is in the Pershing Papers.

The description of the atmosphere and the political situation in Washington after Marshall became Deputy Chief of Staff, in 1938, is reconstructed from contemporary documents. Marshall's first meeting with the President in his new position is based on his own taped account of it. Life for the Marshalls in official Washington is described by Katherine Marshall in *Together* (op. cit.), and it is from this that I have taken the quotations. The letter written by Marshall to an Atlanta newsman, Leo Farrell, bidding him hold back in supporting his chances of becoming Chief of Staff is in MF. The subsequent conversation between the President and Marshall about the job is quoted from Marshall's tapes.

Katherine Marshall's embarrassing attack of poison ivy is described in *Together* (op. cit.), and the Malin Craig telegram comes from the same source.

Chapter 8: The Road to Pearl

The account of the general situation in Washington and the War Department after war began in Europe in 1939 is reconstructed from contemporary newspaper and other sources. Adlai Stevenson's comments on the prevailing climate in the nation are from his oral history in MF.

The President's attempt to get rid of Colonel Truman Smith is described by General Sherman Miles in his oral history in MF, and General Walter Bedell Smith, in another oral history in MF, tells how Marshall resisted all blandishments to draw him into the White House inner circle. Marshall's own account of how he dealt with the President is set out in his tapes.

The extracts from the comments of General Paul M. Robinett come from the Robinett Diaries, deposited in MF. Marshall's frequent clashes with the President, including Roosevelt's reaction to unpalatable news ("his head went back") is to be found in his tapes. Secretary of War Stimson's remark about the "battle tactics" is from his own oral history in MF. The quotation from Pogue about the B-17 bombers comes from Volume II of his official biography.

The comment by Marshall on the Lend-Lease Act and on Harry Hopkins' attitude toward Russia is to be found in his tapes.

The attempt to mirror America's attitude at this time is based on contemporary records and a study of many documents (see the author's biography *Lindbergh* [op. cit.]). The Walter Lippmann comment comes from the New York *Herald Tribune* of September 20, 1941. The subsequent McCloy-Lovett memorandum which Marshall handed to the President is in MF. Efforts by Marshall to beef up Army appropriations and recruitment against much opposition is described in his tapes and contemporary records.

Chapter 9: Bunglers

The description of life in the War Department in the months before the outbreak of World War II is reconstructed from many sources, including oral histories by members of the department such as Walter Bedell Smith, Sherman Miles, Truman Smith. In addition, I have used Truman Smith's long account of this period in the Yale University Library and a long conversation with General Albert C. Wedemeyer at his home in Maryland. General Wedemeyer talked at length about his service in the U.S. Army, his sojourn in Nazi Germany as a student in Berlin and with the Wehrmacht; and I have based my account of the famous "leak" of the Victory Plan to the Chicago *Tribune* on his account of the circumstances, though I have supplemented his remarks with quotations

from Secretary Stimson, Assistant Secretary McCloy, and others in documents to be found in MF and the National Archives (NA).

The documentation and the literature on Pearl Harbor are huge,
and everything pertaining to it so far as Marshall is concerned is to be
found in MF and the Library of Congress (LC), including his memorandums, telegrams, and evidence before the different internal and congressional inquiries into the disaster. I have been very carefully through all
this documentation, and I have also dealt with it at great length in my
biography *Hirohito: Emperor of Japan* (op. cit.). (I have also studied a
document which seems to have received surprisingly little attention in
this country from a famous double agent in World War II, one Dusko
Popov, who reported to J. Edgar Hoover of the FBI in 1941 that he had
been specially asked by the Nazis to report on the defenses of Pearl
Harbor for their Japanese allies. Popov indicated that Pearl Harbor looked
like a prime target for any future Japanese attack. Hoover took no notice
but instead threatened to arrest Popov for taking a woman not his wife
across state lines for supposedly "illegal purposes.") Hoover had been
most authoritatively warned in advance (the British backed up Popov's
report) that Pearl Harbor was being sized up for attack but did nothing
about it. Nevertheless he has never, so far as I know, been accused of
participating in a conspiracy or a cover-up, nor has this matter received
much attention from American writers about the Pearl Harbor attack.
It would hardly fit in with conspiracy theories about President Roosevelt
and his staff, which some of them have advanced.

The description of Marshall's activities during the run-up to the
Pearl Harbor attack is taken from details in MF and LC. So are the
warning telegrams from him and Admiral Harold R. Stark. Stark's own
separate telegram is also to be found in MF and LC. The interview with
Admiral Kimmel in Hawaii on December 5, 1941, by Joseph Harsch is
to be found in the *Christian Science Monitor* of the following day.

The confusion in Hawaii (and Washington) over what Alerts A, B,
and C really meant is clearly set out by General Sherman Miles in his
oral history in MF. His comments on the misunderstanding are also to
be found in the same document. The comments of Colonel Orlando
Ward and his own reply to them are contained in General Walter Bedell
Smith's oral history in MF. Miles's remarks about his subsequent regrets
over the confusion are also in his oral history, and Marshall's comments
on Short's failure to act were made in his testimony before a congressional inquiry.

Chapter 10: Day of Infamous Confusion

The comment at the head of this chapter was made by General Sherman Miles in his oral history in MF.

Admiral Stark's rebuttal of conspiracy charges are made in his oral history in MF.

For fuller details of hour-by-hour Japanese moves both in Tokyo and in Washington in the twenty-four hours before Pearl Harbor, the reader's attention is drawn to the account in the author's *Hirohito* (op. cit.). General Marshall's account of his movements in the same period was made in testimony before a congressional committee inquiring into the Pearl Harbor disaster. It is from General Walter Bedell Smith's oral history in MF that I have taken his report of Bratton's arrival in the War Department with the first thirteen parts of the intercepted Japanese message to Washington. The President's reaction to the message comes from White House documents in NA.

Sergeant Powder's account of his movements on Pearl Harbor Day, and of Bratton's call to him, come from his oral history in MF. Marshall explained in testimony before Congress what he did once he reached the War Department and read the Japanese message. The actions taken in the department to warn U.S. bases are described in oral histories from General Miles, Bedell Smith, General Gerow, all in MF. Gerow also described MacArthur's reaction after he telephoned him in the wake of the Pearl Harbor attack. The story of how the stenographer, Aileen Morgan, botched Marshall's report is told in the oral history of Major (later General) Maxwell Taylor in MF.

Chapter 11: Gearing Up

General Mark Clark, in his oral history in the collection at Carlisle Barracks, relates how he recommended General Dwight Eisenhower for promotion. Marshall tells in his tapes how he came to consider General George S. Patton and details how he controlled his arrogance and exuberance. Eisenhower has described his own promotion in several places, including his memoirs and the Eisenhower Papers at Abilene, and he also relates the story of his arrival at the War Department in his oral history in MF. His attitude (or should it be antipathy?) toward General MacArthur and his recommendation to Marshall that he be left to be captured by the Japanese in the Philippines are related in his diaries, specifically in the entry dated February 23, 1942. See *The Eisenhower Diaries,* edited by Robert H. Ferrell (New York: Norton, 1981). Marshall in his tapes goes on to describe how he ordered MacArthur to leave the islands and arranged for him to receive the Medal of Honor to mask any suggestion he was running out on his troops, and he further mentions in his tapes how he did this without first consulting either with the President or with America's allies.

The description of Admiral Ernest J. King is based on his own autobiography, *Fleet Admiral King: A Naval Record* (New York: Norton, 1952), which deals frankly with his drinking problem, and *Master of Sea Power,* by Thomas B. Buell (Boston: Little, Brown, 1980), which examines his relations with his wife, family, and the Navy. King's comments on promotion, staying power, and the British—particularly the Royal Navy—come from his autobiography.

The first (aborted) meeting between King and Marshall is described at length in one of Marshall's tapes, as is the sequence of his subsequent visit to King's office.

The account of the British attitudes toward the tactics and strategy of the war in Europe is based on documents in the papers of the Combined Chiefs of Staff, plus the Joint Chiefs of Staff reports in the National Archives. I have also consulted Churchill's memoirs and Marshall's memorandums in MF. Roosevelt's stiff note to Marshall after his fit of pique over British hesitations is also in MF.

The report by Mark Clark of his and Dwight Eisenhower's visit to Montgomery's headquarters in England is told in Clark's oral history at Carlisle. Clark also describes the visit to Marshall in London by General de Gaulle (in his oral history in MF), and it is from this same source that I have taken the story of the codes Clark used when communicating with Eisenhower and Washington from North Africa.

Chapter 12: Turning Pro

The description of the North African campaign and the difficulties it caused with the Free French comes from many sources—U.S., British, and French. In a long interview in San Antonio, General Thomas T. Handy, who was Marshall's chief of plans, gave a fascinating account of American doubts over the operation and of Marshall's hesitations and also mentioned his difficulties with the President over timing and his encounter with Steve Early.

Marshall's remark about the necessity for a political leader to "keep the people entertained" comes from his tapes.

The reconstruction of the Free French attitude toward North Africa, and of the difficulties encountered there, is based on the memoirs of General de Gaulle, General Handy's oral history in MF, and General Mark Clark's oral histories in MF and CB. Marshall's letter to Eisenhower about the situation is in the Marshall correspondence in MF. The description of the assassination of Darlan, and Churchill's reaction to it, comes from Clark's oral history in CB. His account of the encounter between De Gaulle and General Giraud comes from his oral history in MF, as does his anecdote about Giraud on the Italian front.

The account of the Casablanca meeting is based on documentation from the Combined Chiefs of Staff, U.S. Joint Chiefs of Staff, memorandums by Admiral Ernest King in the Navy Historical Center, a conversation with General Wedemeyer, and various memoirs.

Marshall's sixty-second birthday party is described in extracts from Stimson's diary in MF. General Hastings Ismay's reactions to Admiral King are to be found in *The Memoirs of General Lord Ismay* (New York: Viking, 1960). Wedemeyer described to the author his journey to India with Field Marshal Dill.

Chapter 13: Great White Stepfather

The anecdote about Marshall's absentmindedness over his wife's name is told by Rose Page Wilson in her memoir (op.cit.).

Katherine Marshall tells the story of her son's Army status in *Together* (op. cit.) and also that about the wandering Dalmatian dog, Fleet.

The stern attitude toward her son's Army life by their stepfather is also mentioned by Katherine, but the letters and telegrams exchanged between Marshall, his stepson Clifton, and his commanding officers in North Africa come from the Marshall official correspondence files in the National Archives. Marshall's chief office aide at this time was Captain (later Brigadier General) Frank McCarthy, with whom I talked in Beverly Hills. McCarthy did his best to ease the tensions inevitably caused by Marshall's determination that no one should accuse him of favoring his stepsons. McCarthy explained how he also had to be ultracareful to show no partiality toward anyone, and what happened after he wrote in 1942 to Ronald Reagan in Hollywood is an illustration of this. The letter comes from McCarthy's files in MF. So does the curt letter to General Brereton from Marshall about handling (or mishandling) secretaries in war zones.

The data about Marshall's concern for servicemen's welfare come from many documents to be found in MF in which he queries his assistants about PX supplies, entertainment, leaves, and recreational services for men overseas. Both Tom Handy and Frank McCarthy told the author how Marshall always, on overseas tours, found occasion to slip away from his officer hosts and mix with the enlisted men to find out how they were feeling.

The correspondence and telegrams referring to General Eisenhower and Mrs. Kay Summersby are taken from the Marshall correspondence files, the McCarthy files, the General Handy files, and General White's files in NA and from the author's conversations with General McCarthy.

Chapter 14: Thwarted

The account of how Marshall failed to become Commander in Chief in Europe and gave up the job to Eisenhower has been told many times in memoirs of generals from Ike down. The new documentation in this account comes from MF. The letters exchanged between General Pershing and President Roosevelt on the subject are in the Pershing Papers.

General Handy described British feeling about the D-Day invasion and Churchill's exchange with Stimson in a conversation with the author in San Antonio and also refers to it in his oral history in MF. The reaction of Admiral King, and his fury over the Japanese code "leaks" in Washington, are to be found in documents in MF about code breaking. General Patch, whose career he almost wrecked, had a distinguished record of fighting in Europe. He died in San Antonio, Texas, in November 1945. Eisenhower's conversation in North Africa with Roosevelt over the C in C appointment comes from Ike's oral history in his files in the Eisenhower Library (EL) at Abilene.

The Cairo Conference has also received a good deal of attention from historians and memoirists. The account is based on wide documentation, Stillwell's oral history, Tom Handy's recollections of Madame Chiang, supplemented by Marshall's tapes and the memories of

Frank McCarthy. Marshall described in his tapes his row with Churchill, his first encounter with Stalin at Teheran, and his final agreement to stay in Washington with the President when D-Day took place.

Frank McCarthy described to the author how Marshall thereupon stole out of Cairo and flew back around the world to the United States.

Chapter 15: Perfidious Allies

The description of Marshall's habits and routine was described by his aide, Frank McCarthy.

There are many references in Marshall's tapes to his friendship and admiration for the British liaison officer in Washington, Field Marshal Sir John Dill. This account is based on these, on descriptions of the association from Tom Handy, and on letters Marshall wrote about Dill (particularly one to the U.S. ambassador to Britain, Wendell Willkie, after Dill's death), all of them in MF. The story of the rebuff to Sholto Douglas and the appointment of Lord Mountbatten to command in Southeast Asia comes from the same sources. Dill's telegram to London on the subject is in MF. Dill's Yale degree and how it came about also come from these sources, supplemented by a more detailed account of it in the oral history of Harvey Bundy, assistant secretary of war, in MF.

The exchange of memorandums between the President and Marshall over Eisenhower's visit to Washington, prior to D-Day, and the President's subsequent views of the Free French problem come from the Marshall correspondence in MF.

Handy, in his conversations with the author and in his oral history in MF, described the row with the Gaullists over the Normandy landings. The description of the incident between Marshall, Churchill, and Eden over De Gaulle comes from the Stimson diaries, and Marshall also mentions the incident in his tapes.

The Anglo-American row over the D-Day and post-D-Day situation in France was watched and commented on at close quarters by the author, who was a correspondent with the Allied forces and was a witness of some of the major quarrels. The description of the general situation comes from contemporary reports, from Marshall's tapes, and from Eisenhower's criticism of Montgomery in his oral history in his files at EL, Abilene. This was supplemented by conversations between the author and the late General Sir Francis de Guingand, Montgomery's chief of staff, during frequent meetings in the south of France.

The letter from Mrs. Kay Summersby to Frank McCarthy is to be found in the file of McCarthy's official correspondence in NA.

Chapter 16: The Bitter End

The quotations from General Handy about Marshall were made to the author in San Antonio in 1980. Eisenhower's quarrel with Churchill over the south of France invasion is described in a letter to Marshall in the EL at Abilene. Ike recalls Marshall's early attitude to the Russians in his oral history in his files at EL.

The letter from Moscow from General John R. Deane is found in the Marshall correspondence in MF, together with Marshall's memorandum to Stimson and Deane's subsequent cable.

The "no bed of roses" comment was made by Marshall to Eisenhower in a letter to SHAEF in February, 1945. The firing of Stilwell is the subject of a stack of letters and memorandums, between Marshall and Stilwell, Marshall and Wedemeyer, and Marshall and Roosevelt in MF and NA. The cable to Stilwell about reconciling with Mountbatten is also in MF and NA.

All the correspondence over Dewey's apparent threat to use the breaking by the United States of the Japanese code in his 1944 presidential election campaign, and of Marshall's determination to stop him, is to be found in the Marshall and Dewey correspondence files in MF.

The death of Sir John Dill and Marshall's reaction to it are also the subject of many memorandums and letters in MF.

Eisenhower's comment to Montgomery over his eagerness to thrust for Berlin comes from Ike's oral history in his files in EL. His remark that "Somebody just ought to smack him down" is in a letter to Marshall in EL.

The "terrible meeting" at Malta is described in a Marshall tape, supplemented by accounts from Churchill, Admiral King, and McCarthy.

Chapter 17: Berlin to the Bomb

The description of Yalta at the beginning of this chapter is based on an oral history in MF made by Sergeant James W. Powder, together with an account of his relationship with the general.

Marshall also deals with Yalta in his tapes, and Admiral King comments in his memoirs (op. cit.).

The discussion in Washington by experts from the Strategic Bombing Survey over the best ways of overcoming Japan was described by one of its members, Paul Nitze, in a conversation with the author in Washington, D.C., in 1980. Churchill's comments are made in his memoirs.

The account of how Marshall heard about Roosevelt's death was told by Frank McCarthy. The description of the funeral ceremonials comes from Sergeant Powder's oral history in MF.

For a full account of the political situation between the Allies at this juncture of the war, and of Stalin's suspicions of the U.S. and British moves, see the author's *Dulles* (op. cit.). Eisenhower mentions slapping down Montgomery over Berlin in his oral history in his files at EL.

The description of the Ninth Army's part in all this was told at some length by its commander, General William Simpson, in a conversation shortly before his death in San Antonio, in the presence of his wife and my fellow researcher, in 1980. Its substance was confirmed by Simpson's chief of staff, General James Moore, in a conversation in Chevy Chase, Maryland, shortly afterward. Between them they sketched in the situation prevailing on the front between their forces bestriding the Elbe and Berlin, fifty miles away. The point they both made was that the road to Berlin was open.

Marshall's comments on the order not to precede the Russians into Berlin are made in one of his tapes, and Eisenhower also comments in his oral history in his files at EL.

Chapter 18: New Direction

The letter from Lady Mary Burghley is in Marshall's correspondence files in MF. So is the letter which Marshall wrote for the President to send to General de Gaulle over the Free French land grab in northern Italy. The ultimatums sent to General Crittenberger by the local Free French commander there are also to be found in Marshall's correspondence file in MF.

Marshall's comments on the rude letter from Stalin which Churchill had received are made in one of his tapes. For a fuller account of the peace overtures Emperor Hirohito made in 1945 through the USSR, see the author's *Hirohito* (op. cit.).

Admiral Leahy's comment on the atom bomb ("biggest bunk in the world") is made in Harvey Bundy's oral history in the Bundy Papers. Bundy also describes the conference between Stimson and Marshall over where the bomb should be dropped, after the successful test at Alamogordo. Marshall's views on the atom bomb attack on Japan appear in one of his tapes. He also discusses at some length the plans which he made for more uses of the bomb if and when it became necessary during an invasion of Japan, and in the same tape he describes the confusion caused when the first bomb on Hiroshima failed to produce the immediate cry for mercy which he and Stimson had anticipated.

In another tape, Marshall comments on the implications of the Allied insistence on unconditional surrender and the difficulties faced by democracies in times of war.

Churchill's message describing Marshall as the "organizer of victory" and his further message in the summer of 1945 ("It has not fallen to your lot . . .") are in Marshall's correspondence files in MF. This last message was never issued publicly and is not to be found in the National Archives, although there is a copy in Churchill's papers in London.

Marshall's resignation letter and the message from the members of the Imperial General Staff ("Friend to truth!") are in Marshall's correspondence files in MF and the BL, London.

The farewell scene for Secretary Stimson when Marshall kept the big brass waiting in the sun is described in Harvey Bundy's oral history in MF.

Chapter 19: Mission Impossible

For the background to the China situation in 1945 I have read most of the relevant books on the subject (and there are scores of them) and additional reports by everybody from Theodore H. "Teddy" White through Jack Belden, Tilman Durdin, John Carter Vincent to John Paton Davies, Jr., and Ambassador Patrick Hurley. There is a voluminous correspondence in NA between Marshall and General Joseph Stilwell, written during World War II, which sets the stormy postwar scene, and there is also a thick file of letters reporting on the situation from General A. C. Wedemeyer, in NA. In addition, there are comments on China from such interested parties as Dean Acheson, William D. Pawley, Walter Robertson, and many others.

The treatment of Admiral Harold R. Stark by Secretary of the Navy Forrestal is described by Admiral Ernest King in *Master of Sea Power* by Thomas Buell (op. cit.). Marshall's letter to Stark is in his correspondence file in the office of Naval Records and Library.

Eisenhower's letter to Marshall about home leave comes from his file in NA and EL at Abilene. Marshall's letter commenting on a forthcoming British divorce suit is to be found among his correspondence in MF.

The description by Cora Thomas, Marshall's secretary, of Kay Summersby's postwar visit to the War Department was given to Forrest Pogue and is now in the FBI files. What happened to the dog Felix is unknown. A report on Mrs. Summersby's visit was subsequently sent to the FBI.

Chapter 20: *Showdown in Shanghai*

The account of General Marshall's arrival in China in December 1945 and of his first twenty-four hours in Shanghai is based on a conversation with General Albert C. Wedemeyer at his farm (Friend's Advice) near Washington, D.C. General Wedemeyer had recently returned from two melancholy events concerning his wartime colleagues: the funerals of Admiral Viscount Mountbatten, under whom he had served for a time in Southeast Asia and with whom he had preserved a lively postwar association, and General William Simpson, who had been buried in Arlington National Cemetery the previous day. It was nearly thirty-five years since Wedemeyer's confrontation with Marshall in the Cathay Hotel, Shanghai, but it was plain that the memory was still vivid and that it still hurt.

The circumstances in which Marshall accepted the China mission are well described in Truman's oral history (in both MF and TL). Readings of the oral histories by Dean Acheson, then a junior assistant in the State Department, and that of Walter Robertson have helped fill out the details. It was, however, Wedemeyer who revealed that Robertson had repeated to him Marshall's critical remarks about his "getting too big for his breeches."

Chapter 21: *"Don't Look Back"*

The description of the ups and downs of the China mission come from a wide reading of documents in the State Department, conversations with those who were involved in it (see also the author's book

Dulles [op. cit.]), and conversations with Ambassador Byroade and General Wedemeyer. I have also had access to Dean Acheson's reports on the subject. Wedemeyer's letters are from the official files in the National Archives.

The letters from Madame Chiang Kai-shek to Marshall, from the time he assumed his mission to China until shortly before his death, are to be found in the State Department files. A rapport was established between them from their first meeting in Cairo in 1943, and it soon became a warm friendship.

The quotation from Ambassador Henry A. Byroade is based on his oral history in the John Foster Dulles Papers at Princeton University, and in conversations with the author during the research for the author's *Dulles* (op. cit.).

Wedemeyer's letter to Marshall accepting the ambassadorship to China is in his files at NA.

Marshall's letter to Eisenhower about the China situation is in EL at Abilene. Acheson's comments are from his oral history in MF, as is his description of Marshall's change of mind over Wedemeyer and Wedemeyer's behavior in reaction.

Wedemeyer discussed this change of mind during conversations with the author and still, thirty-five years later, cannot understand how it came about. His letter to Marshall on May 29, 1946, is in his files in NA, as is his subsequent missive from Washington about writing a book. (There are copies under "China" in the National Archives.)

Marshall's letter to Truman accepting the job of secretary of state—with provisos—is in his correspondence files at the TL. His comments to Eisenhower are part of a memorandum he wrote later, which also included the simple code he and Ike used in their correspondence. Byroade's description of the last days in China is based on his subsequent account in State Department files.

In the author's conversations with Wedemeyer, the general maintains that Marshall asked him to alter his report on China because it disagreed with his own. I can find no confirmation of this in MF or State Department papers on China in the National Archives. The President's message of faith in Marshall was delivered to his aide Colonel Marshall Carter in Washington and is to be found in TL.

Marshall's letters to Eisenhower from China are in his file in the Eisenhower Papers at Abilene. Dean Acheson's view of Marshall's failure with the Chinese is contained in his papers and in his book *Present at the Creation* (New York: Norton, 1969). He also in these documents helps clarify the story told me by Wedemeyer of his own dealings with Marshall in China, particularly the contretemps over the appointment and cancellation of Wedemeyer as envoy to China. Wedemeyer's letters to Marshall, particularly the one dated May 29, 1946, from which I have quoted at some length, are to be found in the National Archives.

Tilman Durdin, of *The New York Times,* an old wartime colleague of the author's in the Far East, described his association with Marshall in the last days of his mission.

The President's message of assurance to Marshall after rumors of Wedemeyer's criticism of it was delivered to his aide General Marshall Carter and sent on to him. A copy is in State Department files.

Chapter 22: Initiation

The afternoon sessions of Secretary Byrnes and Dean Acheson, Chip Bohlen, and Ben Cohen are described by Acheson in the Acheson papers and documents in MF. Bohlen also referred to them in conversations with the author in Paris when Bohlen was U.S. ambassador to France (see *Dulles,* op. cit.). Acheson describes the White House reception when Byrnes learned that Marshall was replacing him. Stimson's letter of congratulation and advice to Marshall is to be found in his file of correspondence in NA. Walter Bedell Smith's letter is in Marshall's correspondence in State Department files.

The description of the prevailing world situation in 1947 comes from a general study of books, documents, and reports on the period as well as the author's own observations; he was a correspondent in Europe at the time. The account of Marshall's first appearance before the joint congressional committee as secretary and Acheson's impressions of it come from his autobiography, *Present at the Creation* (op. cit.).

The segment dealing with the Moscow Conference is based on many documents, including several oral histories by participants in the Dulles Papers at Princeton University and General Mark Clark's oral histories in MF and CB. (See also the author's *Dulles,* op. cit.)

Clark in his oral histories tells the story of his homecoming, his encounters with Eisenhower and Marshall, and his radio speech. Marshall's "I take it all back now" remark is in Clark's file at Carlisle (MHI).

Chapter 23: Marshalling Europe

President Truman's remarks about Marshall come from his oral history, a copy of which is in TL.

Dean Acheson describes Marshall's somber mood on his return from the Moscow Conference in *Present at the Creation* (op. cit.) The account of the conception and delivery of the Marshall Plan speech comes from many sources, including conversations with the late Charles "Chip" Bohlen and Paul Nitze (who wrote parts of the speech), which the author had in Paris with Bohlen and (in 1980) in Washington with Nitze. Acheson talks about it in his oral history in MF, and so does Truman. Acheson confirms that the speech was not completed until just before delivery and that the President was not aware of its specifics beforehand. His description of how he had to telephone at the last minute to get a press copy of the speech is described by Acheson in *Present at the Creation*, and there are further details in his oral history. He also mentions how he alerted British correspondents to its importance. The comment on Bevin's reception of the text comes from *Present at the Creation*, as does Molotov's reaction.

The Washington reaction to the Marshall Plan speech was described to me by Lucius D. Battle in a conversation in Washington, D.C., in 1980. Battle was assistant to Dean Acheson at the time and is now chairman of the Johns Hopkins Foreign Policy Institute in Washington, D.C.

Paul Nitze told me the story of how Marshall dealt with the McCarran Committee in a conversation in Washington, D.C., in 1980.

Katherine Marshall's book *Together* (op. cit.) was published in 1947, and Winston Churchill's letter mentioning it and also commending Marshall on his recovery plan is in Marshall's correspondence in MF. Frank McCarthy told the author the story of his encounter with his old chief in Paris during a conversation in Beverly Hills in 1980.

The exchange of letters with Lady Mary Burghley comes from Marshall's correspondence files in MF. His subsequent meeting with Queen Frederika of Greece at Claridge's Hotel is mentioned in letters which were exchanged between them from this time onward. The correspondence was conducted first through the Greek Embassy in Washington, then, when there were rumors about it, through the U.S. Embassy in Athens, and finally, after this was no longer considered secure, through CIA couriers. After Marshall's death General Omar Bradley, then Chief of Staff, wrote to the queen and told her he was arranging with the CIA to have all her letters returned. Owing to upheavals in Greece, that never happened, and the letters stayed in the CIA files, and copies were sent to the Marshall correspondence files in MF and NA. Ex-Queen Frederika died after a minor operation in Spain in 1980. Her daughter, to whom Marshall refers affectionately in his letters, is now Queen Sophie of Spain.

Chapter 24: Light in the Refrigerator

The account of the Palestine negotiations and the subsequent creation of the independent state of Israel is based on many books and documents, oral histories in both MF and the Dulles Papers at Princeton, and conversations with participants in them, including Dean Rusk, a member of the U.S. delegation to the United Nations (see *Dulles*, op. cit.). The memorandums quoted at the beginning of this chapter come from Frank McCarthy's files at MF. The letter from Marshall to Mrs. Eleanor Roosevelt is in her papers in the FDR Library.

The reactions of the Israeli delegation to Marshall's part in the negotiations was described to the author by Abba Eban (who was one of the two Israeli members of the delegation to Paris, the other being the late Moshe Sharett) during conversations in Herzlia, Israel, in 1980.

The letters between Marshall and Queen Frederika come from her correspondence files in the CIA and NA.

General Lucius D. Clay's reaction to the blockade of Berlin by the Soviets is described in his oral history in MF. Marshall's worry about the situation, and his consultation with the late Bernard Baruch, are to be found in Baruch's oral history in MF and in the Baruch Papers. So is the story Marshall told to illustrate his opposition to "preventive war."

Back to the Palestine negotiations. The descriptions and quotes are based on the author's conversations with Abba Eban, Dean Rusk (see *Dulles*) and Assistant Secretary of War Robert A. Lovett's reflections.

Marshall's trip to Greece is mentioned at some length in letters to him from Queen Frederika, and I have also used contemporary documents.

Mary Burghley's letter is quoted in Marshall's correspondence files in MF, as is Robert Lovett's letter to him describing Truman's triumphal return to Washington after his defeat of the Republican candidate, Thomas Dewey. The letter to Walter Huston from Marshall is to be found in the same files.

Chapter 25: No Respite

Katherine Marshall's telegram to the king and queen of Greece is in Marshall's correspondence file at the State Department. So is Dean Acheson's letter to Marshall. The satirical military report written by Madame Chiang Kai-shek about her stay at Dodona Manor with Katherine Marshall during the general's illness is a much longer document than the extracts quoted. Its heading, "Report for General Flicker," makes her one of the few people in the world to know about Marshall's boyhood nickname and to have the temerity to refer to it in a communication to him.

Truman's reply to Marshall's resignation letter is in his correspondence file at TL.

Marshall's comments on his physical condition ("my clothes are an irritation") were sent to Dean Acheson, who had taken his place as secretary, and are in Acheson's file at the State Department.

Chapter 26: Eminence Grise

Acheson's letter to Marshall on assuming the post of secretary of state is in Acheson's file at the State Department. Marshall's letter to Madame Chiang Kai-shek is in the State Department files, as is Frederika's letter. Marshall's memorandum enclosing it for State perusal produced a reply from Acheson which is in the same file. He faithfully forwarded her subsequent letters, and Acheson's replies are included with them in his files at the State Department.

The dismissal of Louis Johnson as secretary of defense and Assistant Secretary James Webb's role in securing it were described to me in a conversation with Lucius Battle in Washington in 1980. Marshall's appointment to succeed him, and the circumstances in which he accepted the job, are described in one of Marshall's tapes and also in Truman's oral history at TL. Acheson's comments on the appointment appeared in *Present at the Creation* (op. cit.). Marshall's first appearances in the role are based on recollections by Acheson and Luke Battle.

Chapter 27: Front Man

Margaret Chase Smith's remark about "the Four Horsemen of Calumny" was made in a speech before Congress. Jenner's charges against Marshall are taken from the *Congressional Record*. Truman's remarks to Marshall about Jenner were reported by Luke Battle. Anna Rosenberg's experiences as assistant secretary of defense were recounted in her speeches and published recollections.

The exchange of telegrams between Marshall and MacArthur in September 1950 is taken from Marshall's correspondence file at NA. The Korean War situation is reconstructed from a reading of many books on the conflict, a study of the documents in the National Archives, the Dulles Papers at Princeton, and contemporary records. Madame Chiang's letter about MacArthur's visit comes from her files at the State Department, as does Marshall's reply. His letter to Eisenhower about building up the armed forces is in his correspondence files, the Eisenhower Papers, as is his tribute to the qualities of his former commander in Europe.

The account of the 1952 presidential election is based on a wide reading and study, and for a fuller account of it, see the author's *Dulles* (op. cit.). These readings are supplemented by the oral history of William D. Pawley in the Dulles Papers at Princeton and conversations with General A. C. Wedemeyer.

Chapter 28: Clash

Truman's remark about the world situation in 1950 is taken from his notes in the Truman Library. The comment about MacArthur's Inchon success by General Collins comes from his book *Lightning Joe* (Baton Rouge: Louisiana State University Press, 1979). The Wake Island meeting between MacArthur and Truman was marred by charges and countercharges about exactly what was said between the general and the President. Private conversations were reported by an eavesdropping secretary of Truman and denied by MacArthur. So no specifics are used here.

The messages from the Joint Chiefs of Staff to MacArthur are taken from Korean War dispatches in the National Archives. Walter Bedell Smith's CIA memorandums to Marshall about MacArthur's reports were passed on to the author by CIA sources (see *Dulles* [op. cit.]). William Manchester in his biography of MacArthur (*American Caesar* [op. cit.]) refers to the possible espionage intervention of double agent Kim Philby. The author put Manchester and Philby in touch with each other, but there is no reason to believe that Philby had any effect upon the course of the Korean War except to warn the United States of possible Soviet reaction if MacArthur's belligerence persisted.

Adlai Stevenson's comment on Marshall's worry about Korea is made in his oral history in MF and there is a reference to it in his papers. MacArthur's dispatch about the possible end of the war is in the JCS files in the National Archives.

Acheson's report about Marshall's refusal "to give a military judgment" about MacArthur's reversals in Korea is made in his oral history in the State Department. Truman's statement on the situation repudiating the possibility of using the bomb is in the Truman Papers. Acheson describes the panic in Washington over Korea in his oral history and in *Present at the Creation* (op. cit.).

The description of Attlee's rush mission to the United States is based on British documents, supplemented by Dean Acheson's recollections. The replacement of General Walton Walker by General Matthew Ridgway is described by Ridgway in his reports in NA.

The four-point directive to MacArthur from the Joint Chiefs is in the JCS documents in the National Archives. So are MacArthur's counterplan and Ridgway's report on the battlefront situation. MacArthur's riposte of February 11, 1952, is also in the JCS files.

Chapter 29: Crossing the Rubicon

The quote about MacArthur's paranoia over former members of Pershing's General Staff (including Marshall) comes from Manchester's biography *American Caesar* (op. cit.). Marshall's efforts to "play fair" with MacArthur are documented in memorandums in the JCS Papers, in Marshall's wartime dispatches in MF and NA, and in reports in the Naval Research Center. His comment about supporting him "through thick and thin" comes from one of Marshall's tapes.

The quotation from Manchester occurs in *American Caesar*. Truman's remark about MacArthur is in the Truman Papers. MacArthur's interview with Hugh Baillie is taken from contemporary sources, the JCS message about a "presidential announcement" comes from the JCS Papers, and his letter to Congressman Martin was also reported in the newspapers of the day. Marshall's comment on it came later, during a congressional hearing.

Marshall's hesitation about going along with Truman's wish to fire MacArthur is set out in the President's oral history and Acheson's *Present at the Creation* (op. cit.). So is his suggestion that MacArthur be recalled for talks. Truman also describes how Marshall finally agreed with his conclusions and wrote out the recall message to Tokyo. MacArthur's reaction to it ("Marshall pulled the trigger") is in *American Caesar*.

Acheson's summing-up of the dilemma is quoted from his oral history.

Chapter 30: Chinese Laundry

Acheson's story ("Thank God that's over") is told in *Present at the Creation* (op. cit.). The description of MacArthur's homecoming is taken from contemporary records and news reports, and the account of the congressional inquiry comes from official reports and the *Congressional Record*. Both MacArthur's remarks about Marshall's China mission and Marshall's comments on the risks MacArthur was taking in Korea come from these reports.

The exchange between Wayne Morse and Richard Nixon was reported in the Washington *Post*.

Katherine Marshall's remarks about relations between her husband and President Truman come from her oral history in MF. Luke Battle's remarks about Marshall were made during a conversation in Washington, D.C., in 1980.

The letter from Dwight Eisenhower on July 17, 1952, comes from Ike's correspondence file in the Eisenhower Library at Abilene. The description of the Milwaukee speech which was supposed to include the rebuttal of McCarthy is based on contemporary reports and a conversation with Richard Rovere, who covered it. Eisenhower's later comments were made in a telephone conversation with Forrest Pogue. The Eisenhower Library has a full transcript. Truman's remarks come from his oral history, a copy of which is to be found in the Truman Library at Independence, Missouri.

Marshall's congratulatory letter to Eisenhower is in his files at MF and in EL at Abilene, and Katherine Marshall describes subsequent relations with the new President in her oral history in MF.

Chapter 31: Final Chores

The description of Marshall's visit to England for the coronation of Queen Elizabeth II comes from documents in MF by Frank McCarthy and General Omar Bradley. Katherine Marshall's part in the celebrations was described by General Sir Leslie Hollis, the gentleman-in-waiting, in conversations in 1970 at Haywards Heath, England, with the author.

His reunion with Queen Frederika is described in his letters to Madame Chiang Kai-shek and in Katherine Marshall's oral history in MF.

Marshall's letter to Eisenhower about the Nobel Prize is in EL at Abilene. Madame Chiang's birthday letter is in State Department files. The description of his journey and condition was given by General Tom Handy in a conversation with the author in San Antonio in 1980. The exchange of letters with Queen Frederika about her projected visit to the United States comes from CIA files and NA.

Tom Handy described the last time he saw Marshall in a conversation with the author in 1980. The description of Sergeant Powder's last visit comes from his oral history in MF.

The letter to Queen Frederika from Colonel George is to be found in his correspondence file at MF. Queen Frederika's reply from Austria is in her special file at the CIA and NA.

The description of Marshall's last days is reconstructed from many conversations with his family, colleagues, contemporary documents, and Colonel George's letter to Marshall Carter is in MF. Churchill's summing-up of Marshall was made in a statement to British newspapers. Truman's is contained in papers at TL.

Classifications of the Papers Studied in the George Marshall Research Foundations

Fort Benning, 1932
Correspondence, March 1932–June 15, 1932.

Fort Screven, 1932–1933
    Correspondence, June 27, 1932–June 1933.
Fort Moultrie, 1933
    Correspondence, July 1933–October 1933.
Illinois National Guard, 1933–1936
    Correspondence
        General, 1933–October 5, 1936.
        Acknowledgments of Congratulations re Promotion to Brig-
        adier General, 1936.
Vancouver Barracks, 1936–1938
    Correspondence
        General, October 6, 1936–July 1, 1938.
        Invitations, November 1936–June 1938.
Pentagon Office, 1938–1951
    Biographical Material
        Marshall, George C., 1938–1944.
        Marshall, Katherine Tupper, 1939–1947.
    Correspondence
        General, 1938–1951.
        Selected, 1921 (1938–1951).
        Categorical, 1938–1951.
    Shorthand Notebooks
        General, 1940–1949 and n.d.
        Nason, 1942–1946.*
    Speeches, Statements, and Writings
        Marshall, 1908–1951.
        Excerpts from Marshall Speeches, 1939–1951(?)
        Others than Marshall, 1939–1945.
    Testimonies before Congress, 1939–1945
    Engagement and Visitor Records
        Engagement Books, 1940–1949.
        Appointment Calendar, 1946–1948.
        Appointment Lists, 1945–1946.
        Daily Log of Visitors, 1942.
        Calling Cards Left, 1940–1945.
    Financial and Legal Records, 1938–1951.
    Scrapbooks and Scrapbook Materials, 1939–1945.
China Mission, 1945–1947

*Mona Nason was one of Marshall's secretarial assistants.

Correspondence
  General.
  Carter (Marshall S.) Files
    Chronological.
    Classified.
Memorandums, Messages, and Cables
  Memorandums.
  Gold Messages and Memorandum.*
  Radio Messages.
  Cables re Journalists' Commentaries on China.
Writings
Secretary of State, 1947–1948
  Biographical Material.
  Correspondence
    General.
    Categorical.
  Speeches and Statements
    Marshall.
    Others Than Marshall.
  Engagement Records.
  Scrapbooks and Scrapbook Material.
American Battle Monuments Commission, 1949–1959
  Correspondence
    General, 1949–1959.
    Dedication of American Military Cemetery at Suresnes, France, 1952
      General.
      Inspection Trip.
      Trip Details.
  Scrapbook.
American Red Cross, 1949–1950
  Correspondence
    General.
    Subject.
    Categorical.
  Speeches and Statements.
  Travel Schedules.
  Appointment Diary.

*Classified messages with or between heads of state.

Secretary of Defense, 1950–1952
    Biographical Material.
    Correspondence
        Number Indexed.
        Selected.
        Categorical.
        Chronological Files
          Director Executive Office.
          Secretaries.
    Shorthand Notebooks.
    Speeches and Statements
        Marshall.
        Others Than Marshall.
    Engagement, Visitor, and Correspondent Records.
    Financial Records.
    Scrapbooks and Scrapbook Material.
Retirement, 1951–1960.
    Biographical Material.
    Correspondence
        General.
        Chronological.
        Categorical (Index Sheets Only).
    Speeches and Statements
        Marshall.
        Others Than Marshall.
    Engagement and Correspondent Records.

Marshall Tape Recordings Used

All made at Pinehurst, North Carolina, on following dates:
    November 15, 1956
    November 19, 1956
    November 21, 1956
    December 7, 1956
    January 15, 1957
    January 22, 1957
    February 4, 1957
    February 11, 1957
    February 14, 1957

February 20, 1957
March 6, 1957
April 4, 1957
April 11, 1957

Oral Histories

Dean Acheson
Field Marshal Viscount Alanbrooke
Bernard Baruch
General William Bryden
Harvey Bundy
Henry A. Byroade
General Wayne Mark Clark
General J. Lawton Collins
General John R. Deane
General Jacob L. Devers
Anthony Eden (Viscount Avon)
President Dwight D. Eisenhower
General Leonard T. Gerow
General Leslie Groves
Gerhard Gesell
General Thomas T. Handy
General Sir Leslie Hollis
Viscount Ismay
Robert A. Lovett
Mrs. Katherine Marshall
General John J. McCloy
General Frank McCarthy
General Sherman Miles
Sergeant James Powder
William D. Pawley
Speaker of the House Sam Rayburn
Mrs. Eleanor Roosevelt
Walter Robertson
Mrs. Anna Rosenberg
Adlai Stevenson
General Walter Bedell Smith
Admiral Harold R. Stark

Colonel Truman Smith
General Maxwell Taylor
Ms. Cora Thomas
President Harry S. Truman
General Albert C. Wedemeyer

Oral Histories at Military History Institute, Carlisle Barracks, Pennsylvania

General Omar Bradley
General William Bryden
General Lucius Clay
General J. Lawton Collins
General Wayne Mark Clark
General John R. Deane
General John J. McCloy
General Matthew Ridgway

Index